Oxford
Primary
Thesaurus

Chief Editor: Susan Rennie
Literacy Consultant: Kate Ruttle

OXFORD
UNIVERSITY PRESS

OXFORD
UNIVERSITY PRESS

Great Clarendon Street, Oxford OX2 6DP

Oxford University Press is a department of the University of Oxford.
It furthers the University's objective of excellence in research, scholarship,
and education by publishing worldwide in

Oxford   New York

Auckland   Cape Town   Dar es Salaam   Hong Kong   Karachi
Kuala Lumpur   Madrid   Melbourne   Mexico City   Nairobi
New Delhi   Shanghai   Taipei   Toronto

With offices in

Argentina   Austria   Brazil   Chile   Czech Republic   France   Greece
Guatemala   Hungary   Italy   Japan   Poland   Portugal   Singapore
South Korea   Switzerland   Thailand   Turkey   Ukraine   Vietnam

Oxford is a registered trade mark of Oxford University Press
in the UK and in certain other countries

First published 1993
Second edition 1998
Revised second edition 2002
Third edition 2005
Fourth edition 2007

This new illustrated edition 2012

All artwork by Dynamo Design

British Library Cataloguing in Publication
Data available

ISBN: 978-0-19-275689-3

10 9 8 7 6 5 4 3

Printed in Malaysia by Vivar Printing Sdn. Bhd.

Paper used in the production of this book is a natural, recyclable product
made from wood grown in sustainable forests. The manufacturing process
conforms to the enviromental regulations of the country of origin.

Contents

Preface   iv

Introduction   v

How to use the thesaurus   vi

Illustrations   viii

Special panels   ix

Oxford Primary Thesaurus   1–482

Become a Word Explorer!   483

Preface

The Oxford Primary Thesaurus has been specially written for primary school children aged 9+. It is designed to address schools and curriculum needs and has been checked by teachers. It is also designed to complement the Oxford Primary Dictionary which is aimed at the same age range.

A special feature of this edition is the informative illustrations that have been added to provide even more vocabulary and help with creative writing. There is also the *Become a Word Explorer* section at the back of the thesaurus. This includes advice on using synonyms and other types of language, and tips on how to make writing more varied and colourful through the use of a thesaurus.

Susan Rennie

Introduction
What is a thesaurus for?

Here are three good reasons to use your thesaurus:

- *to find a more interesting word*

What words can you use besides *kick* for striking a football? Look up **kick** and **ball** to find some other verbs to describe footwork.

- *to find the right word*

What do you call the home of a fox? Is a young otter known as a cub or a pup? Look up **animal** to find the answers.

- *to give you ideas for writing*

Imagine you are describing a giant's **castle**. Look up **castle** for ideas for the setting, then **big** to find adjectives to describe how *colossal* and *mammoth* everything is in a giant's world.

What is the difference between a thesaurus and a dictionary?

A **dictionary** tells you what a word means, whereas a **thesaurus** tells you what other words have the same meaning, or are related to the word in some way. A **dictionary** gives you a definition of a word; a **thesaurus** gives you synonyms of a word.

For example, if you look up **clothes** in a dictionary, it will tell you that clothes are things that you wear. But a thesaurus will give you some other words for clothes (*garments, dress, attire*) and will list particular types of clothes (*jeans, kilt, pyjamas*).

You often use a dictionary to check the meaning of something you have read or heard. You use a thesaurus to find ways to write or say something yourself.

How to use the thesaurus

Word web panel
gives words that are related to the headword and are useful for project work and story writing. Look for the illustrations which give even more vocabulary—a list is given on the following page.

Overused word panel
offers more interesting alternatives for common words such as **big, bit, happy, nice,** and **sad**

cross reference
points you to another headword in this thesaurus where you will find further useful words or information

Writing tips panel
helps you write creatively by suggesting ways to describe how things look, move, or sound

bit to bitter

A
B
C
D
E
F
G
H
I
J
K
L
M
N
O
P
Q
R
S
T
U
V
W
X
Y
Z

38

SOME TYPES OF BIRD HOME
nest, nesting box; aviary, coop, roost

SOUNDS MADE BY BIRDS
cackle, caw, cheep, chirp, chirrup, cluck, coo, crow, gabble, honk, peep, pipe, quack, screech, squawk, trill, tweet, twitter, warble

A turkey gobbles.
An owl hoots.

SPECIAL NAMES
A female peacock is a peahen.
A young duck is a duckling.
A young goose is a gosling.
A young swan is a cygnet.
An eagle's nest is an eyrie.
A place where rooks nest is a rookery.
●For groups of birds see group

 WRITING TIPS
You can use these words to describe a bird

TO DESCRIBE *HOW A BIRD MOVES*
circle, dart, flit, flutter, fly, glide, hop, hover, peck, perch, preen, skim, soar, swoop, waddle, wheel
The post owls arrived, swooping down through rain-flecked windows, scattering everyone with droplets of water.
— J. K. Rowling, Harry Potter and the Half-Blood Prince

TO DESCRIBE *A BIRD'S FEATHERS*
bedraggled, downy, drab, fluffy, gleaming, iridescent, ruffled, smooth, speckled
The peacock displayed its iridescent tail.

bit noun
1 *Mum divided the cake into eight bits.*
piece, portion, part, section, segment, share, slice
2 *These jeans are a bit long for me.*
a little, slightly, rather, fairly, somewhat, quite

 OVERUSED WORD
Try to vary the words you use for bit. Here are some other words you could use.

FOR A *LARGE BIT* OF SOMETHING
chunk, lump, hunk, wedge, slab
Chunks of rock came tumbling down the mountain.

FOR A *SMALL BIT* OF SOMETHING
fragment, scrap, chip, particle, speck, pinch, touch, dab, atom, iota
(informal) smidgen
The map was drawn on a scrap of old paper.

FOR A *BIT* OF FOOD
morsel, crumb, bite, nibble, taste, mouthful
Please try a morsel of chocolate mousse.

FOR A *BIT* OF LIQUID
drop, dash, dribble, splash, spot
Add a splash of vinegar to the sauce.

bite verb bites, biting, bit, bitten
1 *I bit a chunk out of my apple.*
munch, nibble, chew, crunch, gnaw
(informal) chomp
For other ways to eat see eat
2 *Take care. These animals can bite.*
nip, pinch, pierce, wound
When an animal tries to bite you it snaps ●
at you.
When an insect bites you it stings you.
A fierce animal mauls or savages its prey.

bitter adjective
1 *The medicine had a bitter taste.*
sour, sharp, acid, acrid, tart
opposite sweet
2 *His brother was still bitter about the quarrel.*
resentful, embittered, disgruntled, aggrieved
opposite contented
3 *The wind blowing in from the sea was bitter.*
biting, cold, freezing, icy, piercing, raw, wintry

example sentence
shows you how you might use a word and each meaning of a word has a separate example

special synonyms
words that are similar in meaning to the headword, but can only be used in special cases

label
ells you that certain
ynonyms are only for
nformal or *formal* use

guide words
show the first and
last word on a page

headword
in blue, it is the word
you look up and is in
alphabetical order

highlighted letter
shows you which letter
you are on

(informal) perishing
opposite **mild**

bizarre adjective
'Whiskers' is a bizarre name for a goldfish!
odd, strange, peculiar, weird, extraordinary,
outlandish
opposite **ordinary**

black adjective & noun
The pony had a shiny black coat.
coal-black, jet-black, pitch-black, ebony,
raven
You can also describe a black night as pitch-
dark.
Someone in a bad mood is said to look
as black as thunder.
Common similes are as black as coal and
as black as night.

blame verb
Don't blame me if you miss the bus.
accuse, criticize, condemn, reproach, scold

bland adjective
This cheese has a really bland taste.
mild, dull, weak, insipid
opposites **strong, pungent**

blank adjective
1 *There are no blank pages left in my jotter.*
empty, bare, clean, plain, unmarked,
unused
2 *The old woman gave us a blank look.*
expressionless, faceless, vacant
blank noun
Fill in the blanks to complete the sentence.
space, break, gap

blanket noun
1 *The baby was wrapped in a woollen blanket.*
cover, sheet, quilt, rug, throw
2 *A blanket of snow covered the lawn.*
covering, layer, film, sheet, mantle

blast noun
1 *A blast of cold air came through the door.*
gust, rush, draught, burst
2 *They heard the blast of a trumpet.*
blare, noise, roar

3 *Many people were injured in the blast.*
explosion, shock

blatant adjective
*Do you expect me to believe such a blatant
lie?*
barefaced, flagrant, obvious, shameless,
brazen, unabashed

blaze noun
Firefighters fought the blaze for hours.
fire, flames, inferno
blaze verb
*Within a few minutes the campfire was
blazing.*
burn brightly, flare up

bleak adjective
1 *The countryside was bleak and barren.*
bare, barren, desolate, empty, exposed,
stark
2 *The future looks bleak for the club.*
gloomy, hopeless, depressing, dismal,
grim, miserable
opposite **promising**

blemish noun
This peach has a blemish on the skin.
fault, flaw, defect, imperfection, mark,
spot, stain

blend verb
1 *Blend the flour with a tablespoon of water.*
beat together, mix, stir together, whip,
whisk
2 *The paint colours blend well with each
other.*
go together, match, fit, harmonize
opposite **clash**

blessing noun
1 *The author gave the film her blessing.*
approval, backing, support, consent,
permission
opposite **disapproval**
2 *A warm hat is a blessing in cold weather.*
benefit, advantage, gift, asset,
comfort
opposites **curse, evil**

a
b
c
d
e
f
g
h
i
j
k
l
m
n
o
p
q
r
s
t
u
v
w
x
y
z
39

alphabet
on every page
to help you
find your way
around the
thesaurus easily

synonyms
words that
mean the same,
or nearly the
same, as the
headword

word class
what type of word
it is, for example,
noun, verb, adjective,
or adverb

numbered sense
if a word has more
than one meaning,
they are numbered

opposites
words that are opposite in
meaning to the headword, they
are also called *antonyms*

Illustrations

At the following entries in this thesaurus you will find illustrations with labels, to give you more vocabulary and support your writing:

amphibian	flower	music	shape
armour	game	myth	shoe
athletics	glasses	pirate	snake
chess	hat	polar	theatre
communication	horse	pyramid	time
dinosaur	insect	reptile	transport
drawing	knight	robot	zodiac
drum	medicine	seashore	

helmet

visor

gauntlet

breastplate

greave

armour

Special panels

Throughout this thesaurus, you will see special tinted boxes which give extra help on finding and using words. There are three types of panel, each marked by a special symbol:

Overused words   Writing tips   Word webs

Overused words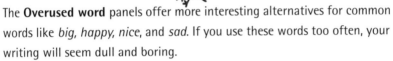

The **Overused word** panels offer more interesting alternatives for common words like *big, happy, nice,* and *sad.* If you use these words too often, your writing will seem dull and boring.

Here is a complete list of all the **overused word panels** in this thesaurus:

bad	good	look	sad
beautiful	happy	lovely	say
big	hard	move	small
bit	like	nice	strong
eat	little	old	walk

Writing tips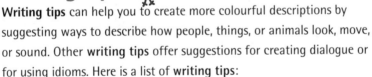

Writing tips can help you to create more colourful descriptions by suggesting ways to describe how people, things, or animals look, move, or sound. Other **writing tips** offer suggestions for creating dialogue or for using idioms. Here is a list of **writing tips**:

afraid	building	hair	sound
angry	clothes	light	surprised
animal	colour	nose	tooth
ball	eye	planet	un-
bell	exclamation	river	voice
bird	face	sea	water
boat	feel	sky	weather
body	food	smell	writing

Word webs

As well as exploring alternative words, you can explore related words. The **word web** panels give lists of words related to a topic word, such as **animal** or **castle**. These can be useful for both project work and for story writing.

accommodation	chess	expression
aircraft	church	eye
alien	cloth	fairy
amphibian	clothes	family
animal	coin	farm
anniversary	colour	fighter
armed services	communication	figure of speech
armour	competition	fish
art	computer	flower
artist	cook	food
astronaut	cricket	football
athletics	criminal	fossil
bear	crockery	fruit
bee	cutlery	furniture
bicycle	dance	game
bird	day	ghost
blue	desert	glasses
boat	detective	green
body	dinosaur	group
bone	disaster	hair
book	dog	hat
brown	dragon	herb
building	drawing	horse
car	drink	hospital
card	drum	house
castle	education	ice
cat	entertainer	illness
cave	explorer	injury

Special panels

insect	plant	space
island	poem	spice
jewel	polar	sport
jewellery	politics	spy
job	pottery	story
jungle	poultry	sweet
kitchen	prehistoric	swim
knife	punctuation	sword
knight	pyramid	tennis
light	railway	tent
magic	red	theatre
mathematics	religion	time
meal	reptile	tool
measurement	restaurant	tooth
meat	road	toy
medicine	robot	transport
metal	rock	travel
moon	room	tree
mountain	royalty	vegetable
music	ruler	vehicle
myth	school	water
needlework	science	weapon
nut	sea	weather
ocean	seashore	wedding
paint	seaside	white
paper	shape	wood
park	shellfish	writing
party	shoe	yellow
pasta	shop	zodiac
pattern	sing	
pet	snake	
pirate	song	
planet	sound	

Aa

abandon verb
1 *The robbers abandoned the stolen car.*
leave, desert, forsake, leave behind, strand
(informal) dump, ditch
2 *We abandoned our picnic because of the rain.*
cancel, give up, scrap, drop, abort, discard

abduct verb
The pirates abducted two members of the crew.
kidnap

ability noun
Skin has a natural ability to heal itself.
capability, competence, aptitude, talent,
expertise, skill

able adjective
1 *Will you be able to come to my party?*
allowed, permitted, free, willing
opposite unable
2 *Penguins are very able swimmers.*
competent, capable, accomplished, expert,
skilful, proficient, talented, gifted
opposite incompetent

abnormal adjective
It's abnormal to have snow in June.
unusual, exceptional, extraordinary,
peculiar, odd, strange, weird, bizarre,
unnatural, freak
opposite normal

abolish verb
I wish someone would abolish homework!
get rid of, do away with, put an end to,
eliminate
opposite create

about preposition
There are about two hundred children in the school.
approximately, roughly, close to, around

to be about something
The film is about a dog called Scruff.
concern, deal with, involve

above preposition
The witch flew above the rooftops on her broom.
over, higher than

abroad adverb
We're planning to go abroad next summer.
overseas, to a foreign country

abrupt adjective
1 *The book came to a very abrupt end.*
sudden, hurried, hasty, quick,
unexpected
opposite gradual
2 *The sales assistant had a very abrupt manner.*
blunt, curt, sharp, rude, gruff, impolite,
tactless, unfriendly
opposite polite

absence noun
There's an absence of salt in the soup.
lack, want, need, deficit
opposite presence

absent adjective
Why were you absent from school yesterday?
away, missing
To be absent from school without a good reason is to play truant.
opposite present

absent-minded adjective
The absent-minded witch had forgotten the spell.
forgetful, careless, inattentive, vague
opposite alert

absolute adjective
The hypnotist asked for absolute silence.
complete, total, utter, perfect

absolutely adverb
This floor is absolutely filthy!
completely, thoroughly, totally, utterly,
wholly, entirely

a
b
c
d
e
f
g
h
i
j
k
l
m
n
o
p
q
r
s
t
u
v
w
x
y
z

absorb verb
A sponge absorbs water.
soak up, suck up, take in, fill up with, hold, retain

absorbed adjective
to be absorbed in something
I was so absorbed in my book that I forgot the time.
be engrossed in, be interested in, be preoccupied with, concentrate on, think about

absorbing adjective
'101 Dalmatians' is an absorbing book.
interesting, fascinating, intriguing, gripping, enthralling, engrossing, captivating

absurd adjective
The idea that little green men live on Mars is absurd.
ridiculous, silly, ludicrous, preposterous, foolish, laughable, nonsensical, idiotic, senseless, stupid, unreasonable, illogical
(informal) daft
opposites sensible, reasonable

abundant adjective
Birds have an abundant supply of food in the summer.
ample, plentiful, generous, profuse, lavish, liberal
opposites meagre, scarce

abuse verb
1 *The rescued dog had been abused by its owners.*
mistreat, maltreat, hurt, injure, damage, harm, misuse
2 *The referee was abused by players from both teams.*
be rude to, insult, swear at
(informal) call someone names

abuse noun
1 *They campaigned against the abuse of animals.*
mistreatment, misuse, damage, harm, injury
2 *A spectator yelled abuse at the referee.*
insults, name-calling, swear words

accelerate verb
The bus accelerated when it reached the motorway.
go faster, speed up, pick up speed
opposite slow down

accent noun
1 *My mum speaks English with a Jamaican accent.*
pronunciation, intonation, tone
2 *Play the first note of each bar with a strong accent.*
beat, stress, emphasis, rhythm, pulse

accept verb
1 *I accepted the offer of a lift to the station.*
take, receive, welcome
opposite reject
2 *The club accepted my application for membership.*
approve, agree to, consent to
opposite reject
3 *Do you accept responsibility for the damage?*
admit, acknowledge, recognize, face up to
opposite deny
4 *They had to accept the umpire's decision.*
agree to, go along with, tolerate, put up with, resign yourself to

acceptable adjective
1 *Would a pound be acceptable as a tip?*
welcome, agreeable, appreciated, pleasant, pleasing, worthwhile
2 *She said my handwriting was not acceptable.*
satisfactory, adequate, appropriate, permissible, suitable, tolerable, passable
opposite unacceptable

access noun
The access to the lighthouse is over those rocks.
entrance, way in, approach

access verb
Can I access my email on this computer?
get at, obtain, reach, make use of

accident noun
1 *There has been an accident at a fireworks display.*
misfortune, mishap, disaster, calamity, catastrophe
A person who is always having accidents is **accident-prone**.
2 *A motorway accident is causing traffic delays.*
collision, crash, smash
An accident involving a lot of vehicles is a **pile-up**.
A railway accident may involve a **derailment**.
3 *It was pure accident that led us to the secret passage.*
chance, luck, a fluke
by accident
I found the piece of paper by accident.
by chance, accidentally, coincidentally, unintentionally

accidental adjective
1 *The damage to the building was accidental.*
unintentional, unfortunate, unlucky
2 *The professor made an accidental discovery.*
unexpected, unforeseen, unplanned, fortunate, lucky, chance
opposite deliberate

accommodate verb
1 *The hotel can accommodate thirty guests.*
house, shelter, lodge, provide for, cater for, put up, take in, hold
2 *If you need anything, we'll try to accommodate you.*
serve, assist, help, aid, oblige, supply, please

accommodation noun
Have you booked your holiday accommodation yet?
housing, lodgings, quarters, premises, shelter, rooms

WORD WEB
PLACES WHERE PEOPLE NORMALLY LIVE
bedsit, flat, house
KINDS OF HOLIDAY ACCOMMODATION
apartment, bed and breakfast, boarding house, chalet, guest house, hotel, motel, self-catering, timeshare, youth hostel

Accommodation for students is in a **hall of residence** or (informal) **digs**. Accommodation for the armed services is in **barracks** or a **billet**.

See also **building, house**

accompany verb
A guide accompanied us through the jungle.
escort, go with, follow, attend, travel with, tag along with

accomplish verb
She accomplished her goal of sailing round the world.
achieve, finish, complete, carry out, perform, succeed in, fulfil

account noun
1 *I wrote an account of our camping trip in my diary.*
report, record, description, history, narrative, story, chronicle, log
(informal) write-up
2 *Money was of no account to him.*
importance, significance, consequence, interest, value

account verb
to account for
Can you account for your strange behaviour?
explain, give reasons for, justify, make excuses for

accumulate verb
1 *Our family has accumulated a lot of rubbish.*
collect, gather, amass, assemble, heap up, pile up, hoard
opposite scatter

a
e
f
g
h
i
j
k
l
m
n
o
p
q
r
s
t
u
v
w
x
y
z

Dust had accumulated on the mantelpiece.
build up, grow, increase, multiply
opposite **decrease**

accurate adjective
1 *The detective took accurate measurements of the room.*
careful, correct, exact, meticulous, minute, precise
opposites **inexact, rough**
2 *Is this an accurate account of what happened?*
faithful, true, reliable, truthful, factual
opposites **inaccurate, false**

accuse verb
accuse of
Miss Sharp accused her opponent of cheating.
charge with, blame for, condemn for, denounce for
opposite **defend**

accustomed adjective
accustomed to
Martians are not accustomed to rain.
acclimatized to, familiar with, used to

ache noun
The ache in my tooth is definitely getting worse.
pain, soreness, throbbing, discomfort, pang, twinge
See also **pain**

ache verb
My legs ached from the long walk.
hurt, be painful, be sore, throb, pound, smart

achieve verb
1 *He achieved his ambition to play rugby for Wales.*
accomplish, attain, succeed in, carry out, fulfil
2 *The singer achieved success with her first CD.*
acquire, win, gain, earn, get, score

achievement noun
To climb Mount Everest would be an achievement.
accomplishment, attainment, success, feat, triumph

acknowledge verb
1 *The queen did not acknowledge her cousin's claim to the throne.*
admit, accept, concede, grant, recognize
opposite **deny**
2 *Please acknowledge my email.*
answer, reply to, respond to

acquire verb
Where can I acquire a copy of this book?
get, get hold of, obtain
To acquire something by paying for it is to buy or purchase it.

across preposition
We could see their camp across the river.
on the other side of, over, beyond

act noun
1 *Rescuing the boy from the river was a brave act.*
action, deed, feat, exploit, operation
2 *The best act at the circus involved three clowns.*
performance, sketch, item, turn

act verb
1 *We must act as soon as we hear the signal.*
do something, take action
2 *Give the medicine time to act.*
work, take effect, have an effect, function
3 *Stop acting like a baby!*
behave, carry on
4 *I acted the part of a pirate in the play.*
perform, play, portray, represent, appear as

action noun
1 *The driver's action prevented an accident.*
act, deed, effort, measure, feat
2 *The fruit ripens through the action of the sun.*
working, effect, mechanism
3 *The film was packed with action.*
drama, excitement, activity, liveliness,

energy, vigour, vitality
4 *He was killed in* action *in the Second World War.*
battle, fighting

active adjective
1 *Mr Aziz is very* active *for his age.*
energetic, lively, dynamic, vigorous, busy
2 *My uncle is an* active *member of the football club.*
enthusiastic, devoted, committed, dedicated, hard-working
opposite inactive

activity noun
1 *The town centre was full of* activity.
action, life, busyness, liveliness, excitement, movement, animation
2 *My mum's favourite* activity *is gardening.*
hobby, interest, pastime, pursuit, job, occupation, task

actor or actress noun
A company of actors *performed a play in the school hall.*
performer, player
The most important actor in a play or film is the lead or the star.
The other actors are the supporting actors.
All the actors in a play or film are the cast or the company.

actual adjective
Did you see the actual *crime?*
real, true, genuine, authentic
opposites imaginary, supposed

actually adverb
What did the teacher actually *say to you?*
really, truly, definitely, certainly, genuinely, in fact

acute adjective
1 *She felt an* acute *pain in her knee.*
intense, severe, sharp, piercing, sudden, violent
opposites mild, slight
2 *There is an* acute *shortage of food.*
serious, urgent, crucial, important, vital
opposite unimportant

3 *Clearly the aliens had an* acute *intelligence.*
keen, quick, sharp, clever, intelligent, shrewd, smart, alert
opposite stupid

adapt verb
1 *I'll* adapt *the goggles so that they fit you.*
alter, change, modify, convert, reorganize, transform
2 *Our family* adapted *quickly to life in the country.*
become accustomed, adjust, acclimatize

add verb
The poet added *an extra line in the last verse.*
join on, attach, append, insert
to add to
The herbs add to *the flavour of the stew.*
improve, enhance, increase
to add up
1 *Can you* add up *these figures for me?*
count up, find the sum of, find the total of
(informal) tot up
2 (informal) *Her story just doesn't* add up.
be convincing, make sense

additional adjective
There are additional *toilets downstairs.*
extra, further, more, supplementary

address verb
The head addressed *us in assembly.*
speak to, talk to, make a speech to, lecture to

adequate adjective
1 *A sandwich will be* adequate, *thank you.*
enough, sufficient, ample
2 *Your work is* adequate, *but I'm sure you can do better.*
satisfactory, acceptable, tolerable, competent, passable, respectable
opposite inadequate

adjust verb
1 *You need to* adjust *the TV picture.*
correct, modify, put right, improve, tune

a b c d e f g h i j k l m n o p q r s t u v w x y z

A

2 *She* adjusted *the central heating thermostat.*
alter, change, set, vary, regulate
to adjust to
I found it hard to adjust to *my new school at first.*
adapt to, get used to, get accustomed to, become acclimatized to, settle in to

admiration noun
I'm full of admiration *for her work.*
praise, respect, approval
opposite contempt

admire verb
1 *I* admire *her skill with words.*
think highly of, look up to, value, have a high opinion of, respect, applaud, approve of, esteem
opposite despise
2 *The travellers stopped to* admire *the view.*
enjoy, appreciate, be delighted by

admission noun
1 *We were surprised by his* admission *of guilt.*
confession, declaration, acknowledgement, acceptance
opposite denial
2 *Admission to the castle is by ticket only.*
entrance, entry, access, admittance

admit verb
1 *The hospital* admitted *all the victims of the accident.*
receive, take in, accept, allow in, let in
opposite exclude
2 *Did he* admit *that he told a lie?*
acknowledge, agree, accept, confess, grant, own up
opposite deny

adopt verb
1 *Our school has* adopted *a healthy eating policy.*
take up, accept, choose, follow, embrace
2 *We have* adopted *a stray kitten.*
foster, take in

adore verb
1 *Rosie* adores *her big sister.*
love, worship, idolize, dote on
2 (informal) *I* adore *chocolate milk shakes!*
love, like, enjoy
opposites hate, detest

adult adjective
An adult *zebra can run at 80km an hour.*
grown-up, mature, full-size, fully grown
opposites young, immature

advance noun
1 *You can't stop the* advance *of science.*
progress, development, growth, evolution
2 *This computer is a great* advance *on our old one.*
improvement

advance verb
1 *As the army* advanced, *the enemy fled.*
move forward, go forward, proceed, approach, come near, press on, progress, forge ahead, gain ground, make headway, make progress
opposite retreat
2 *Mobile phones have* advanced *in the last few years.*
develop, grow, improve, evolve, progress

advantage noun
We had the advantage *of the wind behind us.*
assistance, benefit, help, aid, asset
opposites disadvantage, drawback

adventure noun
1 *He told us about his latest* adventure.
enterprise, exploit, venture, escapade
2 *They travelled the world in search of* adventure.
excitement, danger, risk, thrills

adventurous adjective
1 *I dreamed of being an* adventurous *explorer.*
bold, daring, heroic, enterprising, intrepid
2 *She has led a very* adventurous *life.*
exciting, eventful, dangerous, challenging, risky
opposite unadventurous

amateur noun
All the players in this team are unpaid amateurs.
opposite professional

amaze verb
It amazes me to think that the Earth is billions of years old.
astonish, astound, startle, surprise, stun, shock, stagger, dumbfound
(informal) flabbergast

amazed adjective
I was amazed by the number of emails I received.
astonished, astounded, stunned, surprised, dumbfounded, speechless, staggered
(informal) flabbergasted

amazing adjective
The Northern Lights are an amazing sight.
astonishing, astounding, staggering, remarkable, surprising, extraordinary, incredible, breathtaking, phenomenal, sensational, stupendous, tremendous, wonderful, mind-boggling

ambition noun
1 *She had great ambition when she was young.*
drive, enthusiasm, enterprise, push, zeal
2 *My ambition is to play tennis at Wimbledon.*
goal, aim, intention, objective, target, desire, dream, wish, hope, aspiration

ambitious adjective
1 *If you're ambitious, you will probably succeed.*
enterprising, enthusiastic, committed, go-ahead, keen
opposite unambitious
2 *I think your plan is too ambitious.*
grand, big, large-scale

amend verb
I amended the letter to make it clearer.
change, alter, adjust, modify, revise

among preposition
We played hide-and-seek among the bushes.
between, amid, in, in the middle of, surrounded by

amount noun
1 *Mum wrote a cheque for the correct amount.*
sum, total, whole
2 *There's a large amount of paper in the cupboard.*
quantity, measure, supply, volume, mass, bulk

amount verb
to amount to
What does the bill amount to?
add up to, come to, total, equal, make

amphibian noun

🕸 WORD WEB
SOME ANIMALS WHICH ARE AMPHIBIANS
bullfrog, frog, newt, salamander, toad, tree frog

For other animals see **animal**

bullfrog

newt

treefrog

ample adjective
1 *The car has an ample boot.*
big, large, spacious, roomy
opposite small
2 *We had an ample supply of food.*
abundant, plentiful, generous, substantial,
considerable, profuse, lavish, liberal
opposite meagre
3 *No more juice, thanks—that's ample.*
plenty, sufficient, lots, more than enough
(informal) heaps, masses, loads, stacks
opposite insufficient

amuse verb
I think this joke will amuse you.
make you laugh, entertain, cheer up, divert
(informal) tickle

amusement noun
1 *What's your favourite amusement?*
pastime, recreation, entertainment,
diversion, game, hobby, interest,
leisure activity, sport
2 *We tried not to show our amusement.*
merriment, hilarity, laughter, mirth

amusing adjective
I didn't find his jokes very amusing.
funny, witty, humorous, comic, comical,
hilarious, diverting, entertaining
opposites unamusing, serious

analyse verb
We analysed the results of our experiment.
examine, study, investigate, scrutinize

ancestor noun
Our family's ancestors came from France.
forebear, forefather, predecessor
opposite descendant

ancestry noun
She was proud of her African ancestry.
origins, descent, heredity, heritage, blood,
extraction, pedigree, stock

ancient adjective
1 *Does that ancient car still go?*
old, old-fashioned, antiquated, out of date,
obsolete

2 *In ancient times, our ancestors were hunters.*
early, primitive, prehistoric, remote,
long past, olden
The times before written records were kept
are prehistoric times.
The ancient Greeks and Romans lived in
classical times.
opposite modern

anger noun
I was filled with anger when I read her letter.
rage, fury, indignation
(old use) wrath, ire
An outburst of anger is a tantrum or a
fit of temper.

anger verb
His cruelty towards his dog angered me.
enrage, infuriate, incense, madden, annoy,
irritate, exasperate, antagonize, provoke
(informal) make your blood boil,
make you see red
opposite pacify

angle noun
1 *He wore a top hat set at a slight angle.*
slope, slant, tilt
2 *Let's look at the problem from a different angle.*
viewpoint, point of view, perspective

angry adjective
Miss Potts turns purple when she gets angry.
cross, furious, enraged, infuriated, irate,
livid, annoyed, incensed, exasperated,
fuming, indignant, raging, seething
(informal) mad
To become angry and lose control is to
lose your temper.
opposite calm

angry adjective

WRITING TIPS
SOMEONE WHO GETS ANGRY MIGHT
blow a fuse, blow their top,
fly off the handle,
have a face like thunder,
have steam coming out of their ears,
hit the roof, see red

For things an angry person might say see
exclamation

animal noun
Wild animals roam freely in the safari park.
creature, beast, brute
A word for wild animals in general is **wildlife**.
A scientific word for animals is **fauna**.

VARIOUS KINDS OF ANIMAL
amphibian, arachnid, bird, fish, insect, invertebrate, mammal, marsupial, mollusc, reptile, rodent, vertebrate
An animal that eats meat is a **carnivore**.
An animal that eats plants is a **herbivore**.
An animal that eats many things is an **omnivore**.
Animals that sleep most of the winter are **hibernating animals**.
Animals that are active at night are **nocturnal animals**.

 WORD WEB

SOME ANIMALS THAT LIVE ON LAND
aardvark, antelope, ape, armadillo, baboon, badger, bat, bear, beaver, bison, buffalo, camel, cheetah, chimpanzee, chinchilla, chipmunk, deer, dormouse, elephant, elk, fox, gazelle, gibbon, giraffe, gnu, gorilla, grizzly bear, hare, hedgehog, hippopotamus, hyena, jackal, jaguar, kangaroo, koala, lemming, lemur, leopard, lion, llama, lynx, mongoose, monkey, moose, mouse, ocelot, opossum, orang-utan, otter, panda, panther, platypus, polar bear, porcupine, rabbit, rat, reindeer, rhinoceros, skunk, squirrel, stoat, tapir, tiger, vole, wallaby, weasel, wildebeest, wolf, wolverine, wombat, yak, zebra

For animals commonly kept as pets see **pet**

See also **amphibian, bird, fish, insect, reptile**

SOME ANIMALS THAT LIVE IN THE SEA
dolphin, porpoise, seal, sea lion, walrus, whale

SOME EXTINCT ANIMALS
dinosaur, dodo, quagga
See also **dinosaur**

PARTS OF AN ANIMAL'S BODY
antler, claw, fang, foreleg, hind leg, hoof, horn, jaws, mane, muzzle, paw, snout, tail, trotter, tusk, whisker, fur, coat, fleece, hide, pelt

MALE AND FEMALE ANIMALS
A male elephant or whale is a **bull** and a female is a **cow**.
A male fox is a **dog** and a female is a **vixen**.
A male goat is a **billy goat** and a female is a **nanny goat**.
A male hare or rabbit is a **buck** and a female is a **doe**.
A male horse is a **stallion** and a female is a **mare**.
A female lion is a **lioness**.
A female pig is a **sow**.
A male sheep is a **ram** and a female is a **ewe**.
A female tiger is a **tigress**.
A male wolf is a **dog** and a female is a **bitch**.
See also **cat, cattle, deer, dog**

YOUNG ANIMALS
A young beaver is a **kit**.
A young fox or lion is a **cub**.
A young goat is a **kid**.
A young hare is a **leveret**.
A young horse is a **foal**, **colt** (male), or **filly** (female).
A young pig is a **piglet**.
A young otter or seal is a **pup**.
A young sheep is a **lamb**.
See also **cat, cattle, deer, dog**

HOMES OF WILD ANIMALS
den, lair
A badger lives in a **sett**.
A beaver or otter lives in a **lodge**.

A
B
C
D
E
F
G
H
I
J
K
L
M
N
O
P
Q
R
S
T
U
V
W
X
Y
Z

A fox lives in an **earth**.
A rabbit lives in a **burrow** or **warren**.
A squirrel lives in a **drey**.

SOUNDS MADE BY ANIMALS
bark, bay, bellow, buzz, gnash, growl,
grunt, hiss, howl, jabber, purr, roar,
snap, snarl, snort, snuffle, squeak,
trumpet, whimper, whine, yap, yelp,
yowl

A sheep **bleats**.
A donkey **brays**.
A frog **croaks**.
Cattle **low** or **moo**.
A cat **mews** or **miaows**.
A horse **neighs** or **whinnies**.

For groups of animals see **group**

WRITING TIPS
You can use these words to describe an
animal

TO DESCRIBE HOW AN ANIMAL MOVES
bound, creep, crouch, dart, gallop,
gambol, leap, lumber, nuzzle, pad,
paw, pounce, roam, scuttle, skip, slink,
slither, spring, stamp, stampede, trot,
waddle
The jaguar padded *along silently.*

TO DESCRIBE AN ANIMAL'S BODY
agile, nimble, sinewy, wiry; lumbering,
majestic, mighty, muscular,
powerful
The cheetah stretched its long, sinewy
body.

TO DESCRIBE AN ANIMAL'S SKIN OR COAT
coarse, fluffy, furry, glistening, glossy,
hairy, leathery, matted, prickly, scaly,
shaggy, shiny, silky, sleek, slimy,
slippery, smooth, spiky, thick, thorny,
tough, wiry, woolly, dappled, mottled,
piebald, spotted, striped
She was a strong, well-made animal, of a
bright dun colour, beautifully dappled, and
with a dark-brown mane and tail.
— Anna Sewell, *Black Beauty*

anniversary noun
The anniversary of the day you were born is
your **birthday**.
The anniversary of the day someone was
married is their **wedding anniversary**.

WORD WEB
SPECIAL ANNIVERSARIES
centenary (100 years),
sesquicentenary (150 years),
bicentenary (200 years),
tercentenary (300 years),
quatercentenary (400 years),
quincentenary (500 years),
millenary (1000 years)

SPECIAL WEDDING ANNIVERSARIES
silver wedding (25 years),
ruby wedding (40 years),
golden wedding (50 years),
diamond wedding (60 years)

announce verb
1 *She* announced *that sports day was*
cancelled.
declare, state, proclaim, report
2 *The DJ* announced *the next record.*
present, introduce, lead into

announcement noun
1 *The head reads the* announcements *in*
assembly.
notice
2 *The prime minister issued an*
announcement.
statement, declaration, proclamation,
pronouncement
3 *I heard the* announcement *on TV.*
report, bulletin, news flash

annoy verb
1 *I was* annoyed *that I missed the bus.*
irritate, bother, displease, exasperate,
anger, upset, vex, trouble, worry
opposite **please**
2 *Please don't* annoy *me while I'm working.*
pester, bother, harass, badger, nag, plague,
trouble, try
(informal) **bug**

annoyance noun
1 *Mrs Grant's face showed her annoyance.*
irritation, anger, exasperation, vexation
2 *Is the dog an annoyance to you?*
nuisance, bother, trouble, worry

annoying adjective
My brother has a lot of annoying habits.
irritating, exasperating, maddening,
provoking, tiresome, trying, vexing,
troublesome

anonymous adjective
1 *An anonymous donor gave the school some
money.*
unnamed, nameless, unidentified,
unknown
2 *I received an anonymous letter.*
unsigned

answer noun
1 *Did you get an answer to your letter?*
reply, response, acknowledgement, reaction
A quick or angry answer is a **retort**.
2 *The answers to the quiz are on the next
page.*
solution, explanation

answer verb
1 *You haven't answered my question.*
give an answer to, reply to, respond to,
react to, acknowledge
2 *'I'm quite well,' I answered.*
reply, respond, return
To answer quickly or angrily is to **retort**.
to answer back
She doesn't like it when I answer back.
argue, protest, object

anthology noun
see **collection**

anticipate verb
I anticipate that the result will be a draw.
expect, predict, forecast, foretell

antique adjective
The palace was full of antique furniture.
old, old-fashioned
Antique cars are **veteran** or **vintage** cars.

anxiety noun
1 *We waited for news with a growing sense
of anxiety.*
apprehension, concern, worry, fear,
nervousness, dread, tension, strain, stress,
uncertainty, doubt
opposites **calmness, calm**
2 *In his anxiety to win, he started before the
gun went off.*
eagerness, keenness, desire, impatience,
enthusiasm

anxious adjective
1 *Are you anxious about your exams?*
nervous, worried, apprehensive, concerned,
uneasy, fearful, edgy, fraught, tense,
troubled
(informal) uptight, jittery
opposite **calm**
2 *I'm anxious to do my best.*
eager, keen, impatient, enthusiastic, willing

apologetic adjective
*The shopkeeper was apologetic about his
mistake.*
sorry, repentant, remorseful, regretful,
penitent, contrite
opposite **unrepentant**

apologize verb
The ogre apologized for being rude.
make an apology, say sorry, express regret,
repent, be penitent

appal verb
*They were appalled by conditions in the
prison.*
disgust, revolt, shock, sicken, horrify,
distress

appalling adjective
1 *He suffered appalling injuries in the
accident.*
distressing, dreadful, frightful, gruesome,
horrible, horrific, horrifying, shocking,
sickening, revolting
2 *Your writing is appalling—I can barely
read it.*
bad, awful, terrible, deplorable,

apparent adjective
There was no apparent reason for the crash.
obvious, evident, clear, noticeable, detectable, perceptible, recognizable, conspicuous, visible
opposites concealed, unclear

appeal verb
to appeal for
The prisoners appealed for our help.
request, beg for, plead for, cry out for, entreat, ask earnestly for, pray for
to appeal to
That kind of music doesn't appeal to me.
attract, interest, fascinate, tempt

appeal noun
1 Did you hear their appeal for help?
request, call, cry, entreaty
An appeal signed by a lot of people is a petition.
2 Baby animals always have great appeal.
attractiveness, interest, charm, fascination

appear verb
1 Snowdrops appear in the spring.
come out, emerge, become visible, come into view, develop, occur, show, crop up, spring up, surface
2 Our visitors didn't appear until midnight.
arrive, come, turn up
(informal) show up
3 It appears that the baby is asleep.
seem, look
4 I once appeared in a musical.
act, perform, take part, feature

appearance noun
1 They were startled by the appearance of the ghost.
approach, arrival, entrance, entry
2 Mr Hogweed had a grim appearance.
air, aspect, bearing, look

appetite noun
1 When I was ill, I lost my appetite.
desire to eat, hunger
2 Explorers have a great appetite for adventure.
hunger, desire, eagerness, enthusiasm, passion, keenness, wish, urge, taste, thirst, longing, yearning, craving, lust, zest

appetizing adjective
The appetizing smell of baking filled the house.
delicious, tasty, tempting, mouth-watering
See also food

applaud verb
The audience laughed and applauded.
clap, cheer
opposite boo

application noun
1 Have you sent in our application for a refund?
request, claim
2 The job needs a lot of patience and application.
effort, commitment, dedication, perseverance, persistence, devotion

apply verb
1 The nurse told me to apply the ointment generously.
administer, put on, lay on, spread
2 My brother has applied for a new job.
make an application for, ask for, request
3 The rules apply to all our members.
be relevant, relate, refer
4 The vet applied all her skill to save the animal's life.
use, employ, exercise, utilize

appoint verb
1 The school governors appointed a new teacher.
choose, select, elect, vote for, settle on
2 We appointed a time for our meeting.
arrange, decide on, fix, settle, determine

appointment noun
1 I have an appointment to meet the bank manager.
arrangement, engagement, date

disgraceful, unsatisfactory, atrocious
(informal) abysmal

2 *The team are waiting for the* appointment *of a new captain.*
naming, selection, choice, choosing, election
3 *My uncle got a new* appointment *overseas.*
job, post, position, situation

appreciate verb
1 *He* appreciates *good music.*
enjoy, like, love
2 *I* appreciate *her good qualities.*
admire, respect, regard highly, approve of, value, esteem
opposite despise
3 *I* appreciate *that you can't afford much.*
realize, recognize, understand, comprehend, know, see
4 *Dad hopes that the value of our house will* appreciate.
grow, increase, go up, mount, rise

apprehensive adjective
Are you apprehensive *about your exams?*
worried, anxious, nervous, tense, edgy, uneasy, troubled, frightened, fearful

approach verb
1 *The lioness* approached *her prey.*
draw near to, move towards, come near to, advance on
2 *I* approached *the head to ask if we could have a party.*
speak to, contact, go to
3 *The volunteers* approached *their work cheerfully.*
begin, undertake, embark on, set about

approach noun
1 *We could hear the* approach *of heavy footsteps.*
arrival, advance, coming
2 *Dad made an* approach *to the bank manager for a loan.*
application, appeal, proposal
3 *I like her positive* approach.
attitude, manner, style, way
4 *The easiest* approach *to the castle is from the west.*
access, entry, entrance, way in

appropriate adjective
It's not appropriate *to wear jeans to a wedding.*
suitable, proper, fitting, apt, right, tactful, tasteful, well-judged
opposite inappropriate

approval noun
1 *We cheered to show our* approval.
appreciation, admiration, praise, high regard, acclaim, respect, support
opposite disapproval
2 *The head gave her* approval *to our plan.*
agreement, consent, authorization, assent, go-ahead, permission, support, blessing
opposite refusal

approve verb
The head approved *my request for a day off school.*
agree to, consent to, authorize, allow, accept, pass, permit, support, back
opposite refuse
to approve of
Her family did not approve of *her marriage.*
like, favour, welcome, appreciate, admire, value, praise, commend, applaud, respect, esteem
opposite condemn

approximate adjective
What is the approximate *length of the journey?*
estimated, rough, inexact, near
opposite exact

approximately adverb
The film will finish at approximately *five o'clock.*
roughly, about, around, round about, close to, nearly, more or less

apt adjective
1 *He is* apt *to be careless with money.*
likely, liable, inclined, prone
2 *Your comments on my essay were very* apt.
appropriate, suitable, proper, fitting, right, well-judged, pertinent
(informal) spot on

a
b
c
d
e
f
g
h
i
j
k
l
m
n
o
p
q
r
s
t
u
v
w
x
y
z

A
B
C
D
E
F
G
H
I
J
K
L
M
N
O
P
Q
R
S
T
U
V
W
X
Y
Z

3 *She turned out to be a very* apt *pupil.*
clever, quick, bright, sharp

aptitude noun
He has a remarkable aptitude *for music.*
talent, gift, ability, skill, expertise,
potential, bent

arch verb
The cat arched *its back.*
curve, bend, bow

arch noun
They saw the arch *of a rainbow in the sky.*
curve, arc, bend, bow

archer noun
see arrow

arctic adjective
see polar

area noun
1 *From the plane we saw a big* area *of desert.*
expanse, stretch, tract
A small area is a **patch**.
An area of water or ice is a **sheet**.
2 *I live in an urban* area.
district, locality, neighbourhood, region,
zone, vicinity

arena noun
For places where sport takes place see **sport**

argue verb
1 *You two are always* arguing *over*
something.
quarrel, disagree, differ, fall out, fight,
have an argument, squabble, wrangle,
bicker
opposite **agree**
2 *We* argued *over the price of the cloth.*
bargain, haggle
opposite **agree**
3 *He* argued *that it was my turn to walk the*
dog.
claim, assert, try to prove, maintain,
reason, suggest
to argue about something
We could argue *for hours about football.*
debate, discuss

argument noun
1 *They was an* argument *over who should*
pay for the meal.
disagreement, quarrel, dispute, row, clash,
controversy, debate, difference, fight,
squabble, altercation
2 *Did you follow the* argument *of the book?*
line of reasoning, theme, outline, gist

arid adjective
No plants could grow in the arid *soil.*
dry, parched, barren, waterless, lifeless,
infertile, sterile, unproductive

arise verb
1 *We can phone for help if the need* arises.
occur, emerge, develop, ensue, appear,
come into existence, come up, crop up,
happen
2 (old use) *'*Arise, *Sir Lancelot!' said the King.*
stand up, get up

arm noun
The skeleton held out a bony arm.
For parts of your body see **body**

arm verb
The boys armed *themselves with sticks.*
equip, supply, provide

armed services plural noun

WORD WEB
THE PRINCIPAL ARMED SERVICES ARE
air force, army, navy

People in the services are **troops**.
A new serviceman or servicewoman is a
recruit.
A young person training to be in the
armed services is a **cadet**.

VARIOUS GROUPS IN THE ARMED SERVICES
battalion, brigade, company, corps,
fleet, garrison, legion, patrol, platoon,
regiment, squad, squadron

SERVICEMEN AND SERVICEWOMEN INCLUDE
aircraftman, aircraftwoman, commando,
marine, paratrooper, sailor, soldier

See also **soldier**

armour noun

> **WORD WEB**
> PARTS OF A MEDIEVAL KNIGHT'S ARMOUR
> **breastplate, gauntlet,
> greave (shin guard),
> habergeon (sleeveless coat), helmet,
> visor**
>
> Armour made of linked rings is
> **chain mail.**
> An outfit of armour is a **suit of armour.**
>
> See also **knight**

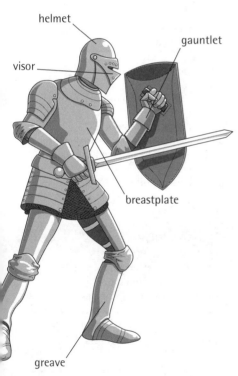

helmet

gauntlet

visor

breastplate

greave

arms plural noun
The bandits were equipped with arms.
weapons, guns, firearms, ammunition

army noun
see **armed services**

aroma noun
The aroma of lavender filled the air.
smell, scent, odour, fragrance, perfume

around preposition
1 *The mermaid wore a coral necklace around her neck.*
about, round, encircling, surrounding
2 *There were around a hundred people in the audience.*
about, approximately, roughly, more or less

arouse verb
The plan to build a supermarket aroused strong feelings.
cause, generate, evoke, stir up, excite, stimulate, incite, provoke, lead to, produce, set off, whip up
opposites **calm, quell**

arrange verb
1 *The books are arranged in alphabetical order.*
sort, order, put in order, group, organize, categorize, classify, collate, display, sort out, set out, lay out, line up
2 *Do you need any help arranging the party?*
plan, organize, prepare, set up, see to

arrangement noun
1 *They have improved the arrangement of the garden.*
layout, organization, design, planning
2 *Did you change the arrangement of my CDs?*
order, grouping, display, distribution, spacing
3 *We have an arrangement to use the swimming pool.*
agreement, deal, bargain, contract, scheme

arrest verb
1 *The police arrested two men yesterday.*
seize, capture, detain, apprehend, hold, take prisoner, take into custody, catch
(informal) **nick**

a
b
c
d
e
f
g
h
i
j
k
l
m
n
o
p
q
r
s
t
u
v
w
x
y
z

2 *Doctors are trying to* arrest *the spread of the disease.*
stop, prevent, halt, hinder, check, delay

arrive verb
When is the train due to arrive?
appear, come, turn up, show up, get in
When a plane arrives, it lands *or* touches down.
to arrive at
We arrived at *the castle before midnight.*
get to, reach

arrogant adjective
His arrogant *manner annoys me.*
boastful, conceited, proud, haughty, self-important, bumptious, pompous, snobbish, superior, vain
(informal) cocky, snooty, stuck-up
opposite **modest**

arrow noun
The spine of an arrow is the **shaft**.
The point of an arrow is the **arrowhead**.
Arrows are shot using a **bow**.
A holder for several arrows is a **quiver**.
The sport of shooting arrows at a target is **archery**.
Someone who practises archery is an **archer**.

art noun
1 *The* art *of writing letters is disappearing fast.*
skill, craft, technique, talent, knack, trick
2 *She took a course in* art *and design.*
artwork, fine art

art noun

WORD WEB
SOME ARTS AND CRAFTS
animation, basketry, batik, beadwork, carpentry, carving, collage, crochet, cross stitch, découpage, drawing, embroidery, enamelling, engraving, etching, graphics, illustration, jewellery, knitting, metalwork, modelling, mosaics, needlework, origami, painting, patchwork, photography, pottery, printing, quilting, screen printing, sculpture, sewing, sketching, spinning, stained glass, stamping, stencilling, tapestry, weaving, woodwork

For people who work in arts and crafts see **artist**

article noun
1 *Have you any* articles *for the jumble sale?*
item, object, thing
2 *Did you read my* article *in the magazine?*
essay, report, piece of writing

artificial adjective
1 *Organic gardeners don't use* artificial *fertilizers.*
man-made, synthetic, unnatural, manufactured
opposite **natural**
2 *She had an* artificial *flower in her buttonhole.*
fake, false, imitation, unreal, bogus, counterfeit
opposites **genuine, real**
3 *Captain Hook gave us an* artificial *smile.*
pretended, sham, affected, simulated
(informal) put on
opposites **genuine, natural**

artist noun

WORD WEB
SOME ARTISTS AND CRAFTSPEOPLE
animator, blacksmith, carpenter, cartoonist, designer, draughtsman, draughtswoman, embroiderer, engraver, goldsmith, graphic designer, illustrator, knitter, mason, painter, photographer, potter, printer, quilter, sculptor, silversmith, weaver

For performing artists see **entertainer**

artistic adjective
Mum's flower arrangements are very artistic.
creative, imaginative, aesthetic, attractive, beautiful, tasteful
opposite **ugly**

ascend verb
1 *It took the rescuers a long time to* ascend *the mountain.*
climb, go up, mount, move up, scale
2 *The plane began to* ascend.
lift off, take off
3 *The eagle* ascended *into the air.*
fly up, rise, soar
opposite descend

ascent noun
The bus moved slowly up the steep ascent.
climb, rise, slope, hill, gradient, incline, ramp
opposite descent

ashamed adjective
He was ashamed *because of what he had done.*
sorry, remorseful, repentant, embarrassed, shamefaced, abashed, mortified, apologetic, penitent
(informal) **red-faced**
opposites unashamed, unrepentant

ashes plural noun
Next morning, the ashes *of the bonfire were still glowing.*
embers, cinders

ask verb
1 *I* asked *them to be careful with the parcel.*
beg, entreat, appeal to, implore, plead with
2 *'Are you ready?' I* asked.
demand, enquire, inquire, query, question
3 *I'm going to* ask *you to my party.*
invite
(formal)
request the pleasure of your company

asleep adjective
I didn't hear the phone because I was asleep.
sleeping, dozing, having a nap, napping
(formal) **slumbering**
A patient asleep *for an operation is* **anaesthetized** *or* **under sedation.**
An animal asleep *for the winter is* **hibernating.**
opposite awake

to fall asleep
We waited until the giant fell asleep.
drop off, doze, nod off
To fall asleep quickly is
to go out like a light.

aspect noun
1 *The book describes some* aspects *of life in ancient Rome.*
part, feature, element, angle, detail, side, facet
2 *The ruined tower had an unfriendly* aspect.
appearance, look, manner, air, expression, face, countenance
3 *The front room has a southern* aspect.
outlook, view, prospect

assault noun
The old lady was the victim of a serious assault.
attack, mugging
assault verb
It's a serious crime to assault *a policeman.*
attack, strike, hit, beat up, mug

assemble verb
1 *A crowd* assembled *to watch the rescue.*
gather, come together, converge, accumulate, crowd together, flock together, meet, convene
opposite disperse
2 *We* assembled *our luggage at the front door.*
collect, gather, bring together, pile up, put together
3 *The general* assembled *his troops.*
round up, rally, muster

assembly noun
There was a large assembly *of people in the market square.*
gathering, meeting, crowd, throng
An assembly *for worship is a* **service.**
A large assembly *to show support for something, often out of doors, is a* **rally.**
An assembly *to discuss political matters is a* **council** *or* **parliament.**
An assembly *to discuss and learn about a particular topic is a* **conference** *or* **congress.**

a
b
c
d
e
f
g
h
i
j
k
l
m
n
o
p
q
r
s
t
u
v
w
x
y
z

A
B
C
D
E
F
G
H
I
J
K
L
M
N
O
P
Q
R
S
T
U
V
W
X
Y
Z

assent noun
The pirates gave their assent to the plan.
agreement, approval, consent, go-ahead,
permission
opposite **refusal**

assert verb
The prisoner asserted that he was innocent.
state, claim, contend, declare, argue, insist,
maintain, proclaim, insist, protest, swear,
testify

assess verb
*The test will assess your knowledge
of French.*
evaluate, determine, judge, estimate,
measure, gauge, value, weigh up

asset noun
Good health is a great asset.
advantage, benefit, help, blessing

assign verb
*He assigned the difficult jobs to the older
children.*
allocate, allot, give, consign, hand over,
distribute, share out

assignment noun
The spy was given a tough assignment.
job, task, piece of work, mission, project,
duty, responsibility

assist verb
*We were asked to assist the gardener with
the weeding.*
help, aid, support, cooperate with,
collaborate with
opposite **hinder**

assistance noun
1 *Do you need assistance with your
luggage?*
help, aid, support, encouragement
2 *We bought new sports equipment with the
assistance of a local firm.*
backing, collaboration, cooperation,
sponsorship, subsidy, support

assistant noun
The magician was training a new assistant.
helper, partner, colleague, associate,
supporter

associate verb
to associate one thing with another
I associate Christmas with holly and snow.
connect with, identify with, link with,
relate to
to associate with someone
You shouldn't associate with those people!
be friends with, go about with, mix with

association noun
1 *We have started a junior tennis association.*
club, society, group, league, fellowship,
partnership, union, alliance
A political association is a **party**.
A business association is a **company** or
organization.
2 *The association between the two men
lasted many years.*
friendship, relationship, link, partnership,
closeness

assorted adjective
*I bought a bag of sweets with assorted
flavours.*
various, different, mixed, diverse,
miscellaneous, several

assortment noun
*There was an assortment of sandwiches to
choose from.*
variety, mixture, selection, array, choice,
collection, diversity

assume verb
1 *I assume you'd like some chocolate.*
suppose, presume, imagine, believe, guess,
expect, gather, suspect, think
2 *The bandit assumed a disguise.*
put on, adopt, dress up in, wear

assure verb
I assure you that I will take care of your dog.
promise, give your word to

astonish verb
It astonished us to learn that the house was haunted.
amaze, astound, surprise, stagger, shock, dumbfound, leave speechless, startle, stun, take aback, take by surprise
(informal) flabbergast,
take your breath away

astonishing adjective
The volcano was an astonishing sight.
amazing, astounding, staggering, remarkable, surprising, extraordinary, incredible, breathtaking, phenomenal, sensational, stupendous, tremendous, wonderful

astound verb
see astonish

astounding adjective
see astonishing

astronaut noun
The astronauts climbed aboard the spacecraft.
spaceman or spacewoman

> **WORD WEB**
>
> THINGS AN ASTRONAUT MIGHT USE OR WEAR
> jet pack, oxygen tank,
> moon boots or space boots,
> space helmet, spacesuit, visor
>
> PLACES AN ASTRONAUT MIGHT VISIT
> alien planet, moon base, space lab,
> space station, star base
>
> See also moon, planet, space

astronomy noun
For words used in astronomy see space

ate
past tense see eat

athlete noun
For events in which athletes take part see athletics

athletic adjective
You need to be athletic to run in a marathon.
fit, active, energetic, strong, muscular, powerful, robust, sturdy, vigorous,
well built
(informal) sporty
opposites feeble, puny

athletics noun

> **WORD WEB**
>
> SOME ATHLETIC EVENTS
> cross-country, decathlon, discus, heptathlon, high jump, hurdles, javelin, long jump, marathon, pentathlon, pole vault, relay race, running, shot, sprinting, steeplechase, triathlon, triple jump
>
> For other sports see sport

discus

high jump

hurdles

javelin

sprinting

pole vault

relay race

shot

a
b
c
d
e
f
g
h
i
j
k
l
m
n
o
p
q
r
s
t
u
v
w
x
y
z

A
B
C
D
E
F
G
H
I
J
K
L
M
N
O
P
Q
R
S
T
U
V
W
X
Y
Z

atmosphere noun
1 *The atmosphere on Mars is unbreathable.*
air, sky
2 *There was a happy atmosphere at the party.*
feeling, mood, spirit

atrocious adjective
Everyone was shocked by the atrocious crime.
wicked, terrible, dreadful, abominable,
brutal, savage, barbaric, bloodthirsty,
callous, cruel, diabolical, evil, fiendish,
horrifying, merciless, outrageous, sadistic,
terrible, vicious, villainous

attach verb
Attach this label to the parcel.
fasten, fix, join, tie, bind, secure, connect,
link, couple, stick, affix, add, append
opposite **detach**

attached adjective
attached to
The twins are very attached to each other.
fond of, close to, dear to, devoted to,
loyal to, affectionate towards,
friendly towards, loving towards
opposite **not close to**

attack noun
1 *The pirates' attack took us by surprise.*
assault, strike, charge, rush, raid, ambush,
invasion, onslaught
An attack with big guns or bombs is a **blitz**
or **bombardment**.
An attack by planes is an **air raid**.
2 *The newspaper published an attack on his
character.*
criticism, outburst, abuse, tirade
3 *I had a sneezing attack in assembly.*
bout, fit, spasm
(informal) **turn**

attack verb
1 *The travellers were attacked by
highwaymen.*
assault, beat up, mug, set on, assail
To attack someone else's territory is to
invade or raid it.
To attack someone from a hidden place is to
ambush them.

To attack the enemy with bombs or heavy
guns is to bombard them.
To attack by rushing at the enemy is to
charge.
To attack a place suddenly is to storm it.
If an animal attacks you, it might savage
you.
2 *He attacked her reputation.*
abuse, criticize, denounce
opposite **defend**

attain verb
*The team attained a total of twelve gold
medals.*
get, obtain, reach, achieve, accomplish,
gain

attempt verb
They will attempt to reconstruct a Viking ship.
try, endeavour, strive, seek, aim,
make an effort

attempt noun
*The pole vaulter cleared the bar at the first
attempt.*
try, effort
(informal) shot, go

attend verb
*Are you going to attend the end-of-term
concert?*
go to, appear at, be present at
to attend to
1 *Please attend carefully to my instructions.*
listen to, pay attention to, follow carefully,
heed, mark, mind, note, notice, observe,
think about
2 *Who will attend to the washing up?*
deal with, see to
3 *The nurses attended to the wounded.*
take care of, care for, look after, help,
mind, tend

attention noun
1 *Give your full attention to the teacher.*
concentration, consideration, thought,
observation, awareness, heed, concern
2 *The survivors need urgent medical
attention.*
treatment, care

attentive adjective
Drivers should be attentive at all times.
alert, paying attention, watchful, vigilant, observant, careful, listening, on the alert, on the lookout, sharp-eyed, wary, wide awake

attitude noun
I'm trying to take a more positive attitude to life.
outlook, approach, behaviour, stance, frame of mind, disposition, view, position, manner, mood

attract verb
1 *Do you think our exhibition will attract people?*
interest, appeal to, fascinate, tempt, entice
2 *Baby animals attract big crowds at the zoo.*
draw, pull in
opposite **repel**

attractive adjective
1 *Miranda was a very attractive young woman.*
beautiful, pretty, good-looking, handsome, gorgeous, glamorous, striking, fetching, charming, lovely, delightful, pleasing, fascinating, captivating, enchanting
See also **beautiful**
opposites **unattractive, repulsive**
2 *There are some attractive bargains in the sale.*
appealing, agreeable, interesting, desirable, tempting, irresistible

audible adjective
see **hear**

audience noun
The audience were enthralled by the jugglers.
crowd, spectators
The audience for a TV programme is the **viewers**.
The audience for a radio programme is the **listeners**.

authentic adjective
1 *That is an authentic painting by Picasso.*
genuine, real, actual
opposite **counterfeit**
2 *The book is an authentic account of life at sea.*
accurate, truthful, reliable, true, honest, dependable, factual
opposite **false**

author noun
see **writer**

authority noun
1 *I have the head's authority to go home early.*
permission, consent, approval
2 *The king had the authority to execute the prisoners.*
power, right, influence
3 *My uncle is an authority on steam trains.*
expert, specialist

automatic adjective
1 *We took our car through the automatic car wash.*
automated, mechanical, programmed, computerized
2 *My sneezing was an automatic response to the pepper.*
instinctive, involuntary, impulsive, spontaneous, reflex, natural, unconscious, unthinking

available adjective
1 *There are no more seats available.*
obtainable, free
2 *Is there a phone available in the library?*
accessible, ready, usable, at hand, handy, within reach, convenient
opposite **unavailable**

average adjective
It was an average kind of day at school.
everyday, ordinary, normal, typical, usual, regular, commonplace, familiar
opposites **unusual, extraordinary**

a
b
c
d
e
f
g
h
i
j
k
l
m
n
o
p
q
r
s
t
u
v
w
x
y
z

A
B
C
D
E
F
G
H
I
J
K
L
M
N
O
P
Q
R
S
T
U
V
W
X
Y
Z

avid adjective
My sister is an avid reader.
keen, eager, enthusiastic, passionate, ardent, fervent, zealous

avoid verb
1 *The driver tried hard to avoid the collision.*
get out of the way of, avert, dodge, keep clear of, steer clear of, fend off, shun
2 *The outlaws avoided capture for months.*
elude, evade, run away from, escape from
3 *How did you manage to avoid the washing up?*
get out of, dodge, shirk

await verb
I await your reply to my letter.
wait for, look out for, be ready for, expect, hope for

awake adjective
Hester lay awake all night worrying.
wide awake, restless, sleepless, conscious, astir
Not being able to sleep is to be suffering from insomnia.
opposite **asleep**

awaken verb
1 *Mum awakened us at seven.*
wake, waken, rouse, arouse, call, alert
2 *The dragon will awaken at dawn.*
wake up, become conscious, stir

award noun
Kirsty got a national award for gymnastics.
prize, trophy, medal

award verb
My friend was awarded first prize in the competition.
give, present, grant

aware adjective
aware of
The spy was aware of the dangers of the mission.
acquainted with, conscious of, familiar with, informed about
opposite **ignorant of**

awful adjective
1 *The weather was awful last weekend.*
bad, dreadful, terrible, appalling, dire, abysmal
(informal) rubbish, lousy
2 *The teacher complained about our awful behaviour.*
disgraceful, shameful, disobedient, naughty
3 *Cinderella's stepmother was an awful woman.*
unpleasant, disagreeable, nasty, horrid, detestable, unkind, unfriendly
4 *The country was shocked by the awful crime.*
horrifying, shocking, atrocious, abominable, outrageous
5 *I feel awful about forgetting your birthday.*
sorry, ashamed, embarrassed, guilty, remorseful
For other ways to describe something bad see **bad**

awkward adjective
1 *The parcel was an awkward shape.*
bulky, inconvenient, unmanageable, unwieldy
opposite **convenient**
2 *The giant was very awkward with his knife and fork.*
clumsy, unskilful, bungling
opposite **skilful**
3 *We found ourselves in a very awkward situation.*
difficult, troublesome, trying, perplexing, tough
opposites **straightforward, easy**
4 *Are you trying to be awkward?*
obstinate, stubborn, uncooperative, unhelpful, exasperating
opposite **cooperative**
5 *I felt awkward as I didn't know anyone at the party.*
embarrassed, uncomfortable, uneasy, out of place
opposites **comfortable, at ease**

Bb

baby noun
infant, child
A baby who has just been born is a
newborn.
A baby just learning to walk is a toddler.
The time when someone is a baby is their
babyhood.
For names of baby animals see animal

babyish adjective
My brother thinks that dolls are babyish.
childish, immature, infantile
opposites grown-up, mature

back noun
We always sit at the back of the bus.
end, rear, tail end
The back of a ship is the stern.
The back of an animal is the hindquarters,
rear, or rump.
The back of a piece of paper is the reverse.
opposite front

back adjective
The back door of the cabin was locked.
end, rear, tail
The back legs of an animal are its hind legs.
opposite front

back verb
1 *A big lorry was backing into our driveway.*
go backwards, reverse
2 *I'm backing the blue team to win the race.*
bet on, put money on
3 *The council is backing the plan to build a
skate park.*
support, sponsor, endorse
to back away
*When the dog growled, the robber backed
away.*
back off, retreat, give way, retire, recoil
opposite approach
to back out of something

*The injured player may have to back out of
the final.*
drop out of, withdraw from
to back someone up
Will you back me up if I need help?
support, second

background noun
1 *I drew a mermaid with the sea in the
background.*
opposite foreground
2 *The first chapter deals with the background
to the war.*
circumstances (of), history (of),
lead-up (to)
3 *My mother's family has a Swedish
background.*
tradition, upbringing, ancestry

bad adjective
This has been a bad week for all of us.
awful, horrible, terrible
opposites good, fine, excellent

bad adjective

OVERUSED WORD

Try to vary the words you use for bad.
Here are some other words you could use.

FOR A **BAD PERSON**
wicked, evil, cruel, malevolent,
malicious, vicious, villainous, mean,
nasty, beastly, monstrous, corrupt,
deplorable, detestable, immoral,
infamous, shameful, sinful
*Gobo was a detestable king who was
loathed by his subjects.*

A bad person is a scoundrel, rogue, or
rascal.
A bad character in a story or film is a
villain or (informal) baddy.
opposites good, virtuous

FOR A **BAD ACCIDENT OR BAD ILLNESS**
serious, severe, grave, distressing, acute
Ingrid has a severe case of chickenpox.
opposite minor

a
b
c
d
e
f
g
h
i
j
k
l
m
n
o
p
q
r
s
t
u
v
w
x
y
z

A
B
C
D
E
F
G
H
I
J
K
L
M
N
O
P
Q
R
S
T
U
V
W
X
Y
Z

FOR BAD BEHAVIOUR
naughty, mischievous, disobedient, disgraceful, wrong
That mischievous *kitten drank my milk!*
opposites **exemplary, angelic**

FOR A **BAD EXPERIENCE** OR BAD NEWS
unpleasant, unwelcome, disagreeable, horrible, awful, terrible, dreadful, horrific, appalling, shocking, hideous, disastrous, ghastly, frightful, abominable, diabolical
The letter contained disagreeable *news.*
opposites **good, excellent**

Another word for a bad experience is an ordeal.

FOR A **BAD HABIT** OR SOMETHING THAT IS BAD FOR YOU
harmful, damaging, dangerous, undesirable, detrimental, injurious
Fizzy drinks can be harmful *to your teeth.*

FOR A **BAD PERFORMANCE** OR BAD WORK
poor, inferior, weak, unsatisfactory, inadequate, incompetent, awful, hopeless, terrible, useless, worthless, abysmal, shoddy
(informal) rubbish
The worst part of the film is the incompetent *acting.*

FOR A **BAD SMELL** OR **BAD TASTE**
disgusting, revolting, repulsive, sickening, nauseating, repugnant, foul, loathsome, offensive, vile
A nauseating *smell wafted from the kitchen.*
opposites **pleasant, appetizing**

FOR BAD TIMING
inconvenient, unsuitable, unfortunate, inappropriate
You've caught me at an inconvenient *moment.*
opposites **convenient, opportune**

FOR BAD WEATHER
harsh, hostile, unfavourable, adverse, miserable
(informal) lousy
Penguins face hostile *weather in the Antarctic.*
opposites **fine, favourable**

FOR FOOD THAT HAS **GONE BAD**
mouldy, rotten, off, decayed, sour, spoiled, rancid
The strawberries have started to go mouldy.
opposite **fresh**

TO **FEEL BAD** ABOUT SOMETHING
guilty, ashamed, sorry, remorseful, repentant
Scrooge feels repentant *by the end of the story.*
opposites **unashamed, unrepentant**

bad-tempered adjective
Trolls are always bad-tempered *before breakfast.*
cross, grumpy, irritable, moody, quarrelsome, fractious, ill-tempered, short-tempered, cantankerous, crotchety, snappy, testy, sullen
opposites **good-tempered, cheerful**

bag noun
I put my wet clothes in a plastic bag.
sack, carrier, holdall, satchel, handbag, shoulder bag
A bag you carry on your back is a backpack or rucksack.

baggage noun
We loaded our baggage *onto a trolley.*
luggage, bags, cases, suitcases, belongings, things
(informal) gear, stuff

baggy adjective
The clown wore a pair of baggy *trousers.*
loose, loose-fitting, roomy

beauty noun
The film star was famous for her beauty.
attractiveness, prettiness, loveliness,
charm, allure, magnificence, radiance,
splendour
opposite ugliness

beckon verb
*The guard was beckoning me to
approach.*
signal, gesture, motion, gesticulate

become verb becomes, becoming,
became, become
1 *I soon became frustrated with the video
game.*
begin to be, turn, get
2 *Eventually, the tadpoles will become
frogs.*
grow into, change into, develop into,
turn into
3 *That style of hat becomes you.*
look good on, suit, flatter

bed noun
1 *The children slept on hard, wooden
beds.*
bunk, mattress
A bed for a baby is a cot, cradle, or crib.
Two single beds one above the other are
bunk beds.
A bed on a ship or train is a berth.
A bed made of net or cloth hung up above
the ground is a hammock.
2 *We planted daffodils in the flower beds.*
plot, patch, border
3 *These creatures feed on the bed of the
ocean.*
bottom, floor
opposite surface

bedraggled adjective
*After its swim, the puppy was wet and
bedraggled.*
messy, scruffy, untidy, dishevelled, dirty,
wet
opposites smart, spruced up

bee noun

> **WORD WEB**
> SOME TYPES OF BEE
> bumblebee, drone, honeybee, worker,
> queen
>
> A young bee after it hatches is a larva.
> A group of bees is a swarm or a colony.
> A place where bees live is a hive.
>
> For other insects see insect

before adverb
1 *Have you used a camera before?*
previously, in the past, earlier, sooner
opposite later
2 *Those people were before us in the queue.*
in front of, ahead of, in advance of
opposite after

beg verb
He begged me not to let go of the rope.
ask, plead with, entreat, implore, beseech

begin verb begins, beginning, began,
begun
1 *The hunters began their search at dawn.*
start, commence, embark on, set about
opposites end, finish, conclude
2 *When did the trouble begin?*
start, commence, arise, emerge, appear,
originate, spring up
opposites end, stop, cease

beginner noun
This swimming class is for beginners.
learner, starter, novice
A beginner in a trade or a job is an
apprentice or trainee.
A beginner in the police or armed services is
a cadet or recruit.

a
b
c
d
e
f
g
h
i
j
k
l
m
n
o
p
q
r
s
t
u
v
w
x
y
z

A
B
C
D
E
F
G
H
I
J
K
L
M
N
O
P
Q
R
S
T
U
V
W
X
Y
Z

beginning noun
The house was built at the beginning of the last century.
start, opening, commencement, introduction, establishment, foundation, initiation, launch, dawn
The beginning of the day is **dawn** *or* **daybreak.**
The beginning of a journey is the **starting point.**
The beginning of a stream or river is the **origin** *or* **source.**
A piece of writing at the beginning of a book is an **introduction, preface,** *or* **prologue.**
A piece of music at the beginning of a musical or opera is a **prelude** *or* **overture.**
opposites end, conclusion

behave verb
Our neighbour is behaving very strangely.
act, react
to behave yourself
We promised to behave ourselves in the car.
be good, be on your best behaviour

behaviour noun
I give my puppy treats for good behaviour.
actions, conduct, manners, attitude

being noun
They looked like beings from another planet.
creature, individual, person, entity

belch verb
The chimney belched clouds of black smoke.
discharge, emit, send out, gush, spew

belief noun
1 *She has strong religious beliefs.*
faith, principle, creed, doctrine
2 *It is my belief that he stole the money.*
opinion, view, conviction, feeling, notion, theory

believable adjective
None of the characters in the book is believable.
credible, plausible
opposites unbelievable, implausible

believe verb
1 *I don't believe anything he says.*
accept, have faith in, rely on, trust
opposites disbelieve, doubt
2 *I believe they used to live in Canada.*
think, assume, feel, presume, reckon, suppose

bell noun

WRITING TIPS
You can use these words to describe how a bell sounds:
chime, clang, jangle, jingle, peal, ring, tinkle, toll
The front-door bell clanged loudly, and the Rat, who was very greasy with buttered toast, sent Billy, the smaller hedgehog, to see who it might be.
— Kenneth Grahame, *The Wind in the Willows*

belong verb
1 *This ring belonged to my grandmother.*
be owned by
2 *Do you belong to the sports club?*
be a member of, be connected with

belongings plural noun
Don't leave any belongings on the bus.
possessions, property, goods, things

below preposition
1 *We saw goldfish swimming below the surface.*
under, underneath, beneath
2 *The temperature never fell below 20 degrees.*
less than, lower than
opposite above

belt noun
1 *The prince wore a belt of pure gold.*
girdle, sash, strap, band
2 *We walked through a belt of woodland.*
strip, band, line, stretch

bench noun
We sat on a bench in the park.
seat, form
A long seat in a church is a **pew**.
For other types of seat see **seat**

bend verb
This drinking straw bends in the middle.
curve, turn, twist, curl, coil, loop, arch, warp, wind
A word to describe things which bend easily is **flexible** or (informal) **bendy**.
opposite **straighten**
to bend down
I bent down to tie my shoelaces.
stoop, bow (rhymes with **cow**), crouch, duck, kneel

bend noun
Watch out for the sharp bend in the road.
curve, turn, angle, corner, twist, zigzag

beneath preposition
The tunnel ran beneath the castle.
under, underneath, below
opposites **above, over**

beneficial adjective
Drinking water is beneficial to your health.
favourable, useful, advantageous, salutary
opposites **harmful, detrimental**

benefit noun
What are the benefits of regular exercise?
advantage, reward, gain, good point
opposites **disadvantage, drawback**

benefit verb
The rainy weather will benefit gardeners.
help, aid, assist, be good for, profit
opposites **hinder, harm**

benevolent adjective
The lady greeted us with a benevolent smile.
friendly, kind, warm-hearted, sympathetic, generous, charitable, benign
opposite **malevolent**

bent adjective
1 *After the crash, the car was a mass of bent metal.*
curved, twisted, coiled, looped, buckled, crooked, arched, folded, warped
(informal) **wonky**
2 *The witch had a bent back and walked with a stick.*
crooked, hunched, curved, arched, bowed (rhymes with **loud**)
opposite **straight**

beside preposition
You can sit beside me if you like.
next to, alongside, by, close to, near
beside the point
The fact that you're ill is beside the point.
irrelevant, neither here nor there, unimportant

besides adverb
1 *No-one knows the secret, besides you and me.*
as well as, in addition to, apart from, other than
2 *It's too cold to go out. Besides, it's dark now.*
also, in addition, additionally, furthermore, moreover

besiege verb
1 *The Greeks besieged Troy for 10 long years.*
blockade, cut off, isolate
2 *The film star was besieged by reporters.*
surround, mob, plague, harass

best adjective
1 *She is our best goalkeeper.*
top, leading, finest, foremost, supreme, star, outstanding, unequalled, unrivalled
opposite **worst**
2 *We did what we thought was best.*
most suitable, most appropriate

bet noun
I had a bet that our team would win.
gamble, wager
(informal) **flutter**

bet verb bets, betting, bet or betted
1 *I bet you 50 pence that it will snow tomorrow.*
gamble, wager, stake, risk

a
b
c
d
e
f
g
h
i
j
k
l
m
n
o
p
q
r
s
t
u
v
w
x
y
z

A

B

C

D

E

F

G

H

I

J

K

L

M

N

O

P

Q

R

S

T

U

V

W

X

Y

Z

2 *I bet my brother forgets my birthday.*
feel sure, be certain, expect

betray verb
1 *He betrayed us by telling the enemy our plan.*
be disloyal to, be a traitor to, cheat, conspire against, double-cross
Someone who betrays you is a **traitor**.
To betray your country is to commit **treason**.
2 *The look in her eyes betrayed her true feelings.*
reveal, show, indicate, disclose, divulge, expose, tell

better adjective
1 *Which of these songs do you think is better?*
superior, finer, preferable
2 *I had a cold, but I'm better now.*
recovered, cured, healed, improved, well

between preposition
Let's divide the chocolate between us.
among, amongst

beware verb
Beware! There are thieves about.
be careful, watch out, look out, take care, be on your guard
beware of
Beware of the bull.
watch out for, avoid, mind, heed, keep clear of

bewilder verb
We were bewildered by the directions on the map.
confuse, puzzle, baffle, bemuse, mystify, perplex, fox
(informal) flummox

beyond preposition
The village lies just beyond those hills.
after, past, the other side of

biased adjective
A referee should not make a biased decision.

prejudiced, partial, one-sided, partisan, unfair
opposite **impartial**

bicycle noun
push bike
(informal) bike
A person who rides a bicycle is a **cyclist**.

WORD WEB
SOME TYPES OF BICYCLE
mountain bike, racing bike, reclining or **recumbent bike, road bike, tandem, trailer bike**

A cycle with one wheel is a **unicycle**.
A cycle with three wheels is a **tricycle** or (informal) **trike**.
A cycle without pedals is a **scooter**.
A type of bicycle used in the past was a **penny-farthing**.

THE MAIN PARTS OF A BICYCLE ARE
brakes, brake lever, chain, crossbar, gear shift, handlebars, pedals, saddle

bid noun
1 *There were several bids for the painting at the auction.*
offer, price, tender
2 *His bid to beat the world record failed.*
attempt, effort, try, go

big adjective
The giant owned three pairs of big boots.
large, huge, great, massive, enormous, gigantic, colossal, mammoth
(informal) whopping, ginormous, humongous
opposites **small, little, tiny**

big adjective

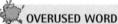 OVERUSED WORD
Try to vary the words you use for **big**.
Here are some other words you could use.

FOR A **BIG PERSON** OR **BIG CREATURE**
burly, giant, hefty, hulking, mighty,
monstrous, towering
The **mighty** *robot clanked as it moved.*

FOR A **BIG OBJECT**
bulky, heavy, hefty, weighty
What could be inside that **bulky** *envelope?*

FOR A **BIG ROOM** OR **BIG BOX**
roomy, sizeable, spacious
Inside, the spaceship was surprisingly
roomy.
opposite cramped

FOR A **BIG DISTANCE**
immense, infinite, vast
A **vast** *stretch of ocean lay before them.*

FOR A **BIG AMOUNT** OR **BIG HELPING**
ample, considerable, substantial
We each got an **ample** *helping of porridge.*
opposites meagre, paltry

FOR A **BIG DECISION** OR **BIG MOMENT**
grave, important, serious, significant
Yesterday was the most **significant** *day in*
my short life.
opposites unimportant, minor

bill noun
My granny offered to pay the **bill.**
account, invoice, statement, charges

billow verb
1 *Smoke* **billowed** *from the mouth of the*
cave.
pour, swirl, spiral
2 *The sheets on the washing line* **billowed**
in the wind.
swell, bulge, puff, balloon

bind verb binds, binding, bound
We **bound** *the sticks together with some rope.*
attach, fasten, tie, secure, join, connect,
lash, rope

bird noun
A female bird is a **hen.**
A male bird is a **cock.**

A young bird is a **chick, fledgling,** or
nestling.
A family of chicks is a **brood.**
A group of birds is a **colony** or **flock.**
A group of flying birds is a **flight** or **skein.**
A person who studies birds is an
ornithologist.

 WORD WEB

SOME COMMON BRITISH BIRDS
**blackbird, blue tit, bullfinch, bunting,
chaffinch, crow, cuckoo, dove,
greenfinch, jackdaw, jay, linnet,
magpie, martin, nightingale, pigeon,
raven, robin, rook, skylark, sparrow,
starling, swallow, swift, thrush, tit,
wagtail, waxwing, woodpecker, wren,
yellowhammer**

BIRDS OF PREY
**buzzard, eagle, falcon, hawk, kestrel,
kite, merlin, osprey, owl, sparrowhawk,
vulture**

FARM AND GAME BIRDS
**chicken, duck, goose, grouse, partridge,
pheasant, quail, turkey**

Birds kept by farmers are called **poultry.**

SEA AND WATER BIRDS
**albatross, auk, bittern, coot, cormorant,
crane, curlew, duck, gannet, goose,
guillemot, gull, heron, kingfisher,
kittiwake, lapwing, mallard, moorhen,
oystercatcher, peewit, pelican, penguin,
puffin, seagull, snipe, stork, swan, teal**

BIRDS FROM OTHER COUNTRIES
**bird of paradise, budgerigar, canary,
cockatoo, flamingo, humming bird,
ibis, kookaburra, macaw, mynah bird,
parakeet, parrot, toucan**

BIRDS WHICH CANNOT FLY
emu, kiwi, ostrich, peacock, penguin

PARTS OF A BIRD'S BODY
**beak, bill; claw, talon; breast, crown,
throat; crest, feather, down, plumage,
plume, wing**

See also **feather**

a
b
c
d
e
f
g
h
i
j
k
l
m
n
o
p
q
r
s
t
u
v
w
x
y
z

A
B
C
D
E
F
G
H
I
J
K
L
M
N
O
P
Q
R
S
T
U
V
W
X
Y
Z

SOME TYPES OF BIRD HOME
nest, nesting box; aviary, coop, roost

SOUNDS MADE BY BIRDS
cackle, caw, cheep, chirp, chirrup, cluck, coo, crow, gabble, honk, peep, pipe, quack, screech, squawk, trill, tweet, twitter, warble

A turkey **gobbles.**
An owl **hoots.**

SPECIAL NAMES
A female peacock is a **peahen.**
A young duck is a **duckling.**
A young goose is a **gosling.**
A young swan is a **cygnet.**
An eagle's nest is an **eyrie.**
A place where rooks nest is a **rookery.**

For groups of birds see **group**

WRITING TIPS
You can use these words to describe a bird

TO DESCRIBE HOW A BIRD MOVES
circle, dart, flit, flutter, fly, glide, hop, hover, peck, perch, preen, skim, soar, swoop, waddle, wheel

The post owls arrived, swooping down through rain-flecked windows, scattering everyone with droplets of water.
— J. K. Rowling, Harry Potter and the Half-Blood Prince

TO DESCRIBE A BIRD'S FEATHERS
bedraggled, downy, drab, fluffy, gleaming, iridescent, ruffled, smooth, speckled
The peacock displayed its iridescent tail.

bit noun
1 *Mum divided the cake into eight bits.*
piece, portion, part, section, segment, share, slice
2 *These jeans are a bit long for me.*
a little, slightly, rather, fairly, somewhat, quite

OVERUSED WORD
Try to vary the words you use for **bit.**
Here are some other words you could use.

FOR A **LARGE BIT** OF SOMETHING
chunk, lump, hunk, wedge, slab
Chunks of rock came tumbling down the mountain.

FOR A **SMALL BIT** OF SOMETHING
fragment, scrap, chip, particle, speck, pinch, touch, dab, atom, iota
(informal) **smidgen**
The map was drawn on a scrap of old paper.

FOR A **BIT** OF FOOD
morsel, crumb, bite, nibble, taste, mouthful
Please try a morsel of chocolate mousse.

FOR A **BIT** OF LIQUID
drop, dash, dribble, splash, spot
Add a splash of vinegar to the sauce.

bite verb bites, biting, bit, bitten
1 *I bit a chunk out of my apple.*
munch, nibble, chew, crunch, gnaw
(informal) **chomp**
For other ways to eat see **eat**
2 *Take care. These animals can bite.*
nip, pinch, pierce, wound
When an animal tries to bite you it **snaps** at you.
When an insect bites you it **stings** you.
A fierce animal **mauls** or **savages** its prey.

bitter adjective
1 *The medicine had a bitter taste.*
sour, sharp, acid, acrid, tart
opposite **sweet**
2 *His brother was still bitter about the quarrel.*
resentful, embittered, disgruntled, aggrieved
opposite **contented**
3 *The wind blowing in from the sea was bitter.*
biting, cold, freezing, icy, piercing,

raw, wintry
(informal) **perishing**
opposite mild

bizarre adjective
'Whiskers' is a bizarre name for a goldfish!
odd, strange, peculiar, weird, extraordinary, outlandish
opposite ordinary

black adjective & noun
The pony had a shiny black coat.
coal-black, jet-black, pitch-black, ebony, raven
You can also describe a black night as **pitch-dark.**
Someone in a bad mood is said to look as **black as thunder.**
Common similes are as **black as coal** and as **black as night.**

blame verb
Don't blame me if you miss the bus.
accuse, criticize, condemn, reproach, scold

bland adjective
This cheese has a really bland taste.
mild, dull, weak, insipid
opposites strong, pungent

blank adjective
1 *There are no blank pages left in my jotter.*
empty, bare, clean, plain, unmarked, unused
2 *The old woman gave us a blank look.*
expressionless, faceless, vacant

blank noun
Fill in the blanks to complete the sentence.
space, break, gap

blanket noun
1 *The baby was wrapped in a woollen blanket.*
cover, sheet, quilt, rug, throw
2 *A blanket of snow covered the lawn.*
covering, layer, film, sheet, mantle

blast noun
1 *A blast of cold air came through the door.*
gust, rush, draught, burst

2 *They heard the blast of a trumpet.*
blare, noise, roar
3 *Many people were injured in the blast.*
explosion, shock

blatant adjective
Do you expect me to believe such a blatant lie?
barefaced, flagrant, obvious, shameless, brazen, unabashed

blaze noun
Firefighters fought the blaze for hours.
fire, flames, inferno

blaze verb
Within a few minutes the campfire was blazing.
burn brightly, flare up

bleak adjective
1 *The countryside was bleak and barren.*
bare, barren, desolate, empty, exposed, stark
2 *The future looks bleak for the club.*
gloomy, hopeless, depressing, dismal, grim, miserable
opposite promising

blemish noun
This peach has a blemish on the skin.
fault, flaw, defect, imperfection, mark, spot, stain

blend verb
1 *Blend the flour with a tablespoon of water.*
beat together, mix, stir together, whip, whisk
2 *The paint colours blend well with each other.*
go together, match, fit, harmonize
opposite clash

blessing noun
1 *The author gave the film her blessing.*
approval, backing, support, consent, permission
opposite disapproval

a
b
c
d
e
f
g
h
i
j
k
l
m
n
o
p
q
r
s
t
u
v
w
x
y
z

A

B

C

D

E

F

G

H

I

J

K

L

M

N

O

P

Q

R

S

T

U

V

W

X

Y

Z

2 *A warm hat is a blessing in cold weather.*
benefit, advantage, gift, asset, comfort
opposites **curse, evil**

blew
past tense see blow

blight noun
The tower block is a blight on the landscape.
menace, nuisance, affliction, curse, evil, plague

blind adjective
Polar bear cubs are born blind.
sightless, unsighted, unseeing
A common simile is as blind as a bat.
opposites **sighted, seeing**
blind to
The captain was blind to his own faults.
ignorant of, unaware of, oblivious to
opposite **aware of**

bliss noun
Having a whole day off school was sheer bliss.
joy, delight, pleasure, happiness, heaven, ecstasy
opposite **misery**

blob noun
The alien left blobs of green slime on the carpet.
drop, lump, spot, dollop, daub, globule

block noun
1 *A block of ice fell from the glacier.*
chunk, hunk, lump, piece
2 *There must be a block in the drainpipe.*
blockage, jam, obstacle, obstruction

block verb
1 *A tall hedge blocked our view of the house.*
obstruct, hamper, hinder, interfere with
2 *A mass of leaves had blocked the drain.*
clog, choke, jam, plug, stop up, congest
(informal) bung up

blockage noun
Dad spent ages clearing the blockage in the drain.
block, obstacle, obstruction, jam

bloodshed noun
In ancient times, this was a scene of bloodshed.
killing, massacre, slaughter, butchery, carnage

bloodthirsty adjective
The bloodthirsty pirates rattled their swords.
brutal, cruel, barbaric, murderous, inhuman, pitiless, ruthless, savage, vicious

bloom noun
The pear tree was covered in white blooms.
flower, blossom, bud

bloom verb
The daffodils bloomed early this year.
blossom, flower, open
opposite **fade**

blossom noun

> **Blossom** usually refers to a mass of flowers rather than a single flower.

I love to see the cherry blossom in spring.
blooms, buds, flowers

blot noun
The old map was covered with ink blots.
spot, blotch, mark, blob, splodge, smudge, smear, stain

blot verb
to blot something out
The new tower block blots out the view.
conceal, hide, mask, obliterate, obscure

blotch noun
The dragon had green skin with purple blotches.
patch, blot, spot, mark, blob, splodge, splash, stain

blow noun
1 *He was knocked out by a blow on the head.*
knock, bang, bash, hit, punch, clout, slap, smack, swipe, thump
(informal) wallop, whack

2 *Losing the hockey match was a terrible blow.*

shock, upset, setback, disappointment, catastrophe, misfortune, disaster, calamity

blow verb blows, blowing, blew, blown
The wind was blowing from the east.

blast, gust, puff, fan

To make a shrill sound by blowing is to whistle.

to blow out
I blew out the candles on my birthday cake.

extinguish

to blow up
1 *I need to blow up the tyres on my bike.*

inflate, pump up, swell, fill out

2 *The soldiers tried to blow up the enemy hideout.*

blast, bomb, destroy

3 *Do you think they could blow up this photograph?*

enlarge

blue adjective & noun

> **WORD WEB**
>
> SOME SHADES OF BLUE
>
> azure, cobalt, indigo, navy blue, sapphire, sky-blue, turquoise

blunder noun
Forgetting her birthday was a terrible blunder.

mistake, error, fault, slip, slip-up, gaffe
(informal) howler

blunt adjective
1 *This pencil is blunt.*

dull, worn, unsharpened
opposites sharp, pointed

2 *Her reply to my question was very blunt.*

abrupt, frank, direct, outspoken, plain, tactless
opposite tactful

blur verb
1 *The steamy windows blurred the view.*

cloud, darken, obscure, smear

2 *The accident blurred her memory.*

confuse, muddle

blurred adjective
The background of the photograph is all blurred.

indistinct, vague, blurry, fuzzy, hazy, out of focus
opposites clear, distinct

blush verb
The actor blushed with embarrassment.

flush, go red, colour

blustery adjective
It was a typical, blustery day in autumn.

gusty, windy, blowy, squally
opposite calm

board noun
The table top was made from a wooden board.

plank, panel, beam, timber

board verb
We boarded the plane for New York.

get on, enter, embark

boast verb
The knight was always boasting about his fencing skills.

brag, show off, crow, gloat, swagger
(informal) blow your own trumpet

boastful adjective
Giants are boastful creatures and brag about everything.

arrogant, big-headed, conceited, vain, bumptious
(informal) cocky, swanky
opposites modest, humble

boat noun
Several fishing boats were moored in the harbour.

ship, craft, vessel

> **WORD WEB**
>
> SOME TYPES OF BOAT OR SHIP
>
> barge, canoe, catamaran, cruise liner, dhow, dinghy, dugout, ferry, freighter, gondola, hovercraft, hydrofoil, junk, kayak, launch, lifeboat, motor boat,

A
B
C
D
E
F
G
H
I
J
K
L
M
N
O
P
Q
R
S
T
U
V
W
X
Y
Z

oil tanker, punt, raft, rowing boat, schooner, skiff, speedboat, steamship, tanker, trawler, tug, yacht

MILITARY BOATS OR SHIPS
aircraft carrier, battleship, destroyer, frigate, gunboat, minesweeper, submarine, warship

SOME BOATS USED IN THE PAST
brigantine, clipper, coracle, cutter, galleon, galley, man-of-war, paddle steamer, schooner, trireme, windjammer

WORDS FOR PARTS OF A BOAT OR SHIP
boom, bridge, bulwark, cabin, crow's nest, deck, engine room, fo'c's'le or forecastle, funnel, galley, helm, hull, keel, mast, poop, porthole, propeller, quarterdeck, rigging, rudder, sail, tiller

SPECIAL NAMES
The front part of a boat is the bow or prow.
The back part of a boat is the stern.
The left-hand side of a boat is called port.
The right-hand side of a boat is called starboard.
A shed where boats are stored is a boathouse.

 WRITING TIPS
You can use these words to describe how a boat moves

cut through the waves or water, drift, float, glide, lurch, pitch, roll, sail, steam, tack
The tiny raft pitched from side to side in the storm.

bob verb
A plastic duck bobbed up and down in the water.
bounce, dance, toss, wobble

body noun
The study of the human body is anatomy.
The main part of your body except your head, arms, and legs is your trunk or torso.
The shape of your body is your build, figure, or physique.
The dead body of a person is a corpse.
The dead body of an animal is a carcass.

 WORD WEB

OUTER PARTS OF THE HUMAN BODY
abdomen, ankle, arm, armpit, breast, buttocks, calf, cheek, chest, chin, ear, elbow, eye, finger, foot, forehead, genitals, groin, hand, head, heel, hip, instep, jaw, knee, kneecap, knuckle, leg, lip, mouth, navel, neck, nipple, nose, pores, shin, shoulder, skin, stomach, temple, thigh, throat, waist, wrist

INNER PARTS OF THE HUMAN BODY
arteries, bladder, bowels, brain, eardrum, glands, gullet, gums, guts, heart, intestines, kidneys, larynx, liver, lung, muscles, nerves, ovaries, pancreas, prostate, sinews, stomach, tendons, tongue, tonsil, tooth, uterus, veins, windpipe, womb

For bones in your body see bone

For parts of animal bodies see animal

WRITING TIPS
You can use these words to describe a person's body

athletic, beefy, brawny, burly, hefty, hulking, muscular, sinewy, squat, stocky, stout; fat, flabby, plump, rotund, well-rounded; lean, petite, short, slight, slender, svelte, thin; bony, gangly, gaunt, lanky, puny, scraggy, scrawny, skinny, spindly, tall, wiry
Hiccup was just absolutely average, the kind of unremarkable, skinny, freckled boy who was easy to overlook in a crowd.
— Cressida Cowell, *How to be a Pirate*

See also thin

bog noun
We felt our boots sinking into the bog.
swamp, quagmire, quicksand, fen

boil verb
1 *Would you like your egg* boiled *or fried?*
For ways to cook food see **cook**
2 *The water must be* boiling *before you add the pasta.*
bubble, seethe, steam

bold adjective
1 *It was a* bold *move to attack the fortress.*
brave, courageous, daring, adventurous, audacious, confident, enterprising, fearless, heroic, valiant, intrepid, plucky
opposite cowardly
2 *The poster uses large letters in* bold *colours.*
striking, strong, bright, loud, showy, conspicuous, eye-catching, noticeable, prominent
opposites inconspicuous, subtle

bolt verb
1 *Did you remember to* bolt *the door?*
fasten, latch, lock, secure, bar
2 *The horses* bolted *when they heard the thunder.*
dash away, dart, flee, sprint, run away, rush off
3 *Don't* bolt *your food.*
gobble, gulp, guzzle, wolf down
For other ways to eat see **eat**

bond noun
1 *The prisoner tried to escape from his* bonds.
chains, fetters, ropes, handcuffs, manacles, shackles, restraints
2 *There was a special* bond *between the twins.*
attachment, connection, tie, link, relationship

bone noun
The bones of your body are your **skeleton**.

WORD WEB

SOME BONES IN THE HUMAN BODY
backbone or **spine, collarbone,**
cranium or skull, pelvis, ribs, shoulder blade, vertebrae

bonus noun
I got a bonus *on top of my pocket money last week.*
extra, supplement, reward, tip, handout

book noun
A book with hard covers is a **hardback**.
A book with soft covers is a **paperback**.
A book which is typed or handwritten but not printed is a **manuscript**.
A thin book in paper covers is a **booklet, leaflet,** or **pamphlet**.
A book which is part of a set is a **volume**.
A large, heavy book is a **tome**.
The person who writes a book is the **author**.
A book which sells a lot of copies is a **bestseller**.

WORD WEB

SOME TYPES OF BOOK
album, annual, anthology, atlas, audiobook, dictionary, directory, e-book, encyclopedia, graphic novel, guidebook, manual, novel, picture book, reading book, reference book, story book, textbook, thesaurus

BOOKS YOU CAN WRITE OR DRAW IN
diary, exercise book, jotter, notebook, scrapbook, sketchbook

SOME PARTS OF A BOOK
appendix, bibliography, blurb, chapters, contents page, cover, foreword, illustrations, index, introduction, preface, prologue, title page

For ways to describe a book or story see **writing**

book verb
1 *Have you* booked *a seat on the train?*
order, reserve
2 *I've* booked *the disco for the party.*
arrange, engage, organize

A
B
C
D
E
F
G
H
I
J
K
L
M
N
O
P
Q
R
S
T
U
V
W
X
Y
Z

boom verb
1 *Miss Barker's voice* boomed *along the corridor.*
shout, roar, bellow, blast, thunder, resound, reverberate
2 *Business was* booming *in the Riverbank Cafe.*
be successful, do well, expand, flourish, grow, prosper, thrive

boost verb
Winning the cup really boosted *the team's morale.*
raise, uplift, improve, increase, bolster, help, encourage, enhance
opposites **lower, dampen**

boot noun
For types of shoe or boot see **shoe**

border noun
1 *The town is on the* border *between France and Germany.*
boundary, frontier
2 *I drew a thin line around the* border *of the picture.*
edge, margin, perimeter
A decorative border round the top of a wall is a **frieze**.
A border round the bottom of a skirt is a **hem**.
A decorative border on fabric is a **frill**, **fringe**, or **trimming**.

bore¹ verb
They bored *a hole right through the outer wall.*
drill, pierce, sink, tunnel

bore²
past tense see **bear¹**

boring adjective
The film was so boring *I fell asleep.*
dull, dreary, tedious, tiresome, unexciting, uninteresting, dry, monotonous, uninspiring, insipid, unimaginative, uneventful, humdrum
opposites **interesting, exciting**

borrow verb
Can I borrow *your pencil?*
use, take, obtain, acquire, cadge
(informal) scrounge
opposite **lend**

boss noun
There is a new boss *at the football club.*
head, chief, manager, leader, director
(informal) gaffer

bossy adjective
Stop being so bossy *towards your sister.*
domineering, bullying, dictatorial, officious, tyrannical
An informal name for a bossy person is **bossy boots**.

bother verb
1 *Would it* bother *you if I played some music?*
disturb, trouble, upset, annoy, irritate, pester, worry, vex, exasperate
(informal) bug, hassle
2 *Don't* bother *to phone tonight.*
make an effort, take the trouble, concern yourself, care, mind

bother noun
It's such a bother *to remember the password.*
nuisance, annoyance, irritation, problem, inconvenience, pest, trouble, difficulty,
(informal) hassle

bottle noun
Bring a bottle *of water with you.*
flask, flagon, jar, pitcher
A bottle for serving water or wine is a **carafe** or **decanter**.
A small bottle for perfume or medicine is a **phial**.

bottle verb
to bottle something up
It's not healthy to bottle up *your anger.*
hold in, cover up, conceal, suppress
opposites **show, express**

bottom noun
1 *We camped at the* bottom *of the mountain.*
foot, base
opposites **top, peak**

2 *The wreck sank to the* **bottom** *of the sea.*
bed, floor
opposite **surface**
3 *A wasp stung me on the* **bottom**.
backside, behind, buttocks, rear, rump, seat
(informal) **bum**

bottom adjective
I got the **bottom** *mark in the maths test.*
least, lowest
opposite **top**

bough noun
The robin perched on a **bough** *of the tree.*
branch, limb

bought
past tense see **buy**

bounce verb
The ball **bounced** *twice before it reached the net.*
rebound, ricochet, spring, leap

bound¹
past tense see **bind**

bound² adjective
1 *It's* **bound** *to rain at the weekend.*
certain, sure
2 *I felt* **bound** *to invite my cousin to the party.*
obliged, duty-bound, committed, compelled, forced, required
3 *The accident was* **bound** *to happen.*
destined, doomed, fated
bound for
The space rocket was **bound for** *Jupiter.*
going to, heading for, making for, travelling towards, off to

bound³ verb
The puppies **bounded** *across the lawn.*
leap, bounce, jump, spring, skip, gambol, caper, frisk

boundary noun
The lamp post marks the **boundary** *of Narnia.*
border, frontier, edge, end, limit, perimeter, dividing line

bout noun
1 *She's recovering from a* **bout** *of flu.*
attack, fit, period, spell
(informal) **turn**
2 *A judo* **bout** *is between two contestants.*
contest, match, round, fight, battle, combat

bow¹ noun (rhymes with **go**)
The archer raised his **bow** *and arrow.*
For words to do with archery see **arrow**

bow² noun (rhymes with **cow**)
The captain stood at the **bow** *of the ship.*
front, prow
For other parts of a boat or ship see **boat**

bow³ verb (rhymes with **cow**)
1 *The prisoner* **bowed** *his head in shame.*
lower, bend, duck
2 *The knight knelt and* **bowed** *in front of the king.*
The corresponding movement of a woman is to **curtsy**.

bowl¹ noun
There was a **bowl** *of fresh fruit on the table.*
basin, dish, vessel
A large bowl for serving soup is a **tureen**.

bowl² verb
Can you **bowl** *a faster ball next time?*
throw, pitch, fling, hurl, toss
For other ways to throw a ball see **ball**

box noun
case, chest, crate, carton, packet
A small box for jewellery or treasure is a **casket**.
A large box for luggage is a **trunk**.

boy noun
lad, youngster, youth
(informal) **kid**

a
b
c
d
e
f
g
h
i
j
k
l
m
n
o
p
q
r
s
t
u
v
w
x
y
z

A
B
C
D
E
F
G
H
I
J
K
L
M
N
O
P
Q
R
S
T
U
V
W
X
Y
Z

brag verb
Flo is still bragging about her swimming medal.
show off, boast, gloat, crow
(informal) blow your own trumpet
A person who is always bragging is a
braggart.

brain noun
You'll need to use your brain to solve this riddle.
intelligence, intellect, mind, reason, sense, wit

branch noun
1 *A robin perched on a branch of the tree.*
bough, limb
2 *I've joined the local branch of the Kennel Club.*
section, division, department, wing

branch verb
Follow the track until it branches into two.
divide, fork

brand noun
Which brand of ice-cream do you like?
make, kind, sort, type, variety, label
The sign of a particular brand of goods is a
trademark.

brandish verb
Captain Hook brandished his cutlass at the crew.
flourish, wield, flaunt, wave

brave adjective
It was brave of you to save the cat from drowning.
courageous, heroic, valiant, fearless,
daring, gallant, intrepid, plucky
A common simile is as brave as a lion.
opposite cowardly

bravery noun
The police dog was awarded a medal for bravery.
courage, heroism, valour, fearlessness,
daring, nerve, gallantry, grit, pluck

(informal) guts, bottle
opposite cowardice

brawl noun
We could hear a brawl on the street outside.
fight, quarrel, scuffle, tussle
(informal) scrap

breach noun
1 *Handling the ball is a breach of the rules.*
breaking, violation
You can also talk about an offence against
the rules.
2 *The storm caused a breach in the sea wall.*
break, split, crack, gap, hole, opening,
fracture, rupture, fissure

break noun
1 *Can you see any breaks in the chain?*
breach, crack, hole, gap, opening, split, rift,
puncture, rupture, fracture, fissure
2 *Let's take a break for coffee.*
interval, pause, rest, lull, time-out
(informal) breather

break verb breaks, breaking, broke, broken
1 *The vase fell off the shelf and broke.*
smash, shatter, fracture, chip, crack, split,
snap, splinter
(informal) bust
2 *The burglar was breaking the law.*
disobey, disregard, violate, flout
3 *In her last race, she broke the world record.*
beat, better, exceed, surpass, outdo
to break down
Our car broke down on the motorway.
fail, go wrong, stop working
(informal) pack in, conk out
to break off
We'll break off for lunch at one o'clock.
have a rest, pause, stop
to break out
A flu epidemic broke out just after Christmas.
begin, spread, start
to break out of
The prisoner tried to break out of jail.
escape from, break loose from,
abscond from

to break up
After the speeches, the crowd broke up.
disperse, scatter, separate, split up, disintegrate

breakable adjective
Be careful! The parcel has breakable things in it.
fragile, delicate, brittle, frail
opposite unbreakable

breakdown noun
1 *There has been a breakdown in the peace talks.*
failure, collapse, fault
2 *Can you give me a breakdown of the figures?*
analysis

break-in noun
There was a break-in at the local bank.
burglary, robbery, theft, raid

breakthrough noun
Scientists have made a breakthrough in medicine.
advance, leap forward, discovery, development, revolution, progress
opposite setback

breath noun
There wasn't a breath of wind in the air.
breeze, puff, waft, whiff, whisper, sigh

breathe verb
To breathe in is to inhale.
To breathe out is to exhale.
To breathe heavily when you have been running is to pant or puff.
The formal word for breathing is respiration.

breathless adjective
Leo was breathless after the race.
out of breath, gasping, panting, puffing, tired out, wheezing

breed verb
1 *Salmon swim upstream to breed every year.*
reproduce, have young, multiply, procreate, spawn

2 *Bad hygiene breeds disease.*
cause, produce, generate, encourage, promote, cultivate, induce

breed noun
What breed of dog is that?
kind, sort, type, variety
The evidence of how a dog has been bred is its pedigree.

breezy adjective
Today the weather was bright and breezy.
windy, blowy, blustery, gusty, fresh, draughty
See also weather

brew verb
1 *I'm just going to brew some tea.*
make, prepare
When you brew beer it ferments.
2 *It looks like a storm is brewing.*
develop, form, loom, build up, gather, threaten

brew noun
The wizard stirred an evil-smelling brew.
mixture, concoction

bridge noun
A bridge you can walk over is a footbridge.
A bridge to carry water is an aqueduct.
A long bridge carrying a road or railway is a viaduct.

brief adjective
1 *We paid a brief visit to our cousins on the way home.*
short, quick, hasty, fleeting, temporary
2 *Give me a brief account of what happened.*
short, concise, abbreviated, condensed, compact, succinct
opposites long, lengthy

bright adjective
1 *We saw the bright lights of the town in the distance.*
shining, brilliant, blazing, dazzling, glaring, gleaming
opposites dull, dim, weak

a
b
c
d
e
f
g
h
i
j
k
l
m
n
o
p
q
r
s
t
u
v
w
x
y
z

A
B
C
D
E
F
G
H
I
J
K
L
M
N
O
P
Q
R
S
T
U
V
W
X
Y
Z

2 *Bright colours will make the poster stand out.*
strong, intense, vivid
Colours that shine in the dark are luminous colours.
opposites **dull, faded, muted**
3 *Her teachers thought she was very* bright.
clever, intelligent, gifted, sharp, quick-witted
(informal) brainy
A common simile is as bright as a button.
opposites **stupid, dull-witted**
4 *Miranda gave me a* bright *smile.*
cheerful, happy, lively, merry, jolly, radiant
opposites **sad, gloomy**
5 *The day was cold, but* bright.
sunny, fine, fair, clear, cloudless
opposites **dull, cloudy, overcast**

brighten verb
It was a cloudy morning, but it brightened *after lunch.*
become sunny, clear up, improve
to brighten up
A new coat of paint will brighten up *the room.*
cheer up, light up, enliven

brilliant adjective
1 *The fireworks gave off a* brilliant *light.*
bright, blazing, dazzling, glaring, gleaming, glittering, glorious, shining, splendid, vivid
opposites **dim, dull**
2 *Brunel was a* brilliant *engineer.*
clever, exceptional, outstanding, gifted, talented
opposites **incompetent, talentless**
3 (informal) *I saw a* brilliant *film last week.*
excellent, marvellous, outstanding, wonderful, superb
(informal) fantastic, fabulous
See also **good**

brim noun
I filled my glass to the brim.
top, rim, edge, brink, lip

bring verb brings, bringing, brought
1 *Can you* bring *the shopping in from the car?*
carry, fetch, deliver, bear, transport
2 *You can* bring *a friend to the party.*
invite, conduct, escort, guide, lead
3 *The war has* brought *great sorrow to our people.*
cause, produce, lead to, result in, generate
to bring something about
The new coach brought about *some changes.*
cause, effect, create, introduce, be responsible for
to bring someone up
In the story, Tarzan is brought up *by apes.*
rear, raise, care for, foster, look after, nurture, educate, train
to bring something up
I wish you hadn't brought up *the subject of money.*
mention, talk about, raise, broach

brink noun
We stood on the brink *of a deep crater.*
edge, lip, rim, verge, brim

brisk adjective
1 *Mr Hastie went for a* brisk *walk every evening.*
lively, fast-paced, energetic, invigorating, vigorous, refreshing, bracing
opposites **slow, leisurely**
2 *The flower shop does a* brisk *trade around Easter.*
busy, lively, bustling, hectic
opposites **quiet, slack, slow**

brittle adjective
The bones of the skeleton were dry and brittle.
breakable, fragile, delicate, frail
opposites **soft, flexible**

broad adjective
1 *The streets in the city were* broad *and straight.*
wide, open, large, roomy, spacious, vast, extensive
opposite **narrow**

2 *Give me a* **broad** *outline of what happened.*
general, rough, vague, loose, indefinite, imprecise
opposites specific, detailed

broaden verb
I'm **broadening** *my interests by listening to jazz.*
widen, extend, enlarge, expand, increase, develop, diversify

brochure noun
We got some holiday **brochures** *from the travel agent.*
leaflet, pamphlet, booklet, catalogue

broke
past tense see **break**

broken adjective
1 *Don't use that computer—it's* **broken.**
faulty, defective, damaged, out of order
opposite working
2 *After losing all his money, Forbes was a* **broken** *man.*
crushed, defeated, beaten, spiritless

brood verb
1 *The hen was* **brooding** *her clutch of eggs.*
hatch, incubate, sit on
2 *He was still* **brooding** *over what I had said.*
fret, mope, worry, dwell on

brought
past tense see **bring**

brown adjective & noun

WORD WEB
SOME SHADES OF BROWN
beige, bronze, buff, chestnut, chocolate, dun, fawn, khaki, russet, sepia, tan, tawny

browse verb
1 *I like* **browsing** *through toy catalogues.*
flick through, leaf through, scan, skim
2 *The cattle were* **browsing** *in the meadow.*
graze, feed

bruise verb
I fell and **bruised** *my knee.*
mark, hurt, injure
For others types of injury see **injury**

brush verb
1 *Jill spent ages* **brushing** *her hair for the party.*
groom, comb, tidy
2 *A bird* **brushed** *against my cheek as it flew past.*
touch, contact, rub, scrape
to brush up
I must **brush up** *my French before we go to Paris.*
revise, improve, go over,
refresh your memory of
(informal) swot up

brutal adjective
The bandits launched a **brutal** *attack.*
savage, vicious, cruel, barbaric, bloodthirsty, callous, ferocious, inhuman, merciless, pitiless, ruthless, sadistic
opposites gentle, humane

bubble noun
The bubbles in a fizzy drink are **effervescence.**
The bubbles made by soap or detergent are **lather** or **suds.**
Bubbles on top of a liquid are **foam** or **froth.**
The bubbles on top of beer are the **head.**

bubble verb
A green liquid **bubbled** *in the witch's cauldron.*
boil, seethe, gurgle, froth, foam

bubbly adjective
1 **Bubbly** *drinks get up my nose.*
fizzy, sparkling, effervescent
2 *Sophie has a bright and* **bubbly** *personality.*
cheerful, lively, vivacious, spirited, animated

bucket noun
We took **buckets** *and spades to the seaside.*
pail, can

a
b
c
d
e
f
g
h
i
j
k
l
m
n
o
p
q
r
s
t
u
v
w
x
y
z

A

B

C

D

E

F

G

H

I

J

K

L

M

N

O

P

Q

R

S

T

U

V

W

X

Y

Z

buckle noun
The pirate wore a belt with a large silver buckle.
clasp, fastener, fastening, clip, catch

buckle verb
1 *Please buckle your seat belts.*
fasten, secure, clasp, clip, do up, hook up
2 *The bridge buckled when the giant stepped onto it.*
bend, warp, twist, crumple, cave in, collapse

bud noun
Buds are appearing on the apple trees.
shoot, sprout

budge verb
The window was stuck and wouldn't budge.
give way, move, shift, stir

budget verb
to budget for
Have you budgeted for a holiday this year?
allow for, plan for, provide for

bug noun
1 *Birds help to control bugs in the garden.*
insect, pest
2 (informal) *I can't get rid of this stomach bug.*
infection, virus, germ, disease, illness
3 *There are a few bugs in the computer program.*
fault, error, defect, flaw
(informal) **gremlin**

bug verb
1 *The spy bugged their telephone conversations.*
tap, listen in to, intercept
2 (informal) *I wish you'd stop bugging me with questions.*
bother, annoy, pester, trouble, harass

build verb builds, building, built
Dad is going to build a shed in the garden.
construct, erect, put together, put up, set up, assemble

to build up
1 *I'm building up a collection of DVDs.*
accumulate, assemble, collect, put together
2 *Tension was building up in the crowd.*
increase, intensify, rise, grow, mount up, escalate

build noun
Charlotte was a girl of slender build.
body, form, frame, figure, physique
See also **body**

building noun
The new building will have seven storeys.
construction, structure, dwelling
A person who designs buildings is an
architect.

WORD WEB

BUILDINGS WHERE PEOPLE LIVE
apartment, barracks, bungalow, castle, cottage, farmhouse, flat, fort, fortress, house, mansion, palace, skyscraper, tenement, terrace, tower, villa
See also **house**

BUILDINGS WHERE PEOPLE WORK
factory, garage, lighthouse, mill, shop, store, warehouse

BUILDINGS WHERE PEOPLE WORSHIP
abbey, cathedral, chapel, church, monastery, mosque, pagoda, shrine, synagogue, temple
See also **church**

OTHER TYPES OF BUILDING
cabin, cafe, cinema, college, gallery, hotel, inn, library, museum, observatory, police station, post office, power station, prison, pub or **public house, restaurant, school, shed, theatre**

PARTS YOU MIGHT FIND INSIDE A BUILDING
balcony, basement, cellar, conservatory, corridor, courtyard, crypt, dungeon, foyer, gallery, lobby, porch, room, staircase, veranda
See also **room**

PARTS YOU MIGHT FIND OUTSIDE A BUILDING
arch, balustrade, bay window,
bow window, buttress, chimney,
colonnade, column, dome,
dormer window, drainpipe, eaves,
foundations, gable, gutter, masonry,
parapet, pediment, pillar, pipes,
quadrangle, roof, tower, turret, vault,
wall, window, window sill
For parts of a castle see **castle**

 WRITING TIPS
You can use these words to describe a
building:

airy, compact, cramped, crumbling,
forbidding, grand, imposing,
ramshackle, ruined, run–down, spacious,
sprawling, squalid, stark, stately

bulge noun
There was a large bulge in the robber's sack.
bump, hump, lump, swelling,
protuberance

bulge verb
The creature had eyes which bulged out of its head.
stick out, swell, puff out, protrude

bulk noun
1 *The sheer bulk of the iceberg was staggering.*
size, dimensions, magnitude, mass,
largeness, immensity
2 *We spent the bulk of our holiday lazing on the beach.*
most, most part, greater part, majority

bulky adjective
The parcel is too bulky to go through the letterbox.
big, large, hefty, substantial, sizeable,
cumbersome, unwieldy
opposites small, compact

bully verb
Some of the children were afraid of being bullied.
persecute, torment, intimidate, terrorize,
push around

bump verb
1 *The baby bumped his head on the table.*
hit, strike, knock, bang
2 *My bicycle bumped up and down over the cobbles.*
bounce, shake, jerk, jolt
to bump into
1 *The taxi bumped into the car in front of it.*
collide with, bang into, run into,
crash into
2 *I bumped into one of my friends in the bookshop.*
meet, come across, run into

bump noun
1 *We felt a bump as the plane landed.*
thud, thump, bang, blow, knock
2 *How did you get that bump on your head?*
lump, swelling, bulge

bumpy adjective
1 *The car jolted up and down on the bumpy road.*
rough, uneven, irregular, lumpy
opposites smooth, even
2 *We had a bumpy ride in a jeep over muddy tracks.*
bouncy, jerky, jolting, lurching, choppy

bunch noun
1 *The jailer jangled a bunch of keys.*
bundle, cluster, collection, set
2 *She picked a bunch of flowers.*
bouquet, posy, spray
3 (informal) *They're a friendly bunch of people.*
group, set, circle, band, gang, crowd

bundle noun
I found a bundle of old newspapers.
bunch, batch, pile, stack, collection,
pack, bale

A
B
C
D
E
F
G
H
I
J
K
L
M
N
O
P
Q
R
S
T
U
V
W
X
Y
Z

bundle verb
1 *We bundled up the papers that were on the desk.*
pack, tie, fasten, bind
2 *The police bundled him into the back of their car.*
move hurriedly, push, jostle

burden noun
1 *Each mule was carrying a heavy burden.*
load, weight, cargo
2 *The captain has the burden of organizing the players.*
responsibility, obligation, duty, pressure, stress, trouble, worry

burden verb
I won't burden you with my own problems.
bother, worry, trouble, distress, encumber, lumber
(informal) saddle

burglar noun
The burglars must have got in through the window.
robber, thief, intruder

burglary noun
see stealing

burn verb burns, burning, burnt or burned
1 *We could see the campfire burning in the distance.*
be alight, be on fire, blaze, flame, flare, flicker
To burn without flames is to glow or smoulder.
2 *The captain ordered them to burn the enemy ship.*
set fire to, incinerate, reduce to ashes
To start something burning is to ignite, kindle, or light it.
To burn something slightly is to char, scorch, or singe it.
To hurt someone with boiling liquid or steam is to scald them.
To burn a dead body is to cremate it.
To burn a mark on an animal is to brand it.

burrow noun
The field was full of rabbit burrows.
hole, tunnel
A piece of ground with many burrows is a warren.
A fox's burrow is called an earth.
A badger's burrow is called an earth or set.
For other animal homes see animal

burrow verb
Rabbits have been burrowing under the fence.
tunnel, dig, excavate, mine

burst verb
The balloon burst when my brother sat on it.
puncture, rupture, break, give way, split, tear

bury verb
1 *The document was buried under a pile of old letters.*
cover, conceal, hide, secrete
2 *They say the old witch was buried in that graveyard.*
inter, entomb

bush noun
Birds often build their nests in bushes.
shrub

bushy adjective
The troll had bushy green eyebrows.
hairy, thick, dense, shaggy, bristly

business noun
1 *My uncle runs a restaurant business.*
company, firm, organization
2 *The new bookshop does a lot of business.*
trade, trading, buying and selling, commerce
3 *What sort of business do you want to go into?*
work, job, career, employment, industry, occupation, profession, trade
4 *He left early to attend to some urgent business.*
matter, issue, affair, problem, point, concern, question

Cc

bustle verb
Miss Flyte bustled about the kitchen making tea.
rush, dash, hurry, scurry, scuttle, fuss

busy adjective
1 *Mum is busy making my birthday cake just now.*
occupied, engaged, employed, working, slaving away, beavering away
(informal) hard at it, up to your eyes
A common simile is as busy as a bee.
opposite idle
2 *Christmas is a very busy time for shops.*
active, hectic, frantic, lively
opposites quiet, restful
3 *Is the town always this busy on Saturdays?*
crowded, bustling, hectic, lively, teeming
opposites quiet, peaceful

butt verb
The Minotaur butted Theseus against the wall.
hit, bump, knock, push, ram, shove
to butt in
Please don't butt in when I'm talking.
interrupt, cut in

buy verb buys, buying, bought
I'm saving up to buy a skateboard.
get, pay for, purchase, acquire
opposite sell

buzz noun & verb
For various sounds see **sound**¹

cabin noun
1 *The outlaws hid in a cabin in the woods.*
hut, shack, shed, lodge, chalet, shelter
2 *The crew assembled in the captain's cabin.*
berth, quarters, compartment

cable noun
1 *The tent was held down with strong cables.*
rope, cord, line, chain
2 *Don't trip over the computer cable.*
flex, lead, wire, cord

cafe noun
We had lunch in a cafe overlooking the river.
cafeteria, coffee shop, tea room, snack bar, buffet, canteen, bistro, brasserie
For other places to eat see **restaurant**

cage noun
A large cage or enclosure for birds is an **aviary**.
A cage or enclosure for poultry is a **coop**.
A cage or enclosure for animals is a **pen**.
A cage or box for a pet rabbit is a **hutch**.

cake noun
Do you prefer carrot cake or chocolate cake?
sponge, flan, gateau
A small individual cake is a **cupcake** or **fairy cake**.

calamity noun
The fire in the warehouse was a calamity.
disaster, catastrophe, tragedy, misfortune, mishap, blow

calculate verb
I calculated that it would take an hour to walk home.
work out, compute, figure out, reckon, add up, count, total
To calculate something roughly is to **estimate**.

a
b
c
d
e
f
g
h
i
j
k
l
m
n
o
p
q
r
s
t
u
v
w
x
y
z

A
B
C
D
E
F
G
H
I
J
K
L
M
N
O
P
Q
R
S
T
U
V
W
X
Y
Z

call noun
1 *We heard a call for help from inside the cave.*
cry, exclamation, scream, shout, yell
2 *Grandad made an unexpected call.*
visit, stop, stay
3 *There's not much call for suncream in winter.*
demand, need

call verb
1 *'Stop that racket!' called the janitor.*
cry out, exclaim, shout, yell
For other ways to say something see **say**
2 *It was too late at night to call my friends.*
phone, ring, telephone
3 *The head teacher called me to her office.*
summon, invite, send for, order
4 *The doctor called to see if I was feeling better.*
visit, pay a visit, drop in, drop by
5 *They called the baby Jessica.*
name, baptize, christen, dub
6 *What is your new book going to be called?*
name, title, entitle
to call something off
It was so rainy that we called off the barbecue.
cancel, abandon, postpone
to call someone names
It's not funny to call people names.
insult, be rude to, make fun of, mock

calm adjective
1 *The weather was too calm to fly our kites.*
still, quiet, peaceful, tranquil, serene, windless
opposites **stormy, windy**
2 *The sea was calm, and we had a pleasant voyage.*
smooth, still, flat, motionless, tranquil
opposites **rough, choppy**
3 *I tried to stay calm before my judo exam.*
cool, level-headed, patient, relaxed, sedate, unemotional, unexcitable, untroubled
opposites **anxious, nervous**

came
past tense see **come**

camel noun
A camel with a single hump is a **dromedary**.
A camel with two humps is a **Bactrian**.

camp noun
From the hill we saw a camp in the field below us.
campsite, camping ground, base
A military camp is an **encampment**.

campaign noun
1 *Will you join our campaign to save the whale?*
movement, crusade, drive, fight, effort, struggle
2 *The army launched a campaign to recapture the city.*
operation, offensive, action, war

cancel verb
We had to cancel the race because of the weather.
abandon, call off, scrap, drop, axe
(informal) **scrub, ditch**
To cancel something after it has already begun is to **abort** it.
To cancel something, but rearrange it for later, is to **postpone** it or **put it off**.
To cancel items on a list is to **cross out**, delete, or erase them.

candidate noun
A candidate for a job is an **applicant**.
A candidate in an examination is an **entrant**.
A person competing with others in a contest is a **competitor, contender**, or **contestant**.

canopy noun
We sheltered from the rain under a canopy.
awning, cover, shade

cap noun
1 *The tennis players wore caps because it was sunny.*
For various kinds of hat see **hat**
2 *Who left the cap off the toothpaste?*
cover, lid, top

cap verb
Mount Everest is always capped with snow.
cover, top, crown

capable adjective
She is a capable ballet dancer.
competent, able, accomplished,
proficient, skilful, skilled, gifted,
talented
opposite **incompetent**
to be capable of
Do you think the professor is capable of murder?
be able to do, be equal to, be up to
opposite **be incapable of**

capacity noun
1 *Alice has a great capacity for making friends.*
ability, power, potential, capability,
competence, talent
(informal) knack
2 *What is the capacity of this glass?*
size, volume, space, extent, room
3 *She spoke in her capacity as team leader.*
position, function, role, office

cape[1] noun
We could see the island from the cape.
headland, promontory, point, head

cape[2] noun
The lady wore a cape of black velvet.
cloak, shawl, wrap, robe
(old use) mantle

capital noun
1 *Paris is the capital of France.*
capital city, centre of government
2 *We have enough capital to start a new business.*
funds, money, finance, cash, assets,
savings, means, resources
capital letter
Start a new sentence with a capital letter.
block capital, block letter

capsize verb
The canoe capsized when it hit a rock.
overturn, tip over, turn over, keel over
(informal) turn turtle

capsule noun
1 *This capsule contains poison.*
pill, tablet, lozenge
2 *The space capsule is designed to orbit Mars.*
module, craft, pod
For other words to do with space travel see
space

captain noun
The captain brought his ship safely into harbour.
commander, commanding officer, master,
skipper

captive noun
The captives were thrown into the dungeon.
prisoner, convict
A person who is held captive until a demand
is met is a **hostage**.

captive adjective
The pirates held the crew captive for ten days.
imprisoned, captured, arrested, detained,
jailed
opposites **free, released**

captivity noun
The hostages have been released from captivity.
imprisonment, confinement, detention,
incarceration
opposite **freedom**

capture verb
1 *The bank robbers were captured by police this morning.*
catch, arrest, apprehend, seize,
take prisoner
(informal) nab, nick
2 *The castle has never been captured by enemy forces.*
occupy, seize, take, take over, win

car noun
Our car is getting repaired in the garage.
motor car, motor, vehicle
(American) automobile
An informal name for an old, noisy car is a
banger.
See the panel on the next page.

a
b
c
d
e
f
g
h
i
j
k
l
m
n
o
p
q
r
s
t
u
v
w
x
y
z

A B **C** D E F G H I J K L M N O P Q R S T U V W X Y Z

WORD WEB

SOME TYPES OF CAR
convertible, coupé, electric car, estate, four-wheel drive, hatchback, (trademark) Jeep, (trademark) Land Rover, limousine or (informal) limo, (trademark) Mini, patrol car or police car, people carrier, racing car, saloon, sports car

Very early cars are **veteran** or **vintage** cars.

THE MAIN PARTS OF A CAR ARE
body, bonnet, boot, bumper, chassis, doors, engine, exhaust pipe, fuel tank, gearbox, headlamps, lights, mirrors, roof, tyres, undercarriage, wheels, windscreen, wings

THE MAIN CONTROLS IN A CAR ARE
accelerator, brake, choke, clutch, gear lever, handbrake, ignition key, indicators, steering wheel, windscreen wipers

For other vehicles see **vehicle**

carcass noun
The lions fed on the carcass of the antelope.
body, corpse, cadaver, remains

card noun
Did you send her a birthday card?

WORD WEB

CARDS TO SEND ON SPECIAL OCCASIONS
birthday card, Christmas card, Diwali card, Easter card, get well card, greetings card, Hanukkah card, invitation, notelet, picture postcard, sympathy card, thank you card, Valentine
The magician shuffled the pack of cards.

SOME CARD GAMES
beggar-my-neighbour, blackjack, bridge, canasta, cribbage, go fish, old maid, patience, poker, pontoon, rummy, snap, solitaire, whist

A complete set of playing cards is a **pack**. All the cards with the same sign on them are a **suit**.

THE SUITS IN A PACK OF CARDS ARE
clubs, diamonds, hearts, spades

NAMES FOR SPECIAL CARDS ARE
king, queen, jack or knave, ace, joker

The king, queen, and jack are called **court cards**.

care noun
1 *The old wizard's face was full of care.*
worry, anxiety, trouble, concern, burden, responsibility, sorrow, stress
2 *I took great care with my handwriting.*
attention, concentration, thoroughness, thought, meticulousness
opposite carelessness
3 *Jake left his pet hamster in my care.*
charge, keeping, protection, safe keeping, supervision
to take care
Please take care crossing the road.
be careful, be on your guard, look out, watch out
to take care of someone or something
My granny takes care of me after school.
care for, look after, mind, watch over, attend to, tend

care verb
Do you care which team wins the World Cup?
mind, bother, worry, be interested, be troubled, be bothered, be worried
to care for someone or something
1 *The veterinary hospital cares for sick animals.*
take care of, look after, attend to, tend, nurse
2 *I don't really care for broccoli.*
like, be fond of, be keen on, love

career noun
Max had a successful career as a lawyer.
job, occupation, profession, trade, business, employment, calling
For various careers see **job**

careful adjective
1 *You must be more careful with your spelling.*
accurate, conscientious, thorough, thoughtful, meticulous, painstaking, precise
opposites **careless, inaccurate**
2 *Dad kept a careful watch on the bonfire.*
attentive, cautious, watchful, alert, wary, vigilant
opposites **careless, inattentive**
to be careful
Please be careful with those scissors.
take care, be on your guard, look out, watch out

careless adjective
1 *This is a very careless piece of work.*
messy, untidy, thoughtless, inaccurate, slapdash, shoddy, scrappy, sloppy, slovenly
opposites **careful, accurate**
2 *I was careless and cut my finger.*
inattentive, thoughtless, absent-minded, heedless, irresponsible, negligent, reckless
opposites **careful, attentive**

caress noun
The mother bear gave each cub a caress.
hug, kiss, embrace, pat, stroke, touch

caress verb
The woman gently caressed her child's hair.
stroke, touch, smooth

cargo noun
Some planes carry cargo instead of passengers.
goods, freight, merchandise

carnival noun
The whole village comes out for the annual carnival.
fair, festival, fête, gala, parade, procession, show, celebration, pageant

carriage noun
For types of vehicle see **vehicle**

carry verb
1 *I helped Mum to carry the shopping to the car.*
take, transfer, lift, fetch, bring, lug
2 *Aircraft carry passengers and goods.*
transport, convey
3 *The rear axle carries the greatest weight.*
bear, support, hold up
to carry on
We carried on in spite of the rain.
continue, go on, persevere, persist, keep on, remain, stay, survive
to carry something out
The soldiers carried out the captain's orders.
perform, do, execute, accomplish, achieve, complete, finish

cart noun
For types of vehicle see **vehicle**

carton noun
I put a carton of juice in my lunch-box.
box, pack, package, packet

carve verb
1 *The statue was carved out of stone.*
sculpt, chisel, hew
2 *Mum carved the chicken for Sunday dinner.*
cut, slice

case¹ noun
1 *I loaded my case into the boot of the car.*
suitcase, trunk, bag, holdall
A number of suitcases that you take on holiday is your **baggage** or **luggage**.
2 *What's in those cases in the attic?*
box, chest, crate, carton, casket

case² noun
1 *This has been a clear case of mistaken identity.*
instance, occurrence, example, illustration
2 *It was one of Sherlock Holmes's most famous cases.*
inquiry, investigation

a
b
c
d
e
f
g
h
i
j
k
l
m
n
o
p
q
r
s
t
u
v
w
x
y
z

A
B
C
D
E
F
G
H
I
J
K
L
M
N
O
P
Q
R
S
T
U
V
W
X
Y
Z

3 *She presented a good* case *for abolishing hunting.*
argument, line of reasoning

cash noun
How much cash *do you have?*
money, change, loose change, ready money, coins, notes, currency

cast verb casts, casting, cast
1 *The child* cast *a penny into the fountain.*
throw, toss, drop, fling, lob, sling
2 *The statue was* cast *in bronze.*
form, mould, shape

castle noun

WORD WEB

CASTLES AND OTHER FORTIFIED BUILDINGS
château, citadel, fort, fortress, motte and bailey, palace, stronghold, tower

PARTS OF A CASTLE
bailey, barbican, battlement, buttress, courtyard, donjon, drawbridge, dungeon, gate, gateway, keep, magazine, moat, motte, parapet, portcullis, postern, rampart, tower, turret, wall, watchtower

casual adjective
1 *It was just a* casual *remark, so don't take it too seriously.*
accidental, chance, unexpected, unintentional, unplanned
opposite **deliberate**
2 *The restaurant had a* casual *atmosphere.*
easy-going, informal, relaxed
opposite **formal**
3 *The teacher complained about our* casual *attitude.*
apathetic, careless, slack, unenthusiastic
opposite **enthusiastic**

casualty noun
Police are reporting heavy casualties *from the fire.*
death, fatality, injury, loss, victim

cat noun
A male cat is a **tom**.
A young cat is a **kitten**.
A cat with streaks in its fur is a **tabby**.
An informal word for a cat is **puss** or **pussy cat**.
A word meaning 'to do with cats' is **feline**.

WORD WEB

SOME BREEDS OF CAT
Abyssinian, Burmese, chinchilla, Manx, Persian, Siamese

SOME WILD ANIMALS OF THE CAT FAMILY
bobcat, cheetah, jaguar, leopard, lion, lynx, ocelot, puma, tiger, wild cat

See also **animal**

catastrophe noun
The drought is a catastrophe *for the farmers.*
disaster, calamity, misfortune, mishap, tragedy

catch verb catches, catching, caught
1 *My friends yelled at me to* catch *the ball.*
clutch, grab, grasp, grip, hang on to, hold, seize, snatch, take
2 *One of the anglers* caught *a fish.*
hook, net, trap
3 *The police hoped to* catch *the thief red-handed.*
arrest, capture, corner
(informal) nab
4 *I hope you don't* catch *my cold.*
become infected by, contract, get
(informal) go down with
5 *You must hurry if you want to* catch *the bus.*
be in time for, get on
to catch on
Their latest record didn't catch on.
become popular, do well, succeed
(informal) make it
to catch up with someone
If we run we'll catch up with *them.*
gain on, overtake

catch noun
1 *The angler got a large* catch *of salmon.*
haul
2 *The car is so cheap that there must be a* catch.
problem, obstacle, snag, difficulty, disadvantage, drawback, trap, trick
3 *All the windows are fitted with safety* catches.
fastening, latch, lock, bolt, hook

catching adjective
Chickenpox is catching.
contagious, infectious

category noun
I won first prize in the under-10s category.
group, section, class, division, set

cater verb
to cater for
The hotel can cater for *a hundred guests.*
cook for, provide food for, serve, supply

cattle plural noun
Male cattle are **bulls, steers,** or **oxen.**
Female cattle are **cows.**
Young male cattle are **calves** or **bullocks.**
Young female cattle are **calves** or **heifers.**
A word meaning 'to do with cattle' is **bovine.**
Farm animals in general are **livestock.**

caught
past tense see **catch**

cause noun
1 *What was the* cause *of the trouble?*
origin, source, start
You can also talk about the **reasons** for the trouble.
2 *You've got no* cause *to complain.*
grounds, basis, motive, reason
3 *The sponsored walk is for a good* cause.
purpose, object

cause verb
A single spark from the fire could cause *an explosion.*
bring about, create, generate, lead to, give rise to, result in, provoke, arouse

caution noun
1 *We decided to proceed with* caution.
care, attention, watchfulness, wariness, vigilance
2 *The traffic warden let him off with a* caution.
warning, reprimand, telling-off
(informal) **ticking-off**

cautious adjective
My grandad is a cautious *driver.*
careful, attentive, watchful, wary, vigilant, hesitant
opposite **reckless**

cave noun
The cave *walls were covered with prehistoric paintings.*
cavern, pothole, underground chamber
A man-made cave with decorative walls is a grotto.

WORD WEB
THINGS YOU MIGHT SEE IN A CAVE
cave painting, stalactite, stalagmite

The entrance to a cave is the **mouth.**
The top of a cave is the **roof** and the bottom is the **floor.**
Prehistoric people who lived in caves were **cavemen** and **cavewomen,** or **troglodytes.**
Someone who enjoys exploring caves is a **potholer.**

cave verb
to cave in
The miners had a lucky escape when the roof caved in.
collapse, fall in

cavity noun
The map was lodged in a secret cavity *in the wall.*
hole, hollow, space, chamber

a
b
c
d
e
f
g
h
i
j
k
l
m
n
o
p
q
r
s
t
u
v
w
x
y
z

A

cease verb
The fighting ceased at midnight.
come to an end, end, finish, stop, halt
opposite begin

ceaseless adjective
*The ceaseless noise of traffic kept me awake
all night.*
constant, continual, continuous,
never-ending, non-stop, incessant,
interminable, endless, everlasting,
permanent, perpetual, unending,
persistent, relentless
opposite brief

celebrate verb
1 *Let's celebrate!*
enjoy yourself, have a good time, be happy,
rejoice
2 *What shall we do to celebrate Granny's
birthday?*
commemorate, observe, keep

celebrated adjective
*Beatrix Potter is a celebrated author of
children's books.*
famous, well-known, respected, renowned,
eminent, distinguished, notable,
outstanding, popular, prominent
opposite unknown

celebration noun
*We had a big celebration for my cousin's
wedding.*
festivity, party, feast, festival, banquet,
jamboree

celebrity noun
*The awards were handed out by a TV
celebrity.*
famous person, personality, public figure,
VIP, star, idol

cellar noun
*We keep our bikes and sports gear in the
cellar.*
basement, vault
See also basement

cemetery noun
*A famous author is buried in the local
cemetery.*
graveyard, burial ground, churchyard
A place where dead people are cremated is a
crematorium.

central adjective
1 *We are now in the central part of the
building.*
middle, core, inner, interior
opposite outer
2 *Who are the central characters in
the story?*
chief, crucial, essential, fundamental,
important, main, major, principal, vital
opposite unimportant

centre noun
The library is in the centre of the town.
*The burial chamber is in the centre of the
pyramid.*
middle, heart, core, inside, interior
The centre of a planet or a piece of fruit is
the core.
The centre of an atom or living cell is the
nucleus.
The centre of a wheel is the hub.
The point at the centre of a see-saw is the
pivot.
The edible part in the centre of a nut is the
kernel.
opposites edge, outside, surface

ceremony noun
1 *We watched the ceremony of the opening
of parliament.*
rite, ritual, formalities
A ceremony where someone is given a prize
is a presentation.
A ceremony where someone is given a
special honour is an investiture.
A ceremony to celebrate something new is
an inauguration or opening.
A ceremony where someone becomes a
member of a society is an initiation.
A ceremony to make a church or other
building sacred is a dedication.

A ceremony to remember a dead person or a past event is a **commemoration**.
A ceremony held in a church is a **service**. For ceremonies which can be held in a church see **church**
2 *They had a quiet wedding without a lot of ceremony.*
formality, pomp, pageantry, spectacle

certain adjective
1 *My mum was certain she would win the cookery competition.*
confident, convinced, positive, sure, determined
opposite uncertain
2 *We have certain proof that the painting is a forgery.*
definite, clear, convincing, absolute, unquestionable, reliable, trustworthy, undeniable, infallible, genuine, valid
opposite unreliable
3 *The damaged plane faced certain disaster.*
inevitable, unavoidable
opposite possible
4 *Her new book is certain to be a bestseller.*
bound, sure
for certain
I'll give you the money tomorrow for certain.
certainly, definitely, for sure, without doubt, sure
to make certain
Please make certain that you switch off the lights.
make sure, ensure

certainly adverb
Baby dragons are certainly not timid.
definitely, undoubtedly, unquestionably, assuredly, without a doubt

certificate noun
At the end of the course, you will receive a certificate.
diploma, document, licence

chain noun
1 *The anchor was attached to a chain.*
One ring in a chain is a **link**.

A chain used to link railway wagons together is a **coupling**.
2 *The police formed a chain to keep the crowd back.*
line, row, cordon
3 *Holmes described the chain of events that led to the murder.*
series, sequence, succession, string

chair noun
For furniture to sit on see **seat**

challenge verb
I challenged Jo not to eat sweets for a week.
dare, defy

champion noun
1 *She is the current world champion at ice-skating.*
title-holder, prizewinner, victor, winner, conqueror
2 *Martin Luther King was a champion of civil rights.*
supporter, advocate, defender, upholder, patron, backer

championship noun
Fifteen schools took part in the karate championship.
competition, contest, tournament

chance noun
1 *They say there's a chance of rain later.*
possibility, likelihood, probability, prospect, danger, risk
2 *I haven't had a chance to reply yet.*
opportunity, time, occasion
3 *The director took a chance in hiring an unknown actor.*
gamble, risk
by chance
I found the house quite by chance.
by accident, accidentally, by coincidence
An unfortunate chance is **bad luck** or a **misfortune**.
A fortunate chance is **good luck** or a **fluke**.

a b c d e f g h i j k l m n o p q r s t u v w x y z

61

A
B
C
D
E
F
G
H
I
J
K
L
M
N
O
P
Q
R
S
T
U
V
W
X
Y
Z

change verb

1 *They've changed the programme for the concert.*
alter, modify, rearrange, reorganize, adjust, adapt, vary
2 *The town has changed a lot since Victorian times.*
alter, become different, develop, grow, move on
3 *Can I change these jeans for a bigger size, please?*
exchange, replace, switch, substitute
(informal) swap
to change into
Tadpoles change into frogs.
become, turn into, be transformed into

change noun

There has been a slight change of plan.
alteration, modification, variation, difference, break
A change to something worse is a deterioration.
A change to something better is an improvement or a reform.
A very big change is a revolution, transformation, or U-turn.
A change in which one person or thing is replaced by another is a substitution.

changeable adjective

The weather has been changeable today.
variable, unsettled, unpredictable, unreliable, inconsistent, erratic, unstable
If your loyalty is changeable you are fickle.
opposite steady

channel noun

1 *The rainwater runs along this channel.*
ditch, duct, gully, gutter, furrow, trough
2 *How many TV channels do you get?*
station

chaos noun

After the earthquake, the city was in chaos.
confusion, disorder, mayhem, uproar, tumult, pandemonium, anarchy, bedlam, muddle, shambles
opposite order

chaotic adjective

Alice finds that life in Wonderland is chaotic.
confused, disorderly, disorganized, muddled, topsy-turvy, untidy, unruly, riotous
opposites orderly, organized

chapter noun

I read a chapter of my book last night.
part, section, division
One section of a play is an act or scene.
One part of a serial is an episode or instalment.

character noun

1 *Her character is quite different from her sister's.*
personality, temperament, nature, disposition, make-up, manner
2 *Our neighbour is a well-known character in our street.*
figure, personality, individual, person
3 *Which character would you like to play in Peter Pan?*
part, role

characteristic noun

The Martians had some odd physical characteristics.
feature, peculiarity, attribute, trait, distinguishing feature

characteristic adjective

Windmills are a characteristic feature of this area.
typical, distinctive, recognizable, particular, special, unique, singular

charge noun

1 *The admission charge is five euros.*
price, rate
The charge made for a ride on public transport is the fare.
The charge made to post a letter or parcel is the postage.
A charge made to join a club is a fee or subscription.
A charge made for certain things by the government is a duty or a tax.

A charge made to use a private road, bridge, or tunnel is a **toll**.
2 *The robbers face several criminal* charges.
accusation, allegation
3 *Many soldiers were killed in the* charge.
assault, attack, onslaught, raid
4 *My best friend left her hamster in my* charge.
care, keeping, protection, custody, trust
to be in charge of something
An experienced sailor was in charge of *the crew.*
manage, lead, command, direct, supervise, run

charge verb
1 *The library* charges *ten pence for a photocopy.*
ask for, make you pay
2 *A man has been* charged *with attempted robbery.*
accuse (of)
3 *The cavalry* charged *the enemy line.*
attack, assault, storm, rush

charm noun
1 *In the painting, the girl's face is full of youthful* charm.
attractiveness, appeal, charisma
2 *The sorcerer recited a magic* charm.
spell, incantation
For other words to do with magic see **magic**
3 *The boy carried a crystal as a lucky* charm.
talisman, mascot, amulet, trinket

charm verb
Winnie the Pooh has charmed *readers all over the world.*
bewitch, captivate, delight, enchant, entrance, fascinate, please

charming adjective
We drove through some charming *scenery.*
delightful, attractive, pleasant, pleasing, likeable, appealing

chart noun
1 *The explorer stopped to consult his* chart.
map
2 *This* chart *shows the average monthly rainfall.*
diagram, graph, table

charter verb
We chartered *a minibus for our trip.*
hire, lease, rent

chase verb
The wolves chased *a deer through the forest.*
pursue, run after, follow, track, trail, hunt

chasm noun
From the bridge, we looked down at a deep chasm.
hole, ravine, crevasse, canyon, gorge, abyss, gulf, fissure, pit, rift

chat or chatter verb
see **talk**

chatty adjective
Frank is usually shy, but today he's quite chatty.
talkative, communicative
opposite silent

cheap adjective
1 *We got a* cheap *flight to London.*
inexpensive, affordable, bargain, cut-price, discount, reasonable
2 *These tyres are made from* cheap *rubber.*
inferior, shoddy, second-rate, worthless, trashy
(informal) **tacky, tatty**
opposites superior, good-quality

cheat verb
1 *She was* cheated *into buying a fake diamond ring.*
deceive, trick, swindle, double-cross, hoax, fool
(informal) **con, diddle, fleece, rip off**
2 *Anyone who* cheats *in the quiz will be disqualified.*
copy, crib

cheat noun
Don't trust him—he's a cheat.
cheater, deceiver, swindler, fraud, impostor, hoaxer

a b c d e f g h i j k l m n o p q r s t u v w x y z

63

A B C D E F G H I J K L M N O P Q R S T U V W X Y Z

check verb

1 *Have you checked your work carefully?*
examine, inspect, look over, scrutinize

2 *The heavy snow checked their progress towards the Pole.*
hamper, hinder, block, obstruct, delay, hold back, slow, slow down, halt, stop

check noun

I need to run some checks on your computer.
test, examination, inspection, check-up

cheeky adjective

Don't be so cheeky!
disrespectful, facetious, flippant, impertinent, impolite, impudent, insolent, insulting, irreverent, mocking, rude, saucy, shameless
opposite **respectful**

cheer verb

1 *We cheered when our team scored a goal.*
clap, applaud, shout, yell
opposite **jeer**

2 *The good news cheered us.*
comfort, console, gladden, delight, please, encourage, uplift
opposite **sadden**

to cheer up
The weather had cheered up by the afternoon.
become more cheerful, brighten

cheerful adjective

The sun was shining, and we set out in a cheerful mood.
happy, good-humoured, light-hearted, merry, jolly, joyful, joyous, glad, pleased, optimistic, lively, elated, animated, bright, buoyant, jovial, gleeful, chirpy
opposite **sad**

chemist noun

pharmacist
(old use) apothecary, alchemist
A chemist's shop is a **dispensary** or pharmacy.

chess noun

WORD WEB

THE PIECES USED IN PLAYING CHESS ARE
bishop, castle or rook, king, knight, pawn, queen

SOME TERMS USED IN PLAYING CHESS
castle, check, checkmate, mate, move, stalemate, take

For other board games see game

pawn

bishop

castle or rook

knight

king

queen

chest noun

I found some old books in a chest in the attic.
box, crate, case, trunk

chew verb
Are you still chewing that toffee?
eat, gnaw, munch
For other ways to eat see **eat**

chicken noun
A female chicken is a **hen**.
A male chicken is a **rooster**.
A young chicken is a **chick**.
A group of chickens is a **brood**.
A farm which keeps chickens is a
poultry farm.

chief noun
The pirates chose Redbeard as their chief.
leader, ruler, head, commander, captain,
chieftain, master, governor, president,
principal
(informal) **boss**

chief adjective
1 *The chief ingredients in a trifle are jelly,
custard, and cream.*
main, central, key, principal, crucial, basic,
essential, important, vital, major, primary,
foremost, fundamental, indispensable,
necessary, significant, predominant,
prominent
opposites unimportant, minor, trivial
2 *Albert was Queen Victoria's chief advisor.*
head, senior

chiefly adverb
Kangaroos are found chiefly in Australia.
mainly, mostly, predominantly, primarily,
principally, especially

child noun
1 *The book festival is aimed especially at
children.*
boy or girl, infant, juvenile, youngster,
youth, lad or lass
(informal) **kid, tot, nipper**
2 *How many children do you have?*
son or daughter, descendant, offspring
A child who expects to inherit a title or
fortune from parents is an **heir** or **heiress**.
A child whose parents are dead is an **orphan**.
A child looked after by a guardian is a **ward**.
See also **baby**

childhood noun
Neil spent much of his childhood by the sea.
infancy, youth, boyhood or girlhood
The time when someone is a baby is their
babyhood.
The time when someone is a teenager is
their **adolescence** or **teens**.
opposite adulthood

childish adjective
It's childish to make rude noises.
babyish, immature, juvenile, infantile
opposite mature

chill verb
Chill the pudding before serving it.
freeze, cool, make cold, refrigerate
opposite warm

chilly adjective
1 *It's a chilly evening, so wrap up well.*
cold, cool, frosty, icy, crisp, fresh, raw,
wintry
(informal) **nippy**
opposite warm
2 *The librarian gave me a very chilly look.*
unfriendly, hostile, unwelcoming,
unsympathetic
opposite friendly

chime verb
The church clock chimed at midnight.
ring, sound, strike, peal, toll
For sounds made by a bell see **bell**

chimney noun
A chimney on a ship or steam engine is a
funnel.
A pipe to take away smoke and fumes is a
flue.

chip noun
1 *There were chips of broken glass on the
pavement.*
bit, piece, fragment, scrap, sliver, splinter,
flake, shaving
2 *This mug's got a chip in it.*
crack, nick, notch, flaw

a
b
c
d
e
f
g
h
i
j
k
l
m
n
o
p
q
r
s
t
u
v
w
x
y
z

A
B
C
D
E
F
G
H
I
J
K
L
M
N
O
P
Q
R
S
T
U
V
W
X
Y
Z

chip verb
I chipped a cup while I was washing up.
crack, nick, notch, damage

choice noun
1 *My bike had a flat tyre, so I had no choice but to walk.*
alternative, option
2 *She wouldn't be my choice as team captain.*
preference, selection, pick, vote
3 *The greengrocer has a good choice of vegetables.*
range, selection, assortment, array, mixture, variety, diversity

choke verb
1 *This tie is so tight it's choking me.*
strangle, suffocate, stifle, throttle
2 *Thick fumes made the firefighters choke.*
cough, gasp

choose verb chooses, choosing, chose, chosen
1 *We had a show of hands to choose a winner.*
select, appoint, elect, vote for
2 *I chose the blue shoes to go with my dress.*
decide on, select, pick out, opt for, plump for, settle on, single out
3 *Lola chose to stay at home.*
decide, make a decision, determine, prefer, resolve

chop verb
1 *Chop the celery into large chunks.*
cut, split
2 *They chopped down the undergrowth to make a path.*
hack, slash
To chop down a tree is to **fell** it.
To chop a branch off a tree is to **lop** it.
To chop off an arm or leg is to **amputate** it.
To chop food into small pieces is to **dice** or **mince** it.

chorus noun
1 *I'm singing in the chorus in the school musical.*
choir

2 *I forgot the words to the song, so I just sang the chorus.*
refrain

chubby adjective
The baby chicks are fluffy and chubby.
plump, tubby, podgy, dumpy

chunk noun
I bit a chunk out of my apple.
piece, portion, lump, block, hunk, slab, wedge

church noun

WORD WEB
PLACES WHERE CHRISTIANS WORSHIP
abbey, cathedral, chapel, meeting house, parish church

For places where people of other religions worship see **building**

PARTS OF A CHURCH
aisle, belfry, chancel, cloister, crypt, nave, spire, steeple, transept, vestry

THINGS YOU MIGHT SEE IN A CHURCH
altar, crucifix, font, lectern, pews, pulpit

SERVICES WHICH MAY BE HELD IN A CHURCH
baptism or christening, communion, confirmation, funeral, mass, wedding

circle noun
1 *We arranged the chairs in a circle.*
ring, round, hoop, loop, band
A flat, solid circle is a **disc**.
A three-dimensional round shape is a **sphere**.
An egg shape is an **oval** or **ellipse**.
For other shapes see **shape**
The distance round a circle is the **circumference**.
The distance across a circle is the **diameter**.
The distance from the centre to the circumference is the **radius**.
A circular movement is a **revolution** or **rotation**.
A circular trip round the world is a **circumnavigation**.

A circular trip round a planet is an **orbit**.
2 *She has a wide circle of friends.*
group, set, crowd

circle verb
The vultures circled overhead.
turn, go round, revolve, rotate, wheel

circular adjective
The flying saucer was circular in shape.
round, ring-shaped, disc-shaped

circulate verb
1 *Blood circulates in the body.*
go round, move round
2 *I asked friends to circulate our newsletter.*
distribute, send round, issue

circumference noun
There is a fence around the circumference of the field.
perimeter, border, boundary, edge, fringe

circumstances plural noun
He described the circumstances which led to the accident.
situation, conditions, background, causes, context, details, facts, particulars

citizen noun
The citizens of New York are proud of their city.
resident, inhabitant

city noun
The main city of a country or region is the **metropolis**.
An area of houses outside the central part of a city is the **suburbs**.
A word meaning 'to do with a town or city' is **urban**.
A word meaning 'to do with a city and its suburbs' is **metropolitan**.
See also **town**

civilization noun
We are studying the civilization of ancient Egypt.
culture, society, achievements, attainments

civilized adjective
Trolls seldom behave in a civilized manner.
polite, well-behaved, well-mannered, orderly, cultured, sophisticated, refined
opposite **uncivilized**

claim verb
1 *You can claim your prize for the raffle here.*
ask for, request, collect, demand, insist on
2 *The professor claims to be an expert on dinosaurs.*
declare, assert, allege, maintain, argue, insist

clamber verb
We clambered over the rocks towards the sea.
climb, scramble, crawl, move awkwardly

clang and clank noun & verb
see sound[1]

clap verb
1 *The audience clapped loudly at the end of the concert.*
applaud, cheer
2 *Suddenly, a hand clapped me on the back.*
slap, hit, pat, smack

clash noun
1 *The clash of cymbals made me jump.*
crash, bang, ringing
2 *There was a clash between rival supporters at the match.*
argument, confrontation, conflict, fight, scuffle
(informal) scrap

clash verb
1 *The cymbals clashed.*
crash, resound
2 *Two good films clash on TV tonight.*
coincide, happen at the same time
3 *Demonstrators clashed with the police.*
argue, fight, get into conflict, squabble

clasp verb
1 *My little brother clasped my hand.*
grasp, grip, hold, squeeze, cling to
2 *She clasped him in her arms.*
embrace, hug

a
b
c
d
e
f
g
h
i
j
k
l
m
n
o
p
q
r
s
t
u
v
w
x
y
z

clasp noun
The cloak was held in place by a gold clasp.
fastener, fastening, brooch, clip, pin, buckle, hook

class noun
1 *There are 26 children in our class.*
form, set, stream
The other pupils in your class are your classmates.
2 *There are many different classes of plants.*
category, group, classification, division, set, sort, type, kind, species
3 *The ancient Romans divided people into social classes.*
level, rank, status

classic adjective

> Notice that **classic** means *excellent of its kind*, while **classical** means either *to do with the ancient Greeks and Romans*, or *to do with serious music written in the past.*

That was a classic tennis final this year.
excellent, first-class, first-rate, top-notch, exceptional, fine, great, admirable, masterly, model, perfect
opposite **ordinary**

claw verb
We could hear the monster clawing at the door.
scratch, scrape, tear, savage

clean adjective
1 *Can you bring me a clean cup, please?*
spotless, washed, scrubbed, swept, tidy, immaculate, hygienic, sanitary
An informal word meaning 'very clean' is squeaky-clean.
A common simile is as clean as a whistle.
opposite **dirty**
2 *I began my diary on a clean piece of paper.*
blank, unused, unmarked, empty, bare, fresh, new
opposite **used**
3 *This plaster will keep the wound clean.*
sterile, sterilized, uninfected

4 *You can get clean water from this tap.*
pure, clear, fresh, unpolluted, uncontaminated
5 *The referee said he wanted a clean fight.*
fair, honest, honourable, sporting, sportsmanlike
opposite **dishonourable**

clean verb
1 *We cleaned the house from top to bottom. I tried to clean the mud off my boots.*
wash, wipe, mop, scour, scrub, polish, dust, sweep, vacuum, rinse, wring out, hose down, sponge, shampoo, swill
To clean clothes is to launder them.
opposites **dirty, mess up**
2 *The nurse cleaned the wound with an antiseptic wipe.*
cleanse, bathe, disinfect, sanitize, sterilize
opposites **infect, contaminate**

clear adjective
1 *We saw fish swimming in the clear pool.*
clean, pure, colourless, transparent
A common simile is as clear as crystal.
opposite **opaque**
2 *It was a beautiful clear day.*
bright, sunny, cloudless, unclouded
A clear night is a moonlit or starlit night.
opposites **cloudy, overcast**
3 *The instructions on the map were quite clear.*
plain, understandable, intelligible, lucid, unambiguous
opposites **ambiguous, confusing**
4 *The actor spoke his words with a clear voice.*
distinct, audible
A common simile is as clear as a bell.
opposite **muffled**
5 *The signature on this letter is not clear.*
legible, recognizable, visible
opposite **illegible**
6 *My camera takes nice clear pictures.*
sharp, well defined, focused
opposite **unfocused**
7 *Are you sure that your conscience is clear?*
innocent, untroubled, blameless
opposite **guilty**

8 *There's a* clear *difference between a male blackbird and a female.*
obvious, definite, noticeable, conspicuous, perceptible, pronounced
opposite imperceptible
9 *They made sure the road was* clear *for the ambulance.*
open, empty, free, passable, uncrowded, unobstructed
opposite congested

clear verb
1 *I* cleared *the weeds from the flower bed.*
get rid of, remove, eliminate, strip
2 *The plumber* cleared *the blocked drain.*
unblock, unclog, clean out, open up
To clear a channel is to **dredge** it.
3 *I* cleared *the misty windows.*
clean, wipe, polish
4 *If the fire alarm goes,* clear *the building.*
empty, evacuate
5 *The fog* cleared *slowly.*
disappear, vanish, disperse, evaporate, melt away
6 *The forecast said that the weather will* clear.
become clear, brighten, brighten up
7 *He was* cleared *of all the charges.*
acquit, free, release
8 *The runners* cleared *the first hurdle.*
go over, get over, jump over, pass over, vault
to clear up
Please clear up *this mess before you go.*
clean up, tidy up, put right, put straight

clench verb
1 *The warrior* clenched *his teeth and gripped his sword.*
close tightly, squeeze together, grit
2 *She* clenched *the coin tightly in her hand.*
clasp, hold, grasp, grip

clever adjective
1 *Dr Hafiz is very* clever *and can read hieroglyphics.*
intelligent, bright, gifted, able, knowledgeable
(informal) brainy, smart
opposite unintelligent

An informal name for a clever person is a **brainbox**.
An uncomplimentary synonym is **clever clogs** or **smarty pants**.
2 *The elves were very* clever *with their fingers.*
accomplished, capable, gifted, skilful, talented
If you are clever at a lot of things you are **versatile**.
opposite unskilful
3 *They are* clever *enough to get away with it.*
quick, sharp, shrewd, smart
Uncomplimentary synonyms are **artful**, **crafty**, **cunning**, **wily**.
opposite stupid

client noun
The shop has a growing number of overseas clients.
customer, user, buyer, consumer

cliff noun
The car rolled over the edge of a cliff.
crag, precipice, rock face

climate noun
see **weather**

climax noun
The climax *of the film is a stunning car chase.*
high point, highlight, peak
opposite anticlimax

climb verb
1 *It took us several hours to* climb *the mountain.*
ascend, clamber up, go up, scale
2 *The plane* climbed *into the clouds.*
lift off, soar, take off
3 *The road* climbs *steeply up to the castle.*
rise, slope
to climb down
1 *It's harder to* climb down *the rock than to get up it.*
descend, get down from
2 *We all told him he was wrong, so he had to* climb down.
admit defeat, give in, surrender

a
b
c
d
e
f
g
h
i
j
k
l
m
n
o
p
q
r
s
t
u
v
w
x
y
z

A
B

C

D
E
F
G
H
I
J
K
L
M
N
O
P
Q
R
S
T
U
V
W
X
Y
Z

climb noun
It's a steep climb up to the castle.
ascent, hill, gradient, rise, slope, incline

cling verb clings, clinging, clung
to cling to someone or something
1 *The baby koala clung to its mother.*
clasp, grasp, clutch, embrace, hug
2 *Ivy clings to the wall.*
adhere to, fasten on to, stick to

clip verb
1 *The sheets of paper were clipped together.*
pin, staple
2 *Dad clipped the hedges in the back garden.*
cut, trim
To cut unwanted parts off a tree or bush is
to **prune** it.

cloak noun
*The girl wrapped her cloak tightly around
herself.*
cape, coat, wrap
(old use) mantle

clock noun
For instruments used to measure time see
time

clog verb
The dead leaves are clogging the drain.
block, choke, congest, obstruct, bung up,
jam, stop up

close¹ adjective (say klohss)
1 *Our house is close to the shops.*
near, nearby, not far
To be actually by the side of something is to
be **adjacent**.
opposites far, distant
2 *Anisha and I are close friends.*
intimate, dear, devoted, fond, affectionate
3 *The police made a close examination of the
stolen car.*
careful, detailed, painstaking, minute,
thorough
opposite casual
4 *It was an exciting race because it was so
close.*
equal, even, level, well-matched

5 *Open the window—it's very close in here.*
humid, muggy, stuffy, clammy, airless,
stifling, suffocating
opposite airy

close² verb (say klohz)
1 *Don't forget to close the lid.*
shut, fasten, seal, secure
2 *The road has been closed to traffic for the
parade.*
barricade, block, obstruct, stop up
3 *The band closed the concert with my
favourite song.*
finish, end, complete, conclude, stop,
terminate
(informal) wind up

clot verb
*If you cut yourself, the blood will clot and
form a scab.*
thicken, solidify

cloth noun
*The curtains were made of striped cotton
cloth.*
fabric, material
A word for cloth in general is **textiles**.

✺ WORD WEB

SOME KINDS OF CLOTH
**canvas, corduroy, cotton, denim, felt,
flannel, jersey, linen, (trademark) Lycra,
muslin, nylon, polyester, rayon, satin,
silk, taffeta, tweed, velvet, wool**

clothe verb
to be clothed in
The bridesmaids were clothed in white.
be dressed in, be wearing

clothes plural noun
What clothes are you taking on holiday?
clothing, garments, outfits, dress, attire,
garb, finery
(informal) gear, togs, get-up
A set of clothes to wear is a **costume, outfit,**
or **suit.**
An official set of clothes worn for school or
work is a **uniform.**

WORD WEB

SOME ITEMS OF CLOTHING
blouse, caftan, camisole, chador or chuddar, dhoti, dress, dungarees, frock, gown, jeans, jersey, jodhpurs, jumper, kilt, kimono, leggings, miniskirt, pinafore, polo shirt, pullover, robe, sari, sarong, shirt, shorts, skirt, slacks, smock, suit, sweater, sweatshirt, trousers, trunks, T-shirt, tunic, waistcoat

OUTER CLOTHES
anorak, apron, blazer, cagoule, cape, cardigan, cloak, coat, dressing gown, duffel coat, fleece, gilet, hoody, greatcoat, jacket, mackintosh, oilskins, overalls, overcoat, parka, poncho, raincoat, shawl, shrug, stole, tracksuit, windcheater

UNDERWEAR
boxer shorts, bra, briefs, crop top, drawers, knickers, pants, petticoat, slip, socks, stockings, tights, underpants, vest

CLOTHES FOR SLEEPING IN
nightdress or (informal) nightie, pyjamas

CLOTHES WORN IN THE PAST
corset, doublet, frock coat, gauntlet, ruff, toga

ACCESSORIES WORN WITH CLOTHES
belt, braces, cravat, earmuffs, gloves, sash, scarf, shawl, tie

See also **hat**, **shoe**

PARTS OF A GARMENT
bodice, button, buttonhole, collar, cuff, hem, lapel, pocket, seam, sleeve, waistband, zip

THINGS USED TO DECORATE CLOTHES
beads, frills, fringes, lace, ruffles, sequins, tassels

WRITING TIPS

You can use these words to describe **clothes**

baggy, casual, chic, dowdy, drab, fashionable, fine, flashy, flattering, frilly, frumpy, glamorous, ill-fitting, loose, luxurious, old-fashioned, ornate, ragged, roomy, shabby, skimpy, smart, sporty, stylish, tattered or in tatters, threadbare, tight-fitting, trendy, worn

The stranger was wearing an extremely shabby set of wizard's robes which had been darned in several places.
— J. K. Rowling, *Harry Potter and the Prisoner of Azkaban*

cloud noun
A **cloud** of steam billowed from the kettle.
billow, puff, haze, mist

cloudy adjective
1 *The day was cold and* **cloudy**.
dull, overcast, grey, dark, dismal, gloomy, sunless
opposite cloudless
See also **weather**
2 *We couldn't see any fish in the* **cloudy** *water.*
muddy, murky, hazy, milky
opposites clear, transparent

club noun
1 *The warrior brandished a wooden* **club**.
stick, baton, truncheon
2 *Would you like to join our book* **club**?
group, society, association, organization, circle, union

club verb
The giant **clubbed** *Jack on the head.*
hit, strike, thump, whack, batter, bash
For other ways of hitting see **hit**

clue noun
1 *I don't know the answer. Can you give me a* **clue**?
hint, suggestion, indication, pointer, tip, idea

a
b
c
d
e
f
g
h
i
j
k
l
m
n
o
p
q
r
s
t
u
v
w
x
y
z

A

2 *'This footprint is an important clue,' said the detective.*
piece of evidence, lead
See also **detective**

B

C

clump noun
The owl flew into a clump of trees on the hill.
group, thicket, cluster, collection
A clump of grass or hair is a **tuft**.

D

E

F

clumsy adjective
The clumsy gnome was always breaking things.
careless, awkward, ungainly, inept
An informal name for a clumsy person is **butterfingers**.
opposite **graceful**

G

H

I

J

cluster noun
A cluster of people waited outside the cinema.
crowd, bunch, collection, assembly, gathering, knot
See also **group**

K

L

M

clutch verb
The mountaineer clutched his rope.
catch, clasp, cling to, grab, grasp, grip, hang on to, hold on to, seize, snatch

N

O

P

clutches plural noun
The evil wizard had us in his clutches.
grasp, power, control

Q

R

clutter noun
We'll have to clear up all this clutter.
mess, muddle, junk, litter, rubbish, odds and ends

S

T

coach noun
1 *We went to Cardiff by coach.*
bus
For other vehicles see **vehicle**
2 *Their football team has a new coach.*
trainer, instructor

U

V

coach verb
He was coached by a former champion.
train, teach, instruct

W

X

Y

Z

coarse adjective
1 *The blanket was made of coarse woollen material.*
rough, harsh, scratchy, bristly, hairy
opposite **soft**
2 *We were shocked by their coarse table manners.*
rude, offensive, impolite, improper, indecent, crude, vulgar
opposites **polite, refined**

coast noun
After the disaster, oil was washed up along the coast.
coastline, shore
See also **seashore**

coast verb
I coasted down the hill on my bike.
cruise, freewheel, glide

coat noun
1 *The detective was wearing a thick winter coat.*
For coats and other garments see **clothes**
2 *The fox had a reddish-brown coat.*
hide, pelt, skin, fur, hair
A sheep's coat is a **fleece**.
3 *The front door needs a coat of paint.*
layer, coating, covering, lick

coat verb
We ate marshmallows coated with chocolate.
cover, spread, smear, glaze

coax verb
Sam coaxed the hamster back into its cage.
persuade, tempt, entice

code noun
1 *There is a strict code of conduct for using the pool.*
rules, regulations, laws
2 *The message was written in a secret code.*
To put a message in code is to **encode** or **encrypt** it.
To understand a message in code is to **decode, decipher**, or (informal) **crack** it.

comb verb
1 *I combed my hair and put it in a ponytail.*
arrange, groom, tidy, untangle
2 *The police combed the house in search of clues.*
search thoroughly, hunt through, scour, ransack, rummage through

combat noun
Two hundred warriors were killed in combat.
battle, war, warfare, fighting
See also **fight**

combat verb
There's a new campaign to combat crime in the city.
fight, oppose, resist, stand up to, tackle, battle against, grapple with

combine verb
1 *We combined our pocket money to buy a kite.*
put together, add together, join, merge, unite, amalgamate
opposite **divide**
2 *Combine the mixture with water to make a paste.*
mix, stir together, blend, mingle, bind
opposite **separate**

come verb comes, coming, came, come
1 *We expect our guests to come in the afternoon.*
arrive, appear, visit
opposite **go**
2 *When you hear a cuckoo, you know that summer is coming.*
advance, draw near
to come about
Can you tell me how the accident came about?
happen, occur, take place, result
to come across
I came across an old friend of mine.
find, discover, chance upon, meet, bump into
to come round or to come to
How long did it take me to come round after the operation?
become conscious, revive, wake up

to come to
1 *Tell me when you come to the last chapter.*
reach, get to, arrive at
2 *What did the repair bill come to?*
add up to, amount to, total

comfort noun
1 *My teddy bear was a comfort to me when I was ill.*
reassurance, consolation, encouragement, support, relief
2 *If I had a million pounds, I could live in comfort.*
ease, luxury, contentment, well-being, prosperity, affluence

comfort verb
The coach tried to comfort the team after they lost.
cheer up, console, reassure, encourage, hearten, sympathize with, soothe

comfortable adjective
1 *The bed was so comfortable that Goldilocks fell fast asleep.*
cosy, snug, relaxing, easy, soft, warm, roomy, padded, plush
(informal) comfy
opposite **uncomfortable**
2 *Wear comfortable clothes for travelling.*
casual, informal, loose-fitting
3 *Our cat leads a comfortable life.*
contented, happy, pleasant, agreeable, well-off, prosperous, luxurious, affluent

comic or comical adjective
We laughed at his comic remarks.
amusing, humorous, funny, hilarious, witty, diverting
(informal) hysterical
To be comical in a cheeky way is to be **facetious**.
To be comical in a silly way is to be **absurd**, **farcical**, **ludicrous**, or **ridiculous**.
To be comical in a hurtful way is to be **sarcastic**.

command noun
1 *The general gave the command to attack.*
order, instruction, commandment, edict

A

B

C

D

E

F

G

H

I

J

K

L

M

N

O

P

Q

R

S

T

U

V

W

X

Y

Z

2 *Captain Nemo has* command *of the whole crew.*
charge, control, authority (over), power (over), management, supervision
3 *My sister has a good* command *of Spanish.*
knowledge, mastery, grasp, understanding, ability (in), skill (in)

command verb
1 *The officer* commanded *his troops to fire.*
order, instruct, direct, tell, bid
2 *The captain* commands *the ship.*
control, direct, be in charge of, govern, head, lead, manage, administer, supervise

commander noun
The commander *decided to abandon the expedition.*
leader, chief, head, officer-in-charge

commence verb
The flag is a signal for the race to commence.
begin, start, embark (on)

commend verb
The head commended *us on our work.*
congratulate, compliment, praise, applaud
opposite **criticize**

comment noun
He made some nasty comments *about his boss.*
remark, statement, observation, opinion, mention, reference
A hostile comment *is a* criticism.

commit verb
The thieves were planning to commit *another robbery.*
carry out, do, perform, execute

commitment noun
1 *Our team certainly has the* commitment *to win.*
determination, dedication, enthusiasm, keenness, passion, resolution
2 *I've made a* commitment *to join the choir.*
promise, pledge, vow, undertaking, guarantee

committee noun
The tennis club is run by a committee *of volunteers.*
board, panel, council, body, cabinet

common adjective
1 *Colds are a* common *complaint in winter.*
commonplace, everyday, frequent, normal, ordinary, familiar, well known, widespread
opposite **rare**
2 *'Good morning' is a* common *way to greet people.*
typical, usual, regular, routine, standard, customary, conventional, habitual, traditional
opposite **uncommon**
3 *My friends and I have a* common *interest in music.*
shared, mutual, joint

commonplace adjective
Computers are now commonplace *in schools.*
common, everyday, frequent, usual, normal, ordinary, routine, familiar

commotion noun
Football supporters were causing a commotion *outside.*
disturbance, row, fuss, trouble, disorder, unrest, agitation, turmoil, uproar, racket, rumpus, upheaval, riot, fracas, furore, hullabaloo, brouhaha, pandemonium, bedlam

communal adjective
The swimming pool has communal *showers.*
shared, public, common
opposite **private**

communicate verb
1 *Steve* communicated *his boredom with a yawn.*
express, make known, indicate, convey, disclose, announce, pass on, proclaim, publish, report
2 *Nowadays, we* communicate *by email.*
contact each other, correspond, be in touch

communication noun
1 *Dolphins use sound for communication.*
communicating, contact, understanding each other
2 *I've received an urgent communication.*
message, dispatch, letter, statement, announcement

communication noun

WORD WEB

SOME FORMS OF SPOKEN COMMUNICATION
chat, conversation, dialogue, gossip, lecture, message, phone call, rumour, speech

SOME FORMS OF WRITTEN COMMUNICATION
blog, cable, correspondence, email, fax, greetings card, letter, memo or **memorandum, note, notice, postcard, telegram, text**

OTHER FORMS OF COMMUNICATION
body language, Braille, hand gesture, the Internet, Morse code, radio, semaphore, sign language or **signing, telepathy, television, webcast, website**
See illustration.

American sign language for 'love'

British sign language for 'walk'

community noun
My uncle grew up in a farming community.
area, district, neighbourhood, locality

compact adjective
This camera is light and compact.
small, portable, petite
opposite large

companion noun
Zak's pony was his favourite companion.
friend, partner, comrade
(informal) **mate, buddy, pal, chum**

company noun
1 *My cousin works for a computer company.*
business, firm, corporation, organization, establishment
2 *Shrek shunned the company of other ogres.*
fellowship, companionship, friendship, society

compare verb
Can you compare these sets of figures?
contrast, juxtapose, relate, set side by side
to compare with
This copy can't compare with the original painting.
compete with, rival, emulate, equal, match

a
b
c
d
e
f
g
h
i
j
k
l
m
n
o
p
q
r
s
t
u
v
w
x
y
z

A B **C** D E F G H I J K L M N O P Q R S T U V W X Y Z

comparison noun
1 *I put the two dresses side by side for comparison.*
comparing, contrast, juxtaposition
2 *There's no comparison between their team and ours.*
similarity, resemblance, likeness, match

compartment noun
The sewing box has compartments for needles and pins.
section, division, area, space

compatible adjective
Miss Scott and her mother were not at all compatible.
well suited, well matched
opposite **incompatible**

compel verb
You can't compel me to come with you.
force, make

compete verb
Five schools will be competing in the hockey tournament.
participate, perform, take part, enter
to compete against
We are competing against a strong team this week.
oppose, play against, contend with

competent adjective
You have to be a competent swimmer to join the club.
able, capable, skilful, skilled, accomplished, proficient, experienced, expert, qualified, trained
opposite **incompetent**

competition noun

> **WORD WEB**
> SOME KINDS OF COMPETITION
> championship, contest, game, knock-out competition, match, quiz, race, rally, series, tournament, trial
>
> See also **sport**

competitor noun
The competitors lined up for the start of the race.
contestant, contender, challenger, participant, opponent, rival
People who take an exam are **candidates** or **entrants**.

complain verb
Miss Grouch spent most of her life complaining.
moan, protest, grumble, grouse, gripe, whinge, make a fuss
to complain about
I wrote a letter complaining about the noise.
protest about, object to, criticize, find fault with
opposite **praise**

complaint noun
1 *They received hundreds of complaints about the film.*
criticism, objection, protest, moan, grumble
2 *You have a nasty stomach complaint.*
disease, illness, ailment, sickness, infection

complement verb
That shade of green complements your eyes.
accompany, go with

complete adjective
1 *Your training as a witch is not yet complete.*
completed, ended, finished, accomplished, concluded
opposite **unfinished**
2 *Have you got a complete set of cards?*
whole, entire, full, intact
opposite **incomplete**
3 *My birthday party was a complete disaster.*
total, utter, sheer, absolute, thorough, downright, perfect, pure

complete verb
We have completed all the tasks on the sheet.
finish, end, conclude, carry out, perform

complex adjective
Defusing a bomb is a complex task.
complicated, difficult, elaborate, detailed, intricate, involved
(informal) fiddly
opposite simple

complexion noun
The elf had a greenish tinge to his complexion.
skin, colour, colouring
For ways to describe complexion see face

complicated adjective
The plot of the film is very complicated.
complex, intricate, involved, difficult, elaborate, convoluted
opposites simple, straightforward

complimentary adjective
1 *My teacher made complimentary remarks on my playing.*
appreciative, approving, admiring, positive, favourable, flattering
opposites critical, insulting, negative
2 *We were given complimentary tickets for the game.*
free, gratis

compliments plural noun
It was nice to get compliments about my cooking.
praise, appreciation, approval, congratulations, tribute
Compliments which you don't deserve are flattery.
opposite insults

component noun
The factory makes components for cars.
part, bit, piece, element, spare part

compose verb
Beethoven composed nine symphonies.
create, devise, produce, make up, think up, write

to be composed of
This quilt is composed of pieces of patchwork.
be made of, consist of, comprise

composition noun
Is the song your own composition?
piece, work, creation
(formal) opus
For types of musical composition see music

comprehend verb
The crowd couldn't comprehend what was happening.
understand, realize, appreciate, figure out, grasp, perceive, follow

comprehensive adjective
She gave us a comprehensive account of her travels.
complete, full, thorough, detailed, extensive, inclusive, exhaustive, wide-ranging, encyclopedic
opposite selective

compress verb
I tried to compress all my clothes into one bag.
press, squeeze, cram, crush, jam, squash, stuff, flatten

comprise verb
The team comprised athletes from several countries.
be composed of, consist of, include, contain

compulsive adjective
1 *Suddenly, I felt a compulsive urge to laugh.*
compelling, overwhelming, overpowering, irresistible, uncontrollable
2 *We knew that the troll was a compulsive liar.*
habitual, obsessive, incurable

compulsory adjective
The wearing of seat belts is compulsory.
required, obligatory, necessary
opposite optional

a
b
c
d
e
f
g
h
i
j
k
l
m
n
o
p
q
r
s
t
u
v
w
x
y
z

A B C D E F G H I J K L M N O P Q R S T U V W X Y Z

computer noun

WORD WEB

SOME KINDS OF COMPUTER
laptop, mainframe, notebook,
PC or personal computer, server

SOME PARTS OF A COMPUTER SYSTEM
CD-ROM drive, DVD drive, hard disk,
keyboard, memory stick, microchip,
microprocessor, modem, monitor,
motherboard, mouse, processor, screen,
terminal, touch pad, USB port, webcam

OTHER TERMS USED IN COMPUTING
back-up, broadband, browser, byte,
cursor, data, database, download,
digital, disk, email, gigabyte, hardware,
Internet, megabyte, memory, menu,
MP3, network, online, printout,
program, RAM, software, upload, virus,
web, window, wireless, word processor

concave adjective
see curved
opposite **convex**

conceal verb
1 *The dog tried to conceal its bone.*
hide, cover up, bury
2 *We tried to conceal our hiding place.*
disguise, mask, screen, camouflage,
make invisible
3 *Don't conceal the truth.*
keep quiet about, keep secret, hush up,
suppress

conceited adjective
He was so conceited when he won first prize!
boastful, arrogant, proud, vain,
self-satisfied
(informal) big-headed, cocky
opposite **modest**

conceive verb
1 *Who conceived this silly plan?*
think up, devise, invent, make up,
originate, plan, produce, work out
(informal) dream up

2 *I could not conceive how the plan would
work.*
imagine, see

concentrate verb
1 *I had to concentrate to hear what she was
saying.*
be attentive, think hard, focus
2 *The crowds concentrated in the middle of
town.*
collect, gather, converge

concept noun
I find the concept of time travel fascinating.
idea, thought, notion

concern verb
1 *This conversation doesn't concern you.*
affect, involve, be important to, matter to,
be relevant to, relate to
2 *It concerns me that we are destroying the
rainforests.*
bother, distress, trouble, upset, worry

concern noun
1 *My private life is no concern of theirs.*
affair, business
2 *Global warming is a great concern to us all.*
worry, anxiety, fear
3 *She's the head of a business concern.*
company, firm, enterprise, establishment

concerned adjective
1 *After waiting an hour, Julia began to feel
concerned.*
worried, bothered, troubled, anxious,
upset, distressed
2 *We're writing a letter to all those
concerned.*
involved, connected, related, affected

concerning preposition
The head spoke to me concerning my future.
about, regarding, relating to,
with reference to, relevant to

concert noun
The jazz band is giving a concert tonight.
recital, performance, show

concise adjective
He gave the police a concise account of what happened.
brief, short, condensed, succinct
A concise account of something is a precis or summary.
opposite long

conclude verb
1 *We concluded the Christmas concert with carols.*
end, finish, complete, round off, wind up
2 *The concert concluded with some carols.*
close, terminate, culminate
3 *They concluded that he was guilty.*
decide, deduce, infer, suppose, assume, gather

conclusion noun
1 *The conclusion of the film was a bit puzzling.*
close, end, finale, finish, completion, culmination
2 *'What is your conclusion, Inspector?'*
decision, judgement, opinion, verdict, deduction

concrete adjective
The police are looking for concrete evidence.
real, actual, definite, firm, solid, substantial, physical, factual, objective
opposite abstract

condemn verb
1 *The manager condemned the behaviour of the players.*
criticize, disapprove of, denounce, deplore, reproach
opposite praise
2 *The judge condemned the men to death.*
sentence
opposite acquit

condense verb
1 *I condensed my poem so that it fitted on one page.*
reduce, shorten, compress, summarize
opposite expand

2 *Steam condenses on a cold window.*
become liquid, form condensation
opposite evaporate

condition noun
1 *Is your bike in good condition?*
state, order, repair
2 *A dog needs exercise to stay in good condition.*
fitness, health, shape
3 *It's a condition of membership that you pay a subscription.*
requirement, obligation, term
on condition that
You can come on condition that you pay your own fare.
provided, providing that, only if

conduct verb
1 *A guide conducted us round the museum.*
guide, lead, take, accompany, escort
2 *We asked the eldest girl to conduct our meeting.*
lead, manage, control, run, administer, supervise, preside over, organize, handle
to conduct yourself
The grown-ups did not conduct themselves well.
behave, act, carry on

conduct noun
Our teacher congratulated us on our good conduct.
behaviour, manners, attitude

confer verb
1 *They conferred the freedom of the city on the victorious team.*
give (to), grant (to), present (to), award (to)
2 *The king conferred with his advisors before making a decision.*
consult, have a discussion, talk things over, converse

conference noun
All the witches were invited to a grand conference.
meeting, consultation, discussion

a
b
c
d
e
f
g
h
i
j
k
l
m
n
o
p
q
r
s
t
u
v
w
x
y
z

A B **C** D E F G H I J K L M N O P Q R S T U V W X Y Z

confess verb
The goblin confessed to stealing the gold.
admit, own up to, acknowledge, reveal

confidence noun
1 *We can face the future with confidence.*
hope, optimism, faith
opposite **doubt**
2 *I wish I had her confidence.*
self-confidence, assurance, boldness,
conviction

confident adjective
1 *I am confident that we will win.*
certain, sure, positive, optimistic
opposite **doubtful**
2 *She is a confident sort of person.*
self-confident, assertive, bold, fearless,
unafraid

confidential adjective
The details of the plan are confidential.
secret, private
opposite **public**

confine verb
1 *They confined their discussion to the
weather.*
limit, restrict
2 *Our farm animals are not confined indoors.*
enclose, surround, fence in, shut in,
coop up, hem in

confirm verb
1 *The strange events confirmed his belief in
ghosts.*
prove, justify, support, back up, reinforce
opposite **disprove**
2 *I phoned to confirm my appointment at the
dentist.*
verify, make official
opposite **cancel**

confiscate verb
The janitor confiscated our ball.
take away, take possession of, seize

conflict noun
There's a lot of conflict in their family.
disagreement, quarrelling, fighting,
hostility, friction, antagonism, opposition,
strife, unrest

conflict verb
to conflict with
*Her account of what happened conflicts
with mine.*
disagree with, differ from, contradict,
contrast with, clash with

conflicting adjective
*My brother and I have conflicting tastes in
music.*
different, contrasting, contradictory,
opposite, incompatible

conform verb
to conform to or with
*The club expels anyone who doesn't conform
with the rules.*
follow, keep to, obey, abide by, agree with,
fit in with, submit to
opposite **disobey**

confront verb
*I decided to confront her and demand an
apology.*
challenge, stand up to, face up to

confuse verb
1 *I was confused by the directions on
the map.*
puzzle, bewilder, mystify, baffle, perplex
2 *You must be confusing me with
someone else.*
mix up, muddle

confusion noun
1 *There was great confusion when the lights
went out.*
chaos, commotion, fuss, uproar, turmoil,
pandemonium, bedlam, hullabaloo
2 *There was a look of confusion on
her face.*
bewilderment, puzzlement, perplexity

congratulate verb
We congratulated the winners.
praise, applaud, compliment
opposite **criticize**

congregate verb
The party guests congregated in the hall.
gather, assemble, collect, come together
opposite disperse

connect verb
1 *What's the best way to connect these wires?*
join, attach, fasten, link, couple, fix together, tie together
opposite separate
2 *The fingerprints connected him with the crime.*
make a connection between, associate, relate

connection noun
There is a close connection between our two families.
association, relationship, link

conquer verb
1 *Extra troops were sent to conquer the enemy forces.*
beat, defeat, overcome, vanquish, get the better of, overwhelm, crush, rout, thrash
2 *Gaul was conquered by Julius Caesar.*
seize, capture, take, win, occupy, possess
3 *Several climbers have conquered Mount Everest.*
climb, reach the top of

conqueror noun
Cheering crowds greeted the conquerors.
victor, winner

conquest noun
The book gave an account of the Norman conquest.
invasion, occupation, capture, possession

conscientious adjective
Elves are very conscientious workers.
hard-working, careful, dependable, reliable, responsible, dutiful, meticulous, painstaking, thorough
opposite careless

conscious adjective
1 *The patient was conscious throughout the operation.*
awake, alert, aware
opposite unconscious
2 *She made a conscious effort to improve her work.*
deliberate, intentional, planned
opposite accidental

consent verb
to consent to
The head has consented to our request.
agree to, grant, approve of, authorize
opposite refuse

consequence noun
1 *He drank the potion without thinking of the consequences.*
effect, result, outcome, upshot, sequel
2 *The loss of a few pence is of no consequence.*
importance, significance

conservation noun
Our group supports the conservation of wildlife.
preservation, protection, maintenance, upkeep
opposite destruction

conservative adjective
1 *Miss Frump has a very conservative taste in clothes.*
old-fashioned, conventional, unadventurous, traditional
opposites progressive, up-to-date
2 *At a conservative estimate, the work will take six months.*
cautious, moderate, reasonable
opposite extreme

conserve verb
The explorers had to conserve their water supply.
save, preserve, be sparing with, use wisely, look after, protect
opposite waste

a
b
c
d
e
f
g
h
i
j
k
l
m
n
o
p
q
r
s
t
u
v
w
x
y
z

consider verb
1 *The detective considered the problem carefully.*
think about, examine, contemplate, ponder on, reflect on, study, weigh up, meditate about
2 *I consider this to be my best work.*
believe, judge, reckon

considerable adjective
1000 dollars is a considerable sum of money.
big, large, significant, substantial, sizeable
opposites **negligible, insignificant**

considerate adjective
It was considerate of you to lend me your umbrella.
kind, kind-hearted, helpful, obliging, sympathetic, thoughtful, unselfish, caring, charitable, neighbourly
opposite **selfish**

consist verb
to consist of
1 *The planet consists largely of craters.*
be made of, be composed of, comprise, contain, include, incorporate
2 *His job consists mostly of answering the phone.*
involve

consistency noun
The mixture had the consistency of porridge.
texture, thickness, density

consistent adjective
1 *These plants need to be kept at a consistent temperature.*
steady, constant, regular, stable, unchanging
2 *Fortunately, our goalkeeper is a consistent player.*
predictable, dependable, reliable
opposite **inconsistent**

console verb
He did his best to console me when my dog died.
comfort, soothe, sympathize with, support

conspicuous adjective
1 *The clock tower is a conspicuous landmark.*
prominent, notable, obvious, eye-catching, unmistakable, visible
2 *I had made some conspicuous mistakes.*
clear, noticeable, obvious, evident, glaring
opposite **inconspicuous**

constant adjective
1 *There is a constant noise of traffic on the motorway.*
continual, continuous, never-ending, non-stop, ceaseless, incessant, interminable, endless, everlasting, permanent, perpetual, unending, persistent, relentless
opposite **changeable**
2 *My dog has been my constant friend for many years.*
faithful, loyal, dependable, reliable, firm, true, trustworthy, devoted
opposite **unreliable**

constitute verb
In rugby, fifteen players constitute a team.
make up, compose, comprise, form

construct verb
We constructed a tree-house in the back garden.
build, erect, assemble, make, put together, put up, set up
opposite **demolish**

construction noun
1 *The construction of the tree-house took all afternoon.*
building, erecting, erection, assembly, setting-up
2 *The hut was a flimsy construction.*
building, structure

consult verb
1 *You should consult the dentist about your sore tooth.*
ask, get advice from, speak to
2 *If you don't know how to spell a word, consult your dictionary.*
refer to

consume verb
1 *The birds consumed all the bread in ten minutes!*
eat, devour, gobble up, guzzle
2 *The truck consumed a great deal of fuel.*
use up
3 *The building was consumed by fire.*
destroy

contact verb
I'll contact you when I have some news.
call, call on, get in touch with, speak to, communicate with, notify, talk to, correspond with, phone, ring, write to

contagious adjective
Mumps is a very contagious disease.
catching, infectious

contain verb
1 *This box contains various odds and ends.*
hold
2 *A dictionary contains words and definitions.*
include, incorporate, comprise, consist of

container noun
Put the left over sauce in a container.
vessel, receptacle, holder, box, case, canister, carton, pot, tub, tin

contaminate verb
The river was contaminated with chemicals.
pollute, poison, infect
opposite **purify**

contemplate verb
1 *Asha contemplated herself in the mirror.*
look at, view, observe, survey, watch, stare at, gaze at
2 *The robbers contemplated what to do next.*
think about, consider, ponder, study, reflect on, weigh up, meditate about

contemporary adjective
Do you like contemporary music?
current, fashionable, modern, up-to-date, the latest
(informal) trendy
opposites **old-fashioned, out-of-date**

contempt noun
The knight stared at his enemy with a look of contempt.
hatred, scorn, loathing, disgust, dislike, distaste
opposite **admiration**

contend verb
I contend that I was right.
declare, claim, argue, assert, maintain
to contend with
1 *The team had to contend with strong opposition.*
compete with, fight against, oppose, grapple with, struggle against, strive against
2 *We had to contend with bad weather and midges!*
cope with, deal with, face, put up with

content adjective
Fergus was perfectly content to sit reading a book.
happy, contented, satisfied, pleased, willing
opposite **unwilling**

contented adjective
After her meal, the cat looked very contented.
happy, pleased, content, satisfied, fulfilled, serene, peaceful, relaxed, comfortable, tranquil, untroubled
opposite **discontented**

contents plural noun
The children tried to guess the contents of the mystery parcel.
elements, ingredients, parts

contest noun
The tennis final was an exciting contest.
competition, challenge, fight, bout, encounter, struggle, game, match, tournament

contest verb
Several players contested the referee's decision.
challenge, disagree with, question, oppose, argue against, quarrel with

a
b
c
d
e
f
g
h
i
j
k
l
m
n
o
p
q
r
s
t
u
v
w
x
y
z

A

B

C

D

E

F

G

H

I

J

K

L

M

N

O

P

Q

R

S

T

U

V

W

X

Y

Z

contestant noun
There are twenty contestants *in the spelling competition.*
competitor, participant, player, contender

continual adjective
I get sick of their continual *arguing.*
constant, persistent, perpetual, repeated, frequent, recurrent, eternal, unending
See also continuous
opposite occasional

continue verb
1 *We* continued *our search until it got dark.*
keep up, prolong, sustain, persevere with, pursue
(informal) stick at
2 *This rain can't* continue *for long.*
carry on, last, persist, endure, keep on, go on, linger
3 *We'll* continue *our meeting after lunch.*
resume, proceed with, pick up

continuous adjective
We had continuous *rain all through our holiday.*
never-ending, non-stop, ceaseless, everlasting, incessant, unbroken, unceasing, uninterrupted
An illness which continues for a long time is a chronic *illness.*
See also continual
opposite intermittent

contract noun
The actress has signed a contract *for a new film.*
agreement, deal, undertaking
A contract between two countries is an alliance *or* treaty.
A contract to end a dispute about money is a settlement.

contract verb
1 *Metal* contracts *when it gets colder.*
reduce, lessen, shrink, tighten
opposite expand
2 *The crew* contracted *a mysterious illness.*
catch, develop, get

contradict verb
I didn't dare to contradict *the witch.*
challenge, disagree with, speak against

contraption noun
The inventor's house was full of weird contraptions.
machine, device, gadget, invention, apparatus, contrivance, mechanism, gizmo

contrary adjective
Griselda had always been a sulky, contrary *child.*
awkward, difficult, stubborn, disobedient, obstinate, uncooperative, unhelpful, wilful, perverse
opposite cooperative
contrary to
Contrary *to popular belief, snakes are not slimy.*
differing from, against, opposing, in the face of, unlike

contrast verb
1 *We were asked to* contrast *two of our favourite poems.*
compare, juxtapose, distinguish between
2 *Her handwriting* contrasts *with mine.*
differ (from), clash

contrast noun
There is a sharp contrast *between the two paintings.*
difference, distinction, opposition
opposite similarity

contribute verb
Will you contribute *something to our charity collection?*
donate, give, provide
(informal) chip in
to contribute to
The sunny weather contributed *to our enjoyment.*
add to, help, aid, encourage, enhance

contrive verb
They contrived *a way to escape from the dungeon.*
think up, plan, make up, create, invent

control noun
The captain had complete control over the crew.
authority, power, command, government, management, direction, leadership, guidance

control verb
1 *The government controls the country's affairs.*
be in control of, be in charge of, manage, run, command, direct, lead, guide, govern, administer, regulate, rule, superintend, supervise
2 *Can't you control that dog?*
manage, handle, restrain
3 *They built a dam to control the floods.*
check, curb, hold back, contain

controversial adjective
The decision to award a penalty was controversial.
debatable, questionable, arguable

controversy noun
There is much controversy about the election results.
disagreement, debate, argument, dispute, quarrelling

convenient adjective
1 *Is there a convenient place to put my umbrella?*
suitable, appropriate, available, nearby, accessible
opposite **inconvenient**
2 *Mum has a convenient tool for opening jars.*
handy, helpful, useful, labour-saving, neat

conventional adjective
The conventional way to greet someone is to shake hands.
customary, traditional, usual, accepted, common, normal, ordinary, everyday, routine, standard, regular, habitual, orthodox
opposite **unconventional**

converge verb
The two rivers converge at this point.
come together, join, meet, merge, combine, coincide
opposite **divide**

conversation noun
An informal conversation is a **chat** or **gossip**.
A more formal conversation is a **discussion**.
A very formal conversation is a **conference**.
Conversation in a play or novel is **dialogue**.

converse verb
The travellers conversed happily for several minutes.
chat, talk, have a conversation, engage in conversation
See also **talk**

convert verb
1 *We have converted our attic into a games room.*
change, adapt, alter, transform
2 *I never used to like football, but my cousin converted me.*
change someone's mind, persuade, convince, win over

convex adjective
see **curved**
opposite **concave**

convey verb
1 *The breakdown truck conveyed our car to a garage.*
bring, carry, deliver, take, move, bear, transfer, transport
To convey something by sea is to **ferry** or **ship** it.
2 *What does his message convey to you?*
communicate, tell, reveal, indicate, signify, mean

convict noun
Four convicts have escaped from the prison.
prisoner, criminal

a
b
c
d
e
f
g
h
i
j
k
l
m
n
o
p
q
r
s
t
u
v
w
x
y
z

convict verb

The thieves were convicted and sent to prison.
condemn, declare guilty, sentence
opposite **acquit**

convince verb

The prisoner convinced them that he was innocent.
persuade, assure, satisfy, make believe, win round

convincing adjective

I tried to think of a convincing excuse.
persuasive, believable, credible, plausible

cook verb

To cook food for guests or customers is to cater for them.
Cooking as a business is catering.
The art or skill of cooking is cookery.

WORD WEB

SOME WAYS TO COOK FOOD
bake, barbecue, boil, braise, brew, broil, casserole, deep-fry, fry, grill, poach, roast, sauté, simmer, steam, stew, toast

OTHER WAYS TO PREPARE FOOD
baste, blend, chop, dice, grate, grind, infuse, knead, liquidize, marinade, mince, mix, peel, purée, sieve, sift, stir, whisk

SOME ITEMS THAT ARE USED FOR COOKING
baking tin or tray, barbecue, blender, bowl, carving knife, casserole, cauldron, chopping board, colander, cooker, dish, food processor, frying pan, grill, ladle, liquidizer, microwave, mincer, oven, pan, pot, rolling pin, saucepan, skewer, spatula, spit, strainer, toaster, whisk, wok, wooden spoon

See also **crockery, cutlery, kitchen**

cook noun

The chief cook in a restaurant or hotel is the chef.
A person who cooks food as a business is a caterer.

cool adjective

1 *The weather is cool for the time of year.*
chilly, coldish
opposites **hot, warm**
2 *Would you like a cool glass of lemonade?*
chilled, iced, refreshing
opposite **hot**
3 *Clifford remained cool when everyone else panicked.*
calm, level-headed, relaxed, unexcitable, unflustered
(informal) laid-back
A common simile is as cool as a cucumber.
opposite **frantic**
4 (informal) *Those roller skates are really cool!*
chic, fashionable, smart
(informal) trendy

cooperate verb

to cooperate with
The scouts cooperated with each other to build a fire.
work with, work together with, collaborate with, aid, assist, support

cope verb

Shall I help you, or can you cope on your own?
manage, carry on, get by, make do, survive
to cope with
I can't cope with all this homework!
deal with, handle, manage, get through

copy noun

That isn't the original painting—it's a copy.
replica, reproduction, duplicate, imitation, likeness
A copy made to deceive someone is a fake or a forgery.
A living organism which is identical to another is a clone.

copy verb

1 *I copied the poem into my planner.*
duplicate, reproduce, write out
To copy something in order to deceive is to fake or forge it.
2 *My parrot can copy my voice.*
imitate, impersonate, mimic

cord noun
The pilot pulled the cord to open his parachute.
string, rope, tape, strap, line, cable, flex

core noun
It is very hot at the earth's core.
centre, middle, inside, heart, nucleus

corn noun
The farmer was growing corn in the field.
grain, cereal, wheat

corner noun
1 *I'll meet you at the corner of the road.*
turn, turning, junction, crossroads, intersection
The place where two lines meet is an **angle.**
2 *I sat in a quiet corner and read her letter.*
alcove, recess, nook

correct adjective
1 *Your answers are all correct.*
right, accurate, exact, faultless
2 *I hope he has given us correct information.*
true, genuine, authentic, precise, reliable, factual
3 *What is the correct way to address this letter?*
proper, acceptable, regular, appropriate, suitable
opposite wrong

correct verb
1 *I have to correct my spelling mistakes.*
alter, put right, make better, improve
2 *Miss Nicol spent the day correcting exam papers.*
mark

correspond verb
to correspond with
1 *Her version of the story doesn't correspond with mine.*
agree with, match, be similar to, be consistent with, tally with
2 *Carol corresponds with a friend in Paris.*
write to, communicate with, send letters to

corrode verb
This acid will corrode metal.
eat away, erode, rot, rust

corrupt adjective
Corrupt officials had accepted millions of pounds in bribes.
dishonest, criminal, untrustworthy
(informal) bent, crooked
opposite honest

cost verb costs, costing, cost
How much do these shoes cost?
be worth, go for, sell for

cost noun
The bill shows the total cost.
price, charge, amount, payment, fee, figure, expense, expenditure, tariff
The cost of travelling on public transport is the **fare.**

costly adjective
It would be too costly to repair the car.
dear, expensive
opposite cheap

costume noun
The Irish dancers were wearing national costumes.
outfit, dress, clothing, suit, attire, garment, garb
(informal) get-up
A costume you dress up in for a party is **fancy dress.**
A set of clothes worn by soldiers or members of an organization is a **uniform.**
See also **clothes**

cosy adjective
It's good to feel cosy in bed when it's cold outside.
comfortable, snug, soft, warm, secure
opposite uncomfortable

couch noun
My brother sat on the couch watching TV all weekend.
settee, sofa
For other types of seat see **seat**

a
b
c
d
e
f
g
h
i
j
k
l
m
n
o
p
q
r
s
t
u
v
w
x
y
z

A B **C** D E F G H I J K L M N O P Q R S T U V W X Y Z

counsel verb
His advisors counselled him to surrender.
advise, guide, direct, encourage,
recommend, urge

count verb
1 *I'm counting the days until my birthday.*
add up, calculate, compute, estimate,
reckon, figure out, work out, total
2 *It's playing well that counts, not winning.*
be important, be significant, matter
to count on
You can count on me to support you.
depend on, rely on, trust, bank on

countless adjective
*Countless people watched the TV
broadcast.*
a great many, numerous,
innumerable
opposite **finite**

country noun
1 *England and Wales are separate
countries.*
nation, state, land, territory
A country ruled by a king or queen is a
kingdom, monarchy, or realm.
A country governed by leaders elected by
the people is a democracy.
A democratic country with a president is a
republic.
2 *We went for a picnic in the country.*
countryside, landscape, outdoors, scenery
opposites **town, city**
A word meaning 'to do with the country' is
rural and its opposite is urban.

coupon noun
*You can exchange these coupons for a
free mug.*
token, voucher, ticket

courage noun
The rescue dogs showed great courage.
bravery, boldness, daring, fearlessness,
nerve, pluck, valour, heroism, grit
(informal) guts
opposite **cowardice**

courageous adjective
*The warriors were always courageous in
battle.*
brave, bold, daring, fearless, heroic,
intrepid, plucky, gallant, valiant
opposite **cowardly**

course noun
1 *The hot-air balloon was drifting off its
course.*
direction, path, route, way, progress,
passage
2 *The war changed the course of history.*
development, progression, sequence,
succession
of course
Of course you can come to my party.
naturally, certainly, definitely, undoubtedly

courteous adjective
I received a courteous reply to my letter.
polite, respectful, well-mannered, civil,
considerate, friendly, helpful
opposite **rude**

cover verb
1 *A coat of paint will cover the graffiti.*
conceal, disguise, hide, obscure, mask,
blot out
2 *She covered her face with her hands.*
shield, screen, protect, shade, veil
3 *The hikers are hoping to cover twenty-five
miles a day.*
progress, travel
4 *An encyclopedia covers many subjects.*
deal with, include, contain, incorporate
5 *Will £50 cover your expenses?*
be enough for, pay for

cover noun
1 *The cover of the book was torn.*
wrapper
A cover for a letter is an envelope.
A cover for a book is a jacket.
A cover to keep papers in is a file or folder.
2 *On the bare hillside, there was no cover
from the storm.*
shelter, protection, defence, shield, refuge,
sanctuary

covering noun
There was a light covering of snow on the hills.
coating, coat, layer, blanket, carpet, film, sheet, skin, veil

cowardly adjective
It was cowardly to run away.
timid, faint-hearted, spineless, gutless
(informal) yellow, chicken
opposite brave

cower verb
A frightened creature was cowering in the corner.
cringe, shrink, crouch, flinch, quail

crack noun
1 *There's a crack in this cup.*
break, chip, fracture, flaw, chink, split
2 *The outlaw hid in a crack between two rocks.*
gap, opening, crevice, rift, cranny
3 *The detective heard the crack of a pistol shot.*
bang, fire, explosion, snap, pop
4 *She gave the robber a crack on the head.*
blow, bang, knock, smack, whack
5 *I had a crack at writing a poem.*
try, attempt, shot, go

crack verb
A brick fell down and cracked the pavement.
break, fracture, chip, split, shatter, splinter

craft noun
1 *I'd like to learn the craft of weaving.*
art, skill, technique, expertise, handicraft
For arts and crafts see art
2 *All sorts of craft were in the harbour.*
boats, ships, vessels
For types of boat or ship see boat

crafty adjective
The evil sorceress had a crafty plan.
cunning, clever, shrewd, scheming, sneaky, sly, tricky, wily, artful

cram verb
1 *We can't cram any more people in— the car is full.*
pack, squeeze, crush, force, jam, compress
2 *My sister is cramming for her maths exam.*
revise, study
(informal) swot

cramped adjective
The seating on the train was a bit cramped.
confined, narrow, restricted, tight, uncomfortable, crowded
(informal) poky
opposite roomy

crash noun
1 *I heard a loud crash from the kitchen.*
bang, smash
For other kinds of sound see sound[1]
2 *We saw a nasty crash on the motorway.*
accident, collision, smash, bump
A crash involving a lot of vehicles is a pile-up.
A train crash may involve a derailment.

crash verb
The car crashed into a lamp post.
bump, smash, collide, knock

crate noun
We packed our belongings into crates.
box, case, chest, packing case

crater noun
The surface of the Moon is full of craters.
pit, hole, hollow, cavity, chasm, opening, abyss

crawl verb
I saw a caterpillar crawling along a leaf.
creep, edge, inch, slither, clamber

craze noun
This game is the latest craze in the playground.
fad, trend, vogue, fashion, enthusiasm, obsession, passion

a
b
c
d
e
f
g
h
i
j
k
l
m
n
o
p
q
r
s
t
u
v
w
x
y
z

A
B
C
D
E
F
G
H
I
J
K
L
M
N
O
P
Q
R
S
T
U
V
W
X
Y
Z

crazy adjective

1 *The dog went crazy when it was stung by a wasp.*
mad, insane, frenzied, hysterical, frantic, berserk, delirious, wild
(informal) loopy, nuts
2 *It was a crazy idea to try to build a space rocket!*
absurd, ridiculous, ludicrous, daft, idiotic, senseless, silly, stupid, foolhardy, preposterous
(informal) bonkers, barmy, wacky
opposite **sensible**

creamy adjective

That ice cream is really creamy!
rich, smooth, thick, velvety

crease noun

Can you iron the creases out of this shirt?
wrinkle, crinkle, pucker, fold, furrow, groove, line
A crease made deliberately in a skirt or other garment is a **pleat**.

crease verb

Pack the clothes carefully, so you don't crease them.
wrinkle, crinkle, crumple, crush, pucker

create verb

1 *The cats were creating a racket outside.*
make, cause, produce
2 *We have created a website for our chess club.*
set up, start up, bring about, bring into existence, originate
You write a poem or story.
You compose music.
You draw or paint a picture.
You carve a statue.
You invent or think up a new idea.
You design a new product.
You devise a plan.
You found a new club or organization.
You manufacture goods.
You generate electricity.
You build or construct a model or a building.
opposite **destroy**

creation noun

1 *The TV programme is about the creation of life on earth.*
beginning, origin, birth, generation, initiation
2 *They raised money for the creation of a sports centre.*
building, construction, establishing, foundation
3 *This pizza recipe is my own creation.*
concept, invention

creative adjective

My aunt is a very creative person.
artistic, imaginative, inventive, original, inspired
opposite **unimaginative**

creator noun

Walt Disney was the creator of Mickey Mouse.
inventor, maker, originator, producer, deviser
The creator of a design is an **architect** or **designer**.
The creator of goods for sale is a **manufacturer**.

creature noun

A wild-looking creature emerged from the swamp.
animal, beast, being
See also **animal**
For creatures found in myths and legends see **myth**

credible adjective

The detective did not find the woman's story credible.
believable, convincing, persuasive, trustworthy, likely, possible, reasonable
opposite **incredible**

credit noun

The author is finally getting the credit she deserves.
recognition, honour, praise, distinction, fame, glory, reputation
opposite **dishonour**

credit verb
It's hard to credit that they are brother and sister.
believe, accept, have faith in, trust
opposite doubt

creed noun
Pupils of all races and creeds attend the school.
religion, doctrine, faith, set of beliefs

creep verb creeps, creeping, crept
1 *I watched the lizard creep back into its hiding place.*
crawl, edge, inch, slither, wriggle
2 *I crept out of bed without waking the others.*
move quietly, sneak, tiptoe, slip, slink, steal

creepy adjective
There were creepy noises coming from the cellar.
scary, frightening, eerie, ghostly, weird, sinister, uncanny, unearthly
(informal) spooky
See also **ghost**

crest noun
1 *The bird had a large red crest on its head.*
comb, plume, tuft
2 *There was a wonderful view from the crest of the hill.*
top, peak, summit, crown, head, brow

crevice noun
Moss was growing in the crevices in the rock.
crack, cranny, gap, opening, rift, split
A deep crack in a glacier is a **crevasse**.

crew noun
For words for groups of people see **group**

cricket noun

WORD WEB
PEOPLE WHO PLAY CRICKET
batsman, bowler, cricketer, fielder or **fieldsman, wicketkeeper**

The official who makes sure players keep to the rules is the **umpire**.

SOME OTHER TERMS USED IN CRICKET
boundary, crease, innings, maiden over, over, pitch, run, stump, wicket

crime noun
Robbing a bank is a serious crime.
offence, lawbreaking, wrongdoing

criminal noun
These men are dangerous criminals.
lawbreaker, offender, wrongdoer
(informal) crook
A criminal who has been sent to prison is a convict.

WORD WEB
SOME TYPES OF CRIMINAL
assassin, bandit, blackmailer, brigand, burglar, cat burglar, con man, gangster, highwayman, hijacker, kidnapper, mugger, murderer, outlaw, pickpocket, pirate, poacher, robber, shoplifter, smuggler, terrorist, thief, thug, vandal

criminal adjective
The gang were involved in many criminal schemes.
illegal, unlawful, corrupt, dishonest, wrong
(informal) bent, crooked
opposite honest

cringe verb
I cringed with embarrassment when my name was called.
shrink, flinch, wince, cower

cripple verb
1 *The fall may have crippled the horse.*
disable, handicap, maim, lame
2 *The country was nearly crippled by the war.*
ruin, destroy, crush, wreck, damage, weaken

crisis noun
The election result caused a crisis in the country.
emergency, problem, difficulty, predicament

a
b
c
d
e
f
g
h
i
j
k
l
m
n
o
p
q
r
s
t
u
v
w
x
y
z

93

A
B
C
D
E
F
G
H
I
J
K
L
M
N
O
P
Q
R
S
T
U
V
W
X
Y
Z

crisp adjective
1 *Fry the bacon until it's crisp.*
crispy, crunchy, brittle
opposites **soft, soggy, limp**
2 *It was a crisp winter morning.*
cold, fresh, frosty

critical adjective
1 *He made critical comments about my hair.*
negative, disapproving, derogatory,
uncomplimentary, unfavourable
opposite **complimentary**
2 *This match is critical for our team's chances of success.*
crucial, important, vital, serious, decisive
opposite **unimportant**

criticism noun
I think his criticism of my singing was unfair.
attack, disapproval, reprimand, reproach

criticize verb
She criticized us for being so careless.
blame, condemn, disapprove of, berate,
find fault with, reprimand, reproach, scold
opposite **praise**

crockery noun
Please put the crockery away.
china, dishes, plates

WORD WEB
SOME ITEMS OF CROCKERY
bowl, butter dish, cup, dinner plate,
gravy boat, milk jug, mug, plate, saucer,
side plate, sugar bowl, teacup, teapot,
tureen

crooked adjective
1 *The wizard bent his wand into a crooked shape.*
bent, twisted, warped, gnarled
opposite **straight**
2 (informal) *The crooked salesman was selling fake diamonds.*
criminal, dishonest, corrupt
(informal) bent
opposite **honest**

crop noun
We had a good crop of apples this year.
harvest, yield, produce
crop verb
Miss Marshall was cropping her garden hedge.
cut, trim, clip, snip, shear
to crop up
Several problems have cropped up.
arise, appear, occur, emerge, come up,
turn up

cross verb
1 *There is a bus stop where the two roads cross.*
criss-cross, intersect
2 *You can cross the river at the footbridge.*
go across, pass over, traverse, ford, span
cross adjective
My mum will be cross if we're late.
angry, annoyed, upset, vexed,
bad-tempered, ill-tempered, irritable,
grumpy, testy, irate
See also **angry**
opposite **pleased**

crouch verb
The outlaws crouched silently in the bushes.
squat, kneel, stoop, bend, duck, bob down,
hunch, huddle

crowd noun
1 *A crowd of people waited outside the theatre.*
gathering, group, assembly, bunch, cluster,
throng, mob, multitude, crush, horde,
swarm
2 *There was a huge crowd for the tennis final.*
audience, spectators, gate, attendance
crowd verb
1 *People crowded on the pavement to watch the parade.*
gather, collect, assemble, congregate,
mass, flock, muster
2 *Hundreds of people crowded into the hall.*
push, pile, squeeze, pack, cram, crush, jam,
bundle, herd

crowded adjective
The shops are always crowded at Christmas time.
full, packed, teeming, swarming, overflowing, jammed, congested
opposite **empty**

crown noun
The royal crown was made of solid gold.
coronet, diadem, tiara

crown verb
Mary was crowned Queen of Scots when she was a baby.
enthrone, anoint
A ceremony at which a king or queen is crowned is a **coronation**.

crucial adjective
We are at a crucial point in our chess game.
important, critical, decisive, vital, serious, momentous
opposite **unimportant**

crude adjective
1 *The refinery processes crude oil.*
raw, natural, unprocessed, unrefined
opposite **refined**
2 *We made a crude shelter out of twigs.*
rough, clumsy, makeshift, primitive
opposite **skilful**
3 *The teacher told them to stop using crude language.*
rude, obscene, coarse, dirty, foul, impolite, indecent, vulgar
opposite **polite**

cruel adjective
I think hunting is a cruel way to kill animals.
brutal, savage, vicious, fierce, barbaric, bloodthirsty, barbarous, heartless, ruthless, merciless, inhuman, sadistic, uncivilized, beastly
opposites **kind, humane, gentle**

crumb noun
We put out some crumbs of bread for the birds.
bit, fragment, scrap, morsel
See also **bit**

crumble verb
1 *The walls of the castle were beginning to crumble.*
disintegrate, break up, collapse, fall apart, decay, decompose
2 *The farmer crumbled some bread into his soup.*
crush, grind, pound, pulverize

crumpled adjective
Your shirt is crumpled.
creased, wrinkled, crinkled, crushed

crunch verb
1 *The dog was crunching on a bone.*
chew, munch, chomp, grind
See also **eat**
2 *I heard heavy footsteps crunching up the path.*
crush, grind, pound, smash

crush verb
1 *He crushed his anorak into his school bag.*
squash, squeeze, mangle, pound, press, bruise, crunch, scrunch
To crush something into a soft mess is to **mash** or **pulp** it.
To crush something into a powder is to **grind** or **pulverize** it.
To crush something out of shape is to **crumple** or **smash** it.
2 *Our soldiers crushed the attacking army.*
defeat, conquer, vanquish, overcome, overwhelm, quash, trounce, rout

crush noun
There was a crush of people at the front gates.
crowd, press, mob, throng, jam, congestion

a
b
c
d
e
f
g
h
i
j
k
l
m
n
o
p
q
r
s
t
u
v
w
x
y
z

A
B
C
D
E
F
G
H
I
J
K
L
M
N
O
P
Q
R
S
T
U
V
W
X
Y
Z

cry verb
1 *Someone was* **crying** *for help from the burning house.*
call, shout, yell, exclaim, roar, bawl, bellow, scream, screech, shriek
2 *The baby started to* **cry**.
sob, weep, bawl, blubber, wail, shed tears, snivel
When someone starts to cry, their eyes well up with tears.

cry noun
The wounded man let out a **cry** *of pain.*
call, shout, yell, roar, howl, exclamation, bellow, scream, screech, shriek, yelp

cuddle verb
My baby brother **cuddles** *a teddy bear in bed.*
hug, hold closely, clasp, embrace, caress, nestle against, snuggle against

cue noun
When I nod, that is your **cue** *to speak.*
sign, signal, reminder

culprit noun
Police are searching for the **culprits**.
criminal, offender, wrongdoer

cultivate verb
1 *Farmers have* **cultivated** *this land for centuries.*
farm, work, till, plough, grow crops on
2 *We want to* **cultivate** *good relations with our neighbours.*
develop, encourage, promote, try to achieve, further, improve

cunning adjective
The pirates had a **cunning** *plan to seize the ship.*
clever, crafty, devious, wily, ingenious, shrewd, artful, scheming, sly, tricky

cup noun
A tall cup with straight sides is a **mug**.
A tall cup without a handle is a **beaker** or **tumbler**.
A decorative drinking cup is a **goblet**.
For other containers for drinks see **drink**

cupboard noun
There are some spare pillows in the **cupboard**.
cabinet, dresser, sideboard
A cupboard for food is a **larder**.
For other items of furniture see **furniture**

curb verb
You must try to **curb** *your anger.*
control, restrain, suppress, check, hold back, limit, moderate, repress, restrict
opposite **encourage**

cure verb
1 *These pills will* **cure** *your headache.*
ease, heal, help, improve, make better, relieve
opposite **aggravate**
2 *No-one can* **cure** *the problem with my computer.*
correct, mend, sort, repair, fix, put an end to, put right

cure noun
I wish they could find a **cure** *for colds.*
remedy, treatment, antidote, medicine, therapy

curiosity noun
Babies are full of **curiosity** *about the world.*
inquisitiveness, interest
Uncomplimentary words are **nosiness**, **prying**, and **snooping**.

curious adjective
1 *We were all very* **curious** *about Joe's secret.*
inquisitive, inquiring, interested, intrigued, agog
An uncomplimentary word is **nosy**.
opposites **uninterested**, **indifferent**
2 *What is that* **curious** *smell?*
odd, strange, peculiar, abnormal, queer, unusual, extraordinary, funny, mysterious, puzzling, weird

curl verb
1 *The snake* **curled** *itself around a branch.*
wind, twist, loop, coil, wrap, curve, turn, twine
2 *Steam* **curled** *upwards from the cauldron.*
coil, spiral, twirl, swirl, furl, snake, writhe, ripple

curl noun
The girl's hair was a mass of golden curls.
wave, ringlet, coil, loop, twist, roll, scroll, spiral

curly adjective
My new doll has curly black hair.
curled, curling, wavy, frizzy, crinkly, ringletted
opposite **straight**

current noun
The wooden raft drifted along with the current.
flow, tide, stream
A current of air is a **draught**.

current adjective
1 *The shop sells all the current teenage fashions.*
modern, contemporary, present-day, up to date, topical, prevailing, prevalent
opposites **past, old-fashioned**
2 *Have you got a current passport?*
valid, usable, up to date
opposite **out of date**
3 *Who is the current prime minister?*
present, existing
opposites **past, former**

curse noun
1 *Long ago, a wizard put a curse on the family.*
jinx, hex
2 *When the gardener hit his finger, he let out a curse.*
swear word, oath

curve noun
Try to draw a straight line without any curves.
bend, curl, loop, turn, twist, arch, arc, bow, bulge, wave
A curve in the shape of a new moon is a **crescent**.
A curve on a road surface is a **camber**.

curve verb
The road ahead curves round to the right.
bend, wind, turn, twist, curl, loop, swerve, veer, snake, meander

curved adjective
The wall was painted with a series of curved lines.
curving, curvy, curled, looped, coiled, rounded, bulging, bent, arched, bowed, twisted, crooked, spiral, winding, meandering, serpentine, snaking, undulating
A surface which is curved like the inside of a circle is **concave**.
A surface which is curved like the outside of a circle is **convex**.

cushion verb
If you fall off the swing, the mat will cushion your fall.
soften, reduce the effect of, absorb, muffle

custom noun
1 *It's our custom to give presents at Christmas.*
tradition, practice, habit, convention, fashion, routine, way
2 *The shop is having a sale to attract more custom.*
customers, buyers, trade, business

customary adjective
It is customary to leave the waiter a tip.
traditional, conventional, usual, normal, common, typical, expected, habitual, routine, regular, everyday, ordinary, prevailing, prevalent
opposite **unusual**

customer noun
There was a queue of customers at the checkout.
buyer, shopper, client

cut verb cuts, cutting, cut
1 *The woodcutter cut the tree trunk to make logs.*
chop, slit, split, chip, notch, axe, hack, hew, cleave
To cut off a limb is to **amputate** or **sever** it.
To cut down a tree is to **fell** it.
To cut branches off a tree is to **lop** them.

a
b
c
d
e
f
g
h
i
j
k
l
m
n
o
p
q
r
s
t
u
v
w
x
y
z

A
B
C
D
E
F
G
H
I
J
K
L
M
N
O
P
Q
R
S
T
U
V
W
X
Y
Z

98

To cut twigs off a growing plant is to **prune** it.

To cut something up to examine it is to **dissect** it.

To cut stone to make a statue is to **carve** it.

To cut an inscription in stone is to **engrave** it.

2 *The cook* cut *the apples into small pieces.*
chop, slice, dice, grate, mince, shred

3 *I'm going to get my hair* cut *in the holidays.*
trim, clip, crop, snip, shave

To cut wool off a sheep is to **shear** it.

To cut grass is to **mow** it.

To cut corn is to **harvest** or reap it.

4 *Josh* cut *his foot on a sharp stone.*
gash, slash, nick, stab, pierce, wound

5 *This letter is too long—I'll need to* cut *it.*
shorten, condense, edit

6 *The shop has* cut *its prices by 10%.*
lower, reduce, decrease

If you cut something by half, you **halve** it.

cut noun

1 *I got a nasty* cut *when I was slicing bread.*
gash, wound, injury, nick, slash, scratch, slit, snip

2 *There has been a* cut *in the price of petrol.*
fall, reduction, decrease

cutlery noun

WORD WEB

SOME ITEMS OF CUTLERY

bread knife, butter knife, carving knife, cheese knife, chopsticks, dessert spoon, fish knife, fork, knife, ladle, spoon, steak knife, tablespoon, teaspoon

cutting adjective
She made a cutting *remark about my dress.*
sharp, hurtful, biting, stinging, vicious

cycle noun
see **bicycle**

Dd

daily adjective
Walking to school is part of my daily *exercise routine.*
everyday, regular
opposites infrequent, irregular

dainty adjective
The doll's hair was tied with a dainty *little ribbon.*
delicate, neat, charming, fine, exquisite, bijou
(informal) cute, dinky
opposite clumsy

dam noun
Some beavers have built a dam *in this river.*
barrier, barrage, embankment, dyke, weir

dam verb
The river was dammed *to make a reservoir.*
block, check, hold back

damage verb
Many books were damaged *in the fire.*
harm, spoil, mar, break, impair, weaken, disfigure, deface, mutilate, scar
To damage something beyond repair is to **destroy, ruin,** or **wreck** it.
To damage something deliberately is to **sabotage** or **vandalize** it.

damp adjective
1 *Don't wear those clothes if they are* damp.
moist, soggy, clammy, dank
2 *I don't like this* damp *weather.*
drizzly, foggy, misty, rainy, wet
Weather which is both damp and warm is **humid** or **muggy** weather.
opposite dry

dampen verb
1 *Dampen the cloth with a little water.*
moisten, wet
2 *Nothing could* dampen *her enthusiasm.*
make less, decrease, reduce

dance noun

WORD WEB

SOME KINDS OF DANCE OR DANCING

ballet, ballroom dancing, barn dance, belly-dancing, bolero, break-dancing, cancan, disco, flamenco, folk dance, Highland dancing, hornpipe, jazz dance, jig, jive dancing, limbo dancing, line-dancing, mazurka, morris dance, quadrille, reel, rumba, samba, (Scottish) country dancing, square dance, step dancing, street dance, tap dancing, tarantella

A person who writes the steps for a dance is a **choreographer**.

SOME BALLROOM DANCES

foxtrot, minuet, polka, quickstep, tango, waltz

GATHERINGS WHERE PEOPLE DANCE

ball, ceilidh, disco

dance verb

I could have danced for joy.
caper, cavort, frisk, frolic, gambol, hop about, jig about, jump about, leap, prance, skip, whirl

danger noun

1 *Who knows what dangers lie ahead?*
peril, jeopardy, trouble, crisis, hazard, menace, pitfall, threat, trap
opposite **safety**
2 *The forecast says there's a danger of frost.*
chance, possibility, risk

dangerous adjective

1 *We were in a dangerous situation.*
hazardous, perilous, risky, precarious, treacherous, unsafe, alarming, menacing
(informal) **hairy**
2 *The police arrested him for dangerous driving.*
careless, reckless
3 *A dangerous criminal had escaped from prison.*
violent, desperate, ruthless, treacherous

4 *It's wicked to empty dangerous chemicals into the river.*
harmful, poisonous, deadly, toxic
opposites **harmless, safe**

dangle verb

There was a bunch of keys dangling from the chain.
hang, swing, sway, droop, wave about, flap, trail

dare verb

1 *I wouldn't dare to make a parachute jump.*
have the courage, take the risk
2 *They dared me to climb the tree.*
challenge, defy

daring adjective

It was a very daring plan.
bold, brave, adventurous, courageous, fearless, intrepid, plucky, valiant
A daring person is a **daredevil**.
opposite **timid**

dark adjective

1 *It was a very dark night.*
black, dim, murky, shadowy, gloomy, dingy
opposite **bright**
2 *She wore a dark green coat.*
opposites **pale, light**

darken verb

The sky darkened.
become overcast, blacken, cloud over
opposite **brighten**

dash noun

1 *When the storm broke, we made a dash for shelter.*
run, rush, race, sprint
2 *I like just a dash of milk in my tea.*
drop, small amount, splash, spot

dash verb

1 *We dashed home because it was raining.*
hurry, run, rush, race, hasten, sprint, speed, tear, zoom
2 *She dashed her cup against the wall.*
throw, hurl, knock, smash

a
b
c
d
e
f
g
h
i
j
k
l
m
n
o
p
q
r
s
t
u
v
w
x
y
z

data plural noun
I entered all the data into the computer.
information, details, facts
Data can be in the form of figures,
numbers, or statistics.

date noun
I have a date with some friends this evening.
meeting, appointment, engagement

dawn noun
1 *I was woken at dawn by the birds singing outside.*
daybreak, sunrise, first light
opposites dusk, sunset
2 *It was the dawn of the modern age.*
beginning, start, birth, origin

day noun
1 *Badgers sleep during the day.*
daytime
opposite night
2 *Things were different in my grandfather's day.*
age, time, era, epoch, period

day noun

🕸 **WORD WEB**

VARIOUS TIMES OF THE DAY

dawn or **daybreak** or **sunrise, morning,
noon** or **midday, afternoon, evening,
nightfall** or **sunset, dusk** or **twilight,
night, midnight**

dazed adjective
He had a dazed expression on his face.
confused, bewildered, muddled, perplexed

dazzle verb
1 *My eyes were dazzled by the bright lights.*
daze, blind
2 *The acrobats dazzled the audience with their skill.*
amaze, astonish, impress, fascinate, awe

dead adjective
1 *A dead fish floated near the river's edge.*
deceased, lifeless

Instead of 'the king who has just died', you
can say 'the late king'.
A dead body is a carcass or corpse.
A common simile is as dead as a doornail.
opposite alive
2 *Latin is a dead language.*
extinct, obsolete
opposite living
3 *This battery is dead.*
flat, not working, worn out
4 *The town centre is dead at this time of night.*
dull, boring, uninteresting, slow
opposite lively

deaden verb
1 *The dentist gave me an injection to deaden the pain.*
anaesthetize, lessen, reduce, suppress
opposite increase
2 *Double glazing deadens the noise of the traffic.*
dampen, muffle, quieten
opposite amplify

deadly adjective
The witch gave her a deadly dose of poison.
lethal, fatal, harmful, dangerous,
destructive
opposite harmless

deafening adjective
We complained about the deafening noise.
loud, blaring, booming, thunderous,
penetrating

deal verb deals, dealing, dealt
1 *Who is going to deal the cards?*
give out, distribute, share out
2 *My uncle used to deal in second-hand cars.*
do business, trade
to deal with something
1 *I can deal with this problem.*
cope with, sort out, attend to, see to,
handle, manage, control, grapple with,
look after, solve
2 *The book deals with the history of Rome.*
be concerned with, cover, explain about

deal noun
She made a deal with the garage for her new car.
arrangement, agreement, contract, bargain
a good deal or **a great deal**
We went to a great deal of trouble to do things properly.
a lot, a large amount

dear adjective
1 *She is a very dear friend.*
close, loved, valued, beloved
opposite **distant**
2 *I didn't buy the watch because it was too dear.*
expensive, costly
(informal) pricey
opposite **cheap**

death noun
1 *The Vikings mourned the death of their chief.*
dying, end, passing
2 *The accident resulted in several deaths.*
fatality

debate noun
We had a debate about animal rights.
discussion, argument, dispute
Something which people argue about a lot is a controversy.

debate verb
1 *We debated whether it is right to kill animals for food.*
discuss, argue
2 *I debated what to do next.*
consider, ponder, deliberate, weigh up, reflect on

debris noun
Debris from the crashed aircraft was scattered over a large area.
remains, wreckage, fragments, pieces

decay verb
Dead leaves fall to the ground and decay.
decompose, rot, disintegrate, break down

deceit noun
I saw through his deceit.
deception, trickery, dishonesty, fraud, duplicity, double-dealing, pretence, bluff, cheating, deceitfulness, lying
opposite **honesty**

deceitful adjective
Don't trust him—he's a deceitful person.
dishonest, underhand, insincere, duplicitous, false, cheating, hypocritical, lying, treacherous, two-faced, sneaky
opposite **honest**

deceive verb
The spy had been deceiving them for years.
fool, trick, delude, dupe, hoodwink, cheat, double-cross, mislead, swindle, take in
(informal) con, diddle

decent adjective
1 *I did the decent thing and owned up.*
honest, honourable
2 *My friend's jokes were not decent.*
polite, proper, respectable, acceptable, appropriate, suitable, fitting
opposite **indecent**
3 *I haven't had a decent meal for ages!*
satisfactory, agreeable, good, nice
opposite **bad**

deception noun
see **deceit**

deceptive adjective
Appearances can be deceptive.
misleading, unreliable, false

decide verb
1 *We decided to finish our work instead of going out to play.*
choose, make a decision,
make up your mind, opt, elect, resolve
2 *The referee decided that the player was offside.*
conclude, judge, rule
3 *The last lap decided the result of the race.*
determine, settle

a
b
c
d
e
f
g
h
i
j
k
l
m
n
o
p
q
r
s
t
u
v
w
x
y
z

A
B
C
D
E
F
G
H
I
J
K
L
M
N
O
P
Q
R
S
T
U
V
W
X
Y
Z

decision noun
1 *Can you tell me what your* decision *is?*
choice, preference
2 *The judge announced his* decision.
conclusion, judgement, verdict, findings

decisive adjective
1 *A* decisive *piece of evidence proved that he was innocent.*
crucial, convincing, definite
2 *A referee needs to be* decisive.
firm, forceful, strong-minded, resolute, quick-thinking
opposite **hesitant**

declare verb
He declared *that he was innocent.*
announce, state, assert, make known, pronounce, proclaim, swear

decline verb
1 *Our enthusiasm* declined *as the day went on.*
become less, decrease, diminish, lessen, weaken, dwindle, flag, wane, tail off
opposite **increase**
2 *Why did you* decline *my invitation to lunch?*
refuse, reject, turn down
opposite **accept**

decode verb
see code

decorate verb
1 *We* decorated *the Christmas tree with tinsel.*
adorn, beautify, prettify, deck, festoon
To decorate a dish of food is to garnish it.
To decorate clothes with lace or ribbon is to trim them.
2 *Dad is going to* decorate *my bedroom next weekend.*
paint, paper, wallpaper
(informal) do up, make over
3 *The firefighters were* decorated *for their bravery.*
award or give a medal to, honour, reward

decorative adjective
The book had a decorative *design on the cover.*
ornamental, elaborate, fancy, attractive, beautiful, colourful, pretty
opposite **plain**

decrease verb
1 *We* decreased *speed.*
reduce, cut, lower, slacken
2 *Our enthusiasm* decreased *as the day went on.*
become less, decline, diminish, lessen, weaken, dwindle, flag, wane, tail off, shrink, subside
opposite **increase**

decrease noun
There has been a decrease *in the number of sparrows this year.*
decline, drop, fall, cut, reduction
opposite **increase**

decree verb
The king decreed *that the day would be a holiday.*
order, command, declare, pronounce, proclaim

dedicate verb
He dedicates *himself entirely to his art.*
commit, devote

dedicated adjective
A group of dedicated *fans waited at the stage door.*
committed, devoted, keen, enthusiastic, faithful, zealous

deduce verb
The detective deduced *that the footprints were fresh.*
conclude, work out, infer, reason, gather

deduct verb
Tax is deducted *from your salary.*
subtract, take away, knock off
opposite **add**

deed noun
The rescue team performed a heroic deed.
act, action, feat, exploit, effort,
achievement

deep adjective
1 *The pond is quite deep in the middle.*
opposite **shallow**
2 *The letter expressed his deep regret.*
intense, earnest, genuine, sincere
opposite **insincere**
3 *Veronica fell into a deep sleep.*
heavy, sound
opposite **light**
4 *The actor spoke in a deep and sombre voice.*
low, bass
opposite **high**

deer noun
A male deer is a **buck**, **hart**, **roebuck**, or
stag.
A female deer is a **doe** or **hind**.
A young deer is a **fawn**.
Deer's flesh used as food is **venison**.

defeat verb
The Greeks attacked and defeated the Trojans.
beat, conquer, vanquish, triumph over,
win a victory over, overcome, overpower,
crush, rout, trounce
To defeat someone in chess is to **checkmate**
them.
To be defeated is to **lose**.

defeat noun
The team suffered a humiliating defeat.
failure, humiliation, rout, trouncing
opposite **victory**

defect noun
*Cars are tested for defects before they leave
the factory.*
fault, flaw, imperfection, shortcoming,
failure, weakness
A defect in a computer program is a **bug**.

defence noun
1 *What was the accused woman's defence?*
justification, excuse, explanation,
argument, case

2 *The castle was built as a defence against
enemy attack.*
protection, guard, safeguard, fortification,
barricade, shield

defend verb
1 *They tried to defend themselves against
the enemy.*
protect, guard, keep safe
opposite **attack**
2 *He gave a speech defending his actions.*
justify, support, stand up for,
make a case for
opposite **accuse**

defer verb
*They deferred their departure until the
weekend.*
delay, put off, postpone

defiant adjective
*The prisoner cursed with a defiant look in
his eye.*
rebellious, insolent, aggressive,
challenging, disobedient, obstinate,
quarrelsome, uncooperative, stubborn,
mutinous
opposites **submissive, compliant**

deficient adjective
Their diet is deficient in vitamins.
lacking, wanting, short of, inadequate,
insufficient, unsatisfactory
opposite **adequate**

define verb
A dictionary defines lots of words.
explain, give the meaning of, interpret,
clarify

definite adjective
1 *Is it definite that we're going to move?*
certain, sure, fixed, settled, decided
2 *The doctor saw definite signs of
improvement.*
clear, distinct, noticeable, obvious, marked,
positive, pronounced, unmistakable
opposite **indefinite**

A

definitely adverb
I'll definitely phone you tomorrow.
certainly, for certain, positively, surely,
unquestionably, without doubt,
without fail
opposite **perhaps**

deflect verb
The goalkeeper was able to deflect the shot.
divert, turn aside, intercept, avert, fend off,
ward off

deft adjective
*She applied the paint with a deft flick of her
brush.*
skilful, agile, nimble, quick, clever, expert,
proficient, adept
(informal) **nifty**
opposite **clumsy**

defy verb
1 *The rebel army decided to defy the king.*
disobey, refuse to obey, resist, stand up to,
confront
opposite **obey**
2 *I defy you to come up with a better idea.*
challenge, dare
3 *The jammed door defied our efforts to open
it.*
resist, withstand, defeat, frustrate, beat

degrading adjective
*Losing by ten goals to nil was a degrading
experience.*
shameful, humiliating, embarrassing,
undignified

degree noun
The gymnast showed a high degree of skill.
standard, level, grade, measure, extent

dejected adjective
I felt dejected when I failed the test.
depressed, disheartened, downhearted,
unhappy, sad, low, gloomy, glum,
melancholy, miserable, downcast,
despondent, woeful, wretched, forlorn
(informal) **fed up, down**
opposites **happy, cheerful**

delay verb
1 *Don't let me delay you.*
detain, hold up, keep waiting, make late,
hinder, slow down
2 *They delayed the race because of bad
weather.*
postpone, put off, defer
3 *You'll miss the bus if you delay.*
hesitate, linger, pause, wait, dawdle, loiter
(informal) **hang about** or **around,**
drag your feet

delay noun
*There has been a delay with the building
work.*
hold-up, wait, pause

delete verb
I deleted your email by mistake.
remove, erase, cancel, cross out

deliberate adjective
1 *That remark was a deliberate insult.*
intentional, planned, calculated, conscious,
premeditated
opposites **accidental, unintentional**
2 *He walked with deliberate steps across the
room.*
careful, steady, cautious, slow, unhurried
opposites **hasty, careless**

deliberately verb
*Did you say that deliberately to hurt my
feelings?*
on purpose, intentionally
opposites **accidentally,
unintentionally**

delicate adjective
1 *The blouse has delicate embroidery on the
cuffs.*
dainty, exquisite, intricate, neat
2 *Take care not to damage the delicate
material.*
fragile, fine, flimsy, thin
3 *Delicate plants should be protected from
frost.*
sensitive, tender
opposites **tough, hardy**

A
B
C
D
E
F
G
H
I
J
K
L
M
N
O
P
Q
R
S
T
U
V
W
X
Y
Z

4 *The child was born with a delicate constitution.*
frail, weak, feeble, sickly, unhealthy
opposite strong
5 *The pianist's fingers had a delicate touch.*
gentle, light, soft
6 *He discussed the matter in a delicate way.*
tactful, sensitive, considerate, diplomatic, careful, discreet
opposite insensitive
7 *Can you help me with a delicate problem?*
awkward, embarrassing

delicious adjective
The food at the banquet was delicious.
tasty, appetizing, mouth-watering, delectable
(informal) scrumptious, yummy
opposites horrible, disgusting
For other ways to describe food see **food**

delight noun
Imagine my delight when I saw my friend again!
happiness, joy, pleasure, enjoyment, bliss, ecstasy

delight verb
The puppet show delighted the children.
please, charm, entertain, amuse, divert, enchant, entrance, fascinate, thrill
opposite dismay

delighted adjective
The delighted crowd cheered the winners.
pleased, happy, joyful, thrilled, ecstatic, elated, exultant

delightful adjective
The poem she wrote was delightful.
lovely, pleasant, pleasing, beautiful, attractive, charming

deliver verb
1 *Does anyone deliver mail to the island?*
convey, bring, hand over, distribute, present, supply, take round
2 *The head delivered a lecture on good behaviour.*
give, make, read out

delude verb
He deluded us into thinking he was very rich.
deceive, fool, trick, mislead, hoax, bluff
(informal) con

delusion noun
Your belief that you are a great writer is a delusion!
fantasy, dream, self-deception

demand verb
1 *I demanded a refund for my train fare.*
insist on, claim, call for, require, want
2 *'What do you want?' demanded a voice inside.*
ask, enquire, inquire

demand noun
1 *The king refused the demands of his people.*
request, claim, requirement
2 *There is not much demand for ice lollies in winter.*
need, call

demanding adjective
1 *Toddlers can be very demanding.*
difficult, trying, tiresome, insistent
2 *The expedition leader had a very demanding job.*
difficult, challenging, exhausting, hard, tough, testing, taxing, onerous
opposite easy

demolish verb
They demolished a building to make way for the road.
destroy, flatten, knock down, level, pull down, tear down, bulldoze
opposites build, construct

demonstrate verb
1 *The teacher demonstrated how warm air rises.*
show, exhibit, illustrate
2 *Animal rights campaigners were demonstrating in the street.*
protest, march, parade

demonstration noun

1 *I watched a demonstration of the new computer game.*
show, display, presentation
2 *Everyone joined the demonstration against world poverty.*
protest, rally, march, parade
(informal) demo

demote verb

The team may be demoted to a lower division.
put down, relegate
opposite **promote**

den noun

We built a den in the garden.
hideout, shelter, hiding place, secret place
The den of a wild animal is its lair.

denote verb

What does this symbol denote?
mean, indicate, signify, stand for,
be a sign of, express

dense adjective

1 *The accident happened in dense fog.*
thick, heavy
2 *A dense crowd waited in the square.*
compact, packed, solid
3 *I'm being rather dense today!*
stupid, slow

dent noun

There was a large dent in the car door.
indentation, depression, hollow, dip,
dimple

dent verb

A football hit the car door and dented it.
make a dent in, knock in, push in

dentist noun

A dentist who specializes in straightening
teeth is an orthodontist.
For other words to do with teeth see tooth

deny verb

1 *The boy denied that he had stolen the money.*
reject, dispute, disagree with,
contradict, dismiss, oppose
opposites **admit, accept**
2 *Her parents don't deny her anything.*
refuse, deprive of, withhold
opposite **give**

depart verb

1 *What time is the train due to depart?*
leave, set off, get going, set out, start,
begin a journey
opposites **arrive, get in**
2 *It looks as if the robbers departed in a hurry.*
leave, exit, go away, retreat, withdraw,
make off
(informal) clear off, scram, scarper
opposite **arrive**

department noun

Mr Taylor works in the sales department.
section, branch, division, office

depend verb

to depend on someone
I depend on you to help me.
rely on, count on, bank on, trust
to depend on something
My success will depend on good luck.
be decided by, rest on, hinge on

dependable adjective

Are these friends of yours dependable?
reliable, trustworthy, loyal, faithful, trusty,
honest, sound, steady
opposite **unreliable**

dependent adjective

dependent on
Everything is dependent on the weather.
determined by, subject to, controlled by,
reliant on

depict verb

1 *She depicted the landscape in watercolours.*
draw, paint, sketch
2 *The film depicts the horror of war.*
show, represent, portray, describe,
illustrate, outline

deplorable adjective
Their rudeness was deplorable.
disgraceful, shameful, scandalous,
shocking, unforgivable, lamentable,
reprehensible, inexcusable
opposite **praiseworthy**

deplore verb
We all deplore cruelty to animals.
condemn, disapprove of, hate

deport verb
He was deported from Australia.
exile, banish, expel, send abroad

deposit noun
1 *Dad paid the deposit on a new car.*
down-payment, first instalment,
initial payment
2 *There was a deposit of mud at the bottom
of the river.*
layer, sediment

depress verb
The miserable weather was depressing us.
sadden, discourage, dishearten, dispirit
opposite **cheer**

depressed adjective
*After his friends left, he began to feel
depressed.*
disheartened, dejected, discouraged,
downcast, downhearted, unhappy, sad,
low, gloomy, glum, melancholy, miserable,
despondent, desolate, in despair
(informal) **down**
opposite **cheerful**

depressing adjective
It was a depressing situation to be in.
discouraging, dispiriting, disheartening,
gloomy, sad, dismal, dreary, sombre, bleak
opposite **cheerful**

depression noun
1 *She sank into a state of depression.*
despair, dejection, sadness, gloom,
unhappiness, hopelessness, low spirits,
melancholy, misery, desolation, pessimism,
glumness
opposite **cheerfulness**
2 *Most businesses do badly during a
depression.*
recession, slump
opposite **boom**
3 *The rain had collected in several
depressions in the ground.*
hollow, indentation, dent, dip, hole, pit, rut
opposite **bump**

deprived adjective
The charity tries to help deprived families.
poor, needy, underprivileged
opposites **wealthy, privileged**

deputy noun
The sheriff appointed a new deputy.
second-in-command, assistant, stand-in,
substitute

Words with the prefix *vice* often mean
'the deputy for a particular person',
e.g. *vice-captain, vice-president.*

derelict adjective
*They plan to pull down those derelict
buildings.*
dilapidated, crumbling, decrepit, neglected,
deserted, abandoned, ruined

deride verb
The book was derided when it first came out.
ridicule, mock, laugh at, dismiss
(informal) **pooh-pooh**
opposite **praise**

derive verb
1 *Bill derives a lot of pleasure from his
garden.*
get, obtain, receive, gain
2 *She derived many of her ideas from books.*
borrow, draw, pick up, take
(informal) **lift**

descend verb
1 *After admiring the view, we began to*

a
b
c
d
e
f
g
h
i
j
k
l
m
n
o
p
q
r
s
t
u
v
w
x
y
z

A

descend *the mountain.*
climb down, come down, go down, move down
To descend through the air is to **drop** or **fall**.
To descend through water is to **sink**.
2 *The road* descends *gradually into the valley.*
drop, fall, slope, dip, incline
opposite ascend
to be descended from someone
She's descended from *a French family.*
come from, originate from

descendant noun

A person's descendants are their **heirs** or **successors**.
opposite ancestor

descent noun

The path makes a steep descent *into the valley.*
drop, fall, dip, incline
opposite ascent

describe verb

1 *An eyewitness* described *the accident.*
report, tell about, depict, explain, outline
2 *Friends* described *him as a quiet, shy man.*
portray, characterize, represent, present

description noun

1 *I wrote a* description *of our day at the seaside.*
report, account, story
2 *Write a* description *of your favourite character in the play.*
portrait, representation, sketch

descriptive adjective

The author writes in a very descriptive *style.*
expressive, colourful, detailed, graphic, vivid

desert noun

🕸 WORD WEB

THINGS YOU MIGHT SEE OR EXPERIENCE IN A DESERT
mirage, oasis, sand dune, sandstorm, whirlwind

SOME ANIMALS WHICH LIVE IN DESERTS
armadillo, camel, chameleon, coyote, desert rat, gerbil, lizard, locust, meerkat, rattlesnake, roadrunner, scorpion, tarantula, vulture

SOME PLANTS WHICH ARE FOUND IN DESERTS
cactus, date palm, grasses, prickly pear, sagebrush, tumbleweed

A group of people travelling together across a desert is a **caravan**.
People who live in the desert are often **nomads**.

For desert islands see **island**

desert verb

He deserted *his friends when they needed him most.*
abandon, leave, forsake, betray
(informal) **walk out on**
To desert someone in a place they can't get away from is to **maroon** or **strand** them.

deserted adjective

By midnight, the streets of the town were deserted.
empty, unoccupied, uninhabited, vacant
opposite crowded

deserve verb

You deserve *a break after all your hard work.*
be worthy of, be entitled to, have earned, merit, warrant

design noun

1 *This is the winning* design *for the new art gallery.*
plan, drawing, outline, blueprint, sketch
A first example of something, used as a model for making others, is a **prototype**.
2 *Do you like the* design *of this wallpaper?*
style, pattern, arrangement, composition

design verb

She designs *all her own clothes.*
create, develop, invent, devise, conceive, think up

desirable adjective
1 *The house has many desirable features.*
appealing, attractive, interesting, tempting
opposite worthless
2 *It is desirable to phone before you arrive.*
advisable, sensible, prudent, wise
opposite unwise

desire verb
The magic mirror will show you what you most desire.
wish for, long for, want, crave, fancy, hanker after, yearn for, pine for, set your heart on, have a yen for

desire noun
My greatest desire is to swim with dolphins.
wish, want, longing, ambition, craving, fancy, hankering, urge, yearning
A desire for food is **appetite** or **hunger**.
A desire for drink is **thirst**.
Excessive desire for money or other things is **greed**.

desolate adjective
1 *Jamie felt desolate when his goldfish died.*
depressed, dejected, miserable, sad, melancholy, hopeless, wretched, forlorn
opposite cheerful
2 *No-one wants to live in that desolate place.*
bleak, depressing, dreary, gloomy, dismal, cheerless, inhospitable, deserted, uninhabited, abandoned, godforsaken
opposite pleasant

despair noun
The defeated knight was overcome by despair.
depression, desperation, gloom, hopelessness, misery, anguish, dejection, melancholy, pessimism, wretchedness
opposite hope

despatch noun & verb
see **dispatch**

desperate adjective
1 *The shipwrecked crew were in a desperate situation.*
difficult, critical, grave, serious, severe, drastic, dire, urgent, extreme
2 *The hills were home to a band of desperate outlaws.*
dangerous, violent, reckless

despicable adjective
The pirates were known for despicable acts of cruelty.
disgraceful, hateful, shameful, contemptible, loathsome, vile

despise verb
I despise people who cheat at cards.
hate, loathe, feel contempt for, deride, have a low opinion of, look down on, scorn, sneer at
opposite admire

despite preposition
We went for a walk despite the rain.
in spite of, regardless of, notwithstanding
opposite because of

dessert noun
For dessert, there's apple pie and ice cream.
pudding, sweet
(informal) **afters**

destination noun
The train arrived at its destination five minutes early.
terminus, stop

destined adjective
1 *It was destined that he would become a famous actor.*
fated, doomed, intended, meant, certain, inevitable, unavoidable, inescapable
2 *This parcel is destined for Japan.*
bound, directed, intended, headed

destiny noun
Was it destiny that brought us together?
fate, fortune

destroy verb
1 *An avalanche destroyed the village.*
demolish, devastate, crush, flatten, knock down, level, pull down, shatter, smash, sweep away

2 *He tried to* **destroy** *the good work we did.*
ruin, wreck, sabotage, undo

destruction noun
1 *The hurricane caused coastal* **destruction.**
devastation, damage, demolition, ruin,
wrecking
opposite **creation**
2 *Global warming may cause the* **destruction**
of many animal species.
elimination, annihilation, obliteration,
extermination, extinction
opposite **conservation**

destructive adjective
Tornadoes have a great **destructive** *power.*
damaging, devastating, catastrophic,
disastrous, harmful, injurious, ruinous,
violent

detach verb
The camera lens can be **detached** *for
cleaning.*
remove, separate, disconnect, take off,
release, undo, unfasten, part
To **detach** a caravan from a vehicle is to
unhitch it.
To **detach** railway wagons from a locomotive
is to uncouple them.
To **detach** something by cutting it off is
to sever it.
opposite **attach**

detail noun
*Her account of what happened was accurate
in every* **detail.**
fact, feature, particular, aspect, item,
point, respect

detailed adjective
This book gives a **detailed** *description of
Victorian London.*
precise, exact, specific, full, thorough,
elaborate, comprehensive, exhaustive
opposites **rough, vague**

detain verb
1 *The police* **detained** *the suspect for over
three days.*
hold, arrest, capture, imprison, restrain
opposite **release**

2 *I'll try not to* **detain** *you for long.*
delay, hold up, hinder, keep waiting

detect verb
I could **detect** *the smell of burning in the air.*
identify, recognize, spot, find, discover,
reveal, diagnose, track down

detective noun
Detective *Dewar solved the case of the stolen
tiara.*
investigator, sleuth
(informal) private eye

WORD WEB
THINGS A DETECTIVE MIGHT LOOK FOR
clues, evidence, eyewitness, fingerprints,
footprints, murder weapon, tracks;
criminal, crook, culprit, felon, suspect,
mastermind
THINGS A DETECTIVE MIGHT DO
analyse, comb (an area),
deduce, deduct, detect, dig up,
ferret out, follow a hunch,
follow a lead or a tip-off,
interrogate or question (a witness),
investigate, pursue,
shadow, solve (a case),
stake out (a hiding place),
tail or track down (a suspect)
An informal name for a story in which a
detective solves a crime is a whodunnit.

deter verb
How can we **deter** *birds from eating the
pears?*
discourage, put off, dissuade, prevent,
stop
opposite **encourage**

deteriorate verb
1 *The queen's health had begun to*
deteriorate.
worsen, decline, degenerate, get worse,
go downhill
2 *The walls will* **deteriorate** *if we don't
maintain them.*
decay, disintegrate, crumble
opposite **improve**

determination noun
Marathon runners show great determination.
resolve, commitment, will-power, courage, dedication, drive, grit, perseverance, persistence, spirit
(informal) guts

determine verb
Our task was to determine the depth of the loch.
calculate, compute, figure out, work out, reckon, decide

determined adjective
1 *Boudicca must have been a determined woman.*
resolute, decisive, firm, strong-minded, assertive, persistent, tough
opposite weak-minded
2 *I'm determined to finish the race.*
committed, resolved

detest verb
I detest the smell of boiled cabbage.
dislike, hate, loathe
Informal expressions are can't bear and can't stand.
opposite love

detour noun
I wasted time by taking a detour.
diversion, indirect route, roundabout route

detrimental adjective
Too much water can be detrimental to plants.
damaging, harmful, destructive, adverse
opposite beneficial

devastate verb
The earthquake devastated the island.
destroy, wreck, ruin, demolish, flatten, level

devastating adjective
The siege had a devastating effect on the town.
overwhelming, stunning, shocking, shattering

develop verb
1 *The zoo is developing its education programme.*
expand, extend, enlarge, build up, diversify
2 *Her piano playing has developed this year.*
improve, progress, evolve, advance, get better
3 *The plants will develop quickly in the spring.*
grow, flourish
4 *How did he develop that posh accent?*
get, acquire, pick up, cultivate

development noun
1 *Were there any developments while I was away?*
event, happening, incident, occurrence, change
2 *We are pleased with the development of our website.*
growth, expansion, improvement, progress, spread

deviate verb
We were forced to deviate from our original plan.
depart, diverge, differ, stray

device noun
The TV comes with a remote control device.
tool, implement, instrument, appliance, apparatus, gadget, contraption
(informal) gizmo

devious adjective
1 *The mad professor had a devious plan to take over the world.*
cunning, deceitful, dishonest, furtive, scheming, sly, sneaky, treacherous, wily
2 *Because of the roadworks, we took a devious route home.*
indirect, roundabout, winding, meandering
opposite direct

devise verb
We need to devise a strategy for Saturday's game.
conceive, form, invent, contrive, formulate, come up with, make up, plan, prepare, map out, think out, think up

a
b
c
d
e
f
g
h
i
j
k
l
m
n
o
p
q
r
s
t
u
v
w
x
y
z

A
B
C
D
E
F
G
H
I
J
K
L
M
N
O
P
Q
R
S
T
U
V
W
X
Y
Z

devote verb
My brother devotes all his free time to football.
set aside, dedicate, assign, commit

devoted adjective
She's a devoted supporter of our team.
loyal, faithful, dedicated, enthusiastic, committed
opposite apathetic

devotion noun
Penguins show great devotion to their offspring.
attachment, fondness, loyalty, dedication, commitment

devour verb
He devoured a whole plateful of sandwiches.
eat, consume, guzzle, gobble up, gulp down, swallow
(informal) scoff, wolf down
See also eat

diagram noun
We drew a diagram of the life cycle of a frog.
chart, plan, sketch, outline

dial verb
I picked up the phone and dialled his number.
phone, call, ring, telephone

dialogue noun
The play consists of a series of dialogues.
conversation, talk, discussion, exchange, debate, chat

diary noun
I wrote about my birthday party in my diary.
journal, daily record
A diary describing a voyage or mission is a log *or* logbook.
A diary in which you insert pictures and souvenirs is a scrapbook.
A diary published on a website is a blog.

dictate verb
to dictate to someone
You've got no right to dictate to me!
order about, give orders to,

command, bully
(informal) boss about, push around, lord it over

die verb
1 *My sister's hamster died last week.*
expire, pass away, perish
(informal) snuff it, kick the bucket, croak
To die of hunger is to starve.
2 *The flowers will die if they don't have water.*
wither, wilt, droop, fade
to die down
The flames will die down eventually.
become less, decline, decrease, subside, weaken, dwindle, fizzle out, wane
to die out
When did the dinosaurs die out?
become extinct, cease to exist, come to an end, disappear, vanish

diet noun
Koalas live on a diet of eucalyptus leaves.
food, nourishment, nutrition
If you choose what to eat in order to lose weight, you are on a slimming *diet.*
A vegetarian *diet excludes meat.*
A vegan *diet excludes all animal products.*
See also food
on a diet
We ate too much on holiday—now we're on a diet
trying to lose weight

differ verb
The two men differed in their beliefs.
disagree, conflict, argue, clash, contradict each other, oppose each other, quarrel
opposite agree
to differ from
My style of painting differs from hers.
be different from, contrast with

difference noun
1 *Can you see any difference between these two colours?*
contrast, distinction
opposite similarity

2 *This money will make a* **difference** *to their lives.*
change, alteration, modification, variation

different adjective
1 *We have* **different** *views about global warming.*
differing, contradictory, opposite, clashing, conflicting
2 *It's important that the teams wear* **different** *colours.*
contrasting, dissimilar, distinguishable
3 *We had sweets of* **different** *flavours.*
various, assorted, mixed, several, diverse, numerous, miscellaneous
4 *Let's go somewhere* **different** *on holiday this year.*
new, original, fresh
5 *Everyone's handwriting is* **different.**
distinct, distinctive, individual, special, unique
opposites identical, similar

difficult adjective
1 *This crossword is really* **difficult.**
We were faced with a **difficult** *problem.*
hard, complicated, complex, involved, intricate, baffling, perplexing, puzzling
(informal) tricky, thorny, knotty
opposite simple
2 *It is a* **difficult** *climb to the top of the hill.*
challenging, arduous, demanding, taxing, exhausting, formidable, gruelling, laborious, strenuous, tough
opposite easy
3 *Mum says I was a* **difficult** *child.*
troublesome, awkward, trying, tiresome, annoying, disruptive, obstinate, stubborn, uncooperative, unhelpful
opposite cooperative

difficulty noun
1 *The explorers were used to facing* **difficulty.**
trouble, adversity, challenges, hardship
2 *There are some* **difficulties** *with your application.*
problem, complication, hitch, obstacle, snag

dig verb digs, digging, dug
1 *We spent the afternoon* **digging** *the garden.*
cultivate, fork over, turn over
2 *Rabbits* **dig** *holes in the ground.*
burrow, excavate, tunnel, gouge out, hollow out, scoop out
3 *Did you* **dig** *me in the back?*
poke, prod, jab

dignified adjective
Lady Snodgrass was a very **dignified** *old lady.*
refined, stately, distinguished, noble, sedate, solemn, proper, grave, grand, august
opposite undignified

dignity noun
1 *Their laughter spoilt the* **dignity** *of the occasion.*
formality, seriousness, solemnity
2 *She handled the problem with* **dignity.**
calmness, poise, self-control

dilute verb
You need to **dilute** *orange squash with water.*
thin, water down, weaken
opposite concentrate

dim adjective
1 *I could see the* **dim** *outline of a figure in the mist.*
indistinct, faint, blurred, fuzzy, hazy, shadowy, vague
opposite clear
2 *The light in the cave was rather* **dim.**
dark, dull, dingy, murky, gloomy
opposite bright

dimensions plural noun
We measured the **dimensions** *of the room.*
measurements, size, extent, capacity
For words used in measuring see **measurement**

diminish verb
1 *Don't* **diminish** *his confidence by making fun of him.*
lessen, reduce, make smaller, minimize

a
b
c
d
e
f
g
h
i
j
k
l
m
n
o
p
q
r
s
t
u
v
w
x
y
z

A

2 *Our water supply was* diminishing *rapidly.*
become less, decrease, decline, subside,
B
dwindle, wane
opposite **increase**

C

din noun
D
I can't hear you because of that awful din!
noise, racket, row, clatter, hullabaloo
E

dine verb
F
We will be dining at eight o'clock.
eat, have dinner, sup
G

dingy adjective
H
How can we brighten up this dingy room?
dull, drab, dreary, dowdy, colourless,
I
dismal, gloomy, murky
opposite **bright**

J

K

L

M

N

O

P

Q

R

S

T

U

V

W

X

Y

Z

dinosaur noun

> **WORD WEB**
>
> SOME TYPES OF DINOSAUR
> **apatosaurus, archaeopteryx,
> brachiosaurus, diplodocus,
> gallimimus, iguanodon, megalosaurus,
> pterodactylus, stegosaurus, triceratops,
> tyrannosaurus rex, velociraptor**
>
> BODY PARTS WHICH A DINOSAUR MAY HAVE
> **dorsal plates, bony frill, fleshy fin, horn,
> wings, crest**
>
> A person who studies dinosaurs and other
> fossils is a **palaeontologist.**
>
> For other prehistoric animals see
> **prehistoric**

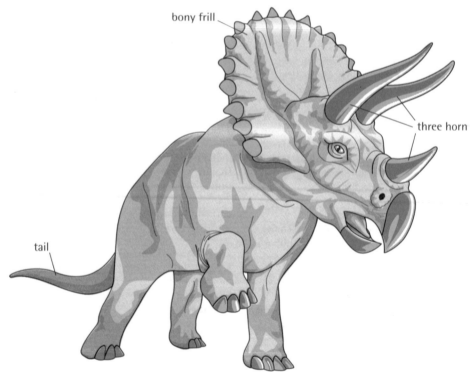

bony frill

three horn

tail

triceratops

discipline noun
Discipline is important in the army.
order, control

disclose verb
He never disclosed the truth.
reveal, tell, make known, confess,
make public
opposite **conceal**

discomfort noun
He experiences discomfort from his injury.
pain, soreness, distress, unease

disconnect verb
Disconnect the cooker before you move it.
detach, cut off, unplug, unhook

discontented adjective
She felt very discontented with her job.
dissatisfied, miserable, unhappy, upset
(informal) fed up
opposites **happy, satisfied**

discontinue verb
That style of shoe has been discontinued.
stop, end, terminate
opposites **introduce, establish**

discount noun
I got a discount on the full price.
deduction, reduction, cut, concession,
allowance

discourage verb
1 *Don't let her criticism discourage you.*
demoralize, depress
(informal) put you off
2 *The burglar alarm will discourage thieves.*
deter, dissuade, prevent, restrain, stop,
hinder
opposite **encourage**

discover verb
I discovered some old toys in the attic.
find, come across, spot, stumble across,
uncover
To discover something that has been buried
is to **unearth** it.

To discover something that has been under
water is to **dredge it up**.
To discover something you have been
pursuing is to **track it down**.
opposite **hide**

discovery noun
*Scientists have made an exciting new
discovery.*
find, breakthrough

discreet adjective
*I asked a few discreet questions about her
illness.*
tactful, sensitive, delicate, careful,
cautious, diplomatic, wary
opposite **tactless**

discriminate verb
*It's sometimes hard to discriminate between
poisonous mushrooms and edible ones.*
distinguish, tell the difference
to discriminate against
*It's wrong to discriminate against people
because of their age.*
be biased against, be intolerant of,
be prejudiced against

discrimination noun
1 *The school has a policy against racial
discrimination.*
prejudice, bias, intolerance, unfairness
Discrimination against people because of
their sex is **sexism**.
Discrimination against people because of
their race is **racism**.
2 *She shows discrimination in her choice of
music.*
good taste, good judgement

discuss verb
I discussed the idea with my parents.
talk about, confer about, debate

discussion noun
*We had a lively discussion about pocket
money.*
conversation, argument, exchange of views
A formal discussion is a **conference** or
debate.

a
b
c
d
e
f
g
h
i
j
k
l
m
n
o
p
q
r
s
t
u
v
w
x
y
z

A
B
C
D
E
F
G
H
I
J
K
L
M
N
O
P
Q
R
S
T
U
V
W
X
Y
Z

disease noun
He was suffering from a serious disease.
illness, ailment, sickness, complaint, affliction
(informal) bug
See also illness

diseased adjective
Gardeners throw away diseased plants.
unhealthy, sickly, infected
opposite healthy

disembark verb
The passengers disembarked from the ferry.
go ashore
opposite embark

disgrace noun
1 *He never got over the disgrace of being caught cheating.*
humiliation, shame, embarrassment, dishonour
2 *The way he treats them is a disgrace!*
outrage, scandal

disgraceful adjective
We were shocked by her disgraceful behaviour.
shameful, shocking, appalling, outrageous, scandalous
opposite honourable

disguise verb
I tried to disguise my feelings.
conceal, hide, cover up, camouflage, mask
to disguise yourself as
The spy disguised himself as a hotel porter.
dress up as, pretend to be

disguise noun
I didn't recognize him in that disguise.
costume, camouflage, make-up, mask

disgust noun
The sight of the carcass filled me with disgust.
repulsion, repugnance, distaste, dislike, horror, loathing, detestation
opposite liking

disgust verb
The smell of rotten eggs disgusts me.
repel, revolt, sicken, appal, offend, distress, shock, horrify
(informal) put you off, turn your stomach
opposite please

disgusting adjective
The brew in the cauldron looked disgusting.
repulsive, revolting, horrible, nasty, loathsome, repellent, repugnant, offensive, appalling, sickening, nauseating
(informal) yucky, icky, gross
opposites delightful, pleasing

dish noun
1 *Mum served the trifle in a large glass dish.*
bowl, basin, plate, platter
A dish to serve soup from is a tureen.
See also crockery
2 *What's your favourite dish?*
food, recipe, meal

dishevelled adjective
His clothes were a mess and his hair was dishevelled.
messy, untidy, scruffy, unkempt, bedraggled, slovenly
opposites neat, tidy

dishonest adjective
1 *They were taken in by a dishonest salesman.*
deceitful, cheating, corrupt, disreputable, untrustworthy, immoral, lying, swindling, thieving
(informal) bent, crooked, dodgy, shady
2 *The author makes some dishonest claims.*
false, misleading, untruthful, fraudulent, devious
opposite honest

dishonesty noun
The MP was accused of dishonesty.
deceit, cheating, corruption, insincerity, lying, deviousness
(informal) crookedness
opposite honesty

disinfect verb
The nurse disinfected my wound.
cleanse, sterilize
opposite infect
To disinfect an infected place is to decontaminate it.
To disinfect a room using fumes is to fumigate it.

disintegrate verb
The cloth is so old that it's starting to disintegrate.
break up, fall apart, break into pieces, crumble, decay, decompose

disinterested adjective
A referee must be disinterested.
impartial, neutral, unbiased, unprejudiced, detached, fair
opposite biased

disk noun
see disc

dislike noun
His colleagues regarded him with intense dislike.
hatred, loathing, detestation, disapproval, disgust, revulsion
opposite liking

dislike verb
I dislike people who hunt wild animals.
hate, loathe, detest, disapprove of
opposite like

dislodge verb
The wind dislodged some tiles on the roof.
displace, move, shift, disturb

disloyal adjective
The rebels were accused of being disloyal to the king.
unfaithful, treacherous, faithless, false, unreliable, untrustworthy
opposite loyal

dismal adjective
1 *How can we brighten up this dismal room?*
dull, drab, dreary, dingy, colourless, cheerless, gloomy, murky
opposites bright, cheerful
2 (informal) *It was a dismal performance by the home team.*
dreadful, awful, terrible, feeble, useless, hopeless
(informal) pathetic
opposites brilliant, splendid

dismantle verb
After the school fair, we had to dismantle all the stalls.
take apart, take down
To dismantle your group's tents is to strike camp.
opposite assemble

dismay noun
We listened with dismay to the bad news.
distress, alarm, shock, concern, anxiety, gloom

dismayed adjective
I was dismayed by the failure of our plan.
distressed, discouraged, depressed, devastated, shocked, appalled
opposite encouraged

dismiss verb
1 *The teacher dismissed the class.*
send away, discharge, free, let go, release
2 *The firm dismissed ten workers.*
sack, give the sack, give notice to, make redundant
(informal) fire
3 *The weather was so bad that we dismissed the idea of having a picnic.*
discard, drop, reject

dismount verb
The knight dismounted from his horse.
descend, get off

disobedient adjective
She said she had never known such a disobedient child.
naughty, badly behaved, undisciplined, uncontrollable, unmanageable, unruly,

a
b
c
d
e
f
g
h
i
j
k
l
m
n
o
p
q
r
s
t
u
v
w
x
y
z

A ungovernable, troublesome, defiant, disruptive, mutinous, rebellious, contrary
B **opposite obedient**

disobey verb
1 *You will be penalized if you* disobey *the rules.*
break, ignore, disregard, defy, violate
2 *Soldiers are trained never to* disobey.
be disobedient, rebel, revolt, mutiny
opposite obey

disorder noun
1 *The public meeting broke up in* disorder.
disturbance, uproar, commotion, quarrelling, rioting, brawling, fighting, lawlessness, anarchy
2 *It's time I tidied up the* disorder *in my room.*
mess, muddle, untidiness, chaos, confusion, clutter, jumble
opposite order

disorderly adjective
The class were behaving in a disorderly *manner.*
badly behaved, disobedient, unruly, uncontrollable, undisciplined, ungovernable, unmanageable
opposite orderly

dispatch noun
The messenger brought a dispatch *from headquarters.*
message, communication, report, letter, bulletin

dispatch verb
The parcel has already been dispatched.
post, send, transmit

dispense verb
to dispense with
Now that I have new trainers, I can dispense *with the old ones.*
get rid of, dispose of, do without, remove

disperse verb
1 *The police* dispersed *the crowd.*
break up, send away, drive away, separate, send in different directions

2 *The crowd* dispersed *quickly after the match.*
scatter, spread out, disappear, dissolve, melt away, vanish
opposite gather

displace verb
1 *The gales have* displaced *some of the roof tiles.*
dislodge, put out of place, shift, disturb
2 *A brilliant new player* displaced *me in the team.*
replace, take the place of, succeed

display verb
We planned the best way to display *our work.*
demonstrate, exhibit, present, put on show, set out, show, show off
To display something boastfully is to flaunt it.

display noun
We set out a display *of our art work.*
exhibition, show, presentation, demonstration

displease verb
I must have done something to displease *her.*
annoy, irritate, upset, anger, exasperate, vex

dispose verb
to dispose of something
Let's dispose *of this old carpet.*
get rid of, discard, throw away, give away, scrap
(informal) dump
to be disposed to do something
He didn't seem disposed *to help us.*
be willing to, be inclined to, be ready to, be likely to

disposition noun
Our labrador has a very friendly disposition.
character, nature, personality

dispute noun
We settled the dispute *about who should wash the dishes.*
argument, disagreement, quarrel, debate, controversy, difference of opinion

disqualify verb
Two athletes have been disqualified from the competition.
bar, prohibit

disregard verb
I disregarded the doctor's advice.
ignore, pay no attention to, take no notice of, reject
opposite **heed**

disrespectful adjective
She was very disrespectful towards her parents.
rude, bad-mannered, insulting, impolite, insolent, cheeky
opposite **respectful**

disrupt verb
Bad weather has disrupted the tennis tournament.
interrupt, upset, interfere with, throw into confusion or disorder

dissatisfied adjective
I was dissatisfied with my piano playing.
displeased, disappointed, discontented, frustrated, annoyed
opposite **satisfied**

dissolve verb
Stir your tea until the sugar dissolves.
disperse, disintegrate, melt

dissuade verb
to dissuade someone from doing something
We tried to dissuade him from going out in the storm.
discourage someone from, persuade someone not to, deter someone from, warn someone against
opposite **persuade**

distance noun
What is the distance from Earth to the Sun?
measurement, space, extent, reach, mileage

The distance across something is the breadth or width.
The distance along something is the length.
The distance between two points is a gap or interval.
For units for measuring distance see **measurement**

distant adjective
1 *I'd love to travel to distant countries.*
faraway, remote, out-of-the-way, inaccessible, exotic
opposite **close**
2 *His distant manner puts me off.*
unfriendly, unapproachable, formal, reserved, withdrawn, cool, haughty, aloof
opposite **friendly**

distinct adjective
1 *There is a distinct improvement in your handwriting.*
definite, evident, noticeable, obvious, perceptible
opposite **imperceptible**
2 *It was a small photo, but the details were quite distinct.*
clear, distinguishable, plain, recognizable, sharp, unmistakable, visible, well defined
opposite **indistinct**
3 *Organize your essay into distinct sections.*
individual, separate

distinction noun
1 *There's a clear distinction between the real diamond and the fake.*
difference, contrast, distinctiveness
2 *He had the distinction of being the team captain.*
honour, glory, merit, credit, prestige

distinctive adjective
We spotted the distinctive footprints of a yeti in the snow.
characteristic, recognizable, unmistakable, special, unique

A
B
C
D
E
F
G
H
I
J
K
L
M
N
O
P
Q
R
S
T
U
V
W
X
Y
Z

distinguish verb
1 *It was impossible to* distinguish *one twin from the other.*
tell apart, pick out, discriminate, differentiate, make a distinction, decide
2 *In the dark we couldn't* distinguish *who was walking past.*
identify, tell, make out, determine, perceive, recognize, single out

distinguished adjective
1 *The school has a* distinguished *academic record.*
excellent, first-rate, outstanding, exceptional
opposite **ordinary**
2 *He is a very* distinguished *actor.*
famous, celebrated, well known, eminent, notable, prominent, renowned
opposites **unknown, obscure**

distort verb
1 *When my bike hit the kerb, it* distorted *the wheel.*
bend, buckle, twist, warp, contort
2 *The newspaper* distorted *the facts of the story.*
twist, slant, misrepresent

distract verb
Don't distract *the bus driver.*
divert the attention of, disturb, put off

distress noun
The trapped animal was clearly in distress.
suffering, torment, anguish, dismay, anxiety, grief, misery, pain, sadness, sorrow, worry, wretchedness

distress verb
We could see that the bad news distressed *her.*
upset, disturb, trouble, worry, alarm, dismay, torment
opposite **comfort**

distribute verb
1 *The coach* distributed *water to the players at half-time.*
give out, hand round, circulate, dispense, issue, share out, take round
(informal) dish out, dole out
2 *Distribute the seeds evenly.*
scatter, spread, disperse

district noun
Granny lives in a quiet district.
area, neighbourhood, locality, region, vicinity

distrust verb
I distrusted *the professor from the moment I met him.*
doubt, mistrust, question, suspect, be suspicious or wary of, be sceptical about, feel uncertain or uneasy or unsure about
opposite **trust**

disturb verb
1 *Don't* disturb *the baby when she's asleep.*
bother, interrupt, annoy, pester
2 *They were* disturbed *by the bad news.*
distress, trouble, upset, worry, alarm, frighten
3 *Please don't* disturb *the papers on my desk.*
muddle, mix up, move around, mess about with

disused adjective
They made the disused *railway line into a cycle track.*
abandoned, unused, closed down

ditch noun
We dug a ditch *to drain away the water.*
trench, channel, drain, gully

dither verb
Stop dithering *and make up your mind!*
hesitate, waver, be in two minds
(informal) shilly-shally

dive verb
1 *The mermaid* dived *into the water.*
plunge, jump, leap
A dive *in which you land flat on your front is a bellyflop.*
2 *The eagle* dived *towards its prey.*
pounce, swoop

diver noun
A diver who wears a rubber suit and flippers and breathes air from a portable tank is a scuba diver or frogman.

diverse adjective
People from many diverse cultures live in the area.
different, differing, varied, various, contrasting

diversion noun
1 *The police had set up a traffic diversion.*
detour, indirect route, roundabout route
2 *There were lots of diversions at the holiday camp.*
entertainment, amusement, recreation

divert verb
1 *They diverted the plane to another airport.*
redirect, switch
2 *She diverted herself by reading.*
entertain, amuse, occupy, interest, keep happy

divide verb
1 *We divided the class into two groups.*
separate, split, break up, move apart, part
opposite **combine**
2 *I divided the cake between my friends.*
distribute, share out, give out, allot, deal out, dispense
3 *Which way do we go? The path divides here.*
branch, fork
opposite **converge**

divine adjective
1 *The temple is used for divine worship.*
holy, religious, sacred, spiritual
2 *The Greeks believed divine beings lived on Mount Olympus.*
godlike, immortal, heavenly
3 (informal) *These fairy cakes taste divine!*
excellent, wonderful, superb

division noun
1 *The map shows the division of Europe after the war.*
dividing, splitting, separation, partition

2 *There was a division in the government.*
disagreement, split, feud
3 *There is a movable division between the two classrooms.*
partition, divider, dividing wall, screen
4 *They work in different divisions of the same company.*
branch, department, section, unit

dizzy adjective
Going on a roundabout makes me feel dizzy.
dazed, giddy, faint, reeling, unsteady

do verb does, doing, did, done
1 *My friend always knows what to do in a crisis.*
act, behave, conduct yourself
2 *The vet has a lot of work to do this morning.*
attend to, cope with, deal with, handle, look after, perform, undertake
3 *It took me half an hour to do the washing-up.*
accomplish, achieve, carry out, complete, execute, finish
4 *I need to do all of these sums.*
answer, puzzle out, solve, work out
5 *Staring at the sun can do damage to your eyes.*
bring about, cause, produce, result in
6 *If you don't have lemonade, water will do.*
be acceptable, be enough, be satisfactory, be sufficient, serve
to do away with
I wish our school would do away with homework.
get rid of, abolish, eliminate, end, put an end to
to do up
These jeans are too tight to do up.
button up, fasten

docile adjective
Don't be afraid of the dog—he's quite docile.
tame, gentle, meek, obedient, manageable, safe, submissive
opposite **fierce**

a
b
c
d
e
f
g
h
i
j
k
l
m
n
o
p
q
r
s
t
u
v
w
x
y
z

dock noun
A boat was waiting for us at the end of the dock.
harbour, quay, jetty, wharf, landing stage, dockyard, pier, port, marina

dock verb
We can't disembark until the ship docks.
moor, tie up

doctor noun
For people who practise medicine see **medicine**

document noun
The library contains many old documents.
paper, record, file, certificate, deed

dodge verb
I just managed to dodge the snowball.
avoid, evade, side-step

dog noun
A female dog is a **bitch**.
A young dog is a **pup**, **puppy**, or **whelp**.
Informal words for a dog are **mutt** and **pooch**.
An uncomplimentary word for a dog is **cur**.
A dog of pure breed with known ancestors has a **pedigree**.
A dog of mixed breeds is a **mongrel**.
A dog used for hunting is a **hound**.
A word meaning 'to do with dogs' is **canine**.

WORD WEB

SOME BREEDS OF DOG
Afghan hound, Alsatian, basset hound, beagle, bloodhound, boxer, bulldog, bull terrier, cairn terrier, chihuahua, cocker spaniel, collie, corgi, dachshund, Dalmatian, Doberman, fox terrier, Great Dane, greyhound, husky, Irish Setter, Labrador, mastiff, Pekinese or Pekingese, Pomeranian, poodle, pug, golden retriever, Rottweiler, St Bernard, Schnauzer, setter, sheepdog, spaniel, terrier, West Highland terrier, whippet, wolfhound, Yorkshire terrier

domestic adjective
1 *At weekends I do various domestic chores.*
household, family
2 *Cats and dogs are popular domestic animals.*
domesticated, tame

dominant adjective
1 *The captain plays a dominant role in the team.*
leading, main, chief, major, powerful, principal, important, influential
opposite **minor**
2 *The castle is a dominant feature in the landscape.*
conspicuous, prominent, obvious, large, imposing, eye-catching
opposite **insignificant**

dominate verb
The visiting team dominated the game.
control, direct, monopolize, govern, take control of, take over

donate verb
Will you donate something to our collection?
give, contribute

donation noun
The museum relies on donations from the public.
contribution, gift, offering

done adjective
1 *All my thank-you letters are done now.*
finished, complete, over
2 *The cake will be brown on top when it's done.*
cooked, ready

donor noun
A generous donor gave us money for new sports equipment.
benefactor, contributor, sponsor

doomed adjective
The expedition was doomed from the start.
ill-fated, condemned, fated, cursed, jinxed, damned

A
B
C
D
E
F
G
H
I
J
K
L
M
N
O
P
Q
R
S
T
U
V
W
X
Y
Z

door noun

A door in a floor or ceiling is a hatch or trapdoor.
The plank or stone underneath a door is the threshold.
The beam or stone above a door is the lintel.
The device on a door swings is the hinge.

dose noun

The nurse gave me a dose of the medicine.
measure, correct amount, dosage, portion

dot noun

She was furious when she saw dots of paint on the carpet.
spot, speck, fleck, point, mark
The dot you always put at the end of a sentence is a full stop.
on the dot (informal)
We left the house at nine o'clock on the dot.
exactly, precisely

double adjective

You enter the room through a double set of doors.
dual, twofold, paired, twin, matching, duplicate

double noun

She's so like you—she's almost your double.
twin
(informal) lookalike, spitting image, dead ringer
A living organism created as an exact copy of another living organism is a clone.

doubt noun

1 *Have you any doubt about his honesty?*
distrust, suspicion, mistrust, hesitation, reservation, scepticism
opposite confidence
2 *There is no doubt that you will pass your exam.*
question, uncertainty, ambiguity, confusion
opposite certainty

doubt verb

There is no reason to doubt her story.
distrust,
feel uncertain or uneasy or unsure about,
question, mistrust, suspect,
be sceptical about, be suspicious or wary of
opposite trust

doubtful adjective

1 *He looked doubtful, but agreed to let us go.*
unsure, uncertain, unconvinced, hesitant, distrustful, sceptical, suspicious
opposite certain
2 *The referee made a doubtful decision there.*
questionable, debatable, arguable

downfall noun

After the government's downfall, there was a general election.
collapse, fall, ruin

downward adjective

We took the downward path into the valley.
downhill, descending
opposite upward

doze verb

Dad often dozes in the evening.
rest, sleep, nod off
(informal) drop off

drab adjective

That dress is too drab to wear to the party.
dull, dingy, dreary, cheerless, colourless, dismal, gloomy, grey
opposites bright, cheerful

draft noun

I jotted down a draft of my story.
outline, plan, sketch, rough version

draft verb

I began to draft my story.
outline, plan, prepare, sketch, work out

drag verb

The tractor dragged the car out of the ditch.
pull, tow, tug, draw, haul, lug
opposite push

a
b
c
d
e
f
g
h
i
j
k
l
m
n
o
p
q
r
s
t
u
v
w
x
y
z

A
B
C
D
E
F
G
H
I
J
K
L
M
N
O
P
Q
R
S
T
U
V
W
X
Y
Z

dragon noun

A fearsome dragon once lived in these hills.

 WORD WEB

SOME WAYS TO DESCRIBE A DRAGON
ancient, fearsome, fiery, fire-breathing, legendary, mighty, monstrous, scaly, winged

BODY PARTS A DRAGON MIGHT HAVE
barbed tail, bat-like wings, claws, crest, forked tail or **tongue, pointed teeth, scales, spikes** or **spines**

A DRAGON'S SCALES MIGHT BE
dazzling, iridescent, patterned, shimmering

A DRAGON'S BREATH MIGHT BE
fiery, flaming, scorching, searing

THINGS A DRAGON MIGHT DO
breathe fire, change shape, curl its body or **tail, furl** or **unfurl its wings, puff smoke, roar, snort, soar, swoop**

PLACES WHERE A DRAGON MIGHT LIVE
cave, den, lair

For other creatures found in myths and legends see **myth**

drain noun

Surplus water runs away along a drain.
ditch, channel, drainpipe, gutter, pipe, sewer

drain verb

1 *If they drain the marsh, lots of waterbirds will die.*
dry out, remove water from
2 *She drained the oil from the engine.*
draw off, empty
3 *The water slowly drained away.*
trickle, ooze, seep
4 *The tough climb drained my energy.*
use up, consume, exhaust

drama noun

1 *Drama is one of my favourite subjects.*
acting
See also **theatre**

2 *I witnessed the drama of a real robbery.*
action, excitement, suspense, spectacle

dramatic adjective

We watched the dramatic rescue on TV.
exciting, eventful, thrilling, sensational, spectacular, gripping

drank

past tense see **drink**

drastic adjective

After being without food for three days, the explorers needed to take drastic action.
desperate, extreme, radical, harsh, severe
opposite **moderate**

draught noun

I felt a draught of air from the open window.
breeze, current, movement, puff

draw verb draws, drawing, drew, drawn

1 *I drew some pictures of the flowers in our garden.*
sketch, trace, doodle
2 *I'm not very good at drawing faces.*
depict, portray, represent
3 *The horse was drawing a cart.*
pull, tow, drag, haul, tug, lug
4 *We expect tomorrow's match to draw a big crowd.*
attract, bring in, pull in
5 *The two teams drew 1-1.*
finish equal, tie
to draw near
As the spaceship drew near, I began to get nervous.
approach, advance, come near

draw noun

Kinds of prize draw are a lottery and a raffle.

drawback noun

It's a drawback to be small if you play basketball.
disadvantage, difficulty, handicap, obstacle, inconvenience, hindrance, downside, snag

drawing noun

> **WORD WEB**
>
> SOME TYPES OF DRAWING
> caricature, cartoon, design, doodle, illustration, outline, sketch
>
> TOOLS USED FOR DRAWING
> chalk, charcoal, crayon, ink, pastel, pen, pencil
>
> See also **picture**

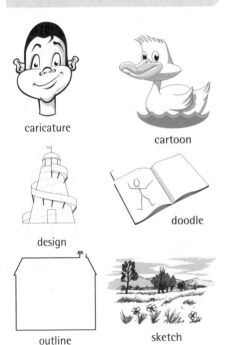

caricature

cartoon

design

doodle

outline

sketch

dread noun
Our teacher has a dread of spiders.
fear, horror, terror, phobia (about), anxiety (about)

dreadful adjective
1 *There has been a dreadful accident at sea.*
horrible, terrible, appalling, horrendous, distressing, shocking, upsetting, tragic, grim

2 *The weather at the weekend was dreadful.*
bad, awful, terrible, abysmal, abominable, dire, foul, nasty
opposites good, pleasant

dream noun
A bad dream is a **nightmare**.
A dreamlike experience you have while awake is a **daydream**, **fantasy**, or **reverie**.
Something you see in a dream or daydream is a **vision**.
The dreamlike state when you are hypnotized is a **trance**.
Something you think you see that is not real is a **hallucination** or **illusion**.

dream verb dreams, dreaming, dreamt or dreamed
I dreamed that I was a mermaid.
daydream, imagine, fancy, fantasize

dreary adjective
1 *The newsreader had a very dreary voice.*
dull, boring, flat, tedious, unexciting, uninteresting
opposite lively
2 *When will this dreary weather end?*
depressing, dismal, dull, gloomy, cheerless, murky, overcast
opposites bright, sunny

drench verb
The rain drenched me to the skin.
soak, wet thoroughly

dress noun
1 *What kind of dress are you wearing to the party?*
frock, gown
2 *The invitation said to wear casual dress.*
clothes, clothing, outfit, costume, garments
See also **clothes**

dress verb
1 *I helped to dress my little brother.*
clothe, put clothes on
opposite undress
2 *A nurse dressed my wound.*
bandage, put a dressing on, bind up

a
b
c
d
e
f
g
h
i
j
k
l
m
n
o
p
q
r
s
t
u
v
w
x
y
z

A

dressing noun
The nurse put a dressing on the wound.
bandage, plaster

B

C

drew
past tense see **draw**

D

dribble verb
1 *Careful, the baby's dribbling on your jumper.*
drool
2 *Water dribbled out of the hole in the tank.*
drip, trickle, leak, ooze, seep

E

F

G

H

drift verb
1 *The boat drifted downstream.*
float, be carried, move slowly
2 *The crowd lost interest and drifted away.*
stray, wander, meander, ramble, walk aimlessly
3 *The snow will drift in this wind.*
pile up, accumulate, make drifts

I

J

K

L

drift noun
1 *The car was stuck in a snow drift.*
bank, heap, mound, pile, ridge
2 *Did you understand the drift of the speech?*
gist, main idea, point

M

N

O

drill noun
1 *There will be a fire drill at school next week.*
practice, training
2 *Do you all know the drill for erecting a tent?*
procedure, routine, system

P

Q

R

S

drill verb
It took a long time to drill through the wall.
bore, penetrate, pierce

T

drink noun

U

WORD WEB

SOME HOT DRINKS
chocolate, cocoa, coffee, tea

SOME NON-ALCOHOLIC COLD DRINKS
barley water, cola, cordial, fruit juice, ginger beer, iced tea, lemonade, milk, milkshake, mineral water, orangeade,

V

W

X

Y

Z

smoothie, soda water, squash, tonic water, water

SOME ALCOHOLIC DRINKS
beer, brandy, champagne, cider, gin, mead, port, punch, rum, shandy, sherry, whisky, wine

Very strong alcoholic drinks are **spirits**.

CONTAINERS FOR DRINKS
beaker, bottle, can, cup, glass, goblet, mug, tankard, tumbler, wine glass

See also **bottle**, **cup**

drink verb drinks, drinking, drank, drunk
To drink greedily is to **gulp**, **guzzle**, or **swig**.
To drink noisily is to **slurp**.
To drink a small amount at a time is to **sip**.
To drink with the tongue as a cat does is to **lap**.

drip noun
Dad was worried by the drips of oil underneath the car.
spot, dribble, splash, trickle

drip verb
The oil dripped onto the garage floor.
drop, leak, dribble, splash, trickle

drive verb drives, driving, drove, driven
1 *The dog drove the sheep through the gate.*
direct, guide, herd
2 *I couldn't drive the spade into the hard ground.*
push, thrust, hammer, plunge, ram
3 *When can I learn to drive a car?*
control, handle, manage
4 *Lack of money drove him to steal.*
force, compel, oblige
to drive someone out
The invading soldiers drove the people out.
eject, expel, throw out
To drive people out of their homes is to **evict** them.
To drive people out of their country is to **banish** or **exile** them.

drive noun
1 *We went for a* **drive** *in the country.*
ride, trip, journey, outing, excursion, jaunt
2 *Have you got the* **drive** *to succeed?*
ambition, determination, keenness,
motivation, energy, zeal

driver noun
Many **drivers** *go too fast.*
motorist
A person who drives someone's car as a job
is a **chauffeur**.

droop verb
Plants tend to **droop** *in dry weather.*
sag, wilt, bend, flop, be limp

drop noun
1 *Large* **drops** *of rain began to fall.*
drip, droplet, spot, bead, blob
2 *Could I have another* **drop** *of milk in my tea?*
dash, small quantity
3 *We expect a* **drop** *in the price of fruit in the summer.*
decrease, reduction, cut
4 *There's a* **drop** *of two metres on the other side of the wall.*
fall, descent, plunge

drop verb
1 *The hawk* **dropped** *onto its prey.*
descend, dive, plunge, swoop
2 *I* **dropped** *to the ground exhausted.*
collapse, fall, sink, subside, slump, tumble
3 *Why did you* **drop** *me from the team?*
omit, eliminate, exclude, leave out
4 *They* **dropped** *the plan for a new bypass.*
abandon, discard, reject, give up, scrap
to drop in
Drop in *on your way home.*
visit, call, pay a call
to drop out
Why did you **drop out** *of the race at the last minute?*
withdraw, back out, pull out
(informal) quit

drove
past tense see **drive**

drown verb
The music from upstairs **drowned** *our conversation.*
overwhelm, overpower, drown out

drowsy adjective
If you feel **drowsy**, *why not go to bed?*
sleepy, tired, weary

drug noun
A new **drug** *has been discovered for back pain.*
medicine, remedy, treatment
A drug which relieves pain is an **analgesic** or **painkiller**.
A drug which calms you down is a **sedative** or **tranquillizer**.
Drugs which make you more active are **stimulants**.

drum noun

> ### WORD WEB
> SOME TYPES OF DRUM
> **bass drum, bongo drum,**
> **kettledrum** or **timpani, snare drum,**
> **tabor, tambour, timpani, tom-tom**
>
> For other musical instruments see **music**

kettledrum   djembe

bongo drums

A
B
C
D
E
F
G
H
I
J
K
L
M
N
O
P
Q
R
S
T
U
V
W

dry adjective
1 *Nothing will grow in this dry soil.*
arid, parched, moistureless, waterless, dehydrated, desiccated, barren
opposite **wet**
A common simile is as dry as a bone.
2 *He gave rather a dry speech.*
dull, boring, dreary, tedious, uninteresting
opposite **interesting**
3 *I can't understand his dry sense of humour.*
ironic, wry, witty, subtle

dry verb
1 *If it's sunny, I'll hang the clothes out to dry.*
get dry, dry out
2 *Will you please dry the dishes?*
wipe dry
When you dry food to preserve it, you dehydrate it.
When your throat feels very dry, you are parched.

dual adjective
The building has a dual purpose: it can be either a cinema or a theatre.
double, twofold, twin, combined

dubious adjective
I'm a bit dubious about getting a snake for a pet.
doubtful, uncertain, unsure, hesitant
opposites **certain, sure**

duck noun
A male duck is a drake.
A young duck is a duckling.

duck verb
1 *Oliver ducked to avoid the snowball.*
bend down, bob down, crouch, stoop
2 *My friends threatened to duck me in the pool.*
dip, immerse, plunge, submerge

due adjective
1 *The train is due in five minutes.*
expected, anticipated
2 *Subscriptions are now due.*
owed, owing, payable

3 *I give her due credit for what she did.*
fitting, proper, appropriate, suitable, deserved, well-earned

dug
past tense see **dig**

dull adjective
1 *I don't like the dull colours in this room.*
dim, dingy, drab, dreary, dismal, faded, gloomy, sombre, subdued
opposites **bright, colourful**
2 *The sky was dull that day.*
cloudy, overcast, grey, sunless, murky
opposite **clear**
3 *I heard a dull thud from upstairs.*
indistinct, muffled, muted
opposite **distinct**
4 *He's rather a dull student.*
stupid, slow, unintelligent, dim, unimaginative, dense, obtuse
(informal) thick
opposite **clever**
5 *The play was so dull that I fell asleep.*
boring, dry, monotonous, tedious, uninteresting, unexciting, lacklustre
opposite **interesting**
A common simile is as dull as ditchwater.

dumb adjective
1 *She was struck dumb with amazement.*
If you do not speak, you are mute or silent.
If you cannot speak because you are surprised, confused, or embarrassed, you are speechless or tongue-tied.
If you find it hard to express yourself, you are inarticulate.
2 (informal) *He's too dumb to understand.*
stupid, unintelligent, dim, slow, dense, obtuse
(informal) thick

dummy adjective
There was a dummy door at the side of the stage.
imitation, fake, copy, toy

dump verb
1 *I decided to dump some of my old toys.*
get rid of, throw away, throw out, discard,

dispose of, scrap
2 *Just* dump *your things in the bedroom.*
put down, set down, deposit, place, drop, throw down, tip

duplicate noun
We made a duplicate *of the original document.*
copy, photocopy, reproduction, replica
An exact copy of a historic document or manuscript is a **facsimile**.
A person who looks like you is your **double** or **twin**.
A living organism which is a duplicate of another living organism is a **clone**.

duration noun
We slept in a tent for the duration *of the holiday.*
length, period, extent

dusk noun
Bats begin to emerge at dusk.
twilight, nightfall, sunset, sundown
opposite dawn

dust noun
There was a lot of dust *on the furniture.*
dirt, grime, particles, powder, grit

dust verb
1 *I* dusted *the bookshelves.*
wipe over, clean, polish
2 *Mum* dusted *the top of the cake with icing sugar.*
powder, sprinkle

dusty adjective
The books we found in the attic were very dusty.
dirty, grimy
opposite clean

duty noun
1 *I have a* duty *to help my parents.*
responsibility, obligation
2 *I carried out my* duties *conscientiously.*
job, task, assignment, chore

3 *The government has increased the* duty *on petrol.*
charge, tax

dwell verb dwells, dwelling, dwelt
to dwell in
It is said that bandits dwell *in these caves.*
live in, inhabit, occupy, reside in
to dwell on
Try not to dwell *on things that happened in the past.*
keep thinking about, worry about, brood over

dwelling noun
see **house**

dwindle verb
Our enthusiasm dwindled *as the day went on.*
become less, diminish, decline, decrease, lessen, subside, wane, weaken
opposite increase

dynamic adjective
The team has a new, dynamic *captain.*
energetic, lively, enthusiastic, vigorous, active, forceful, powerful
opposite apathetic

Ee

eager adjective
He is always eager *to help.*
keen, enthusiastic, desperate, anxious
opposite unenthusiastic

early adjective
1 *The bus was* early *today.*
ahead of time, ahead of schedule
opposite late
2 *The* early *computers were huge machines.*
first, old, primitive, ancient
opposites recent, new

a
b
c
d
e
f
g
h
i
j
k
l
m
n
o
p
q
r
s
t
u
v
w
x
y
z

A
B
C
D
E
F
G
H
I
J
K
L
M
N
O
P
Q
R
S
T
U
V
W
X
Y
Z

earn verb

1 *Bob earns extra pocket money washing cars.*
work for, receive, get, make, obtain, bring in
2 *She trained hard and earned her success.*
deserve, merit

earnest adjective

He's a terribly earnest young man.
serious, sincere, solemn, thoughtful, grave
opposites casual, flippant

earth noun

The earth was so dry that many plants died.
ground, land, soil
Rich, fertile earth is loam.
The top layer of fertile earth is topsoil.
Rich earth consisting of decayed plants is humus.
A heavy, sticky kind of earth is clay.

earthquake noun

When there is an earthquake, you feel a shock or tremor.
An instrument which detects and measures earthquakes is a seismograph.

ease noun

1 *She swam ten lengths of the pool with ease.*
facility, skill, speed
opposite difficulty
2 *Lady Deadwood leads a life of ease.*
comfort, contentment, leisure, peace, quiet, relaxation, rest, tranquillity
opposite stress

ease verb

1 *The doctor gave her some pills to ease her pain.*
relieve, lessen, soothe, moderate
opposite aggravate
2 *After taking the pills, the pain began to ease.*
decrease, reduce, slacken
opposite increase
3 *We eased the piano into position.*
edge, guide, manoeuvre, inch, slide, slip

east noun, adjective, & adverb

The parts of a country or continent in the east are the eastern parts.
In the past, the countries of east Asia, east of the Mediterranean, were called oriental countries.
To travel towards the east is to travel eastward or eastwards or in an easterly direction.
A wind from the east is an easterly wind.

easy adjective

1 *Tonight's homework is really easy.*
undemanding, effortless, light
An informal word for an easy task is a doddle.
2 *The instructions were easy to understand.*
simple, straightforward, clear, plain, elementary
A common simile is as easy as ABC.
3 *Our cat has an easy life.*
carefree, comfortable, peaceful, relaxed, leisurely, restful, tranquil, untroubled
opposite difficult

eat verb eats, eating, ate, eaten

Hannah was eating a cheese sandwich.
consume, devour
(informal) scoff
When cattle eat grass they are grazing.
A person who eats a large amount is said to eat like a horse.
For various things to eat see food

eat verb

OVERUSED WORD

Try to vary the words you use for **eat**.
Here are some other words you could use.

TO **EAT GREEDILY** OR QUICKLY
bolt down, gobble, gulp, guzzle, gorge, polish off, wolf down
I was so hungry, I wolfed down a whole pizza.

TO **EAT NOISILY**
chomp, crunch, gnash, gnaw, munch, slurp
Rabbits like to chomp raw carrots.

TO EAT IN SMALL AMOUNTS
nibble, peck, pick at or pick away at, taste
Do you have any biscuits we could nibble?

TO EAT WITH ENJOYMENT
relish, savour, tuck into
Mr Hogg was savouring *a sausage roll.*

TO EAT A FORMAL MEAL
banquet, dine, feast
The guests will be dining *in the great hall.*

ebb verb
1 *The fishermen waited for the tide to* ebb.
recede, retreat, flow back, fall, go down
2 *She fell ill and her strength began to* ebb.
decline, weaken, lessen, fade, wane

eccentric adjective
What is the reason for his eccentric *behaviour?*
odd, peculiar, strange, weird, abnormal, unusual, curious, unconventional, unorthodox, quirky, zany
(informal) way-out, dotty
opposites conventional, orthodox

echo verb
1 *The sound* echoed *across the valley.*
resound, reverberate
2 *'He's gone home.' 'Gone home?' she* echoed.
repeat, imitate, mimic

edge noun
The edge of a cliff or other steep place is the brink.
The edge of a cup or other container is the brim or rim.
The line round the edge of a circle is the circumference.
The line round the edge of any other shape is its outline.
The distance round the edge of an area is the perimeter.
The stones along the edge of a road are the kerb.
Grass along the edge of a road is the verge.

The space down the edge of a page is the margin.
The space round the edge of a picture is a border.
Something that fits round the edge of a picture is a frame.
The edge of a garment is the hem.
An edge with threads or hair hanging loosely down is a fringe.
The edge of a crowd is the fringe of the crowd.
The area round the edge of a city is the outskirts or suburbs.
The edge of a cricket field is the boundary.
The edge of a football pitch is the touchline.

edge verb
1 *We* edged *away from the lion's den.*
creep, inch, move stealthily, steal, slink
2 *Her bonnet was* edged *with black lace.*
trim, hem

edgy adjective
Horses become edgy *during thunderstorms.*
nervous, restless, anxious, agitated, excitable, tense, jumpy, fidgety
(informal) uptight, jittery
opposite calm

edible adjective
Are these toadstools edible?
eatable, fit to eat, good to eat, safe to eat
opposites poisonous, uneatable

edit verb
The letters were edited *before they were published.*
revise, correct, adapt, rework, rewrite, rephrase

edition noun
We're preparing a Christmas edition *of our magazine.*
copy, issue, number, version

educate verb
The job of a school is to educate *young people.*
teach, train, inform, instruct, tutor

A B C D

F G H I J K L M N O P Q R S T U V W X Y Z

educated adjective
She is an educated woman.
knowledgeable, learned, literate, well read, well informed, cultivated, cultured

education noun
This school is for the education of young witches and wizards.
schooling, teaching, training, instruction, tuition, tutoring, coaching
A programme of education is the curriculum or syllabus.

WORD WEB
PEOPLE WHO PROVIDE EDUCATION
coach, counsellor, governess, head teacher, instructor, lecturer, professor, teacher, trainer, tutor
PLACES TO RECEIVE EDUCATION
academy, college, kindergarten, nursery, playgroup, primary school, secondary school, sixth-form college, university

eerie adjective
I heard some eerie sounds in the night.
strange, weird, uncanny, mysterious, frightening, creepy, ghostly, sinister, unearthly, unnatural
(informal) scary, spooky

effect noun
1 *The effect of eating too much was that I became fat!*
result, consequence, outcome, sequel, upshot
2 *Does this music have any effect on you?*
impact, influence
3 *The lighting gives an effect of warmth.*
feeling, impression, sense, illusion

effective adjective
1 *I wish they could find an effective cure for colds.*
successful
2 *Our team needs an effective goalkeeper.*
competent, able, capable, proficient, skilled

3 *He presented an effective argument against hunting.*
convincing, persuasive, compelling, impressive, telling
opposite useless

efficient adjective
1 *An efficient worker can do the job in an hour.*
effective, competent, able, capable, proficient
2 *Dad tried to work out an efficient way of heating our house.*
economic, productive
opposite inefficient

effort noun
1 *A lot of effort went into making the film.*
work, trouble, exertion, industry, labour, toil
2 *She congratulated us on a good effort.*
attempt, try, endeavour, go, shot

eject verb
1 *Lava was ejected from the volcano when it erupted.*
discharge, emit
2 *The caretaker ejected an intruder from the building.*
remove, expel, evict, banish, kick out, throw out, turn out

elaborate adjective
The plot of the book is so elaborate that I got lost halfway through.
complicated, complex, detailed, intricate, involved, convoluted
opposite simple

elated adjective
We were elated when we won the match.
delighted, pleased, thrilled, joyful, ecstatic, gleeful, exultant, delirious
(informal) over the moon

elbow verb
Miss Crook elbowed her way to the front of the queue.
push, shove, nudge, jostle

enclose verb
1 *The documents were* enclosed *in a brown paper envelope.*
contain, insert, wrap, bind, sheathe
2 *The animals were* enclosed *within a wire fence.*
confine, restrict, fence in, shut in, imprison

enclosure noun
An animal's enclosure with bars is a **cage**.
An enclosure for chickens is a **coop** *or* **run**.
An enclosure for cattle and other animals is a **pen** *or* **corral**.
An enclosure for horses is a **paddock**.
An enclosure for sheep is a **fold**.

encounter verb
1 *He* encountered *her outside the station.*
meet, come across, run into, bump into, come face to face with
2 *We* encountered *some problems.*
experience, come upon, confront, be faced with

encourage verb
1 *We went to the match to* encourage *our team.*
inspire, support, motivate, cheer, spur on, egg on
2 *The poster* encourages *people to eat healthily.*
persuade, urge
3 *Is advertising likely to* encourage *sales?*
increase, boost, stimulate, further, promote, help, aid
opposite **discourage**

encouragement noun
Our team needs some encouragement.
reassurance, inspiration, incitement, stimulation, urging, incentive, stimulus, support

encouraging adjective
The results of the tests were encouraging.
hopeful, positive, promising, reassuring, optimistic, cheering, favourable

end noun
1 *The fence marks the* end *of the garden.*
boundary, limit
2 *The* end *of the film was very exciting.*
ending, finish, close, conclusion, culmination
The last part of a show or piece of music is the **finale**.
A section added at the end of a letter is a **postscript**.
A section added at the end of a story is an **epilogue**.
3 *I was tired by the time we got to the* end *of the journey.*
termination, destination
4 *We arrived late and found ourselves at the* end *of the queue.*
back, rear, tail
5 *What* end *did you have in view when you started?*
aim, purpose, intention, objective, plan, outcome, result

end verb
1 *The meeting should* end *in time for lunch.*
finish, complete, conclude, break off, halt
(informal) **round off**
2 *When did they* end *public executions?*
abolish, do away with, get rid of, put an end to, discontinue, eliminate
3 *The festival* ended *with a show of fireworks.*
close, come to an end, stop, cease, terminate, culminate, wind up

endanger verb
Bad driving endangers *other people.*
put at risk, threaten
opposite **protect**

endeavour verb
Please endeavour *to behave well.*
try, attempt, aim, strive, make an effort

ending noun
The ending *of the film was very exciting.*
end, finish, close, conclusion, culmination, last part
The ending *of a show or piece of music is the* **finale**.

a
b
c
d
e
f
g
h
i
j
k
l
m
n
o
p
q
r
s
t
u
v
w
x
y
z

A B C D E F G H I J K L M N O P Q R S T U V W X Y Z

endless adjective
1 *Teachers need endless patience.*
unending, limitless, infinite, inexhaustible, unlimited
2 *There's an endless procession of cars along the main road.*
continual, continuous, constant, incessant, interminable, perpetual, unbroken, uninterrupted, everlasting, ceaseless

endurance noun
The climb was a test of their endurance.
perseverance, persistence, determination, resolution, stamina

endure verb
1 *She had to endure a lot of pain.*
bear, stand, suffer, cope with, experience, go through, put up with, tolerate, undergo
2 *These traditions have endured for centuries.*
survive, continue, last, persist, carry on, keep going

enemy noun
They used to be friends but now they are bitter enemies.
opponent, adversary, foe, rival
opposites **friend, ally**

energetic adjective
1 *She's a very energetic person.*
dynamic, spirited, enthusiastic, animated, active, zestful
opposites **inactive, lethargic**
2 *It was a very energetic exercise routine.*
lively, vigorous, brisk, fast, quick moving, strenuous
opposites **slow-paced, sluggish**

energy noun
1 *The dancers had tremendous energy.*
liveliness, spirit, vitality, vigour, life, drive, zest, verve, enthusiasm, dynamism
(informal) get-up-and-go, zip
opposite **lethargy**
2 *Wind power is a renewable source of energy.*
power, fuel

enforce verb
The umpire's job is to enforce the rules.
carry out, administer, apply, implement, put into effect, impose, insist on

engage verb
1 *The builder engaged extra workers in order to complete the job on time.*
employ, hire, take on
2 *The general decided to engage the enemy at dawn.*
attack, start fighting

engaged adjective
1 *The painter was engaged in his work.*
busy, occupied, employed, tied up, immersed, absorbed, engrossed
2 *I tried to phone but the line was engaged.*
busy, being used, unavailable
opposites **free, available**

engagement noun
She has a business engagement this afternoon.
meeting, appointment, commitment, date

engine noun
The lawnmower needs a new engine.
motor, mechanism, turbine
A railway engine is a locomotive.

engrossed adjective
Aunt Peggy was engrossed in her knitting.
absorbed, busy, occupied, preoccupied, engaged, immersed

engulf verb
The floods engulfed several villages.
flood, drown, immerse, inundate, overwhelm, submerge, swallow up, swamp

enhance verb
The team's victory enhanced their reputation.
improve, strengthen

enjoy verb
I really enjoyed the film.
like, love, get pleasure from, be pleased by,
admire, appreciate

enjoyable adjective
It was an enjoyable party.
pleasant, agreeable, delightful,
entertaining, amusing
opposite **unpleasant**

enlarge verb
The zoo is going to enlarge the lion enclosure.
expand, extend, develop, make bigger
To make something wider is to **broaden** or
widen it.
To make something longer is to **extend**,
lengthen, or **stretch** it.
To make something seem larger is to
magnify it.
opposite **reduce**

enormous adjective
Enormous waves battered the ship.
huge, gigantic, immense, colossal, massive,
monstrous, monumental, mountainous,
towering, tremendous, vast
(informal) ginormous, humongous
opposite **small**

enough determiner
Is there enough food for ten people?
sufficient, adequate, ample

enquire verb
to enquire about
I enquired about train times to Bristol.
ask for, get information about, request,
investigate

enquiry noun
The librarian helped me with my enquiry.
question, query, request, investigation,
research

enrage verb
I was enraged by their stupidity.
anger, infuriate, madden, incense,
exasperate, provoke
opposite **pacify**

enrol verb
*I enrolled as a member of the drama
club.*
join, sign up, put your name down,
volunteer

ensure verb
Please ensure that you lock the door.
make certain, make sure, confirm, see

enter verb
1 *Silence fell as I entered the room.*
come in, walk in
opposite **leave**
To enter a place without permission
is to **invade** it.
2 *The arrow entered his shoulder.*
go into, penetrate, pierce
3 *Can I enter my name on the list?*
insert, record, register, put down,
set down, sign, write, inscribe
opposite **cancel**
4 *Our class decided to enter the
competition.*
take part in, enrol in, sign up for,
go in for, join in, participate in,
volunteer for
opposite **withdraw from**

enterprise noun
1 *She showed enterprise in starting her
own business.*
drive, initiative
2 *The expedition was a very rash
enterprise.*
adventure, operation, project, undertaking,
venture, effort, mission

entertain verb
1 *The storyteller entertained us with scary
ghost stories.*
amuse, divert, keep amused,
make you laugh, please, cheer up
opposite **bore**
2 *You can entertain friends in the private
dining room.*
receive, welcome, cater for,
give hospitality to

a
b
c
d
e
f
g
h
i
j
k
l
m
n
o
p
q
r
s
t
u
v
w
x
y
z

A B C D E F G H I J K L M N O P Q R S T U V W X Y Z

entertainer noun

WORD WEB

SOME KINDS OF ENTERTAINER

acrobat, actor, actress, ballerina, busker, clown, comedian or comic, conjuror, dancer, disc jockey or DJ, escape artist or escapologist, juggler, magician, mime artist, musician, singer, street entertainer, stunt man or stunt woman, trapeze artist, TV presenter, ventriloquist

A famous entertainer is a **star** or **superstar**.

For types of musician see **music**

ENTERTAINERS IN THE PAST

fool or jester, gladiator, minstrel

entertainment noun

Our hosts had arranged some entertainment for us.

amusements, recreation, diversions, enjoyment, fun, pastimes

enthusiasm noun

1 *The young athletes showed plenty of enthusiasm.*
keenness, commitment, ambition, drive, zeal, zest
opposite **apathy**
2 *Collecting fossils is one of my enthusiasms.*
interest, passion, pastime, hobby, craze, diversion, fad

enthusiast noun

My brother is a football enthusiast.
fan, fanatic, devotee, lover, supporter, addict
(informal) freak, nut

enthusiastic adjective

1 *He's an enthusiastic supporter of our local team.*
keen, passionate, avid, devoted, energetic, fervent, zealous

2 *The audience burst into enthusiastic applause.*
eager, excited, lively, vigorous, exuberant, hearty
opposites **unenthusiastic, apathetic**

entire adjective

Donald spent the entire evening watching television.
complete, whole, total, full

entirely adverb

I'm not entirely sure that I agree with you.
completely, absolutely, wholly, totally, utterly, fully, perfectly, quite

entitle verb

The voucher entitles you to claim a discount.
permit, allow, enable, authorize

entrance[1] noun

1 *Please pay at the entrance.*
entry, way in, access, door, gate
When you go through the entrance to a building, you cross the **threshold**.
2 *I'll meet you in the entrance.*
entrance hall, foyer, lobby, porch
3 *Her sudden entrance took everyone by surprise.*
entry, arrival, appearance
opposite **exit**

entrance[2] verb

The crowd were entranced by the fireworks display.
charm, delight, please, enchant

entrant noun

A prize will be awarded to the winning entrant.
contestant, competitor, contender, candidate, participant

entry noun

1 *A van was blocking the entry to the school.*
way in, entrance, access, door, gate
2 *Every evening I write an entry in my diary.*
item, note

envelop verb
Mist enveloped the top of the mountain.
cover, hide, mask, conceal

envious adjective
He was envious of his brother's success.
jealous, resentful

environment noun
*Animals should live in their natural
environment, not in cages.*
habitat, surroundings, setting, conditions,
situation
the environment
*We must do all we can to protect the
environment.*
the natural world, nature, the earth,
the world

envy noun
*I didn't feel any envy, even when I saw how
rich she was.*
jealousy, resentment, bitterness

envy verb
The evil queen envied Snow White's beauty.
be jealous of, begrudge, grudge, resent

episode noun
1 *I paid for the broken window, and I want to
forget the whole episode.*
event, incident, experience
2 *I missed last night's episode of 'Dr Who'.*
instalment, part

equal adjective
1 *Give everyone an equal amount.*
equivalent, identical, matching, similar,
corresponding, fair
2 *The scores were equal at half-time.*
even, level, the same, square
To make the scores equal is to **equalize**.

equip verb
*All the bedrooms are equipped with a colour
television.*
provide, supply
To equip soldiers with weapons is to **arm**
them.

To equip a room with furniture is to **furnish**
it.

equipment noun
The shed is full of gardening equipment.
apparatus, gear, kit, tackle, tools,
implements, instruments, materials,
machinery, paraphernalia, things
Computing equipment is **hardware**.

equivalent adjective
*A metre is equivalent to a hundred
centimetres.*
matching, similar, corresponding, identical,
the same as

era noun
Shakespeare lived in the Elizabethan era.
age, period, time, epoch

erase verb
I erased the writing on the blackboard.
delete, remove, rub out, wipe out,
get rid of

erect adjective
The dog stood with its ears erect.
upright, vertical, perpendicular

erect verb
The town hall was erected in 1890.
build, construct, raise, put up, set up
To erect a tent is to **pitch** it.

erode verb
The flood water eroded the river bank.
wear away, eat away, destroy

errand noun
I went on an errand to the corner shop.
job, task, assignment, trip, journey

erratic adjective
*The team's performance has been erratic this
season.*
inconsistent, irregular, uneven, variable,
changeable, fluctuating, unpredictable
opposite consistent

a
b
c
d
e
f
g
h
i
j
k
l
m
n
o
p
q
r
s
t
u
v
w
x
y
z

A
B
C
D
E
F
G
H
I
J
K
L
M
N
O
P
Q
R
S
T
U
V
W
X
Y
Z

error noun

1 *The accident was the result of an* error *by the driver.*

mistake, fault, lapse, blunder

2 *I think there is an* error *in your argument.*

flaw, inaccuracy, misunderstanding, inconsistency

The error of leaving something out is an **omission** or **oversight**.

erupt verb

Smoke began to erupt *from the volcano.*

be discharged, be emitted, pour out, issue, spout, gush, spurt, belch

escape verb

1 *Why did you let him* escape*?*

get away, get out, run away, break free, break out

(informal) **give you the slip**

A performer who escapes from chains, etc., is an **escape artist** or **escapologist**.

2 *She always escapes the nasty jobs.*

avoid, get out of, evade, dodge, shirk

escape noun

1 *The prisoner's* escape *was filmed by security cameras.*

getaway, breakout, flight

2 *The explosion was caused by an* escape *of gas.*

leak, leakage, seepage

escort noun

1 *The president always has an* escort *to protect him.*

bodyguard, guard

2 *The actress arrived with her* escort*.*

companion, partner

escort verb

The queen was escorted *by a number of attendants.*

accompany, guard, protect, look after

especially adverb

I like apple pie, especially *with ice-cream.*

above all, chiefly, most of all

espionage noun

see **spy**

essential adjective

Fruit and vegetables are an essential *part of our diet.*

important, necessary, basic, vital, principal, fundamental, chief, crucial, indispensable

establish verb

1 *He plans to* establish *a new business.*

set up, start, begin, create, found, initiate, institute, introduce, launch, originate

2 *The police have not managed to* establish *his guilt.*

prove, show to be true, confirm, verify

estate noun

1 *There's a new housing* estate *near our school.*

area, development, scheme

2 *The castle is sited on a large* estate*.*

land, grounds

3 *The millionaire left his* estate *to charity.*

property, fortune, wealth, possessions

estimate noun

What is your estimate *of how much it will cost?*

assessment, calculation, evaluation, guess, judgement, opinion

An official estimate of the value of something is a **valuation**.

An official estimate of what a job is going to cost is a **quotation** or **tender**.

estimate verb

The builders estimate *that the work will take four months.*

calculate, assess, work out, compute, count up, evaluate, judge, reckon, think out

eternal adjective

1 *The magic fountain was said to give* eternal *youth.*

everlasting, infinite, lasting, unending, timeless

Beings with eternal life are said to be **immortal**.

2 *I'm sick of your* eternal *quarrelling!*
constant, continual, never-ending,
non-stop, persistent, perpetual, endless,
ceaseless, incessant, unceasing

evacuate verb
1 *The firefighters* evacuated *everyone from
the building.*
remove, clear, send away, move out
2 *We were told to* evacuate *the building.*
leave, quit, abandon, withdraw from,
empty, vacate

evade verb
Don't try to evade *your responsibilities.*
avoid, dodge, shirk, escape from,
steer clear of, fend off
opposite confront

even adjective
1 *You need an* even *surface for ice-skating.*
level, flat, smooth, straight
opposite uneven
2 *The runners kept up an* even *pace.*
regular, steady, unvarying, rhythmical,
monotonous
opposite irregular
3 *Mr Humphreys has an* even *temper.*
calm, cool, placid, unexcitable
opposite excitable
4 *The scores were* even *at half time.*
equal, level, matching, identical, the same,
square
opposite different
5 *The numbers 2, 4, and 6 are* even *numbers.*
opposite odd

even verb
to even something up
Join their team and even *up the numbers.*
equalize, level, balance, match, square

evening noun
Towards evening *it clouded over and began
to rain.*
dusk, nightfall, sundown, sunset, twilight

event noun
1 *Her autobiography describes the main
events of her life.*

happening, incident, occurrence
2 *There was an* event *to mark the launch of
the new film.*
function, occasion, ceremony,
entertainment, party, reception
3 *The World Cup is an important* event *for
football fans.*
competition, contest, fixture, engagement,
meeting, game, match, tournament

eventful adjective
We had an eventful *journey.*
interesting, exciting, busy, lively, active
opposites uneventful, dull

eventual adjective
We were happy with our eventual *score.*
final, ultimate, resulting, overall, ensuing

eventually adverb
The journey took ages, but eventually *we
arrived safely.*
finally, at last, in the end, ultimately

evergreen adjective
Most pine trees are evergreen.
opposite deciduous

everyday adjective
Don't dress up—just wear your everyday
clothes.
normal, ordinary, usual, regular, customary

evidence noun
This piece of paper is evidence *that he is
lying.*
proof, confirmation
Evidence that someone accused of a
crime was not there when the crime was
committed is an alibi.
Evidence given in a law court is a testimony.
To give evidence in court is to testify.

evident adjective
It was evident *that someone had been in the
room.*
clear, obvious, apparent, plain, certain,
unmistakable, undeniable, noticeable,
perceptible, visible

a
b
c
d
e
f
g
h
i
j
k
l
m
n
o
p
q
r
s
t
u
v
w
x
y
z

A

evidently adverb
The woman was evidently *upset.*
clearly, obviously, apparently, plainly,
undoubtedly

B

C

evil adjective
1 *The charm was used to keep away* evil
spirits.
malevolent, fiendish, diabolical
2 *Who would do such an* evil *deed?*
wicked, immoral, cruel, sinful, villainous,
malicious, foul, hateful, vile
opposite **good**

D

E

F

G

evil noun
1 *The good witch tried to fight against* evil.
wickedness, badness, wrongdoing, sin,
immorality, villainy, malevolence, malice
2 *They had to endure the* evils *of famine and
drought.*
disaster, misfortune, suffering, pain,
affliction, curse

H

I

J

K

L

evolve verb
Life evolved *on Earth over millions of years.*
develop, grow, progress, emerge, mature

M

N

exact adjective
1 *I gave the police an* exact *account of what
happened.*
accurate, precise, correct, true, faithful,
detailed, meticulous, strict
2 *Is this an* exact *copy of the original
document?*
identical, perfect, indistinguishable
opposite **inaccurate**

O

P

Q

R

S

exactly adverb
At what time exactly *did you leave the house?*
precisely, specifically, accurately, correctly,
strictly
opposites **roughly, inaccurately**
A phrase meaning 'exactly on time' is to be
on the dot.

T

U

V

W

exaggerate verb
He tends to exaggerate *his problems.*
magnify, inflate, overdo, make too much of
opposite **minimize**

X

Y

Z

examination noun
1 *The results of the* examinations *will be
announced next month.*
test, assessment
(informal) **exam**
2 *The judge made a thorough* examination *of
the facts.*
investigation, inspection, study, analysis,
survey, review, appraisal
3 *He was sent to hospital for an*
examination.
check-up
A medical examination of a dead person is a
post-mortem.

examine verb
1 *The judge* examined *the evidence.*
inspect, study, investigate, analyse,
look closely at, pore over, scrutinize, probe,
survey, review, weigh up, sift
2 *They were* examined *on their knowledge of
history.*
question, interrogate, quiz
To examine someone rigorously is to **grill**
them.

example noun
1 *Give me an* example *of what you mean.*
instance, illustration, sample, specimen,
case
2 *She's an* example *to us all.*
model, ideal

exasperate verb
Her constant questions began to exasperate
me.
annoy, irritate, upset, frustrate, anger,
madden, vex

exceed verb
She exceeded *the previous race record by two
seconds.*
beat, better, outdo, pass, surpass, go over

excel verb
She's a good all-round athlete, but she excels
at sprinting.
do best, stand out, shine

excellent adjective
That's an excellent idea!
first-class, first-rate, outstanding,
exceptional, remarkable, tremendous,
wonderful, superb, great, fine,
marvellous, superior, superlative,
top-notch, (informal) brilliant,
fantastic, terrific, fabulous,
sensational, super
For other ways to describe something good
see **good**
opposites **bad, awful, second-rate**

except preposition
Everyone got a prize except me.
apart from, but, with the exception of,
excluding

exception noun
to take exception to something
*She took exception to what he said about
her clothes.*
dislike, object to, complain about,
disapprove of, be upset by

exceptional adjective
*It is exceptional to have such cold weather
in June.*
unusual, extraordinary, uncommon,
unexpected, amazing, rare, odd,
peculiar, strange, surprising, special,
abnormal, phenomenal, unheard-of,
bizarre
opposites **normal, usual**

excerpt noun
She recited an excerpt from the poem.
extract, passage, part, section
A short excerpt is a **quotation**.
The most interesting excerpts from
something are the **highlights**.
Excerpts from a film are **clips**.

excess noun
If there is an excess of something, so that it
is hard to sell it, there is a **glut**.
When a business has an excess of income
over its expenses, it has a **profit** or a
surplus.

excessive adjective
1 *I think his enthusiasm for football
is excessive.*
extreme, exaggerated, fanatical
2 *Mum prepared excessive amounts of food
for the party.*
unnecessary, needless, superfluous,
extravagant, wasteful, unreasonable

exchange verb
The shop will exchange faulty goods.
change, replace
To exchange goods for other goods without
using money is to **barter**.
To exchange an old thing for part of the
cost of a new one is to **trade** it **in**.
To exchange things with your friends is to
swap them.
To exchange players for other players in a
football match, etc., is to **substitute** them.

excite verb
The prospect of going to Italy excited Ali.
thrill, enthuse, stimulate, electrify, rouse,
stir up
opposite **calm**

excited adjective
*On Christmas Eve, my little brother was too
excited to sleep.*
agitated, lively, enthusiastic, exuberant,
thrilled, elated, eager, animated
opposite **calm**

excitement noun
I could hardly bear the excitement!
suspense, tension, drama, thrill

exciting adjective
*The last minutes of the match were the most
exciting of all!*
dramatic, eventful, thrilling, gripping,
sensational, stirring, rousing, stimulating,
electrifying
opposites **dull, boring**

exclaim verb
'Get out of my house!' she exclaimed.
call, shout, cry out, yell
For other ways to say something see **say**

a
b
c
d
e
f
g
h
i
j
k
l
m
n
o
p
q
r
s
t
u
v
w
x
y
z

A
B
C
D
E
F
G
H
I
J
K
L
M
N
O
P
Q
R
S
T
U
V
W
X
Y
Z

exclamation noun
Dr Doyle gave an exclamation of surprise.
cry, shout, yell
An impolite exclamation is an **oath** or **swear word**.

WRITING TIPS
SOMEONE WHO IS **ANGRY** OR **ANNOYED** MIGHT SAY
blast, bother, drat, fiddlesticks
'Fiddlesticks!' said Merlin. 'I've forgotten the spell!'
SOMEONE WHO IS **SURPRISED** OR **ALARMED** MIGHT SAY
blimey, crikey, golly, goodness me, good gracious, good heavens, gosh, my word, yikes
'My word, is that a dinosaur bone?' asked Dr Doyle.

exclude verb
1 *Adults are excluded from joining our club.*
ban, bar, prohibit, keep out, banish, reject
2 *She had to exclude dairy products from her diet.*
leave out, omit
opposite **include**

excluding preposition
The gardens are open every day excluding Christmas.
except, except for, with the exception of, apart from, bar

exclusive adjective
They stayed at a very exclusive hotel.
select, private, snobbish, upmarket
(informal) **posh, fancy**

excursion noun
We went on an excursion to the seaside.
trip, journey, outing, expedition, jaunt

excuse noun
What is your excuse for being so late?
reason, explanation, defence, justification

excuse verb
I can't excuse his bad behaviour.
forgive, overlook, pardon
opposite **punish**
to be excused something
May I be excused swimming?
be exempt from, be let off, be released from

execute verb
1 *In some countries, criminals may still be executed.*
put to death
Someone who executes people is an **executioner**.
To execute someone unofficially without a proper trial is to **lynch** them.
2 *She executed a perfect somersault.*
perform, carry out, produce, complete, accomplish

exercise noun
1 *Exercise helps to keep you fit.*
physical activity, working out, keep-fit, training
2 *Doing exercises will improve your guitar playing.*
practice, training, drill

exercise verb
1 *If you exercise regularly, you will keep fit.*
keep fit, train, exert yourself
2 *I sometimes exercise our neighbour's dog.*
take for a walk, take out, walk
3 *We must exercise patience.*
show, use, apply, display, employ

exert verb
He exerted all his strength to lift the box.
use, apply, employ

exertion noun
The exertion of climbing the stairs made him sweat.
effort, hard work, labour, toil

exhale verb
The doctor asked me to exhale slowly.
breathe out
opposite **inhale**

exhaust noun
The exhaust from cars damages the environment.
fumes, smoke, emissions, gases

exhaust verb
1 *The steep climb up the hill exhausted me.*
tire, wear out
2 *We had exhausted our food supply by midday.*
finish, go through, use up, consume
(informal) **polish off**

exhausted adjective
After a hard race, we lay exhausted on the grass.
tired, weary, worn out, fatigued, breathless, gasping, panting
(informal) **all in, done in, bushed, zonked**

exhausting adjective
Digging the garden is exhausting work.
tiring, demanding, hard, laborious, strenuous, difficult, gruelling, wearisome
opposite **easy**

exhaustion noun
He was overcome by sheer exhaustion.
tiredness, fatigue, weariness, weakness

exhibit verb
1 *Her paintings were exhibited in galleries all over Europe and America.*
display, show, present, put up, set up, arrange
2 *He was exhibiting signs of anxiety.*
show, demonstrate, reveal
opposite **hide**

exhibition noun
We went to see an exhibition of paintings by Picasso.
display, show

exile verb
As a result of the war, many people were exiled from their own country.
banish, expel, drive out, deport, eject, send away

exile noun
He returned to his country after 24 years of exile.
banishment, expulsion, deportation
A person who has been exiled is an exile or a refugee.

exist verb
1 *Some people claim that ghosts actually exist.*
be real, occur
2 *We can't exist without food.*
live, remain alive, survive, keep going, last, continue, endure

existence noun
1 *Do you believe in the existence of ghosts?*
reality
2 *Most plants depend on sunlight for their existence.*
life, survival

existing adjective
1 *There are only two existing species of elephants.*
surviving, living, remaining
2 *Next year, the existing rules will be replaced by new ones.*
present, current

exit noun
1 *I'll wait for you by the exit.*
door, way out, doorway, gate, barrier
opposite **entrance**
2 *The robbers made a hurried exit.*
departure
opposite **entrance**

exit verb
The actors exited from the left of the stage.
go out, leave, depart, withdraw
opposite **enter**

exotic adjective
My aunt has travelled to many exotic places.
remote, foreign, alien, different, exciting, romantic, strange, unfamiliar, wonderful
opposite **familiar**

a
b
c
d
e
f
g
h
i
j
k
l
m
n
o
p
q
r
s
t
u
v
w
x
y
z

A B C D **E** F G H I J K L M N O P Q R S T U V W X Y Z

expand verb
Their computer business is expanding rapidly.
increase, enlarge, extend, build up, develop, make bigger
To become larger is to **grow** or **swell**.
To become wider is to **broaden**, **thicken**, or **widen**.
To become longer is to **extend**, **lengthen**, or **stretch**.
opposites contract, reduce

expanse noun
The explorers crossed a large expanse of desert.
area, stretch, tract
An expanse of water or ice is a **sheet**.

expect verb
1 *I expect that it will rain today.*
anticipate, imagine, forecast, predict, foresee, prophesy
2 *She expects me to do everything for her!*
require, want, count on, insist on, demand
3 *I expect they missed the bus.*
believe, imagine, guess, suppose, presume, assume, think

expedition noun
An expedition into unknown territory is an **exploration**.
An expedition to carry out a special task is a **mission**.
An expedition to find something is a **quest**.
An expedition to worship at a holy place is a **pilgrimage**.
An expedition to see or hunt wild animals is a **safari**.
See also **explorer**

expel verb
1 *A fan expels the stale air and fumes.*
send out, force out
2 *He was expelled from school.*
dismiss, ban, remove, throw out, send away
To expel someone from their home is to **eject** or **evict** them.
To expel someone from their country is to **banish** or **exile** them.
To expel evil spirits is to **exorcise** them.

expense noun
She was worried about the expense of the holiday.
cost, charges, expenditure

expensive adjective
Houses are very expensive in this area.
dear, costly
opposite cheap

experience noun
1 *Have you had any experience of singing in a choir?*
practice, involvement, participation
2 *I had an unusual experience today.*
happening, event, occurrence, incident
An exciting experience is an **adventure**.
An unpleasant experience is an **ordeal**.

experienced adjective
He's an experienced actor who has been in many films.
skilled, qualified, expert, knowledgeable, trained, professional
opposite inexperienced

experiment noun
We carried out a scientific experiment.
test, trial
A series of experiments is **research** or an **investigation**.

experiment verb
They experimented to see if their robot would work.
do tests
To experiment on or with something is to **test it** or **try it out**.

expert noun
He's an expert at chess.
specialist, authority, genius, wizard
(informal) **dab hand, whizz**

expert adjective
Only an expert sailor could cross the ocean.
brilliant, capable, clever, competent, experienced, knowledgeable, professional, proficient, qualified, skilful, skilled, specialized, trained
opposites amateur, unskilful

expertise noun
Do you have the expertise *to restore the painting?*
skill, ability, competence, knowledge, know-how, training

expire verb
1 *The television licence* expires *next month.*
finish, run out, come to an end, become invalid
2 *The animal* expired *before the vet arrived.*
die, pass away

explain verb
1 *The doctor* explained *the procedure carefully.*
make clear, give an explanation of, clarify, describe
2 *Can you* explain *your strange behaviour?*
give reasons for, account for, excuse, make excuses for, justify

explanation noun
1 *They could find no* explanation *for the accident.*
reason, excuse, justification
2 *He gave a brief* explanation *of how his invention worked.*
account, description, demonstration

explode verb
1 *The firework* exploded *with a bang.*
blow up, make an explosion, go off, burst, shatter
2 *The slightest movement might* explode *the bomb.*
detonate, set off

exploit noun
The book describes her exploits *as a secret agent.*
adventure, deed, feat, venture, escapade

exploit verb
They plan to exploit *the area as a tourist attraction.*
make use of, take advantage of, use, develop, profit from
(informal) cash in on

explore verb
1 *The spacecraft will* explore *the solar system.*
search, survey, travel through, probe
2 *We must* explore *all the possibilities.*
examine, inspect, investigate, look into, research, analyse, scrutinize

explorer noun
The explorers *were looking for the legendary Lost City.*
traveller, voyager, discoverer, wanderer

WORD WEB
THINGS AN EXPLORER MIGHT FIND
catacombs, cave, cavern, chest, hieroglyphics, inscription, labyrinth, maze, mummy, parchment, pyramid, riddle, sarcophagus, seal, secret passage, skeleton, stone tablet, temple, tomb, treasure, tunnel, underground chamber

THINGS AN EXPLORER MIGHT USE OR CARRY
binoculars, chart, compass, machete, map, penknife, rope, rucksack, telescope, tent, torch, water bottle

For explorers in polar regions see polar

For explorers in space see astronaut

explosion noun
The explosion *rattled the windows.*
blast, bang
An explosion from a volcano is an eruption.
An explosion of laughter is an outburst.
The sound of a gun going off is a report.

export verb
The factory exports *most of the cars it makes.*
sell abroad, send abroad, ship overseas
opposite import

expose verb
1 *He yawned,* exposing *a set of white teeth.*
uncover
2 *The truth about his past was* exposed *in the newspaper.*
make known, publish, reveal, disclose

a
b
c
d
e
f
g
h
i
j
k
l
m
n
o
p
q
r
s
t
u
v
w
x
y
z

A
B
C
D
E
F
G
H
I
J
K
L
M
N
O
P
Q
R
S
T
U
V
W
X
Y
Z

express verb

He's always quick to express his opinions.

voice, communicate, convey,
put into words, phrase

To express yourself by word of mouth is to speak.

To express yourself on paper is to write.

To express your feelings forcefully is to give vent to them.

expression noun

1 *'Tickled pink' is a colloquial expression.*

phrase, saying, term, wording

An expression that people use too much is a cliché.

2 *Did you see her expression when I told her the news?*

look, appearance, countenance, face

3 *Rhona plays the piano with great expression.*

feeling, emotion, sympathy, understanding

expression noun

WORD WEB

EXPRESSIONS YOU MIGHT SEE ON A FACE

beam, frown, glare, glower, grimace, grin, laugh, leer, long face, poker-face, pout, scowl, smile, smirk, sneer, wide-eyed look, wince, yawn

See also **face**

expressive adjective

1 *The old wizard gave me an expressive look.*

meaningful, significant, revealing, telling

2 *An actor needs to have an expressive voice.*

lively, varied, eloquent

opposites **expressionless, flat**

exquisite adjective

There was some exquisite lace on the collar.

beautiful, fine, delicate, intricate, dainty

extend verb

1 *Stopping for lunch will extend our journey by an hour.*

lengthen, make longer, prolong, delay, draw out

opposite **shorten**

2 *They have recently extended their website.*

enlarge, expand, increase, build up, develop, add to, widen the scope of

opposite **reduce**

3 *He sat back and extended his legs.*

stretch out, hold out, put out, reach out, stick out

4 *We extended a warm welcome to the visitors.*

give, offer

extension noun

They are building an extension to the runway.

continuation, addition

extensive adjective

The palace gardens cover an extensive area.

big, large, broad, wide, spread out

opposite **small**

extent noun

1 *The map shows the extent of the island.*

area, dimensions, expanse, spread, breadth, length, limits, measurement

2 *After the storm we went out to see the extent of the damage.*

amount, degree, level, size, scope, magnitude, range

exterior noun

He painted the exterior of his house.

outside

opposite **interior**

exterminate verb

They used poison to exterminate the rats.

destroy, kill, get rid of, annihilate, wipe out

external adjective

In external appearance, the house was rather gloomy.

exterior, outside, outer

opposite **internal**

extinct adjective
An extinct species is one that has **died out** or **vanished**.
An extinct volcano is an **inactive** volcano.

extinguish verb
We **extinguished** *the campfire before we went to bed.*
put out, quench, smother
opposite ignite

extra adjective
1 *There is an* **extra** *charge for taking your bike on the train.*
additional, further, added, supplementary, excess
2 *There is* **extra** *food in the kitchen if you need it.*
more, spare, surplus, reserve

extract noun
There's an **extract** *from the new Jacqueline Wilson book in the magazine.*
excerpt, passage, part, section
A short extract is a **quotation**.
Especially interesting extracts from something are the **highlights**.
An extract from a newspaper is a **cutting**.
An extract from a film is a **clip**.

extract verb
1 *The dentist decided to* **extract** *my tooth.*
pull out, remove, take out, draw out, withdraw
(informal) **whip out**
2 *The following passages are* **extracted** *from the book.*
derive, get, gather, obtain, quote, select

extraordinary adjective
The astronauts saw many **extraordinary** *sights.*
amazing, astonishing, remarkable, outstanding, exceptional, incredible, fantastic, marvellous, miraculous, phenomenal, rare, special, strange, surprising, unheard of, unusual, weird, wonderful, abnormal, curious
opposite ordinary

extravagant adjective
He held a large, **extravagant** *party for all his friends.*
expensive, lavish, wasteful
Someone who spends money in an extravagant way is a **spendthrift**.
opposite modest

extreme adjective
1 *Polar bears can withstand* **extreme** *cold.*
great, intense, severe, acute, excessive
2 *She lives on the* **extreme** *edge of the town.*
farthest, furthest

eye noun

WORD WEB
PARTS OF YOUR EYE
cornea, eyeball, eyebrow, eyelash, eyelid, iris, lens, pupil, retina
A person who tests your eyesight is an **optician**.
A word meaning 'to do with eyes' is **optical**.
A person with good eyesight is said to have **eyes like a hawk**.

WRITING TIPS
You can use these words to describe **eyes**
beady, bulbous, bulging, deep-set, glassy, heavy-lidded, hooded, protuberant, saucer-like, sunken; cloudy, misty, moist, piercing, steely, tearful, watery
Bod did not look up. If he had, he would have seen a pair of watery blue eyes watching him intently from a bedroom window.
— Neil Gaiman, *The Graveyard Book*

eye verb
The dog **eyed** *the sausages hungrily.*
look at, regard, stare at, watch, gaze at, contemplate

a
b
c
d
e
f
g
h
i
j
k
l
m
n
o
p
q
r
s
t
u
v
w
x
y
z

A
B
C
D
E
F
G
H
I
J
K
L
M
N
O
P
Q
R
S
T
U
V
W
X
Y
Z

Ff

fabric noun

This fabric *will make a lovely dress for my doll.*

cloth, material, stuff

A plural word for different kinds of fabric is textiles.

See also **cloth**

fabulous adjective

1 (informal) *We had a* fabulous *time at the party.*

excellent, first-class, marvellous, outstanding, superb, tremendous, wonderful

(informal) brilliant, fantastic, smashing

2 *Dragons are* fabulous *creatures.*

fictitious, imaginary, legendary, mythical

face noun

1 *We saw the anger in the witch's* face.

expression, features, look, countenance

2 *The* face *of the clock had been smashed.*

front

3 *A cube has six* faces.

side, surface

WRITING TIPS

You can use these words to describe a face

TO DESCRIBE ITS SHAPE

flat, long, oval, round, rounded; lantern-jawed, square-jawed

TO DESCRIBE ITS FEATURES

chiselled, chubby, craggy, delicate, fine, gaunt, haggard, hollow, pinched, prominent, puffy, skeletal, sunken

Their faces were gaunt *and* pinched *from hunger.*

TO DESCRIBE ITS SKIN OR COLOUR

clear, dark, fair, flushed, freckled, fresh, glowing, healthy, rosy, ruddy, tanned; ashen, grey, leaden, pale, pallid, pasty, sallow, sickly, unhealthy, wan; flabby, saggy, shrivelled, weather-beaten, wizened, wrinkled, wrinkly; disfigured, pimply, pock-marked, scarred, spotty

Peering between the baskets, the children saw the woman for the first time. She was painfully thin, with a pinched, weather-beaten face and tightly frizzed hair.

— David Miller, *Shark Island*

TO DESCRIBE THE LOOK ON A FACE

cheeky, cheerful, radiant, sunny; grave, grim, serious; sulky, sullen, surly; blank, deadpan, faceless, impassive, unmoving, vacant

The guard stared ahead, his face unmoving.

See also **expression**

For parts of a face see **eye** and **nose**

face verb

1 *Stand and* face *your partner.*

be opposite to, look towards

2 *The astronauts had to* face *many dangers.*

cope with, deal with, face up to, stand up to, tackle, meet, encounter, confront

opposite avoid

fact noun

It is a fact *that dodos are now extinct.*

reality, truth, certainty

opposite fiction

the facts

The detective considered the facts *in the case.*

details, particulars, information, data

Facts which are useful in trying to prove something are **evidence**.

Facts expressed as numbers are **statistics**.

factual adjective

Anne Frank wrote a factual account of her life during the war
real, true, truthful, accurate, authentic, faithful, genuine, objective, reliable
A film or story based on a person's life is biographical.
A film or story based on history is historical.
A film telling you about real events is a documentary.
opposites made-up, fictional

fade verb

1 *Sunlight has faded the curtains.*
make paler, bleach, blanch, whiten, dim
opposite brighten
2 *Those flowers will fade in a few days.*
wither, wilt, droop, flag, shrivel
opposite flourish
3 *Gradually, the light began to fade.*
weaken, decline, diminish, dwindle, fail, wane, disappear, melt away, vanish
opposite increase

fail verb

1 *Their plan to steal the crown jewels failed miserably.*
be unsuccessful, go wrong, fall through, founder, come to grief, miscarry
(informal) flop, bomb
opposite succeed
2 *The rocket engine failed before take-off.*
break down, cut out, give up, stop working
3 *By late afternoon, the light had begun to fail.*
weaken, decline, diminish, dwindle, fade, get worse, deteriorate
opposite improve
4 *The professor failed to warn us of the danger.*
neglect, forget, omit
opposite remember
5 *I hope I don't fail my violin exam.*
(informal) flunk
opposite pass

failure noun

1 *The storm caused a power failure.*
breakdown, fault, malfunction, crash, loss, collapse, stoppage
2 *Their attempt to reach the North Pole was a failure.*
defeat, disappointment, disaster, fiasco
(informal) flop, wash-out
opposite success

faint adjective

1 *The details in the photograph are very faint.*
faded, dim, unclear, indistinct, vague, blurred, hazy, pale, shadowy, misty
opposites clear, distinct
2 *There was a faint smell of burning in the air.*
delicate, slight
opposite strong
3 *We heard a faint cry for help.*
weak, low, muffled, distant, hushed, muted, soft, thin
opposite loud
4 *Gordon was so hungry that he felt faint.*
dizzy, giddy, light-headed, unsteady, weak, exhausted, feeble
(informal) woozy

faint verb

The explorers nearly fainted from exhaustion.
become unconscious, collapse, pass out, black out, swoon

fair¹ adjective

1 *I think the referee made a fair decision.*
just, proper, right, fair-minded, honest, honourable, impartial, unbiased, unprejudiced, disinterested
opposite unfair
2 *The twins both have fair hair.*
blond or blonde, light, golden, yellow
opposite dark
3 *Our team has a fair chance of winning the cup.*
reasonable, moderate, average, acceptable, adequate, satisfactory, passable, respectable, tolerable
4 *The weather should be fair today.*
dry, fine, sunny, bright, clear, cloudless, pleasant, favourable

a
b
c
d
e
f
g
h
i
j
k
l
m
n
o
p
q
r
s
t
u
v
w
x
y
z

A
B
C
D
E
F
G
H
I
J
K
L
M
N
O
P
Q
R
S
T
U
V
W
X
Y
Z

fair² noun
1 *My sister won a teddy bear at the* fair.
fairground, funfair, carnival, fete, gala
2 *Our school is holding a book* fair *next week.*
show, exhibition, display, market, bazaar

fairly adverb
1 *The competition will be judged* fairly.
honestly, properly, justly, impartially
2 *The ground is still* fairly *wet.*
I'm fairly *certain that we are heading north.*
quite, rather, somewhat, slightly, moderately, up to a point, reasonably, tolerably
(informal) pretty

fairy noun

🕸 **WORD WEB**

THINGS A FAIRY MIGHT HAVE OR USE
fairy dust, lantern, wand, wings

A FAIRY'S WINGS OR CLOTHES MIGHT BE
diaphanous, feathery, glittering, glowing, gossamer, lustrous, sheer, sparkling, translucent, transparent

PLACES WHERE A FAIRY MIGHT LIVE
dell, glen, magic forest, magic tree, glade, mound, toadstool

SOME CREATURES SIMILAR TO FAIRIES
brownie, elf, imp, leprechaun, nymph, pixie, sprite

For other creatures found in myths and legends see myth

faith noun
1 *The acrobat had complete* faith *in his assistant.*
belief, trust, confidence
opposite doubt
2 *In our school, we have pupils of many different* faiths.
religion, creed, doctrine, belief

faithful adjective
1 *My dog, Scruffy, is my* faithful *friend.*
loyal, devoted, reliable, trustworthy, dependable, firm, constant, close
opposite unfaithful
2 *Is this a* faithful *copy of the map?*
accurate, exact, precise, true

fake noun
That's not a real Roman coin—it's a fake.
copy, imitation, reproduction, replica, forgery
(informal) phoney
An event that is a fake is a hoax, sham, or simulation.
A person who pretends to be another person is an impostor.

fake verb
The spy tried to fake *a foreign accent.*
imitate, copy, pretend, put on, reproduce, simulate
To fake someone's signature is to forge it.

fall verb falls, falling, fell, fallen
1 *Sam* fell *off a ladder and broke his leg.*
tumble, topple, crash down, pitch, plunge
2 *Snow was beginning to* fall *quite thickly.*
drop, come down, descend, rain down, plummet
3 *The level of the river had* fallen *since March.*
go down, subside, recede, sink, ebb
4 *The temperature in the cave* fell *to below freezing.*
go down, become lower, decrease, decline, lessen, diminish, dwindle
5 *After a long siege, the town* fell *to the enemy.*
give in, surrender
6 *Millions of soldiers* fell *in the war.*
die, be killed, perish
(old use) be slain
7 *We arrived at the camp as night was* falling.
happen, occur, come, take place
to fall in
The roof of the cabin fell in *during the storm.*
cave in, collapse, give way

to fall out
The twins are always falling out *with each other.*
argue, disagree, quarrel, squabble, bicker
to fall through
Our holiday plans have fallen through *again.*
come to nothing, fail, collapse, founder

fall noun
1 *Ellen had a* fall *and cut her knee.*
tumble
2 *We noticed a sharp* fall *in the temperature.*
drop, lowering
opposite rise
3 *There has was a* fall *in the price of coffee.*
decrease, reduction, decline
opposite increase
4 *This is a story about the* fall *of Troy.*
defeat, surrender

false adjective
1 *They gave us* false *information about the treasure.*
wrong, incorrect, untrue, inaccurate, mistaken, erroneous, faulty, invalid, misleading, deceptive
opposite correct
2 *The spy was travelling with a* false *passport.*
fake, bogus, sham, counterfeit, forged
opposites genuine, authentic
3 *Mrs Gummidge put in her* false *teeth.*
artificial, imitation
opposites real, natural
4 *The Black Knight turned out to be a* false *ally.*
unfaithful, disloyal, unreliable, untrustworthy, deceitful, dishonest, treacherous
opposites faithful, loyal

falter verb
1 *The horse* faltered *as it approached the jump.*
hesitate, flinch, hold back, pause, stumble, waver, get cold feet
To falter in your speech is to stammer *or* stutter.

2 *The knight's courage began to* falter.
weaken, diminish, flag, wane

fame noun
Her Olympic medal brought her international fame.
celebrity, stardom, renown, glory, reputation, name, standing, stature, prominence
Fame that you get for doing something bad is notoriety.

familiar adjective
1 *Seagulls are a* familiar *sight on the beach.*
common, everyday, normal, ordinary, usual, regular, customary, frequent, mundane, routine
opposite rare
2 *It seems a bit* familiar *to call her by her first name.*
informal, friendly, intimate, relaxed, close
opposites formal, unfriendly
to be familiar with something
Are you familiar with *the rules of chess?*
be acquainted with, be aware of, know

family noun
Some members of my family *live in New Zealand.*
relations, relatives
An old-fashioned term for your family is your kin.
The official term for your closest relative is next of kin.
A group of related Scottish families is a clan.
A succession of people from the same powerful family is a dynasty.
In certain societies, a group of families living together is a tribe.
A single stage in a family is a generation.
The line of ancestors from which a family is descended is its ancestry.
A diagram showing how people in your family are related is a family tree.
The study of family history is genealogy.
A family of young birds is a brood.
A family of kittens or puppies is a litter.

a
b
c
d
e
f
g
h
i
j
k
l
m
n
o
p
q
r
s
t
u
v
w
x
y
z

WORD WEB

MEMBERS OF A FAMILY MAY INCLUDE
adopted child, aunt, brother, child, cousin, daughter, father, foster-child, foster-parent, grandchild, grandparent, guardian, husband, mother, nephew, niece, parent, sister, son, spouse, step-child, step-parent, uncle, ward, wife

famished adjective
What's for dinner? I'm famished!
hungry, ravenous, starving
If you are slightly hungry, you are **peckish**.

famous adjective
Pele is a very famous football player.
well-known, celebrated, renowned, acclaimed, notable, prominent, distinguished, eminent
To be famous for doing something bad is to be **notorious**.
opposites unknown, obscure

fan¹ noun
Can you switch on the fan, please?
ventilator, blower, extractor, air-conditioner

fan² noun
I used to be a fan of jazz music.
enthusiast, admirer, devotee, follower, supporter

fanatic noun
My brother is a rugby fanatic.
enthusiast, addict, devotee
(informal) **freak, nut**

fanatical adjective
Wayne is fanatical about football.
enthusiastic, extreme, fervent, over-enthusiastic, passionate, rabid, zealous
opposite moderate

fanciful adjective
I like reading fanciful stories about dragons.
fantastic, unrealistic, whimsical, imaginary, fictitious, made-up
opposite realistic

fancy adjective
Alice bought a fancy hat for her friend's wedding.
elaborate, decorative, ornamental, ornate
opposite plain

fancy verb
1 *What do you fancy to eat?*
feel like, want, wish for, desire, prefer
2 *I fancied I heard a noise downstairs.*
imagine, think, believe, suppose

fantastic adjective
1 *The story is full of fantastic creatures.*
fanciful, extraordinary, strange, odd, weird, outlandish, far-fetched, incredible, imaginative
opposite realistic
2 (informal) *We had a fantastic time at camp.*
excellent, first-class, outstanding, superb, wonderful, tremendous, marvellous
(informal) **brilliant, fabulous, smashing**

fantasy noun
Rosie had a fantasy about being a mermaid.
dream, daydream, delusion, fancy

far adjective
1 *The castle stood in the far north of the country.*
distant, faraway, remote
opposite nearby
2 *The ferry took us to the far side of the river.*
opposite, other
opposite near

fare noun
Do you have enough money for the bus fare?
price, charge, cost, payment, fee

farm noun
The formal word for farming is **agriculture**.

A farm which uses no artificial fertilizers or chemicals is an **organic farm**.
A very small farm is a **smallholding**.
A small farm growing fruit and vegetables is a **market garden**.
A small farm in Scotland is a **croft**.
A large cattle farm in America is a **ranch**.

 WORD WEB

FARM BUILDINGS
barn, byre or **cowshed, dairy, farmhouse, granary, milking parlour, outhouse, pigsty, stable**

OTHER PARTS OF A FARM
barnyard or **farmyard, cattle pen, fields, haystack, meadow, paddock, pasture, rick, sheep fold, silo**

ITEMS OF FARM EQUIPMENT
baler, combine harvester, cultivator, drill, harrow, harvester, mower, planter, plough, tractor, trailer

PEOPLE WHO WORK ON A FARM
agricultural worker, (old use) **dairymaid, farmer, farm labourer, ploughman, shepherd, stockbreeder, tractor driver**

SOME FARM ANIMALS
bull, bullock, chicken or **hen, cow, duck, goat, goose, horse, pig, sheep, turkey**

Birds kept on a farm are **poultry**.
Cows kept for milk or beef are **cattle**.
Farm animals in general are **livestock**.

farm verb
The MacDonalds had farmed the land for centuries.
cultivate, work, till, plough

fascinate verb
We were fascinated by the inventor's workshop.
interest, engross, captivate, enthrall, absorb, beguile, entrance, attract, charm, enchant, delight
opposite bore

fashion noun
1 *The Martians behaved in a peculiar fashion.*
way, manner
2 *Zoe dresses according to the latest fashion.*
trend, vogue, craze, fad, style, look

fashionable adjective
Megan has a fashionable new hairstyle.
stylish, chic, up-to-date, popular, elegant, smart
(informal) trendy, hip, in
opposites unfashionable, out-of-date

fast adjective
The robber made a fast exit when he heard us coming.
quick, rapid, speedy, swift, brisk, hurried, hasty, high-speed, headlong, breakneck
(informal) nippy
opposites slow, unhurried
Something which goes faster than sound is **supersonic**.
A common simile is **as fast as lightning**.

fast adverb
1 *Mr Toad was driving too fast in his motor car.*
quickly, speedily, swiftly, rapidly, briskly
2 *The boat was stuck fast on the rocks.*
firmly, securely, tightly
3 *Be quiet! The baby is fast asleep.*
deeply, sound, soundly, completely

fasten verb
1 *They fastened their ropes to the rock face.*
tie, fix, attach, connect, join, link, bind, hitch, clamp, pin, clip, tack, stick
To fasten a boat is to **anchor** or **moor** it.
To fasten an animal is to **tether** it.
2 *They fastened the gate with a heavy chain.*
secure, seal, lock, bolt, make fast

fat adjective
1 *You'll get fat if you eat too many crisps!*
overweight, obese, chubby, plump, podgy, dumpy, flabby, portly, stout, round, rotund
2 *The witch opened a big, fat book of spells.*
thick, bulky, chunky, weighty, substantial
opposite thin

a
b
c
d
e
f
g
h
i
j
k
l
m
n
o
p
q
r
s
t
u
v
w
x
y
z

A
B
C
D
E
F
G
H
I
J
K
L
M
N
O
P
Q
R
S
T
U
V
W
X
Y
Z

fatal adjective
1 *The knight delivered a* fatal *wound to his enemy.*
deadly, lethal, mortal
A fatal *illness is an* incurable *or* terminal *illness.*
2 *Leaving the door unlocked was a* fatal *mistake.*
disastrous, catastrophic, dreadful, calamitous

fate noun
1 *The shipwrecked crew were in the hands of* fate.
fortune, destiny, providence, chance, luck
2 *The prisoner met with a terrible* fate.
death, end

fatigue noun
Some of the runners were overcome with fatigue.
exhaustion, tiredness, weariness, weakness

fatigued adjective
We were all fatigued *by the time we got home.*
exhausted, tired, worn out, weary
(informal) **all in**

fault noun
1 *This DVD has a* fault *in it.*
defect, flaw, malfunction, snag, problem, weakness
2 *It was my* fault *that we missed our bus.*
responsibility, liability

faultless adjective
The dancer's movements were faultless.
perfect, flawless, ideal, impeccable
opposite **imperfect**

faulty adjective
The TV was faulty, *so we took it back to the shop.*
broken, not working, defective, out of order, unusable, damaged
opposite **perfect**

favour noun
1 *I asked my friend to do me a* favour.
good deed, good turn, kindness, service, courtesy
2 *The captain's plan found* favour *with most of the crew.*
approval, support, liking, goodwill
to be in favour of something
We're all in favour of *longer holidays.*
agree to, approve of, support, like the idea of

favour verb
Do you favour *the idea of free school meals?*
approve of, support, back, advocate, choose, like, opt for, prefer
(informal) **fancy, go for**
opposite **oppose**

favourable adjective
1 *The weather conditions are* favourable *for sailing.*
advantageous, helpful, beneficial
opposite **unfavourable**
2 *The film has received* favourable *reviews.*
good, positive, complimentary, encouraging, enthusiastic, sympathetic, approving, agreeable
opposites **critical, hostile, negative**

favourite adjective
What is your favourite *book?*
best-loved, preferred, treasured, dearest, special, top

fear noun
When Garth heard the monster, he trembled with fear.
fright, terror, horror, alarm, panic, dread, anxiety, apprehension, trepidation
opposite **courage**
A formal word for a special type of fear is **phobia.**
A fear of open spaces is **agoraphobia.**
A fear of spiders is **arachnophobia.**
A fear of enclosed spaces is **claustrophobia.**
A fear or dislike of foreigners is **xenophobia.**

fear verb
1 *My sister fears snakes and spiders.*
be frightened of, be afraid of, be scared of, dread
2 *I fear we may be too late.*
suspect, expect, anticipate

fearful adjective
1 *The warrior had a fearful look in his eyes.*
frightened, scared, terrified, afraid, panicky, nervous, anxious, timid
opposite brave
2 *The erupting volcano was a fearful sight.*
frightening, terrifying, shocking, fearsome, ghastly, dreadful, appalling, terrible

fearless adjective
The fearless explorers entered the dark cave.
brave, courageous, daring, heroic, valiant, intrepid, plucky
opposite cowardly

fearsome adjective
The dragon revealed a fearsome set of teeth.
frightening, fearful, horrifying, terrifying, dreadful, awesome
(informal) scary

feasible adjective
Is it feasible to fly to Paris and back in a day?
possible, practicable, practical, achievable, realistic, workable
opposites impractical, impossible

feast noun
The king held a great feast to celebrate his birthday.
banquet, dinner
(informal) spread

feat noun
The trapeze artists performed many daring feats.
act, action, deed, exploit, achievement, performance

feather noun
A large feather is a **plume**.
All the feathers on a bird are its **plumage**.
Soft, fluffy feathers are **down**.
A feather used as a pen is a **quill**.
For ways to describe a bird's feathers see **bird**

feature noun
1 *The room has several unusual features.*
characteristic, detail, point, aspect, quality, peculiarity, trait, facet
A person's features are their **face**.
For ways to describe facial features see **face**
2 *There was a feature about our school in the newspaper.*
article, report, story, item, piece

feature verb
1 *The film features some thrilling car chases.*
give prominence to, highlight, spotlight, show off
2 *A new cartoon character features in this film.*
appear, take part, figure, star

fee noun
The club charges an annual membership fee.
charge, cost, payment, price
A fee to use a private road or bridge is a **toll**.

feeble adjective
1 *The elderly knight looked tired and feeble.*
weak, frail, infirm, delicate, poorly, sickly, puny, weary, weedy
opposites strong, powerful
2 *I made a feeble attempt to stop the ball.*
Do you expect me to believe that feeble excuse?
weak, poor, ineffective, inadequate, unconvincing, tame, flimsy, lame

feed verb feeds, feeding, fed
We have enough sandwiches to feed six people.
provide for, cater for, give food to, nourish
to feed on
The leopard was feeding on its prey.
eat, consume, devour

feel verb feels, feeling, felt
1 *I felt the llama's soft, woolly fur.*
touch, caress, stroke, fondle

a
b
c
d
e
f
g
h
i
j
k
l
m
n
o
p
q
r
s
t
u
v
w
x
y
z

A
B
C
D
E
F
G
H
I
J
K
L
M
N
O
P
Q
R
S
T
U
V
W
X
Y
Z

2 *When the candle went out, we had to* feel *our way out of the cave.*
grope, fumble

3 *It* feels *colder today.*
appear, seem, strike you as

4 *Older people tend to* feel *the cold.*
notice, be aware of, be conscious of, experience, suffer from

5 *I* feel *that it's time we made a start.*
think, believe, consider

to feel like
Do you feel like *going for a walk?*
fancy, want, wish for, desire

feel verb

WRITING TIPS

You can use these words to describe
how something feels

bristly, coarse, creamy, crinkly, crunchy, dry, feathery, fibrous, fine, fluffy, grainy, hairy, knobbly, lumpy, moist, papery, rough, rubbery, runny, silky, smooth, soft, spongy, springy, squashy, sticky, stiff, stringy, velvety, watery, woolly
Sylvia was too sleepy to study her surroundings before she was placed between soft, smooth sheets and sank deep into dreamless slumber.
— Joan Aiken, *The Wolves of Willoughby Chase*

feel noun
I love the feel *of warm sand between my toes.*
feeling, sensation, touch

feeling noun
1 *The cat had lost all* feeling *in its paw.*
sense of touch, sensation, sensitivity

2 *I didn't mean to hurt your* feelings.
emotion, passion, sentiment

3 *I have a* feeling *that something is wrong.*
suspicion, notion, inkling, hunch, idea, impression, fancy, intuition

4 *There was a good* feeling *at the party.*
atmosphere, mood, air, aura

fell
past tense see **fall**

female adjective
For female human beings see **woman**
For female animals see **animal**
opposite **male**

feminine adjective
Lisa likes to dress in a feminine *style.*
womanly, ladylike, girlish
(informal) girly
opposite **masculine**

fence noun
The mansion was surrounded by a tall fence.
railing, barrier, wall, paling, stockade, hedge

fence verb
The field was fenced *with a thorn hedge.*
enclose, surround, bound, encircle

fend verb
to fend for yourself
The lion cubs will soon have to fend *for themselves.*
look after, take care of, care for

to fend someone or something off
The knight raised his shield to fend *off the blow.*
repel, resist, ward off, fight off, hold off, thwart

ferment verb
The sorcerer left the potion to ferment *in a jar.*
bubble, fizz, foam, seethe

ferment noun
Before the revolution, the country was in a state of ferment.
turmoil, unrest, upheaval, agitation, excitement, commotion, turbulence, confusion, disorder, tumult

ferocious adjective
The mansion was guarded by a ferocious *dog.*
fierce, fearsome, savage, wild, vicious, violent, bloodthirsty, brutal
opposite **tame**

fertile adjective
The surrounding countryside was green and fertile.
fruitful, productive, rich, fecund
opposites barren, sterile

fertilize verb
If you want good crops, you must fertilize the soil.
enrich, feed, manure

fervent adjective
My gran is a fervent supporter of the local team.
eager, keen, avid, ardent, committed, enthusiastic, fanatical, passionate, zealous
opposites apathetic, lukewarm

festival noun
The town holds a festival every summer.
carnival, fiesta, fête, gala, fair, celebration, jamboree
A celebration of a special anniversary is a jubilee.
For religious festivals see **religion**

festive adjective
Chinese New Year is a festive occasion.
cheerful, happy, merry, jolly, cheery, joyful, joyous, jovial, light-hearted, celebratory
opposites gloomy, sombre

fetch verb
1 *I fetched the shopping from the car.*
get, bring, carry, collect, transfer, transport, convey, pick up, retrieve, obtain
2 *If we sell our car, how much will it fetch?*
make, raise, sell for, go for, bring in, earn

feud noun
There has been a feud between our families for years.
quarrel, dispute, conflict, hostility, enmity, rivalry, strife, antagonism
A feud that lasts a long time is a vendetta.

feverish adjective
1 *I felt feverish with the cold.*
When you are feverish you are **hot** and shivery.

With a bad fever you may become **delirious**.
2 *There was feverish activity in the kitchen.*
frenzied, frantic, frenetic, excited, agitated, hectic, busy, hurried, impatient, restless

few determiner
1 *I've only been abroad a few times.*
a small number of, a handful of
2 *Few astronauts have walked on the Moon.*
not many, hardly any
opposite many

fibre noun
Rope is made by twisting fibres together.
thread, strand, hair, filament

fickle adjective
Some fickle supporters deserted the team when they lost.
changeable, disloyal, unfaithful, unreliable, erratic, inconsistent, unpredictable, inconstant
opposite loyal

fiction noun
1 *Roald Dahl wrote fiction for both children and adults.*
For various kinds of literature see **writing**
2 *Her account of what happened was pure fiction.*
fantasy, invention, fabrication, lies
opposite fact

fictional adjective
Harry Potter is a fictional character.
imaginary, made-up, invented, fanciful
opposites factual, real

fictitious adjective
The spy was using a fictitious name.
false, fake, fabricated, fraudulent, bogus, assumed, spurious, unreal
opposites genuine, real

a
b
c
d
e
f
g
h
i
j
k
l
m
n
o
p
q
r
s
t
u
v
w
x
y
z

A
B
C
D
E
F
G
H
I
J
K
L
M
N
O
P
Q
R
S
T
U
V
W
X
Y
Z

fiddle verb
1 *Who's been fiddling with the DVD player?*
tinker, meddle, tamper, play about, mess about, twiddle
2 (informal) *Mr Filch had been fiddling the bank account for years.*
falsify, alter, rig
(informal) **cook the books**

fiddly adjective
Icing a cake can be a fiddly job.
intricate, complicated, awkward, involved
opposite simple

fidget verb
I begin to fidget when I'm bored.
be restless, fiddle about, play about, mess about

fidgety adjective
After waiting an hour, we began to get fidgety.
restless, unsettled, impatient, agitated, jumpy, nervy
opposite calm

field noun
1 *Cattle were grazing in the field.*
meadow, pasture
A small field for horses is a **paddock**.
An area of grass in a village is a **green**.
2 *The field is too wet to play football.*
ground, pitch, playing field
3 *Electronics is not my field.*
special interest, speciality, area of study

fierce adjective
1 *The travellers were killed in a fierce attack by armed bandits.*
vicious, ferocious, savage, brutal, violent, wild, cruel, merciless, ruthless, pitiless
2 *Our team will face fierce opposition in the final.*
strong, keen, eager, aggressive, competitive, passionate, relentless
3 *The explorers braved the fierce heat of the desert sun.*
blazing, intense, raging

fiery adjective
1 *It's best to avoid the fiery heat of the midday sun.*
blazing, burning, hot, intense, fierce, raging, flaming, red-hot, glowing
2 *My great aunt has always had a fiery temper.*
violent, passionate, excitable, angry, furious

fight noun
1 *The warriors faced each other for a fight to the death.*
Fighting is **combat** or **hostilities**.
A fight between armies is a **battle**.
A minor unplanned battle is a **skirmish**.
A series of battles is a **campaign** or **war**.
A minor fight is a **brawl, scrap, scuffle,** or **tussle**.
A fight arranged between two people is a **duel**.
2 *We support the fight to save the rainforest.*
campaign, crusade, struggle

fight verb fights, fighting, fought
1 *Two seagulls were fighting over a scrap of bread.*
have a fight, scrap, scuffle, exchange blows, come to blows
2 *The two countries fought each other in the war.*
do battle with, wage war with, attack
Fighting with swords is **fencing**.
Fighting with fists is **boxing**.
Fighting in which you try to throw your opponent to the ground is **wrestling**.
Fighting sports such as karate and judo are **martial arts**.
3 *We will fight the decision to close our local library.*
protest against, oppose, resist, make a stand, take a stand against, campaign against

fighter noun

WORD WEB

PEOPLE WHO FIGHT IN A WAR OR CONFLICT
guerrilla, soldier, warrior

See also **armed services**

PEOPLE WHO FOUGHT IN PAST TIMES
archer, gladiator, knight, swordsman or **swordswoman**

PEOPLE WHO FIGHT AS A SPORT
boxer, fencer, kick-boxer, wrestler

figure noun
1 *Please write the figure '8' on the board.*
number, numeral, digit, integer
2 *What figure would you put on your old bike?*
price, value, amount, sum, cost
3 *Ballet dancers need to have a good figure.*
body, build, form, shape
4 *Inside the temple were several clay figures.*
statue, carving, sculpture
5 *The figure on page 22 shows the annual rainfall for Wales.*
diagram, graph, illustration, drawing

figure verb
Donald Duck figures in many cartoons.
appear, feature, take part
to figure out
We couldn't figure out what the riddle meant.
work out, make out, understand, see

figure of speech noun

WORD WEB

SOME COMMON FIGURES OF SPEECH
alliteration, metaphor, onomatopoeia, personification, simile

file noun
1 *I keep all my award certificates in a file.*
folder, binder, cover
A file containing information, especially secret information, is a **dossier**.
2 *Please walk in a single file.*
line, row, column, rank, queue, procession

file verb
1 *I file all my letters in a pink folder.*
organize, put away, store

2 *We filed into the hall for assembly.*
walk in a line, march, troop, parade

fill verb
1 *Dad filled the trolley with shopping.*
load, pack, stuff, cram, top up
To fill a tyre with air is to **inflate** it.
opposite empty
2 *What can I use to fill this hole?*
close up, plug, seal, block up, stop up
3 *Sightseers filled the streets.*
crowd, jam, block, obstruct
(informal) **bung up**

filling noun
The filling started to ooze out of my sandwich.
stuffing, insides, innards, padding

film noun
1 *There is a good film on TV tonight.*
movie, picture, video, DVD
A long film is a **feature film**.
A short excerpt from a film is a **clip**.
A script for a film is a **screenplay** and a writer of screenplays is a **screenwriter**.
A well-known film actor is a **film star**.
A theatre where films are shown is a **cinema**, **picture house**, or (American) **movie theatre**.
2 *There was a film of oil on the water.*
coat, coating, layer, covering, sheet, skin
A large patch of oil floating on water is a **slick**.

filth noun
The walls of the dungeon were covered with filth.
dirt, grime, muck, mess, mud, sludge, scum, slime

filthy adjective
1 *Those trainers are filthy!*
dirty, mucky, messy, grimy, grubby, muddy, soiled, stained
opposite clean
2 *Don't drink the filthy water from the well.*
cloudy, contaminated, foul, impure, polluted, slimy, smelly, stinking
opposite pure

a
b
c
d
e
f
g
h
i
j
k
l
m
n
o
p
q
r
s
t
u
v
w
x
y
z

final adjective
1 *The final moments of the match were very tense.*
last, closing, concluding
opposite opening
2 *What was the final result?*
eventual, ultimate

finally adverb
I've finally managed to finish my book.
eventually, at last, in the end

finances plural noun
Are your finances doing well?
money, bank account, funds, resources, assets, wealth

find verb finds, finding, found
1 *Did you find any fossils on the beach?*
come across, discover, see, spot, locate, encounter, stumble across, unearth
2 *The children never found the secret door again.*
trace, track down, recover, retrieve
opposite lose
3 *Did the doctor find what was wrong?*
find out, detect, identify, diagnose, ascertain
4 *You will find that building a tree house is hard work.*
find out, become aware, realize, learn, recognize, notice, observe

findings plural noun
The detective told us of his findings.
judgement, conclusion, verdict, decision

fine¹ adjective
1 *The young musicians gave a fine performance.*
excellent, first-class, superb, splendid, admirable, commendable, good
opposite bad
2 *As the weather was fine, we took a picnic.*
sunny, fair, bright, clear, cloudless, pleasant
opposite dull

3 *Spiders spin very fine thread for their webs.*
delicate, fragile, thin, flimsy, slender, slim
opposite thick
4 *The desert dunes were made of fine sand.*
dusty, powdery
opposite coarse

fine² noun
The boy had to pay a fine for dropping litter.
penalty, charge, damages

finger noun
Your short fat finger is your thumb.
The finger next to your thumb is your index finger, because it is the finger you point with or indicate things with.
The next finger is your middle finger.
The next finger is your ring finger, because you can wear a wedding or engagement ring on that finger of your left hand.
Your small thin finger is your little finger or (Scottish) pinkie.
The joints in your fingers are your knuckles.

finger verb
Please don't finger the food on the table.
touch, feel, poke, fondle

finish verb
1 *When are you likely to finish your homework?*
complete, reach the end of, cease, round off
2 *The film should finish around nine o'clock.*
end, stop, conclude, terminate
(informal) wind up
3 *I've already finished my bag of crisps.*
consume, use up, get through, exhaust
(informal) polish off
opposite start

finish noun
We stayed to watch the parade until the finish.
end, close, conclusion, completion, result, termination
opposite start

A
B
C
D
E
F
G
H
I
J
K
L
M
N
O
P
Q
R
S
T
U
V
W
X
Y
Z

fire noun
We toasted marshmallows in the fire.
blaze, flames, burning, combustion
A very big hot fire is an **inferno.**
An open fire out of doors is a **bonfire.**
An enclosed fire which produces great heat
is a **furnace.**
An enclosed fire for cooking food is an **oven.**
An enclosed fire for making pottery is a **kiln.**
A team of people whose job is to put out
fires is a **fire brigade.**
A member of a fire brigade is a **firefighter.**

fire verb
1 *The clay will harden if you fire it in a kiln.*
bake, harden, heat
2 *The soldier aimed his rifle and fired two
shots.*
shoot, discharge, let off, set off
To fire a missile is to **launch** it.
3 (informal) *Miss Stark fired her assistant for
being late for work.*
dismiss, sack

firm noun
Mr Perkins owns a firm that makes biscuits.
company, business, organization, enterprise

firm adjective
1 *The surface of the planet was dry and firm.*
hard, solid, dense, compact, rigid, set
opposite soft
2 *Make sure the knots in the rope are firm.*
**secure, tight, strong, stable, fixed, sturdy,
steady**
3 *Zelda had a firm belief in the power of
magic.*
**definite, certain, sure, decided, determined,
resolute, unshakeable, unwavering**
opposite unsure
4 *The two girls have become firm friends.*
**close, devoted, faithful, loyal, constant,
dependable, reliable**

first adjective
1 *The first inhabitants of the area were Picts.*
earliest, original
2 *The first thing to do in an emergency is to
keep calm.*
**principal, key, main, fundamental, basic,
chief**

at first
At first, we thought the dog was asleep.
**at the beginning, to start with, initially,
originally**

first-class or first-rate adjective
That was a first-class game of chess.
**excellent, first rate, outstanding, superb,
exceptional, superior, superlative,
top-notch**
opposites second-rate, mediocre

fish noun

WORD WEB
SOME TYPES OF FISH
**brill, carp, catfish, chub, cod, conger eel,
cuttlefish, dace, eel, flounder, goldfish,
grayling, gudgeon, haddock, hake,
halibut, herring, jellyfish, lamprey, ling,
mackerel, minnow, mullet, perch, pike,
pilchard, piranha, plaice, roach,
salmon, sardine, sawfish, shark, skate,
sole, sprat, squid, starfish, stickleback,
sturgeon, swordfish, trout, tuna, turbot,
whitebait, whiting**

For types of shellfish see **shellfish**

Young fish are **fry.**
An informal word for a very small fish is
a **tiddler.**
A large number of fish swimming
together is a **shoal.**
A person who sells fish is a **fishmonger.**
The sport or job of catching fish is
fishing.
Fishing with a rod and a line is **angling**
and a person who does this is an **angler.**
Fishing with nets from a boat is **trawling.**
Fishing equipment is **tackle.**

fit¹ adjective
1 *Cinderella's gown was fit for a princess.*
**suitable, appropriate, fitting, right,
good enough, worthy**
opposite unsuitable
2 *I walk to school every day to keep fit.*
healthy, well, strong, robust,

a
b
c
d
e
f
g
h
i
j
k
l
m
n
o
p
q
r
s
t
u
v
w
x
y
z

(old use) **hale and hearty**
opposite unhealthy
A common simile is as **fit as a fiddle**.
3 *After a long ride, the horses were* fit *to collapse.*
ready, liable, likely, about

fit¹ verb
1 *We need to* fit *a new lock on the door.*
install, put in place, position
2 *This key doesn't* fit *the lock.*
He fits *the description of the wanted criminal.*
match, correspond to, go together with, tally with
3 *Her speech perfectly* fitted *the occasion.*
be suitable for, be appropriate to, suit

fit² noun
My friend and I had a fit *of the giggles.*
attack, bout, outburst, spell

fitting adjective
Scoring the winning goal was a fitting *end to his career.*
suitable, appropriate, apt, proper
opposite inappropriate

fix verb
1 *The soldier* fixed *a bayonet to the end of his rifle.*
fasten, attach, connect, join, link
2 *We* fixed *the tent poles in the ground.*
set, secure, make firm, stabilize
3 *Let's* fix *a time for the party.*
decide on, agree on, set, arrange, settle, determine, specify, finalize
4 (informal) *Dad says he can* fix *my bike.*
repair, mend, (informal) **sort, put right**

fix noun
(informal) *Can you help me? I'm in a* fix.
difficulty, mess, predicament, plight
(informal) **jam, hole**

fizz verb
The lemonade fizzed *when I opened the bottle.*
hiss, bubble, foam, froth

fizzy adjective
Could I have a bottle of fizzy *water, please?*
sparkling, bubbly, effervescent, gassy, foaming
opposite still

flabby adjective
This exercise is good for flabby *thighs.*
fat, fleshy, sagging, slack, loose, floppy, limp
opposite firm

flag noun
The street was decorated with flags *for the carnival.*
banner, pennant, streamer
The flag of a regiment is its **colours** or **standard**.
A flag flown on a ship is an **ensign**.
Decorative strips of small flags are **bunting**.

flag verb
By evening, our energy was starting to flag.
diminish, lessen, decrease, decline, weaken, slump, fade, dwindle, wane

flap verb
The sail flapped *in the wind.*
flutter, sway, swing, wave about, thrash about

flare verb
to flare up
1 *The fire* flared up *when we blew on it.*
blaze, burn brightly, flame
2 *My sister* flares up *at the slightest thing.*
become angry, lose your temper

flash verb
We saw a light flash *from an upstairs window.*
shine, beam, blaze, flare, glare, gleam, glint, flicker, glimmer, sparkle

flash noun
There were flashes *of lightning in the sky.*
blaze, flare, beam, ray, shaft, burst, gleam, glint, flicker, glimmer, sparkle
For other ways to describe light see **light¹**

flat adjective
1 *You need a flat surface to write on.*
even, level, smooth, plane
A common simile is **as flat as a pancake.**
opposite uneven
2 *I lay flat on the ground.*
horizontal, outstretched, spread out
To be lying face downwards is to be **prone.**
To be lying face upwards is to be **supine.**
opposite upright
3 *The robot spoke in a flat, electronic voice.*
dull, boring, lifeless, uninteresting,
monotonous, tedious
opposite lively
4 *The front tyre of my bike was flat.*
deflated, punctured
opposite inflated
5 *Our request met with a flat refusal.*
outright, straight, positive, absolute, total,
utter, point-blank

flat
For places where people live see **building**

flatten verb
1 *We flattened the crumpled map on the
desk.*
smooth, press, roll out, iron out
2 *The earthquake flattened several buildings.*
demolish, destroy, knock down, pull down,
level
3 *The young plants were flattened by the
rain.*
squash, crush, trample, (informal) squish

flaunt verb
*She's always flaunting her expensive
jewellery.*
show off, display, parade, exhibit

flavour noun
1 *I don't like the flavour of raw onions.*
taste, tang
For ways to describe flavour see **food**
2 *Which flavour of ice cream do you like best?*
kind, sort, variety

flavour verb
*The sauce was flavoured with garlic and
herbs.*
season, spice

flaw noun
1 *Pride was the only flaw in his character.*
weakness, fault, shortcoming, failing, lapse
2 *I can see a flaw in your argument.*
error, inaccuracy, mistake, slip
3 *There is a tiny flaw in this glass.*
imperfection, defect, blemish, break, chip,
crack

fleck noun
*There were a few flecks of paint on the
carpet.*
spot, speck, flake, dot, dab
See also **bit**

flee verb flees, fleeing, fled
When they heard the alarm, the robbers fled.
run away, bolt, fly, escape, get away,
take off, hurry off
(informal) clear off, make off, scarper

fleet noun
A fleet of boats or small ships is a **flotilla.**
A fleet of warships is an **armada.**
A military fleet belonging to a country is its
navy.

fleeting adjective
I only caught a fleeting glimpse of the badger.
brief, momentary, quick, short, passing
opposites lengthy, lasting

flesh noun
tissue, muscle, fat
An animal's flesh used for food is **meat.**
The decaying flesh of a dead animal is
carrion.

flew
past tense see **fly²**

flex noun
Don't trip over the flex of the iron!
cable, lead, wire

flexible adjective
1 *I need a pair of trainers with flexible soles.*
bendable, supple, pliable, bendy, elastic,
springy
opposites rigid, inflexible

a
b
c
d
e
f
g
h
i
j
k
l
m
n
o
p
q
r
s
t
u
v
w
x
y
z

167

A B C D E **F** G H I J K L M N O P Q R S T U V W X Y Z

2 *My working hours are very flexible.*
adjustable, adaptable, variable, open
opposite **fixed**

flicker verb
The candlelight flickered in the draught.
twinkle, glimmer, waver, flutter, blink, shimmer

flight noun
1 *He is an expert on the history of flight.*
flying, aviation, aeronautics
For other words to do with flying see **aircraft**
2 *No-one saw the king's flight from the battlefield.*
escape, getaway, retreat

flimsy adjective
1 *The kite was so flimsy that it broke apart.*
fragile, delicate, frail, brittle, weak, wobbly, shaky, rickety,
opposites **sturdy, robust**
2 *The fairy wore a dress of the flimsiest silk.*
thin, fine, light, lightweight, floaty

flinch verb
He flinched as an arrow flew past his head.
back off, draw back, falter, recoil, shrink back, start, wince

fling verb flings, flinging, flung
I flung a stone into the pond.
throw, cast, sling, toss, hurl, pitch
(informal) chuck, bung

flip verb
We flipped a coin to decide who should go first.
toss, flick, spin

float verb
We watched the twigs float gently down the river.
sail, drift, glide, slip, slide, waft

flock noun
For groups of animals see **group**

flock verb
People flocked round to see what was happening.
crowd, gather, collect, herd, jostle

flood noun
1 *The flood of water swept away the bridge.*
deluge, inundation, rush, torrent, spate
2 *The restaurant has received a flood of complaints.*
succession, barrage, storm, volley

flood verb
1 *The river burst its banks and flooded the valley.*
drown, swamp, inundate, submerge, immerse, engulf
2 *We have been flooded with entries for our competition.*
overwhelm, swamp, besiege

floor noun
1 *The children in the audience sat on the floor.*
ground, flooring, base
A floor on a ship is a **deck**.
2 *Doreen's flat is on the top floor.*
storey, level, tier, stage

flop verb
1 *I was so tired that I just flopped onto my bed.*
collapse, drop, fall, slump
2 *The plants will flop if you don't water them.*
dangle, droop, hang down, sag, wilt
3 (informal) *The first film flopped, but the sequel was a big hit.*
be unsuccessful, fail, founder, fall flat

floppy adjective
The dog had long, floppy ears.
droopy, limp, saggy, soft
opposites **stiff, rigid**

flounder verb
The soldiers floundered through the mud.
struggle, stumble, stagger, fumble, wallow, blunder, falter

flourish verb
1 *My tomato plants are flourishing this year.*
grow well, thrive, bloom, blossom, flower
opposite die
2 *Sales on our website have continued to flourish.*
be successful, do well, prosper, thrive, boom, succeed, progress, develop, increase
opposite fail
3 *Ted flourished a newspaper to attract my attention.*
wave, brandish, wield, shake

flow verb
The rain water flowed along the gutter.
run, stream, pour, glide
To flow slowly is to dribble, drip, ooze, seep, or trickle.
To flow fast is to cascade, gush, or sweep.
To flow with sudden force is to spurt or squirt.
To flow over the edge of something is to overflow or spill.
When blood flows from someone, they bleed.
When the tide flows out, it ebbs.

flow noun
1 *It's hard work rowing against the flow.*
current, tide, drift
2 *There was a steady flow of water into the pond.*
stream, flood, cascade, gush, rush, spate

flower noun
A single flower is a bloom.
A mass of small flowers growing together is blossom.
Flowers in a vase are an arrangement.
A bunch of flowers arranged for a special occasion is a bouquet, posy, or spray.
Flowers arranged in a circle are a garland or wreath.
A person who sells and arranges flowers is a florist.

 WORD WEB
SOME WILD FLOWERS
bluebell, buttercup, catkin, cornflower, cowslip, daisy, dandelion, foxglove, harebell, orchid, poppy, primrose
SOME POPULAR CULTIVATED FLOWERS
azalea, begonia, carnation, chrysanthemum, crocus, cyclamen, daffodil, dahlia, forget-me-not, freesia, fuchsia, geranium, gladiolus, hollyhock, hyacinth, iris, lilac, lily, lupin, marigold, nasturtium, pansy, peony, petunia, phlox, rose, snowdrop, sunflower, tulip, violet, water lily
THE MAIN PARTS OF A FLOWER ARE
anther, filament, ovary, petal, pistil, pollen, sepal, stamen, stigma, style

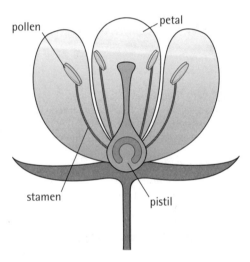

pollen · petal · stamen · pistil

flower verb
Most plants flower in the summer.
bloom, blossom, bud

fluffy adjective
Four fluffy ducklings were swimming in the pond.
feathery, downy, furry, fuzzy, hairy, woolly, shaggy, soft

fluid noun
An oily fluid oozed from the pipe.
liquid, solution, juice
opposite solid

a b c d e f g h i j k l m n o p q r s t u v w x y z

A
B
C
D
E
F
G
H
I
J
K
L
M
N
O
P
Q
R
S
T
U
V
W
X
Y
Z

fluke noun
It was a fluke that the ball went into the net.
chance, accident, stroke of good luck

flush verb
Rory flushed with embarrassment.
blush, go red, colour, redden, burn

flustered adjective
I get flustered when I have to read in assembly.
confused, upset, bothered, agitated, unsettled, ruffled
(informal) rattled
opposite **calm**

flutter verb
A moth fluttered about the light bulb.
flap, beat, flicker, quiver, tremble, vibrate

fly¹ noun
For various insects see **insect**

fly² verb flies, flying, flew, flown
1 *Two swallows were flying high in the sky.*
glide, swoop, flit, hover, float
For ways to describe how birds move see **bird**
2 *Suddenly the eagle flew into the air.*
rise, soar, mount, take off
3 *The ship was flying the British flag.*
display, show, hoist, raise
4 *Doesn't time fly!*
go quickly, pass quickly, rush by

foam noun
The bath water was covered with pinkish foam.
bubbles, froth, suds, lather
Foam made by sea water is **surf** or **spume**.

foam verb
The mixture in the cauldron foamed and gurgled.
froth, bubble, fizz, boil, seethe, ferment, lather

focus noun
1 *Can you adjust the focus on your camera?*
clarity, sharpness

2 *The new lion cubs were the focus of everyone's attention.*
centre, focal point, target, core, pivot

focus verb
to focus on
Our teacher wants us to focus on our spelling.
concentrate on, think about, examine, look at

fog noun
The mountain-top was covered with fog.
Thin fog is **haze** or **mist**.
A thick mixture of fog and smoke is **smog**.

foggy adjective
1 *It was too foggy to see through the windows.*
misty, hazy, murky, cloudy, smoggy
2 *My photo of the horses came out foggy.*
blurred, fuzzy, indistinct, out of focus
opposites **clear, in focus**

foil verb
The dog foiled their plan to burgle the house.
frustrate, thwart, block, prevent, obstruct, stop, check, halt

fold¹ verb
Fold the paper along the dotted line.
bend, double over, crease, pleat

fold¹ noun
She smoothed the soft folds of her dress.
crease, furrow, layer
A fold which is pressed into a garment is a **pleat**.

fold² noun
The dog drove the sheep into the fold.
enclosure, pen

folder noun
I keep all my art work in a folder.
file, binder, wallet, portfolio

follow verb
1 *Why does thunder always follow lightning?*
come after, succeed, replace
opposite **precede**

2 *I think that car is following us!*
go after, chase, pursue, track, trail, tail, stalk, hunt, shadow
3 Follow *this path until you reach the river.*
go along, keep to
4 *I followed the instructions on the packet.*
carry out, comply with, heed, obey, observe
5 *Which football team do you* follow?
be a fan of, support
6 *We found it hard to* follow *what the creature was saying.*
understand, comprehend, grasp, take in, catch
7 *Although we are the same age, it doesn't* follow *that we are friends.*
mean, happen, result, ensue, arise, come about

follower noun
Someone who follows you in a job is your **successor**.
Someone who follows a person or animal to try to catch them is a **hunter** or **pursuer**.
Someone who continually follows a person about is a **stalker**.
Someone who follows a person's teaching is a **disciple**.
Someone who follows a football team, etc., is a **fan** or **supporter**.

fond adjective
1 *Mrs Walker gave her pet poodle a* fond *kiss.*
loving, tender, affectionate
2 *Anna had a* fond *hope that she would become a film star.*
foolish, silly, unrealistic, fanciful
to be fond of
I'm very fond *of chocolate cake.*
be keen on, be partial to, like, love

food noun
The banquet table was laid out with all kinds of food.
foodstuffs, rations, provisions, refreshments, eatables, nourishment, nutrition
(informal) grub, nosh

The food that you normally eat or choose to eat is your **diet**.

A diet which includes no meat is a **vegetarian** diet.
A diet which includes no animal products is a **vegan** diet.
Food which includes fish or shellfish is **seafood**.
Foods made from milk, butter, cheese, or eggs are **dairy foods**.
Food for farm animals is **fodder**.
For meat and foods made from meat see **meat**

WORD WEB
SOME TYPES OF SEAFOOD
bloater, bream, caviare, cod, crab, eel, haddock, halibut, herring, kipper, lobster, mackerel, monkfish, mussels, oysters, pilchard, plaice, prawn, salmon, sardine, scampi, sea bass, shrimp, sole, sprat, trout, tuna, whelks, whitebait, whiting

SOME DAIRY FOODS
butter, cheese, cream, curds, eggs, ice-cream, milk, yoghurt

For fruits and vegetables see **fruit**, **vegetable**

FOODS MADE FROM FLOUR OR CEREALS
batter, biscuits, bread, bun, cornflakes, cracker, crispbread, muesli, noodles, oatcake, pancake, pastry, popcorn, porridge, rice cake, roll, scone, toast

SOME PREPARED DISHES OF FOOD
balti, bhaji, broth, casserole, chilli, chips, chop suey, chow mein, curry, dhal, fritters, goulash, houmous, hotpot, omelette, pakora, panini, pasta, pie, pizza, quiche, samosa, sandwich, soufflé, soup, stew, stir-fry, sushi

For types of pasta see **pasta**

SOME PUDDINGS AND OTHER SWEET FOODS
brownie, cake, chocolate, flan, gateau, honey, jam, jelly, marmalade, marzipan, meringue, mousse, muffin, sponge, steamed pudding, sugar, tart, treacle, trifle

a
b
c
d
e
f
g
h
i
j
k
l
m
n
o
p
q
r
s
t
u
v
w
x
y
z

A
B
C
D
E
F
G
H
I
J
K
L
M
N
O
P
Q
R
S
T
U
V
W
X
Y
Z

SOME FLAVOURINGS AND SAUCES FOR FOOD
chilli, chutney, French dressing, garlic, gravy, herbs, ketchup, mayonnaise, mustard, pepper, pickle, salsa, salt, spices, vinegar

Things like salt and pepper which you add to food are condiments or seasoning.

WRITING TIPS

You can use these words to describe food

TO DESCRIBE HOW IT LOOKS OR FEELS
chewy, creamy, crispy, crumbly, crunchy, dry, flaky, greasy, juicy, leathery, lumpy, milky, mushy, rubbery, runny, slimy, sloppy, smooth, soggy, soupy, spongy, sticky, stodgy, stringy, syrupy, velvety, watery
The pudding was a sloppy, watery mess.

TO DESCRIBE HOW IT TASTES
bitter, bland, fiery, flavoursome, fresh, fruity, hot, mellow, mild, peppery, piquant, pungent, refreshing, salty, savoury, sharp, sour, spicy, strong, sugary, sweet, syrupy, tangy, tart, vinegary
The sauce was hot, but not too spicy.

For ways to describe how food smells see smell

TO DESCRIBE FOOD YOU LIKE
delicious, appetizing, tasty, tempting, mouth-watering, well-cooked
(informal) scrummy, scrumptious, yummy

Something especially tasty to eat is a delicacy.

TO DESCRIBE FOOD YOU DO NOT LIKE
disgusting, flavourless, indigestible, inedible, nauseating, stomach-turning, tasteless, unappetizing, uneatable; charred, mouldy, overcooked, stale, undercooked
(informal) yucky

Measle didn't think the food was very good. The stew was watery and tasteless and the vegetables were soggy and overcooked.
— Ian Ogilvy, *Measle and the Doompit*

fool noun
1 *Only a fool would believe that story.*
idiot, dope, ass, clown, halfwit, dimwit, dunce, simpleton, blockhead, buffoon, clot, dunderhead, imbecile, moron
(informal) twit, chump, nitwit, nincompoop
2 (old use) *The king's fool entertained the court.*
jester, clown

fool verb
The spy fooled everyone with his disguises.
deceive, trick, mislead, hoax, dupe, hoodwink
(informal) con, kid, have you on, take you in, pull the wool over your eyes
to fool about or around
We were told not to fool about in the swimming pool.
play about, mess about, misbehave

foolish adjective
It would be foolish to stand too close to the lions.
stupid, silly, idiotic, senseless, ridiculous, nonsensical, unwise, ill-advised, half-witted, unintelligent, absurd, crazy, mad, hare-brained
(informal) daft
opposite sensible

foot noun
1 *Rhona walked on the sand in her bare feet.*
The foot of an animal that has claws is a paw.
The foot of a cow, deer, or horse is a hoof.
A pig's foot is a trotter.
A bird's feet are its claws.
The feet of a bird of prey are its talons.
2 *We set up camp at the foot of the mountain.*
base, bottom

football noun
Football is also known as soccer.
Someone who plays football is a **footballer**.
Football is played on a **field** or **pitch** in a **ground**, **park**, or **stadium**.

WORD WEB

MEMBERS OF A FOOTBALL TEAM
captain, defender, full back, forward, goalkeeper or (informal) goalie, midfielder, striker, substitute, sweeper, winger

OTHER PEOPLE INVOLVED IN FOOTBALL
ballboy or ballgirl, coach, linesman, manager, referee

SOME MOVES A FOOTBALLER MIGHT MAKE
chip, dribble, dummy, header, kick, mazy run, miss, pass, score, shot, tackle, volley

For ways to hit or kick a ball see **ball**

SOME OTHER TERMS USED IN FOOTBALL
corner, crossbar, deflection, dugout, equalizer, extra time, final whistle, foul, free kick, goal, goalposts, half-time, kick-off, net, offside, penalty, penalty shoot out, red or yellow card, sending off, throw-in

footprint noun
We followed the footprints in the snow.
footmark, track, print
The tracks left by an animal are also called a **spoor**.

footstep noun
I heard footsteps crunching up the garden path.
step, footfall, tread

forbidden adjective
Skateboarding is forbidden in the playground.
banned, barred, prohibited, disallowed, outlawed
opposite allowed

forbidding adjective
The haunted tower had a dark, forbidding look.
gloomy, grim, menacing, ominous, stern, threatening, unfriendly, unwelcoming
opposite friendly

force noun
1 *The firefighters had to use force to open the door.*
strength, power, might, muscle, vigour, effort, energy
2 *The force of the explosion broke all the windows.*
impact, effect, shock, intensity
3 *The soldiers are part of a peace-keeping force.*
group, unit, team, corps, army, troops

force verb
1 *The slaves were forced to work in the mines.*
compel, make, order, require, oblige, pressurize, coerce
2 *The king forced a new law upon the country.*
impose, inflict
3 *The firefighters had to force the door.*
break open, burst open, prise open, smash, wrench
(informal) **yank**

forceful adjective
My great aunt has a very forceful personality.
strong, powerful, dynamic, commanding, assertive, overbearing
opposite weak

forecast noun
The weather forecast is for snow tomorrow.
outlook, prediction

forecast verb forecasts, forecasting, forecast or forecasted
Snow has been forecast for Tuesday.
foresee, foretell, predict

foreground noun
I took a photo of our house with my mum in the foreground.
front
opposite background

a
b
c
d
e
f
g
h
i
j
k
l
m
n
o
p
q
r
s
t
u
v
w
x
y
z

A
B
C
D
E
F
G
H
I
J
K
L
M
N
O
P
Q
R
S
T
U
V
W
X
Y
Z

foreign adjective

1 *Lots of* foreign *tourists visit Edinburgh in the summer.*
overseas, international
opposites **native, domestic**
2 *I like travelling to* foreign *countries.*
overseas, distant, faraway, exotic, remote, far-flung
3 *The idea of work was completely* foreign *to the princess.*
unnatural, unfamiliar, strange, alien

foreigner noun

Many foreigners *have come to live in the city.*
overseas visitor, stranger, outsider, newcomer
A formal word is **alien**.
A word describing people who come from abroad to live in a country is **immigrant**.

foremost adjective

Hans Christian Andersen was one of the foremost *writers of fairy tales.*
best known, leading, most important, greatest, principal, chief, major

foresee verb foresees, foreseeing, foresaw, foreseen

Do you foresee *any problems with our plan?*
anticipate, expect, predict, forecast, prophesy, foretell

forest noun

For places where trees grow see **tree**

foretell verb foretells, foretelling, foretold

1 *The fortune-teller* foretold *that I would go on a voyage.*
predict, prophesy, forecast, foresee
2 *The cold wind* foretold *a change in the weather.*
herald, signify

forever adverb

Timmy is forever *complaining about something.*
constantly, continually, always, perpetually

forge¹ verb

1 *The blacksmith* forged *a new horseshoe.*
cast, hammer out, beat into shape
2 *That signature has been* forged.
fake, copy, counterfeit

forge² verb

to forge ahead
After a slow start, the rowing team was forging ahead.
advance, make progress, make headway

forgery noun

One of these paintings is a forgery.
fake, copy, imitation, reproduction, replica
(informal) phoney

forget verb forgets, forgetting, forgot, forgotten

1 *I* forgot *my toothbrush when I packed my suitcase.*
leave out, leave behind, overlook
2 *I* forgot *to switch off the computer.*
omit, neglect, fail
opposite **remember**

forgetful adjective

As the professor grew older, he became more forgetful.
absent-minded, careless, inattentive, oblivious, vague, dreamy, lax

forgive verb forgives, forgiving, forgave, forgiven

Please forgive *me for being so rude.*
excuse, pardon, let off, overlook, spare

fork verb

The path ahead widened and then forked *into two.*
split, branch, divide

forlorn adjective

Aisha felt forlorn *after her friends had left.*
sad, unhappy, lonely, dejected, miserable, sorrowful
opposite **cheerful**

form noun

1 *I made out the form of a man through the mist.*
shape, figure, outline, silhouette
2 *Ice is a form of water.*
kind, sort, type, variety
3 *My brother moves up into a higher form next term.*
class, year, grade, set
4 *If you want to join the club, sign this form.*
document, paper, sheet, questionnaire

form verb

1 *The sculptor formed the clay into the shape of a bird.*
shape, mould, model, fashion, work, cast
2 *My friends and I have formed a chess club.*
set up, establish, found, create, start
3 *Icicles had formed on the roof of the cave.*
appear, develop, grow, emerge, take shape

formal adjective

1 *I was invited to the formal opening of the museum.*
official, ceremonial
2 *The letter was written in a very formal style.*
correct, proper, conventional, dignified, solemn
opposites informal, casual

former adjective

In former times, the castle was surrounded by a moat.
earlier, previous, past, bygone

formula noun

The inventor was working on a new formula for toothpaste.
recipe, prescription

forsake verb forsakes, forsaking, forsook, forsaken

Ben knew that his old sheepdog would never forsake him.
abandon, desert, leave

fort noun

A few soldiers were left to defend the fort.
fortress, fortification, stronghold, castle, citadel, tower
See also castle

fortify verb

1 *The townspeople built fences to fortify the town.*
defend, protect, secure, reinforce
2 *Breakfast will fortify you for the morning.*
strengthen, support, sustain, bolster, boost, invigorate
opposite weaken

fortunate adjective

We were fortunate to have good weather.
lucky, in luck
opposites unfortunate, unlucky

fortune noun

1 *By good fortune, I stumbled across a secret doorway.*
chance, luck, accident, fate
2 *The millionairess left her fortune to charity.*
wealth, riches, possessions, property, assets, estate
(informal) millions

fortune–teller noun

The fortune-teller gazed into her crystal ball.
clairvoyant, soothsayer, seer

forward adjective

1 *We need to do some forward planning for the camping trip.*
advance, early, future
2 *Would it be too forward to send him an email?*
bold, cheeky, brash, familiar, impudent, presumptuous

forwards adverb

1 *The queue moved forwards very slowly.*
on, onwards, along
2 *Will you all face forwards, please.*
to or toward the front, ahead
opposite backwards

a
b
c
d
e
f
g
h
i
j
k
l
m
n
o
p
q
r
s
t
u
v
w
x
y
z

A
B
C
D
E
F
G
H
I
J
K
L
M
N
O
P
Q
R
S
T
U
V
W
X
Y
Z

fossil noun

Isla found a fossil *on the beach.*

WORD WEB

SOME TYPES OF FOSSIL
ammonite, dinosaur bone, petrified wood, trilobite

A person who looks for fossils is a **fossil hunter.**
A person who studies fossils is a **palaeontologist.**

foster verb

My aunt has decided to foster *a child.*
bring up, rear, raise, care for, look after, take care of
To **adopt** a child is to make the child legally a full member of your family.

fought
past tense see **fight**

foul adjective

1 *The knight fainted at the* foul *smell of the dragon's breath.*
disgusting, revolting, repulsive, rotten, stinking, offensive, unpleasant, loathsome, nasty, horrible, vile
opposite pleasant
2 *The walls and floor of the dungeon were* foul.
dirty, unclean, filthy, mucky, messy
opposites clean, pure
3 *The player was sent off for using* foul *language.*
rude, offensive, insulting, abusive, improper, indecent, obscene
4 *The referee blew her whistle for a* foul *tackle.*
illegal, prohibited, unfair
opposite fair

found¹ verb

The school was founded *a hundred years ago.*
establish, set up, start, begin, create, originate, initiate, institute

found²
past tense see **find**

foundation noun

1 *There's no* foundation *for the rumour they are spreading.*
basis, grounds
2 *It's a hundred years since the* foundation *of the museum.*
founding, beginning, establishment, setting up

founder verb

1 *The ship struck a rock and* foundered.
go under, sink, submerge
2 *The project* foundered *because of lack of money.*
fail, fall through, collapse, come to nothing
(informal) **fold, flop, bomb**

fountain noun

A fountain *of water shot into the air.*
jet, spout, spray, spring

fox noun

A male fox is a **dog.**
A female fox is a **vixen.**
A young fox is a **cub.**
A fox lives in an **earth.**

fox verb

The last clue in the crossword foxed *me completely.*
puzzle, baffle, bewilder, mystify, perplex
(informal) **flummox, floor**

fraction noun

Only a fraction *of an iceberg shows above the water.*
bit, part, portion

fracture verb

Steve fell off his bike and fractured *his wrist.*
break, crack, split, splinter

fracture noun

The X-ray showed a fracture *in the bone.*
break, breakage, crack, split, fissure

fragile adjective
Fossil dinosaur bones are very fragile.
breakable, delicate, frail, brittle,
easily damaged, weak
opposite strong

fragment noun
1 *I dug up a fragment of broken pottery.*
bit, piece, chip, sliver, shard
2 *She overheard fragments of their conversation.*
part, portion, scrap, snippet

fragrant adjective
The room was fragrant with the smell of roses.
sweet-smelling, perfumed, scented,
aromatic

frail adjective
1 *My grandad felt frail after his illness.*
weak, infirm, feeble
2 *That step-ladder looks a bit frail.*
flimsy, fragile, delicate, rickety, unsound
opposites strong, robust

frame noun
1 *The frame of the house is made of timber.*
framework, structure, shell, skeleton
2 *I put the photo of my friend in a frame.*
mount, mounting, surround, border,
setting, edging

frank adjective
We had a very frank discussion about money.
honest, direct, sincere, genuine, candid,
outspoken, plain, blunt, straightforward,
truthful
opposite insincere

frantic adjective
1 *I was frantic with worry when our kitten got lost.*
beside yourself, fraught, desperate,
distraught, hysterical, worked up, berserk
2 *There was frantic activity on the day of the wedding.*
excited, hectic, frenzied, feverish, wild, mad
opposite calm

fraud noun
1 *The bank manager was found guilty of fraud.*
deceit, deception, dishonesty, swindling,
cheating
2 *The prize draw was just a fraud—nobody won anything.*
swindle, trick, hoax, pretence, sham
(informal) con, scam
3 *The salesman turned out to be a fraud.*
cheat, swindler, trickster, hoaxer
(informal) con man, phoney

fraudulent adjective
Beware of fraudulent email messages.
dishonest, illegal, criminal, corrupt,
swindling, bogus, sham
(informal) crooked, phoney
opposite honest

frayed adjective
The old woman wore a cloak of frayed tartan cloth.
tattered, ragged, worn, threadbare

free adjective
1 *You are free to wander anywhere in the building.*
able, allowed, permitted, at liberty
opposite restricted
2 *After ten years in jail, the prisoners were free at last.*
freed, liberated, released, emancipated,
at large, on the loose
A common simile is as free as a bird.
opposites imprisoned, enslaved
3 *I got a free drink with my sandwich.*
complimentary, free of charge, gratis,
on the house
4 *Are you free this weekend?*
available, unoccupied
opposites busy, occupied
5 *The bathroom is free now.*
available, unoccupied, vacant, empty
opposite engaged
6 *Uncle Jack is very free with his money.*
generous, lavish, liberal
opposite mean

a
b
c
d
e
f
g
h
i
j
k
l
m
n
o
p
q
r
s
t
u
v
w
x
y
z

A B C D E **F** G H I J K L M N O P Q R S T U V W X Y Z

free verb
1 *The soldiers freed the prisoners of war.*
release, liberate, set free, deliver
To free slaves is to emancipate them.
To free prisoners by paying money to their captors is to ransom them.
opposite imprison
2 *We freed the dogs and let them run about.*
loose, turn loose, let go, untie, unchain
opposite confine
3 *The escapologist tried to free his arms from the chains.*
undo, untangle, work loose

freedom noun
The animals have a lot of freedom in the safari park.
liberty, independence

freeze verb freezes, freezing, froze, frozen
1 *Water begins to freeze at 0°C.*
become ice, ice over, harden, solidify
2 *If you freeze food, you can store it for a long time.*
deep-freeze, chill, refrigerate
3 *Season-ticket prices have been frozen for another year.*
fix, hold, peg, keep as they are

freezing adjective
It's freezing outside in winter.
chilly, frosty, icy, wintry, raw, bitter

frequent adjective
1 *I send frequent email messages to my friends.*
numerous, constant, continual, recurring, recurrent, repeated, countless
opposite infrequent
2 *Badgers are frequent visitors to the garden.*
regular, habitual, common, familiar, persistent
opposite rare

frequent verb
Office workers frequent the park at lunchtime.
visit, attend, haunt

fresh adjective
1 *This pudding is made with fresh fruit.*
natural, raw, unprocessed
2 *The shop bakes fresh bread every day.*
new
opposites old, stale
3 *Sally went outside to get some fresh air.*
clean, cool, crisp, refreshing
opposite stuffy
4 *Have you put fresh sheets on the bed?*
new, clean, laundered, washed
opposite dirty
5 *Having a shower makes me feel nice and fresh.*
refreshed, revived, restored, invigorated
6 *We need some fresh ideas for our magazine.*
new, original, different, novel, innovative
opposite old

fret verb
My sister is fretting about her piano exam.
worry, fuss, agonize, become stressed, get worked up

friction noun
1 *You can make fire from the friction of rubbing sticks together.*
rubbing, chafing, abrasion
2 *There was some friction between the two teams.*
conflict, disagreement, hostility, rivalry, antagonism, discord, quarrelling

friend noun
I am inviting four friends to my birthday party.
companion, comrade
(informal) mate, pal, buddy, chum
A friend you play games with is a playmate.
A friend you write to but do not normally meet is a penfriend.
A friend you know only slightly is an acquaintance.
opposite enemy

friendly adjective
1 *Our neighbour's pet dog is very friendly.*
affectionate, loving, good-natured, likeable, amiable, approachable,

kind-hearted, kindly, amicable, genial, sociable, outgoing, sympathetic
2 *Those two are very* friendly *with each other.*
close, familiar, intimate (informal) pally, chummy
3 *I like this cafe—it has a very* friendly *atmosphere.*
warm, welcoming, hospitable, cordial, neighbourly
opposites unfriendly, hostile

friendship noun
Their friendship *has lasted for many years.*
closeness, affection, fondness, familiarity, intimacy, attachment, comradeship, fellowship
A formal friendship between countries or parties is an alliance.
opposite hostility

fright noun
1 *The girl jumped up in* fright *and began to scream.*
fear, terror, alarm, horror, panic, dread
2 *The explosion gave us an awful* fright!
scare, shock, surprise, start, turn, jolt

frighten verb
Sorry—I didn't mean to frighten *you.*
scare, terrify, startle, alarm, shock, panic, petrify

frightened adjective
Mia always felt frightened *in the dark.*
afraid, scared, terrified, alarmed, fearful, panicky, petrified
See also afraid

frightening adjective
The ghost story she told was quite frightening.
terrifying, horrifying, alarming, nightmarish, chilling, spine-chilling, hair-raising, blood-curdling, eerie, sinister, fearsome
(informal) scary, creepy, spooky

frill noun
1 *My party dress has a* frill *round the hem.*
ruffle, ruff, flounce, fringe
2 *Our hotel was basic with no* frills.
extra, luxury

fringe noun
1 *My scarf has a beaded* fringe *at each end.*
border, edging, frill, trimming
2 *We live on the* fringe *of the town.*
edge, border, margin, outskirts

frisky adjective
The new lion cubs in the zoo are very frisky.
playful, lively, high-spirited, sprightly

fritter verb
to fritter away
Luke frittered away *his pocket money on sweets.*
waste, squander, spend unwisely, use up

frivolous adjective
1 *We were in a* frivolous *mood before we went on holiday.*
playful, lively, high-spirited, jaunty
opposites serious, sombre
2 *Don't waste my time asking* frivolous *questions.*
foolish, silly, ridiculous, shallow, superficial, pointless, unimportant, trivial, petty
opposites serious, important

frock noun
For items of clothing see clothes

frog noun
A young frog is a tadpole.
Frogs' eggs are frogspawn.
The sound a frog makes is a croak *or* ribbit.

frolic verb
Lambs were frolicking *in the field.*
jump about, leap about, bound, caper, prance, gambol, romp, skip

front noun
1 *We stood at the* front *of the queue.*
head, start, beginning, lead, top

a
b
c
d
e
f
g
h
i
j
k
l
m
n
o
p
q
r
s
t
u
v
w
x
y
z

A
B
C
D
E
F
G
H
I
J
K
L
M
N
O
P
Q
R
S
T
U
V
W
X
Y
Z

2 *The* front *of the house was painted white.*
face, facing, frontage, facade
opposites **back, rear**
The front of a ship is the **bow** or **prow**.
The front of a picture is the **foreground**.

front adjective
1 *The* front *runners came into sight round the corner.*
first, leading, most advanced
opposite **back**
2 *The horse had injured one of its* front *legs.*
fore
opposites **back, rear, hind**

frontier noun
We crossed the frontier *between France and Belgium.*
border, boundary

frosty adjective
1 *It was a clear,* frosty *night.*
cold, crisp, icy, freezing, wintry
2 *The shopkeeper gave us a* frosty *stare.*
unfriendly, unwelcoming, cold, cool, stony
opposites **warm, friendly**

froth noun
I like a lot of froth *on my hot chocolate.*
foam, bubbles, head
The froth on top of soapy water is **lather** or **suds**.
Dirty froth is **scum**.

frown noun
On Christmas Eve, Scrooge had a frown *on his face.*
scowl, glare, grimace, glower, black look
For other facial expressions see **expression**

frown verb
The witch frowned *when her spell didn't work.*
scowl, glare, grimace, glower,
knit your brow, look sullen

frugal adjective
1 *Mr Skinflint was always* frugal *with his money.*
thrifty, sparing, economical, prudent
opposites **wasteful, spendthrift**

2 *Cinderella ate a* frugal *meal of bread crusts.*
meagre, paltry, plain, simple
opposite **lavish**

fruit noun

> **WORD WEB**
>
> SOME COMMON VARIETIES OF FRUIT
> apple, apricot, avocado, banana, bilberry, blackberry, blackcurrant, blueberry, cherry, coconut, cranberry, damson, date, fig, gooseberry, grape, guava, kiwi fruit, loganberry, lychee, mango, melon, nectarine, pawpaw or papaya, peach, pear, pineapple, plum, pomegranate, quince, raspberry, redcurrant, rose hip, sloe, strawberry, tomato
>
> CITRUS FRUITS
> clementine, grapefruit, kumquat, lemon, lime, mandarin, orange, satsuma, tangerine
>
> DRIED FRUITS
> currant, prune, raisin, sultana
>
> **Rhubarb** is not a fruit, although it is cooked and eaten like one.
> A person who sells fruit and vegetables is a **greengrocer**.

fruitful adjective
Did you have a fruitful *shopping trip?*
successful, productive, useful, worthwhile, profitable, rewarding
opposite **fruitless**

fruitless adjective
They spent a fruitless *morning searching for clues.*
unsuccessful, unprofitable, unproductive, futile, pointless, useless, vain
opposites **fruitful, successful**

frustrate verb
1 *It* frustrated *us to have to wait in the long queue.*
exasperate, discourage, dispirit, irritate

2 *Our plans were* frustrated *by the weather.*
block, foil, thwart, defeat, check, hinder, prevent

fry verb
For ways to cook things see **cook**

fugitive noun
Police searched everywhere for the fugitives.
runaway, escapee, outlaw, deserter
Someone who is a fugitive from war or persecution is a **refugee**.

fulfil verb
1 *She* fulfilled *her ambition to play tennis at Wimbledon.*
achieve, realize, accomplish, attain, carry out, complete, succeed in
2 *To join the club, you must* fulfil *these conditions.*
meet, satisfy, conform to

full adjective
1 *My suitcase is* full *to the brim.*
filled, loaded, topped up
opposite **empty**
2 *The shopping centre was* full *on Saturday.*
busy, crowded, jammed, packed, crammed, congested
opposite **empty**
3 *The detective gave a* full *account of his findings.*
complete, detailed, comprehensive, thorough, exhaustive
opposite **incomplete**
4 *The horses were galloping at* full *speed.*
top, maximum, greatest, highest
opposite **minimum**
5 *The wedding dress has a very* full *skirt.*
wide, broad, voluminous
opposite **tight**

fun noun
We had great fun *at the beach on our holiday.*
amusement, diversion, enjoyment, entertainment, games, jokes, laughter, merriment, play, pleasure, recreation, sport
to make fun of someone

It was cruel to make fun of *her when she fell over.*
jeer at, laugh at, mock, ridicule, taunt, tease

function noun
1 *The* function *of a vet is to cure sick animals.*
duty, role, task, job, responsibility, purpose
2 *The hall is being used for an official* function.
event, occasion, party, reception

function verb
This camera doesn't function *properly.*
work, go, operate, run, perform

fundamental adjective
He taught me the fundamental *rules of chess.*
basic, elementary, essential, important, main, necessary, principal

funds plural noun
The school used some of its funds *to buy a minibus.*
money, cash, savings, capital, reserves

funny adjective
1 *There are some very* funny *jokes in the film.*
amusing, humorous, comic, comical, hilarious, witty, entertaining, diverting
(informal) hysterical, priceless
opposite **serious**
2 *There's a* funny *smell in here.*
strange, odd, peculiar, curious, puzzling, weird, queer, bizarre

fur noun
Arctic foxes have thick white fur *in the winter*
hair, coat, hide, pelt

furious adjective
1 *The manager was* furious *when his team lost.*
angry, mad, enraged, infuriated, incensed, livid, fuming, raging, seething
2 *The elves worked at a* furious *rate to finish their work.*
frantic, hectic, frenzied, extreme, intense
opposite **calm**

a
b
c
d
e
f
g
h
i
j
k
l
m
n
o
p
q
r
s
t
u
v
w
x
y
z

A
B
C
D
E
F
G
H
I
J
K
L
M
N
O
P
Q
R
S
T
U
V
W
X
Y
Z

furniture noun

WORD WEB

SOME ITEMS OF FURNITURE

armchair, bed, bookcase, bureau, chair, chest of drawers, coffee table, couch, cupboard, desk, dresser, dressing table, filing cabinet, settee, sideboard, sofa, sofa bed, stool, table, wardrobe

The soft covering on a chair or sofa is upholstery.
Old and valuable pieces of furniture are antiques.

furrow noun
The tractor wheels had made deep furrows in the mud.
groove, rut, ditch, channel, trench

furry adjective
A small, furry creature was curled inside the box.
hairy, fleecy, woolly, fuzzy, downy, feathery

further adjective
Look on our website for further information.
more, extra, additional, supplementary

furtive adjective
The spy cast a furtive glance around the room.
secretive, stealthy, surreptitious, underhand, crafty, sneaky, sly

fury noun
1 *The fury of the creature showed in its eyes.*
anger, rage, wrath, indignation
2 *There was no shelter from the fury of the storm.*
ferocity, fierceness, intensity, severity, violence, turbulence, savagery

fuse verb
The metals had fused together into a solid mass.
blend, combine, merge, unite, join, melt
To fuse metals together when you are making or mending something is to solder or weld them.

fuss noun
There was a lot of fuss when the queen arrived.
bother, commotion, excitement, trouble, hullabaloo

fuss verb
Please don't fuss!
worry, fret, bother, get worked up

fussy adjective
1 *Our cat is fussy about her food.*
finicky, hard to please, particular
(informal) choosy, picky
An informal name for a fussy person is a fusspot.
2 *I don't like clothes with fussy designs.*
fancy, elaborate, ornate, florid

futile adjective
They made a futile attempt to put out the fire.
fruitless, pointless, unsuccessful, useless, ineffectual, vain, wasted
opposite successful

future noun
She has a bright future as a tennis player.
outlook, prospects
opposite past

fuzzy adjective
1 *The TV picture has gone fuzzy.*
blurred, bleary, unfocused, unclear, indistinct, hazy, cloudy
opposite clear
2 *Mia was wearing a fuzzy cardigan.*
fluffy, frizzy, furry, woolly, fleecy

Gg

gadget noun
My pocket torch is a handy little gadget.
tool, instrument, implement, device, contraption, gizmo

gain verb
1 *Martha gained a reputation as an excellent cook.*
get, acquire, obtain, earn, win
opposite lose
2 *We gained our target of raising £200.*
reach, get to, arrive at, achieve, attain

game noun
1 *My favourite game is hide-and-seek.*
amusement, pastime, sport, activity, recreation
2 *The big game is on this Saturday.*
match, contest, competition, tournament

 WORD WEB

INDOOR GAMES
backgammon, bagatelle, battleships, billiards, bingo, cards, chess, Chinese checkers, computer game, cribbage, dice, dominoes, draughts, go, hangman, lotto, ludo, pool, snakes and ladders, snooker, table tennis or (informal) ping-pong, tiddlywinks, video game

For names of card games see **card**

PARTY GAMES
charades, hide-and-seek, I-spy, musical chairs, pass the parcel

PLAYGROUND AND OTHER OUTDOOR GAMES
conkers, hopscotch, leapfrog, marbles, skipping, skittles, tag

For more indoor and outdoor games see **sport**

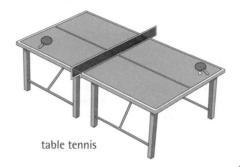

table tennis

computer game

skipping

dominoes

gang noun
1 *The sea was swarming with gangs of pirates.*
group, band, crowd, pack, set, mob
2 *A gang of workmen dug a hole in the road.*
team, unit, crew, squad, party

gap noun
1 *The animals escaped through a gap in the fence.*
opening, space, hole, breach, break, crack, rift
2 *She returned to work after a gap of two years.*
break, interval, interruption, pause, lull

a
b
c
d
e
f
g
h
i
j
k
l
m
n
o
p
q
r
s
t
u
v
w
x
y
z

A B C D E F **G** H I J K L M N O P Q R S T U V W X Y Z

gaping adjective
The meteor left a gaping hole in the ground.
wide, broad, yawning, vast, cavernous

garden noun
A small area of garden is a plot or patch.
A rented garden for growing vegetables is an allotment.
A garden planted with trees is an orchard.
A formal word for gardening is horticulture.
A word meaning 'to do with gardens or gardening' is horticultural.
For tools used for gardening see tool

garment noun
see clothes

gas noun
The mixture gave off an evil-smelling gas.
vapour, fumes

gash noun
The broken glass made a nasty gash in my foot.
cut, slash, wound, slit

gasp verb
At the end of the race we lay gasping for breath.
gulp, pant

gate noun
People waited at the gate to be let in.
gateway, doorway, entrance, portal

gather verb
1 *A crowd gathered to watch the performers.*
assemble, collect, come together, congregate
opposite disperse
2 *The captain gathered her team to give them a talk.*
bring together, round up, muster
3 *We gathered daisies to make into chains.*
pick, pluck, collect, harvest
4 *I gather that you've been on holiday.*
understand, hear, learn, believe

gathering noun
There was a family gathering for granny's birthday.
assembly, meeting, crowd, party, get-together

gaudy adjective
The newsreader wore a rather gaudy tie.
flashy, showy, loud, glaring, garish, lurid

gauge verb
They're trying to gauge the size of the volcano.
measure, calculate, judge, assess, estimate, reckon

gaunt adjective
The sorceress had a gaunt face and stringy hair.
haggard, drawn, thin, skinny, scraggy, scrawny, wasted, skeletal

gave
past tense see give

gaze verb
The dog gazed hungrily at the food.
stare, look, gape

gear noun
We put our fishing gear in the back of the car.
equipment, stuff, things, paraphernalia, tackle

gem noun
The crown was made of solid gold, studded with gems.
jewel, precious stone
For names of gem stones see jewel

general adjective
1 *There was a general air of gloom about the abbey.*
widespread, extensive, broad, sweeping, overall, prevalent
2 *I've only got a general idea of where we are.*
rough, approximate, indefinite, vague, loose

generally adverb
I generally travel to school by bus.
usually, normally, as a rule, chiefly, mostly, mainly, commonly, on the whole

generate verb
Our website has generated a lot of interest.
create, produce, bring about, give rise to

generous adjective
1 *It was generous of you to give me your seat.*
unselfish, charitable, kind-hearted
opposite **selfish**
2 *We each got a generous helping of ice-cream.*
ample, large, lavish, plentiful
opposite **meagre**

genial adjective
The housekeeper greeted us with a genial smile.
friendly, kind, warm, warm-hearted, kindly, good-natured, pleasant, agreeable, cordial
opposite **unfriendly**

genius noun
Nila is a genius at maths.
expert, master, mastermind, wizard, ace

gentle adjective
1 *The vet is very gentle with sick animals.*
kind, tender, good-tempered, humane
2 *Grasses swayed in the gentle breeze.*
light, slight, mild, soft, faint
opposite **strong**
3 *There is a gentle slope to the top of the hill.*
slight, gradual, easy
opposite **steep**

genuine adjective
1 *Is that a genuine diamond?*
real, actual, true, authentic
opposite **fake**
2 *Your friend seems like a very genuine person.*
honest, sincere, frank, earnest
opposite **false**

gesture noun
She opened her arms in a gesture of welcome.
sign, signal, motion, movement

get verb gets, getting, got
1 *We're getting a goldfish for our class.*
acquire, obtain, buy, purchase
2 *Can you get me another blanket, please?*
bring, fetch, collect, pick up, retrieve
3 *Cara got a medal for swimming.*
receive, gain, earn, win, achieve
4 *What time did you get home?*
arrive at, reach, come to
opposite **leave**
5 *It was starting to get dark outside.*
become, grow, turn
6 *I got a stomach bug on holiday last year.*
catch, develop, pick up, come down with
7 *You'll never get Oscar to eat celery.*
persuade, urge, influence, coax
8 *I don't get the point of that film.*
understand, follow, comprehend, grasp
to get on or along
How are you getting on with playing the guitar?
manage, fare, cope, prosper, succeed
to get out of
My brother got out of doing the washing up.
avoid, evade, shirk
to get over
He hasn't got over the accident yet.
get better from, recover from, shake off, survive

ghastly adjective
The boy's face turned a ghastly shade of green.
appalling, awful, dreadful, frightful, grim, grisly, horrible, horrifying, shocking, monstrous, terrible

ghost noun
Meldrop House was haunted by several ghosts.
spirit, spectre, phantom, ghoul, apparition, shade, wraith
(informal) spook

a
b
c
d
e
f
g
h
i
j
k
l
m
n
o
p
q
r
s
t
u
v
w
x
y
z

A ghost that makes a lot of noise is a poltergeist.

WORD WEB

A GHOST OR GHOSTLY EXPERIENCE MIGHT BE
blood curdling, chilling, grisly, gruesome, hair-raising, macabre, nightmarish, spine-chilling, spine-tingling

THINGS A GHOST MIGHT DO
flit, float, glide, glow, haunt a person or place, hover, lurk, materialize, pass through walls, rattle chains, shimmer, vanish, waft

NOISES A GHOST MIGHT MAKE
cackle, clang, clank, creak, groan, hoot, howl, moan, screech, sigh, sob, wail

PLACES A GHOST MIGHT BE FOUND
catacombs, crypt, haunted house or mansion, graveyard, sepulchre, tomb, vault

OTHER THINGS THAT MIGHT BE IN A HAUNTED HOUSE
bats, candles, cellar, cobwebs, dungeon, gargoyle, mummy, owl, secret door or passage, skeleton, skull, trap door, turret

ghostly adjective
The candlelight cast ghostly shadows on the wall.
spectral, phantom, ghoulish, unearthly, eerie, sinister, uncanny
(informal) spooky, creepy

giant noun
The castle belonged to a fearsome giant.
For creatures found in myths and legends see **myth**

giant adjective
A giant tree towered above us.
gigantic, huge, enormous, massive, immense, mammoth, colossal, monstrous
See also **big**
opposite **tiny**

giddy adjective
I felt giddy when I stood at the edge of the cliff.
dizzy, faint, unsteady

gift noun
1 *I received some nice gifts on my birthday.*
present
2 *Elsa has a gift for music.*
talent, ability, flair, knack, genius

gifted adjective
There are some gifted players in the team.
talented, able, accomplished, capable, skilful, expert

gigantic adjective
The dragon reared its gigantic head.
huge, giant, enormous, massive, colossal, immense, mammoth, monstrous
(informal) whopping, humongous
opposite **tiny**

giggle verb
Ailsa and I couldn't stop giggling.
snigger, titter, chuckle, laugh

girl noun
A synonym used in some parts of Britain is lass.
Old-fashioned words are damsel, maid, and maiden.

give verb gives, giving, gave, given
1 *Santa Claus gave each child a present.*
deal out, distribute, issue, supply, offer, present, hand over, pass, award
2 *Will you give something to our collection for charity?*
contribute, donate
3 *The giant gave a loud sneeze.*
utter, emit, let out
4 *We are giving a concert at the end of term.*
present, put on, lay on, organize, arrange
5 *Will this branch give if I sit on it?*
collapse, give way, bend, break, buckle
to give in
The boxer gave in after a long fight.
surrender, yield, submit, quit

to give up
He gave up trying to start the car.
abandon, stop, cease, quit

glad adjective
I'm glad to hear that you're feeling better.
pleased, happy, delighted, thrilled
opposite sad

glamorous adjective
She looked very glamorous in a long black dress.
beautiful, attractive, gorgeous, elegant, stylish, fashionable

glance verb
The bus driver glanced quickly at his watch.
look quickly, peek, peep, glimpse

glare verb
The troll glared at us from under his bushy eyebrows.
stare, frown, scowl, glower

glare noun
1 *The glare of the lights dazzled me.*
dazzle, blaze, brightness, brilliance
2 *Miss Frump silenced the children with an angry glare.*
stare, scowl, glower, frown, nasty look

glasses plural noun
She put on her glasses to read the letter.
spectacles, (informal) specs

WORD WEB

OTHER INSTRUMENTS WITH LENSES
binoculars, magnifying glass, microscope, telescope

An old word for a telescope is a spyglass.

binoculars

magnifying glass

microscope

telescope

a
b
c
d
e
f
g
h
i
j
k
l
m
n
o
p
q
r
s
t
u
v
w
x
y
z

A B C D E F **G** H I J K L M N O P Q R S T U V W X Y Z

gleam noun
I saw a gleam of moonlight between the clouds.
glimmer, glint, flash, ray, shaft

gleam verb
The lights gleamed on the water.
glimmer, glint, glisten, shimmer, shine

glide verb
The boat glided gently across the lake.
move smoothly, slide, slip, drift, float, coast

glimmer verb
The city lights glimmered in the distance.
gleam, glint, glow, glisten, shimmer, flicker, blink

glimpse verb
I glimpsed a deer running through the forest.
catch sight of, spot, spy, sight

glimpse noun
We caught a glimpse of a dolphin's tail.
peek, peep, glance, sighting, view

glint verb
Sunlight glinted on the windows.
flash, glitter, sparkle, twinkle

glisten verb
The pavement glistened with frost.
gleam, shine, glint, shimmer, glimmer

glitter verb
The jewels glittered under the bright lights.
sparkle, twinkle, shimmer, glimmer, glint, glisten, flash, shine

gloat verb
He was gloating about winning the poetry prize.
boast, brag, crow, show off

global adjective
The Internet is a global network of computers.
worldwide, international, universal

globe noun
1 *I'd like to travel all round the globe.*
world, planet, earth

2 *The fortune teller used a crystal globe.*
ball, sphere, orb

gloom noun
1 *We could hardly see in the gloom of the cave.*
darkness, dimness, shade, shadow, murk
The gloomy light late in the evening is **dusk** or **twilight**.
2 *There was an air of gloom in the abandoned tower.*
depression, sadness, unhappiness, melancholy, misery, despair

gloomy adjective
1 *It was cold and gloomy in the cellar.*
dark, dingy, dim, dismal, dreary, sombre, cheerless, murky, shadowy
opposite **bright**
2 *Eeyore was feeling gloomy again.*
depressed, sad, unhappy, glum, miserable, melancholy, low, downcast, dejected
(informal) **down in the dumps**
opposite **cheerful**

glorious adjective
Look at that glorious sunset!
magnificent, splendid, stunning, spectacular, superb, magnificent, wonderful, marvellous

glossy adjective
The bear had a thick, glossy coat of black fur.
shiny, sleek, silky, shining, gleaming, lustrous
opposite **dull**

glove noun
For items of clothing see **clothes**

glow noun
The soft glow of burning candles lit the room.
brightness, shine, gleam, radiance

glow verb
The embers of the bonfire were still glowing.
shine, gleam, burn
Something that glows in the dark is **luminous** or **phosphorescent**.

glower verb
The jailer glowered at the prisoners.
glare, scowl, frown, stare angrily

glue noun
Put a blob of glue on each corner of the paper.
adhesive, paste, gum

glue verb
Glue the edges of the box together.
stick, paste, bond, seal

glum adjective
Why are you looking so glum?
depressed, sad, unhappy, gloomy, miserable, melancholy, low, downcast, dejected
opposite **cheerful**

gnarled adjective
The branches of the tree were gnarled with age.
bent, twisted, crooked, distorted, knobbly, knotty

gnaw verb
The wolves gnawed at a pile of bones.
chew, bite, nibble, munch

go verb goes, going, went, gone
1 *A carriage was going slowly along the road.*
move, progress, proceed
See also **move**
2 *My granny has always wanted to go to China.*
travel, journey
3 *Some of the guests had already gone.*
leave, depart, get away, withdraw
4 *By morning, the ice had all gone.*
disappear, vanish
5 *The canal goes all the way from Inverness to Fort William.*
extend, lead, reach, stretch, run
6 *The mountaineer's face went blue with cold.*
become, turn, grow
7 *Is that old grandfather clock still going?*
function, operate, work, run
8 *Cups and saucers go on the bottom shelf.*
belong, be kept, be placed
9 *Time goes slowly when you're stuck indoors.*
pass, go by, elapse
to go back
Sarah has gone back to the house.
return, retreat, retrace your steps
to go in for
I'm not going in for the race this year.
enter, take part in, participate in
to go off
1 *A bomb went off nearby.*
explode, blow up, detonate
2 *The milk will go off if it's not in the fridge.*
turn sour, go bad, rot
to go on
1 *What's going on over there?*
happen, occur, take place
2 *Please go on with your story.*
carry on, continue, keep going, proceed
to go with
Do these shoes go with my dress?
match, suit, blend with

go noun
Would you like to have a go on my computer?
try, turn, chance, opportunity
(informal) shot, bash, stab

goal noun
1 *The goal of the society is to protect wildlife.*
aim, ambition, intention, object, objective, purpose, target
2 *We managed to get a goal just before half-time.*
Three goals scored by the same player is known as a **hat-trick**.

gobble verb
Ladybirds love to gobble greenfly.
guzzle, gulp, bolt, devour

god or **goddess** noun
Zeus was one of the gods of ancient Greece.
deity
A word meaning 'to do with a god or goddess' is **divine**.

gold noun
Something that is made of gold is **golden** or **gilded**.
A thin covering of gold is **gilt**.

a b c d e f g h i j k l m n o p q r s t u v w x y z

A B C D E F **G** H I J K L M N O P Q R S T U V W X Y Z

good adjective
That is a really good idea!
excellent, fine, lovely, nice, wonderful
(informal) fantastic, great, super, cool
opposite **bad**

OVERUSED WORD
Try to vary the words you use for good.
Here are some other words you could use.

FOR A GOOD PERSON
honest, worthy, honourable, moral,
decent, virtuous, noble, kind, humane,
charitable, merciful
*The virtuous knight defeated the evil
queen.*
opposites **evil, wicked**

A good character in a story or film is a
hero or **heroine** or (informal) **goody**.

FOR GOOD BEHAVIOUR
well-behaved, obedient, angelic,
exemplary
The twins are surprisingly well-behaved.
opposites **naughty, disobedient**

A common simile is as good as gold.

FOR A GOOD FRIEND
true, loyal, loving, reliable, trusty,
trustworthy
My dog, Rusty, is a loyal companion.

FOR A GOOD FEELING OR GOOD MOOD
happy, cheerful, light-hearted, positive,
contented
*Mr Fox was in a cheerful mood after his
tea.*

FOR A GOOD EXPERIENCE OR GOOD NEWS
pleasant, enjoyable, delightful,
agreeable, pleasing
*The girls had an enjoyable time at
the party.*
The letter contained some pleasing news.
opposites **unpleasant, disagreeable**

FOR A GOOD PERFORMER OR GOOD WORK
capable, skilful, clever, able, talented,
competent, commendable, sound
My friend, Chris, is a talented dancer.
opposites **poor, awful**

FOR GOOD FOOD OR A GOOD MEAL
delicious, healthy, nourishing,
nutritious, tasty, well-cooked,
wholesome, substantial, hearty
The crew ate a hearty breakfast together.

FOR A GOOD EXCUSE OR GOOD REASON
acceptable, valid, proper, satisfactory,
legitimate
*I hope you have a valid excuse for being
late.*
opposites **poor, unacceptable**

FOR GOOD TIMING
convenient, suitable, fortunate,
appropriate, opportune
Is this a convenient time for a chat?
opposites **inconvenient, unsuitable**

FOR GOOD WEATHER
fine, favourable
We are hoping for fine weather tomorrow.
opposites **harsh, adverse**

goodbye noun
The astronauts said goodbye to their families.
farewell
(informal) cheerio
A formal phrase meaning 'to say goodbye' is
to bid farewell.

good–looking adjective
I think your cousin is quite good-looking.
attractive, handsome, pretty
opposite **ugly**

goods plural noun
The smugglers hid the stolen goods in a cave.
property, merchandise, wares, cargo

gorgeous adjective
The gardens look gorgeous in the summer.
beautiful, glorious, dazzling, stunning,
splendid, superb, glamorous, handsome

gossip verb
Two neighbours were gossiping over the fence.
chatter, tell tales
(informal) natter

gossip noun
1 *Don't believe all the gossip you hear.*
chatter, rumour, hearsay, scandal
(informal) tittle-tattle
2 *Our next-door neighbour is a dreadful gossip.*
busybody, chatterbox, telltale, scandalmonger

gouge verb
The builders gouged a hole in the wall.
dig, hollow out, scoop out, excavate

govern verb
The ancient Romans governed a vast empire.
rule, run, administer, direct, command, manage, be in charge of

gown noun
The mermaid wore a gown made of seaweed and pearls.
dress, robe, frock

grab verb
The cowboy grabbed the reins of the runaway horse.
seize, grasp, catch, clutch, grip, get hold of, snatch

graceful adjective
The gymnast made a graceful landing.
elegant, beautiful, stylish, smooth, flowing, agile, nimble
opposites clumsy, graceless

gracious adjective
The film star waved and gave a gracious smile.
polite, courteous, good-natured, pleasant, agreeable, civil

grade noun
My sister has reached the top grade in judo.
class, standard, level, stage, rank, degree

grade verb
Eggs are graded according to size.
group, sort, classify

gradual adjective
There's been a gradual change in the weather.
steady, slow, gentle, moderate, regular, even
opposite sudden

grain noun
1 *Some grains of sand stuck to my toes.*
bit, particle, speck, granule
2 *The grain will be made into bread.*
cereals, corn

grand adjective
1 *The wedding was a grand occasion.*
magnificent, splendid, stately, impressive, big, great, important, imposing
2 (informal) *Keep going—you're doing a grand job!*
excellent, fine, good, first-class

grant verb
The king granted the prisoners their freedom.
give, allow, permit, award

grapple verb
Sam grappled with the thief, but he got away.
struggle, wrestle, fight, tussle

grasp verb
1 *The climber grasped the end of the rope.*
clutch, grab, grip, seize, catch, snatch, take hold of, hang on to
2 *The ideas were quite difficult to grasp.*
understand, comprehend, follow, take in

grasp noun
Rita has a good grasp of mathematics.
understanding, comprehension, knowledge, mastery

grass noun
People were told not to walk on the grass.
lawn, turf, green

grate verb
1 *I grated the cheese onto the pizza.*
shred, grind

a
b
c
d
e
f
g
h
i
j
k
l
m
n
o
p
q
r
s
t
u
v
w
x
y
z

2 *The chalk grated on the blackboard.*
scrape, scratch
to grate on
That man's voice grates on my nerves.
annoy, irritate, jar on

grateful adjective
I'm grateful for your help.
thankful, appreciative, obliged, indebted
opposite **ungrateful**

gratitude noun
We sent some flowers to show our gratitude.
thanks, appreciation

grave¹ noun
see tomb

grave² adjective
1 *They looked grave when they heard the news.*
grim, sad, serious, thoughtful
opposite **cheerful**
2 *She made a grave mistake.*
crucial, important, serious, vital
opposite **trivial**

graveyard noun
He was buried in the local graveyard.
burial ground, cemetery, churchyard

graze verb
I grazed my knee when I fell off my bike.
scrape, cut, scratch, scuff

greasy adjective
I don't like greasy food.
fatty, oily

great adjective
1 *The inventor had made a great discovery.*
important, significant, major, leading, noteworthy
opposites **insignificant, minor**
2 *Mozart was a great composer.*
famous, notable, celebrated, eminent, distinguished, outstanding, brilliant
3 *Their voices echoed round the great hall.*
big, huge, large, enormous, vast, immense,

gigantic, extensive, cavernous
opposite **small**
4 *Beth took great care over her knitting.*
considerable, extreme, exact
opposite **little**
5 (informal) *That is a great idea!*
very good, excellent, marvellous, outstanding, superb, tremendous, wonderful
(informal) brilliant, fantastic, super, smashing, terrific
opposites **bad, awful**

greed noun
The king wanted more gold to satisfy his greed.
avarice, selfishness, hunger, craving, gluttony

greedy adjective
1 *The boys were so greedy that they ate all the cakes.*
gluttonous
(informal) piggish
A common simile is as greedy as a pig.
2 *Mr Skimp is very greedy with his money.*
selfish, miserly, tight-fisted, grasping

green adjective & noun

WORD WEB
SOME SHADES OF GREEN
bottle-green, emerald, jade, khaki, lime, olive, pea-green

greens plural noun
see vegetable

greet verb
My aunt greeted us with a friendly wave.
welcome, hail, receive, salute

grew
past tense see grow

grey adjective
1 *The old wizard had a bushy grey beard.*
silver, silvery, grizzly, hoary, whitish

A B C D E F G H I J K L M N O P Q R S T U V W X Y Z

2 *The mother's face was* **grey** *with worry.*
ashen, pale, leaden, wan
3 *The day began cold and* **grey.**
dull, cloudy, overcast

grief noun
He couldn't hide his **grief** *at his friend's death.*
sorrow, sadness, mourning, unhappiness, distress, anguish, heartache
opposite **joy**

grieve verb
1 *The family is still* **grieving** *over her death.*
mourn, lament, weep
opposite **rejoice**
2 *It* **grieves** *me to leave so soon.*
sadden, upset, distress, hurt
opposite **please**

grim adjective
1 *The judge wore a* **grim** *expression on his face.*
stern, severe, harsh, bad-tempered, sullen
opposite **cheerful**
2 *The detective made the* **grim** *discovery of the body.*
unpleasant, horrible, dreadful, terrible, hideous, shocking, gruesome, grisly
opposite **pleasant**

grime noun
There was nearly an inch of **grime** *on the floor.*
dirt, filth, muck, mire, mess

grimy adjective
Don't wipe those **grimy** *feet on the carpet!*
dirty, filthy, grubby, mucky, soiled
opposite **clean**

grin noun & verb
Mark arrived with a silly **grin** *on his face.*
smile, beam, smirk
A large grin is a **broad**, **wide**, or **cheesy** grin.

grind verb grinds, grinding, ground
1 **Grind** *the spices into a fine powder.*
crush, pound, powder, pulverize, mill

2 *This tool is used for* **grinding** *knives.*
sharpen, file, hone, whet

grip verb
1 **Grip** *the handle tightly.*
grasp, seize, clutch, clasp, hold
2 *The audience was* **gripped** *by the film.*
fascinate, engross, absorb, enthrall

grisly adjective
We found the **grisly** *remains of a dead sheep.*
gruesome, gory, ghastly, hideous, nasty, revolting, sickening

grit noun
1 *I've got some* **grit** *in my shoe.*
gravel, dust, sand
2 *The marathon runners showed real* **grit.**
bravery, courage, toughness, spirit, pluck
(informal) guts

groan verb
The wounded soldier **groaned** *with pain.*
cry out, moan, sigh, wail

groove noun
Thick **grooves** *had been carved in the stone wall.*
channel, furrow, rut, cut, scratch, slot

grope verb
I **groped** *in the dark for the light switch.*
fumble, feel about, flounder

gross adjective
1 *That is a* **gross** *exaggeration!*
extreme, glaring, obvious, sheer, blatant, outright
2 *Most ogres have* **gross** *table manners.*
offensive, rude, coarse, vulgar

ground¹ noun
1 *I planted some seeds in the* **ground.**
earth, soil, land
2 *The* **ground** *was too wet to play on.*
field, pitch, park, stadium, arena

ground²
past tense see **grind**

A
B
C
D
E
F
G
H
I
J
K
L
M
N
O
P
Q
R
S
T
U
V
W
X
Y
Z

group noun

1 *Japan consists of a group of islands.*
collection, set, batch, cluster, clump
2 *A group of children was waiting at the bus stop.*
crowd, bunch, gathering, band, body, gang
3 *The book group meets once a month.*
club, society, association, circle
4 *We sorted the fossils into different groups.*
category, class, type, kind, sort

WORD WEB

WORDS FOR GROUPS OF PEOPLE
a **band** of musicians
a **class** of pupils
a **company** or **troupe** of actors
a **congregation** of worshippers in church
a **coven** of witches
a **crew** of sailors
a **gang** of workers
a **horde** of invaders
a **team** of players

WORDS FOR GROUPS OF ANIMALS
an **army** or **colony** of ants
a **band** of gorillas
a **brood** of chicks
a **covey** of partridges
a **flock** of sheep or birds
a **gaggle** of geese
a **herd** of cattle or elephants
a **litter** of pigs or puppies
a **pack** of wolves
a **pride** of lions
a **school** or **pod** of dolphins or whales
a **shoal** of fish
a **swarm** of insects
a **troop** of monkeys

WORDS FOR GROUPS OF THINGS
a **battery** of guns
a **bunch** of flowers
a **clump** of trees
a **clutch** of eggs in a nest
a **constellation** or **galaxy** of stars
a **convoy** or **fleet** of ships

grow verb grows, growing, grew, grown

1 *I've grown an inch taller since last summer.*
get bigger, put on growth, spring up, sprout
2 *The number of children in the school has grown.*
increase, develop, enlarge, expand, build up
opposite **decrease**
3 *Our neighbour grows orchids in her greenhouse.*
cultivate, produce, raise, farm
4 *It is growing dark outside.*
become, get, turn

grown-up adjective

The female cheetah has two grown-up cubs.
adult, mature, fully grown
opposite **young**

growth noun

1 *There's been a growth of interest in golf for kids.*
increase, rise, spread, expansion, development, enlargement
2 *The doctor examined the growth on my foot.*
lump, swelling, tumour

grub noun

I found a grub on the cabbage leaf.
larva, maggot, caterpillar

grubby adjective

My hands were grubby from working in the garden.
dirty, filthy, grimy, messy, mucky, soiled
opposite **clean**

grudge noun

Captain Hook bore a grudge against Peter Pan.
grievance, bitterness, resentment, hard feelings, ill-will, spite

gruelling adjective

The marathon is a gruelling race.
hard, tough, demanding, exhausting,

challenging, difficult, laborious, strenuous, back breaking, punishing
opposite **easy**

gruesome adjective
The battlefield was a gruesome sight.
grisly, gory, ghastly, hideous, monstrous, revolting, sickening, appalling, dreadful, frightful, shocking, abominable

gruff adjective
The ogre spoke in a gruff voice.
harsh, rough, hoarse, husky, throaty

grumble verb
You're always grumbling about the weather!
complain, moan, groan, protest, whine, gripe

grumpy adjective
Marge was grumpy because she had a headache.
bad-tempered, cross, irritable, testy, tetchy, cantankerous
(informal) grouchy
opposite **good-humoured**

guarantee verb
I guarantee that you will enjoy the show.
promise, assure, pledge, vow

guard verb
The cave was guarded by a one-eyed giant.
protect, defend, stand guard over, patrol, safeguard, shield, watch over

guard noun
A guard was on duty at the gate.
sentry, sentinel, warder, lookout, watchman

guardian noun
The guardian of the treasure was a fierce dragon.
defender, protector, keeper, minder, custodian

guess noun
My guess is that it will rain tomorrow.
estimate, prediction, feeling, hunch

guess verb
1 *There was a prize for guessing the weight of the cake.*
estimate, judge, work out, gauge, predict, reckon
2 *I guess you must be tired after your journey.*
suppose, imagine, expect, assume, think

guest noun
We are having guests for tea on Sunday.
visitor, caller, company

guide noun
1 *Our guide showed us around the zoo.*
courier, escort, leader, chaperone
2 *We bought a useful guide to the city.*
guidebook, handbook, manual

guide verb
The explorers used the stars to guide them at night.
direct, lead, steer, conduct, escort, show the way

guilt noun
1 *The prisoner admitted his guilt.*
responsibility, liability, blame, wrongdoing
opposite **innocence**
2 *You could see the look of guilt on her face.*
shame, remorse, regret, penitence, disgrace, dishonour

guilty adjective
1 *The prisoner was found guilty of the crime.*
responsible, to blame, at fault, in the wrong, liable
opposite **innocent**
2 *You have a guilty look on your face!*
ashamed, guilt-ridden, remorseful, sorry, conscience-stricken, repentant, shamefaced, sheepish
opposite **unrepentant**

gulp verb
Peter gulped down the cake in one go.
swallow, bolt, gobble, guzzle, devour
For other ways to eat see **eat**

a
b
c
d
e
f
g
h
i
j
k
l
m
n
o
p
q
r
s
t
u
v
w
x
y
z

A B C D E F G H I J K L M N O P Q R S T U V W X Y Z

gulp noun
Amanda took a long gulp *of lemonade.*
swallow, mouthful
(informal) swig

gun noun
For various weapons see weapon

gurgle verb
The mountain stream gurgled *over the rocks.*
burble, babble

gush noun
There was a gush *of water from the pipe.*
rush, stream, torrent, cascade, flood, jet,
spout, spurt

gush verb
Water gushed *from the broken pipe.*
rush, stream, flow, pour, flood, spout,
spurt, squirt

gust noun
A gust *of wind carried the kite into the sky.*
blast, rush, puff, squall, flurry

guzzle verb
The seagulls guzzled *all the bread.*
gobble, gulp, bolt, devour
For other ways to eat see eat

Hn

habit noun
1 *It's her* habit *to go for a walk each morning.*
custom, practice, routine, rule
2 *My dog has a* habit *of scratching his ear.*
mannerism, way, tendency, inclination,
quirk

hack verb
The explorers hacked *their way through the
jungle.*
chop, cut, hew, slash, lop

had
past tense see have

haggard adjective
The warriors looked haggard *after the battle.*
drawn, gaunt, thin, pinched, wasted,
shrunken, wan
opposite healthy

haggle verb
The men haggled *over the price of the gems.*
bargain, negotiate, argue, wrangle

hair noun
Rapunzel's hair *reached down to the ground.*
locks, tresses
(informal) mop
A single piece of hair is a strand.
A bunch of hair is a hank, lock, or tress.
False hair is a hairpiece, toupee, or wig.
An area without hair is a bald patch.
The way hair is cut is a hairstyle or
(informal) hairdo or (formal) coiffure.
Hair is cut or styled by a hairdresser or
hairstylist.
Men's hair is also cut by a barber.

 WORD WEB

SOME HAIRSTYLES
**Afro, bob, braids, bun, bunches,
chignon, corn rows, crew cut,
curls, dreadlocks, fishtail,
French braid or plait, fringe, Mohican,
perm, pigtail, plaits, ponytail, quiff,
ringlets, short back and sides, sideburns,
skinhead, topknot**

HAIR ON AN ANIMAL
**bristles, coat, down, fleece, fur, mane,
whiskers**

 WRITING TIPS

You can use these words to describe hair

TO DESCRIBE ITS **COLOUR**
auburn, blond or **blonde, brunette**
(informal) **carroty**

dark, fair, flaxen, ginger, grey, grizzled, hoary, mousy, platinum blonde, raven, red, silver

TO DESCRIBE HOW IT **LOOKS** OR **FEELS**
bushy, coarse, curly, dishevelled, fine, frizzy, glossy, greasy, lank, limp, matted, ringletted, shaggy, shiny, silky, spiky, straggly, straight, stringy, tangled,

thick, tousled, tuggy, unkempt, wavy, windswept, wispy
The hair on Mr Twit's face didn't grow smooth and matted as it does on most hairy-faced men. It grew in spikes that stuck out straight like the bristles of a nailbrush.
— Roald Dahl, *The Twits*

For ways to describe animal hair see **animal**

hairy adjective
Mammoths were like elephants with thick hairy coats.
shaggy, bushy, bristly, woolly, fleecy, furry, fuzzy, long-haired, hirsute

hall noun
1 *The hall was full for the concert.*
assembly hall, auditorium, concert hall, theatre
2 *You can use the coat stand in the hall.*
entrance hall, hallway, lobby, foyer

halt verb
1 *The car halted at the red light.*
stop, come to a halt, draw up, pull up, wait
2 *A traffic jam halted the traffic.*
stop, check, obstruct
3 *Work halted when the whistle went.*
end, cease, terminate, break off
opposites **start, go**

halve verb
1 *Halve the tomatoes and scoop out the seeds.*
cut in half, divide into halves, split in two

2 *The workforce has been halved in the last five years.*
cut by half, reduce by half

hammer verb
I hammered on the door, but no one came.
strike, beat, knock, batter, pummel, pound

hamper verb
Bad weather hampered the rescuers.
hinder, hold up, obstruct, impede, restrict, handicap, frustrate
opposite **help**

hand noun
When you clench your hand you make a **fist**.
The flat part of the inside of your hand is the **palm**.
Work that you do with your hands is **manual** work.

hand verb
The postman handed me several letters.
give, pass, present, offer, deliver
to hand something down
This brooch has been handed down from generation to generation.
pass down, pass on, bequeath

handicap noun
1 *Lack of experience can be a handicap in some jobs.*
disadvantage, drawback, hindrance, obstacle, problem, difficulty, limitation
opposite **advantage**
2 *He was born with a visual handicap.*
disability, impairment

handicap verb
The search was handicapped by bad weather.
hamper, hinder, hold up, restrict, impede
opposite **help**

handle noun
The door handle is broken.
grip, handgrip, knob, shaft
The handle of a sword is the **hilt**.

handle verb
1 *Please don't handle the exhibits.*
touch, feel, hold, stroke, fondle, finger, grasp

a
b
c
d
e
f
g
h
i
j
k
l
m
n
o
p
q
r
s
t
u
v
w
x
y
z

A
B
C
D
E
F
G
H
I
J
K
L
M
N
O
P
Q
R
S
T
U
V
W
X
Y
Z

2 *The referee* handled *the game well.*
manage, control, conduct, deal with, cope with, tackle

handsome adjective
1 *Prince Charming was very* handsome.
attractive, good-looking, nice-looking, gorgeous
(informal) dishy
opposites **ugly, unattractive**
2 *They sold their house for a* handsome *profit.*
big, large, substantial, sizeable
opposite **slight**

handy adjective
1 *This* handy *gadget is for peeling potatoes.*
useful, helpful, convenient, practical
opposite **awkward**
2 *I always keep my umbrella* handy.
accessible, available, close at hand, nearby, ready
opposite **inaccessible**

hang verb hangs, hanging, hung
1 *A monkey was* hanging *from the tree branch.*
dangle, be suspended, swing, sway
2 *The dog had hair* hanging *down over his eyes.*
droop, drape, flop, trail, cascade
3 *I* hung *the picture on the wall.*
fix, attach, fasten, stick, peg
4 *Smoke* hung *in the air.*
float, hover, drift, linger, cling
to hang about or around
Don't hang about; *we'll miss the bus.*
delay, dawdle, linger, loiter
to hang on (informal)
Try to hang on *a bit longer.*
carry on, continue, stay, remain, persist, keep going, persevere
to hang on to something
1 Hang on to *the rope.*
hold, grip, grasp
2 Hang on to *your bus ticket.*
keep, retain, save

happen verb
Did anything interesting happen *today?*
take place, occur, arise, come about, crop up, emerge, result

happening noun
There have been strange happenings *here lately.*
event, occurrence, incident, phenomenon

happiness noun
The bride's face glowed with happiness.
joy, joyfulness, delight, jubilation, pleasure, contentment, gladness, cheerfulness, merriment, ecstasy, bliss
opposite **sorrow**

happy adjective

OVERUSED WORD

Try to vary the words you use for **happy**. Here are some other words you could use.

FOR A **HAPPY MOOD** OR **HAPPY PERSON**
cheerful, joyful, jolly, merry, light-hearted, contented, gleeful, delighted
The girls look really cheerful *in the photograph.*
opposites **unhappy, sad**

A common simile is as happy as a lark.

FOR A **VERY HAPPY MOOD**
thrilled, ecstatic, elated, overjoyed
(informal) over the moon, thrilled to bits, tickled pink
Sandy was ecstatic *when she won first prize.*

FOR A **HAPPY TIME** OR **HAPPY EXPERIENCE**
enjoyable, joyous, glorious, blissful, heavenly, idyllic
They spent a glorious *summer on the island.*

FOR A **HAPPY COINCIDENCE**
lucky, fortunate, favourable
By a lucky *coincidence, we took the same train.*
opposite **unfortunate**

TO BE **HAPPY TO DO SOMETHING**
pleased, glad, willing, delighted
I would be glad to help organize the party.
opposite unwilling

harass verb
I keep being harassed with junk email.
pester, trouble, bother, annoy, disturb, plague, torment, badger, hound, hassle

harbour noun
Several yachts were tied up in the harbour.
port, dock, mooring, quay, pier, wharf

hard adjective

OVERUSED WORD
Try to vary the words you use for **hard**. Here are some other words you could use.

FOR **HARD GROUND** OR A **HARD SURFACE**
solid, firm, dense, compact, rigid, stiff
The ground was solid and covered with frost.

Common similes are **as hard as nails** and **as hard as a rock**.
opposite soft

FOR A **HARD PULL** OR **HARD PUSH**
strong, forceful, heavy, powerful, violent
Try giving the door a heavy push.
opposite light

FOR **HARD WORK**
tough, gruelling, strenuous, tiring, exhausting, laborious, back-breaking
Digging the tunnel was strenuous work.
opposite easy

FOR A **HARD WORKER**
energetic, keen, diligent
The elves are very diligent workers.
opposite lazy

FOR A **HARD PERSON** OR **HARD TREATMENT**
strict, stern, harsh, severe, cruel, hard-hearted, heartless, unfeeling, unkind
Cinderella's sisters were heartless and selfish.
opposite mild

FOR A **HARD PROBLEM** OR **HARD QUESTION**
difficult, complicated, complex, intricate, perplexing, puzzling, baffling, knotty, thorny
None of us could solve the complex riddle.
opposite simple

hard adverb
1 *Ros is working hard at learning French.*
strenuously, energetically, diligently, keenly, intently
2 *It has been raining hard all afternoon.*
heavily, steadily
(informal) **cats and dogs**

harden verb
We left the cement to harden.
set, solidify, stiffen
If you harden clay in a kiln, you **bake** or **fire** it.
opposite soften

hardly adverb
I could hardly see in the fog.
barely, scarcely, only just, with difficulty

hardship noun
They suffered years of hardship during the war.
suffering, trouble, difficulty, distress, misery, misfortune, need, want

hardy adjective
You must be hardy to go camping in winter.
tough, strong, robust, sturdy, hearty, rugged
opposite tender

harm verb
1 *His captors didn't harm him.*
hurt, injure, ill-treat, wound

A B C D E F G **H** I J K L M N O P Q R S T U V W X Y Z

2 *Too much sunlight may* harm *this plant.*
damage, spoil, ruin

harm noun
I didn't mean to cause him any harm.
damage, hurt, injury, pain
opposite **benefit**

harmful adjective
Junk food can be harmful *to your health.*
damaging, dangerous, destructive, injurious, unhealthy
opposites **harmless, beneficial**

harmless adjective
1 *You can drink the potion—it is quite* harmless.
safe, non-toxic, innocuous
opposites **harmful, dangerous**
2 *It was just a bit of* harmless *fun.*
innocent, inoffensive

harsh adjective
1 *The trumpet sounded loud and* harsh.
rough, rasping, grating, jarring, shrill, raucous
opposites **soft, gentle**
2 *We blinked in the* harsh *light.*
bright, brilliant, dazzling, glaring
opposites **soft, subdued**
3 *The rescue team braved the* harsh *weather.*
severe, strict, cruel, hard, tough, bleak
opposite **mild**
4 *The coach had some* harsh *words to say.*
strong, sharp, unkind, unfriendly, strict

harvest noun
There was a good harvest *of apples this year.*
crop, yield, return
Things grown on a farm are **produce**.
A plentiful harvest is a **bumper harvest**.

haste noun
The elves worked with great haste.
hurry, rush, speed, urgency

hasty adjective
1 *The robbers made a* hasty *exit.*
fast, hurried, quick, sudden, swift, rapid, speedy
opposite **slow**

2 *The king regretted his* hasty *decision.*
rash, reckless, impatient, foolhardy, thoughtless
opposites **careful, measured**

hat noun

WORD WEB

SOME KINDS OF HAT
balaclava, baseball cap, beanie, bearskin, beret, bicycle helmet, bonnet, bowler hat, cap, deerstalker, fez, hard hat, helmet, kufi, mitre, mortar board, panama hat, skullcap, sombrero, sou'wester, Stetson, sun hat, tam o' shanter, top hat, trilby, turban, woolly hat

baseball cap

woolly hat

fascinator

beanie

bicycle helmet

hard hat

hatch verb
The gang hatched a plot to rob a bank.
plan, develop, conceive, think up, devise
(informal) cook up, dream up

hate verb
1 *Eddie hates broccoli and peas.*
dislike, detest, despise, loathe
2 *I hate to bother you.*
be sorry, be reluctant, regret
opposites like, love

hate noun
Washing dishes is one of my pet hates.
dislike

hatred noun
The evil wizard stared with hatred in his eyes.
hate, loathing, dislike, hostility, enmity,
contempt, detestation
opposite love

haughty adjective
Celia sniffed and gave us a haughty look.
proud, arrogant, conceited, lofty, superior,
pompous, disdainful
(informal) stuck-up
opposite modest

haul verb
Eric hauled his bike out of the shed.
drag, pull, tow, draw

haunt verb
For things a ghost might do see **ghost**

have verb has, having, had
1 *I have my own CD player.*
own, possess
2 *Our house has three bedrooms.*
consist of, comprise, include, incorporate
3 *We are having a barbecue at the weekend.*
hold, organize, provide, host, throw
4 *Dad had trouble finding a place to park.*
experience, go through, meet with,
run into, face, suffer
5 *The girls had a great time at the party.*
experience, enjoy
6 *The BBC has had lots of email messages.*
receive, get, be given, be sent

7 *Sharon had the last toffee.*
take, consume, eat
8 *One of the giraffes has had a baby.*
give birth to, bear, produce
9 *I have to be home by six o'clock.*
must, need, ought, should

haven noun
The lake is a haven for wild birds.
refuge, shelter, retreat, sanctuary

havoc noun
The pixies were causing havoc in the kitchen.
chaos, mayhem, disorder, disruption

hazard noun
The road through the mountains is full of hazards.
danger, risk, threat, trap, pitfall, snag

hazardous adjective
They made the hazardous journey to the South Pole.
dangerous, risky, unsafe, perilous, precarious
opposite safe

haze noun
I could hardly see through the haze.
fog, mist, cloud, steam, vapour

hazy adjective
1 *The face in the photograph was rather hazy.*
blurred, misty, unclear, dim, faint
opposites clear, sharp
2 *I have a hazy memory of that day.*
uncertain, vague
opposites clear, strong

head noun
1 *My dad hit his head on the attic ceiling.*
skull, crown
(informal) nut
For other parts of your body see **body**
2 *Can you add up these figures in your head?*
brain, mind, intellect, intelligence
3 *There is a new head of the music department.*
chief, leader, manager, director, controller
(informal) boss

a
b
c
d
e
f
g
h
i
j
k
l
m
n
o
p
q
r
s
t
u
v
w
x
y
z

A

4 *The girls waited at the head of the queue.*
front, lead, top
opposites **back, rear**

B

head verb
The professor was chosen to head the expedition.
lead, be in charge of, direct, command, manage, oversee, supervise
to head for
At the end of the day we headed for home.
go towards, make for, aim for

C

D

E

F

G

heading noun
Each chapter had a different heading.
title, caption, headline

H

headlong adjective
We made a headlong dash to get under cover.
quick, hurried, hasty, breakneck

I

J

K

headquarters plural noun
The spy contacted headquarters for instructions.
base, head office
(informal) **HQ**

L

M

N

head teacher noun
The head teacher runs the school.
headmaster or headmistress, principal

O

P

heal verb
1 *It took two months for my leg to heal properly.*
get better, mend, recover
2 *Part of a vet's job is to heal sick animals.*
cure, make better, treat, restore

Q

R

S

T

health noun
The puppies are in excellent health.
condition, fitness, shape, strength, vigour, well-being
For various medical treatments see **medicine**

U

V

W

healthy adjective
1 *Neil has always been a healthy child.*
well, fit, strong, sturdy, vigorous, robust
(informal) **in good shape**
opposites **ill, sickly**

X

Y

Z

2 *Porridge makes a very healthy breakfast.*
health-giving, wholesome, invigorating
opposite **unhealthy**

heap noun
There was an untidy heap of clothes on the floor.
mound, pile, stack, mountain, collection, mass

heap verb
We heaped up all the rubbish in the corner.
pile, stack, collect, bank, mass

hear verb hears, hearing, heard
1 *Did you hear what she said?*
catch, listen to, make out, pick up, overhear, pay attention to
A sound that you can hear is audible.
A sound that you cannot hear is inaudible.
2 *Have you heard the news?*
be told, discover, find out, learn, gather

heart noun
1 *Have you no heart?*
compassion, feeling, sympathy, tenderness, affection, humanity, kindness, love
2 *The hotel is located right in the heart of the city.*
centre, middle, hub
3 *They tried to get to the heart of the problem.*
core, essence

heartless adjective
How could she be so heartless?
hard-hearted, callous, cruel, inhuman, unfeeling, unkind, pitiless, ruthless
opposite **kind**

hearty adjective
1 *He gave me a hearty slap on the back.*
strong, forceful, vigorous
opposite **feeble**
2 *The girls had a hearty appetite after their walk.*
big, healthy
opposite **poor**
3 *Our friends gave us a hearty welcome.*
enthusiastic, sincere, warm
opposite **unenthusiastic**

heat noun
1 *The cat basked in the heat of the fire.*
warmth, glow
2 *Last summer, the heat made me feel ill.*
hot weather, high temperatures, closeness
A long period of hot weather is a **heatwave.**

heave verb
The men heaved the sacks onto a lorry.
haul, drag, pull, draw, tow, tug, hoist, lug,
lift, raise, throw

heavy adjective
1 *The box was too heavy for me to lift.*
weighty, massive, dense, bulky
2 *Digging the garden is heavy work.*
hard, tough, gruelling, back-breaking,
strenuous
3 *This book makes heavy reading.*
serious, intense, demanding
4 *The rain has caused heavy flooding.*
severe, extreme, torrential
5 *Both sides suffered heavy losses in the
battle.*
large, substantial, considerable
6 *A heavy mist hung over the landscape.*
dense, thick
opposite light
with a heavy heart
She said goodbye with a heavy heart.
unhappily, sadly, sorrowfully, gloomily,
in low spirits

hectic adjective
The days before the wedding were hectic.
busy, frantic, feverish, frenzied, chaotic
(informal) manic
opposites quiet, leisurely

heed verb
The sailors didn't heed the captain's warning.
listen to, pay attention to, take notice of,
attend to, regard, obey, follow, mark, mind,
note
opposite ignore

hefty adjective
1 *The postman was carrying a hefty parcel.*
big, large, weighty, massive, bulky

2 *The wrestler was a hefty man.*
strong, sturdy, muscular, powerful, brawny,
burly, hulking
(informal) beefy
opposite slight

height noun
1 *The plane was flying at its normal height.*
altitude, elevation
2 *His height wasn't a problem.*
tallness, size, stature

held
past tense see **hold**

help noun
1 *Thank you for your help.*
aid, assistance, support, guidance,
cooperation, advice
opposite hindrance
2 *Would a torch be of any help to you?*
use, benefit

help verb
1 *Could you please help me with my luggage?*
aid, assist, cooperate with
(informal) give a hand to
2 *The Red Cross is an organization that helps
people in need.*
be helpful to, support, serve, stand by
3 *This medicine will help your cough.*
make better, cure, ease, relieve, improve
opposites aggravate, worsen
4 *I can't help coughing.*
stop, avoid, prevent, refrain from

helpful adjective
1 *The staff were friendly and helpful.*
obliging, cooperative, kind, considerate,
thoughtful, sympathetic
opposite unhelpful
2 *The waiter gave us some helpful advice.*
useful, valuable, worthwhile, beneficial,
profitable
opposite worthless

helping noun
I got a huge helping of ice cream.
serving, portion, plateful, amount, share,
ration

a
b
c
d
e
f
g
h
i
j
k
l
m
n
o
p
q
r
s
t
u
v
w
x
y
z

A

helpless adjective
Kittens are born blind and helpless.
powerless, weak, feeble, dependent,
defenceless, vulnerable
opposites **independent, strong**

B

C

D

hem verb
to hem someone in
The bus was hemmed in *by some parked cars.*
shut in, box in, encircle, enclose,
surround

E

F

G

herb noun

H

WORD WEB

SOME COMMON HERBS
basil, chamomile, caraway, chervil,
chicory, chive, coriander, cumin, dill,
fennel, fenugreek, hyssop, lemon balm,
liquorice, lovage, marjoram, mint,
oregano, parsley, peppermint, rosemary,
sage, tarragon, thyme

I

J

K

L

M

N

herd noun
For groups of animals see **group**

O

heroic adjective
The firefighters made a heroic *effort to put out the blaze.*
bold, brave, courageous, daring, fearless,
noble, selfless, valiant
opposite **cowardly**

P

Q

R

hesitant adjective
The puppy was hesitant *about going outside.*
uncertain, unsure, doubtful, cautious,
tentative, timid, shy, wary
opposite **confident**

S

T

U

hesitate verb
I hesitated *for a moment before ringing the doorbell.*
pause, delay, wait, hold back, dither,
falter, waver
(informal) think twice

V

W

X

Y

Z

hidden adjective
1 *The giant kept his gold* hidden *in a wooden chest.*
concealed, out of sight, unseen, invisible,
covered, disguised
opposite **visible**
2 *There's a* hidden *message in the riddle.*
secret, mysterious, obscure, coded, cryptic
opposite **obvious**

hide verb hides, hiding, hid, hidden
1 *Quick! Someone's coming—we'd better* hide.
go into hiding, take cover, take refuge,
keep out of sight, lie low, go to ground
2 *They hid the jewels in a secret drawer.*
conceal, secrete, bury
(informal) stash
opposite **expose**
3 *The clouds hid the sun.*
blot out, cover, screen, shroud, veil, mask
opposite **uncover**
4 *I tried to* hide *my feelings.*
disguise, keep secret, suppress,
camouflage, cloak
opposite **show**

hideous adjective
The troll had a hideous *grin on his face.*
repulsive, revolting, ugly, grotesque,
monstrous, ghastly, gruesome, horrible,
appalling, dreadful, frightful
opposite **beautiful**

high adjective
1 *The castle was surrounded by a* high *wall.*
tall, towering, elevated, lofty
opposite **low**
2 *Sir Grinalot was a knight of* high *rank and status.*
senior, top, leading, important, prominent,
powerful
opposites **low, junior**
3 *House prices are very* high *at the moment.*
expensive, dear, costly, excessive
opposite **low**
4 *A* high *wind was blowing.*
strong, powerful, forceful, extreme
opposite **gentle**

5 *The pixie spoke in a* **high** *squeaky voice.*
high-pitched, sharp, shrill, piercing
opposite deep
A high singing voice is **soprano** or **treble**.

highlight noun
The **highlight** *of the holiday was spotting a wild dolphin.*
high point, high spot, best moment, climax

highly adverb
It is **highly** *unusual to see badgers during the day.*
very, extremely, exceptionally, considerably, decidedly

hike verb & noun
We often go **hiking** *across the moors.*
trek, walk, ramble, tramp

hilarious adjective
The boys thought the cartoon was **hilarious**.
funny, amusing, comical
(informal) **hysterical**

hill noun
1 *From the top of this* **hill** *you can see for miles.*
mount, peak, ridge
A small hill is a **hillock** or **mound**.
The top of a hill is the **summit**.
2 *Jenny pushed her bike up the steep* **hill**.
slope, rise, incline, ascent, gradient

hinder verb
The snowstorm **hindered** *the rescue attempt.*
hamper, hold up, obstruct, impede, slow down, stand in the way of, restrict, handicap
opposite help

hindrance noun
The sharks were a **hindrance** *to the divers.*
obstacle, obstruction, handicap, drawback, inconvenience, difficulty, disadvantage,
opposite help

hint noun
1 *I don't know the answer—can you give me a* **hint**?
clue, indication, sign, suggestion, inkling

2 *The magazine offers handy* **hints** *for decorating.*
tip, pointer

hint verb
Mum **hinted** *that we might be getting a puppy.*
give a hint, suggest, imply, indicate

hire verb
If you hire a bus or aircraft you **charter** it.
If you hire someone to do a job you **engage** or **employ** them.
If you hire a building for a time you **lease** or **rent** it.

historic adjective

Take care not to confuse **historic**, which means famous or important in history, with **historical**, which simply refers to anything that happened in the past.

The first landing on the Moon was a **historic** *event.*
famous, notable, celebrated, important, renowned, momentous, significant, major
opposite unimportant

historical adjective

See note at **historic**.

Robin Hood may have been a **historical** *character.*
real, real-life, true, actual, authentic
opposite fictitious

history noun
1 *Dr Rice is an expert on Egyptian* **history**.
heritage, past, antiquity, past times, olden days
2 *He wrote a* **history** *of the First World War.*
account, chronicle, record
The history of a person's life is their **biography**.
The history of your own life is your **autobiography** or **memoirs**.

a
b
c
d
e
f
g
h
i
j
k
l
m
n
o
p
q
r
s
t
u
v
w
x
y
z

hit noun

1 *Matt got a nasty hit on the head.*
bump, blow, bang, knock, whack
A hit with your fist is a punch.
A hit with your open hand is a slap or smack.
A hit with a bat or club is a drive, stroke, or swipe.
2 *Their new CD was an instant hit.*
success, triumph
(informal) winner

hit verb hits, hitting, hit

1 *Auntie Flo hit the burglar on the head with her umbrella.*
strike, knock, bang, bash, thump, bump, crack, rap, slam, swipe, slog, cuff
(informal) whack, wham, wallop, sock, clout, clobber, belt, biff
(old use) smite
To hit with your fist is to punch.
To hit with the palm of your hand is to slap or smack.
To punish someone by hitting them is to beat them.
To hit someone with a stick is to club them.
To hit your toe on something is to stub it.
To kill an insect by hitting it is to swat it.
To hit something repeatedly is to batter, buffet, or pound it.
To hit something gently is to tap it.
For ways to hit a ball see ball
2 *The drought has hit many farms in the area.*
affect, damage, harm, hurt

hoard noun

Hamish keeps a hoard of sweets in his desk.
cache, store, stock, supply, pile, stockpile
A hoard of treasure is a treasure trove.

hoard verb

Squirrels hoard nuts for the winter.
store, collect, gather, save, put by, pile up, stockpile
(informal) stash away

hoarse adjective

Mr Barker's voice was hoarse from shouting.
rough, harsh, husky, croaky, throaty, gruff, rasping, gravelly

hoax noun

The telephone call was a hoax.
joke, practical joke, prank, trick, spoof
(informal) con, scam

hobby noun

My favourite hobby is snorkelling.
pastime, pursuit, interest, activity, recreation

hoist verb

The crane hoisted the crates onto a ship.
lift, pull up, raise, heave, winch up

hold noun

The vet took a firm hold of the dog's collar.
grip, grasp, clutch, clasp

hold verb holds, holding, held

1 *Please hold the dog's lead.*
clasp, grasp, grip, cling to, hang on to, clutch, seize
2 *Can I hold the baby?*
embrace, hug, cradle
3 *They held the suspect until the police arrived.*
confine, detain, keep
4 *Will the ladder hold my weight?*
bear, support, carry, take
5 *If our luck holds, we could reach the final.*
continue, last, carry on, persist, stay
6 *She holds strong opinions.*
believe in, maintain, stick to
to hold out
1 *The robot held out one of his arms.*
extend, reach out, stick out, stretch out
2 *Our supplies won't hold out much longer.*
keep going, last, carry on, continue, endure
to hold something up
1 *Please hold up your hand.*
lift, put up, raise
2 *The accident held up the traffic.*
delay, hinder, slow down

hole noun

1 *The meteor created a massive hole in the ground.*
pit, hollow, crater, dent, depression, cavity, chasm, abyss

A
B
C
D
E
F
G
H
I
J
K
L
M
N
O
P
Q
R
S
T
U
V
W
X
Y
Z

2 *The rabbits escaped through a* **hole** *in the fence.*
gap, opening, breach, break, cut, slit, gash, split, tear, vent

holiday noun
We spent our summer **holiday** *in Ireland.*
vacation, break, leave, time off

hollow adjective
Tennis balls are **hollow.**
empty, unfilled
opposite **solid**

hollow noun
The ball rolled into a **hollow** *in the ground.*
dip, dent, depression, hole, pit, crater
A **hollow** *between two hills is a* **valley.**

hollow verb
We **hollowed** *out a pumpkin to make a Halloween lantern.*
dig, excavate, gouge, scoop

holy adjective
1 *The pilgrims knelt to pray in the* **holy** *shrine.*
sacred, blessed, revered
2 *The pilgrims were* **holy** *people.*
religious, spiritual, devout, pious, godly, saintly

home noun
The hurricane forced people to flee their **homes.**
house, residence, dwelling, abode, lodging
A **home** *for the sick is a* **convalescent home** *or* **nursing home.**
A place where a bird or animal lives is its **habitat.**
See also **house**
For homes of wild animals see **animal**

homely adjective
The hotel was small with a **homely** *atmosphere.*
friendly, informal, cosy, familiar, relaxed, easy-going, comfortable, simple

honest adjective
1 *He's an* **honest** *boy, so he gave the money back.*
good, honourable, law-abiding, moral,
trustworthy, upright, virtuous
opposite **dishonest**
2 *Please give me your* **honest** *opinion.*
sincere, genuine, truthful, direct, frank, candid, plain, straightforward, unbiased
opposite **insincere**

honour noun
1 *Her success brought* **honour** *to the school.*
credit, good reputation, good name, respect, praise, acclaim
2 *It's an* **honour** *to meet you.*
privilege, distinction

honour verb
The winners were **honoured** *at a special ceremony.*
praise, celebrate, salute, give credit to, pay tribute to, glorify

honourable adjective
1 *The knight was an* **honourable** *man.*
good, honest, sincere, noble, principled, moral, righteous, trustworthy, upright, virtuous, worthy, decent, fair, trusty
2 *It was an* **honourable** *thing to do.*
noble, admirable, praiseworthy, decent
opposite **unworthy**

hook verb
1 *Dad* **hooked** *the trailer to the car.*
attach, fasten, hitch, connect, couple
2 *The angler* **hooked** *an enormous fish.*
catch, land, take

hop verb
The goblins **hopped** *about in excitement.*
jump, leap, skip, spring, prance, caper, bound, dance

hope verb
I **hope** *to see you again soon.*
wish, trust, expect, look forward

hope noun
1 *Her dearest* **hope** *was to see her family again.*
ambition, dream, desire, wish
2 *There's* **hope** *of better weather tomorrow.*
prospect, expectation, likelihood

a
b
c
d
e
f
g
h
i
j
k
l
m
n
o
p
q
r
s
t
u
v
w
x
y
z

A B C D E F G H I J K L M N O P Q R S T U V W X Y Z

hopeful adjective
1 *I am feeling* hopeful *about tomorrow's match.*
optimistic, confident, positive, expectant
opposite **pessimistic**
2 *The future is beginning to look more hopeful.*
promising, encouraging, favourable, reassuring
opposite **discouraging**

hopeless adjective
1 *The shipwrecked crew were in a* hopeless *situation.*
desperate, wretched, beyond hope
opposite **hopeful**
2 *I'm* hopeless *at ice-skating.*
bad, poor, incompetent
(informal) useless, rubbish
opposites **good, competent**

horde noun
Hordes of people were queuing for tickets.
crowd, throng, mob, swarm, gang, group

horizontal adjective
Lay the pole on the ground in a horizontal *position.*
flat, level
opposite **vertical**

horrible adjective
What a horrible *smell!*
awful, terrible, dreadful, appalling, unpleasant, disagreeable, offensive, objectionable, disgusting, repulsive, revolting, horrendous, horrid, nasty, hateful, odious, loathsome, beastly, ghastly
opposite **pleasant**

horrific adjective
The film has some horrific *scenes of battle.*
horrifying, terrifying, shocking, gruesome, dreadful, appalling, ghastly, hideous, atrocious, grisly, sickening

horrify verb
We were horrified *by the sight of the monster.*
appal, shock, terrify, frighten, alarm, scare, sicken, disgust

horror noun
1 *Ingrid screamed in* horror *when she saw the snake.*
terror, fear, fright, alarm, dread
2 *The film depicts the full* horror *of war.*
awfulness, hideousness, gruesomeness, ghastliness, frightfulness

horse noun
A male horse is a stallion and a female is a mare.
A young horse is a foal, colt (male), or filly (female).
An uncomplimentary word for a horse is nag.
A poetic word for a horse is steed.
A word meaning 'to do with horses' is equine.
A cross between a donkey and a horse is a mule.

WORD WEB

SOME TYPES OF HORSE
bronco, carthorse, Clydesdale, mustang, piebald, pony, racehorse, Shetland pony, shire horse, warhorse

NOISES MADE BY A HORSE
neigh, snicker, snort, whinny

WAYS A HORSE CAN MOVE
canter, gallop, trot, walk

PARTS OF A HORSE'S HARNESS
bit, blinker, bridle, girth, noseband, pommel, rein, saddle, stirrups

SPORTS AND ACTIVITIES INVOLVING HORSES
gymkhana, horse-racing, jousting, rodeo, polo, showjumping, steeplechase

A person who rides a horse in a race is a jockey.
A word meaning 'to do with horse riding' is equestrian.
Soldiers who fight on horseback are cavalry.
An old word for a cavalry horse was a charger.
Please see illustration on following page.

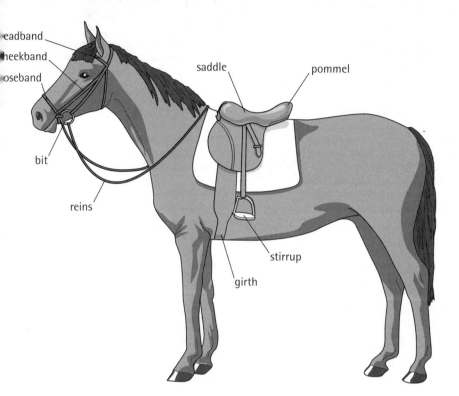

headband
cheekband
noseband
saddle
pommel
bit
reins
stirrup
girth

a
b
c
d
e
f
g
h
i
j
k
l
m
n
o
p
q
r
s
t
u
v
w
x
y
z

hospital noun

WORD WEB

PLACES WHERE PEOPLE GO FOR MEDICAL TREATMENT
clinic, convalescent home, hospice, infirmary, nursing home, sanatorium

PARTS OF A HOSPITAL
accident and emergency, dispensary, intensive care unit, operating theatre, outpatients, pharmacy, X-ray department, ward

See also **medicine**

hostile adjective
1 *The warriors shook their weapons in a* hostile *manner.*
aggressive, antagonistic, unfriendly, unwelcoming, warlike, malevolent
opposite friendly

2 *The North Pole has a very* hostile *climate.*
harsh, unfavourable, adverse, bad
opposite favourable

hostility noun
The hostility *between the two players was obvious.*
dislike, enmity, hate, hatred, aggression, antagonism, bad feeling, detestation, ill-will, unfriendliness, malice
opposite friendship

hot adjective
1 *The weather has been* hot *this summer.*
warm, balmy, blazing, roasting, scorching, blistering, sweltering, stifling
opposites cold, cool
2 *Careful—the soup's really* hot.
burning, boiling, baking hot, piping hot, scalding, searing, sizzling, steaming
opposites cold, cool

A B C D E F G **H** I J K L M N O P Q R S T U V W X Y Z

3 *I like curry, but only if it's not too* hot.
spicy, peppery, fiery
opposite **mild**
4 *My sister, Diana, has a* hot *temper.*
fierce, fiery, violent, passionate, raging, angry, intense
opposites **calm, mild**

house noun

WORD WEB

WORDS FOR THE PLACE YOU LIVE IN
abode, dwelling, home, lodging, quarters, residence

BUILDINGS WHERE PEOPLE LIVE
apartment, bungalow, chalet, cottage, council house, croft, detached house, farmhouse, flat, hovel, hut, igloo, lodge, manor, manse, mansion, rectory, semi-detached house, shack, shanty, tenement, terraced house, thatched house, vicarage, villa

For rooms in a house see room

house verb
The farm animals are housed *indoors during the winter.*
accommodate, lodge, shelter, take in, quarter, board

hover verb
1 *A flock of seagulls* hovered *overhead.*
fly, flutter, float, hang, drift
2 *He* hovered *outside the room, afraid to knock.*
linger, pause, wait about, hesitate, dally, loiter, dither
(informal) hang about

however adverb
1 *I couldn't lift the stone,* however *hard I tried.*
no matter how
2 *Spiders' silk is thin;* however*, it is also strong.*
nevertheless, nonetheless, yet, still, even so

howl verb
1 *The injured boy* howled *in pain.*
cry, yell, scream, yelp, shriek, wail
2 *They heard wolves* howling *in the night.*
bay, yowl

huddle verb
The penguins huddled *together to get warm.*
crowd, gather, flock, cluster, squeeze, pack, nestle, cuddle, snuggle
opposite **scatter**

hue noun
The alien's face turned a strange hue *of green.*
colour, shade, tint, tone, tinge
For various colours see colour

hug verb
Ellie was hugging *her favourite teddy bear.*
cuddle, clasp, embrace, cling to, squeeze

huge adjective
Elephants are huge *animals.*
enormous, gigantic, massive, colossal, giant, immense, vast, mighty, mammoth, monumental, hulking, great, big, large
(informal) whopping, ginormous, humongous
opposites **small, little, tiny**

hum verb
We heard insects humming *in the air.*
buzz, drone, murmur, purr, whirr

humane adjective
A humane *society should treat animals well.*
kind, compassionate, sympathetic, civilized, benevolent, kind-hearted, charitable, loving, merciful
opposite **cruel**

humans plural noun
Humans have smaller brains than whales.
human beings, the human race, humanity, mankind, people

humble adjective
1 *The gentle giant was both* humble *and kind.*
modest, meek, unassuming, polite, respectful, submissive
opposite **proud**

2 *Hansel and Gretel lived in a* humble *cottage.*
simple, modest, plain, ordinary,
commonplace, lowly
opposite grand

humid adjective
I don't like this humid *weather.*
muggy, clammy, close, sticky, steamy,
sweaty
opposite fresh

humiliate verb
He humiliated her in front of her friends.
embarrass, disgrace, shame, make ashamed,
humble, crush, degrade
(informal) put you in your place,
take you down a peg

humiliating adjective
The team suffered a humiliating *defeat.*
embarrassing, crushing, degrading,
humbling, undignified
opposite glorious

humorous adjective
My friend told me a humorous *story.*
amusing, funny, comic, witty,
entertaining
opposite serious

humour noun
1 *I liked the* humour *in the film.*
comedy, wit, amusement, jokes
2 *The ogre was in a very bad* humour.
mood, temper, disposition, frame of mind,
spirits

hump noun
Camels have humps *on their backs.*
bump, lump, bulge, swelling

hunch¹ noun
The detective had a hunch *about the murder.*
feeling, intuition, inkling, guess,
impression, suspicion, idea

hunch² verb
Will hunched *his shoulders to keep out the
cold.*
arch, bend, curve, hump, shrug, curl up

hung
past tense see hang

hunger noun
*After a week without food, the crew were
faint with* hunger.
lack of food, starvation, famine
Bad health caused by not having enough
food is **malnutrition**.

hungry adjective
Our dog always seems to be hungry.
starving, famished, ravenous
(informal) peckish

hunt noun
Police have begun the hunt *for clues.*
search, quest, chase, pursuit

hunt verb
1 *Some Native Americans used to* hunt
buffalo.
chase, pursue, track, trail, hound, stalk
An animal which hunts other animals for
food is a **predator**.
2 *I* hunted *in the attic for our old photos.*
search, seek, look, rummage, ferret,
root around

hurdle noun
1 *The horse jumped over the* hurdle
easily.
fence, barrier, jump, barricade,
obstacle
2 *The biggest* hurdle *facing the team is lack
of experience.*
difficulty, problem, handicap, hindrance,
snag, stumbling block

hurl verb
I hurled *the ball as far as I could.*
throw, fling, pitch, toss, cast, sling, launch
(informal) chuck

hurry verb
1 *If you want to catch the bus, you'd better
hurry.*
be quick, hasten, make speed
(informal) get a move on, step on it
opposite dawdle

a
b
c
d
e
f
g
h
i
j
k
l
m
n
o
p
q
r
s
t
u
v
w
x
y
z

2 *Alice saw the White Rabbit* hurrying *past.*
rush, dash, fly, speed, hurtle, scurry
opposites **amble, stroll**
3 *It's no good trying to* hurry *a donkey.*
quicken, speed up, urge on
opposite **slow down**

hurry noun
In our hurry, *we forgot the tickets.*
rush, haste, speed, urgency

hurt verb
1 *Be careful not to* hurt *yourself with the scissors.*
harm, injure, damage, wound, maim
To hurt someone deliberately is to **torment** or **torture** them.
2 *My feet* hurt.
be sore, be painful, ache, throb, sting, smart
3 *Your letter* hurt *me deeply.*
upset, distress, offend, grieve

hurtful adjective
That was a very hurtful *remark.*
upsetting, unkind, cruel, mean, painful, spiteful, nasty

hurtle verb
The train hurtled *along at top speed.*
rush, speed, race, dash, fly, charge, tear, shoot, zoom

husband noun
Hugh is Mrs Hart's fourth husband.
Another word for a person's husband or wife is spouse.

hush verb
The speaker tried his best to hush *the crowd.*
silence, quieten, settle, still, calm
to hush something up
They tried to hush up *the scandal.*
cover up, hide, conceal, keep quiet, keep secret, suppress

husky adjective
The wizard spoke in a husky *voice.*
hoarse, throaty, gruff, rasping, gravelly, rough, croaky

hut noun
The walkers came across a hut *in the forest.*
shed, shack, cabin, den, shelter, shanty, hovel

hygienic adjective
Always use a hygienic *surface for chopping food.*
sanitary, clean, disinfected, sterilized, sterile, germ-free, healthy
opposite **unhygienic**

hysterical adjective
1 *The fans became* hysterical *when the band appeared.*
crazy, frenzied, mad, delirious, raving, wild, uncontrollable
2 *(informal) We laughed at the* hysterical *jokes in the film.*
hilarious, funny, amusing, comical

I i

ice noun

WORD WEB

VARIOUS FORMS OF ICE
black ice, floe, frost, glacier, iceberg, ice sheet, icicle

WAYS TO DESCRIBE ICE
brittle, cracked, frozen solid, glacial, glassy, gleaming, glinting, hard, packed, slippery or (informal) **slippy, smooth, treacherous**

THINGS YOU MIGHT DO ON ICE
glide, skate, skid, slide, slip, slither

SPORTS THAT ARE PLAYED ON ICE
curling, figure skating, ice skating, ice hockey, speed skating

Ice sports are played on an **ice rink**.

icy adjective
1 *You need to dress warmly in* icy *weather.*
cold, freezing, frosty, wintry, arctic, bitter, biting
2 *Icy roads are dangerous.*
frozen, slippery, glacial, glassy
(informal) slippy

idea noun
1 *I've got a great* idea!
plan, scheme, proposal, suggestion, inspiration
2 *She has some funny* ideas *about life.*
belief, notion, opinion, view, theory, concept, conception, hypothesis
3 *What's the main* idea *of this poem?*
point, meaning, intention, thought
4 *Give me an* idea *of what you are planning.*
clue, hint, inkling, impression

ideal adjective
It's ideal *weather for a picnic.*
perfect, excellent, the best, faultless, suitable

identical adjective
The twins were wearing identical *clothes.*
matching, similar, alike, indistinguishable
opposite different

identify verb
1 *The police asked if I could* identify *the thief.*
recognize, name, distinguish, pick out, single out
2 *The doctor couldn't* identify *what was wrong.*
diagnose, discover, spot
(informal) put a name to
to identify with
Can you identify with *the hero of the story?*
sympathize with, feel for, understand
(informal) put yourself in the shoes of

idiotic adjective
That was an idiotic *thing to do.*
stupid, silly, foolish, unwise, senseless, ridiculous, half-witted, unintelligent, crazy, mad, hare-brained, daft
opposite sensible

idle adjective
1 *The ogre was an* idle, *foul-smelling creature.*
lazy, indolent, slothful, work-shy
opposite hard-working
2 *The computers lay* idle *all week.*
inactive, unused, inoperative
opposites busy, active

idol noun
1 *The floor of the temple was littered with broken* idols.
god, deity, image, statue
2 *He was a pop* idol *of the fifties.*
star, celebrity, icon, pin-up, favourite

idolize verb
Kirsty idolizes *her big brother.*
adore, love, worship, be devoted to, look up to

ignite verb
The matches were wet and would not ignite.
light, catch fire, burn, kindle, spark

ignorant adjective
Trolls are often described as ignorant *creatures.*
uneducated, simple, stupid
ignorant of
Detective Miles was ignorant of *the facts in the case.*
unaware of, unfamiliar with, unacquainted with
opposite aware of

ignore verb
Ignoring the weather, Lynn went for a walk.
disregard, take no notice of, overlook, neglect, spurn, snub
(informal) turn a blind eye to

ill adjective
1 *I missed school for a week when I was* ill.
sick, unwell, poorly, sickly, ailing, infirm, unfit, indisposed, diseased, infected, nauseous, queasy, off colour, peaky
(informal) under the weather
For common illnesses see illness
opposites healthy, well

a
b
c
d
e
f
g
h
i
j
k
l
m
n
o
p
q
r
s
t
u
v
w
x
y
z

213

A B C D E F G H I J K L M N O P Q R S T U V W X Y Z

2 *Did the plants suffer* ill *effects in the frost?*
bad, harmful, adverse, damaging
opposite **good**

illegal adjective
Stealing is illegal.
unlawful, against the law, banned,
prohibited, criminal, forbidden, wrong
opposite **legal**

illegible adjective
The signature on the letter was illegible.
unreadable, indecipherable, unclear,
indistinct
opposites **legible, readable**

illness noun
What kind of illness *is he suffering from?*
abnormality, affliction, ailment, attack,
complaint, condition, disability, disease,
disorder, health problem, infection,
infirmity, sickness
(informal) bug, upset
A sudden illness is an attack or fit.
A period of illness is a bout of illness.
A general outbreak of illness in a particular
area is an epidemic.

WORD WEB
SOME COMMON ILLNESSES
allergy, appendicitis, asthma,
bronchitis, chickenpox, chill, cold,
cough, diarrhoea, eczema, fever, flu,
glandular fever, hay fever, headache,
indigestion, influenza, jaundice,
laryngitis, measles, migraine, mumps,
stomach-ache, tonsillitis, ulcer,
whooping cough

For ways to treat illness see medicine

illustrate verb
1 *I used some photos to* illustrate *my story.*
depict, picture, portray
2 *The accident* illustrates *the importance
of road safety.*
show, demonstrate, make clear

illustration noun
1 *I like cookery books with lots of
illustrations.*
picture, photograph, drawing, sketch,
diagram
2 *I'll give you an* illustration *of what I mean.*
example, instance, demonstration,
specimen

image noun
1 *The film contained frightening* images *of
war.*
picture, portrayal, depiction, representation
2 *The temple contained* images *of the gods.*
figure, idol, statue, carving
3 *You can see your* image *in the mirror.*
reflection, likeness
4 *Alice is the* image *of her mother.*
double, twin

imaginary adjective
The story takes place in an imaginary
universe.
imagined, non-existent, unreal, made up,
invented, fanciful, fictitious, fictional
opposite **real**

imagination noun
Use your imagination *to draw an alien
spaceship.*
creativity, inventiveness, ingenuity,
inspiration, originality, vision, artistry,
fancy

imaginative adjective
Roald Dahl wrote highly imaginative
stories.
creative, inventive, inspired, original,
artistic, fanciful, ingenious, clever
opposites **unimaginative, dull**

imagine verb
1 Imagine *what it would be like to visit
Mars.*
picture, visualize, pretend, think up,
dream up, fancy, conjure up
2 *I* imagine *you'd like something to eat.*
suppose, assume, presume, believe, guess

imitate verb
Parrots can imitate the human voice.
copy, reproduce, mimic, mirror, echo,
simulate, impersonate, follow, match
(informal) send up, take off

imitation adjective
The coat was made from imitation leather.
artificial, synthetic, fake, sham, mock
opposites real, genuine

imitation noun
This is an imitation of a Viking helmet.
copy, replica, reproduction, duplicate
An imitation made to deceive someone is a
fake or a forgery.

immature adjective
Tess is quite immature for her age.
childish, babyish, infantile, juvenile
opposite mature

immediate adjective
1 *Please can I have an immediate reply.*
instant, instantaneous, prompt, speedy,
swift, urgent, quick, direct
(informal) snappy
opposite slow
2 *Are you friends with your immediate
neighbours?*
closest, nearest, adjacent, next
opposite distant

immediately adverb
You must fetch a doctor immediately!
at once, now, straight away, right away,
instantly, promptly, directly

immense adjective
The giant wiggled one of his immense toes.
huge, great, massive, enormous, colossal,
vast, giant, gigantic, mighty, mammoth,
monumental, humongous
(informal) whopping, ginormous
opposite tiny

immobile adjective
The knight stood immobile at the castle gate.
unmoving, motionless, stationary, still
opposite mobile

immoral adjective
It would be immoral to steal the money.
wrong, wicked, bad, sinful, dishonest,
corrupt
opposites moral, right

immortal adjective
*The ancient Greeks believed their gods were
immortal.*
undying, ageless, eternal, everlasting
opposite mortal

impact noun
1 *The crater was caused by the impact of a
meteor.*
crash, collision, smash, blow, bump,
bang, knock, jolt
2 *Computers have a big impact on our lives.*
effect, influence

impair verb
Very loud noise can impair your hearing.
damage, harm, injure, weaken

impartial adjective
Referees must be impartial.
neutral, detached, objective, unbiased,
unprejudiced, disinterested,
independent, fair, fair-minded, just,
even-handed, open-minded
opposite biased

impatient adjective
1 *As time went on, Henry grew more and
more impatient.*
restless, agitated, anxious, edgy, fidgety,
irritable, snappy, testy, jumpy
opposite patient
2 *The crowd were impatient for the show to
begin.*
anxious, eager, in a hurry, keen
(informal) itching

imperfect adjective
The items on this shelf are imperfect.
damaged, faulty, defective, flawed, broken,
incomplete
opposite perfect

a
b
c
d
e
f
g
h
i
j
k
l
m
n
o
p
q
r
s
t
u
v
w
x
y
z

impertinent adjective
The elf made some rather impertinent *remarks.*
rude, cheeky, impolite, impudent, insolent, disrespectful
opposites **respectful, polite**

implement noun
The shed is full of garden implements.
tool, appliance, device, utensil, gadget, instrument
See also **tool**

implore verb
Jack implored *the giant not to eat him.*
beg, entreat, plead with

imply verb

> See note at **infer**.

Are you implying *that I am a liar?*
suggest, hint, indicate

impolite adjective
It would be impolite *to refuse the invitation.*
rude, bad-mannered, discourteous, disrespectful, insulting
opposite **polite**

import verb
The UK imports *tea and coffee.*
bring in, ship in
opposite **export**

important adjective
1 *The World Cup is an* important *sporting event.*
major, significant, big, central, momentous, outstanding, historic
2 *I have some* important *business to attend to.*
serious, urgent, pressing, weighty, vital, essential, crucial
3 *The prime minister is an* important *person.*
prominent, powerful, influential, notable, eminent, distinguished
opposites **unimportant, minor**

impose verb
The government imposed *a tax on fuel.*
introduce, enforce, fix, inflict, prescribe, set
to impose on
I don't want to impose on *you.*
inconvenience, intrude on, take advantage of

imposing adjective
The castle is an imposing *building.*
grand, great, impressive, stately, magnificent, splendid, majestic, dignified, striking
opposite **insignificant**

impossible adjective
We used to think that space travel was impossible.
impractical, unthinkable, unrealistic, unachievable, unworkable, out of the question
opposite **possible**

impress verb
Frank impressed *the coach with his football skills.*
make an impression on, influence, leave its mark on, stick in your mind

impression noun
1 *I had the* impression *that something was wrong.*
feeling, idea, sense, notion, suspicion, hunch
2 *The film made a big* impression *on them.*
effect, impact, influence, mark
3 *My sister does a good* impression *of the Queen.*
imitation, impersonation, (informal) **send-up**

impressive adjective
The film includes some impressive *special effects.*
striking, effective, powerful, remarkable, spectacular, exciting, inspiring
opposites **unimpressive, uninspiring**

A B C D E F G H I J K L M N O P Q R S T U V W X Y Z

imprison verb
The thief was imprisoned for two years.
send to prison, jail, lock up, incarcerate, confine, detain
(informal) put away, send down, put under lock and key
opposite **liberate**

improve verb
1 *Her work improved during the term.*
get better, advance, progress, develop, move on
opposite **deteriorate**
2 *Has he improved since his illness?*
get better, recover, recuperate, pick up, rally, revive
opposite **get worse**
3 *How can I improve this story?*
make better, enhance, refine, amend, revise, correct, upgrade

improvement noun
1 *Your handwriting shows signs of improvement.*
getting better, advance, progress, development, recovery, upturn
2 *The author made some improvements to the book.*
amendment, correction, revision, modification, enhancement

impudent adjective
The pixie had an impudent grin on his face.
cheeky, insolent, rude, impolite, impertinent, disrespectful
opposites **respectful, polite**

impulse noun
I had a sudden impulse to sing out loud.
desire, instinct, urge

impulsive adjective
She regretted her impulsive decision to dye her hair.
hasty, rash, reckless, sudden, spontaneous, thoughtless, unthinking, impetuous
opposite **deliberate**

inaccessible adjective
The caves were in an inaccessible part of the island.
unreachable, isolated, remote, out of the way, hard to find
opposite **accessible**

inaccurate adjective
That spelling of my surname is inaccurate.
wrong, incorrect, mistaken, false, inexact, untrue
opposite **accurate**

inadequate adjective
They had brought an inadequate supply of matches.
insufficient, not enough, limited, scarce, scanty, meagre
opposite **adequate**

inappropriate adjective
It's inappropriate to call the teacher by her first name.
unsuitable, improper, out of place, unfitting, unseemly
opposite **appropriate**

inaudible adjective
see **hear**

incapable adjective
incapable of
Miss Havers is incapable of making a decision.
unable to, incompetent at, unfit to, unsuited to, ineffective at
opposite **capable of**

incident noun
There was an amusing incident at school this morning.
event, happening, occurrence, episode, affair

incidental adjective
Tell us the main story without the incidental details.
unimportant, minor, inessential, secondary, subordinate
opposite **essential**

a
b
c
d
e
f
g
h
i
j
k
l
m
n
o
p
q
r
s
t
u
v
w
x
y
z

A

B

C

D

E

F

G

H

I

J

K

L

M

N

O

P

Q

R

S

T

U

V

W

X

Y

Z

incline noun
The house was at the top of a steep incline.
hill, slope, rise, gradient

inclined adjective
to be inclined to
Ogres are inclined to eat too much.
be disposed to, have a habit of, be liable to, tend to

include verb
Does the cost include postage and packing?
contain, incorporate, comprise, involve, take in, allow for, take into account, cover
opposite exclude

income noun
What is your average monthly income?
pay, salary, wages, earnings
opposite expenditure

incompetent adjective
The actor was so incompetent that he forgot his lines.
unskilful, inept, ineffective, unsatisfactory, useless, hopeless
opposite competent

incomplete adjective
The new football stadium is still incomplete.
unfinished, uncompleted, not ready
opposite complete

inconsiderate adjective
It's inconsiderate to play the radio so loudly.
selfish, unthinking, thoughtless, insensitive, rude, tactless, unkind, uncaring
opposite considerate

inconsistent adjective
1 *His performance has been inconsistent this season.*
changeable, unreliable, variable, unpredictable, erratic, fickle

2 *The stories of the two witnesses are inconsistent.*
contradictory, conflicting, different
opposite consistent

inconspicuous adjective
The spy wore plain clothes to be inconspicuous.
unnoticed, unobtrusive, camouflaged, out of sight
opposite conspicuous

inconvenient adjective
The guests arrived at an inconvenient moment.
awkward, difficult, unsuitable, unfortunate, untimely, inopportune
opposite convenient

incorporate verb
The show incorporates some well-known tunes.
include, contain, embrace, take in
opposite exclude

incorrect adjective
Nine out of ten of his answers were incorrect.
wrong, mistaken, inaccurate, false
opposite correct

increase verb
1 *They've increased the size of the tennis courts.*
make bigger, enlarge, expand, develop, add to, widen, broaden
2 *She increased the cooking time in the recipe.*
extend, lengthen, prolong
3 *The police increased their efforts to find the murderer.*
intensify, step up
4 *Will you be increasing the bus fares?*
put up, raise
5 *Can you increase the volume of the TV?*
turn up, amplify, boost
6 *The number of cars on the roads continues to increase.*
grow, mount, go up, rise, soar, build up, escalate, multiply
For opposites see decrease

incredible adjective
1 *Do you expect us to believe that* incredible *story?*
unbelievable, unlikely, improbable, far-fetched, absurd, implausible
opposite **credible**
2 *The Forth Bridge is an* incredible *feat of engineering.*
extraordinary, amazing, astounding, magnificent, marvellous, spectacular

independence noun
The islanders value their independence.
freedom, liberty, autonomy
opposite **dependence**

independent adjective
1 *My granny is a very* independent *person.*
free, liberated, self-sufficient, self-reliant
opposite **dependent**
2 *Luxembourg is an* independent *country.*
autonomous, self-governing
3 *We need an* independent *opinion on the matter.*
impartial, neutral, objective, unbiased
opposite **biased**

indicate verb
1 *The usher* indicated *where we should sit.*
point to or out, specify, show, reveal, make known
2 *A red light* indicates *danger.*
mean, stand for, denote, express, signal, signify, communicate, convey

indication noun
He gave no indication *that he felt ill.*
sign, signal, hint, clue, inkling, evidence, warning, symptom, token

indifferent adjective
1 *I felt* indifferent *as I watched the game.*
uninterested, detached, uncaring, unenthusiastic, unmoved, uninvolved, unconcerned
opposite **enthusiastic**
2 *The food in the restaurant was* indifferent.
mediocre, ordinary, unexciting, average
opposite **excellent**

indignant adjective
The player was indignant *when he was sent off.*
annoyed, angry, cross, affronted, offended, outraged, piqued

indirect adjective
The bus took an indirect *route into town.*
roundabout, winding, meandering, rambling, zigzag
opposite **direct**

indistinct adjective
1 *The photo was rather* indistinct.
unclear, blurred, blurry, fuzzy, hazy, vague, indefinite, obscure, shadowy
opposite **clear**
2 *They heard* indistinct *sounds of people talking.*
muffled, mumbled, muted, faint, weak, inaudible, unintelligible, incoherent
opposite **distinct**

individual adjective
Her singing has an individual *style.*
characteristic, distinct, distinctive, special, unique, personal, singular

individual noun
Who was that odd individual?
person, character, man, woman

induce verb
1 *I couldn't* induce *her to come to the party.*
persuade, convince, prevail on, coax, tempt
2 *Some headaches are* induced *by stress.*
cause, produce, provoke, bring on, lead to, give rise to

indulge verb
They indulged *their children too much.*
spoil, pamper, mollycoddle
to indulge in
I indulged *in a nice hot bath.*
enjoy, revel in, wallow in

indulgent adjective
They are very indulgent *towards their grandchildren.*
tolerant, patient, permissive, lenient,

a
b
c
d
e
f
g
h
i
j
k
l
m
n
o
p
q
r
s
t
u
v
w
x
y
z

A

easy-going, generous, liberal
opposite **strict**

B

industry noun

C

1 *Many people in the area work in the car industry.*
business, trade, commerce, manufacturing, production

D

2 *The elves' workshop was a hive of* industry.
hard work, effort, energy, diligence, application, busyness
opposite **laziness**

E

F

G

ineffective adjective

H

He was an ineffective *captain of the team.*
incompetent, inadequate, unsuccessful, inept,
(informal) useless, hopeless
opposite **effective**

I

J

inefficient adjective

K

1 *Our old vacuum cleaner was very* inefficient.
ineffective, unproductive, useless, slow, sloppy
2 *The car is* inefficient *in its use of fuel.*
wasteful, uneconomical, extravagant
opposite **efficient**

L

M

N

O

inevitable adjective

P

If it rains, it is inevitable *that the pitch will get wet.*
certain, sure, definite, unavoidable, inescapable

Q

R

inexpensive adjective

S

We bought some inexpensive *clothes in the market.*
cheap, low-priced, low-cost, cut-price, affordable
opposite **expensive**

T

U

infamous adjective

V

Dick Turpin was an infamous *highwayman.*
notorious, villainous, wicked

W

infant noun

X

He had blond, curly hair as an infant.
baby, small child, tot, toddler

Y

Z

infect verb

A virus may have infected *the water supply.*
contaminate, pollute, poison

infection noun

The infection *spread rapidly.*
disease, virus, contagion, contamination

infectious adjective

Chickenpox is highly infectious.
contagious, catching

infer verb

Notice that **infer** and **imply** are not synonyms.

What can you infer *from the tone of her letter?*
conclude, deduce, gather, assume, guess, work out

inferior adjective

1 *The clothes were of* inferior *quality.*
poor, bad, second-rate, mediocre, cheap, shoddy
2 *Officers can give orders to those of* inferior *rank.*
lesser, lower, junior, subordinate

infested adjective

The attic was infested *with mice.*
swarming, teeming, crawling, overrun, plagued

infiltrate verb

Spies infiltrated *the enemy's camp.*
enter secretly, penetrate

infinite adjective

You need infinite *patience to train a puppy.*
endless, limitless, unlimited, boundless, never-ending, unending, inexhaustible
opposite **finite**

infirm adjective

Most of the patients are elderly and infirm.
frail, weak, feeble, poorly, ill, unwell
opposite **healthy**
People who have to stay in bed are bedridden.

inflammation noun
This ointment will soothe the inflammation.
swelling, redness, soreness, infection

inflate verb
The tyres need to be inflated.
blow up, pump up
opposite deflate

inflict verb
I hate seeing anyone inflict pain on an animal.
administer, deal out, apply, impose

influence noun
Rock music had a big influence on her life.
effect, impact, power, dominance, guidance, authority, control

influence verb
The money he was offered influenced his decision.
affect, have an effect on, direct, guide, control, motivate

influential adjective
She knows some very influential people.
important, leading, powerful, significant
opposite unimportant

inform verb
Please inform us if you move house.
tell, let know, notify, advise

informal adjective
1 *The party will be a very informal event.*
casual, relaxed, easy-going, friendly, homely, natural
2 *Emails are usually written in an informal style.*
colloquial, familiar, chatty, personal
opposite formal

information noun
There is more information on our website.
details, particulars, facts, data, advice, guidance, knowledge
(informal) info

informative adjective
That book you lent me was very informative.
helpful, useful, instructive, illuminating, revealing
opposite unhelpful

infuriate verb
He was infuriated by the umpire's decision.
anger, enrage, incense, madden, exasperate

ingenious adjective
It seemed like an ingenious plan.
clever, brilliant, inspired, inventive, imaginative, original, crafty, cunning, shrewd

inhabit verb
People inhabited the caves thousands of years ago.
live in, occupy, dwell in, reside in, populate, settle in

inhabitant noun
The island has fewer than thirty inhabitants.
resident, dweller, native, occupier, occupant
An inhabitant of a particular city or country is a citizen.
The inhabitants of a place are its population.

inhabited adjective
Is the island inhabited?
occupied, lived-in
opposite uninhabited

inherit verb
She inherited the farm from her uncle.
succeed to, be left, come into

inherited adjective
Eye colour is an inherited characteristic.
hereditary, passed down

inhuman adjective
I think it's inhuman to hunt animals.
barbaric, cruel, inhumane, merciless, heartless
opposite humane

a
b
c
d
e
f
g
h
i
j
k
l
m
n
o
p
q
r
s
t
u
v
w
x
y
z

221

A
B
C
D
E
F
G
H
I
J
K
L
M
N
O
P
Q
R
S
T
U
V
W
X
Y
Z

initial adjective
My initial *reaction was to run away and hide.*
first, earliest, preliminary, opening, introductory
opposites final, eventual

initially adverb
Initially, I didn't like swimming.
at first, in the beginning, to begin with, to start with, at the outset

initiative noun
You must use your initiative *on the treasure hunt.*
resourcefulness, inventiveness, originality, enterprise

injection noun
The nurse gave me an injection.
inoculation, vaccination
(informal) **jab**

injure verb
Was anyone injured *in the accident?*
hurt, harm, wound
To injure someone causing permanent damage is to **maim** *them.*

injury noun
She escaped without any serious injury.
wound, harm, hurt

🕸 WORD WEB

SOME TYPES OF INJURY
bite, bruise, burn, cut, fracture, gash, graze, scald, scratch, sprain, sting, strain

inner adjective
1 *A passageway led to the* inner c hamber.
central, inside, interior, internal, middle
opposites outer, exterior
2 *She tries to hide her* inner *feelings.*
innermost, inward, personal, private, intimate, secret, hidden, concealed
opposites outward, external

innocent adjective
1 *The jury found the man* innocent.
guiltless, blameless, free from blame
opposite guilty
2 *Baby tigers look so innocent.*
angelic, harmless, faultless, virtuous, pure, simple, inexperienced, naive
opposite wicked

innumerable adjective
There are innumerable stars in the sky.
countless, numberless, uncountable, untold

inquire verb
to inquire into
Detectives are inquiring into the robbery.
look into, investigate, examine, explore

inquiry noun
There will be an official inquiry into the accident.
investigation, inspection, examination

inquisitive adjective
Chimpanzees are naturally inquisitive.
curious, questioning, inquiring, probing
For uncomplimentary synonyms see **nosy**

insane adjective
1 *It was rumoured that the king had gone* insane.
mentally ill, mad, crazy, deranged, demented, disturbed, unhinged
(informal) **off your head, out of your mind**
opposite sane
2 *It would be* insane *to swim in the sea in January!*
crazy, mad, daft, senseless, stupid, foolish, idiotic
opposites sensible, wise

inscription noun
The professor read the inscription on the tomb.
engraving, carving, writing

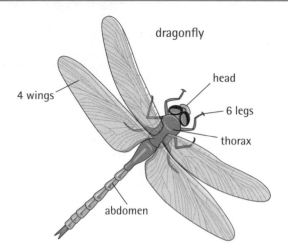

dragonfly

head

6 legs

thorax

4 wings

fly

abdomen

ladybird

a
b
c
d
e
f
g
h
i
j
k
l
m
n
o
p
q
r
s
t
u
v
w
x
y
z

insect noun

🕸 **WORD WEB**

SOME TYPES OF INSECT
ant, aphid, bee, beetle, bluebottle,
bumble-bee, butterfly, cicada,
cockroach, crane fly or daddy-long-legs,
cricket, dragonfly, earwig, firefly, flea,
fly, glow-worm, gnat, grasshopper,
greenfly, hornet, horsefly, ladybird,
locust, louse, mantis, mayfly, midge,
mosquito, moth, stick insect, termite,
tsetse fly, wasp, weevil

See also **bee**

For groups of insects see **group**

LIFE STAGES OF SOME INSECTS
caterpillar, chrysalis, grub, larva,
maggot, pupa

PARTS OF INSECTS' BODIES
abdomen, antennae, head, legs, thorax,
wings

SOME CREATURES SIMILAR TO INSECTS
centipede, earthworm, mite, slug,
spider, woodlouse, worm

insecure adjective

1 *Be careful—that scaffolding is insecure.*
unsafe, unsteady, unstable, loose, shaky,
wobbly, dangerous, hazardous, precarious

2 *Colin felt insecure on his first day at school.*
anxious, nervous, worried, apprehensive,
uneasy, uncertain, unconfident
opposite secure

insensitive adjective
I'm sorry if my comments were insensitive.
thoughtless, tactless, unfeeling, uncaring,
unsympathetic, callous
opposite sensitive

insert verb
Please insert a coin in the slot.
put in, place, push in, stick in, install,
implant

inside adjective
The inside doors are all painted green.
indoor, inner, interior, internal
opposite outside

inside noun
The inside of the nest was lined with feathers.
interior, inner surface, centre, core, heart,
middle
opposite outside

insignificant adjective
The author made a few insignificant changes.
unimportant, minor, trivial, negligible,
slight, meaningless
opposite significant

A
B
C
D
E
F
G
H
I
J
K
L
M
N
O
P
Q
R
S
T
U
V
W
X
Y
Z

insincere adjective
The butler welcomed us with an insincere *smile.*
false, pretended, hypocritical, dishonest, deceitful, deceptive, lying
(informal) two-faced
opposite sincere

insist verb
Griselda insisted *that she was not a witch.*
declare, state, assert, maintain, stress, emphasize, swear, vow, claim
to insist on
The magician insisted on *silence before he began.*
demand, require

insolent adjective
The boy gave the teacher an insolent *stare.*
rude, impudent, disrespectful, impolite, impertinent, arrogant, brazen
(informal) cheeky
opposites polite, respectful

inspect verb
They inspected *the damage done by the storm.*
check, examine, investigate, look over, study, survey, scrutinize

inspection noun
There will be a safety inspection *this afternoon.*
check, check-up, examination, review, survey

inspiration noun
1 *What was the* inspiration *behind your story?*
impulse, motivation, stimulus
2 *The scientist had a sudden* inspiration.
idea, thought

inspire verb
The crowd inspired *the team to play well.*
motivate, prompt, stimulate, encourage, stir, arouse, spur on

install verb
We are getting a new bathroom installed.
put in, set up, fix, place, position, establish
opposite remove

instalment noun
I missed the first instalment *of 'Dr Who'.*
episode, part

instance noun
Give me an instance *of what you mean.*
example, illustration, case, sample

instant adjective
Gardeners don't expect instant *results.*
immediate, quick, rapid, fast, prompt, snappy, speedy, swift, direct

instant noun
The shooting star was gone in an instant.
moment, second, split second, flash
(informal) tick, jiffy

instinct noun
The detective always followed his instincts.
impulse, inclination, intuition, hunch, feeling, urge

instinctive adjective
Most people have an instinctive *fear of sharks.*
intuitive, natural, innate, inherent, automatic, involuntary, reflex, spontaneous, impulsive, unconscious, unthinking
opposites deliberate, conscious

instruct verb
1 *All the staff are* instructed *in first aid.*
teach, train, coach, tutor
2 *The police* instructed *the cars to wait.*
tell, order, direct, command

instructions plural noun
Please follow the instructions *carefully.*
directions, guidelines, orders, commands

instructor noun
The swimming instructor *teaches life-saving.*
teacher, trainer, coach

instrument noun
Dentists use special instruments to check your teeth.
tool, implement, utensil, appliance, device, gadget, contraption
For musical instruments see **music**

insufficient adjective
The plants died because they had insufficient water.
inadequate, deficient, not enough, too little, scant, scanty
opposites **enough, excessive**

insult verb
He was insulted not to be invited to the party.
offend, outrage, be rude to, hurt, injure, slight, snub

insult noun
It is considered an insult to refuse a gift.
rudeness, offence, affront, slight, slur, snub

insulting adjective
She made an insulting comment about my clothes.
offensive, rude, impolite, derogatory, scornful
opposite **complimentary**

intact adjective
The vase has remained intact for centuries.
unbroken, whole, undamaged, unharmed, complete, perfect
(informal) in one piece

integrate verb
They decided to integrate the two orchestras.
bring together, combine, join, merge, unite, unify, amalgamate
opposite **separate**

integrity noun
Do you have any reason to doubt his integrity?
honesty, honour, loyalty, trustworthiness, reliability, goodness, sincerity, virtue, fidelity
opposite **dishonesty**

intelligence noun
1 *The robot shows some signs of intelligence.*
cleverness, understanding, comprehension, reason, sense, wisdom, brainpower, wits
(informal) **brains**
2 *The spy was sent to gather secret intelligence.*
information, knowledge, data, facts, reports

intelligent adjective
The aliens from Planet Zog are highly intelligent.
clever, bright, smart, quick, sharp, perceptive, shrewd, able, brilliant, rational, thinking
(informal) **brainy**
opposites **unintelligent, stupid**

intelligible adjective
The language of the Martians was not intelligible.
understandable, comprehensible, meaningful, straightforward, unambiguous, clear, legible, plain, lucid
opposite **incomprehensible**

intend verb
1 *What do you intend to do?*
plan, aim, mean, have in mind, plot, propose
2 *The class is intended for non-swimmers.*
design, set up, aim (at)

intense adjective
1 *I felt a sudden, intense pain in my chest.*
extreme, acute, severe, sharp, great, strong, violent
opposites **slight, mild**
2 *The contest aroused intense feelings.*
deep, passionate, powerful, strong, profound
opposite **mild**

intensive adjective
Police carried out an intensive search of the area.
detailed, thorough, concentrated
opposite **superficial**

a
b
c
d
e
f
g
h
i
j
k
l
m
n
o
p
q
r
s
t
u
v
w
x
y
z

A B C D E F G H I J K L M N O P Q R S T U V W X Y Z

intent adjective
He read the letter with an intent look on his face.
concentrating, absorbed, engrossed, preoccupied, interested
intent on
The detective was intent on solving the crime.
determined to, resolved to, eager to, fixed on, bent on

intention noun
It's his intention to play cricket for Australia.
aim, objective, target, goal, ambition, plan, intent

intentional adjective
He was penalized for an intentional foul.
deliberate, conscious, calculated, planned, intended, wilful
opposite **accidental**

intercept verb
The defender managed to intercept the pass.
check, stop, catch, cut off, head off, deflect

interest verb
Politics doesn't interest me at all.
appeal to, attract, capture your imagination, excite, fascinate, stimulate, absorb
opposite **bore**

interest noun
1 *The dog showed no interest in the bone.*
curiosity, attention, concern, involvement
2 *The information was of no interest to anyone.*
importance, significance, consequence, value
3 *My interests include judo and playing the trombone.*
hobby, pastime, pursuit, activity, diversion

interesting adjective
Everyone wanted to hear about our interesting adventures.
fascinating, absorbing, enthralling, intriguing, engrossing, stimulating, riveting, gripping, entertaining, diverting
opposites **boring, dull**

interfere verb
to interfere in
Don't interfere in other people's affairs.
intervene in, intrude in, meddle in, pry into, encroach on, butt in on
to interfere with
The bad weather interfered with our plans.
hamper, hinder, get in the way of, obstruct

interior adjective & noun
see inside

intermediate adjective
Should I join the intermediate or the advanced class?
middle, midway, halfway, transitional

internal adjective
Scoop out the internal parts of the tomato.
inner, inside, interior
opposite **external**

international adjective
Interpol is an international police organization.
global, worldwide, intercontinental

interpret verb
Can you interpret this old writing?
explain, make sense of, make clear, translate, clarify, decipher, decode

interrogate verb
The police interrogated the suspect for several hours.
question, interview, examine, cross-examine
(informal) quiz, grill

interrupt verb
1 *Please don't interrupt while I am speaking.*
intervene, interject, break in, butt in, cut in
2 *Heavy rain interrupted the tennis match.*
stop, suspend, disrupt, break off, cut short
3 *The new houses will interrupt the view.*
get in the way of, obstruct, spoil

interruption noun
He wrote for an hour without any interruption.
break, pause, stop, gap, halt, disruption, suspension

interval noun
1 *There will be a short interval after the first act.*
break, pause, wait, delay, lapse, lull
Another word for an interval in a play or film is interlude or intermission.
An interval in a meeting is a recess.
An interval when you take a rest is a breather or breathing space.
2 *There were signs at regular intervals along the road.*
space, gap, distance

intervene verb
A man intervened to stop the fight.
step in, interfere, interrupt, butt in

interview verb
He interviewed the author about her new book.
question, talk to, interrogate, examine

intimate adjective
1 *They have been intimate friends for years.*
close, cherished, dear, friendly, informal
opposite distant
2 *The newspaper printed intimate details about her life.*
personal, private, confidential, secret

intimidate verb
You can't intimidate me into telling a lie.
bully, threaten, frighten, menace, scare, terrify, terrorize, persecute

intrepid adjective
The intrepid explorers finally reached the North Pole.
daring, bold, fearless, courageous, brave, valiant, heroic, plucky

intricate adjective
The clock has an intricate mechanism.
complex, complicated, elaborate, sophisticated, involved
opposite simple

intriguing adjective
The results of the experiment are intriguing.
interesting, attractive, fascinating, captivating, beguiling

introduce verb
1 *Let me introduce you to my friend.*
present, make known
2 *The director stood up to introduce the film.*
give an introduction to, announce, lead into
3 *They are introducing a new bus service next year.*
set up, start, begin, create, establish, initiate, bring in

introduction noun
Something which happens as an introduction to a bigger event is a prelude.
An introduction to a book is a preface.
An introduction to a play is a prologue.
A piece played as an introduction to a concert or opera is an overture.

intrude verb
to intrude on
I don't mean to intrude on your privacy.
break in on, encroach on, interrupt, butt in on, interfere with, intervene in

intruder noun
Some intruders broke into the building last night.
trespasser, prowler, burglar

invade verb
The Vikings invaded many parts of Europe.
attack, enter, occupy, overrun, march into, raid

a
b
c
d
e
f
g
h
i
j
k
l
m
n
o
p
q
r
s
t
u
v
w
x
y
z

A B C D E F G **I** J K L M N O P Q R S T U V W X Y Z

invalid adjective
1 *The ticket is* invalid *because it is out of date.*
unacceptable, unusable, worthless
2 *That is an* invalid *argument.*
false, unsound, unreasonable, illogical, irrational, unconvincing
opposite **valid**

invaluable adjective
Reena is an invaluable *member of the hockey team.*
indispensable, irreplaceable, crucial, essential, useful, valuable
opposite **worthless**

invasion noun
Fortunately, the Martian invasion *never happened.*
attack, raid

invent verb
James Dewar invented *the Thermos flask.*
create, devise, think up, conceive, design, originate

invention noun
1 *This computer program is my own* invention.
creation, design, discovery
(informal) brainchild
2 *Her account of what happened was pure* invention.
fantasy, fiction, lies, deceit

inventive adjective
Roald Dahl's stories are full of inventive *characters.*
creative, original, imaginative, ingenious, inspired

inventor noun
James Dewar was the inventor *of the Thermos flask.*
creator, designer, originator, discoverer

investigate verb
Police are investigating *the accident.*
examine, explore, inquire into, look into, study, consider, follow up, probe, research, scrutinize

investigation noun
An investigation *showed how the accident happened.*
examination, inquiry, inspection, study, review, survey

invigorating adjective
We had an invigorating *walk before breakfast.*
refreshing, stimulating, reviving, bracing, healthy
opposite **tiring**

invisible adjective
The wizard was invisible *when he wore his magic cloak.*
out of sight, unseen, unnoticed, hidden, concealed, covered, obscured, camouflaged, disguised, undetectable, unnoticeable, inconspicuous
opposite **visible**

invite verb
Our neighbours invited *us round for tea.*
ask, request your company, welcome, summon

inviting adjective
An inviting *smell came from the kitchen.*
attractive, appealing, pleasant, welcoming, agreeable, appetizing, tempting
opposite **repulsive**

involve verb
1 *My job* involves *a lot of travel.*
include, comprise, require, demand, necessitate, mean
2 *Protecting the environment* involves *us all.*
affect, concern, interest, touch

involved adjective
1 *The film has a long and* involved *plot.*
complex, complicated, elaborate, intricate, confusing, difficult, convoluted
opposite **simple**

2 *Are you* involved *in the theatre?*
concerned, participating, engaged,
caught up, mixed up

irrational adjective
My aunt has an irrational *fear of hamsters.*
unreasonable, illogical, senseless,
nonsensical, absurd, crazy
opposite rational

irregular adjective
1 *The bricks were arranged in an* irregular
pattern.
varying, erratic, haphazard, random,
unpredictable, fitful
opposite regular
2 *It is highly* irregular *to eat pizza with a
spoon!*
abnormal, unusual, exceptional,
unconventional, improper
opposite normal

irrelevant adjective
Some of the information in the book is
irrelevant.
inappropriate, unnecessary, inessential,
pointless, unrelated, unconnected,
beside the point
opposite relevant

irresistible adjective
I had an irresistible *urge to laugh.*
overwhelming, overpowering,
uncontrollable, unavoidable, powerful,
compelling

irresponsible adjective
It's irresponsible *to drive too fast.*
reckless, rash, thoughtless, inconsiderate,
uncaring, unthinking, negligent
opposite responsible

irritable adjective
After a bad night, he woke in an irritable
mood.
bad-tempered, grumpy, short-tempered,
cross, impatient, snappy, touchy, testy,
prickly, peevish
(informal) stroppy, shirty
opposites good-humoured, cheerful

irritate verb
The noise from next door began to irritate *me.*
annoy, bother, exasperate, anger, provoke,
madden, vex
(informal) get on your nerves, bug

island noun
A small island is an **islet**.
A coral island is an **atoll**.
A group of islands is an **archipelago**.
An uninhabited island is a **desert island**.
An island which is not on a map is
uncharted.
A person who is stranded on a desert island
is a **castaway**.

WORD WEB
ON A DESERT ISLAND YOU MIGHT BE
**cast adrift, beached, marooned,
shipwrecked, stranded, washed ashore**

THINGS YOU MIGHT FIND OR USE ON A
DESERT ISLAND
**beach, cave, driftwood, flotsam,
footprints, lagoon, message in a bottle,
palm trees, raft, shelter, tree-house**

isolated adjective
1 *They sheltered in an* isolated *cave in the
mountains.*
remote, out-of-the-way, secluded,
outlying, inaccessible, cut off, deserted
opposite accessible
2 *There have been a few* isolated *cases of
cheating.*
single, uncommon, unusual, abnormal,
exceptional, unique
opposite common

issue verb
1 *They* issued *blankets to the refugees.*
give out, distribute, supply
2 *They have* issued *a new set of stamps.*
bring out, put out, produce, publish,
release, circulate, print
3 *Green smoke* issued *from the dragon's
nostrils.*
come out, emerge, appear, flow out, gush,
erupt

a
b
c
d
e
f
g
h
i
j
k
l
m
n
o
p
q
r
s
t
u
v
w
x
y
z

issue noun
1 *The new issue of the magazine comes out this week.*
edition, number, instalment, copy
2 *They print stories about local issues in the magazine.*
matter, subject, topic, affair, concern, question, problem

itch noun
1 *I had an annoying itch on my foot.*
tickle, tingling, prickle
2 *Olga had a great itch to travel.*
desire, longing, urge, wish, yearning, ache, impulse

item noun
1 *I bought a few items in the jumble sale.*
thing, object, article
2 *There was an item about our school in the paper.*
article, piece, report, feature

Jj

jab verb
A passer-by jabbed me in the ribs.
poke, prod, elbow, nudge, stab, thrust

jagged adjective
This dinosaur had jagged teeth.
rough, uneven, ragged, spiky, toothed, serrated
opposite **smooth**

jail noun
see prison

jam noun
1 *We got stuck in a jam on the motorway.*
traffic jam, hold-up, tailback, blockage
2 (informal) *I'm in a bit of a jam.*
difficulty, mess, predicament, plight
(informal) fix, tight corner

jam verb
1 *Someone had jammed the door open.*
prop, wedge, stick
2 *The roads are jammed at rush hour.*
block, clog, obstruct, congest
(informal) bung up
3 *I jammed my things into a backpack.*
cram, pack, stuff, squeeze, squash, crush, ram, crowd

jangle verb
Silver bracelets jangled on her wrists.
jingle, chink, clink, tinkle

jar[1] noun
We collected some tadpoles in a glass jar.
pot, jug, pitcher, vase

jar[2] verb
1 *He jarred his back badly when he fell.*
jolt, jerk, shake, shock
2 *Those paint colours jar with each other.*
clash, conflict, be at odds

jaunty adjective
The seven dwarves whistled a jaunty tune.
cheerful, lively, bright, jolly, perky, breezy, sprightly
opposite **gloomy**

jealous adjective
Cinderella's sisters were jealous of her beauty.
envious, resentful, grudging

jeer verb
Some of the audience whistled and jeered.
boo, hiss, sneer, taunt, mock, scoff, ridicule
opposite **cheer**

jerk verb
The rider jerked on the horse's reins.
pull, tug, yank, pluck, wrench, tweak

jerky adjective
The stagecoach drew to a jerky halt.
jolting, jumpy, shaky, bouncy, bumpy, uneven
opposite **steady**

A B C D E F G H I J K L M N O P Q R S T U V W X Y Z

jester noun
The king's jester kept the court amused.
fool, joker, clown

jet noun
A jet of water shot high in the air.
spout, spurt, squirt, gush, stream, fountain

jewel and jewellery noun

WORD WEB

SOME ITEMS OF JEWELLERY
anklet, bangle, beads, bindi, bracelet, brooch, chain, charm, choker, clasp, crown, cufflinks, earring, engagement ring, locket, necklace, pendant, pin, ring, tiara, tie pin, wedding ring

STONES OR GEMS USED TO MAKE JEWELLERY
agate, amber, amethyst, aquamarine, carnelian or cornelian, coral, diamond, emerald, garnet, jade, jasper, jet, lapis lazuli, onyx, opal, pearl, ruby, sapphire, topaz, turquoise

METALS USED TO MAKE JEWELLERY
gold, platinum, silver

jingle verb
Some coins jingled in his back pocket.
jangle, chink, clink, tinkle

job noun
1 My sister has a job as a TV reporter.
post, position, profession, occupation, employment, trade, work, career
The job you particularly want to do is your **mission** or **vocation**.
2 Whose job is it to do the washing-up?
duty, task, assignment, chore, errand

job noun

WORD WEB

SOME JOBS
actor, architect, artist, astronaut, banker, barber, bookseller, builder, bus driver, chef, cleaner, coach, cook, curator, dancer, dentist, designer, detective, diver, doctor, editor, electrician, engineer, explorer, farmer, firefighter, fisherman, flight attendant, florist, footballer, gardener, hairdresser, imam, janitor, joiner, journalist, lawyer, librarian, mechanic, midwife, miner, minister, model, musician, nurse, office worker, optician, painter, pharmacist, photographer, pilot, plumber, police officer, politician, postman, priest, professor, programmer, psychiatrist, rabbi, receptionist, reporter, sailor, scientist, secretary, shepherd, shopkeeper, singer, soldier, solicitor, surgeon, tailor, teacher, traffic warden, train driver, TV presenter, undertaker, vet, waiter or waitress, web designer, writer, zookeeper

jog verb
1 He jogs round the park every morning.
go jogging, run, trot
2 A boy sitting next to me jogged my elbow.
nudge, prod, jolt, knock, bump, jar, jostle
3 The photograph may jog her memory.
prompt, stir, arouse, set off, stimulate

join verb
1 Our families joined together to buy the present.
combine, come together, merge, unite, amalgamate
opposite separate
2 Join one piece of rope to the other.
connect, fasten, attach, fix, link, put together, tack on
opposite detach
3 The two roads join here.
meet, merge, converge
opposite divide

a
b
c
d
e
f
g
h
i
j
k
l
m
n
o
p
q
r
s
t
u
v
w
x
y
z

4 *I joined the crowd going into the cinema.*
follow, go with, tag along with
opposite **leave**
5 *We have joined a local sports club.*
become a member of, enrol in, sign up for
To join the army is to enlist.
opposites **leave, resign from**

join noun
If you look hard, you can still see the join.
joint, connection, link, mend, seam

joint adjective
The preparation of the meal was a joint effort.
combined, shared, common, communal,
cooperative, united, collective, mutual
opposite **individual**

joke noun
Do you know any good jokes?
jest, quip, crack, witticism, wisecrack
(informal) gag

joke verb
Those two are always laughing and joking.
jest, clown, have a laugh, make jokes

jolly adjective
We had a jolly time on holiday.
cheerful, merry, happy, joyful, pleasant,
enjoyable
opposite **gloomy**

jolt verb
The car jolted over the bumps in the road.
jerk, jog, bump, bounce, shake, shudder

jostle verb
The film star ʹ ... ʹ?d by photographers.
push, shove, hustle, press, crowd in on

jot verb
to jot down
I quickly jotted down some ideas.
make a note of, write down, take down,
note, scribble

journal noun
1 *The newsagent sells a few journals.*
magazine, newspaper, paper, periodical,
publication

2 *The captain kept a journal of the voyage.*
diary, log, record, account, chronicle

journalist noun
She works as a journalist on the local paper.
reporter, correspondent, columnist, writer

journey noun
*On their journey, the astronauts will pass the
Moon.*
voyage, trip, expedition, travels, tour, route

jovial adjective
Our guests were in a jovial mood.
cheerful, happy, jolly, good-humoured,
merry, joyful
opposite **sad**

joy noun
I remember the sheer joy of scoring a goal!
happiness, joyfulness, delight,
cheerfulness, gladness, mirth, glee,
jubilation, gaiety, rejoicing, bliss, ecstasy,
elation
opposite **sorrow**

joyful adjective
The wedding was a joyful occasion.
happy, cheerful, merry, joyous, jolly, jovial,
good-humoured
opposite **sad**

judge noun
A judge in a local court is a magistrate.
A judge in a competition is an adjudicator.
A judge in a sport is a referee or umpire.

judge verb
1 *The umpire judged that the ball was out.*
rule, decide, decree, adjudicate
2 *Who's judging the flower show this year?*
decide on, assess, evaluate, appraise
3 *He judged the coin to be about a thousand
years old.*
reckon, suppose, consider, gauge, guess,
estimate

judgement noun
1 *What is the judgement of the court?*
decision, finding, ruling, verdict, decree

A
B
C
D
E
F
G
H
I
J
K
L
M
N
O
P
Q
R
S
T
U
V
W
X
Y
Z

2 *His comments show a lack of* **judgement.**
wisdom, common sense, understanding, discrimination
3 *In my* **judgement,** *you're making a big mistake.*
opinion, view, belief, assessment, estimate

juice noun
Squeeze the **juice** *from the lemons.*
liquid, fluid, sap

jumble noun
There was a **jumble** *of clothes on the floor.*
mess, muddle, clutter, chaos, confusion, disorder

jumble verb
Please don't **jumble** *the pages.*
muddle, mix up, mess up, disorganize, shuffle
opposite arrange

jump verb
1 *Suddenly a rabbit* **jumped** *in front of us.*
leap, spring, bound, bounce, hop
When a cat jumps it **pounces.**
2 *All the horses* **jumped** *the first hurdle.*
leap over, vault, clear
3 *The loud bang made them all* **jump.**
start, flinch, jolt

jump noun
1 *With a* **jump,** *the grasshopper landed on the leaf.*
leap, spring, bound, vault, hop
2 *The horse easily cleared the last* **jump.**
hurdle, fence, gate, barrier, obstacle

junction noun
There are traffic lights at the road **junction.**
intersection, crossing, interchange

jungle noun
One of my dreams is to be a **jungle** *explorer.*
rainforest, tropical forest

WORD WEB
THINGS YOU MIGHT SEE IN THE JUNGLE
canopy, foliage, forest floor, swamp, undergrowth

SOME ANIMALS WHICH LIVE IN THE JUNGLE
alligator, ant, anteater, armadillo, bird of paradise, butterfly, chameleon, crocodile, gorilla, hummingbird, jaguar, leopard, macaw, monkey, mosquito, parrot, piranha, porcupine, snake, tarantula, tiger, toucan, tree frog
SOME PLANTS WHICH ARE FOUND IN THE JUNGLE
banana tree, cacao, creeper or liana, mangrove, orchid, palm tree, rubber tree

See also **explorer**

junior adjective
1 *I'm a member of the* **junior** *hockey team.*
younger
2 *He's only a* **junior** *employee in the firm.*
low-ranking, minor, lesser, subordinate
opposite senior

junk noun
The garage is full of old **junk.**
rubbish, clutter, garbage, jumble, trash, waste, scrap, odds and ends

just adjective
It was a **just** *punishment for the crime.*
fair, fitting, appropriate, deserved, proper, reasonable, justified
opposites unjust, unfair

justice noun
1 *The prisoners demanded* **justice.**
fairness, justness, fair play, right, honesty, impartiality
opposite injustice
2 *They were tried in a court of* **justice.**
law

justify verb
Can you **justify** *spending so much money?*
defend, excuse, account for, explain

jut verb
to jut out
A large nail **jutted out** *from the wall.*
stick out, project, protrude, extend, overhang

A B C D E F G H I J K L M N O P Q R S T U V W X Y Z

Kk

juvenile adjective
1 *This book shelf is for* juvenile *fiction.*
children's, young people's
opposite **adult**
2 *His jokes are really* juvenile.
childish, babyish, immature
opposite **mature**

keen adjective
1 *Rhona is a* keen *hockey player.*
enthusiastic, eager, fervent, avid, devoted, committed, motivated
A common simile is as keen as mustard.
opposite **unenthusiastic**
2 *A carving knife should have a* keen *edge.*
sharp, razor-sharp, cutting
opposite **blunt**
3 *Owls have* keen *eyesight.*
sharp, acute, piercing
opposite **poor**
4 *A* keen *wind was blowing from the east.*
bitter, cold, icy, penetrating
opposite **mild**

keep verb keeps, keeping, kept
1 *Let's* keep *the rest of the cake for later.*
save, conserve, preserve, retain, hang on to, hold on to, guard, store
2 *Please* keep *still.*
stay, remain
3 *A man in the audience* kept *coughing.*
persist in, go on, carry on, continue
4 *You're late. What* kept *you?*
delay, detain, hold up, keep waiting
5 *Where do you* keep *the knives and forks?*
store, house, put, stow
6 *Will the milk* keep *until tomorrow?*
last, be usable, stay good
7 *It costs money to* keep *a pet.*
support, maintain, provide for, pay for
to keep something up
Keep up *the good work!*
carry on, continue, maintain

key noun
Have you found the key *to the riddle?*
answer, solution, explanation, clue

kick noun
Ben closed the gate with a kick.
strike, boot, hit, blow

kick verb
The goalkeeper kicked *the ball into the air.*
strike, boot, hit, drive, send

kidnap verb
In the story, a boy is kidnapped *by bandits.*
abduct, capture, seize, carry off, snatch

kill verb
Several people were killed *in the explosion.*
(informal) **bump off, do away with**
(old use) **slay**
To kill someone deliberately is to **murder** them.
To kill someone brutally is to **butcher** them.
To kill large numbers of people is to massacre or slaughter them.
To kill someone as a punishment is to **execute** them or **put them to death.**
To kill someone for political reasons is to assassinate them.

kind¹ noun
What kind *of music do you like to play?*
sort, type, variety, style, category, class, set

kind² adjective
It was very kind *of you to help me.*
kind-hearted, caring, good-natured, kindly, affectionate, warm, genial, loving, sweet, gentle, lenient, amiable, friendly, generous, sympathetic, thoughtful, obliging, considerate, understanding, compassionate, unselfish, giving, gracious, merciful, benevolent, charitable, humane, neighbourly
opposite **unkind**

king noun
Neptune is the mythological King *of the Sea.*
monarch, sovereign

kingdom noun
King Brian ruled over a vast kingdom.
realm, monarchy

kiss noun
The princess gave the frog a kiss on the cheek.
(informal) **peck**

kit noun
I've forgotten my games kit.
gear, outfit, equipment, paraphernalia, tools, tackle

kitchen noun

WORD WEB

EQUIPMENT YOU MIGHT FIND IN A KITCHEN
apron, blender, bread bin, cooker, crockery, cutlery, dishwasher, draining board, food processor, freezer, fridge, grill, kettle, liquidizer, microwave, mixer, oven, oven gloves, refrigerator, scales, sink, toaster

For other things used for cooking see
cook, cutlery

knack noun
George has a knack for taking photographs.
skill, talent, gift, flair

knead verb
Knead the dough until it is smooth.
work, press, squeeze, pummel

knew
past tense see **know**

knife noun

WORD WEB

SOME KINDS OF KNIFE
cleaver, dagger, dirk, machete, penknife, scalpel

For kitchen knives see **cutlery**

knight noun

WORD WEB

THINGS A MEDIEVAL KNIGHT MIGHT WEAR OR CARRY
armour, baldric (leather belt), coat of arms, falcon or hawk, lance, mace (metal club), pennant, shield, surcoat, sword, tabard, tunic

For parts of a suit of armour
see **armour**

A fight between knights on horseback was a **joust**.
A series of sporting contests between knights was a **tournament**.
A boy training to be a knight was first a **page** and then a **squire**.
An expedition made by a knight was a **quest**.

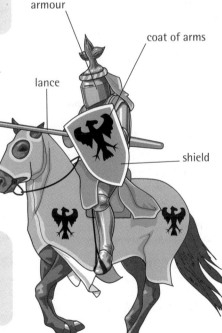

armour

coat of arms

lance

shield

a
b
c
d
e
f
g
h
i
j
k
l
m
n
o
p
q
r
s
t
u
v
w
x
y
z

A
B
C
D
E
F
G
H
I
J
K
L
M
N
O
P
Q
R
S
T
U
V
W
X
Y
Z

knob noun
1 *The knob had fallen off the door.*
handle
2 *Melt a knob of butter in a pan.*
lump, piece, bit

knobbly adjective
Crocodiles have thick and knobbly skin.
lumpy, bumpy, gnarled

knock verb
I knocked my head as I came out of the car.
bump, bang, hit, strike, thump
(informal) bash

knot verb
The sailors knotted the two ropes together.
tie, bind, fasten, join, entwine, lash
opposite untie

know verb knows, knowing, knew, known
1 *Do you know how to mend a puncture?*
understand, have knowledge of, comprehend
2 *As soon as she saw the unicorn, she knew what it was.*
recognize, realize, appreciate, be aware of
3 *Do you know Stewart well?*
be acquainted with, be familiar with, be a friend of

knowledge noun
1 *She has a good knowledge of Italian.*
understanding, grasp, command, familiarity (with)
2 *An encyclopedia contains a lot of knowledge.*
information, data, facts, learning, know-how, wisdom, scholarship

knowledgeable adjective
My dad is very knowledgeable about guitars.
familiar (with), well informed, educated, learned
opposite ignorant

L

label noun
The washing instructions are on the label.
tag, ticket, sticker

label verb
I've labelled all the boxes, so we'll know what's in them.
put a label on, tag, mark, name, identify

laborious adjective
It was a laborious climb to the top of the hill.
hard, tough, strenuous, difficult, stiff, tiring, exhausting, gruelling
opposite easy

labour noun
1 *The workers were paid for their labour.*
work, effort, industry, exertion, toil
2 *The factory took on extra labour.*
workers, employees

labour verb
They laboured to get the job finished on time.
work hard, exert yourself, toil
(informal) slave away

lack noun
The judge dismissed the case because of a lack of evidence.
absence, shortage, scarcity, want
A general lack of food is a famine.
A general lack of water is a drought.
opposite abundance

lack verb
The game lacked excitement.
be short of, be without, want, need, require, miss

lady noun
see woman

lag verb
One runner was lagging behind the others.
straggle, trail, fall behind, drop behind, dawdle, linger, loiter

laid
past tense see lay[1]

lair noun
The hunters tracked the animal back to its lair.
den, refuge, shelter, hideout, hiding place

lake noun
We rowed across the lake.
pond, pool, (Scottish) loch
A salt-water lake is a lagoon.
A lake used to supply water is a reservoir.

lame adjective
1 *The* lame *horse had to be withdrawn from the race.*
disabled, handicapped, crippled, limping
2 *I didn't believe her* lame *excuse.*
feeble, flimsy, poor, unconvincing, inadequate, weak, tame

lamp noun
see light[1]

land noun
1 *The castle is surrounded by several acres of* land.
grounds, estate, property
2 *The* land *here is good for growing strawberries.*
ground, soil, earth
3 *China is a* land *with an ancient history.*
country, nation, state, region, territory

land verb
1 *The plane* landed *exactly on time.*
touch down, arrive
opposite take off
2 *The ship will* land *at Dover.*
dock, berth, come ashore
3 *How did these papers* land *on my desk?*
arrive, turn up, end up, wind up, settle

landscape noun
We sat on the hill and admired the landscape.
countryside, scenery, view, scene, outlook, prospect

lane noun
see road

language noun
1 *The scroll was written in an ancient* language.
tongue, speech, dialect
2 *The author uses very poetic* language.
wording, phrasing, vocabulary, expression, style
The words of a language are its vocabulary.
See also writing

lap noun
1 *My cat, Snowy, likes to sit on my* lap.
knee, knees, thighs
2 *The cars were on the last* lap *of the race.*
circuit, round, loop

lapse noun
1 *They made a mistake because of a* lapse *in concentration.*
failure, error, fault, slip, flaw, weakness, shortcoming
2 *I've started swimming again after a* lapse *of a year.*
break, gap, interval, interruption, lull, pause

large adjective
1 *Elephants are* large *animals.*
big, huge, enormous, colossal, giant, gigantic, immense, great, massive, bulky, heavy, hefty, weighty, mighty, towering
(informal) whopping, ginormous
2 *The cook gave me a* large *helping of pudding.*
ample, generous, plentiful, abundant, lavish
3 *Is this room* large *enough for dancing in?*
spacious, roomy, sizeable
4 *The gales caused damage over a* large *area.*
wide, broad, extensive, widespread, vast
5 *The meeting was attended by a* large *number of people.*
considerable, substantial
opposite small

a
b
c
d
e
f
g
h
i
j
k
l
m
n
o
p
q
r
s
t
u
v
w
x
y
z

A

largely adverb
The driver was largely to blame for the accident.
mainly, chiefly, mostly, principally, to a large extent

B

C

D

last¹ adjective
1 *Z is the last letter of the alphabet.*
final, closing, concluding, terminating, ultimate
opposite first
2 *Did you see his last film?*
latest, most recent
opposite next

E

F

G

H

last noun
at last
The holidays are here at last!
finally, eventually, in the end

I

J

last² verb
1 *Let's hope the fine weather lasts.*
carry on, continue, keep on, stay, remain, persist, endure, hold
2 *The plants won't last long without water.*
hold out, keep going, live, survive

K

L

M

late adjective
1 *The bus is late.*
delayed, overdue
opposites early, punctual, on time
2 *Mr Pettigrew showed us a portrait of his late wife.*
dead, deceased, departed

N

O

P

Q

R

lately adverb
There has been a lot of snow lately.
recently, latterly, of late

S

T

later adjective
We'll study that poem in a later class.
future, following, subsequent

U

V

later adverb
I'm busy now, but I'll phone you later.
afterwards, in a while, subsequently, next

W

X

laugh verb
1 *The children laughed when the clown fell over.*
chuckle, chortle, giggle, titter,

Y

Z

**burst out laughing,
roar** or **scream with laughter,
roll** or **fall about laughing, guffaw**
(informal) **have hysterics, be in stitches**
2 *It's rude to laugh at his way of singing.*
make fun of, mock, ridicule, scoff at, tease, deride

laughter noun
We heard laughter coming from the kitchen.
laughing, amusement, hilarity, mirth, merriment

launch verb
1 *The space shuttle will be launched tomorrow.*
send off, set off, blast off, fire
2 *The new website was launched yesterday.*
begin, start, set up, open, establish, found, initiate

lavatory noun
The girls' lavatories are over there.
toilet, bathroom, WC, cloakroom, washroom
(informal) **loo**

lavish adjective
The king put on a lavish feast for his birthday.
generous, extravagant, sumptuous, luxurious, opulent, grand, abundant, copious, plentiful, bountiful
opposites meagre, paltry

law noun
A law passed by parliament is an **act**.
A proposed law to be discussed by parliament is a **bill**.
The laws of a game are **regulations** or **rules**.
A regulation which must be obeyed is a **commandment, decree, edict,** or **order.**

lay¹ verb **lays, laying, laid**
1 *He laid the parchment carefully on his desk.*
put down, set down, place, position, spread, deposit, leave
2 *Please lay the table for dinner.*
set out, arrange

lay²
past tense see **lie¹**

layer noun
1 *The walls needed two* **layers** *of paint.*
coat, coating, covering, thickness, film, sheet, skin
2 *You can see various* **layers** *of rock in the cliff.*
seam, stratum

laze verb
We spent the day **lazing** *in the garden.*
be lazy, idle, loaf, lounge, lie about, relax, loll

lazy adjective
My **lazy** *little brother stayed in bed all day!*
idle, inactive, lethargic, slack, slothful, indolent
An informal name for a lazy person is **lazybones**.

lead verb leads, leading, led
1 *The rescuers* **led** *the climbers to safety.*
guide, conduct, escort, usher, steer, pilot, shepherd
opposite **follow**
2 *Dr Martez will* **lead** *the expedition to Peru.*
be in charge of, direct, command, head, manage, supervise
3 *The British cyclist* **led** *from the start of the race.*
be in front, be in the lead, head the field
4 *The animals in the zoo* **lead** *a peaceful life.*
have, pass, spend, experience

lead noun
1 *The team followed the captain's* **lead**.
example, guidance, leadership, direction
2 *The Australian swimmer is in the* **lead**.
first place, front position
3 *Charlie was given the* **lead** *in the play.*
main part, starring role, title role
4 *Keep the dog on a* **lead**.
leash, strap, chain, tether, rein
5 *Don't trip over the electrical* **lead**.
cable, flex, wire

leader noun
The **leader** *of the pirates was Captain Cutlass.*
head, chief, commander, captain, director, principal, ruler
(informal) boss
The leader of a group of wrongdoers is the **ringleader**.

leaf noun
1 *Deciduous trees lose their* **leaves** *in autumn.*
A mass of leaves is **foliage** or **greenery**.
2 *A single* **leaf** *had been torn out of the book.*
page, sheet

leak noun
The plumber mended a **leak** *in the water tank.*
crack, hole, opening, drip
A leak in a tyre is a **puncture**.

leak verb
1 *The juice had* **leaked** *all over my school bag.*
escape, drip, seep, ooze, trickle
2 *Details of a secret plan were* **leaked** *to the newspaper.*
reveal, disclose, make known, pass on, give away, let out

lean¹ verb leans, leaning, leaned or leant
1 *I* **leaned** *against the wall.*
recline, rest, prop yourself, support yourself
2 *The yacht* **leaned** *to one side in the wind.*
slope, tilt, tip, incline, slant, list, bank

lean² adjective
The athlete has a strong, **lean** *figure.*
slim, slender, thin, wiry
opposite **fat**

leap verb leaps, leaping, leapt or leaped
The dog **leaped** *in the air to catch the ball.*
jump, spring, bound, vault

learn verb learns, learning, learnt or learned
1 *We are* **learning** *about the Vikings this term.*
discover, find out, gather, grasp, pick up
2 *I've got to* **learn** *the words of this song.*
learn by heart, memorize, master

a
b
c
d
e
f
g
h
i
j
k
l
m
n
o
p
q
r
s
t
u
v
w
x
y
z

learner noun
This swimming class is for learners only.
beginner, starter, novice
Someone learning things at school or
college is a pupil or student.
Someone learning a trade is an
apprentice or trainee.

least adjective & determiner
1 *Who got the least number of points?*
fewest, lowest
2 *The least amount of this poison
is deadly.*
slightest, smallest, tiniest

leave verb leaves, leaving, left
1 *Do you have to leave now?*
go, go away, depart, withdraw,
take your leave, go out, set off,
say goodbye
(informal) take off, disappear
opposite arrive
2 *The doctor left the room in a hurry.*
exit, go out of, depart from, quit, vacate
opposite enter
3 *Don't leave me here on my own!*
abandon, desert, forsake
4 *The crew left the sinking ship.*
evacuate, get out of
5 *My sister has left her job at the bank.*
give up, quit, resign from
(informal) walk out of
6 *Leave the milk bottles by the front door.*
place, position, put down, set down,
deposit
7 *I'll just leave all the arrangements
to you.*
pass on, hand over, refer, entrust
8 *Lady Bigwig left all her money to charity.*
bequeath, hand down, will, endow
to leave someone or something out
Eric was left out of the basketball team.
miss out, omit, exclude, reject

leave noun
1 *The prime minister is away on leave.*
holiday, vacation, time off
2 *Will you give me leave to speak?*
permission, freedom, liberty

lecture noun
1 *There is a lecture about dinosaurs at the
museum today.*
talk, lesson, speech, address
2 *The teacher gave us a lecture on how to
behave.*
reprimand, warning
(informal) telling off

led
past tense see lead

ledge noun
The climbers rested on a ledge of rock.
shelf, projection
A ledge under a window is a windowsill.

left¹ adjective
The left side of a ship when you face
forwards is the port side.
opposite right

left²
past tense see leave

leg noun
1 *Boris fell and bruised his leg.*
For parts of your body see body
2 *The rowers completed the first leg of the
race.*
part, stage, section, phase, stretch

legal adjective
Is it legal to park here on Sundays?
lawful, legitimate, permissible, permitted,
allowed
opposite illegal

legend noun
I like reading legends about ancient heroes.
myth, story, folk tale, fairy tale, fable,
tradition
For creatures found in myths and legends
see myth

legendary adjective
Unicorns are legendary beasts.
mythical, fabulous, fabled, fictional,
fictitious, invented, made-up
opposite real

A
B
C
D
E
F
G
H
I
J
K
L
M
N
O
P
Q
R
S
T
U
V
W
X
Y
Z

legible adjective
Although the letter is old, the handwriting is legible.
readable, clear, distinct, neat
opposite **illegible**

legitimate adjective
Are you the legitimate owner of this car?
legal, proper, rightful, authorized, licensed, permitted

leisure noun
Grandad has plenty of leisure since he retired.
free time, spare time, relaxation, recreation, rest

leisurely adjective
We went for a leisurely stroll in the park.
gentle, relaxed, relaxing, unhurried, restful, slow
opposite **fast**

lend verb
Can you lend me some money until the weekend?
loan, advance, let someone have
opposite **borrow**

length noun
1 *My heart sank when I saw the length of the queue.*
extent, size
2 *We only had to wait a short length of time.*
space, period, stretch

lengthen verb
1 *Is it possible to lengthen these curtains?*
extend, make longer, increase, stretch
2 *The days lengthen in spring.*
draw out, get longer, stretch out
opposite **shorten**

lengthy adjective
There was a lengthy argument over who was to blame.
long, drawn out, extended, prolonged, time-consuming
opposite **short**

lenient adjective
The teacher was lenient and let us off.
easy-going, soft-hearted, tolerant, forgiving, indulgent, kind, merciful
opposite **strict**

lessen verb
1 *The nurse used ointment to lessen the pain.*
minimize, reduce, relieve
2 *The strong winds lessened during the night.*
diminish, decrease, dwindle, subside, weaken, ease off, tail off, die away or down
opposite **increase**

lesson noun
My piano lesson is on Friday afternoon.
class, period, tutorial, instruction

let verb lets, letting, let
1 *Abby's parents let her go to the party.*
allow, give permission to, permit, consent to, agree to
opposite **forbid**
2 *Our friends are letting their house for the summer.*
lease, rent out, hire out

lethal adjective
This bottle contains a lethal potion.
deadly, fatal, mortal, poisonous

letter noun
1 *There are twenty-six letters in the alphabet.*
character, symbol, sign, figure
The letters a, e, i, o, u, and sometimes y are vowels.
The other letters are consonants.
2 *Did you remember to sign your letter?*
note, message, communication
Letters that people send each other are correspondence.

level adjective
1 *You need a level field for playing rounders.*
even, flat, horizontal, smooth
opposite **uneven**
2 *At half-time the scores were level.*
equal, even, the same, matching
(informal) neck-and-neck

a
b
c
d
e
f
g
h
i
j
k
l
m
n
o
p
q
r
s
t
u
v
w
x
y
z

A

level verb
1 *Dad* levelled *the garden to make a lawn.*
even out, flatten, smooth
2 *A serious earthquake* levelled *the town.*
knock down, demolish, destroy, devastate

level noun
1 *The water had reached a high* level.
height
2 *The lift takes you up to the sixth* level.
floor, storey, tier
3 *What* level *have you reached in judo?*
grade, standard, stage, rank, degree

lever verb
Slowly, I levered *open the lid of the chest.*
prise, wrench, force

liable adjective
1 *You're* liable *to make mistakes when you're tired.*
likely, inclined, disposed, prone, ready
opposite unlikely
2 *If you break anything, you'll be* liable *for the cost.*
responsible, answerable, accountable

liberal adjective
1 *We each got a* liberal *helping of ice cream.*
generous, ample, plentiful, lavish, abundant, copious, bountiful
opposites meagre, miserly
2 *She has a* liberal *attitude towards things.*
broad-minded, easy-going, lenient, tolerant, permissive
opposite strict

liberate verb
The prisoners were liberated *at the end of the war.*
free, release, set free, emancipate, discharge, let go, set loose
opposite imprison

liberty noun
1 *The animals have* liberty *to wander around the park.*
freedom, independence
2 *The king granted the prisoners their* liberty.
liberation, release, emancipation

licence noun
He has a licence *to practise as a doctor.*
permit, certificate, authorization, warrant

license verb
Are you licensed *to drive this vehicle?*
permit, allow, authorize, entitle

lid noun
Can you help me get the lid *off this jar?*
cap, cover, covering, top

lie[1] verb lies, lying, lay, lain
1 *It's twelve o'clock and he's still* lying *in bed!*
recline, stretch out, lounge, sprawl, rest
To lie *face down is to be* **prone.**
To lie *face upwards is to be* **supine.**
2 *The castle* lies *in a valley.*
be sited, be situated, be located, be found

lie[2] noun
He accused the newspaper of printing lies.
deceit, falsehood, dishonesty
(informal) **fib**
opposite truth

lie verb lies, lying, lied
I don't trust her—I think she's lying.
deceive someone, bluff
(informal) **fib**

life noun
1 *My hamster, Fluffy, leads a very easy* life.
existence, being, way of life
2 *Our* lives *depended on finding water.*
survival
3 *You seem to be full of* life *today!*
energy, liveliness, vigour, vitality, spirit, sprightliness, animation
4 *I'm reading a* life *of Elvis Presley.*
life story, autobiography, biography

lift verb
1 *The removal men* lifted *the piano carefully.*
pick up, raise, elevate, pull up, hoist
2 *The plane* lifted *off the ground.*
rise, ascend, soar

B C D E F G H I J K **L** M N O P Q R S T U V W X Y Z

light¹ noun

WORD WEB

SOME KINDS OF NATURAL LIGHT
daylight, moonlight, starlight, sunlight, twilight

SOURCES OF ARTIFICIAL LIGHT
bulb, candle, chandelier,
floodlight, fluorescent lamp,
headlamp or headlight, lamp, lantern,
laser, neon light, searchlight, spotlight,
street light, torch

VARIOUS FORMS OF LIGHT
beam, flash, flicker, glow, halo, lustre,
radiance, ray, reflection, shaft

WRITING TIPS

You can use these words to describe
light:

TO DESCRIBE HOW LIGHT APPEARS
bright, brilliant, harsh, luminous,
lustrous, strong; diffused, dim, muted,
soft, warm

LIGHT MAY
beam, blaze, dazzle, flash, flicker, glare,
gleam, glimmer, glint, glisten, glitter,
glow, shimmer, shine, sparkle, twinkle
*Beyond the woods and the strawberry
fields, the Long Island Sound glittered in
the last light of the sun.*
– Rick Riordan, *Percy Jackson and the
Lightning Thief*

light¹ adjective
1 *The artist worked in a* light *and airy studio.*
bright, well-lit, illuminated
opposites **dim, gloomy**
2 *She was wearing* light *blue jeans.*
pale
opposite **dark**

light¹ verb **lights, lighting, lit** or **lighted**
1 *We* lit *the candles on my birthday cake.*
ignite, kindle, set alight, set fire to,
switch on
opposite **extinguish**

2 *The fireworks* lit *the sky.*
light up, brighten, illuminate,
shed light on, shine on
opposite **darken**

light² adjective
1 *The parcel looks big, but it is quite*
light.
lightweight, portable, weightless, slight
A common simile is **as light as a feather.**
opposite **heavy**
2 *A* light *wind rippled the water.*
gentle, faint, slight
opposite **strong**
3 *We had a* light *meal before we went out.*
small, modest, simple, insubstantial
opposites **heavy, substantial**
4 *I brought a book for some* light *reading.*
undemanding, entertaining, lightweight
opposite **serious**

like¹ verb

OVERUSED WORD

Try to vary the words you use for like.
Here are some other words you could use.

TO **LIKE A PERSON** OR **ANIMAL**
admire, adore, be attached to,
be fond of, care for, cherish, esteem,
hold dear, love
(informal) have a soft spot for
Lauren is very attached *to her new puppy.*

TO **LIKE SOMETHING** OR **LIKE DOING
SOMETHING**
appreciate, be interested in, be keen on,
be partial to, delight in, enjoy, prefer,
relish
Alex is very partial *to chocolate cake.*
What sort of films do you enjoy?

opposite **dislike**

like² preposition
The witch's hand looked like *a knobbly
tree.*
similar to, the same as, resembling,
identical to
opposite **unlike**

a
b
c
d
e
f
g
h
i
j
k
l
m
n
o
p
q
r
s
t
u
v
w
x
y
z

A

likely adjective
It's likely *that the shop will be closed tomorrow.*
probable, expected, anticipated, predictable, foreseeable
opposite **unlikely**

B

C

D

likeness noun
1 *There's a strong* likeness *between the two sisters.*
resemblance, similarity, correspondence
opposite **difference**
2 *This photo is a good* likeness *of my grandfather.*
image, representation, picture, portrait, copy

E

F

G

H

I

liking noun
Ray has a liking *for classical music.*
fondness, taste, love, affection, preference
opposite **dislike**

J

K

L

limb noun
Your limbs *are your* arms *and* legs.
Birds have wings.
Seals, whales, and dolphins have flippers.
An octopus has tentacles.
The limbs *of a tree are its* boughs *or* branches.

M

N

O

P

limit noun
1 *There is a* limit *of twenty pupils for this class.*
maximum, restriction, threshold, ceiling, cut-off point
A limit *on time is a* deadline *or* time limit.
2 *The fence marks the* limit *of the school grounds.*
border, boundary, edge, perimeter, frontier

Q

R

S

T

U

limit verb
I had to limit *the invitations to my party.*
put a limit on, restrict, control, ration

V

W

X

limited adjective
1 *The crew had a* limited *supply of water.*
restricted, short, inadequate, insufficient, rationed, finite, fixed

Y

Z

2 *It was hard to move about in the* limited *space.*
small, cramped, narrow, confined
opposite **limitless**

limp¹ verb
She limped *off the pitch with an injured ankle.*
hobble, hop, falter, stumble

limp² adjective
The leaves on the plant are looking limp.
drooping, floppy, sagging, wilting, soft, flabby, slack
opposite **rigid**

line noun
1 *I drew a pencil* line *across the page.*
stroke, rule, underline, stripe, streak, band, bar, dash
A line *that is cut into a surface is a* groove, score, *or* scratch.
A line *on a person's skin is a* wrinkle.
A deep groove or wrinkle is a furrow.
A line *on fabric is a* crease
2 *There was a long* line *of people waiting at the bus stop.*
queue, row, file, column, rank, procession, chain
A line *of police officers forming a barrier is a* cordon.
A line *of schoolchildren walking in pairs is a* crocodile.
3 *The clothes were drying on the washing* line.
cord, rope, string, thread, wire, cable, flex, lead

linger verb
1 *The smell of burning wood* lingered *in the air.*
continue, remain, stay, last, persist
opposite **disappear**
2 *Don't* linger *outside in this cold weather.*
hang about, wait about, loiter, dawdle, dally, delay
opposite **hurry**

link noun
The two schools have close links with each other.
relationship, association, connection, bond, tie

link verb
They linked the trailer to the tractor.
attach, connect, fasten, join, couple
opposite separate

lion noun
A female lion is a **lioness**.
A young lion is a **cub**.
A group of lions is a **pride**.
The fur collar on a male lion is its **mane**.

liquid adjective
Pour the liquid jelly into a mould.
runny, watery, wet, fluid, flowing, running, sloppy
To make something liquid by heating it is to **melt** it.
Liquid metal or rock is **molten**.
opposite solid

liquid noun
The flask contained a frothy green liquid.
fluid, solution, juice, liquor
The liquid inside a plant is **sap**.

list¹ noun
A list of people's names is a **roll** or **register**.
A list of people who have tasks to do is a **rota**.
A list of books in the library or of goods for sale is a **catalogue**.
A list of topics mentioned in a book is an **index**.
A list of things to choose from is a **menu**.
A list of things to do or remember is a **checklist**.

list¹ verb
I helped to list the books in the library.
record, write down, catalogue, index, register

list² verb
The damaged ship listed to one side.
lean, tilt, tip, slope, incline

listen verb
to listen to something
The spy listened carefully to the instructions.
pay attention to, take notice of, attend to, heed
To listen secretly to a private conversation is to **eavesdrop**.

literature noun
1 *The bookshop specializes in children's literature.*
books, writing
For various kinds of literature see **writing**
2 *The travel agent gave us some literature to read.*
brochures, leaflets, pamphlets, handouts

litter noun
The street was covered with litter.
rubbish, waste, refuse, garbage, junk, clutter, mess, odds and ends

litter verb
The desk was littered with scrunched-up paper.
scatter, strew

little adjective & determiner

OVERUSED WORD

Try to vary the words you use for **little**. Here are some other words you could use.

FOR SOMETHING **LITTLE IN SIZE**
compact, mini, miniature, minute, petite, small, tiny, teeny, (Scottish) wee
The camera is so tiny it will fit in your pocket.
opposites big, large

FOR SOMEONE **LITTLE IN AGE**
small, young, (Scottish) wee
My granny lived in India when she was young.
opposites big, old

FOR A **LITTLE TIME** OR A **LITTLE WHILE**
brief, fleeting, passing, short

a
b
c
d
e
f
g
h
i
j
k
l
m
n
o
p
q
r
s
t
u
v
w
x
y
z

It was a short while before our friends arrived.
opposites **lengthy, long**

FOR **LITTLE FOOD** OR **LITTLE MONEY**
hardly any, insufficient, meagre, paltry, scarcely any
There was scarcely any food left in the house.
opposites **ample, plenty**

a little
1 *Would you like a little milk in your tea?*
some, a bit of, a spot of, a touch of
2 *I'm feeling a little tired now.*
a bit, slightly, rather, somewhat

live¹ (rhymes with **give**) verb
Will these plants live through the winter?
stay alive, survive, exist, flourish, last, continue, remain
opposite **die**
to live in a place
They live in a basement flat.
inhabit, occupy, dwell in, reside in
to live on
Koalas live on eucalyptus leaves.
eat, feed on

live² (rhymes with **hive**) adjective
The fishermen caught a live octopus in their nets.
alive, living, breathing
opposite **dead**

lively adjective
1 *The toddlers were in a lively mood.*
active, energetic, animated, spirited, boisterous, excited, vivacious, sprightly, frisky, chirpy, perky
opposite **inactive**
2 *The city centre is always lively at night.*
busy, bustling, crowded, exciting, buzzing
opposites **quiet, dead**

livid adjective
Gary was livid when he saw the damage to his bike.
angry, furious, fuming, incensed, enraged, seething, raging

living adjective
1 *Miss Millicent had no living relatives.*
alive
opposite **dead**
2 *There are no dinosaurs still living.*
existing, surviving
opposite **extinct**

living noun
1 *He makes a living from painting.*
income, livelihood
2 *What does she do for a living?*
job, occupation, profession, trade, career

load noun
1 *Camels can carry heavy loads.*
burden, weight
2 *The lorry delivered its load to the supermarket.*
cargo, consignment, goods, freight

load verb
1 *We loaded the suitcases into the car.*
pack, pile, heap, stow
2 *He was loaded with shopping bags.*
weigh down, burden, saddle

loan noun
She needs a loan to pay for her holiday.
advance
A system which allows you to pay for something later is **credit**.
A loan to buy a house is a **mortgage**.

loathe verb
My brother loathes the colour pink.
hate, detest, dislike, despise
opposites **love, adore**

local adjective
Our local shop delivers newspapers.
neighbourhood, nearby, neighbouring

A B C D E F G H I J K **L** M N O P Q R S T U V W X Y Z

locate verb
1 *I can't locate the book you asked for.*
find, discover, track down, detect, unearth, lay your hands on
opposite lose
2 *The art gallery is located in the city centre.*
place, position, put, situate, set up, build, establish, station

location noun
The pilot made a note of his location.
position, situation, whereabouts, place, spot

lock¹ noun
There was a heavy lock on the lid of the chest.
fastening, clasp, padlock, bolt, latch

lock¹ verb
Make sure you lock the door when you go out.
fasten, secure, bolt, close, shut, seal

lock² noun
The princess cut a lock from her hair.
tress, curl, tuft

lodge verb
1 *Where are you lodging at present?*
live, stay, reside, dwell
2 *The animals are lodged indoors in the winter.*
house, accommodate, board, put up
3 *The ball was lodged in a tree.*
get caught, get stuck, jam, wedge, fix, embed

log noun
1 *They collected logs to burn on the fire.*
For various types of wood see **wood**
2 *The astronauts kept a log of their voyage.*
diary, journal, record, account

logical adjective
The robot always gave a logical answer.
rational, reasonable, sensible, sound, valid, intelligent, clear, lucid, methodical, systematic
opposite illogical

lone adjective
A lone rider galloped past.
single, solitary, unaccompanied, isolated

lonely adjective
1 *Cara felt lonely while her friends were away.*
alone, friendless, lonesome, solitary, abandoned, neglected, forlorn, forsaken
2 *The climbers sheltered in a lonely hut.*
deserted, isolated, remote, secluded, out of the way

long¹ adjective
It seemed a long time before the bus came.
lengthy, prolonged, extended, extensive, long-lasting
opposite short

long² verb
to long for something
I'm longing for a drink.
yearn for, crave, want, wish for, desire, fancy, hunger for, pine for, hanker after, itch for
(informal) be dying for

look verb
1 *If you look carefully, you'll see an owl in the tree.*
watch, observe, view, regard, keep your eyes open
2 *My pet snake looks a bit hungry.*
appear, seem
to look after someone or something
We looked after their house when they went on holiday.
care for, keep an eye on, mind, tend, watch, watch over, guard, protect
To look after sick people is to **nurse** them.
to look for something
He spent ages looking for his keys.
hunt for, search for, seek
to look out
If you don't look out, you'll get wet.
beware, pay attention, take care, watch out, keep an eye open
See the panel on the next page.

a b c d e f g h i j k l m n o p q r s t u v w x y z

A
B
C
D
E
F
G
H
I
J
K
L
M
N
O
P
Q
R
S
T
U
V
W
X
Y
Z

OVERUSED WORD

Try to vary the words you use for look.
Here are some other words you could use.

TO **LOOK QUICKLY**
glance, glimpse, peek, peep
The secret agent glanced at her watch.

TO **LOOK CAREFULLY** OR **INTENTLY**
stare, peer, study, scrutinize, examine, inspect, take a good look at
The fossil hunters peered at the rocks.

TO **LOOK ANGRILY**
glare, glower, grimace, frown, scowl
The grumpy knight glowered at his servant.

To look steadily is to **gaze**.
To look in amazement is to **gape**.
To look over a wide area is to **scan** or **survey** it.

look noun
1 *Did you have a look at what she was wearing?*
glance, glimpse, peep, sight, view
2 *The guard had an unfriendly look.*
appearance, bearing, manner, air, expression, face

lookout noun
Lookouts were posted along the wall.
sentry, guard, sentinel, watchman

loom verb
1 *A figure loomed out of the mist.*
appear, emerge, arise, take shape
2 *The haunted mansion loomed above us.*
rise, tower, stand out, hang over

loop noun
Make a loop in the string and then tie a knot.
coil, hoop, circle, ring, noose, bend, curl, kink, twist

loop verb
The cowboy looped the reins round a fence post.
coil, wind, curl, bend, turn, twist

loose adjective
1 *Some of the cobbles on the road are loose.*
insecure, unfixed, movable, unsteady, shaky, wobbly
opposites firm, secure
2 *The fire was started by a loose wire.*
disconnected, unattached, detached
3 *These jeans are loose around the waist.*
slack, baggy, roomy, loose-fitting
opposite tight
4 *The chickens wander loose about the farm.*
free, at large, at liberty, on the loose, unconfined, unrestricted
opposite confined

loosen verb
Can you loosen these knots?
undo, unfasten, untie, free, loose, slacken, release, ease
opposite tighten

loot noun
The thieves buried their loot in a safe place.
haul, plunder, takings

loot verb
Rioters looted the shops.
raid, ransack, rob, steal from, pillage, plunder

lorry noun
For types of vehicle see **vehicle**

lose verb loses, losing, lost
1 *Debbie has lost one of her gloves.*
be unable to find, mislay, misplace
opposite find
2 *Unfortunately, we lost the game on Saturday.*
be defeated, get beaten, suffer a defeat
opposite win

loss noun
1 *She is suffering from loss of memory.*
failure, disappearance, deprivation
2 *The farmer was upset by the loss of his sheepdog.*
death, decease, passing

lot noun
We are having another lot of visitors this weekend.
group, batch, set, crowd, collection
a lot of
My brother needs a lot of help with his spelling.
a large amount of, a good or great deal of, plenty of
lots of
There are lots of toys to choose from in the shop.
a great number of, many, numerous, plenty of
(informal) loads of, tons of, masses of, oodles of, hundreds of

loud adjective
1 *The whole house was kept awake by the loud music.*
noisy, blaring, booming, deafening, rowdy, resounding, thunderous, penetrating, piercing
A noise which is loud enough to hear is audible.
opposites **quiet, soft**
2 *The tourists wore rather loud shirts.*
bright, gaudy, garish, showy, flashy
opposites **muted, subdued**

lounge verb
They lounged in the garden all day.
relax, be lazy, idle, laze, sprawl, lie around, loll, take it easy, waste time

lovable adjective
Our friends have a lovable new kitten.
adorable, dear, sweet, charming, likeable, lovely, appealing, attractive, cuddly, enchanting, endearing
opposite **hateful**

love noun
She often mentions her love of the outdoors.
liking, passion, fondness, affection, devotion, admiration, adoration
(informal) soft spot for

love verb
1 *They love each other and want to get married.*
be in love with, care for, adore, cherish, hold dear, treasure, worship, idolize
A relationship between two people who love each other is a romance.
2 *My friend, Dot, loves knitting.*
like, have a passion for, be fond of, be partial to, enjoy
opposite **hate**

lovely adjective

OVERUSED WORD

Try to vary the words you use for lovely. Here are some other words you could use.

FOR A **LOVELY PERSON**
charming, delightful, lovable, likeable, dear, sweet, enchanting, endearing
Jemma is a charming girl.

FOR A **LOVELY DAY** OR **LOVELY VIEW**
fine, glorious
It's a glorious day for a bicycle trip.

FOR A **LOVELY EXPERIENCE**
pleasant, pleasing, enjoyable
The girls had an enjoyable time camping.
opposite **nasty**

FOR SOMETHING THAT **LOOKS LOVELY**
appealing, attractive, beautiful, pretty
The roses look attractive in that vase.

loving adjective
Erin gave her teddy bear a loving hug.
affectionate, kind, friendly, warm, tender, fond, devoted, passionate
opposite **unfriendly**

low adjective
1 *The garden is surrounded by a low wall.*
short, shallow, sunken
2 *They were soldiers of low rank in the army.*
junior, inferior, lowly, modest, humble
3 *We spoke in low whispers.*
quiet, soft, muted, subdued, muffled

a
b
c
d
e
f
g
h
i
j
k
l
m
n
o
p
q
r
s
t
u
v
w
x
y
z

A B C D E F G H I J K

L

M N O P Q R S T U V W X Y Z

4 *The tuba plays* low *notes.*
bass, deep
opposite **high**

lower verb
1 *The supermarket* lowered *its prices.*
reduce, cut, bring down, decrease, lessen,
(informal) **slash**
2 *Please* lower *the volume of your radio.*
quieten, turn down
3 *At the end of the Olympic Games, they*
lower *the flag.*
take down, let down, dip
opposite **raise**

loyal adjective
Sir Valiant had always been a loyal *knight.*
true, trusty, faithful, steadfast, reliable,
dependable, devoted, constant, sincere
opposite **disloyal**

luck noun
1 *He found the secret entrance by* luck.
accident, chance, coincidence, fluke, fate,
destiny
2 *She had a bit of* luck *today.*
good fortune, success

lucky adjective
1 *I got the right answer by a* lucky *guess.*
accidental, chance, unintentional,
unplanned
2 *Some* lucky *person won a million
pounds.*
fortunate, favoured, successful
opposite **unlucky**

ludicrous adjective
They laughed at such a ludicrous *idea.*
ridiculous, absurd, laughable, idiotic,
foolish, crazy, daft, senseless

luggage noun
The luggage *can go in the boot of the car.*
baggage, cases, suitcases, bags

lull verb
She lulled *the baby by rocking it gently.*
calm, soothe, hush, quieten, pacify,
subdue

lull noun
There was a brief lull *in the conversation.*
pause, break, gap, interval, calm
(informal) **let-up**

lumber verb
1 *A rhinoceros* lumbered *towards them.*
move clumsily, trundle, trudge, tramp,
blunder, shamble
2 (informal) *Why am I* lumbered *with the
washing up?*
burden
(informal) **saddle**

lump noun
1 *Lumps of sticky clay stuck to his boots.*
chunk, piece, cluster, clump, wad, mass,
hunk, wedge, block
A round lump of something is a **ball**.
A lump of gold is a **nugget**.
A lump of earth is a **clod**.
A lump of blood is a **clot**.
2 *I could feel a* lump *where I'd bumped my
head.*
bump, swelling, bulge, protrusion

lump verb
to lump things together
The books and CDs were all lumped together.
put together, combine, merge, bunch up

lunge verb
Robin lunged *at the sheriff with his sword.*
thrust, charge, rush, dive, pounce,
throw yourself

lurch verb
1 *The bus passengers* lurched *from side to
side.*
reel, sway, rock, stagger, stumble, totter
2 *The ship* lurched *as the waves pounded it.*
pitch, roll, heave, lean, list

lure verb
Spiders lure *insects into their webs.*
attract, entice, tempt, coax, draw, invite,
persuade
Something used to lure an animal into a
trap is **bait**.

lurk verb
The jaguar lurked in wait for its prey.
skulk, loiter, prowl, crouch, hide,
lie in wait, lie low

lush adjective
Rainforests have lush vegetation.
rich, dense, thick, rampant, abundant

luxurious adjective
The dress was trimmed with luxurious lace.
grand, lavish, lush, rich, expensive, costly,
de luxe, plush, magnificent, splendid,
sumptuous
opposites simple, austere

luxury noun
The millionaire lived a life of luxury.
affluence, wealth, richness, splendour,
comfort, ease
opposite poverty

Mm

machine noun
Do you know how this machine works?
apparatus, appliance, device, engine,
contraption

mad adjective
1 *You must be mad to go out on a day like this.*
crazy, daft, insane, senseless, stupid,
foolish, idiotic
(informal) out of your mind, potty, nuts
opposites sensible, wise
2 *The emperor was mad with rage.*
angry, furious, beside yourself, frenzied,
hysterical
3 (informal) *Sandra is mad about horses.*
enthusiastic, fanatical, passionate

made
past tense see **make**

magazine noun
I bought a magazine to read on the train.
journal, periodical, paper, comic

magic adjective
1 *My uncle taught me some magic tricks.*
conjuring
2 *The castle was surrounded by a magic spell.*
magical, supernatural

magic noun
Do you believe in magic?
sorcery, witchcraft, wizardry, spells, charms,
enchantments

> ### WORD WEB
>
> PEOPLE WHO USE MAGIC
> **enchanter** or **enchantress, magician,**
> **sorcerer** or **sorceress, warlock, witch,**
> **wizard**
>
> See also **fairy**
>
> THINGS WHICH A SORCERER MIGHT DO
> **bewitch, enchant, cast** or **undo a spell,**
> **become invisible** or **vanish,**
> **brew a potion, put a curse on you**
>
> THINGS A SORCERER MIGHT HAVE OR USE
> **apprentice, cauldron, elixir, charm,**
> **magic potion, magic spell** or
> **incantation, talisman, wand**
>
> For magical creatures see **myth**

magical adjective
see **magic**

magician noun
1 *The magician pulled a scarf out of his hat.*
conjuror
2 *King Arthur was helped by the magician, Merlin.*
sorcerer, witch, wizard

magnificent adjective
1 *The mountain scenery was magnificent.*
beautiful, glorious, splendid,
spectacular, impressive, majestic

a
b
c
d
e
f
g
h
i
j
k
l
m
n
o
p
q
r
s
t
u
v
w
x
y
z

251

A
B
C
D
E
F
G
H
I
J
K
L

M

N
O
P
Q
R
S
T
U
V
W
X
Y
Z

2 *The film star lived in a* magnificent *house.*
grand, imposing, stately
(informal) posh
3 *That was a* magnificent *meal!*
excellent, first-class, marvellous, superb
(informal) fabulous, fantastic
opposite ordinary

magnify verb
Objects are magnified *through binoculars.*
enlarge, make larger
(informal) blow up
opposites reduce, minimize

mail noun
The mail *arrived early this morning.*
post, delivery, letters and parcels

mail verb
Can you mail *this letter for me?*
post, send, dispatch

maim verb
see injure

main adjective
1 *What was the* main *point of the story?*
central, chief, most important, basic,
essential, fundamental, primary,
predominant
2 *This is the* main *shopping area in the town.*
major, principal, biggest, foremost, largest,
leading, prime
opposites minor, unimportant

mainly adverb
Chimpanzees eat mainly *fruit and vegetables.*
largely, mostly, chiefly, principally,
predominantly, primarily

maintain verb
1 *The referee tried to* maintain *order.*
keep, preserve
2 *A team of gardeners* maintain *the grounds.*
look after, take care of, keep in order
3 *How much does it cost to* maintain *a family?*
support, keep, provide for
4 *He still* maintains *that he's innocent.*
claim, declare, assert, insist, state, contend

majestic adjective
The town was dominated by the majestic *castle.*
grand, magnificent, splendid, impressive,
stately, imposing, noble

major adjective
1 *There are delays on all the* major *roads into the city.*
chief, principal, primary, leading
2 *Writing her first novel was a* major *achievement.*
big, great, considerable, significant,
important
opposite minor

majority noun
the majority of
The majority of *children walk to school.*
the greater number of, the bulk of, most
opposite minority

make verb makes, making, made
1 *We* made *a shelter out of leaves and branches.*
build, construct, assemble, put together,
produce, manufacture
2 *Those two are always* making *trouble.*
cause, bring about, give rise to, provoke
3 *They* made *me captain.*
appoint, elect, nominate
4 *They've* made *the attic into a games room.*
change, turn, convert, modify, transform,
alter
5 *She'll* make *a good actress when she's older.*
become, grow into, turn into, change into
6 *The regulations were* made *to protect children.*
establish, fix, decide on, agree
7 *You* made *me jump!*
cause somebody to
8 *We can't* make *her go if she doesn't want to.*
force, compel, order
9 *He* made *a lot of money last year.*
gain, get, obtain, acquire, receive, earn,
win
10 *The ship finally* made *land.*
reach, arrive at, get to, get as far as

11 *What time do you make it?*
calculate, estimate, reckon
12 *2 and 2 make 4.*
add up to, come to, total
13 *I'll make you an offer for your old bike.*
propose, suggest
14 *Have you made your bed this morning?*
arrange, tidy
to make off
The thieves made off in a stolen car.
leave, escape, get away, run away,
disappear
(informal) clear off
to make someone or something out
I can't make out why everything went wrong.
understand, work out, comprehend,
fathom, make sense of
to make up
I made up a new flavour of ice-cream.
create, invent, think up, concoct

make noun
What make of computer do you have?
brand, model, label

male adjective
For male human beings see **man**
For male animals see **animal**
opposite **female**

malicious adjective
Someone had spread a malicious rumour.
malevolent, hostile, malign, spiteful,
vindictive, vicious, hurtful

mammal noun
For various kinds of animal see **animal**

man noun
A polite word for a man is **gentleman**.
Informal words are **bloke**, **chap**, **fellow**, and
guy.
A married man is a **husband**.
A man who has children is a **father**.
An unmarried man is a **bachelor**.
A man whose wife has died is a **widower**.
A man on his wedding day is a **bridegroom**.
A man who is engaged to be married is a
fiancé.
Words for a young man are **boy**, **lad**, and
youth.

manage verb
1 *His eldest son manages the business now.*
be in charge of, run, direct, lead,
control, govern, rule, supervise, oversee,
preside over
2 *I can't manage any more work this week.*
cope with, deal with, take on, carry out
3 *We'll have to manage without the car.*
cope, make do, get along, get by

manager noun
If you have a problem, talk to the manager.
chief, director, proprietor
(informal) boss

mania noun
*A mania for the pop group swept the
country.*
craze, hysteria, obsession, passion,
fixation, fad

manipulate verb
1 *He manipulated the dials on the robot.*
operate, work, handle, control
(informal) twiddle
2 *She uses her charm to manipulate people.*
take advantage of, use, exploit, impose on

manner noun
1 *They did the work in an efficient
manner.*
way, style, fashion, method
2 *I was put off by her frosty manner.*
behaviour, conduct, attitude, disposition,
air, look, bearing
manners
Trolls have no manners at all!
politeness, courtesy, graces

manoeuvre noun
1 *Parking a bus is a difficult manoeuvre.*
move, operation
2 *The opposing team used a clever
manoeuvre.*
strategy, tactic, trick, dodge, plan, plot,
scheme

manoeuvre verb
How do you manoeuvre a hot-air balloon?
guide, move, pilot, steer, navigate

a
b
c
d
e
f
g
h
i
j
k
l
m
n
o
p
q
r
s
t
u
v
w
x
y
z

A B C D E F G H I J K L **M** N O P Q R S T U V W X Y Z

manufacture verb
The factory manufactures pine furniture.
make, build, assemble, fabricate

many determiner
I've been on an aeroplane many times.
a lot of, plenty of, numerous, frequent, countless, innumerable, untold
(informal) **umpteen, lots of**
opposite **few**

map noun
The travel agent gave us a free map of Paris.
chart, diagram, plan
A book of maps is an **atlas**.
A person who draws maps is a **cartographer**.

mar verb
The film was marred by a terrible soundtrack.
spoil, ruin, harm, impair, tarnish

march verb
The brass band marched down the High Street.
parade, file, troop, stride, pace

margin noun
Don't write in the margin of the paper.
border, edge

marginal adjective
There is a marginal difference between the two signatures.
slight, small, minimal, minor, unimportant, negligible, borderline
opposite **great**

mark noun
1 *There were muddy paw marks all over the kitchen floor.*
spot, stain, blemish, blotch, blot, smear, smudge, streak
A mark left by a pen or pencil is a **scribble**.
A mark left by fingers is a **fingermark**.
A mark on your skin that you are born with is a **birthmark**.
2 *They stood in silence as a mark of respect.*
sign, token, indication, symbol, emblem
3 *What mark did you get in the spelling test?*
score, grade

mark verb
1 *Please be careful not to mark the photographs.*
stain, smudge, dirty, blot
2 *The teacher had a pile of essays to mark.*
correct, grade, assess
3 *There will be trouble, you mark my words!*
mind, heed, attend to, listen to, note, take note of

marked adjective
There's a marked difference in style between the paintings.
noticeable, considerable, pronounced, clear, obvious, distinct, decided
opposites **slight, minor**

market noun
see **shop**

marriage noun
1 *My grandparents celebrated 40 years of marriage.*
matrimony, wedlock
2 *Today is the anniversary of their marriage.*
wedding
See also **wedding**

marry verb
In what year did your grandparents marry?
get married, wed
(informal) **tie the knot, get hitched**
A couple who have promised to marry are **engaged** to each other.
A man who is engaged to be married is a **fiancé** and the woman he is engaged to is his **fiancée**.

marsh noun
Wading birds are found in coastal marshes.
swamp, bog, wetland, marshland, fen

marvel noun
the marvels of modern science
wonder, miracle

marvel verb
to marvel at
The crowd marvelled at the juggler's skill.
admire, wonder at, be amazed by,
be astonished by

marvellous adjective
1 *The professor showed us his marvellous inventions.*
amazing, remarkable, extraordinary,
incredible, miraculous, astonishing,
phenomenal
opposite ordinary
2 *We had a marvellous day at the zoo.*
excellent, superb, tremendous, wonderful,
splendid
(informal) brilliant, fantastic, terrific, super,
smashing
opposites bad, awful

masculine adjective
The singer had a deep, masculine voice.
male, manly, macho, virile
opposite feminine

mash verb
Mash *the potatoes until they're smooth.*
crush, pound, pulp, smash, squash
To make something into powder is to grind
or pulverize it.

mask verb
The entrance was masked by an overhanging tree.
conceal, hide, cover, obscure, screen, veil,
shroud, camouflage

mass noun
She sifted through the mass of papers on her desk.
heap, pile, mound, stack, collection,
quantity, accumulation
(informal) load

massacre verb
see kill

massive adjective
see huge

master noun
1 *We played a game in which I was master of the castle.*
lord, ruler, governor, chief
2 *Sherlock Holmes was a master of disguises.*
expert (at), genius, ace, wizard

master verb
1 *Have you mastered chess yet?*
grasp, learn, understand
(informal) get the hang of,
get to grips with
2 *I've managed to master my fear of heights.*
overcome, conquer, defeat, triumph over,
get the better of, control, curb, subdue,
tame

match noun
1 *The semi-final was a really exciting match.*
game, contest, competition, fixture,
tournament, tie
2 *The hat and gloves are a good match.*
combination, pair

match verb
Does this tie match my shirt?
go with, suit, fit with, blend with,
tone in with
opposite contrast with

matching adjective
The hat comes with matching gloves.
coordinating, corresponding,
complementary, twin
opposite contrasting

mate noun (informal)
1 *Gary is one of my best mates.*
friend, pal, chum, buddy
2 *He's got a job as a plumber's mate.*
assistant, helper, apprentice

material noun
1 *I'm collecting material for the school magazine.*
information, facts, data, ideas, notes
2 *The cleaning materials are in the cupboard.*
stuff, substances, things
3 *The kite is made of lightweight material.*
cloth, fabric
For kinds of fabric see cloth

a
b
c
d
e
f
g
h
i
j
k
l
m
n
o
p
q
r
s
t
u
v
w
x
y
z

A
B
C
D
E
F
G
H
I
J
K
L
M
N
O
P
Q
R
S
T
U
V
W
X
Y
Z

mathematics noun
This computer game makes mathematics *fun!*
sums
(informal) maths

WORD WEB

BRANCHES OF MATHS
algebra, arithmetic, geometry, statistics

THINGS YOU MIGHT DO IN MATHS
adding, calculating, counting, dividing,
measuring, multiplying, subtracting

SOME INSTRUMENTS USED FOR MATHS
calculator, compasses, computer,
dividers, ruler, set square

For other words used in maths see
measurement, shape

matted adjective
The dog's coat was dirty and matted.
knotted, tangled, uncombed

matter noun
1 *The manager will deal with this* matter.
affair, concern, issue, business, situation,
incident, subject, topic, thing
2 *Peat consists mainly of plant* matter.
material, stuff, substance
3 *What's the* matter *with the car?*
problem, difficulty, trouble, worry

matter verb
Will it matter *if I'm late?*
be important, count, make a difference

mature adjective
1 *The zoo has two* mature *gorillas.*
adult, fully grown, well developed
opposite young
2 *He is very* mature *for his age.*
grown-up, responsible, sensible
opposites immature, childish

maximum adjective
What is the maximum *speed of the rocket?*
greatest, top, highest, fullest, biggest,
largest
opposite minimum

maximum noun
The heat is at its maximum *at midday.*
highest point, peak, top, upper limit,
ceiling

maybe adverb
Maybe *you'll be picked for the football team.*
perhaps, possibly
opposite definitely

maze noun
We were lost in a maze *of underground
tunnels.*
labyrinth, network, web, tangle

meadow noun
Cows were grazing in the meadow.
field, pasture

meagre adjective
The prisoners were given meagre *rations of
food.*
scant, sparse, poor, scanty, inadequate,
insufficient, skimpy, paltry
(informal) measly, stingy
opposites generous, ample

meal noun

WORD WEB

MEALS YOU HAVE AT VARIOUS TIMES OF DAY
breakfast, brunch, dinner,
(informal) elevenses, high tea,
lunch or luncheon, supper, tea

A big formal meal is a banquet or feast.
A quick informal meal is a snack.
A meal you eat out of doors is a
barbecue or picnic.
A meal where you help yourself to food
is a buffet.
A meal you buy ready cooked is a
takeaway.

VARIOUS COURSES OF A MEAL
starter; main course; dessert, pudding,
sweet, (informal) afters

See also food

mean¹ verb means, meaning, meant
1 *A red traffic light* means *that cars have to stop.*
indicate, signify, denote, express, imply, convey, communicate, stand for, symbolize
2 *I* mean *to get better at swimming this year.*
intend, plan, aim, propose, want

mean² adjective
1 *Scrooge was too* mean *to buy any presents.*
selfish, miserly, uncharitable
(informal) stingy, tight-fisted, penny-pinching
opposite generous
2 *That was a* mean *trick to play.*
unkind, unpleasant, nasty, spiteful, vicious, cruel, malicious
opposite kind

meaning noun
What is the meaning *of this riddle?*
sense, significance, explanation, interpretation, definition

meaningful adjective
The two friends exchanged a meaningful *look.*
pointed, suggestive, significant, expressive
opposite meaningless

means plural noun
1 *Email is a popular* means *of communication.*
method, mode, medium, channel, course, way
2 *They don't have the* means *to buy a house.*
money, resources, funds, finance, income, wherewithal

measure verb
Measure the height of the wall.
calculate, gauge, assess, survey
To measure the weight of something is to weigh it.

measure noun
1 *At least we now know the* measure *of the problem.*
size, extent, magnitude
2 *They are taking* measures *to improve the park.*
step, action, course, procedure, means

measurement noun
What are the measurements *of this room?*
dimensions, size, extent, proportions

WORD WEB

UNITS FOR MEASURING DISTANCE
millimetre, centimetre, metre, kilometre; inch, foot, yard, mile

The distance of an object in space is measured in light years.
The depth of the sea is measured in fathoms.

UNITS FOR MEASURING AREA
square centimetre or square metre, hectare; square inch or square foot, acre

UNITS FOR MEASURING VOLUME
millilitre, litre, kilolitre; pint, quart, gallon

UNITS FOR MEASURING WEIGHT
milligram, gram, kilo or kilogram, tonne; ounce, pound, stone, ton

UNITS FOR MEASURING TIME
second, minute, hour, day, week, month, year, decade, century

UNITS FOR MEASURING SPEED
kilometres per hour, miles per hour

The speed of a boat or ship is measured in knots.

UNITS FOR MEASURING TEMPERATURE
degrees Celsius, degrees centigrade, degrees Fahrenheit

OTHER MEASUREMENTS USED IN COOKING
cup or cupful, dessertspoon, pinch, spoonful, teaspoon, tablespoon

a
b
c
d
e
f
g
h
i
j
k
l
m
n
o
p
q
r
s
t
u
v
w
x
y
z

A
B
C
D
E
F
G
H
I
J
K
L
M
N
O
P
Q
R
S
T
U
V
W
X
Y
Z

meat noun

WORD WEB

SOME KINDS OF MEAT
bacon, beef, chicken, duck, game, gammon, goose, ham, lamb, mutton, pork, turkey, veal, venison

CUTS OR JOINTS OF MEAT
breast, brisket, chop, cutlet, fillet, leg, loin, rib, rump, sirloin, steak

FOODS MADE FROM MEAT
burger, chop, corned beef, cutlet, haggis, hamburger, kebab, meatball, mince, pasty, paté, pie, rissole, sausage, sausage roll

medal noun

Our team won a bronze medal in the relay race.
award, prize, trophy
A person who wins a medal is a **medallist**.

meddle verb

1 *He is always meddling in other people's affairs.*
interfere, intrude, intervene, pry
(informal) **poke your nose in**
2 *Don't meddle with my things.*
fiddle about, tinker

medicine noun

Did you take your cough medicine?
drug, medication, treatment, remedy
An amount of medicine taken at one time is a **dose**.
Medicine which a doctor gives you is a **prescription**.
My cousin is studying herbal medicine.
therapy, treatment, healing

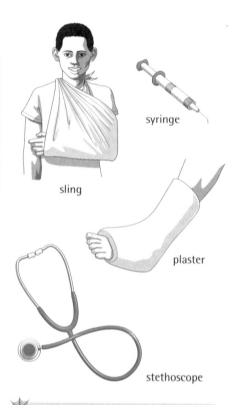

syringe

sling

plaster

stethoscope

WORD WEB

SOME TYPES OF MEDICINE
anaesthetic, antibiotic, antidote, antiseptic, gargle, painkiller, sedative, tincture, tonic, tranquillizer

FORMS IN WHICH YOU TAKE MEDICINE
capsule, inhaler, injection, lotion, lozenge, ointment, pill, tablet

INSTRUMENTS AND OTHER THINGS USED IN MEDICINE
bandage, dressing, forceps, gauze, lint, plaster, poultice, scalpel, sling, splint, stethoscope, syringe, thermometer, tweezers

PLACES WHERE YOU CAN GET MEDICAL TREATMENT
clinic, doctor's surgery, health centre, hospital, infirmary, nursing home, sickbay

thermometer

dressing

message noun
Did you get my message?
note, letter, communication
For types of message see
communication
For secret messages see **code**

messy adjective
My bedroom is really messy!
muddled, untidy, disorderly, chaotic,
dirty, filthy, grubby, mucky
(informal) higgledy-piggledy
opposite neat

met
past tense see **meet**

metal noun

> **WORD WEB**
> SOME COMMON METALS
> aluminium, brass, bronze, copper, gold,
> iron, lead, magnesium, mercury, nickel,
> pewter, platinum, silver, steel, tin, zinc
>
> A bar of metal is an **ingot**.
> A lump of metal is a **nugget**.
> Something that looks or sounds like
> metal is **metallic**.

method noun
*My granny has a secret method for
making jam.*
technique, way, procedure, process
An especially skilful method for doing
something is a **knack**.

methodical adjective
*Inspector Dixon is always very
methodical.*
organized, orderly, systematic,
meticulous, careful, deliberate,
efficient, businesslike,
painstaking
opposite careless

middle adjective
The middle lane is reserved for buses.
central, inner, inside, midway

middle noun
*A scarecrow stood in the middle of
the field.*
centre, core, heart, midpoint
The middle of a wheel is the **hub**.
The middle part of an atom or cell is the
nucleus.

might noun
I banged at the door with all my might.
strength, power, energy, force, vigour

mighty adjective
The dragon let out a mighty roar.
powerful, forceful, vigorous, ferocious,
violent, great, enormous, hefty
opposite weak

mild adjective
1 *He's a mild person who never complains.*
amiable, docile, easy-going, gentle,
good-tempered, harmless, kind, lenient,
merciful, placid, soft-hearted
2 *The weather has been mild for this time of
year.*
pleasant, warm, temperate
opposite severe

milk noun
Foods made from milk are **dairy products**.
See also **food**

milky adjective
The flask contained a milky liquid.
whitish, cloudy, misty, chalky, opaque
opposite clear

mimic verb
My dad is good at mimicking famous people.
do impressions of, imitate, impersonate,
pretend to be
(informal) take off
If you mimic people especially to make fun
of them, you **caricature** or **parody** them.

mind noun
1 *Her mind was as sharp as ever.*
brain, intelligence, intellect, head,
sense, understanding, wits, judgement,
mental powers, reasoning

2 *Are you sure you won't change your* mind*?*
wishes, intention, fancy, inclination, opinion, outlook, point of view

mind verb
1 *Will you* mind *my bag for a minute?*
guard, look after, watch, care for
(informal) keep an eye on
2 Mind *the step.*
look out for, watch out for, beware of, pay attention to, heed, note
3 *They won't* mind *if I'm late.*
bother, care, worry, be upset, take offence, object, disapprove

mine noun
A coal mine is a colliery or pit.
A place where coal is removed from the surface of the ground is an opencast mine.
A place where stone or slate is removed is a quarry.

mingle verb
The secret agent mingled *with the crowd.*
mix in, circulate, blend, combine, merge, fuse

miniature adjective
A piccolo looks like a miniature *flute.*
tiny, minute, diminutive, small-scale, baby, mini
See also small

minimum adjective
Set the oven to the minimum *temperature.*
least, smallest, littlest, lowest
opposite maximum

minor adjective
I only had a minor *part in the play.*
small, unimportant, insignificant, inferior, subordinate, trivial, petty
opposite major

minute adjective
You can hardly see the minute *crack.*
tiny, minuscule, microscopic, negligible
opposite large

miraculous adjective
The patient made a miraculous *recovery.*
amazing, astonishing, astounding, extraordinary, incredible, marvellous, unbelievable, wonderful, mysterious, inexplicable

misbehave verb
My puppy has been misbehaving *again!*
behave badly, be naughty, be disobedient, get up to mischief
opposite behave

miscellaneous adjective
The bag contained miscellaneous *balls of wool.*
assorted, various, different, mixed

mischief noun
The twins are always getting up to mischief.
naughtiness, bad behaviour, disobedience, playfulness, roguishness

miserable adjective
1 *You look* miserable*—what's the matter?*
sad, unhappy, sorrowful, gloomy, glum, downhearted, despondent, dejected, depressed, melancholy, mournful, tearful
opposites cheerful, happy
2 *The animals lived in* miserable *conditions.*
distressing, uncomfortable, wretched, pitiful, pathetic, squalid
opposite comfortable
3 *The weather was cold and* miserable.
dismal, dreary, depressing, unpleasant
opposite pleasant

miserly adjective
He was too miserly *to donate any money.*
mean, selfish
(informal) grasping, stingy, tight-fisted, penny-pinching
opposite generous

misery noun
The slaves must have led a life of misery.
sadness, sorrow, unhappiness, grief, distress, despair, anguish, wretchedness, suffering, torment, heartache, depression
opposite happiness

A
B
C
D
E
F
G
H
I
J
K
L
M
N
O
P
Q
R
S
T
U
V
W
X
Y
Z

misfortune noun
I heard about her family's misfortune.
bad luck, trouble, hardship, adversity,
affliction, setback, mishap
opposite **good luck**

mishap noun
Dad had a slight mishap with the car.
accident, problem, difficulty, setback

mislay verb mislays, mislaying, mislaid
I seem to have mislaid my purse.
lose
opposite **find**

misleading adjective
The directions he gave were quite misleading.
confusing, unreliable, deceptive,
ambiguous, unclear

miss verb
1 *I missed the bus.*
be too late for
2 *The arrow missed the target.*
fall short of, go wide of
3 *If we leave now, we should miss the traffic.*
avoid
4 *I missed Dad when he was in hospital.*
long for, yearn for, pine for
to miss something out
I missed out the boring bits of the story.
leave out, omit, ignore, overlook, skip

missile noun
see **weapon**

missing adjective
She found the missing keys in a drawer.
lost, mislaid, misplaced, absent, straying

mission noun
1 *Her mission in life was to help those in need.*
aim, purpose, objective, task, job,
campaign
2 *The astronauts are on a mission to Mars.*
expedition, journey, voyage, exploration

mist noun
1 *We drove slowly through the mist.*
fog, haze, cloud, drizzle
2 *I can't see because of the mist on my glasses.*
condensation, steam

mistake noun
This piece of writing is full of mistakes.
error, inaccuracy, blunder, slip, slip-up,
lapse
A spelling mistake is a **misspelling**.
A mistake where something is left out is an
omission.
A mistake in a printed book is a **misprint**.

mistake verb mistakes, mistaking,
mistook, mistaken
She mistook my meaning entirely.
misunderstand, get wrong, mix up

mistrust verb
Do you have any reason to mistrust him?
distrust, have doubts about, suspect
opposite **trust**

misty adjective
1 *If it's misty outside, take a torch.*
foggy, hazy
2 *I can't see through the misty window.*
steamy, cloudy, smoky, opaque
3 *We saw a misty shape approaching.*
faint, fuzzy, blurred, dim, indistinct,
shadowy, vague
opposite **clear**

misunderstand verb
misunderstands, misunderstanding,
misunderstood
I think you misunderstood what I said.
mistake, get wrong, miss the point of
opposite **understand**

mix verb
Mix the ingredients in a bowl.
combine, blend, mingle
to mix something up
Please don't mix up my CDs.
muddle, jumble, confuse
To mix up playing cards is to **shuffle** them.

a
b
c
d
e
f
g
h
i
j
k
l
m
n
o
p
q
r
s
t
u
v
w
x
y
z

A B C D E F G H I J K L **M** N O P Q R S T U V W X Y Z

mixed adjective
Add a teaspoon of mixed *herbs.*
assorted, various, different, miscellaneous
opposite **separate**

mixture noun
1 *Put the cake* mixture *in a baking tin.*
mix, blend, combination
A mixture of metals is an alloy.
A mixture of two different species of plant or animal is a hybrid.
2 *There's an odd* mixture *of things in the drawer.*
assortment, collection, variety, jumble
A confused mixture is a mishmash.

moan verb
1 *The wounded warrior* moaned *in pain.*
cry, groan, sigh, wail, howl, whimper
2 *Ned's always* moaning *about the food.*
complain, grumble, grouse, whine
(informal) whinge

mob noun
An angry mob *stormed the castle.*
crowd, horde, throng, mass, rabble, gang, pack, herd, bunch

mob verb
Autograph hunters mobbed *the pop star.*
crowd round, swarm round, surround, besiege, hem in, jostle

mobile adjective
1 *A* mobile *library visits once a fortnight.*
movable, travelling
Something that you can carry about is portable.
opposite **stationary**
2 *A week after the injury, he was* mobile *again.*
moving about, active
(informal) up and about
opposite **immobile**

mock verb
It was mean of them to mock *his singing.*
jeer at, laugh at, make fun of, scoff at, sneer at, ridicule, scorn, deride
(informal) take the mickey out of

model adjective
1 *We went to an exhibition of* model *railways.*
miniature, toy
2 *She's a* model *pupil.*
ideal, perfect

model noun
1 *I'm building a* model *of a space rocket.*
copy, replica, toy
2 *This is the latest* model *of skateboard.*
design, type, version
3 *She's a* model *of good behaviour.*
example, ideal

model verb
The artist models *figures in clay.*
make, mould, shape, construct, fashion

moderate adjective
Her first book was a moderate *success.*
average, fair, modest, medium, reasonable, passable, tolerable
opposite **exceptional**

moderately adverb
He answered the questions moderately *well.*
fairly, reasonably, quite, rather, somewhat
(informal) pretty

modern adjective
1 *All the equipment in their kitchen was* modern.
up to date, contemporary, advanced, the latest
opposite **out of date**
2 *She always dresses in* modern *clothes.*
fashionable, stylish, modish
(informal) trendy, hip
opposite **old-fashioned**

modest adjective
1 *He's very* modest *about his success.*
humble, quiet, reserved, shy, bashful, coy
opposite **conceited**
2 *There has been a* modest *increase in sales.*
moderate, reasonable, average, medium

modify verb
We've had to modify *our travel plans.*
adapt, alter, change, adjust, refine, revise, vary

moist adjective
1 *The walls of the dungeon were* moist.
damp, wet, watery, clammy, dank
2 *Tropical plants grow well in a* moist *atmosphere.*
humid, muggy, steamy, rainy
opposite **dry**

moisture noun
There is still a lot of moisture *on the ground.*
wetness, dampness, damp, dew, condensation, humidity

moment noun
1 *I'll be ready in a* moment.
minute, second, instant, flash
(informal) jiffy, tick
2 *It was a great* moment *in the history of space travel.*
time, occasion, period

momentary adjective
He felt a momentary *stab of pain.*
brief, short, fleeting, temporary
opposite **permanent**

monarch noun
see **ruler**

money noun
How much money *do you have with you?*
cash, currency, funds, finance
(informal) dough, dosh
A large amount of money is a fortune, riches, *or* wealth.

monster noun
A sea monster *reared its head above the waves.*
beast, giant, ogre, brute

monstrous adjective
1 *The town was engulfed by a* monstrous *wave.*
huge, gigantic, enormous, immense, massive, colossal, great, hulking, mighty, towering, vast

2 *The nation was shocked by the* monstrous *crime.*
horrifying, shocking, wicked, evil, hideous, horrible, terrible, atrocious, dreadful, gruesome, outrageous, scandalous

mood noun
What sort of mood *is he in today?*
temper, humour, state of mind, disposition

moody adjective
She's been moody *and withdrawn for weeks.*
sulky, sullen, grumpy, bad-tempered, temperamental, touchy, miserable, gloomy, glum
opposite **cheerful**

moon noun

> **WORD WEB**
>
> FORMS IN WHICH WE SEE THE MOON
> **crescent moon, full moon, new moon; moonbeam, moonlight**
>
> THINGS YOU MIGHT FIND OR DO ON THE MOON
> **crater, moon dust, moon rock, moonscape, moonwalk**
>
> A word meaning 'to do with the Moon' is **lunar**.
>
> See also **astronaut, space**

moor¹ noun
The tower stood on a windswept moor.
moorland, heath, fell

moor² verb
We moored *the boat in the harbour.*
tie up, secure, fasten, anchor, berth, dock

moral adjective
She tried her best to lead a moral *life.*
good, honest, truthful, upright, decent, honourable, principled, ethical, virtuous, righteous
opposite **immoral**

a
b
c
d
e
f
g
h
i
j
k
l
m
n
o
p
q
r
s
t
u
v
w
x
y
z

moral noun
The moral of this story is that crime doesn't pay.
lesson, message, meaning

morale noun
The new coach has improved the team's morale.
confidence, spirit, state of mind, attitude, mood

more determiner
The soup needs more pepper.
extra, further, added, additional
opposite **less**

morning noun
The expedition set off in the early morning.
daybreak, dawn, first light, sunrise
For other times of the day see **day**

morsel noun
They hadn't eaten a morsel of food all day.
bite, crumb, mouthful, taste, nibble, piece, scrap, fragment

mortal adjective
1 *All human beings are mortal.*
opposite **immortal**
2 *The knight had received a mortal wound.*
deadly, fatal, lethal

mostly adverb
I spend my money mostly on books and CDs.
mainly, largely, chiefly, primarily, generally, usually, normally, typically, principally, predominantly

motion noun
He summoned the waiter with a motion of his hand.
gesture, movement

motivate verb
What motivated you to write a book?
prompt, drive, stimulate, urge, provoke, spur, influence, induce

motive noun
The police can find no motive for the crime.
cause, motivation, reason, purpose, grounds

motor noun
The toy train had an electric motor.
engine

motto noun
Her motto has always been, 'Keep smiling'.
catchphrase, proverb, saying, slogan, golden rule

mould verb
The sculptor moulded the figures from clay.
shape, form, fashion, model, cast

mouldy adjective
All I found in the fridge was some mouldy cheese.
rotten, rotting, decaying, musty, damp

mound noun
1 *Her desk was covered with mounds of paper.*
heap, pile, stack, mass
2 *There used to be a castle on top of that mound.*
hill, hillock, rise, hump
An ancient mound of earth over a grave is a **barrow**.

mount verb
1 *She mounted the pony and rode off.*
get on, jump onto
2 *The butler slowly mounted the stairs.*
go up, climb, ascend
3 *The gallery is mounting a new exhibition.*
put up, set up, display
4 *The tension began to mount in the crowd.*
grow, increase, rise, intensify

mountain noun
The top of a mountain is the **peak** or **summit**.
A line of mountains is a **range**.
A long, narrow mountain is a **ridge**.

A B C D E F G H I J K L **M** N O P Q R S T U V W X Y Z

A mountain with a hole at the top caused by an eruption is a **volcano**.

WORD WEB

THINGS YOU MIGHT SEE ON OR NEAR A MOUNTAIN

avalanche, boulder, cave, cliff, crag, crevice, glacier, gorge, ledge, mountain pass, mountain stream, precipice, rocks, slope, valley or (Scottish) **glen**

SOME WORDS TO DESCRIBE A MOUNTAIN

barren, craggy, forbidding, jagged, lofty, massive, misty, rocky, rugged, snow-capped, soaring, towering, treacherous

An area of land with many mountains is **mountainous**.

mourn verb

He was still mourning the loss of his friend.
grieve for, lament for

mouth noun

1 *The crocodile slept with its mouth wide open.*
jaws
A dog's nose and mouth is its **muzzle**.
A word meaning 'to do with your mouth' is **oral**.
2 *They lived in a village at the mouth of the river.*
outlet
A wide river mouth is an **estuary** or (Scottish) **firth**.
3 *The mouth of the cave was hidden by trees.*
entrance, opening

move noun

1 *Don't make a move!*
movement
2 *The spy was watching their every move.*
action, step, deed, manoeuvre
3 *Is it my move next?*
turn, go, chance, opportunity

move verb

OVERUSED WORD

Try to vary the words you use for **move**. Here are some other words you could use.

TO MOVE FROM ONE PLACE TO ANOTHER
carry, remove, transfer, transport, shift
They shifted the piano into the front room.

TO MOVE FROM A POSITION
go, leave, depart, quit, budge
The camel stared and refused to budge.

TO MOVE RESTLESSLY
toss, turn, stir, twist, shake, fidget, twitch, flap
Please stop twitching in your seat.

TO MOVE FROM SIDE TO SIDE
sway, swing, wave, wag, wiggle
The knight swung a sword above his helmet.

TO MOVE ALONG
travel, walk, proceed
Few people travel on these roads after dark.

TO MOVE ALONG QUICKLY
hurry, dash, race, run, rush, hasten, hurtle, career, fly, speed, sweep, shoot, zoom
A boy went careering past on a scooter.
See also **run**

TO MOVE ALONG SLOWLY
amble, stroll, saunter, dawdle, crawl, drift
The tortoise sauntered down the path.

TO MOVE TOWARDS SOMETHING
advance, approach, come, proceed, progress
The lookout saw a pirate ship approaching.

TO MOVE BACK OR MOVE AWAY
back, retreat, reverse, withdraw
The serpent retreated, hissing, into its lair.

TO MOVE DOWNWARDS
drop, descend, fall, sink, swoop
A vulture swooped down from the sky.

a
b
c
d
e
f
g
h
i
j
k
l
m
n
o
p
q
r
s
t
u
v
w
x
y
z

A
B
C
D
E
F
G
H
I
J
K
L
M
N
O
P
Q
R
S
T
U
V
W
X
Y
Z

TO MOVE UPWARDS
rise, ascend, climb, mount, soar, arise
A hot-air balloon mounted *into the air.*

TO MOVE GRACEFULLY
flow, glide, dance
Some swans glided *gently across the pond.*

TO MOVE CLUMSILY
stumble, stagger, flounder, lurch, lumber, shuffle, totter, trundle, trip
The ogre stumbled *up the narrow steps.*

TO MOVE STEALTHILY
creep, crawl, edge, inch, slink
The secret agent edged *carefully along the wall.*

For ways to describe how an animal or bird moves see **animal, bird**

movement noun
1 *The robot made a sudden, jerky movement.*
motion, move, action, gesture
2 *Has there been any* movement *in their attitude?*
progress, development, change, shift
3 *She was involved in the peace* movement.
organization, group, party, campaign

movie noun
see **film**

moving adjective
The story was so moving that I started to cry.
emotional, inspiring, stirring, touching
(informal) **tear-jerking**

muck noun
They cleared the muck out of the stable.
dirt, filth, grime, mud, sludge, dung, manure

mucky adjective
My football boots are all mucky.
dirty, messy, muddy, grimy, grubby, filthy, foul, soiled, squalid
opposite **clean**

mud noun
The tractor left a trail of mud on the road.
dirt, muck, mire, sludge, clay, soil

muddle noun
1 *There was a muddle over the date of the party.*
confusion, misunderstanding
(informal) **mix-up**
2 *There was a muddle of clothes on the floor.*
jumble, mess, tangle

muddle verb
1 *Who muddled the papers on my desk?*
mix up, mess up, disorder, jumble up, shuffle, tangle
opposite **tidy**
2 *They got muddled and took the wrong turning.*
confuse, bewilder, puzzle, perplex

muddy adjective
1 *Take off your muddy shoes before you come in.*
dirty, messy, mucky, filthy, caked, soiled
opposite **clean**
2 *I got filthy walking across the muddy ground.*
boggy, marshy, waterlogged, wet, sodden
opposites **dry, firm**

muffle verb
1 *We muffled ourselves up to play in the snow.*
wrap, cover
2 *She tried to muffle her sneeze.*
stifle, smother, suppress, silence, deaden, dull

muffled adjective
They heard muffled voices from the next room.
faint, indistinct, unclear, muted, deadened
opposite **clear**

muggy adjective
The weather is often muggy before a storm.
humid, close, clammy, sticky, moist, damp, oppressive
opposite **fresh**

multiply verb
Her problems seemed to be multiplying.
increase, grow, spread, mount up

mumble verb
We couldn't hear the actor as he was mumbling.
mutter, talk indistinctly

munch verb
Kim sat munching popcorn all through the film.
chew, crunch
For other ways to eat see **eat**

murder verb
see **kill**

murky adjective
A creature loomed out of the murky waters of the loch.
dark, clouded, cloudy, dim, dull, dingy, gloomy, grey, foggy, misty
opposite clear

murmur verb
We heard voices murmuring in the room above.
mutter, mumble, whisper

muscular adjective
The wrestler had a muscular body.
brawny, beefy, athletic, sinewy, strapping, strong, well-built
opposites puny, weak

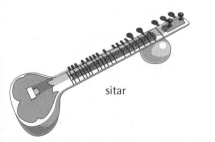
sitar

music noun

WORD WEB

VARIOUS KINDS OF MUSIC
blues, classical music, country and western, dance music, disco music, folk music, gospel, hip hop, jazz, orchestral music, pop music, punk, ragtime, rap, reggae, rock, soul, swing

TYPES OF MUSICAL COMPOSITION
anthem, ballad, carol, concerto, folk song, fugue, hymn, lullaby, march, melody, musical, opera, operetta, sonata, song, symphony, tune

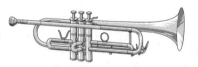
trumpet

harp

guitar

MUSICAL INSTRUMENTS

FAMILIES OF MUSICAL INSTRUMENTS
brass, keyboard, percussion, strings, woodwind

STRINGED INSTRUMENTS THAT CAN BE PLAYED WITH A BOW
cello, double bass, viola, violin or fiddle

a
b
c
d
e
f
g
h
i
j
k
l
m
n
o
p
q
r
s
t
u
v
w
x
y
z

A
B
C
D
E
F
G
H
I
J
K
L
M
N
O
P
Q
R
S
T
U
V
W
X
Y
Z

STRINGED INSTRUMENTS PLAYED BY PLUCKING OR STRUMMING
banjo, cittern, guitar, harp, lute, lyre, mandolin, sitar, ukulele, zither

BRASS INSTRUMENTS
bugle, cornet, euphonium, flugelhorn, French horn, trombone, trumpet, tuba

OTHER INSTRUMENTS PLAYED BY BLOWING
bagpipes, bassoon, clarinet, cor anglais, flute, harmonica or mouth organ, oboe, piccolo, recorder, saxophone

KEYBOARD INSTRUMENTS
accordion, harmonium, harpsichord, keyboard, organ, piano, synthesizer

tambourine

bagpipes

keyboard

bass drum

tuba

saxophone

PERCUSSION INSTRUMENTS
bass drum, bongo drum, castanets, cymbals, drum, glockenspiel, gong, kettledrum, maracas, marimba, rattle, snare drum, tabor, tambour, tambourine, timpani, tom-tom, triangle, tubular bells, vibraphone, xylophone

PEOPLE WHO PLAY VARIOUS INSTRUMENTS
bugler, cellist, clarinettist, drummer, fiddler, flautist, guitarist, harpist, lutenist, oboist, organist, percussionist, pianist, piper, timpanist, trombonist, trumpeter, violinist

SOME OTHER MUSICIANS
accompanist, composer, conductor, instrumentalist, singer, vocalist

For types of singing voice see sing

GROUPS OF MUSICIANS
band, choir or chorus, duet or duo, ensemble, group, orchestra, quartet, quintet, trio

TERMS USED IN MUSIC
chord, counterpoint, discord, harmony, melody, note, octave, pitch, rhythm, scale, semitone, tempo, theme, tone, tune

NAMES OF NOTES AND SIGNS IN WRITTEN MUSIC
clef, crotchet, flat, key signature, minim, natural, quaver, semibreve, semiquaver, sharp, stave, time signature

musical adjective
Helena has a very musical voice.
tuneful, melodic, melodious, harmonious, sweet-sounding

musty adjective
There was a musty smell in the cellar.
damp, dank, mouldy, stale, stuffy, airless
opposite fresh

mute adjective
We stared in mute amazement at the volcano.
silent, speechless, dumb, tongue-tied

mutilate verb
His right hand was mutilated by a firework.
maim, disfigure, injure, wound, mangle

mutiny noun
The crew were plotting a mutiny against the captain.
rebellion, revolt, uprising

mutter verb
The goblin sat muttering to himself in the corner.
mumble, murmur, whisper

mutual adjective
It is in our mutual interest to work together.
joint, common, shared, reciprocal

mysterious adjective
They uncovered a mysterious sign on the wall.
strange, puzzling, baffling, mystifying, perplexing, obscure, unexplained, incomprehensible, inexplicable, curious, weird

mystery noun
What really happened was a mystery.
puzzle, riddle, secret

mystify verb
We were mystified by the curious message.
puzzle, baffle, bewilder, perplex

myth noun

WORD WEB
CREATURES FOUND IN MYTHS AND LEGENDS
basilisk, brownie, chimera, centaur, cyclops, dragon, dwarf, elf, fairy, genie, giant, gnome, goblin, gremlin, gryphon, imp, kelpie, leprechaun, mermaid, nymph, ogre, phoenix, pixie, sea monster, selkie, serpent, sphinx, siren, sprite, troll, unicorn, vampire, werewolf, winged horse, yeti

See also **dragon**, **fairy**

unicorn

phoenix

genie

mythical adjective
The unicorn is a mythical beast.
fabulous, fanciful, imaginary, invented, fictional, legendary, mythological, non-existent, unreal
opposite real

a b c d e f g h i j k l m n o p q r s t u v w x y z

271

Nn

nag verb
He was always nagging her to work harder.
badger, pester, scold

naive adjective
He's so naive that he believes her promises.
innocent, inexperienced, unsophisticated, artless, gullible, simple

naked adjective
He walked naked into the bathroom.
bare, nude, unclothed, undressed
opposite clothed

name noun
The official names you have are your first names or forenames, and surname.
Names a Christian is given at baptism are Christian names.
A false name is an alias.
A name people use instead of your real name is a nickname.
A false name an author uses is a pen name or pseudonym.
The name of a book or film is its title.

name verb
The zoo named the new lion cubs Kiara and Kovu.
call
To name someone at the ceremony of baptism is to baptize or christen them.

nap noun
Granny always takes a nap on Sunday afternoons.
rest, sleep, doze, lie-down, siesta
(informal) snooze, forty winks

narrate verb
The famous actor narrated the story of his life.
tell, recount, relate

narrative noun
The sailor wrote an exciting narrative of his voyage.
account, history, story, tale, chronicle
(informal) yarn

narrow adjective
The rabbit squeezed through a narrow opening in the fence.
thin, slender, slim
opposite wide

nasty adjective
1 *Ogres have a thoroughly nasty temper.*
unkind, unpleasant, unfriendly, disagreeable, objectionable, odious, mean, malicious, cruel, spiteful, vicious
2 *A nasty smell wafted from the laboratory.*
unpleasant, offensive, disgusting, repulsive, revolting, horrible, foul, rotten, sickening
opposites agreeable, pleasant
3 *The weather suddenly turned nasty.*
unpleasant, rough, stormy, squally
For other ways to describe something you don't like see bad

nation noun
People from many nations compete in the Olympic Games.
country, state, land, race, population

national adjective
The programme will be broadcast on national television.
nationwide
opposite local

natural adjective
1 *Karen has a natural gift for music.*
born, inborn, instinctive, intuitive, native
2 *It's only natural to be nervous before an exam.*
normal, common, understandable, reasonable, predictable
opposite unnatural

nature noun
1 *I like TV programmes about nature.*
natural history, wildlife

A B C D E F G H I J K L M N O P Q R S T U V W X Y Z

2 *The old sheepdog has a very kind* **nature.**
character, disposition, personality, manner
3 *I collect coins, medals, and things of that* **nature.**
kind, sort, type, description, variety

naughty adjective
The puppies were quite naughty when they were young.
bad, badly behaved, disobedient, mischievous, uncontrollable, unmanageable, troublesome, unruly
opposite well behaved
to be naughty
misbehave, behave badly, disobey

navigate verb
The captain navigated his ship between the dangerous rocks.
steer, direct, guide, manoeuvre, pilot

navy noun
see **fleet**

near adjective
1 *We get on well with our* **near** *neighbours.*
next-door, nearby, close, adjacent, surrounding
2 *My birthday is* **near.**
approaching, coming
(informal) round the corner
3 *We sent cards to all our* **near** *relatives.*
close, dear, familiar, intimate
opposite distant

nearly adverb
Thank goodness, it's nearly dinner time!
almost, practically, virtually, just about, approaching

neat adjective
1 *Please leave the room as* **neat** *as possible.*
clean, orderly, tidy, uncluttered, immaculate
(informal) spick and span
2 *Craig always looks* **neat** *in his school uniform.*
smart, elegant, spruce, trim

3 *Her handwriting is very* **neat.**
precise, skilful, well formed
opposite untidy

necessary adjective
The recipe lists all the necessary ingredients.
essential, required, needed, needful, compulsory, obligatory, unavoidable
opposite unnecessary

need noun
There's a need for more shops in our area.
call, demand, requirement

need verb
1 *I need a pound coin for the locker.*
require, want, be short of, lack
2 *The charity needs our support.*
depend on, rely on

needless adjective
They went to a lot of needless expense.
unnecessary, unwanted, uncalled for, excessive, superfluous

needlework noun
You need good eyesight for needlework.
sewing

> ### WORD WEB
> SOME TYPES OF NEEDLEWORK
> **appliqué, beadwork, cross-stitch, embroidery, patchwork, quilting, tapestry**
> For other arts and crafts see **art**

needy adjective
They set up a fund to help needy children.
poor, deprived, badly off, hard up
opposite rich

negative adjective
He has a very negative attitude to his job.
pessimistic, uncooperative, unenthusiastic, grudging, unhelpful, unwilling
opposite positive

a
b
c
d
e
f
g
h
i
j
k
l
m
n
o
p
q
r
s
t
u
v
w
x
y
z

A

neglect verb
She's been neglecting her work.
forget, ignore, overlook, abandon,
disregard, pay no attention to, shirk

B

C

negligible adjective
There is a negligible difference in price.
tiny, slight, insignificant, unimportant,
trivial
opposite **considerable**

D

E

F

negotiate verb
1 *She negotiated with the car salesman.*
bargain, haggle, deal, confer
2 *The skier negotiated the course with ease.*
get past, get round, manoeuvre round

G

H

I

neighbourhood noun
They live in a very nice neighbourhood.
area, district, community, locality, vicinity

J

K

neighbouring adjective
*The journey will take them to Mexico and
neighbouring countries.*
nearby, bordering, adjacent, adjoining,
surrounding, nearest, next-door

L

M

N

O

neighbourly adjective
*It was very neighbourly of her to offer to
feed the cat.*
friendly, helpful, kind, obliging, sociable
opposite **unfriendly**

P

Q

R

nerve noun
1 *Acrobats need to have a lot of nerve.*
bravery, courage, daring, pluck
(informal) **bottle**
2 *He had the nerve to ask for more money!*
cheek, impudence, rudeness, impertinence

S

T

U

nervous adjective
She always feels nervous before an exam.
anxious, worried, apprehensive, concerned,
uneasy, fearful, edgy, fraught, tense
(informal) **uptight, jittery**
opposite **calm**

V

W

X

Y

nestle verb
The cubs nestled against their mother.
cuddle, curl up, snuggle

Z

neutral adjective
1 *A referee has to be neutral.*
impartial, unbiased, unprejudiced,
even-handed
opposites **biased, prejudiced**
2 *The room was decorated in neutral
colours.*
dull, drab, indefinite, colourless
opposites **vibrant, distinctive**

new adjective
1 *Start on a new sheet of paper.*
clean, fresh, unused, brand-new
Something new and unused is
in mint condition.
2 *They went to the motor show to see the
new models.*
latest, current, modern, recent,
up to date
3 *They've found a new bug in the
computer program.*
additional, extra, unexpected, unfamiliar
4 *Haven't you got any new ideas?*
fresh, original, novel, innovative, creative,
different
opposite **old**

news noun
What's the latest news?
information, word, report, bulletin
(old use) **tidings**

next adjective
1 *He lives in the house next to the chip
shop.*
adjacent, closest, nearest
opposite **distant**
2 *If you miss this bus, you can catch the
next one.*
following, subsequent
opposite **previous**

nice adjective
1 *That's not a very nice thing to say!*
pleasant, agreeable
opposite **nasty**
2 *There is a nice distinction between
borrowing and stealing.*
delicate, fine, precise, subtle

OVERUSED WORD

Try to vary the words you use for nice.
Here are some other words you could use.

FOR A NICE PERSON
good, kind, friendly, helpful, generous, likeable, amiable, charming, polite, genial
Our singing teacher is very likeable.

FOR A NICE EXPERIENCE
delightful, enjoyable, wonderful, marvellous, splendid
Did you have an enjoyable time in France?

FOR SOMETHING THAT LOOKS NICE
beautiful, attractive, pleasing, lovely
There is an attractive view from the upstairs window.

FOR A NICE SMELL
agreeable, fragrant, sweet-smelling
The fragrant scent of lavender filled the garden.

FOR NICE FOOD
delicious, tasty, appetizing, satisfying
They serve tasty sandwiches in the cafe.

FOR NICE WEATHER
fine, sunny, warm
The weather has been fine all week.

For other ways to describe something you like see **good**

night noun
Badgers usually come out at night.
night-time, dark
Animals which are active at night are nocturnal animals.

nimble adjective
The elves sewed the shoes with their nimble fingers.
agile, skilful, quick, deft
opposite **clumsy**

nip verb
1 *She nipped her finger in the door.*
pinch, squeeze, clip, catch

2 *The dog nipped my leg.*
bite, peck, snip
3 (informal) *I'll just nip along to the shop.*
dash, run, rush
(informal) **pop**

noble adjective
1 *The knight belonged to an ancient noble family.*
aristocratic, high-born, upper-class
2 *The rescuers were congratulated for their noble efforts.*
brave, heroic, courageous, honourable, worthy, virtuous, gallant
opposites **cowardly, unworthy**

nod verb
Simon nodded his head in agreement.
bob, bow, dip, lower
to nod off
He sometimes nods off in front of the television.
fall asleep, doze off, drop off, have a nap

noise noun
Where is that dreadful noise coming from?
din, racket, row, uproar, commotion, tumult, hullabaloo, pandemonium
For various noises see **sound**[1]

noisy adjective
1 *The people next door were playing noisy music.*
loud, blaring, booming, deafening, ear-splitting, thunderous
2 *The children are very noisy this morning.*
rowdy, raucous, chattering, talkative
opposite **quiet**

nominate verb
They nominated her as captain.
appoint, elect, choose, select, name

nonsense noun
Stop talking nonsense!
rubbish, drivel, balderdash, piffle, gibberish, claptrap, gobbledegook
(informal) **rot, tripe, twaddle**

a b c d e f g h i j k l m n o p q r s t u v w x y z

A
B
C
D
E
F
G
H
I
J
K
L
M
N
O
P
Q
R
S
T
U
V
W
X
Y
Z

non-stop adjective
1 *Their* non-stop *chattering annoyed her.*
constant, continual, continuous, endless, ceaseless, incessant, never-ending
2 *They took a* non-stop *train from Glasgow to Edinburgh.*
direct, express, fast

normal adjective
1 *He had a* normal *kind of day at work.*
average, common, customary, familiar, habitual, ordinary, predictable, regular, routine, standard, typical, unsurprising, usual
2 *No* normal *person would sleep on a bed of nails.*
healthy, rational, reasonable, sane
opposite **abnormal**

north noun, adjective, & adverb
The parts of a continent or country in the north are the **northern** parts.
To travel towards the north is to travel **northward** or **northwards** or in a **northerly** direction.
A wind from the north is a **northerly** wind.
A person who lives in the north of a country is a **northerner**.

nose noun
1 *Someone punched Roger on the* nose.
(informal) hooter
The openings in your nose are your nostrils.
A word meaning 'to do with your nose' is nasal.
Words for an animal's nose are muzzle and snout.
2 *I sat in the* nose *of the boat hoping to spot a dolphin.*
front, bow, prow

🐭 WRITING TIPS
You can use these words to describe a nose

beak-like, bulbous, button, classical or **Roman, crooked, pointed, snub, upturned**
The troll had bushy eyebrows and a red, bulbous nose.

nosy adjective (informal)
Stop being so nosy and asking all these questions!
inquisitive, curious, prying, snooping, intrusive
An informal name for a nosy person is a nosy parker.

notable adjective
1 *Many* notable *artists lived and worked in Paris.*
famous, celebrated, renowned, noted, distinguished, eminent, prominent
2 *The fireworks concert this year was a* notable *event.*
memorable, noteworthy, significant, major, important, remarkable
opposites **insignificant, minor**

notch noun
The woodsman cut a notch in the tree trunk.
cut, nick, groove, score, incision

note noun
1 *I sent a* note *thanking him for the present.*
message, letter, communication
2 *There was a* note *of anger in her voice.*
sound, tone, feeling, quality

note verb
1 *The detective* noted *the address on a scrap of paper.*
jot down, make a note of, write down, record, scribble
2 *Did you* note *what she was wearing?*
notice, see, take note of, pay attention to, heed, mark, observe

nothing noun
Four minus four equals nothing.
nought, zero
In cricket a score of nothing is a **duck**, in tennis it is **love**, and in football it is **nil**.

notice noun
Someone put up a notice *about the meeting.*
sign, advertisement, placard, poster, warning
to take notice of something
They took no notice *of the warning.*
heed, pay attention to

notice verb
1 *Did you notice what he was wearing?*
note, see, take note of, pay attention to,
heed, mark, observe
2 *I noticed a funny smell in the room.*
become aware of, detect

noticeable adjective
1 *There has been a noticeable improvement
in the weather.*
definite, distinct, notable, measurable,
perceptible, significant
2 *The tower is noticeable for miles
around.*
visible, conspicuous
3 *He spoke with a noticeable foreign
accent.*
obvious, pronounced, unmistakable,
audible
opposite imperceptible

notion noun
*Uncle Ollie has some strange notions
about life.*
belief, idea, view, thought, opinion, theory,
concept

notorious adjective
He is a notorious liar as well as a thief.
infamous, well-known, disgraceful,
scandalous

nought noun
see nothing

nourish verb
*Plants are nourished by water drawn up
through their roots.*
feed, sustain, support

nourishing adjective
*The penguins live on a nourishing diet of
fish and squid.*
nutritious, wholesome, healthy,
health-giving

novel adjective
*The inventor had a novel idea for building
a robot.*
original, new, innovative, fresh,
different, imaginative, creative, unusual,
unconventional
opposite familiar

novel
For various forms of writing see writing

now adverb
1 *My cousins are now living in Melbourne.*
at present, at the moment, currently,
nowadays
2 *I'll give them a ring now.*
immediately, at once, straight away,
without delay, instantly

nude adjective
The artist painted from a nude model.
naked, bare, undressed, unclothed
opposite clothed

nudge verb
She nudged me with her elbow.
poke, prod, shove, bump, jog, jolt

nuisance noun
The traffic noise is a real nuisance.
annoyance, irritation, inconvenience,
bother, menace, pest, drawback

numb adjective
My toes are numb with cold.
unfeeling, deadened, frozen, insensitive,
paralysed
opposite sensitive

number noun
1 *Add the numbers together to get the
answer.*
figure, numeral
Any of the numbers from 0 to 9 is a digit.
A negative or positive whole number is an
integer.
An amount used in measuring or counting
is a unit.
2 *A large number of people applied for the
job.*
amount, quantity, collection, crowd
3 *I've ordered the latest number of the
magazine.*
edition, issue

a
b
c
d
e
f
g
h
i
j
k
l
m
n
o
p
q
r
s
t
u
v
w
x
y
z

A

4 *The band played some well-known numbers.*
song, piece, tune

B

C

numerous adjective
There are numerous spelling mistakes on this page.
many, plenty of, countless, innumerable, untold, abundant
opposite **few**

D

E

F

nurse noun
For people who practise medicine see medicine

G

nurse verb
The aid workers nursed the sick children.
look after, care for, tend, treat

H

I

J

nut noun

K

WORD WEB
SOME KINDS OF NUT
almond, Brazil nut, cashew, chestnut, coconut, hazelnut, macadamia, peanut, pecan, pistachio, walnut

L

M

N

O

O

P

Q

R

S

oath noun
1 *The knights swore an oath of honour.*
pledge, promise, vow
2 *He let out an oath when he banged his head.*
swear word, curse, blasphemy

T

U

V

obedient adjective
The dog seems very obedient.
well-behaved, disciplined, manageable, dutiful, docile
opposite **disobedient**

W

X

Y

Z

obey verb
1 *The dog obeyed his owner's commands.*
follow, carry out, execute, implement, observe, adhere to, heed
2 *The soldiers obeyed without question.*
do what you are told, take orders, be obedient, conform
opposite **disobey**

object noun
1 *We saw some strange objects in the museum.*
article, item, thing
2 *What is the object of this exercise?*
point, purpose, aim, goal, intention, objective

object verb
to object to something
Several residents have objected to the plan.
complain about, be opposed to, disapprove of, take exception to, protest against
opposites **accept, agree to**

objection noun
Do you have any objection to my sitting here?
protest, complaint, disapproval, opposition

objectionable adjective
The drains were giving off an objectionable smell.
unpleasant, disagreeable, disgusting, foul, offensive, repellent, revolting, obnoxious, nasty
opposite **acceptable**

objective adjective
He gave an objective account of what happened.
disinterested, factual, impartial, rational, unbiased, unemotional, unprejudiced
opposite **subjective**

objective noun
Their objective was to reach the top of the hill.
aim, goal, intention, target, ambition, object, purpose

obligatory adjective
The wearing of seat belts is obligatory.
compulsory, necessary, required
opposite optional

oblige verb
Would you oblige me by watering the plants?
help, assist, do you a favour

obliged adjective
1 *He felt obliged to help them.*
bound, compelled, expected, required
2 *I'm much obliged to you for your kindness.*
thankful, grateful, indebted

oblong noun
rectangle
For other shapes see **shape**

obscene adjective
The film contains some obscene language.
offensive, rude, indecent, improper,
shocking, coarse, crude, foul
opposite decent

obscure adjective
1 *An obscure figure emerged from
the mist.*
dim, murky, shadowy, misty, blurred,
unclear, vague, indistinct
opposite clear
2 *His joke seemed rather obscure.*
confusing, puzzling, incomprehensible
opposite obvious
3 *Henry Kirke White is an obscure poet.*
unknown, unheard of, unimportant,
forgotten, minor
opposite famous

obscure verb
A tall hedge obscured the view.
block out, cover, hide, mask, screen, shroud
opposite reveal

observant adjective
*If you're observant, you might see a badger
tonight.*
alert, attentive, sharp-eyed, vigilant,
watchful
opposite inattentive

observation noun
1 *They took him to hospital for observation.*
study, watching, scrutiny
2 *The detective made an interesting
observation.*
comment, remark, statement

observe verb
1 *Astronomers observed the eclipse last
night.*
watch, look at, view, study
2 *I have observed a change in his behaviour.*
notice, note, see, detect, spot, discern,
perceive, witness
3 *It's important to observe the rules.*
follow, abide by, adhere to, heed, keep to,
obey
4 *My friend observed that I had grown taller.*
mention, say, comment, remark, declare

obsession noun
Football is Frank's obsession.
passion, fixation, addiction, mania

obsolete adjective
That computer software is now obsolete.
out of date, outdated, outmoded,
antiquated, dated
opposite current

obstacle noun
1 *I drove around the obstacles in the road.*
obstruction, barrier, barricade
2 *His age proved to be an obstacle.*
problem, difficulty, hindrance, hurdle,
snag, catch

obstinate adjective
The obstinate camel refused to budge.
stubborn, uncooperative, wilful,
headstrong, pig-headed
opposite cooperative

obstruct verb
The path was obstructed by a fallen tree.
block, jam, make impassable

obstruction noun
The fallen tree was causing an obstruction.
blockage, barrier, barricade

a
b
c
d
e
f
g
h
i
j
k
l
m
n
o
p
q
r
s
t
u
v
w
x
y
z

obtain verb
You must obtain a permit before you can park here.
get, get hold of, acquire
(informal) pick up

obvious adjective
1 *It was silly to make so many obvious mistakes.*
glaring, noticeable, pronounced
2 *The castle is an obvious landmark.*
conspicuous, notable, prominent, visible
opposite **inconspicuous**
3 *It was obvious that the woman was a spy.*
clear, evident, apparent, plain, undeniable, unmistakable
opposite **hidden**

occasion noun
1 *I've been to Italy on several occasions.*
time, moment, instance, opportunity, chance
2 *The wedding was a happy occasion.*
affair, event, happening, incident, occurrence

occasional adjective
The weather forecast said there would be occasional showers.
intermittent, odd, scattered, irregular, infrequent
opposites **frequent, regular**

occasionally adverb
The dragon occasionally lifted its head and roared.
sometimes, now and again, once in a while, every so often
opposites **frequently, often**

occupant noun
The only occupants of the castle were a family of bats.
inhabitant, occupier, resident, tenant

occupation noun
1 *He's not happy with his present occupation.*
job, post, employment, profession, trade, work
For various occupations see **job**

2 *Vita's favourite occupation is reading.*
activity, hobby, pastime, pursuit

occupied adjective
She's very occupied in her work just now.
absorbed, involved, engrossed, busy, engaged
opposite **idle**

occupy verb
1 *They occupy the house next door.*
live in, reside in, dwell in, inhabit
2 *We sold the piano because it occupied too much space.*
fill, take up, use up
3 *The rebel army occupied the town.*
capture, seize, take over, conquer, invade

occur verb
1 *She told us what had occurred.*
happen, take place, come about, arise
2 *The disease only occurs in certain plants.*
develop, crop up, turn up

occurrence noun
An eclipse of the sun is an unusual occurrence.
event, happening, incident, phenomenon

ocean noun

WORD WEB
THE OCEANS OF THE WORLD ARE
Antarctic, Arctic, Atlantic, Indian, Pacific

For creatures that live in the ocean
see **sea**

odd adjective
1 *Her behaviour seemed very odd.*
strange, unusual, abnormal, peculiar, curious, puzzling, queer, unconventional, eccentric, funny, weird
opposite **normal**
2 *He could only find a couple of odd socks.*
left over, single, spare
3 *He does odd jobs to earn money.*
occasional, casual, irregular, various

odour noun
There's a nasty odour *coming from the fridge.*
A nice smell is a **fragrance** or **perfume**.
A nasty smell is a **reek**, **stench**, or **stink**.
See also **smell**

offence noun
1 *The thief was punished for his* offence.
crime, wrongdoing, misdeed, fault, sin
In games, an offence is a **foul** or an **infringement**.
2 *I didn't mean to cause any* offence.
hurt, anger, annoyance, displeasure, hard feelings, disgust

offend verb
1 *I hope my letter didn't* offend *you.*
give or **cause offence to, insult, upset, hurt your feelings, anger, displease, annoy, affront, disgust, vex**
2 *You'll be punished if you* offend *again.*
break the law, do wrong

offensive adjective
1 *The gas produces an* offensive *smell.*
unpleasant, repellent, disgusting, revolting, nasty
opposite pleasant
2 *He apologized for his* offensive *remarks.*
insulting, impolite, rude, abusive

offer verb
1 *A reward was* offered *for the capture of the outlaws.*
propose, put forward, suggest, make available
2 *He* offered *to help with the washing-up.*
volunteer

offer noun
Their offer *of help was gratefully received.*
proposal, suggestion

office noun
1 *The boss won't be in the* office *today.*
workplace, bureau, department
2 *Penny will take up the* office *of treasurer.*
post, position, appointment, role, function

officer noun
For officers in the police force
see **police officer**

official adjective
The official *opening of the museum is next month.*
formal, authentic, authorized, legitimate, proper, genuine, approved
opposite unofficial

official noun
We spoke to an official *of the organization.*
officer, office-holder, representative, executive

often adverb
It often *rains in April.*
frequently, regularly, repeatedly, time after time, many times, again and again, constantly

oil verb
He oiled *the hinge to stop it squeaking.*
grease, lubricate

oily adjective
Fried food is too oily *for me.*
fatty, greasy

ointment noun
The chemist gave her some ointment *for the rash.*
cream, lotion

old adjective

> **OVERUSED WORD**
> Try to vary the words you use for old.
> Here are some other words you could use.
>
> FOR AN **OLD PERSON**
> **elderly, aged**
> *Bus tickets are free for* elderly *people.*
> **opposite young**
>
> FOR AN **OLD BUILDING** OR **OLD DOCUMENT**
> **ancient, historical, original**
> *The* ancient *Norman church is to be restored.*

a
b
c
d
e
f
g
h
i
j
k
l
m
n
o
p
q
r
s
t
u
v
w
x
y
z

A
B
C
D
E
F
G
H
I
J
K
L
M
N
O
P
Q
R
S
T
U
V
W
X
Y
Z

Something that you respect because it is old is **venerable**.

FOR **OLD CLOTHES** OR **OLD SHOES**
worn, scruffy, shabby, threadbare
I put on scruffy jeans to do some gardening.
opposite new

FOR AN **OLD MACHINE**
old-fashioned, out of date, antiquated, early, obsolete
The museum has a display of early computers.
opposites up to date, current

Valuable old cars are **veteran** or **vintage** cars.
Other things which are valuable because they are old are **antique**.

FOR **THE OLD DAYS** OR **OLD TIMES**
past, former, earlier, previous, bygone, olden
We did a project on how children lived in former times.
opposite modern

Times before written records were kept were **prehistoric** times.

old-fashioned adjective
That hairstyle is quite old-fashioned now.
out of date, outdated, outmoded, antiquated
opposites modern, up to date

omit verb
1 *His article was omitted from the magazine.*
exclude, leave out, miss out, cut, eliminate, overlook, skip
2 *Don't omit to turn off the lights.*
forget, fail, neglect

one-sided adjective
The driver gave a one-sided account of the accident.
biased, prejudiced, unbalanced, unfair

ooze verb
The filling started to ooze out my sandwich.
leak, seep, escape, dribble, drip

opaque adjective
The dirt had turned the window opaque.
cloudy, obscure, unclear, dull, hazy, muddy, murky
opposite transparent

open adjective
1 *The puppy escaped through the open door.*
unlocked, unfastened, ajar, gaping
opposite closed
2 *The jam jar had been left open.*
uncovered, unsealed
3 *There is a view of open country from the back window.*
clear, unrestricted, unenclosed, extensive
opposite enclosed
4 *He was open about what he had done wrong.*
frank, honest, sincere, straightforward, candid
opposite deceitful
5 *The captain faced open rebellion from the crew.*
unconcealed, undisguised, obvious, plain
opposite concealed

open verb
1 *Please open the door.*
unfasten, unlock, unbolt
2 *I can't wait to open my birthday presents!*
undo, unwrap, untie, unseal
To open an umbrella is to **unfurl** it.
To open a wine bottle is to **uncork** it.
To open a map is to **unfold** or **unroll** it.
3 *The jumble sale opens at 10 a.m.*
begin, start, commence
(informal) **get going**
opposite close

opening noun
1 *The sheep got out through an opening in the fence.*
gap, hole, breach, break, split
2 *The film has a very dramatic opening.*
beginning, start, commencement

3 *We are invited to the opening of the new sports centre.*
launch, initiation
4 *The job offers a good opening for a keen young person.*
chance, opportunity

operate verb
1 *This watch operates even under water.*
work, function, go, perform
2 *Do you know how to operate this machine?*
use, work, drive, handle, manage, deal with
3 *The surgeon operated to remove her appendix.*
carry out an operation, perform surgery

operation noun
1 *Astronauts control the operation of the spacecraft.*
performance, working, functioning
2 *He had an operation to remove his appendix.*
surgery
3 *Trying to defuse a bomb is a dangerous operation.*
task, activity, action, exercise, manoeuvre, process, procedure

opinion noun
What was your honest opinion of the film?
view, judgement, impression, belief, attitude, point of view, thought, idea, conclusion, assessment, notion, feeling,

opponent noun
The knight fought bravely against his opponent.
enemy, foe, rival, adversary, challenger
Your opponents in a game are the opposition.
opposite **ally**

opportunity noun
1 *There were few opportunities to relax.*
chance, occasion, moment, time
2 *The job offers a good opportunity for a keen young person.*
opening
(informal) **break**

oppose verb
Many people opposed the building of the new road.
object to, disapprove of, be against, be hostile towards, argue against, fight against, attack, resist
opposites **support, defend**

opposite adjective
1 *They have opposite views about politics.*
contrasting, conflicting, contradictory, opposed, opposing, different, contrary
opposite **similar**
2 *My friend lives on the opposite side of the road.*
facing

opposite noun
She says one thing and does the opposite.
contrary, reverse, converse

opposition noun
1 *There was fierce opposition to the new road.*
hostility, resistance, disapproval, unfriendliness, scepticism
opposite **support**
2 *The opposition were stronger than our team expected.*
opponents, rivals

optical adjective
For optical instruments see **glasses**

optimistic adjective
She's optimistic about her chances of success.
hopeful, positive, confident, expectant, cheerful, buoyant
opposite **pessimistic**

option noun
He had the option of staying or leaving.
choice, alternative, possibility

optional adjective
The holiday includes an optional tour of the city.
voluntary, possible
opposite **compulsory**

a
b
c
d
e
f
g
h
i
j
k
l
m
n
o
p
q
r
s
t
u
v
w
x
y
z

A

oral adjective
She had to take an oral exam in French.
spoken, verbal
opposite **written**

B

C

orbit verb
The earth orbits the sun in about 365 days.
circle, travel round

D

E

ordeal noun
The shipwrecked sailor told us about his ordeal.
suffering, troubles, trial, anguish, torture, nightmare

F

G

H

order noun
1 *The captain gave the order to abandon ship.*
command, instruction, direction
2 *I've put in an order for the new book.*
request, demand, reservation, booking
3 *The police restored order after the riot.*
peace, calm, control, quiet, harmony, law and order
4 *The CDs are arranged in alphabetical order.*
arrangement, sequence, series, succession
5 *She keeps her bike in good order.*
condition, state

I

J

K

L

M

N

O

order verb
1 *She ordered them to be quiet.*
command, instruct, require, tell
2 *He ordered the new magazine.*
request, reserve, apply for, book

P

Q

orderly adjective
1 *The library has an orderly system for sorting books.*
organized, ordered, tidy, neat, systematic, methodical
opposite **untidy**
2 *Please form an orderly queue.*
well behaved, controlled, disciplined
opposite **disorderly**

R

S

T

U

V

W

ordinary adjective
1 *It was just an ordinary sort of day.*
normal, typical, usual, customary, habitual, everyday
2 *This is more than just an ordinary robot.*
standard, average, common, conventional, regular

X

Y

Z

3 *It was a very ordinary game.*
mediocre, unexceptional, run-of-the-mill, routine
opposites **special, unusual**

organization noun
1 *She works for a charitable organization.*
institution, operation, enterprise, company
(informal) outfit, set-up
2 *Who was responsible for the organization of the conference?*
coordination, planning, arrangement, running

organize verb
1 *It took her ages to organize the party.*
coordinate, plan, make arrangements for, see to, set up, run
2 *The librarian has to organize the books in the library.*
arrange, put in order, classify, sort out, tidy up

origin noun
1 *We know very little about the origin of life on earth.*
beginning, creation, start, birth, source, cause
opposite **end**
2 *He became very rich, despite his humble origins.*
background, ancestry, descent, family, parentage, pedigree, stock

original adjective
1 *The settlers drove out the original inhabitants.*
earliest, first, initial, native, aboriginal
2 *The story was very original.*
inventive, new, novel, creative, fresh, imaginative, unusual, unconventional
3 *Is that an original work of art or a copy?*
genuine, real, authentic, unique

originate verb
1 *Where did the idea originate?*
begin, start, commence, emerge, crop up
2 *They originated a new style of dancing.*
invent, create, design, conceive, introduce, launch

ornament noun
A few ornaments will make the room more attractive.
decoration, adornment, trinket, bauble

ornamental adjective
There were a few ornamental statues in the garden.
decorative, fancy, pretty, ornate

ornate adjective
The furniture in the palace was very ornate.
elaborate, fancy, showy, ornamental, decorative

orthodox adjective
She wasn't taught to play the piano in the orthodox way.
conventional, accepted, customary, usual, standard, traditional, regular, established, approved, recognized, official
opposites unorthodox, unconventional

outbreak noun
1 *The townspeople feared an outbreak of violence.*
outburst, upsurge (in), flare-up, spate
An outbreak of disease that spreads quickly is an epidemic.
2 *The armies prepared for the outbreak of war.*
beginning, start, onset

outburst noun
There was an outburst of laughter from the next room.
explosion, eruption, outbreak, storm

outcome noun
What was the outcome of the meeting?
result, consequence, effect, upshot

outcry noun
There was an outcry over the closure of the hospital.
protest, complaint, uproar, fuss, furore

outdoor adjective
The hotel had an outdoor swimming pool.
open-air, out of doors, outside

outer adjective
The fishermen wore waterproof outer garments.
external, exterior, outside
opposite inner

outfit noun
1 *Katie bought a new outfit for the wedding.*
clothes, costume, suit, ensemble
(informal) get-up
2 *The puncture repair outfit is in the boot.*
equipment, kit, gear

outing noun
They've gone on their annual outing to London.
trip, excursion, expedition, jaunt

outlaw noun
A band of outlaws held up the train.
bandit, brigand, robber, highwayman, criminal, fugitive

outlet noun
1 *The basin has an outlet for excess water.*
opening, vent, channel, way out, exit, mouth
opposite inlet
2 *The company has outlets throughout the UK.*
shop, store, market

outline noun
1 *We could see the outline of some trees in the distance.*
profile, shape, silhouette, form, shadow
2 *He gave us a brief outline of his plan.*
summary, sketch, framework, precis, rough idea

outline verb
The detective outlined his plan.
summarize, sketch out

a
b
c
d
e
f
g
h
i
j
k
l
m
n
o
p
q
r
s
t
u
v
w
x
y
z

A

B

C

D

E

F

G

H

I

J

K

L

M

N

O

P

Q

R

S

T

U

V

W

X

Y

Z

outlook noun
1 *The cottage has a beautiful* outlook *over the loch.*
view, prospect, sight, vista
2 *He has a rather gloomy* outlook *on life.*
point of view, view, attitude, frame of mind
3 *The* outlook *for the weekend is bright and sunny.*
forecast, prediction, prospect

outrage noun
1 *There was public* outrage *at the government's decision.*
anger, fury, disgust, indignation, horror
2 *He said it was an* outrage *that so much money has been wasted.*
disgrace, scandal, crime, atrocity

outrageous adjective
1 *The behaviour of the trolls was* outrageous.
disgraceful, scandalous, shocking, atrocious, appalling, monstrous, shameful
2 *They charge* outrageous *prices at that shop.*
excessive, unreasonable
opposites acceptable, reasonable

outside adjective
Lookouts were stationed on the outside *wall of the castle.*
exterior, external, outer

outside noun
Insects have their skeletons on the outside *of their bodies.*
exterior, shell, surface
opposite inside

outsider noun
She's lived in the village for years, but still feels like an outsider.
newcomer, stranger, alien, foreigner, immigrant, incomer

outskirts plural noun
We live on the outskirts *of town.*
edge, fringe, outer areas
The outskirts *of a big town are the suburbs.*
opposite centre

outspoken adjective
She's always been outspoken *in her views.*
frank, honest, plain, blunt, straightforward

outstanding adjective
1 *She will be an* outstanding *tennis player in a few years.*
excellent, exceptional, superb, extraordinary, superlative, brilliant, great, fine, distinguished, celebrated, remarkable, superior, striking, notable
opposite ordinary
2 *There are still some* outstanding *bills to pay.*
overdue, unpaid, owing

outward adjective
In outward *appearance, the castle was dark and dingy.*
outer, outside, external, exterior, visible

outwit verb
Ewan managed to outwit *his dad at chess.*
outsmart, get the better of, beat, defeat

oval adjective
The sandwiches were arranged on an oval *platter.*
egg-shaped, elliptical

oven noun
The meat was roasting in the oven.
cooker, stove
A special oven *for firing pottery is a* kiln.

overcast adjective
The sky has been overcast *all day.*
cloudy, dull, grey, sunless, dark, leaden
See also **weather**

overcome verb overcomes, overcoming, overcame, overcome
1 *He managed to* overcome *his fear of flying.*
conquer, defeat, master, get the better of
2 *Some people in the building were* overcome *by fumes.*
overpower, overwhelm

overflow verb
Someone left the tap on and the bath overflowed.
spill over, run over, pour over, flood

overgrown adjective
The back garden was completely overgrown.
unkempt, untidy, tangled, weedy, wild

overhaul verb
The boiler was recently overhauled.
service, check over, inspect, repair, restore, refurbish

overhead adverb
A flock of geese flew overhead.
above, high up, in the sky

overlook verb
1 *He seems to have overlooked one important fact.*
miss, fail to see
2 *She's always willing to overlook his faults.*
excuse, forget about, ignore, disregard, pardon, pay no attention to
(informal) turn a blind eye to
3 *The front room of the house overlooks the garden.*
have a view of, look on to, face

overpowering adjective
I felt an overpowering urge to giggle.
overwhelming, powerful, strong, compelling, irresistible, uncontrollable

overrun verb overruns, overrunning, overran, overrun
The barn was overrun with rats and mice.
invade, take over, spread over, swarm over

overtake verb overtakes, overtaking, overtook, overtaken
We overtook the car in front.
pass, leave behind, pull ahead of, outstrip

overthrow verb overthrows, overthrowing, overthrew, overthrown
The rebels overthrew the President.
bring down, topple, oust, defeat, drive out, depose

overturn verb
1 *The boat overturned.*
capsize, tip over, turn over, turn turtle
2 *She leapt to her feet, overturning her chair.*
knock over, tip over, topple, upset, spill

overwhelm verb
1 *The troops were overwhelmed by the enemy forces.*
defeat, overcome, overpower, crush
2 *A tidal wave overwhelmed the village.*
engulf, flood, inundate, submerge, swallow up, bury

overwhelming adjective
He was elected by an overwhelming majority.
decisive, devastating, crushing, huge, massive, great
An overwhelming victory at an election is a landslide.

owe verb
If you owe money to someone, you are in debt.

owing adjective
owing to
Owing to the rain, the match is cancelled.
because of, on account of, as a result of, thanks to

own verb
It was the first bike she had owned.
be the owner of, have, possess
to own up to
No one owned up to breaking the window.
confess to, admit to, tell the truth about
(informal) come clean about

a
b
c
d
e
f
g
h
i
j
k
l
m
n
o
p
q
r
s
t
u
v
w
x
y
z

A
B
C
D
E
F
G
H
I
J
K
L
M
N
O
P
Q
R
S
T
U
V
W
X
Y
Z

Pp

pace noun
1 *Move forward two* paces.
step, stride
2 *The front runner set a fast* pace.
rate, speed
A formal word is velocity.

pacify verb
The zookeeper managed to pacify *the polar bear.*
calm, quieten, soothe, humour, appease
opposites anger, annoy

pack noun
1 *There were four candles in each* pack.
package, packet, bundle, bale
2 *The hikers picked up their* packs *and trudged off.*
rucksack, backpack, haversack, knapsack

pack verb
1 *She* packed *her suitcase and called a taxi.*
fill, load up
2 *I forgot to* pack *my hairdryer.*
stow away, wrap up
3 *They tried to* pack *too many passengers onto the train.*
cram, crowd, squeeze, stuff, jam, wedge

package noun
The postman delivered a big package.
parcel, packet, bundle

pad noun
1 *She put a* pad *of cotton wool over the wound.*
wad
A pad to make a chair or bed comfortable is a cushion or pillow.
2 *There's a* pad *for messages next to the phone.*
jotter, notebook, writing pad

pad verb
The seats are padded *with foam rubber.*
stuff, fill, pack
To put covers and padding on furniture is to upholster it.

padding noun
The padding *is coming out of this cushion.*
stuffing, filling
The covers and padding on furniture are upholstery.

paddle verb
1 *The children* paddled *at the water's edge.*
dabble, splash about
To walk through deep water is to wade.
2 *He* paddled *his canoe along the canal.*
To move a boat along with two oars is to row it.

page noun
1 *Several* pages *were torn out of the book.*
sheet, leaf
2 *He wrote two* pages *of notes.*
side

paid
past tense see pay

pain noun
Dirk felt a sudden jabbing pain *in his foot.*
anguish, suffering
A dull pain is an ache or soreness.
Severe pain is agony, torment, or torture.
A slight pain is discomfort.
A slight pain which doesn't last long is a twinge.
A sudden pain is a pang or stab.
Pain in your head is a headache.
Pain in your teeth is toothache.

painful adjective
1 *My shoulder is still really* painful.
sore, aching, tender, hurting, smarting, stinging, throbbing
opposite painless
2 *The conversation brought back many* painful *memories.*
unpleasant, upsetting, distressing, disagreeable, traumatic

painless adjective
1 *The treatment is quite* painless.
comfortable, pain-free
opposite painful
2 *This is a quick and* painless *way to make a cake.*
easy, simple, effortless, undemanding

paint noun

> 🕸 **WORD WEB**
>
> KINDS OF PAINT FOR DECORATING
> **emulsion, undercoat, whitewash**
>
> A layer of paint is a **coat** of paint.
> Paint which stays shiny when it dries is **gloss** paint.
> Paint which goes dull when it dries is **matt** paint.
>
> KINDS OF PAINT FOR ARTWORK
> **acrylic, finger paint, oil paint, poster paint, watercolour**

paint verb
1 *The bedroom walls were* painted *green.*
colour, decorate
2 *Samantha* painted *the flowers in bright colours.*
depict, portray, represent

painter noun
A person who paints houses is a **decorator**.
A person who paints pictures is an **artist**.

painting noun
A picture painted on a wall is a **fresco** or a **mural**.
A picture painted by a famous artist of the past is an **old master**.
See also **picture**

pair noun
A pair of people who go out together are a **couple**.
Two people who sing or play music together are a **duet** or a **duo**.
Two people who work together are **partners** or a **partnership**.
Two babies born together are **twins**.

palace noun
For types of building see **building**

pale adjective
1 *Are you all right? You're looking a little* pale.
white, pallid, pasty, wan, ashen, sallow, anaemic
opposites ruddy, flushed
To go pale with fear is to **blanch**.
2 *That shade of pink is too* pale.
light, pastel, faded, faint, dim, bleached, colourless
opposite bright

pamper verb
The twins' grandparents liked to pamper *them.*
spoil, indulge, cosset, mollycoddle, humour

pamphlet noun
We were given a pamphlet *about road safety.*
leaflet, booklet, brochure

pan noun
For things used for cooking see **cook**

panel noun
A panel *of experts judged the contest.*
group, team, board, committee

panic noun
People fled the streets in panic.
alarm, fright, terror, frenzy, hysteria

panic verb
If a fire starts, don't panic*!*
be alarmed, take fright, become hysterical
(informal) lose your head, get in a flap
To panic is also to be **panic-stricken**.

pant verb
Some of the runners were panting.
breathe quickly, gasp, wheeze, puff

pants plural noun
For underwear see **clothes**

paper noun
1 *She started her diary on a fresh sheet of* paper.
A piece of paper is a **leaf** or a **sheet**.

a
b
c
d
e
f
g
h
i
j
k
l
m
n
o
p
q
r
s
t
u
v
w
x
y
z

A
B
C
D
E
F
G
H
I
J
K
L
M
N
O

P

Q
R
S
T
U
V
W
X
Y
Z

2 *The doctor had some important* **papers** *to sign.*
document, deed, certificate
3 *The story made the front page of the local paper.*
newspaper, journal
(informal) rag

paper noun

> **WORD WEB**
>
> MATERIALS FOR WRITING OR DRAWING ON
> **card, cardboard, cartridge paper, notepaper, postcard, stationery, tracing paper, writing paper**
>
> EARLY MATERIALS FOR WRITING ON
> **papyrus, parchment, vellum**
>
> OTHER KINDS OF PAPER
> **greaseproof paper, tissue paper, toilet paper, wallpaper, wrapping paper**

parade noun
A circus **parade** *passed along the street.*
procession, march, spectacle, show, display
A **parade** *of vehicles or of people on horseback is a* cavalcade.
A **parade** *of people in costume is a* pageant.

parade verb
The brass band **paraded** *through the town.*
march, troop, file past

paralyse verb
His right arm was **paralysed** *in the accident.*
disable, immobilize, cripple, deaden, numb

parcel noun
The postman delivered a bulky **parcel.**
package, packet

parched adjective
1 *Nothing was growing in the* **parched** *earth.*
dry, arid, baked, scorched, barren, sterile, waterless
2 *I need a drink of water—I'm* **parched**!
thirsty

pardon verb
The king decided to **pardon** *the prisoners.*
release, free, set free, let off, spare, excuse, forgive
To **pardon** *someone who is condemned to death is to* reprieve *them.*

parent noun
For family relationships see family

park noun
At lunchtime, we went for a walk in the **park.**
public gardens, recreation ground
A **park** *with fields and trees around a big house is an* estate *or* parkland.

> **WORD WEB**
>
> SOME KINDS OF PARK
> **adventure park, amusement park, arboretum, botanical gardens, forest park, nature reserve, play park** or **playground, safari park, skate park, theme park**
>
> EQUIPMENT YOU MIGHT FIND IN A PLAY PARK
> **chute** or **slide, climbing frame, flying fox, monkey bars, rope ladder, roundabout, sandpit, see-saw, swings, trapeze**

park verb
The postman **parked** *his van around the corner.*
leave, position, station

part noun
1 *All the* **parts** *of the engine are now working properly.*
bit, component, constituent
2 *I only saw the first* **part** *of the programme.*
section, piece, portion, element
3 *Which* **part** *of the business do they own?*
branch, department, division
4 *Granny lives in another* **part** *of the town.*
area, district, region, neighbourhood, sector
5 *He's just right to act the* **part** *of Peter Pan.*
character, role

part verb
1 *It was the first time she'd been* parted *from her parents.*
separate, divide, remove
opposite join
2 *They exchanged a final kiss before parting.*
go away, leave, depart, say goodbye
opposite meet

partial adjective
The play was only a partial *success.*
limited, imperfect, incomplete
opposite complete
to be partial to
Becky is very partial to *chocolate cake.*
be fond of, be keen on, enjoy, like

participate verb
Our school is participating *in the mini-marathon.*
take part, join in, be involved, cooperate, help, share

particle noun
The camera lens was covered with particles *of dust.*
speck, grain, fragment, bit, piece, scrap, shred, sliver
See also bit

particular adjective
1 *The tickets must be used on a* particular *day.*
specific, certain, distinct, definite, exact
2 *She took* particular *care not to damage the parcel.*
special, exceptional, unusual, extreme, marked, notable
3 *The cat's very* particular *about his food.*
fussy, finicky, hard to please
(informal) choosy, picky

particulars plural noun
The police officer took down all the particulars.
details, facts, information, circumstances

partition noun
A partition *separates the two classrooms.*
room divider, screen

partly adverb
It was partly *my fault that we were late.*
in part, to some extent, up to a point
opposite entirely

partner noun
The two women have been business partners *for years.*
colleague, associate, ally
In marriage, your partner is your spouse, or your husband or wife.
An animal's partner is its mate.

party noun
1 *We had a class* party *at the end of term.*
celebration, festivity, function, gathering, reception
(informal) get-together, do
2 *A* party *of tourists was going round the museum.*
group, band, crowd, gang
3 *They have formed a new political party.*
alliance, association, faction, league

party noun

WORD WEB
SOME KINDS OF PARTY
ball, banquet, barbecue, birthday party, ceilidh, Christmas party, cocktail party, dance, dinner party, disco, fancy-dress party, garden party, Halloween party, house-warming, picnic, pot luck, reunion, sleepover, tea party, wedding

THINGS YOU MIGHT SEE AT A PARTY
balloons, birthday cake, birthday candles, bunting, party bags, poppers, sparklers, streamers

For party games see game

a
b
c
d
e
f
g
h
i
j
k
l
m
n
o
p
q
r
s
t
u
v
w
x
y
z

A
B
C
D
E
F
G
H
I
J
K
L
M
N
O
P
Q
R
S
T
U
V
W
X
Y
Z

pass verb
1 *We watched the parade as it passed.*
go by, move past
2 *She tried to pass the car in front.*
overtake, go ahead of
3 *We passed over the bridge.*
go, advance, proceed, progress
4 *Could you pass me the sugar, please?*
hand, give, deliver, offer, present
5 *Do you think you will pass your music exam?*
be successful in, get through, succeed in
6 *How did you pass the time on holiday?*
spend, use, occupy, fill, while away
7 *Three years passed before we met again.*
go by, elapse
8 *The pain will soon pass.*
go away, come to an end, disappear, fade
to pass out
One of the runners passed out in the heat.
faint, lose consciousness, black out

pass noun
1 *We had a pass to get into the concert for free.*
permit, licence, ticket
2 *The horses filed through a pass between the hills.*
gap, gorge, ravine, canyon, valley

passage noun
1 *A secret passage led from the chamber to the outside.*
passageway, corridor, tunnel
2 *The guards forced a passage through the crowd.*
path, route, way
3 *A sea passage takes longer than going by air.*
journey, voyage, crossing
4 *Our homework is to choose a favourite passage from a book.*
episode, excerpt, extract, piece, quotation, section
5 *He hadn't changed, despite the passage of time.*
passing, progress, advance

passenger noun
The bus has seats for 55 passengers.
traveller
Passengers who travel regularly to work are commuters.

passion noun
1 *'Romeo and Juliet' is a story of youthful passion.*
love, emotion
2 *She has a passion for sports.*
enthusiasm, eagerness, appetite, desire, craving, urge, zest, thirst, mania

passionate adjective
1 *The captain gave a passionate speech before the battle.*
emotional, intense, moving, heartfelt
opposite unemotional
2 *He is a passionate follower of football.*
eager, keen, avid, enthusiastic, fanatical, fervent
opposite apathetic

passive adjective
Owls are normally passive during the daytime.
inactive, docile
opposite active

past noun
In the past, things were different.
past times, old days, olden days, days gone by
The study of what happened in the past is history.
The things and ideas that have come down to us from the past are our heritage or traditions.
opposite future

past adjective
Things were very different in past centuries.
earlier, former, previous, old
opposite future

pasta noun

WORD WEB

SOME TYPES OF PASTA
cannelloni, lasagne, macaroni, noodles,
penne, ravioli, spaghetti, tagliatelle,
tortellini

For other kinds of food see **food**

paste noun
I used some paste to stick things into my scrapbook.
glue, gum, adhesive

pastime noun
Shona's favourite pastime is swimming.
activity, hobby, recreation, amusement,
diversion, entertainment, relaxation,
game, sport
See also **game, sport**

pasture noun
Cattle were grazing on the pasture.
field, meadow, grassland

pat verb
Andy patted the Shetland pony on the head.
tap, touch, stroke, pet
To touch something quickly and lightly
is to **dab** it.
To stroke someone with an open hand
is to **caress** them.

patch verb
I need some material to patch my jeans.
mend, repair
Another way to mend holes in clothes is to
darn them or **stitch** them up.

patchy adjective
There will be patchy outbreaks of rain overnight.
irregular, inconsistent, uneven,
varying, unpredictable

path noun
Keep to the path as you tour the gardens.
pathway, track, trail, footpath, walk,
walkway, lane
A path for horse-riding is a **bridleway**.
A path by the side of a road is a **pavement**.
A path above a beach is an **esplanade** or
promenade.
A path along a canal is a **towpath**.
A path between buildings is an **alley**.
See also **road**

pathetic adjective
1 *The abandoned kittens were a pathetic sight.*
moving, touching, pitiful, distressing,
heartbreaking, sad, sorry
2 *The goalie made a pathetic attempt to stop the ball.*
hopeless, useless, weak, feeble, inadequate,
incompetent

patience noun
She waited with great patience for an hour.
calmness, tolerance, self-control,
endurance, restraint, perseverance,
persistence, resignation
opposite **impatience**

patient adjective
1 *The nurse was very patient with us.*
calm, composed, even-tempered,
easy-going, tolerant, lenient, mild, quiet,
uncomplaining, resigned, long-suffering
2 *It took hours of patient work to restore the painting.*
persevering, persistent, unhurried,
untiring, steady, determined
opposite **impatient**

patrol verb
Police patrolled the area all night.
guard, keep watch over, inspect, tour

patter noun & verb
For various sounds see **sound**[1]

a
b
c
d
e
f
g
h
i
j
k
l
m
n
o
p
q
r
s
t
u
v
w
x
y
z

A B C D E F G H I J K L M N O P Q R S T U V W X Y Z

pattern noun
Do you like the pattern on this wallpaper?
design, decoration

WORD WEB
SOME KINDS OF PATTERN
checked, criss-cross, dotted or **dotty, floral** or **flowery, geometric, gingham, paisley, polka dot, spotted** or **spotty, striped** or **stripey, tartan, wavy, zigzag**

pause noun
There was a pause while the singers got their breath back.
break, gap, halt, rest, lull, stop, wait, interruption, stoppage
A pause in the middle of a performance is an **interlude** or **interval**.
A pause in the middle of a cinema film is an **intermission**.

pause verb
1 *The stranger paused at the door before knocking.*
hesitate, wait, delay, hang back
2 *The cyclists paused to let the others catch up.*
halt, stop, rest, take a break, break off

paw noun
The cat had a mouse under its paw.
foot
A horse's foot is a **hoof**.
A pig's feet are its **trotters**.
A bird's feet are its **claws**.

pay verb pays, paying, paid
1 *How much did you pay for your new bike?*
spend, give out, hand over
(informal) **fork out**
2 *Who's going to pay the bill?*
pay off, repay, settle, clear, refund
3 *They had to pay for all the damage they caused.*
compensate, pay back
4 *Do you think the new business is likely to pay?*
be profitable

5 *I'll make you pay for this!*
suffer

pay noun
We should get an increase in pay next year.
wages, salary, income, earnings
A payment you get for doing a single job is a **fee**.

payment noun
A voluntary payment to a charity is a **contribution** or **donation**.
The payment you make to travel on public transport is the **fare**.
A payment you have to make as a punishment is a **fine**.
A payment made to free a hostage or prisoner is a **ransom**.
A payment you get as a prize is a **reward**.
A payment to join a club is a **subscription**.
A voluntary payment to a waiter, etc., is a **tip**.
Payment that you receive regularly from your parents is **pocket money**.
A payment you get if you paid too much for something is a **refund**.

peace noun
1 *After the war there was a period of peace.*
agreement, harmony, friendliness
2 *She enjoys the peace of the countryside.*
calmness, peacefulness, quiet, tranquillity, calm, stillness, serenity, silence

peaceful adjective
They enjoyed a peaceful day fishing.
calm, quiet, relaxing, tranquil, restful, serene, undisturbed, untroubled, gentle, placid, soothing, still
opposites noisy, troubled

peak noun
1 *The peak of the mountain was covered in snow.*
summit, cap, crest, crown, pinnacle, top, tip, point
2 *She is at the peak of her career.*
top, height, highest point, climax

peal verb
For sounds made by a bell see **bell**

peculiar adjective
1 *What's that peculiar smell?*
strange, unusual, odd, curious, extraordinary, abnormal, funny, weird, bizarre
opposite ordinary
2 *He recognized her peculiar way of writing.*
characteristic, distinctive, individual, particular, personal, special, unique, identifiable

pedigree noun
They have a complete record of the dog's pedigree.
ancestry, descent, family history

peel noun
Orange peel is used in marmalade.
rind, skin

peep and peer verb
see look

peg noun
Leave your coat and scarf on the peg.
hook, knob

pelt verb
1 *The boys pelted each other with snowballs.*
attack, bombard, shower
See also throw
2 *The rain was pelting down outside.*
pour, teem

pen¹ noun
My pen has run out of ink.
ballpoint, (trademark) biro, felt-tipped pen, fountain pen

pen² noun
The dog drove the sheep into the pen.
enclosure, fold

penalize verb
In football, you are penalized if you handle the ball.
punish

penalty noun
The penalty for this crime is ten years in prison.
punishment
opposite reward

penetrate verb
1 *The bullet had penetrated the man's chest.*
make a hole in, pierce, bore through
When something penetrates a tyre, it punctures it.
2 *The soldiers penetrated the enemy's defences.*
get past, get through, infiltrate

penniless adjective
The family was left penniless and without a home.
poor, impoverished, poverty-stricken
opposite rich

people plural noun
1 *How many people are you inviting?*
persons, individuals
People as opposed to animals are humans, human beings, or mankind.
2 *The government is elected by the people of the country.*
population, citizens, the public, society, nation, race

perceive verb
1 *They perceived a figure moving along the horizon.*
make out, notice, become aware of, catch sight of, recognize
2 *I began to perceive what she meant.*
realize, understand, comprehend, grasp

perceptive adjective
It was very perceptive of you to spot my mistake.
observant, clever, sharp, shrewd, quick, alert
opposite unobservant

perch verb
A robin was perching on top of the postbox.
sit, settle, rest, balance

a
b
c
d
e
f
g
h
i
j
k
l
m
n
o
p
q
r
s
t
u
v
w
x
y
z

A
B
C
D
E
F
G
H
I
J
K
L
M
N
O
P
Q
R
S
T
U
V
W
X
Y
Z

percussion noun
For percussion instruments see **music**

perfect adjective
1 *Each petal on the flower was* perfect.
faultless, flawless, ideal, intact,
undamaged, complete, whole
2 *The dress is a* perfect *fit.*
exact, faithful, precise, accurate,
correct
opposite **imperfect**
3 *I received a letter from a* perfect
stranger.
complete, total, absolute, utter

perfect verb
Gymnasts spend years perfecting *their
technique.*
make perfect, improve, refine, polish

perform verb
1 *Is this your first time* performing
on stage?
act, appear, play, dance, sing
2 *The children* performed *a play about
Cinderella.*
present, stage, produce, put on
3 *Soldiers are expected to* perform *their duty.*
do, carry out, execute, fulfil
To perform a crime is to commit a crime.

performance noun
1 *Tonight's* performance *is already sold out.*
show, production, presentation
2 *He congratulated the players on their
outstanding* performance.
effort, work, endeavour, exertion,
behaviour, conduct

performer noun
see entertainer

perfume noun
The perfume *of roses filled the room.*
smell, scent, fragrance

perhaps adverb
Perhaps *the weather will improve soon.*
maybe, possibly
opposite **definitely**

peril noun
The crew faced many perils *on their voyage.*
danger, hazard, risk, menace, threat
opposite **safety**

perimeter noun
There is a fence round the perimeter *of the
field.*
edge, border, boundary
The distance round the edge of something is
the circumference.

period noun
1 *After a long* period *of hard work they had
a rest.*
time, span, spell, stretch
2 *The book is about the Victorian* period.
age, era, epoch

perish verb
1 *Many birds* perish *in cold weather.*
die, be killed, pass away
2 *The tyres have started to* perish *with age.*
disintegrate, crumble away, rot, decay,
decompose

permanent adjective
1 *Sugar can do* permanent *damage to your
teeth.*
lasting, long-lasting, long-term,
everlasting, enduring
2 *Traffic noise is a* permanent *problem in the
city centre.*
never-ending, perpetual, persistent,
chronic, perennial
3 *She has been offered a* permanent *job in
the firm.*
stable, steady, fixed, lifelong
opposite **temporary**

permission noun
They had the teacher's permission *to leave.*
consent, agreement, approval
(informal) go-ahead

permit verb
The council doesn't permit *fishing in the lake.*
allow, consent to, give permission for,
authorize, license, grant, tolerate, admit

permit noun
You need a permit to fish in the river.
licence, pass, ticket

perpetual adjective
The machine produces a perpetual hum.
constant, continual, continuous,
never-ending, non-stop, endless, ceaseless,
incessant, persistent, unceasing, unending
opposite **temporary**

perplexing adjective
*'This is the most perplexing case I've seen,'
said the detective.*
puzzling, confusing, bewildering, baffling,
mystifying

persecute verb
*People were persecuted for their religious
beliefs.*
oppress, discriminate against, harass,
intimidate, bully, terrorize, torment

persevere verb
*The rescuers persevered despite the bad
weather.*
continue, carry on, keep going, persist
(informal) keep at it, stick at it
opposite **give up**

persist verb
*If your headache persists, you should see a
doctor.*
continue, carry on, last, linger, remain,
endure
opposite **stop**
to persist in
He persists in wearing that awful tie!
keep on, insist on

persistent adjective
1 *There was a persistent drip from the tap in
the kitchen.*
constant, continual, incessant,
never-ending, steady, non-stop
2 *That dog is very persistent—he won't go
away.*
determined, persevering, tireless, resolute,
steadfast, stubborn, obstinate

person noun
*Not a single person has replied to my
email.*
individual, human being, character, soul

personal adjective
1 *The book is based on the writer's personal
experience.*
own, individual, particular
2 *The contents of the letter are personal.*
confidential, private, secret, intimate

personality noun
1 *Like all ogres, he has an ugly personality.*
character, nature, disposition,
temperament, make-up
2 *The show was introduced by a TV
personality.*
celebrity, star, VIP

perspire verb
He perspires a lot in hot weather.
sweat

persuade verb
I persuaded my friend to join the choir.
convince, coax, induce
To persuade someone to do something is
also to talk them into doing it.
opposite **dissuade**

persuasive adjective
She used some very persuasive arguments.
convincing, effective, sound, strong,
forceful, compelling, valid
opposite **unconvincing**

pessimistic adjective
*The players are pessimistic about their
chances of winning.*
negative, unhopeful, gloomy, despairing,
resigned, cynical
opposite **optimistic**

pest noun
1 *I'm trying an organic method to get rid of
garden pests.*
Pests in general are vermin.
An informal word for insect pests is bugs.

a
b
c
d
e
f
g
h
i
j
k
l
m
n
o
p
q
r
s
t
u
v
w
x
y
z

297

A pest which lives on or in another creature is a **parasite**.
2 *Don't be a pest!*
nuisance, bother, annoyance
(informal) **pain**

pester verb
Please don't pester me while I'm busy!
annoy, bother, trouble, harass, badger, hound, nag
(informal) **bug**

pet noun

> ### 🕸 WORD WEB
>
> SOME ANIMALS COMMONLY KEPT AS PETS
> **budgerigar, canary, cat, dog, ferret, fish, gerbil, goldfish, guinea pig, hamster, mouse, parrot, pigeon, rabbit, rat, tortoise**

petrified adjective
Jack stood petrified as the monster lumbered towards him.
terrified, horrified, terror-struck, paralysed, frozen
See also **afraid**

petty adjective
There were a lot of annoying petty rules.
minor, trivial, unimportant, insignificant
opposite **important**

phase noun
Going to school is the start of a new phase in your life.
period, time, stage, step

phenomenal adjective
The winner of the quiz had a phenomenal memory.
amazing, incredible, outstanding, remarkable, exceptional, extraordinary
(informal) **fantastic**
opposite **ordinary**

phenomenon noun
1 *Snow is a common phenomenon in winter.*
happening, occurrence, event, fact

2 *The six-year-old pianist was quite a phenomenon.*
wonder, curiosity, marvel

phobia noun
see **fear**

phone verb
I'll phone you later this evening.
telephone, call, ring, dial

photograph noun
I put my holiday photographs in an album.
photo, snap or snapshot, shot, picture
The photographs you get on paper are prints.
Before digital photography, a photograph on the film from which prints were made was a negative.
A small frame containing a photograph for projecting onto a screen is a slide or transparency.

photograph verb
Rachel photographed some animals in the zoo.
take a picture of, shoot, snap

phrase noun
'Bon voyage' is a French phrase meaning 'have a good journey'.
expression, saying

phrase verb
I tried to phrase my letter carefully.
express, put into words

physical adjective
1 *There's a lot of physical contact in rugby.*
bodily
Physical punishment is corporal punishment.
2 *Ghosts have no physical presence.*
earthly, material, solid, substantial

pick verb
1 *They've picked the players for the hockey team.*
choose, select, decide on, settle on, opt for, single out
2 *Irene picked some flowers from the garden.*
gather, collect, cut

A B C D E F G H I J K L M N O P Q R S T U V W X Y Z

3 *I picked an apple off the tree.*
pluck, pull off, take
to pick up
1 *He was too weak to pick up the box.*
lift, raise, hoist
2 *I'll pick up some milk on the way home.*
get, collect, fetch

picture noun
1 *There's a picture of a pyramid in this book.*
illustration, image, print
A picture which represents a particular
person is a **portrait**.
A picture which represents the artist himself
or herself is a **self-portrait**.
A picture which represents a group of
objects is a **still life**.
A picture which represents a country scene
is a **landscape**.
Pictures on a computer are **graphics**.
See also **painting, portrait**
2 *Mum took some pictures of us building a
sandcastle.*
photo, photograph, snapshot, snap

picture verb
1 *The girl is pictured against a background
of flowers.*
depict, illustrate, represent, show, portray
2 *Can you picture what the world will be like
in a hundred years?*
imagine, visualize

picturesque adjective
1 *They stayed in a picturesque thatched
cottage.*
attractive, pretty, charming, quaint
opposite ugly
2 *She wrote a picturesque account of her trip
to Morocco.*
colourful, descriptive, imaginative,
expressive, lively, poetic, vivid

piece noun
1 *They collected pieces of wood to build a
raft.*
bar, block, length, stick, chunk, lump,
hunk, bit, chip, fragment, particle, scrap,
shred

2 *I've only got two pieces of chocolate left.*
bit, portion, part, section, segment, share,
slice
3 *I always have a piece of fruit in my snack
box.*
item
A piece of clothing is an **article** of clothing.
4 *I've lost one of the pieces of the jigsaw.*
part, element, unit, component,
constituent
5 *There's a piece about our school in the local
paper.*
article, item, report, feature

pier noun
*The passengers waited at the pier to board
the ship.*
quay, wharf, jetty, landing stage

pierce verb
The arrow had pierced the knight's armour.
enter, go through, make a hole in,
penetrate, bore through
To pierce a hole through paper is to **punch** a
hole in it or **perforate** it.
To pierce a hole in a tyre is to **puncture** it.
To pierce someone with a spike is to **impale**
or **spear** them.

piercing adjective
*When she saw the dragon, she let out a
piercing scream.*
high-pitched, shrill, penetrating, loud,
shattering, deafening, ear-splitting

pig noun
An old word for pigs is **swine**.
A wild pig is a **wild boar**.
A male pig is a **boar** or **hog**.
A female pig is a **sow**.
A young pig is a **piglet**.
A family of piglets is a **litter**.
The smallest piglet in a litter is the **runt**.

pile noun
1 *Where did this pile of rubbish come from?*
heap, mound, mountain, stack, hoard,
mass, quantity, collection, assortment

a
b
c
d
e
f
g
h
i
j
k
l
m
n
o
p
q
r
s
t
u
v
w
x
y
z

A
B
C
D
E
F
G
H
I
J
K
L
M
N
O
P
Q
R
S
T
U
V
W
X
Y
Z

2 *I've still got* piles *of homework to do.*
plenty, a lot, a great deal
(informal) lots, masses

pile verb
Pile everything in the corner and we'll sort it out later.
heap, stack, collect, gather, assemble, hoard
to pile up
The bills are beginning to pile up.
build up, mount up, accumulate

pill noun
Take one pill *every four hours.*
tablet, capsule, pellet

pillar noun
The roof was supported by tall pillars.
column, pier, post, prop, support

pillow noun
A long kind of pillow is a **bolster**.
A kind of pillow for a chair or sofa is a **cushion**.

pilot verb
He piloted *the hot-air balloon back to safety.*
fly, steer, guide, lead, navigate

pimple noun
The troll had a pimple *on the end of his nose.*
spot, boil, swelling

pin noun
A decorative pin to wear is a **brooch**.
A pin to fix something on a noticeboard is a **drawing pin**.
A pin to fix clothing in place is a **safety pin**.

pinch verb
1 *The baby* pinched *my arm.*
nip, squeeze, press, tweak, grip
2 (informal) *Who's* pinched *my calculator?*
steal, take, snatch, pilfer
(informal) nick, swipe, make off with

pine verb
The dog pined *when its master died.*
mope, languish, sicken, waste away

to pine for
She was pining for *her old house by the sea.*
long for, yearn for, miss, crave, hanker after

pip noun
Make sure there are no pips *in the lemon juice.*
seed

pipe noun
The water flows away along this pipe.
tube
A pipe used for watering the garden is a **hose**.
A pipe in the street which supplies water for fighting fires is a **hydrant**.
A pipe which carries oil, etc., over long distances is a **pipeline**.
The system of water pipes in a house is the **plumbing**.

pipe verb
1 *Water is* piped *from the reservoir to the town.*
carry, convey, channel, funnel
2 *She began to* pipe *a tune on her recorder.*
play, blow, sound, whistle

pirate noun
The ship was overrun by bloodthirsty pirates.
buccaneer, marauder

WORD WEB

THINGS YOU MIGHT FIND ON A PIRATE SHIP
barrels, cabin, crow's nest, deck, hammock, lantern, mast, plank, pirate flag, rigging, sail, treasure chest, wheel

A pirate flag is a **Jolly Roger** or **skull-and-crossbones**.
A pirate ship might sail on the **high seas** or the **Spanish Main**.
See also **boat**

PEOPLE YOU MIGHT FIND ON A PIRATE SHIP
cabin boy or **girl, captain, captives, cook, crew, first mate, lookout, stowaway**

pit noun
1 *They dug a deep* **pit** *to bury the treasure.*
hole, crater, cavity, hollow, depression, pothole, chasm, abyss
2 *Coal used to be mined from the* **pits** *in this area.*
mine, coal mine, colliery, quarry

pitch noun
1 *The* **pitch** *was waterlogged, so the match was called off.*
ground, field, playing field
2 *She can sing at a very high* **pitch.**
tone, frequency

pitch verb
1 *Scott* **pitched** *the ball back over the fence.*
throw, toss, fling, hurl, sling, cast, lob
(informal) chuck
2 *It was hard trying to* **pitch** *the tent in the rain!*
erect, put up, set up
3 *He lost his balance and* **pitched** *headlong into the water.*
plunge, dive, drop, topple, plummet
4 *The rowing boat* **pitched** *about in the storm.*
lurch, rock, roll, toss

a
b
c
d
e
f
g
h
i
j
k
l
m
n
o
p
q
r
s
t
u
v
w
x
y
z

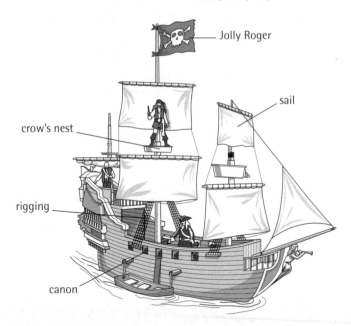

Jolly Roger

sail

crow's nest

rigging

canon

301

A
B
C
D
E
F
G
H
I
J
K
L
M
N
O

P

Q
R
S
T
U
V
W
X
Y
Z

pitfall noun
The author described some of the pitfalls *of being famous.*
difficulty, problem, hazard, danger, snag, catch, trap

pitiful adjective
1 *We could hear* pitiful *cries for help.*
sad, sorrowful, mournful, pathetic, plaintive, heart-rending, moving, touching
2 *The goalie made a* pitiful *attempt to stop the ball.*
hopeless, useless, feeble, inadequate, incompetent, pathetic

pity noun
The pirates showed no pity *towards the captives.*
mercy, compassion, sympathy, humanity, kindness, concern, feeling
opposite **cruelty**
a pity
It's a pity *that you have to leave so early.*
a shame, unfortunate, bad luck

pity verb
We pitied *anyone who was caught up in the storm.*
feel sorry for, feel for, sympathize with, take pity on

pivot noun
The point on which a lever turns is the
fulcrum.
The point on which a spinning object turns is its axis.
The point on which a wheel turns is the axle or hub.

place noun
1 *This is a good* place *to park.*
site, venue, spot, location, position, situation
2 *They are looking for a quiet* place *to live.*
area, district, locality, neighbourhood, region, vicinity
3 *Save me a* place *on the bus.*
seat, space

place verb
1 *The hotel is* placed *next to the beach.*
locate, situate, position, station
2 *You can* place *your coats on the bed.*
put down, set down, leave, deposit, lay
(informal) **dump, plonk**

placid adjective
1 *The dog has a* placid *nature and would make an ideal pet.*
calm, composed, unexcitable, even-tempered
opposite **excitable**
2 *The sea was* placid *at that time of the day.*
calm, quiet, tranquil, peaceful, undisturbed, unruffled
opposite **stormy**

plague noun
1 *Doctors worked hard to prevent the* plague *from spreading.*
pestilence, epidemic, contagion, outbreak
2 *There was a* plague *of wasps this summer.*
invasion, infestation, swarm

plague verb
1 *Stop* plaguing *me with questions!*
bother, pester, trouble, annoy, badger, harass
(informal) **nag, bug**
2 *Celia has been* plagued *by bad luck recently.*
afflict, beset, torment, hound

plain adjective
1 *The furniture in the room was very* plain.
simple, modest, basic
opposite **elaborate**
2 *Some people say she looks* plain *compared with her sister.*
unattractive, ordinary
opposite **attractive**
3 *It is* plain *to me that you are not interested.*
clear, evident, obvious, apparent, unmistakable
opposite **unclear**

4 *She told us what she thought in very* **plain** *terms.*

direct, frank, blunt, outspoken, honest, sincere, straightforward

5 *We need to wear a* **plain** *T-shirt for sports.*

self-coloured

plain noun

A grassy plain in a hot country is called **savannah**.

The large plains of North America are the **prairies**.

The large plains of Russia are the **steppes**.

plan noun

1 *The captain explained her* **plan** *to the rest of the team.*

idea, proposal, scheme, strategy, project, suggestion, proposition

A plan to do something bad is a **plot**.

2 *They looked at the* **plans** *for the new sports centre.*

design, diagram, chart, map, drawing, blueprint

plan verb

1 *The outlaws* **planned** *an attack upon the sheriff.*

scheme, design, devise, work out, formulate, prepare, organize

To plan to do something bad is to **plot**.

2 *What do you* **plan** *to do next?*

aim, intend, propose, mean

plane noun

see **aircraft**

planet noun

The new space probe will travel to far-off planets.

world

WORD WEB

THE PLANETS OF THE SOLAR SYSTEM (IN ORDER FROM THE SUN) ARE

Mercury, Venus, Earth, Mars, Jupiter, Saturn, Uranus, Neptune

The path followed by a planet is its **orbit**.

Minor planets orbiting the sun are **asteroids**.

Pluto is classified as a **dwarf planet**.

Something which orbits a planet is a **satellite**.

The earth's large satellite is the **Moon**.

See also **space**

WRITING TIPS

You can use these words to describe an **alien planet**

Earth-like, gaseous, inhospitable, uninhabitable

TO DESCRIBE ITS **SURFACE**

barren, desolate, dusty, frozen, icy, molten, rocky, volcanic

TO DESCRIBE ITS **ATMOSPHERE** OR AIR

airless, noxious, poisonous, thin, unbreathable

plant noun

WORD WEB

SOME TYPES OF PLANT

algae, bush, cactus, cereal, evergreen, fern, flower, fungus, grass, herb, house plant, lichen, moss, pot plant, shrub, tree, vegetable, vine, weed, wildflower

See also **flower, fruit, herb, tree, vegetable**

PARTS OF VARIOUS PLANTS

bloom, blossom, branch, bud, flower, fruit, leaf, petal, pod, root, shoot, stalk, stem, trunk, twig

A piece cut off a plant to form a new plant is a **cutting**.

A young plant is a **seedling**.

A word for plants in general is **vegetation**.

A person who studies plants is a **botanist**.

A word meaning 'to do with plants' is **botanical**.

A
B
C
D
E
F
G
H
I
J
K
L
M
N
O
P
Q
R
S
T
U
V
W
X
Y
Z

plant verb
These seeds should be planted *in the spring.*
sow, put in the ground
To move a plant from where it was growing
and plant it somewhere else is to
transplant it.

plaster noun
The nurse put a plaster *on the cut.*
dressing, sticking plaster, bandage

plate noun
1 *She piled their* plates *with food.*
For items of crockery see **crockery**
2 *The robot's body was formed of metal*
plates.
panel, sheet
3 *The book includes colour* plates *of various*
flowers.
illustration, photo, picture

platform noun
The conductor stood on a platform *to address*
the audience.
dais, podium, stage, stand

play noun
1 *There was a good* play *on TV last night.*
drama, performance, production
2 *It is important to balance work and* play.
playing, recreation, amusement, fun,
games, sport
For various games and sports see **game,**
sport

play verb
1 *The children went out to* play.
amuse yourself, have fun, romp about
2 *Do you like* playing *basketball?*
take part in, participate in, compete in
3 *We are* playing *the home team next week.*
compete against, oppose, challenge,
take on
4 *Mira* played *the piano at the school*
concert.
perform on
5 *My sister* played *Goldilocks in the school*
play.
act, take the part of, portray,
represent

player noun
1 *You need four* players *for this game.*
contestant, participant, competitor
2 *How many* players *are in the orchestra?*
performer, instrumentalist, musician
Someone who plays music on their own is a
soloist.
For various performers see **entertainer,**
music

playful adjective
The kittens were in a playful *mood.*
lively, spirited, frisky, mischievous, roguish,
impish, joking, teasing
opposite serious

playground noun
For playground games see **game**

playing field noun
There is a training session on the playing
field *tomorrow.*
ground, pitch, sports ground

play park noun
see **park**

plea noun
The king ignored the captives' plea *for*
mercy.
appeal, request, entreaty, petition

plead verb
to plead with
The children pleaded with *the witch to let*
them go.
beg, entreat, implore, appeal to, ask,
request, petition

pleasant adjective
1 *The owner of the shop is always* pleasant
to us.
kind, friendly, likeable, charming, amiable,
amicable, cheerful, genial, good-natured,
good-humoured, approachable, hospitable,
welcoming
2 *We spent a very* pleasant *evening playing*
cards.
pleasing, enjoyable, agreeable, delightful,
lovely, entertaining

3 *The weather is quite* pleasant *today.*
fine, mild, sunny, warm
opposite unpleasant

please verb
1 *I hope my present will* please *you.*
give pleasure to, make happy, satisfy, delight, amuse, entertain
2 *Do as you* please.
want, wish

pleased adjective
Why do you look so pleased *today?*
contented, delighted, elated, glad, grateful, happy, satisfied, thankful, thrilled
opposite annoyed

pleasure noun
1 *Mrs Ramsay gets a lot of* pleasure *from her garden.*
delight, enjoyment, happiness, joy, satisfaction, comfort, contentment, gladness
Very great pleasure is bliss or ecstasy.
2 *He talked about the* pleasures *of living in the country.*
joy, comfort, delight

pleat noun
It takes ages to iron the pleats *in the skirt.*
crease, fold, tuck

pledge noun
The knights swore a pledge *of loyalty to the king.*
oath, vow, promise, word

plentiful adjective
There is a plentiful *supply of berries in the forest.*
abundant, ample, generous, inexhaustible, lavish, liberal, profuse
opposite scarce

plenty noun
Don't buy any milk—there's plenty *in the fridge.*
a lot, a large amount, an abundance, a profusion

A lot more than you need is a glut or surplus.
opposite scarcity
plenty of
We've still got plenty of *time.*
a lot of, lots of, ample, abundant
(informal) loads of, masses of, tons of

plight noun
He was concerned about the plight *of the homeless.*
predicament, trouble, difficulty, problem, dilemma

plod verb
1 *The hikers* plodded *on through the mud.*
tramp, trudge, lumber
2 *She's still* plodding *away at her violin lessons.*
slog, labour, persevere

plot noun
1 *Guy Fawkes was part of a* plot *against the government.*
conspiracy, scheme, secret plan
2 *It was hard to follow the* plot *of the film.*
story, storyline, narrative, thread
3 *They bought a* plot *of ground to build a new house.*
area, piece, lot, patch
A plot of ground for growing flowers or vegetables is an allotment.
A large plot of land is a tract of land.

plot verb
1 *The gang were* plotting *a daring bank raid.*
plan, devise, concoct, hatch
(informal) cook up
2 *They were accused of* plotting *against the queen.*
conspire, intrigue, scheme
3 *The captain* plotted *the course of the ship.*
chart, map, mark

plough verb
1 *Tractors are used to* plough *the fields.*
cultivate, till, turn over
2 *Are you still* ploughing *through that book?*
wade, labour, toil

a b c d e f g h i j k l m n o **p** q r s t u v w x y z

A B C D E F G H I J K L M N O

Q R S T U V W X Y Z

pluck verb
1 *They* plucked *the apples off the tree.*
pick, pull off, gather, collect, harvest
2 *A seagull* plucked *the sandwich out of her hand.*
grab, seize, snatch, jerk, pull, tug, yank
3 *The guitarist* plucked *the strings very gently.*
To run your finger or plectrum across the strings of a guitar is to strum.
To pluck the strings of a violin or cello is to play pizzicato.

plug noun
They removed the plug *in the side of the barrel.*
stopper, cork, bung

plug verb
1 *Dad managed to* plug *the leak in the pipe.*
stop up, block, close, fill, seal, bung up
2 (informal) *We asked the local radio station to* plug *our concert.*
advertise, publicize, promote, push

plump adjective
The goblin was short and plump, *with pointy ears.*
chubby, dumpy, fat, tubby, podgy, round, stout, portly
opposite skinny

plunder verb
Viking raiders plundered *the village.*
loot, pillage, raid, ransack, rob, steal from

plunge verb
1 *One by one, the girls* plunged *into the pool.*
dive, jump, leap, throw yourself
2 *As the wind died down, the kite* plunged *to the ground.*
drop, fall, pitch, tumble, plummet, swoop
3 *I* plunged *my hand in the cold water.*
dip, lower, sink, immerse, submerge
4 *Finn* plunged *his spear into the dragon's throat.*
thrust, stab, push, stick, shove, force

plural adjective
opposite singular

poem noun
We each wrote a poem *about the seaside.*
rhyme
Poems are poetry or verse.
A group of lines forming a section of a poem is a stanza.
A pair of rhyming lines within a poem is a couplet.
The rhythm of a poem is its metre.

WORD WEB
SOME KINDS OF POEM
ballad, cinquain, clerihew, concrete poem, elegy, epic, free verse, haiku, limerick, lyric, narrative poem, nonsense verse, nursery rhyme, ode, sonnet, tanka

poetic adjective
The book is written in a poetic *style.*
expressive, imaginative, lyrical, poetical
An uncomplimentary synonym is flowery.

point noun
1 *Be careful—that knife has a very sharp point.*
tip, end, spike, prong
2 *The stars looked like* points *of light in the sky.*
dot, spot, speck, fleck
3 *He marked on the map the exact* point *where the treasure lay.*
location, place, position, site
4 *At that* point *the rain started to come down.*
moment, instant, time
5 *I agree with your last* point.
idea, argument, thought
6 *His sense of humour is one of his good* points.
characteristic, feature, attribute
7 *There is no* point *in phoning at this hour.*
purpose, reason, aim, object, use, usefulness
8 *I think I missed the* point *of that film.*
meaning, essence, core, gist

point verb
1 *She pointed the way.*
draw attention to, indicate, point out, show, signal
2 *Can you point me in the right direction for the station?*
aim, direct, guide, lead, steer

pointless adjective
It's pointless to argue with him—he's so stubborn.
useless, futile, vain
opposite worthwhile

poise noun
The young actress showed great poise for her age.
calmness, composure, assurance, self-confidence

poised adjective
The jaguar was poised to pounce on its prey.
ready, waiting, prepared, set

poison noun
A poison to kill plants is **herbicide** or **weedkiller**.
A poison to kill insects is **insecticide** or **pesticide**.
The poison in a snake bite is **venom**.
A substance which can save you from the effects of a poison is an **antidote**.

poisonous adjective
Some of those mushrooms may be poisonous.
toxic, venomous, deadly, lethal

poke verb
Someone poked me in the back with an umbrella.
prod, dig, jab, stab, thrust
to poke out
The kitten's head was poking out of the basket.
stick out, project, protrude

polar adjective
The polar expedition will study birds and sea life.
Antarctic or Arctic

WORD WEB
THINGS YOU MIGHT SEE IN POLAR REGIONS
glacier, iceberg, ice field or ice cap, moss, permafrost, pack ice, sheet ice, tundra
See also **ice**

SOME ANIMALS WHICH LIVE IN POLAR REGIONS
albatross, arctic fox, arctic tern, narwhal, penguin, polar bear, reindeer, seal, walrus, whale, wolf

THINGS A POLAR EXPLORER MIGHT USE
goggles, huskies, ice-pick, kayak, mittens, parka, skis, ski pole, sledge, snowmobile, snowshoes

polar bear

penguin

seal

A
B
C
D
E
F
G
H
I
J
K
L
M
N
O
P
Q
R
S
T
U
V
W
X
Y
Z

pole noun
Four poles marked the corners of the field.
post, bar, rod, stick, shaft
A pole that you use when walking or as a weapon is a **staff**.
A pole for a flag to fly from is a **flagpole**.
A pole to support sails on a boat or ship is a **mast** or **spar**.
A pole with a pointed end to stick in the ground is a **stake**.
Poles which a circus entertainer walks on are **stilts**.

police officer noun
Several police officers were patrolling the football ground.
policeman or policewoman, officer, constable
(informal) cop, copper
Police officers of higher rank are **sergeant, inspector,** and **superintendent**.
The head of a police force is the chief constable.
Someone training for the police force is a cadet.
Someone who investigates crimes is a detective.
See also **detective**

policy noun
The leaflet explains the school's policy on bullying.
approach, strategy, stance, plan of action

polish verb
Beeswax is used to polish furniture.
rub down, shine, buff, burnish, wax
to polish something off
The girls polished off a whole plate of sandwiches.
finish, get through, eat up

polish noun
The silverware had been cleaned to give it a good polish.
shine, sheen, gloss, lustre, sparkle, brightness, glaze, finish

polished adjective
1 *She could see her face in the polished surface.*
shining, shiny, bright, glassy, gleaming, glossy, lustrous
opposites dull, tarnished
2 *The orchestra gave a polished performance.*
accomplished, skilful, faultless, perfect, well prepared

polite adjective
My aunt is always polite to visitors.
courteous, well-mannered, respectful, civil, well-behaved, gracious, gentlemanly or ladylike, chivalrous, gallant
opposites rude, impolite

politics noun

WORD WEB
SOME WORDS USED IN POLITICS
alliance, ballot, cabinet, campaign, devolution, election, government, left-wing, lobby, majority, manifesto, parliament, party, policy, referendum, right-wing, vote

poll noun
The result of the poll has been declared.
election, vote, ballot
A vote on a particular question by all the people in a country is a **referendum**.
An official survey to find out about the population is a **census**.

pollute verb
The river has been polluted by chemicals.
contaminate, infect, poison

pompous adjective
The giant spoke in a rather pompous manner.
arrogant, self-important, haughty, snobbish
(informal) stuck-up
opposite modest

pond noun
see pool

pool noun
1 *The surface of the* pool *was covered with frogspawn.*
pond
A larger area of water is a **lake** or (in Scotland) a **loch**.
A small shallow area of water is a **puddle**.
A pool of water in the desert is an **oasis**.
A pool among rocks on a seashore is a **rock pool**.
2 *The sports centre has an indoor and an outdoor* pool.
swimming pool, swimming baths

poor adjective
1 *You can't afford luxuries if you're* poor.
impoverished, poverty-stricken, penniless, needy, badly off, hard-up
opposite rich
2 *His handwriting is very* poor.
bad, inferior, inadequate, incompetent, unsatisfactory, shoddy, weak, worthless
opposites good, superior
3 *They pitied the* poor *animals standing in the rain.*
unlucky, unfortunate, pitiful, wretched
opposite lucky

poorly adjective
He stayed at home because he felt poorly.
ill, sick, unwell, unfit
opposite well

pop noun & verb
For various sounds see **sound**[1]

popular adjective
1 *Disney has made a lot of* popular *children's films.*
well-liked, well-loved, celebrated, favourite
opposite unpopular
2 *Rollerblades are very* popular *just now.*
fashionable, widespread, current, in demand
(informal) **trendy**
opposite unpopular

population noun
About ten per cent of the world's population *is left-handed.*
inhabitants, residents, occupants, citizens, people, community

pore verb
to pore over
The detective pored over *the evidence on his desk.*
examine, study, inspect, look closely at, scrutinize

port noun
A large cruise ship sailed into the port.
harbour, dock, anchorage
A harbour for yachts and pleasure boats is a **marina**.

portable adjective
They took a portable *TV on holiday.*
transportable, mobile, compact, lightweight
A portable phone is a **mobile phone** or **mobile**
A portable computer is a **laptop** or **notebook**.

portion noun
Violet asked for a large portion *of trifle.*
helping, serving, ration, share, quantity, piece, part, bit, slice

portrait noun
There's a portrait *of the Queen on every stamp.*
picture, image, likeness, representation
A portrait which shows a side view of someone is a **profile**.
A portrait which shows just the outline of someone is a **silhouette**.
A portrait which exaggerates some aspect of a person is a **caricature**.

portray verb
The film portrays *life in Victorian England.*
depict, represent, show, describe, illustrate

a
b
c
d
e
f
g
h
i
j
k
l
m
n
o
p
q
r
s
t
u
v
w
x
y
z

A
B
C
D
E
F
G
H
I
J
K
L
M
N
O
P
Q
R
S
T
U
V
W
X
Y
Z

pose verb
The film star posed in front of the camera.
model, sit
to pose as someone
The spy posed as a newspaper reporter.
impersonate, pretend to be,
pass yourself off as

posh adjective (informal)
We went to a posh restaurant for a treat.
smart, stylish, high-class, elegant,
fashionable, up-market, luxurious,
luxury, de luxe, plush
(informal) classy, swanky, swish,
snazzy

position noun
1 *Mark the position on the map.*
location, place, point, spot, site,
whereabouts
2 *He shifted his position to avoid getting
cramp.*
pose, posture, stance
3 *Losing all her money put her in a difficult
position.*
situation, state, condition, circumstances
4 *A referee should adopt a neutral position.*
opinion, attitude, outlook, view
5 *Being a head teacher is an important
position.*
job, post, appointment, function

positive adjective
1 *The detective was positive that the cook
was lying.*
certain, sure, convinced, assured, confident
opposite **uncertain**
2 *Miss Andrews made some positive
comments on my singing.*
helpful, useful, worthwhile, beneficial,
constructive
opposite **negative**

possess verb
1 *They don't possess a computer.*
have, own
2 *What possessed you to take up diving?*
make you think of, come over you

possessions plural noun
*The refugees had lost all of their
possessions.*
belongings, goods, property

possibility noun
There's a possibility that it may rain later.
chance, likelihood, danger, risk

possible adjective
1 *Is it possible that life exists on other
planets?*
likely, probable, conceivable,
credible
2 *It wasn't possible to shift the piano.*
feasible, practicable, practical
opposite **impossible**

possibly adverb
*'Will you finish your homework today?'
'Possibly.'*
maybe, perhaps

post[1] noun
*The farmer put up some posts for a
new fence.*
pole, pillar, shaft, stake, support, prop
post[1] verb
*The names of the winners will be posted on
the noticeboard.*
display, put up, announce, advertise

post[2] noun
The post was delivered late.
mail, letters, delivery
post[2] verb
Did you post those letters?
mail, send, dispatch

post[3] noun
Are you thinking of applying for the post?
job, position, situation, appointment,
vacancy

poster noun
We saw a poster about a missing cat.
advertisement, announcement, bill,
notice, sign, placard

postpone verb
*They **postponed** the match because of bad weather.*
put off, defer, delay
To stop a meeting or game that you intend to start again is to **adjourn** or **suspend** it.

pot noun
*On the table were little **pots** of jam and honey.*
jar, dish, bowl, pan

potent adjective
1 *The magic potion is very **potent**, so you only need a single drop.*
strong, powerful, intoxicating, pungent, heady
2 *She persuaded us with her **potent** arguments.*
effective, forceful, strong, compelling
opposite weak

potential adjective
1 *He's a **potential** champion.*
budding, future, likely, possible, probable, promising
2 *These floods are a **potential** disaster.*
looming, threatening

potion noun
*A magic **potion** was brewing in the wizard's cauldron.*
drug, medicine, mixture

pottery noun

WORD WEB
Someone who creates pottery is a **potter**.
A formal word for pottery is **ceramics**.
TYPES OF POTTERY
bone china, china, earthenware, porcelain, stoneware, terracotta
The kind of pottery we eat and drink from is **crockery**.

pouch noun
*The pirate kept his gunpowder in a **pouch**.*
bag, purse, sack

poultry noun

WORD WEB
KINDS OF POULTRY
bantam, chicken, duck, fowl, goose, guinea fowl, hen, pullet, turkey
A male chicken specially fattened for eating is a **capon**.

pounce verb
to pounce on
*The cat **pounced on** the mouse.*
jump on, leap on, spring on, swoop down on, lunge at, ambush, attack

pound verb
*Huge waves **pounded** the stranded ship.*
beat, hit, batter, smash
To pound something hard until it is powder is to **crush**, **grind**, or **pulverize** it.
To pound something soft is to **knead**, **mash**, or **pulp** it.

pour verb
1 *Water **poured** through the hole.*
flow, run, gush, stream, spill, spout
2 *I **poured** some milk into my cup.*
tip, serve

poverty noun
*Many people were living in **poverty**.*
pennilessness, hardship, need, want
Extreme poverty is **abject** poverty.
opposite wealth

powder noun
*The fairy sprinkled some magic **powder** in the air.*
dust, particles

powdery adjective
*The wind blew the **powdery** soil away.*
dusty, fine, loose, grainy, sandy

power noun
1 *They were amazed by the **power** of the robot.*
strength, force, might, energy

A
B
C
D
E
F
G
H
I
J
K
L
M
N
O

P

Q
R
S
T
U
V
W
X
Y
Z

2 *The storyteller has the* power *to enthrall an audience.*
skill, talent, ability, competence
3 *A policeman has the* power *to arrest someone.*
authority, right
4 *The empress had* power *over all the people.*
authority, command, control, dominance, domination

powerful adjective
1 *Sir Joustalot was the most* powerful *knight in the kingdom.*
influential, leading, commanding, dominant, high-powered
2 *The wrestler had a* powerful *punch.*
strong, forceful, hard, mighty, vigorous, formidable, potent
3 *He used some* powerful *arguments.*
strong, convincing, effective, persuasive, impressive
opposite **weak**

powerless adjective
The good fairy was powerless *to undo the spell.*
helpless, ineffective, weak, feeble, defenceless

practical adjective
1 *I'll ask Katie what to do—she is always very* practical.
down-to-earth, matter-of-fact, sensible, level-headed
opposite **impractical**
2 *The robbers' plan was not very* practical.
workable, realistic, sensible, feasible, viable, achievable
opposite **impractical**
3 *Do you have any* practical *experience of child-minding?*
real, actual, hands-on
opposite **theoretical**

practically adverb
Keep going—we're practically *there!*
almost, just about, nearly, virtually

practice noun
1 *We have extra football* practice *this week.*
training, exercises, preparation, rehearsal, drill
2 *Is it the* practice *amongst ogres to eat grubs for breakfast?*
custom, habit, convention, routine
in practice
What will the plan involve in practice?
in effect, in reality, actually, really

practise verb
1 *My piano teacher asked me to* practise *for longer.*
do exercises, rehearse, train, drill
To practise just before the start of a performance is to **warm up**.
2 *My sister wants to* practise *veterinary medicine.*
do, perform, carry out, put into practice, follow, pursue, work in

praise verb
The critics praised *the actress for her outstanding performance.*
commend, applaud, admire, compliment, congratulate, pay tribute to
(informal) **rave about**
opposite **criticize**

praise noun
She received a lot of praise *for her painting.*
approval, admiration, compliments, congratulations, applause

prance verb
Milly started prancing *about in a silly way.*
dance, skip, hop, leap, romp, cavort, caper, frolic, gambol

precarious adjective
1 *The diver was in a* precarious *situation, surrounded by sharks.*
dangerous, perilous, risky
opposite **safe**
2 *Take care—that ladder looks* precarious!
unsafe, unstable, unsteady, insecure, shaky, wobbly, rickety
opposite **secure**

precede verb
A fireworks display preceded the concert.
come before, go before, lead
opposites **follow, succeed**

precious adjective
1 *Her most precious possession was an old photograph.*
treasured, cherished, valued, prized, dearest, beloved
2 *The throne glittered with precious gems.*
valuable, costly, expensive, priceless
For precious stones see **jewel**
opposite **worthless**

precise adjective
1 *Can you tell me the precise time, please?*
exact, accurate, correct, true, right
opposite **rough**
2 *The map gave precise directions for finding the treasure.*
careful, detailed, specific, particular, definite
opposite **vague**

predict verb
You can't predict what may happen.
forecast, foresee, foretell, prophesy

predictable adjective
It was predictable that it would rain.
expected, foreseeable, likely, probable
opposite **unpredictable**

preface noun
The story behind the book is explained in the preface.
introduction, prologue

prefer verb
Would you prefer juice or lemonade?
rather have, go for, opt for, plump for, choose, fancy

preferable adjective
preferable to
She finds country life preferable to living in the city.
better than, superior to, more attractive than, more suitable than

preference noun
1 *Sandy has a preference for sweet things.*
liking, fancy, inclination
2 *My preference is to walk rather than run.*
choice, option, selection, pick, wish

prefix noun
opposite **suffix**

pregnant adjective
One of the giraffes in the zoo is pregnant.
expecting a baby, carrying a baby, expecting
A pregnant woman is an **expectant mother**.

prehistoric adjective

WORD WEB
PREHISTORIC REMAINS YOU MIGHT VISIT
barrow or **tumulus,**
cromlech or **stone circle, dolmen,**
hill fort, menhir or **standing stone**

A person who studies prehistory by excavating and analysing remains is an **archaeologist.**

NAMES OF PREHISTORIC PERIODS
The best tools and weapons were made of stone in the **Stone Age,** of bronze in the **Bronze Age,** and of iron in the **Iron Age.** Formal names for the Old, Middle, and New Stone Ages are **Palaeolithic, Mesolithic,** and **Neolithic** periods. Prehistoric people who lived during the Stone Age were **Neanderthals.**

Most of the earth's surface was covered with ice in the **Ice Age.**

See also **cave**

SOME PREHISTORIC ANIMALS
cave bear, dinosaur, glyptodont, ground sloth, sabre-toothed cat or **smilodon, sabre-toothed squirrel, woolly mammoth, woolly rhinoceros**

A person who studies fossils of prehistoric life is a **palaeontologist.**

See also **dinosaur**

a
b
c
d
e
f
g
h
i
j
k
l
m
n
o
p
q
r
s
t
u
v
w
x
y
z

A
B
C
D
E
F
G
H
I
J
K
L
M
N
O
P
Q
R
S
T
U
V
W
X
Y
Z

prejudice noun
The school has a policy against racial prejudice.
bias, discrimination, intolerance, narrow-mindedness, bigotry
Prejudice against other races is racism.
Prejudice against other nations is xenophobia.
Prejudice against the other sex is sexism.
opposites fairness, tolerance

preliminary adjective
They were knocked out in the preliminary round of the competition.
first, initial, introductory, early, opening, preparatory

prelude noun
see introduction

premises plural noun
Keep out—these are private premises.
buildings, property, grounds

preoccupied adjective
preoccupied with something
She was so preoccupied with her work that she forgot the time.
absorbed in, engrossed in, wrapped up in, intent on, obsessed with

prepare verb
The museum staff are preparing for the new exhibition.
get ready, make arrangements for, organize, plan, set up
To prepare for a play is to rehearse.
To prepare to take part in a sport is to train.

prepared adjective
The knights were prepared to fight for the Queen.
be able, be ready, be willing

presence noun
Your presence is required upstairs.
attendance

present¹ adjective
1 *Is everyone present?*
here, in attendance, at hand
2 *Who is the present world chess champion?*
current, existing

present² noun
What would you like for your birthday present?
gift
(informal) **prezzie**

present² verb
1 *The head presents the prizes on sports day.*
award, hand over
2 *Our class is presenting a play about the Vikings.*
put on, perform, stage, mount
3 *Dr Smart presented her amazing invention to the world.*
put forward, show, display, exhibit, make known

preserve verb
1 *It's more difficult to preserve food in hot weather.*
keep, save, store
2 *It's important to preserve wildlife.*
look after, protect, conserve, defend, safeguard, maintain

press verb
1 *Press the fruit through a sieve to get r id of the seeds.*
push, force, squeeze, squash, crush, shove, cram, compress
2 *She pressed her blouse for the party.*
iron, flatten, smooth
3 *Our friends pressed us to stay a bit longer.*
beg, urge, entreat, implore

press noun
1 *We read about the competition in the press.*
newspapers, magazines
2 *The press came to the opening of the new arts centre.*
journalists, reporters, the media

pressure noun
1 *The nurse applied pressure to the wound.*
force, compression, squeezing, weight, load
2 *In the final, the home team were under a lot of pressure.*
stress, strain, tension

prestige noun
There's a lot of prestige in winning an Olympic medal.
credit, glory, fame, honour, renown, distinction, status, kudos

presume verb
1 *I presume you'd like something to eat.*
assume, take it, imagine, suppose, think, believe, guess
2 *He wouldn't presume to tell her what to do!*
be bold enough, dare, venture

pretend verb
She's not really crying—she's only pretending.
put on an act, bluff, fake, sham, pose
(informal) kid, put it on

pretend adjective
That's not a real spider—it's just a pretend one!
fake, false, artificial, made-up
opposite real

pretty adjective
The doll was dressed in a pretty blue outfit.
attractive, beautiful, lovely, nice, pleasing, charming, dainty, picturesque, quaint
(informal) cute
A common simile is as pretty as a picture.
opposite ugly

prevent verb
1 *The driver could do nothing to prevent the accident.*
stop, avert, avoid, head off
2 *The police prevented an attempted bank raid.*
block, foil, frustrate, thwart
3 *There's not much you can do to prevent colds.*
stave off, ward off

previous adjective
1 *The couple had met on a previous occasion.*
earlier, former, preceding
2 *The previous owners of the house have gone abroad.*
former
opposite subsequent

prey noun
The lion killed its prey.
quarry, victim

prey verb
to prey on
Owls prey on small animals.
hunt, kill, feed on

price noun
What is the price of a return ticket to Sydney?
cost, amount, figure, expense, payment, sum, charge, rate
The price you pay for a journey on public transport is the fare.
The price you pay to send a letter is the postage.
The price you pay to use a private road, bridge, or tunnel is a toll.

priceless adjective
1 *The museum contained many priceless antiques.*
precious, rare, valuable, costly, expensive, dear
2 (informal) *The joke she told was priceless.*
funny, amusing, comic, hilarious, witty

prick verb
Jamie burst the balloon by pricking it with a pin.
pierce, puncture, stab, jab, perforate

prickle noun
A hedgehog uses its prickles for defence.
spike, spine, needle, barb, thorn
The prickles on a hedgehog or porcupine are also called quills.

a
b
c
d
e
f
g
h
i
j
k
l
m
n
o
p
q
r
s
t
u
v
w
x
y
z

A
B
C
D
E
F
G
H
I
J
K
L
M
N
O

P

Q
R
S
T
U
V
W
X
Y
Z

prickly adjective
Holly leaves are very prickly.
spiky, spiny, thorny, bristly, sharp, scratchy

pride noun
1 *Mr Dodds takes great pride in his garden.*
satisfaction, pleasure, delight
2 *The medal winner was a source of great pride to his family.*
self-esteem, self-respect, dignity, honour
3 *Pride comes before a fall.*
arrogance, conceit, big-headedness, vanity, snobbery
opposite **humility**

priest noun
The priest conducted the wedding ceremony.
minister, vicar, pastor, padre
A Buddhist religious leader is a lama.
A Hindu or Sikh religious leader is a guru.
A Jewish religious leader is a rabbi.
A Muslim religious leader is an imam.
An ancient Celtic priest was a Druid.

prim adjective
Aunt Jemima is always very prim and proper.
prudish, strait-laced, formal, demure

primarily adverb
The website is aimed primarily at teenagers.
chiefly, especially, mainly, mostly, predominantly, principally, above all

primary adjective
Their primary aim was to win the match.
main, chief, principal, foremost, major, most important, top, prime
For primary colours see **colour**

prime adjective
1 *The penguins' prime concern is to protect their chicks.*
see **primary**
2 *The dish is made with prime cuts of meat.*
best, superior, first-class, choice, select, top

primitive adjective
1 *Primitive humans were hunters rather than farmers.*
ancient, early, prehistoric, primeval
opposite **civilized**
2 *These days steam engines seem very primitive.*
crude, basic, simple, rudimentary, undeveloped
opposite **advanced**

prince and **princess** noun
see **royalty**

principal adjective
The principal aim of the race is to raise money for charity.
main, chief, primary, foremost, most important, leading, major, dominant, fundamental, supreme, top

principle noun
Both teams agreed to follow the principles of fair play.
rule, standard, code, ethic

print noun
1 *She found the tiny print difficult to read.*
lettering, letters, printing, type, characters
2 *The detective searched the building for prints.*
mark, impression, footprint, fingerprint
3 *Is that a print or an original painting?*
copy, reproduction, duplicate

priority noun
Traffic on the main road has priority.
precedence, right of way

prise verb
He tried to prise the lid off the treasure chest.
lever, force, wrench

prison noun
He was sentenced to six months in prison.
jail, imprisonment, confinement

prisoner noun
The prisoner tried to escape from jail.
convict, captive, inmate

A person who is held prisoner until a demand is met is a **hostage**.

private adjective
1 *Everything I write in my diary is* private.
secret, confidential, personal, intimate
Secret official documents are **classified** documents.
2 *Can we go somewhere a little more private?*
quiet, secluded, hidden, concealed
opposite public

privilege noun
Club members enjoy special privileges.
advantage, benefit, concession, right

privileged adjective
She comes from a privileged *family background.*
advantaged, wealthy, fortunate, affluent, prosperous

prize noun
Our team won first prize *in the relay race.*
award, reward, trophy
Money that you win as a prize is your **winnings**.
Prize money that keeps increasing until someone wins it is a **jackpot**.

prize verb
Chrissie prized *her grandmother's ring above all else.*
treasure, value, cherish, hold dear, esteem, revere
opposite dislike

probable adjective
A burst pipe was the most probable *cause of the flood.*
likely, feasible, possible, predictable, expected
opposite improbable

probe verb
1 *The submarine can* probe *the depths of the ocean.*
explore, penetrate, see into, plumb

2 *Detectives* probed *the circumstances surrounding the crime.*
investigate, inquire into, look into, examine, study

problem noun
1 *Our maths teacher set us a difficult problem.*
puzzle, question
(informal) brain-teaser, poser
2 *I'm having a* problem *with my computer.*
difficulty, trouble, snag, worry
(informal) headache

procedure noun
The recipe explains the procedure *for making bread.*
method, process, system, technique, way
A procedure which you follow regularly is a **routine**.

proceed verb
1 *The sheep* proceeded *slowly along the path.*
go on, advance, move forward, progress
2 *We advised them not to* proceed *with their plan.*
go ahead, carry on

proceedings plural noun
A thunderstorm interrupted the day's proceedings.
events, happenings, activities, affairs
(informal) goings-on

proceeds plural noun
They added up the proceeds *from the jumble sale.*
income, takings, money, earnings, profit

process noun
The inventor showed us a new process *for creating electricity.*
method, procedure, operation, system, technique

process verb
The dairy processes *milk to make butter and cheese.*
deal with, prepare, treat, refine, transform

a
b
c
d
e
f
g
h
i
j
k
l
m
n
o
p
q
r
s
t
u
v
w
x
y
z

A
B
C
D
E
F
G
H
I
J
K
L
M
N
O
P
Q
R
S
T
U
V
W
X
Y
Z

procession noun
The procession *made its way slowly down the hill.*
parade, march, column, line

proclaim verb
The judges proclaimed *that the winner was disqualified.*
declare, announce, pronounce

prod verb
Someone prodded *me in the back with an umbrella.*
poke, dig, jab, nudge, push

produce verb
1 *Some lorries* produce *a lot of fumes.*
create, generate, cause, give rise to
2 *The tree* produced *a good crop of apples this year.*
yield, grow
3 *The factory* produces *cars and vans.*
make, manufacture, construct
4 *The referee's decision* produced *whistles from the crowd.*
provoke, result in, arouse, stimulate
5 *The writers have* produced *an award-winning comedy.*
compose, invent, think up
6 *The magician* produced *a rabbit from his hat.*
bring out, present, reveal

produce noun
The shop sells organic produce.
food, crops, fruit and vegetables

product noun
1 *The company launched a new range of beauty* products.
item, article, substance
2 *The famine is the* product *of years of drought.*
result, consequence, outcome, upshot

production noun
1 Production *at the factory has increased this year.*
output

2 *We went to see a* production *of 'The Sound of Music'.*
performance, show

productive adjective
1 *The soil here is rich and* productive.
fertile, fruitful
2 *It wasn't a very* productive *meeting.*
useful, valuable, worthwhile, constructive, profitable, fruitful
opposite **unproductive**

profession noun
Nursing is a worthwhile profession.
career, job, occupation, work, employment, business

professional adjective
1 *The plans were drawn by a* professional *architect.*
qualified, skilled, trained, experienced
2 *This is a very* professional *piece of work.*
skilled, expert, proficient, competent, efficient
opposite **incompetent**
3 *His ambition is to be a* professional *footballer.*
paid, full-time
opposite **amateur**

proficient adjective
Olga is a proficient *tap dancer.*
skilful, skilled, accomplished, capable, expert, able
opposite **incompetent**

profile noun
see portrait

profit noun
They sold the business and bought a yacht with the profit.
gain, surplus, excess
The extra money you get on your savings is interest.
opposite **loss**

programme noun
1 *We worked out a* programme *for sports day.*
plan, schedule, timetable
A list of things to be done at a meeting is an agenda.
2 *There was a really good* programme *on TV.*
broadcast, show, production, transmission

progress noun
1 *I traced their* progress *on the map.*
journey, route, movement, travels
2 *I'm not making much* progress *learning Dutch.*
advance, development, growth, improvement, headway
An important piece of progress is a breakthrough.

progress verb
Work on the new building is progressing *well.*
proceed, advance, move forward, make progress, make headway, continue, develop, improve
(informal) come along

prohibit verb
Skateboarding is prohibited *at school.*
ban, forbid, outlaw, rule out, veto
opposites permit, allow

project noun
1 *We did a history* project *on the Victorians.*
activity, task, assignment, piece of research
2 *There is a* project *to create a bird sanctuary in the area.*
plan, proposal, scheme

project verb
1 *A narrow ledge* projects *from the cliff.*
extend, protrude, stick out, jut out, overhang
2 *The lighthouse* projects *a beam of light.*
cast, shine, throw out

prolong verb
We prolonged *their visit by a few days.*
extend, lengthen, make longer, stretch out, draw out
opposite shorten

prominent adjective
1 *The clown had a very* prominent *nose.*
noticeable, conspicuous, obvious, striking, eye-catching
opposite inconspicuous
2 *He is a prominent* Hollywood *actor.*
well-known, famous, celebrated, major, leading, notable, distinguished, eminent
opposite unknown

promise noun
1 *We had* promises *of help from many people.*
assurance, pledge, guarantee, commitment, vow, oath, word of honour
2 *That young pianist shows* promise.
potential, talent

promise verb
Dad promised *that we'd go camping this summer.*
assure someone, give your word, guarantee, swear, take an oath, vow

promising adjective
1 *The weather looks* promising *for tomorrow.*
encouraging, hopeful
2 *Sheena is a* promising *young singer.*
bright, talented, gifted, budding
(informal) up-and-coming

promote verb
1 *Gareth has been* promoted *to captain.*
move up, advance, upgrade, elevate
2 *The singer is here to* promote *her new album.*
advertise, publicize, market, push, sell
(informal) plug
3 *The school is trying to* promote *healthy eating.*
encourage, foster, advocate, back, support

prompt adjective
I received a prompt *reply to my email.*
punctual, quick, rapid, swift, immediate, instant
opposite delayed

a
b
c
d
e
f
g
h
i
j
k
l
m
n
o
p
q
r
s
t
u
v
w
x
y
z

A
B
C
D
E
F
G
H
I
J
K
L
M
N
O
P
Q
R
S
T
U
V
W
X
Y
Z

prompt verb
Having a dog prompted her to take more exercise.
cause, lead, induce, motivate, stimulate, encourage, provoke

prone adjective
1 *The victim was lying prone on the floor.*
face down, on the front
To lie face upwards is to be **supine**.
2 *He is prone to exaggerate his health problems.*
inclined, apt, liable, likely

pronounce verb
1 *Try to pronounce the words clearly.*
say, speak, utter, articulate, sound
2 *The doctor pronounced her fully recovered.*
declare, announce, proclaim, judge

pronounced adjective
She spoke with a pronounced Australian accent.
clear, marked, distinct, definite, noticeable, obvious, striking, unmistakable, prominent
opposite imperceptible

proof noun
There is no proof that he is a secret agent.
evidence, confirmation

prop noun
The bridge is supported by steel props.
support, strut
A stick to prop yourself on when you hurt a leg is a **crutch**.
Part of a building which props up a wall is a **buttress**.

prop verb
Kenny propped his bike against the kerb.
lean, rest, stand
to prop something up
The shelf was propped up with sticks.
support, hold up, reinforce

propel verb
The steamboat was propelled by a huge paddle wheel.
drive forward, push forward, power, impel

proper adjective
1 *The nurse showed them the proper way to tie a bandage.*
correct, right, accurate, precise, true, genuine
opposites wrong, incorrect
2 *It's only proper that he should pay for the broken window.*
fair, just, fitting, appropriate, deserved, suitable
opposite inappropriate
3 *It's not proper to speak with your mouth full.*
decent, respectable, tasteful
opposite rude
4 (informal) *I looked a proper idiot wearing two different socks!*
complete, total, utter, absolute, thorough

property noun
1 *This office deals with lost property.*
belongings, possessions, goods
2 *The website lists property that is for sale in the city.*
buildings, houses, land, premises
3 *Many herbs have healing properties.*
quality, characteristic, feature, attribute, trait

prophecy noun
The witch's prophecy came true.
prediction, forecast

prophesy verb
The witch prophesied that there would be a great battle.
predict, forecast, foresee, foretell

proportion noun
1 *A large proportion of wild elephants live on nature reserves.*
part, section, share, fraction
2 *What is the proportion of girls to boys in your class?*
balance, ratio
proportions
The dining hall was a room of large proportions.
measurements, size, dimensions

proposal noun
What do you think of the proposal to build a skate park?
plan, project, scheme, suggestion, recommendation

propose verb
1 *He proposed a change in the rules.*
suggest, ask for, recommend
2 *How do you propose to pay for the holiday?*
intend, mean, plan, aim
3 *The class proposed two pupils to represent them on the school council.*
nominate, put forward

proprietor noun
Who is the proprietor of the bicycle shop?
manager, owner
(informal) boss

prosecute verb
Anyone caught shoplifting will be prosecuted.
bring to trial, charge, take to court
To take someone to court to try to get money from them is to sue them.

prospect noun
1 *What are their prospects of winning the tournament?*
chance, hope, expectation, likelihood, possibility, probability
2 *The hotel has a lovely prospect across the valley.*
outlook, view, vista

prosper verb
We expect our business to prosper this year.
do well, be successful, flourish, succeed, thrive, grow, boom
opposite fail

prosperity noun
Tourism has brought prosperity to the region.
wealth, affluence, growth, success
(informal) boom

prosperous adjective
She is married to a prosperous businessman.
wealthy, rich, well-off, well-to-do, affluent, successful, thriving
opposite poor

protect verb
1 *A sentry was posted outside to protect the palace.*
defend, guard, safeguard, keep safe, secure
2 *I wore a hat to protect myself from the sun.*
shield, shade, screen, insulate

protection noun
The hood gives protection from the rain.
shelter, cover, defence, insulation

protest noun
1 *There were protests at the plan to close the cinema.*
complaint, objection
A general protest is an outcry.
2 *Some streets will be closed for a protest in the city centre.*
demonstration, march, rally
(informal) demo

protest verb
We wrote a letter protesting about the closure of the cinema.
complain, make a protest, object (to), take exception (to), express disapproval (of)

protrude verb
His stomach protrudes above his waistband.
stick out, poke out, bulge, swell, project, stand out, jut out

proud adjective
1 *Jennie's father was very proud when she passed her music exam.*
delighted (with), pleased (with)
A common simile is as proud as a peacock.
2 *He's too proud to mix with the likes of us!*
conceited, big-headed, arrogant, vain, haughty, self-important, snobbish, superior
(informal) stuck-up
opposite humble

A
B
C
D
E
F
G
H
I
J
K
L
M
N
O
P
Q
R
S
T
U
V
W
X
Y
Z

prove verb
The evidence will prove that he is innocent.
confirm, demonstrate, establish, verify
opposite **disprove**

proverb noun
see saying

provide verb
1 *We'll provide the juice if you bring the sandwiches.*
bring, contribute, arrange for, lay on
To provide food and drink for people is to cater for them.
2 *The ski centre can provide you with boots and skis.*
supply, equip, furnish

provisions plural noun
We had enough provisions for two weeks.
food, rations, stores, supplies

provoke verb
1 *Don't do anything to provoke the lions!*
annoy, irritate, anger, incense, infuriate, exasperate, tease, taunt, goad
(informal) wind up
opposite **pacify**
2 *The referee's decision provoked anger.*
arouse, produce, prompt, cause, generate, induce, stimulate, spark off, stir up, whip up

prowl verb
Guard dogs prowled about the grounds of the palace.
roam, slink, sneak, creep, steal

prudent adjective
It would be prudent to start saving some money.
wise, sensible, shrewd, thoughtful, careful, cautious
opposites **reckless, unwise**

prune verb
Mum prunes her roses every spring.
cut back, trim

pry verb
I didn't mean to pry, but I overheard your conversation.
be curious, be inquisitive, interfere
(informal) be nosy, nose about or around, snoop
to pry into something
Mrs Snout was always prying into other people's business.
interfere in, meddle in, spy on
(informal) poke your nose into

psychological adjective
The doctor thinks her illness is psychological.
mental, emotional
opposite **physical**

public adjective
1 *The public entrance is at the front of the gallery.*
common, communal, general, open, shared
opposite **private**
2 *The name of the author is now public knowledge.*
well-known, acknowledged, published, open, general, universal
opposite **secret**

public noun
the public
This part of the castle is not open to the public.
people in general, everyone, the community, society, the nation

publication noun
She's celebrating the publication of her first novel.
issuing, printing, production
Various publications are books and magazines.

publicity noun
1 *Did you see the publicity for the book fair?*
advertising, advertisements, promotion
2 *Famous people don't always enjoy publicity.*
fame, exposure, limelight

publish verb
1 *The magazine is* published *every week.*
issue, print, produce, bring out, release, circulate
2 *When will they* publish *the results?*
announce, declare, disclose, make known, make public, report, reveal
To publish information on radio or TV is to broadcast it.

pudding noun
Do you want any pudding?
dessert, sweet
(informal) afters
For types of pudding see food

puff noun
1 *A* puff *of wind caught his hat.*
gust, breath, flurry
2 *A* puff *of smoke rose from the chimney.*
cloud, whiff

puff verb
1 *The dragon* puffed *green smoke from its nostrils.*
blow out, send out, emit, belch
2 *By the end of the race I was* puffing.
breathe heavily, pant, gasp, wheeze
3 *The sails* puffed *out as the wind rose.*
become inflated, billow, swell

pull verb
1 *She* pulled *her chair nearer to the desk.*
drag, draw, haul, lug, trail, tow
opposite push
2 *Be careful—you nearly* pulled *my arm off!*
tug, rip, wrench, jerk, pluck
to pull out
1 *The dentist* pulled out *one of my teeth.*
extract, take out, remove
2 *He had to* pull out *of the race.*
back out, withdraw, retire
to pull someone's leg
I hope you aren't pulling my leg!
make fun of, play a trick, tease
to pull through
It was a bad accident, but the doctors expect him to pull through.
get better, recover, revive, survive

to pull up
The bus pulled up *at the traffic lights.*
draw up, stop, halt

pulse noun
You can feel the pulse *of blood in your veins.*
beat, throb, drumming

pump verb
The fire brigade pumped *water out of the cellar.*
drain, draw off, empty
To move liquid from a higher container to a lower one through a tube is to siphon it.

punch verb
1 *Mrs Rafferty* punched *the robber on the nose.*
jab, poke, prod, thump
For other ways of hitting see hit
2 *I need to* punch *a hole through the card.*
bore, pierce

punctual adjective
The bus was punctual *today.*
in good time, on time, prompt
opposite late

punctuation noun

WORD WEB
PUNCTUATION MARKS
apostrophe, brackets, colon, comma, dash, exclamation mark, full stop, hyphen, question mark, quotation marks or speech marks, semicolon, square brackets

OTHER MARKS USED IN WRITING
accent, asterisk or star, bullet point, slash

puncture noun
1 *I had a* puncture *on the way home.*
burst tyre, flat tyre
2 *I found the* puncture *in my tyre.*
hole, leak

a
b
c
d
e
f
g
h
i
j
k
l
m
n
o
p
q
r
s
t
u
v
w
x
y
z

323

A
B
C
D
E
F
G
H
I
J
K
L
M
N
O
P
Q
R
S
T
U
V
W
X
Y
Z

puncture verb
A nail punctured my tyre.
perforate, pierce, deflate, let down

punish verb
Those responsible for the crime will be punished.
penalize, discipline, chastise

punishment noun
The punishment for dropping litter is a fine.
penalty
Punishing someone by taking their life is capital punishment or execution.

puny adjective
Miles was rather a puny child.
delicate, weak, feeble, frail, weedy
opposites **strong, sturdy**

pupil noun
There are 33 pupils in our class.
schoolchild, student, learner, scholar
Someone who follows a great teacher is a disciple.

purchase verb
I'm saving my money to purchase a bike.
buy, pay for, get, obtain, acquire

purchase noun
1 *She opened her bag and examined her purchases.*
acquisition
2 *The climbers had difficulty getting any purchase on the ice.*
grasp, hold, leverage

pure adjective
1 *The bracelet is made of pure gold.*
authentic, genuine, real
2 *He was talking pure nonsense.*
complete, absolute, utter, sheer, total
3 *All our dishes are made from pure ingredients.*
natural, wholesome
4 *They swam in the pure, clear water of the lake.*
clean, fresh, unpolluted
opposite **impure**

purify verb
You can't drink this water unless you purify it.
clean, make pure
You destroy germs by disinfecting or sterilizing things.
You take solid particles out of a liquid by filtering it.
To purify water by boiling it and condensing the vapour is to distil it.
To purify crude oil is to refine it.

purpose noun
1 *Have you got a particular purpose in mind?*
intention, aim, end, goal, target, objective, outcome, result
2 *What's the purpose of your invention?*
point, use, usefulness, value

purposeful adjective
Sam barged into the room with a purposeful look on her face.
determined, decisive, positive
opposite **aimless**

purse noun
I always keep some loose change in my purse.
money bag, pouch
A purse which holds paper money and credit cards is a wallet.

pursue verb
1 *The thief ran off, pursued by two police officers.*
chase, follow, run after, tail, track, hunt, trail, shadow
2 *She wants to pursue a career as a dancer.*
follow, undertake, practise, conduct, carry on, continue, maintain, proceed with

pursuit noun
1 *The pursuit of the criminals lasted for months.*
hunt (for), search (for), tracking, chase, trail
2 *The family enjoy many outdoor pursuits.*
activity, pastime, hobby, interest

push verb
1 *We pushed our way through the crowd.*
shove, thrust, force, propel, barge, elbow, jostle
opposite **pull**
2 *Pete pushed his things into a bag.*
pack, press, cram, crush, compress, ram, squash, squeeze
3 *They pushed him to work even harder.*
pressurize, press, drive, urge, compel, bully
(informal) **lean on**
4 *The actress is pushing her latest film.*
promote, publicize, advertise
(informal) **plug**

put verb puts, putting, put
1 *You can put your school bags in the corner.*
place, set down, leave, deposit, dump, stand
2 *The dog put its head on my lap.*
lay, lean, rest
3 *I'll put some pictures on the wall.*
attach, fasten, fix, hang
4 *Where are they planning to put the car park?*
locate, situate
5 *They put guards outside the bank.*
position, post, station
6 *I'm not sure of the best way to put this.*
express, word, phrase, say, state
to put someone off
The colour of the food put me off eating.
deter, discourage, distract
to put something off
They put off their journey because of the fog.
delay, postpone, defer
to put something out
The firefighters quickly put out the blaze.
extinguish, quench, smother
to put something up
1 *It doesn't take long to put up the tent.*
set up, construct, erect
2 *I'm going to buy a new bike before they put up the price.*
increase, raise

to put up with something
I don't know how you put up with that noise.
bear, stand, tolerate, endure

puzzle noun
Has anyone managed to solve the puzzle?
question, mystery, riddle, conundrum, problem
(informal) **brain-teaser, poser**

puzzle verb
1 *Phil was puzzled by the mysterious message.*
confuse, baffle, bewilder, bemuse, mystify, perplex, fox
2 *We puzzled over the problem for hours.*
ponder, think, meditate, worry, brood

puzzled adjective
Why are you looking so puzzled?
confused, baffled, bewildered, mystified, perplexed

puzzling adjective
There was something puzzling about the signature on the letter.
confusing, baffling, bewildering, mystifying, perplexing, mysterious, inexplicable
opposite **straightforward**

pyramid noun

WORD WEB
THINGS FOUND INSIDE ANCIENT EGYPTIAN PYRAMIDS
burial chamber, Canopic jar, hieroglyphics, mummy (of a pharaoh), papyrus, sarcophagus

A pyramid which does not have smooth sides is a **stepped pyramid.**

For an illustration of a burial chamber, please see following page.

a
b
c
d
e
f
g
h
i
j
k
l
m
n
o
p
q
r
s
t
u
v
w
x
y
z

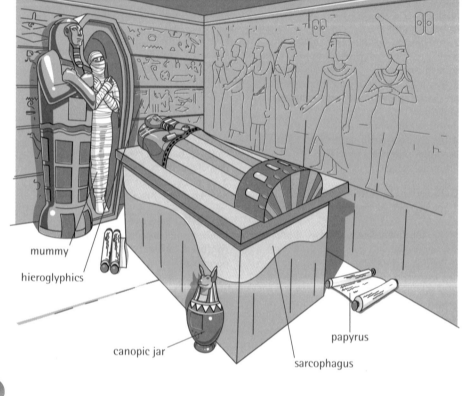

mummy

hieroglyphics

canopic jar

papyrus

sarcophagus

Qq

quaint adjective
They stayed in a quaint thatched cottage.
charming, picturesque, sweet,
old-fashioned, old-world

quake verb
*The ground quaked with the thud of the
giant's footsteps.*
shake, shudder, tremble, quiver, shiver,
vibrate, rock, sway, wobble

qualification noun
1 *What kind of qualification do you need to
be a vet?*
diploma, certificate, degree, knowledge,
training, skill
2 *The committee approved the plan, but with
some qualifications.*
condition, reservation

qualified adjective
1 *This job needs a qualified electrician.*
experienced, skilled, trained, professional
opposite amateur
2 *He received qualified praise for his
efforts.*
limited, cautious, half-hearted

qualify verb
1 *The licence* qualifies *him to work as a private detective.*
authorize, permit, allow, entitle
2 *The first three runners will* qualify *to take part in the final.*
get through, pass, be eligible
3 *She felt the need to* qualify *her remarks.*
limit, modify, restrict, soften, weaken

quality noun
1 *We only use ingredients of the highest quality.*
grade, class, standard
2 *The most obvious* quality *of rubber is that it stretches.*
characteristic, feature, property, attribute, trait

quantity noun
1 *She receives a huge* quantity *of fan mail every week.*
amount, mass, volume, bulk, weight
(informal) **load**
2 *We recycled a large* quantity *of empty bottles.*
number
When you add up numbers, you get a **sum** or **total**.

quarrel noun
We have quarrels, *but really we are good friends.*
argument, disagreement, dispute, tiff, difference of opinion, row, squabble, clash
Continuous quarrelling is **strife**.
A long-lasting quarrel is a **feud** or **vendetta**.
A quarrel in which people become violent is a **brawl** or **fight**.

quarrel verb
The twins quarrelled *over who should sit in the front.*
disagree, argue, row, squabble, bicker, clash, fight, fall out
to quarrel with something
I can't quarrel *with your decision.*
disagree with, object to, take exception to, oppose

quarrelsome adjective
Goblins can be very quarrelsome *creatures.*
bad-tempered, irritable, aggressive, argumentative
opposite **placid**

quaver verb
The boy's voice quavered *with fear.*
shake, tremble, waver, quake, quiver, falter

quay noun
The ship unloaded its cargo onto the quay.
dock, harbour, pier, wharf, jetty, landing stage

queer adjective
1 *The engine made a* queer *rattling noise.*
curious, strange, unusual, weird, funny, mysterious, puzzling
2 *There's something* queer *going on.*
odd, peculiar, abnormal, suspicious, shady
(informal) **fishy**
opposites **normal, ordinary**

quench verb
1 *The iced lemonade soon* quenched *her thirst.*
cool, satisfy
2 *They dumped sand on the embers to* quench *the fire.*
extinguish, put out, smother

query noun
If you have any queries, *please phone this number.*
question, enquiry, problem

query verb
The manager queried *the referee's decision.*
question, challenge, dispute, argue over, quarrel with, object to

quest noun
The knights set out on a quest *to find the enchanted tower.*
search, hunt, expedition, mission

question noun
1 *Does anyone have any* questions?
enquiry, query, problem

a
b
c
d
e
f
g
h
i
j
k
l
m
n
o
p
q
r
s
t
u
v
w
x
y
z

A question which someone sets as a puzzle is a **brain-teaser, conundrum,** or **riddle.**
A series of questions asked as a game is a **quiz.**
A set of questions which someone asks to get information is a **questionnaire** or **survey.**

2 *There's some* question *over the player's fitness.*
uncertainty, doubt, argument, debate, dispute

question verb
1 *The detective decided to* question *the suspect.*
ask, examine, interview, quiz, interrogate
To question someone intensively is to **grill** them.
2 *He* questioned *the referee's decision.*
challenge, dispute, argue over, quarrel with, object to, query

queue noun
There was a queue *of people outside the cinema.*
line, file, column, string
A long queue of traffic on a road is a **tailback.**

queue verb
Please queue *at the door.*
line up, form a queue

quick adjective
1 *You'd better be* quick—*the bus leaves in 10 minutes.*
fast, swift, rapid, speedy, hasty
(informal) **nippy**
A common simile is **as quick as a flash.**
opposite slow
2 *Do you mind if I make a* quick *phone call?*
short, brief, momentary, immediate, instant, prompt, snappy
opposites long, lengthy
3 *She's very* quick *at mental arithmetic.*
bright, clever, sharp, acute, alert
(informal) **on the ball**
opposite slow

quicken verb
The front runners quickened *their pace.*
accelerate, speed up, hurry up, hasten

quiet adjective
1 *The deserted house was still and* quiet.
silent, noiseless, soundless
A common simile is **as quiet as a mouse.**
opposite noisy
2 *The children spoke in* quiet *whispers.*
hushed, low, soft
Something that is so quiet that you can't hear it is **inaudible.**
opposite loud
3 *Amy has always been a* quiet *child.*
shy, reserved, subdued, placid, uncommunicative, retiring, withdrawn,
opposite talkative
4 *We found a* quiet *place for a picnic.*
peaceful, secluded, isolated, restful, tranquil, calm, serene
opposite busy

quieten verb
1 *The mother tried to* quieten *her baby.*
calm, soothe, hush, pacify
2 *Turn this dial to* quieten *the volume.*
deaden, muffle, mute, soften, suppress

quit verb quits, quitting, quitted or quit
1 *She* quit *her teaching job to travel round the world.*
leave, give up, resign from
(informal) **pack in**
2 (informal) Quit *pushing me!*
stop, cease, leave off

quite adverb

Take care how you use **quite**, as the two senses are almost opposites.

1 *The two puppies have* quite *different personalities.*
completely, totally, utterly, entirely, absolutely, very, wholly
2 *They played* quite *well, but far from their best.*
fairly, reasonably, moderately, rather

A B C D E F G H I J K L M N O P Q R S T U V W X Y Z

Rr

quiver verb
The jelly quivered when the table was banged.
shake, wobble, quake, shiver, quaver, tremble, shudder, vibrate

quiz noun
Our class took part in a general knowledge quiz.
test, competition, questionnaire, exam, examination

quiz verb
The teacher quizzed us on our times tables.
question, ask, examine, interrogate

quota noun
I've had my quota of chocolate for this week.
ration, share, portion, allowance, helping

quotation noun
I copied a short quotation from the book.
extract, excerpt, passage, piece
A piece taken from a newspaper is a **cutting**.
A piece taken from a film or TV programme is a **clip**.

quote verb
He quoted some lines from a poem.
recite, repeat

race¹ noun
We had a race to see who was the fastest runner.
competition, contest, chase
A race to decide who will take part in the final is a **heat**.

race¹ verb
1 *We raced each other to the end of the road.*
have a race with, run against, compete with
2 *She had to race home because she was late.*
run, rush, dash, hurry, sprint, fly, tear, whizz, zoom

race² noun
We belong to different races but we're all humans.
nation, people, ethnic group

rack noun
Cooking pots hung from a rack on the wall.
frame, framework, shelf, support

racket¹ noun
A racket is used to hit the ball in tennis.
In cricket and some other games you hit the ball with a **bat**.
In golf you hit the ball with a **club**.

racket² noun
Please stop making that awful racket!
noise, row, din, commotion, disturbance, uproar, rumpus

radiate verb
1 *This fire radiates a lot of heat.*
give off, send out, emit
2 *The bus routes radiate from the centre of town.*
spread out

a
b
c
d
e
f
g
h
i
j
k
l
m
n
o
p
q
r
s
t
u
v
w
x
y
z

A
B
C
D
E
F
G
H
I
J
K
L
M
N
O
P
Q
R
S
T
U
V
W
X
Y
Z

radical adjective
1 *They made radical changes to school meals.*
fundamental, drastic, thorough, sweeping
opposite superficial
2 *The politician was known for her radical views.*
extreme, revolutionary
opposite moderate

rage noun
Derek slammed the door in a show of rage.
anger, fury, indignation
(old use) **wrath**
A child's rage is a **tantrum** or fit of **temper**.

rage verb
1 *He was still raging about the cost of the meal.*
be angry, be fuming, seethe, rant
2 *The hurricane raged for three days.*
blow, storm, rampage

ragged adjective
1 *They met a traveller wearing ragged clothes.*
tattered, tatty, threadbare, torn, frayed, patched, ripped, shabby, worn out
2 *A ragged line of people waited in the rain.*
irregular, uneven

raid noun
The enemy raid caught them by surprise.
attack, assault, strike, onslaught, invasion, blitz

raid verb
1 *Long ago, Vikings raided the towns on the coast.*
attack, invade, ransack, plunder, loot, pillage
Someone who raids ships at sea is a **pirate**.
Someone who raids and steals cattle is a **rustler**.
2 *Police raided the house at dawn.*
descend on, rush, storm, swoop on

rail noun
The fence was made of iron rails.
bar, rod, spar
A fence made of rails is also called **railings**.

railway noun

🕸 WORD WEB

VARIOUS TYPES OF RAILWAY
branch line, cable railway, funicular, main line, metro, monorail, mountain railway, tramway, underground railway

TYPES OF RAILWAY TRAIN
diesel, electric train, express, freight train or **goods train, intercity, sleeper, steam train, tram, underground train**

Vehicles which run on the railway are **locomotives** and **rolling stock**.

PARTS OF A RAILWAY TRAIN
buffet car, carriage or **coach, dining car, engine, goods van, guard's van, locomotive, sleeping car**

THINGS YOU MIGHT SEE ON OR NEAR A RAILWAY
buffers, cutting, level crossing, platform, points, signals, signal box, sleepers, station, track, trolley, tunnel, viaduct

The rails which trains run on are the **line** or **track**.
The end of the line is the **terminus**.

PEOPLE WHO WORK ON A TRAIN OR RAILWAY
conductor, driver, engineer, guard, porter, signalman, station manager, stationmaster, steward

rain noun
A formal word for rain is **precipitation**.
The rainy season in south and south-east Asia is the **monsoon**.
When there is no rain for a long time there is a **drought**.
For ways to describe rain see **weather**

raise verb
1 *Raise your hand if you need help.*
hold up, put up, lift

2 *The box was too heavy for him to* **raise.**
lift, pick up, elevate, hoist, jack up
3 *The Post Office is* **raising** *the price of stamps.*
increase, put up
4 *The runners hope to* **raise** *£1000 for charity.*
collect, gather, take in, make
5 *He* **raised** *some objections to the plan.*
bring up, mention, put forward, present, introduce
6 *The doctor didn't want to* **raise** *their hopes.*
encourage, build up, arouse
7 *It's hard work trying to* **raise** *a family.*
bring up, care for, look after, nurture, rear

rally noun
Some demonstrators held a **rally** *in the town square.*
demonstration, meeting, march, protest
(informal) **demo**

ram verb
The car skidded and **rammed** *into a lamp post.*
bump, hit, strike, crash into, collide with, smash into

ramble verb
1 *They* **rambled** *round the country park.*
walk, stroll, wander, roam, rove, range, hike, trek
2 *The speaker* **rambled** *on for hours.*
chatter, babble, drift
(informal) **rabbit, witter**

rampage verb
An angry mob **rampaged** *through the streets.*
run riot, run amok, go berserk, go wild, race about, rush about

ran
past tense see **run**

random adjective
They picked a **random** *selection of pupils.*
arbitrary, chance, haphazard, casual, unplanned
opposite deliberate

rang
past tense see **ring²**

range noun
1 *There is a* **range** *of mountains to the south.*
chain, line, row, series, string
2 *Supermarkets sell a wide* **range** *of goods.*
variety, assortment, selection, choice, spectrum
3 *The shop caters for all age* **ranges** *from toddlers to teenagers.*
span, scope

range verb
1 *Prices* **range** *from five to twenty euros.*
vary, differ, extend, fluctuate
2 *Rows of jam jars were* **ranged** *on the shelf.*
arrange, order, lay out, set out, line up
3 *Wild deer* **range** *over the hills.*
wander, ramble, roam, rove, stray

rank noun
1 *The soldiers formed themselves into* **ranks.**
column, line, file, row
2 *A black belt is the highest* **rank** *in judo.*
grade, level, position, status
To raise someone to a higher rank is to **promote** them.
To reduce someone to a lower rank is to **demote** them.

ransack verb
1 *Mrs Hogg* **ransacked** *the house looking for her keys.*
search, scour, rummage through, comb
(informal) **turn upside down**
2 *Thieves had* **ransacked** *the building.*
loot, pillage, plunder, wreck

rap verb
Someone **rapped** *urgently on the door.*
knock, tap

rapid adjective
The cyclists set off at a **rapid** *pace.*
fast, quick, speedy, swift, brisk
opposite slow

a b c d e f g h i j k l m n o p q r s t u v w x y z

A
B
C
D
E
F
G
H
I
J
K
L
M
N
O
P
Q
R
S
T
U
V
W
X
Y
Z

rare adjective
1 *These flowers are now very rare in the wild.*
uncommon, unusual, infrequent, scarce, sparse
opposite **common**
2 *He has a rare ability to make people laugh.*
exceptional, remarkable, special

rarely adverb
Our next-door neighbour rarely goes out.
seldom, infrequently, hardly ever
opposite **often**

rash¹ adjective
Don't make any rash promises.
reckless, foolhardy, hasty, hurried, impulsive, unthinking
opposite **careful**

rash² noun
1 *Rory had an itchy red rash on his leg.*
spots
2 *There has been a rash of break-ins lately.*
outbreak, series, succession, spate

rate noun
1 *The cyclists were pedalling at a furious rate.*
pace, speed
2 *What's the usual rate for washing a car?*
charge, cost, fee, payment, price, figure, amount

rate verb
How do you rate their chance of winning?
judge, regard, consider, estimate, evaluate

rather adverb
1 *It's rather chilly today.*
quite, fairly, moderately, slightly, somewhat, a bit, a little
2 *I'd rather not go out tonight.*
preferably, sooner

ratio noun
The ratio of boys to girls is about 50-50.
proportion, balance
You can express a ratio as a **percentage**.

ration noun
The pirates each had a daily ration of rum.
portion, quota, share, allowance, helping, measure
rations
The astronauts took enough rations to last a month.
food, provisions, stores, supplies

ration verb
During the war, the government had to ration food.
limit, restrict, share out, allot

rattle noun & verb
For various sounds see **sound¹**

rave verb
1 *Connie raved about the film.*
be enthusiastic, talk wildly
2 *The head raved on about their bad behaviour.*
shout, rage, storm, yell, roar

ravenous adjective
The children were ravenous after their walk.
hungry, starved, starving, famished

raw adjective
1 *Raw vegetables are supposed to be good for you.*
uncooked
opposite **cooked**
2 *The factory imports a lot of raw materials from abroad.*
crude, natural, unprocessed, untreated
opposites **manufactured, processed**
3 *Her knee felt raw after she fell off her bike.*
red, rough, sore, tender, inflamed
4 *There was a raw wind blowing from the east.*
bitter, cold, chilly, biting, freezing, piercing

ray noun
A ray of light shone into the dark cave.
beam, shaft, stream

reach verb
1 *They hoped to reach Oxford by lunch time.*
arrive at, go as far as, get to, make

2 *The appeal fund has* **reached** *its target.*
achieve, attain
3 *I'm not tall enough to* **reach** *the top shelf.*
get hold of, grasp, touch
to reach out
Reach out your hands.
extend, hold out, put out, stick out, stretch out

reach noun
1 *The shelf was just within his* **reach.**
grasp
2 *The shops are within easy* **reach.**
distance, range

react verb
How did he **react** *when he read the letter?*
respond, behave, answer, reply

reaction noun
What was her **reaction** *when you said you were sorry?*
response, answer, reply

read verb reads, reading, read
They couldn't **read** *the doctor's handwriting.*
make out, understand, decipher
To read through something very quickly is to **skim through** it.
To read here and there in a book is to **dip into** it.
To read something intently is to **pore over** it.

readily adverb
1 *My friends* **readily** *agreed to help.*
willingly, gladly, happily, eagerly
2 *The recipe uses ingredients which are* **readily** *available.*
easily, conveniently, quickly

ready adjective
1 *When will tea be* **ready?**
prepared, set, done, available, in place
opposite **not ready**
2 *He's always* **ready** *to help.*
willing, glad, pleased, happy, keen, eager
opposite **reluctant**
3 *She's always got a* **ready** *reply.*
quick, prompt, immediate
opposite **slow**

real adjective
1 *History is about* **real** *events.*
actual, true, factual, verifiable
opposites **fictitious, imaginary**
2 *The necklace was made from* **real** *rubies.*
authentic, genuine, bona fide, natural
opposites **artificial, fake**
3 *She doesn't often show her* **real** *feelings.*
true, honest, sincere, genuine, heartfelt
opposite **insincere**

realistic adjective
1 *The portrait of the artist is very* **realistic.**
lifelike, true to life, faithful, convincing, recognizable
2 *It's not* **realistic** *to expect a puppy to be quiet.*
feasible, practical, sensible, possible, workable
opposite **unrealistic**

reality noun
Stop daydreaming and face **reality.**
the facts, the real world, the truth

realize verb
It took him a long time to **realize** *what she meant.*
understand, appreciate, grasp, comprehend, recognize, see
(informal) catch on to, tumble to, twig

really adverb
1 *Are you* **really** *going to Peru?*
actually, definitely, truly, in fact, certainly, genuinely, honestly
2 *I saw a* **really** *good film last night.*
very, extremely, exceptionally

realm noun
The king ruled the **realm** *for fifty years.*
country, kingdom, domain, empire

rear¹ adjective
They found seats in the **rear** *coach of the train.*
back, end, last
The **rear** legs of an animal are its **hind** legs.
opposite **front**

a
b
c
d
e
f
g
h
i
j
k
l
m
n
o
p
q
r
s
t
u
v
w
x
y
z

A
B
C
D
E
F
G
H
I
J
K
L
M
N
O
P
Q
R
S
T
U
V
W
X
Y
Z

rear¹ noun
The buffet car is at the rear of the train.
back, end, tail-end
The rear of a ship is the stern.

rear² verb
1 *The couple have reared three children.*
bring up, raise, nurture
2 *The deer reared their heads when they caught his scent.*
hold up, lift, raise

reason noun
1 *What was the reason for the delay?*
cause, grounds, explanation, motive, justification, excuse
2 *It was clear that the poor woman had lost her reason.*
mind, sanity, senses, wits
(informal) marbles
3 *They tried to make him see reason.*
sense, common sense, logic

reason verb
to reason with someone
We tried to reason with him, but he wouldn't change his mind.
argue with, persuade, talk round

reasonable adjective
1 *That seems like a reasonable plan.*
sensible, intelligent, rational, logical, sane, sound
opposite **irrational**
2 *They bought the house for a reasonable price.*
fair, acceptable, average, moderate, respectable, normal, proper
opposite **excessive**

reassure verb
The doctor reassured her that the wound was not serious.
calm, comfort, encourage, hearten, give confidence to
opposite **threaten**

rebel verb
The king feared that the people would rebel.
revolt, rise up

To rebel against the captain of a ship is to mutiny and someone who does this is a mutineer.
opposite **obey**

rebellion noun
The protest soon became a widespread rebellion.
revolt, revolution, uprising, resistance
A rebellion on a ship is a **mutiny**.

rebound verb
The ball rebounded off the wall.
bounce back, spring back
If a bullet rebounds off a surface, it ricochets.

recall verb
Try to recall what happened.
remember, recollect, think back to

recede verb
When the rain stopped, the flood receded.
go back, retreat, decline, subside, ebb

receive verb
1 *The captain went up to receive the winners' cup.*
collect, take, accept, be given
opposites **give, present**
2 *Some passengers received minor injuries.*
experience, suffer, undergo, sustain
opposite **inflict**
3 *We went to the front door to receive our visitors.*
greet, meet, welcome

recent adjective
We watch the news to keep up with recent events.
current, up-to-date, contemporary, new, the latest, fresh

reception noun
1 *The home crowd gave the team a friendly reception.*
greeting, welcome

2 *Who are they inviting to the wedding reception?*
party, gathering, celebration, function (informal) do

recipe noun
I followed my granny's recipe for making apple pie.
directions, instructions
The items you use for a recipe are the ingredients.

recital noun
There will be a short recital of piano music at noon.
concert, performance

recite verb
Zoe recited a poem she had written.
say aloud, read out, narrate

reckless adjective
A man has been charged with reckless driving.
careless, irresponsible, mindless, thoughtless, negligent, foolhardy, rash, wild
opposite careful

reckon verb
1 *I tried to reckon how much she owed me.*
calculate, work out, add up, figure out, assess, estimate
2 *Do you reckon it's going to rain?*
think, believe, guess, imagine, feel

recline verb
Paula reclined lazily on the sofa.
lean back, lie, lounge, rest, stretch out, sprawl, loll

recognize verb
1 *I didn't recognize her with her new haircut.*
identify, know, distinguish, make out, recall, recollect, remember
2 *He refused to recognize that he was to blame.*
acknowledge, admit, accept, grant, concede, confess, realize

recoil verb
Chloe recoiled as a spider scuttled towards her.
draw back, flinch, quail, wince, shrink back

recollect verb
1 *Do you recollect what happened?*
remember, recall, have a memory of
2 *The two friends sat for hours recollecting the past.*
reminisce about, think back to, cast your mind back to
opposite forget

recommend verb
1 *The doctor recommended complete rest.*
advise, counsel, propose, suggest, advocate, prescribe, urge
2 *The restaurant was recommended by a friend of mine.*
approve of, endorse, praise, commend

record noun
The zookeepers keep a record of the animals' diet.
account, report
A record of daily events is a diary or journal.
The record of a voyage at sea or in space is the log.
The record of what happened at a meeting is the minutes.
A record of people's names is a register.
Records consisting of historical documents are archives.

record verb
1 *The concert is being recorded by the BBC.*
tape, video, film
2 *She recorded our interview in a notebook.*
write down, note, set down, put down, enter

recover verb
1 *It took a long time to recover after my illness.*
get better, heal, improve, recuperate, pick up, mend, come round, pull through, revive, rally

a
b
c
d
e
f
g
h
i
j
k
l
m
n
o
p
q
r
s
t
u
v
w
x
y
z

A
B
C
D
E
F
G
H
I
J
K
L
M
N
O
P
Q

R

S
T
U
V
W
X
Y
Z

2 *The police have* recovered *the stolen vehicles.*
get back, retrieve, reclaim, repossess, find, trace

recovery noun
The doctors were surprised at her speedy recovery.
healing, cure, revival, recuperation, convalescence

recreation noun
What do you do for recreation *around here?*
fun, enjoyment, pleasure, relaxation, leisure, amusement, diversion, entertainment, play
A particular activity you do as recreation is a hobby or pastime.

recruit noun
The police recruits *were very inexperienced.*
beginner, learner, novice
A recruit learning a trade is an apprentice or trainee.
A recruit training to be in the armed services is a cadet.

recruit verb
The book club has recruited *two new members.*
bring in, take on, attract, enrol
To be recruited into the armed services is to enlist or sign up.

rectangle noun
oblong

recur verb
Go to the doctor if the symptoms recur.
happen again, come again, reappear, return

recycle verb
You can recycle *glass by putting it in the bottle bank.*
reuse, reprocess, salvage, use again

red adjective & noun
1 *I chose a* red *ribbon for my doll.*
Something which is rather red is reddish.
A common simile is as red as a beetroot.
2 *My nose and cheeks were* red *with cold.*
flushed, glowing, rosy, ruddy, blushing
3 *Her eyes were* red *from lack of sleep.*
bloodshot, inflamed, red-rimmed
4 *The fairy queen had flaming* red *hair.*
ginger, auburn, coppery
(informal) carroty

> **WORD WEB**
>
> SOME SHADES OF RED
> brick red, cherry, crimson, maroon, pillar-box red, pink, rose, ruby, scarlet, vermilion

reduce verb
She's reduced *the amount of sugar in her diet.*
decrease, lessen, lower, cut, cut back, slash
To reduce something by half is to halve it.
To reduce the width of something is to narrow it.
To reduce the length of something is to shorten or trim it.
To reduce speed is to decelerate.
To reduce the strength of a liquid is to dilute it.
opposite increase

reel noun
I bought a reel *of white cotton thread.*
spool

reel verb
1 *The blow made his head* reel.
spin, whirl
2 *The injured man* reeled *as if he was drunk.*
stagger, stumble, sway, rock, totter, lurch, roll
to reel off
The chef reeled off *a long list of ingredients.*
recite, rattle off, fire off

refer verb
The shop assistant referred me to another department.
hand over, pass on, direct, send
to refer to
1 *Please don't refer to this matter again.*
mention, speak of, make reference to, allude to, bring up
2 *If you can't spell a word, refer to a dictionary.*
look up, consult, go to, turn to

referee noun
The referee blew his whistle.
umpire, adjudicator
(informal) **ref**
A person who helps the referee in football is a **linesman** or **touch judge.**

refill verb
The waiter refilled our glasses of water.
top up
To refill a fuel tank is to **refuel.**

reflect verb
1 *Catseyes™ reflect the light from car headlights.*
send back, throw back, shine back
2 *Their success reflects their hard work.*
show, indicate, demonstrate, exhibit, reveal
to reflect on
We need time to reflect on what to do next.
think about, contemplate, consider, ponder, mull over

reflection noun
1 *Gus could see his reflection in the pond.*
image, likeness
2 *Their success is a reflection of their hard work.*
indication, demonstration, evidence, result
3 *We need more time for reflection.*
thinking, contemplation, meditation

reform noun
They're making reforms to the school curriculum.
change, improvement, modification, amendment

refrain verb
to refrain from
Please refrain from talking in the library.
avoid, abstain from, stop
(informal) **leave off, quit**

refresh verb
1 *They refreshed themselves with a glass of lemonade.*
cool, freshen, revive, restore, invigorate, stimulate
2 *Let me refresh your memory.*
jog, prompt, prod

refreshing adjective
We went for a refreshing dip in the pool.
reviving, invigorating, restorative, bracing, stimulating

refuge noun
1 *The climbers looked for refuge from the blizzard.*
shelter, cover, protection, safety
2 *The outlaws stayed hidden in their mountain refuge.*
hideaway, hideout, retreat, haven, sanctuary

refund verb
She asked them to refund her money.
give back, pay back, repay, return

refuse verb
1 *Why did you refuse my offer of help?*
decline, reject, turn down, say no to
opposite **accept**
2 *They were refused permission to enter the building.*
deny, deprive of
opposites **give, allow**

refuse noun
The refuse was taken to the local tip.
rubbish, garbage, trash, waste, litter, junk

regain verb
The patient began to regain consciousness.
get back, get back to, return to

a
b
c
d
e
f
g
h
i
j
k
l
m
n
o
p
q
r
s
t
u
v
w
x
y
z

A

regard verb
1 *Do you still regard him as your friend?*
think of, consider, judge, value
2 *The cat regarded us curiously.*
look at, gaze at, stare at, eye, view,
scrutinize, watch

B

C

D

regarding preposition
I must speak with you regarding a private matter.
about, concerning, on the subject of,
with reference to, with regard to

E

F

G

region noun
1 *The Arctic and Antarctic are polar regions.*
area, place, land, territory,
part of the world
2 *There are two local radio stations serving this region.*
area, district, neighbourhood, locality,
vicinity, zone

H

I

J

K

register verb
1 *The parents registered the birth of their child.*
record, set down, write down
2 *The thermometer registered a very high temperature.*
show, indicate, display, read

L

M

N

O

P

regret verb
She regretted her decision to leave Ireland.
be sorry for, repent, feel sad about

Q

R

regular adjective
1 *Signs are placed at regular intervals along the cycle path.*
evenly spaced, fixed
opposites **irregular, uneven**
2 *The drummer kept up a regular rhythm.*
constant, consistent, steady, uniform,
unvarying
opposite **erratic**
A common simile is
as regular as clockwork.
3 *Is this your regular route to school?*
normal, usual, customary, habitual,
ordinary, routine
opposite **unusual**

S

T

U

V

W

X

Y

Z

4 *Craig is a regular customer at the sweet shop.*
frequent, familiar, persistent
opposites **rare, unusual**

regulate verb
1 *Just turn the knob to regulate the volume.*
control, set, adjust, alter, change, moderate
2 *The new roundabout is meant to regulate the traffic.*
control, manage, direct, govern, monitor

regulation noun
There are new regulations on school uniform.
rule, law, order, decree, requirement

rehearsal noun
The actors had to learn their words before the rehearsal.
practice, preparation
(informal) **try-out**
A final rehearsal in which actors wear their
costumes is a **dress rehearsal.**

rehearse verb
We had to rehearse the scene all over again.
go over, practise, try out

reign verb
Which British monarch reigned the longest?
be king or queen, be on the throne, govern,
rule

reject verb
1 *At first, she rejected their offer of help.*
decline, refuse, turn down, say no to
opposite **accept**
2 *As we picked the berries, we rejected any bad ones.*
discard, get rid of, throw out, scrap

rejoice verb
The people rejoiced when the wicked queen died.
celebrate, delight, be happy, exult
opposite **grieve**

relate verb
1 *Do you think the two crimes are related?*
connect, link, associate

2 *The travellers* related *the story of their adventures.*
tell, narrate, report, describe
relate to
The letter relates to *your great grandfather.*
be about, refer to, have to do with, concern

relation noun
1 *The stolen car has no* relation *to the robbery.*
connection, link, association, bond
2 *Are you a* relation *of hers?*
relative, member of the family, kinsman *or* kinswoman
For members of a family see **family**

relationship noun
1 *There is a* relationship *between your diet and health.*
connection, link, association, bond
The relationship *between two numbers is a* ratio.
2 *The twins have a close* relationship.
friendship, attachment, understanding

relative noun
see **relation**

relax verb
1 *I like to* relax *by listening to music.*
unwind, rest, take it easy
2 *This exercise will* relax *your shoulder muscles.*
loosen, ease
opposite **tighten**
3 *He* relaxed *his hold on the dog's leash.*
slacken, loosen, ease, lessen, reduce
opposite **tighten**

relaxed adjective
They liked the relaxed *atmosphere of village life.*
informal, casual, carefree, leisurely, easy-going, peaceful, restful, unhurried, calm
(informal) laid-back
opposites **tense, stressful**

release verb
1 *The prisoners were* released *early.*
free, let go, discharge, liberate, set free
To release slaves is to **emancipate** them.
opposite **imprison**
2 *The dog was tied up—who* released *him?*
let loose, set loose, unfasten, unleash, untie
3 *The band will* release *their album in April.*
issue, publish, put out

relent verb
Her parents relented *and let her stay up late.*
give in, give way, yield, soften, weaken

relentless adjective
The footballer faced relentless *questions from the press.*
constant, continuous, incessant, perpetual, persistent, never-ending, unrelenting, remorseless, ruthless

relevant adjective
1 *The detective noted everything that was* relevant *to the case.*
applicable, pertinent, appropriate, suitable, significant, related, connected
2 *Don't interrupt unless your comments are* relevant.
to the point, pertinent
opposite **irrelevant**

reliable adjective
1 *The king summoned his most* reliable *knights.*
faithful, dependable, trustworthy, loyal, constant, devoted, staunch, true
2 *The secret agent always sent* reliable *information.*
dependable, valid, trustworthy, safe, sound, steady, sure
opposite **unreliable**

relief noun
1 *The pills gave some* relief *from the pain.*
comfort, ease, help, release
2 *I watched a film for some light* relief *after work.*
relaxation, rest

a
b
c
d
e
f
g
h
i
j
k
l
m
n
o
p
q
r
s
t
u
v
w
x
y
z

A
B
C
D
E
F
G
H
I
J
K
L
M
N
O
P
Q

R

S
T
U
V
W
X
Y
Z

relieve verb
1 *The doctor said the pills would relieve the pain.*
ease, help, lessen, diminish, relax, soothe, comfort
2 *We played cards to relieve the boredom of waiting.*
reduce, lighten, dispel, counteract
opposite **intensify**

religion noun
People from all religions went to the service.
faith, belief, creed, denomination, sect

WORD WEB

MAJOR WORLD RELIGIONS
Buddhism, Christianity, Hinduism, Islam, Judaism, Shintoism, Sikhism, Taoism, Zen

MAJOR RELIGIOUS FESTIVALS
Buddhist: Buddha Day, Nirvana Day; Christian: Lent, Easter, Christmas Day; Hindu: Holi, Diwali; Muslim: Ramadan, Eid; Jewish: Passover, Rosh Hashanah, Yom Kippur, Hanukkah; Sikh: Baisakhi, Birth of Guru Nanak

The study of religion is **divinity** or **theology.**

For religious leaders see **priest**

---

religious adjective
1 *The choir sang a selection of religious music.*
sacred, holy, divine
opposite **secular**
2 *My grandparents were very religious.*
devout, pious, reverent, spiritual, godly
opposite **ungodly**

relish verb
He would relish the chance to appear on television.
enjoy, delight in, appreciate

reluctant adjective
The old woman was reluctant to open the door.
unwilling, hesitant, slow, grudging, half-hearted, resistant
opposite **eager**

rely verb
Are you sure that we can rely on their help?
depend on, count on, have confidence in, trust
(informal) **bank on**

remain verb
1 *The boys were told to remain behind after school.*
stay, wait, linger
(informal) **hang about**
2 *It will remain warm and sunny all weekend.*
continue, persist, keep on, carry on
3 *Little remained of the house after the fire.*
be left, survive

remainder noun
We played games for the remainder of the afternoon.
rest, what is left, surplus, remains

remains plural noun
They cleared away the remains of the picnic.
remnants, leftovers, fragments, traces, scraps, debris
The remains at the bottom of a cup are the **dregs.**
Remains still standing after a building has collapsed are **ruins.**
Historic remains are **relics.**

remark verb
He remarked that it was a nice day.
say, state, comment, note, declare, mention, observe
See also **say**

remark noun
They exchanged a few remarks about the weather.
comment, observation, word, statement, thought, mention

remarkable adjective

1 *He described his remarkable escape from the island.*
amazing, extraordinary, astonishing, memorable, wonderful, incredible, unforgettable, breathtaking
2 *The young violinist shows remarkable skill for her age.*
exceptional, notable, noteworthy, striking, outstanding, impressive, phenomenal
opposite ordinary

remedy noun

1 *There is no known remedy for his illness.*
cure, treatment, medicine, therapy, relief
A remedy to act against a poison is an **antidote**.
2 *We may have found a remedy for the problem.*
solution, answer

remember verb

1 *Can you remember what she looked like?*
recall, recollect, recognize, place
2 *He was trying to remember his lines for the play.*
learn, memorize, keep in mind
opposite forget
3 *My granny likes to remember the old days.*
reminisce about, think back to

remind verb

Remind me to buy a newspaper.
prompt, jog your memory
to remind you of something
What does this tune remind you of?
make you think of, take you back to

reminder noun

1 *They sent him a reminder to pay the bill.*
prompt, cue, hint, nudge
2 *The photographs are a reminder of our holiday.*
souvenir, memento

reminiscent adjective

be reminiscent of something
The tune is reminiscent of an old folk song.
remind you of, make you think of, call to mind

remnants plural noun

They had to clear up the remnants of the party.
remains, scraps, traces, fragments, debris, leftovers

remorse noun

He showed no remorse for stealing the money.
regret, repentance, guilt, guilty conscience, sorrow, shame

remote adjective

1 *The tour will explore a remote part of Brazil.*
distant, faraway, isolated, cut-off, inaccessible, out-of-the-way, unfrequented
opposite accessible
2 *The chances of us winning are remote.*
poor, slender, slight, small, faint, doubtful
opposite likely

remove verb

1 *Please remove your rubbish.*
clear away, take away
2 *The rowdy passengers were removed from the bus.*
throw out, turn out, eject, expel
(informal) **kick out**
To remove people from a house where they are living is to **evict** them.
To remove a monarch from the throne is to **depose** him or her.
3 *The author decided to remove the last paragraph.*
cut out, delete, erase, get rid of, do away with, eliminate
4 *The dentist removed my bad tooth.*
extract, pull out, take out, withdraw
5 *The divers slowly removed their wetsuits.*
take off, peel off, strip off, shed, cast off

render verb

1 *The shock rendered her speechless.*
make, leave, cause to be
2 *Many volunteers rendered their assistance.*
give, provide, offer, furnish, supply

renew verb
1 The church roof has been completely renewed.
repair, renovate, restore, replace, rebuild, reconstruct, revamp, refurbish, overhaul
(informal) do up
2 We stopped for a cup of tea to renew our energy.
refresh, revive, restore, replenish, revitalize
3 You must renew your passport before you go abroad.
bring up to date, update

rent verb
We rented a couple of bikes to tour the Lake District.
hire, charter, lease

repair verb
It took them a week to repair the damaged car.
mend, fix, put right, patch up

repay verb repays, repaying, repaid
1 I can repay you the money next week.
pay back, refund
2 How can we ever repay your kindness?
return, reciprocate

repeat verb
1 The parrot repeated everything he said.
say again, copy, duplicate, reproduce, echo
2 The actors had to repeat the opening scene.
do again, redo

repeatedly adverb
We warned them repeatedly about the danger.
again and again, over and over, regularly, time after time, frequently, often

repel verb
1 The humans managed to repel the Martian invasion.
drive back, beat back, push back, fend off, resist
2 This spray will repel wasps and other insects.
keep away, scare off, deter, ward off

3 They were repelled by the smell of the dragon's lair.
disgust, revolt, sicken, offend
(informal) turn you off

repellent adjective
The princess found the ogre quite repellent.
disgusting, repulsive, revolting, hideous, horrible, loathsome, objectionable, foul, offensive, vile
opposite attractive

replace verb
1 The spy carefully replaced the missing document.
put back, return, restore, reinstate
2 Who will replace the head teacher when she retires?
follow, succeed, take over from, take the place of
3 I need to replace one of the tyres on my bike.
change, renew

replacement noun
They found a replacement for the injured player.
substitute, standby, stand-in, reserve
Someone who can take the place of an actor is an understudy.

replica noun
In the garden, there's a replica of a Roman statue.
copy, reproduction, duplicate, model, imitation, likeness
An exact copy of a document is a facsimile.

reply noun
He has received no replies to his email.
response, answer, reaction, acknowledgement
An angry reply is a retort.

reply verb
to reply to
She took a long time to reply to my letter.
answer, respond to, give a reply to, react to, acknowledge

A B C D E F G H I J K L M N O P Q **R** S T U V W X Y Z

report verb

1 *The newspapers reported what happened.*
give an account of, record, state, describe, announce, publish
2 *We were told to report to reception when we arrived.*
present yourself, make yourself known, check in
3 *If you cause any damage, I'll report you to the police.*
complain about, inform on, denounce

report noun

1 *There was a report in the paper about the crash.*
account, record, story, article, description
2 *The deer were startled by the report of the gun.*
bang, blast, crack, noise

reporter noun

The film star was being interviewed by a TV reporter.
journalist, correspondent

represent verb

1 *The picture represents an ancient legend.*
depict, illustrate, portray, picture, show, describe
2 *A dove is often said to represent peace.*
stand for, symbolize
3 *He appointed a lawyer to represent him.*
speak for

reprimand verb

He reprimanded them for their bad behaviour.
reproach, scold, criticize
(informal) tell off, tick off
opposite praise

reproduce verb

1 *The robot can reproduce a human voice.*
copy, duplicate, imitate, simulate, mimic
2 *Mice reproduce very quickly.*
breed, produce offspring, multiply, procreate
Fish reproduce by **spawning**.
To reproduce plants is to **propagate** them.

reproduction noun

1 *Vets have to know about animal reproduction.*
breeding, procreation
2 *Is that an original painting or a reproduction?*
copy, replica, imitation, likeness, duplicate, print
A reproduction of something which is intended to deceive people is a **fake** or **forgery**.
An exact reproduction of a document is a **facsimile**.

reptile noun

WORD WEB

SOME ANIMALS WHICH ARE REPTILES
alligator, chameleon, crocodile, gecko, iguana, lizard, salamander, slow-worm, snake, terrapin, tortoise, turtle

See also **snake**

A reptile found in myths and legends is a **basilisk**.

For other animals see **animal**

iguana

turtle

slow-worm

a
b
c
d
e
f
g
h
i
j
k
l
m
n
o
p
q
r
s
t
u
v
w
x
y
z

A
B
C
D
E
F
G
H
I
J
K
L
M
N
O
P
Q
R
S
T
U
V
W
X
Y
Z

repulsive adjective
We were put off eating by the repulsive smell.
disgusting, revolting, offensive, repellent, disagreeable, foul, repugnant, obnoxious, sickening, hateful, hideous, horrible, loathsome, objectionable, vile
opposite **attractive**

reputation noun
The singer's reputation spread throughout the world.
fame, celebrity, name, renown, eminence, standing, stature

request verb
Sh requested a transfer to a different job.
ask for, appeal for, apply for, beg for, call for, entreat, implore, invite, pray for, seek

request noun
They have ignored our request for help.
appeal, plea, entreaty, call, cry
A request for a job or membership is an **application.**
A request signed by a lot of people is a **petition.**

require verb
1 *They require a draw to win the championship.*
need, must have
2 *Visitors are required to sign the register.*
instruct, oblige, request, direct, order, command

rescue verb
1 *A helicopter was sent to rescue the climbers.*
free, liberate, release, save, set free
To rescue someone by paying money is to **ransom** them.
2 *The divers rescued some items from the sunken ship.*
retrieve, recover, salvage

resemblance noun
It's easy to see the resemblance between the two sisters.
likeness, similarity, closeness
opposite **difference**

resemble verb
The twins closely resemble their mother.
look like, be similar to
(informal) **take after**

resent verb
She resents having to work such long hours.
be annoyed about, take exception to, be resentful about, begrudge, grudge

reservation noun
1 *We have a reservation for two nights in the hotel.*
booking
2 *She had reservations about whether the plan would work.*
doubt, misgiving, hesitation, qualm
If you have reservations about something, you are **sceptical** about it.
3 *They saw giraffes on the wildlife reservation.*
reserve, park, preserve, sanctuary

reserve verb
1 *The astronauts had to reserve fuel for the return voyage.*
keep, put aside, set aside, save, preserve, retain, hold back
2 *Have you reserved your seats on the train?*
book, order, secure

reserve noun
1 *The climbers kept a reserve of food in their base camp.*
stock, store, supply, hoard, stockpile
A reserve of money is a **fund** or **savings.**
2 *They put him down as a reserve for Saturday's game.*
substitute, standby, stand-in, replacement
Someone who can take the place of an actor is an **understudy.**
3 *The wildlife reserve has a new baby rhino.*
reservation, park, preserve, sanctuary

reserved adjective
1 *These seats are reserved.*
booked, set aside, ordered

2 *She is too reserved to speak up for herself.*
shy, timid, quiet, bashful, modest, retiring, reticent
opposite **outgoing**

residence noun
The palace is the official residence of the queen.
dwelling, home, house
(old use) abode

resident noun
The residents of New York are proud of their city.
citizen, inhabitant, occupant
A temporary resident in a hotel is a **guest**.
A resident in rented accommodation is a **boarder**, **lodger**, or **tenant**.

resign verb
The manager of the football team was forced to resign.
leave, quit, stand down, step down, give in your notice
When a monarch resigns from the throne, he or she **abdicates**.

resist verb
1 *They were too weak to resist the sorcerer's magic.*
stand up to, defend yourself against, withstand, defy, oppose, fend off
opposites **yield to, surrender to**
2 *I couldn't resist having another piece of chocolate.*
avoid, hold back from, refuse
opposites **give in, accept**

resolve verb
1 *I resolved to try harder next time.*
decide, determine, make up your mind
2 *They held a meeting to try to resolve the dispute.*
settle, sort out, straighten out, end, overcome

resort noun
As a last resort, we could always walk.
option, choice, course of action

resort verb
He didn't want to resort to violence.
start using, turn to, fall back on, rely on, stoop to

resound verb
The howling of the wolves resounded through the forest.
echo, boom

resources plural noun
1 *The country is rich in natural resources.*
materials, raw materials, reserves
2 *The library has limited resources for buying CDs.*
funds, money, capital, assets, means, wealth

respect noun
1 *Her colleagues have the deepest respect for her.*
admiration, esteem, regard, reverence, honour
2 *Have some respect for other people's feelings.*
consideration, sympathy, thought, concern
3 *In some respects, he's a better player than I am.*
way, point, aspect, feature, characteristic, detail, particular

respect verb
1 *Everyone respects her for her courage.*
admire, esteem, revere, honour, look up to, value
opposites **scorn, despise**
2 *She tried to respect the wishes of her dead husband.*
obey, follow, observe, adhere to, comply with
opposite **ignore**

respectable adjective
1 *He came from a very respectable family.*
decent, honest, upright, honourable, worthy
2 *I finished the race in a respectable time.*
reasonable, satisfactory, acceptable, passable, adequate, fair, tolerable

a
b
c
d
e
f
g
h
i
j
k
l
m
n
o
p
q
r
s
t
u
v
w
x
y
z

A B C D E F G H I J K L M N O P Q **R** S T U V W X Y Z

respective adjective
We all returned to our respective homes.
separate, individual, own, particular, personal, specific

respond verb
to respond to
He didn't respond to my question.
reply to, answer, react to, acknowledge

response noun
Did you get a response to your letter?
reply, answer, reaction, acknowledgement
An angry response is a **retort**.

responsible adjective
1 *Parents are legally responsible for their children.*
in charge
opposite not responsible
2 *He's a very responsible sort of person.*
reliable, sensible, trustworthy, dependable, conscientious, dutiful, honest
opposite irresponsible
3 *Looking after people's money is a responsible job.*
important, serious
4 *Who is responsible for all this mess?*
to blame, guilty (of), at fault

rest¹ noun
1 *The actors had a short rest in the middle of the rehearsal.*
break, breather, breathing-space, pause, respite, lie-down, nap
2 *The doctor said the patient needed complete rest.*
relaxation, leisure, inactivity, ease, quiet, time off

rest¹ verb
1 *I think we should stop and rest for a while.*
have a rest, lie down, relax, lounge, have a nap
2 *Rest the ladder against the wall.*
lean, prop, stand, place, support

rest² noun
the rest
Take a few sweets now, but leave the rest for later.
the remainder, the surplus, the others, the remains

restaurant noun

WORD WEB
SOME TYPES OF RESTAURANT
buffet, cafe, cafeteria, canteen, carvery, chip shop, coffee shop, diner, grill, ice-cream parlour, snack bar, steakhouse, takeaway, tea room, wine bar

A French-style restaurant is a **bistro**.
A restaurant serving pizza is a **pizzeria**.

restful adjective
We spent a restful Sunday morning reading magazines.
peaceful, quiet, relaxing, leisurely, calm, tranquil, undisturbed
opposite stressful

restless adjective
1 *The animals became restless during the storm.*
agitated, nervous, anxious, edgy, fidgety, excitable, jumpy, jittery
opposite relaxed
2 *I'm tired—I had a restless night.*
sleepless, troubled, disturbed, unsettled, interrupted
opposite restful

restore verb
1 *Please restore the book to its proper place on the shelf.*
put back, replace, return
2 *They are restoring the Sunday bus service.*
bring back, reinstate
3 *My uncle loves to restore old cars.*
renew, repair, renovate, fix, mend, rebuild
To restore someone to health is to **cure** them.

restrain verb
1 *Dogs must be restrained on a lead in the park.*
hold back, keep back, keep under control, subdue, repress, restrict
2 *She tried to restrain her anger.*
control, curb, suppress, stifle

restrict verb
The new law restricts the sale of fireworks.
control, limit, regulate
to restrict to
In a safari park, animals are not restricted to enclosures.
confine to, enclose in, keep in, shut in, imprison in

result noun
1 *The water shortage is a result of a long drought.*
consequence, effect, outcome, sequel, upshot
The result of a game is the **score**.
The result of a trial is the **verdict**.
2 *If you multiply 9 by 12, what is the result?*
answer, product

result verb
The bruising on his leg resulted from a bad fall.
come about, develop, emerge, happen, occur, follow, ensue, take place, turn out
to result in
Severe flooding resulted in chaos on the roads.
cause, bring about, give rise to, lead to, develop into

resume verb
We'll resume work after lunch.
restart, start again, recommence, proceed with, continue, carry on

retain verb
1 *Please retain your ticket.*
hold on to, keep, preserve, reserve, save
(informal) hang on to
opposite **surrender**

2 *This type of soil is good at retaining water.*
hold in, keep in, hold back
opposite **release**

retire verb
1 *The manager plans to retire.*
give up work, stop working
To leave your job voluntarily is to **resign**.
2 *She retired to her room with a headache.*
withdraw, adjourn

retort verb
'There's no need to be rude!' retorted Hannah.
reply, answer, respond, react
For other ways to say something see **say**

retreat verb
1 *The army retreated to a safe position.*
move back, draw back, fall back, withdraw, retire
To retreat in a shameful way is to **run away** or (informal) **turn tail**.
2 *The snail retreated into its shell.*
shrink back, recoil

retrieve verb
I had to climb the fence to retrieve our ball.
get back, bring back, fetch, recover, rescue, salvage

return verb
1 *We hope to return to Paris next summer.*
go back, revisit
2 *My husband returns on Friday.*
get back, come back, come home
3 *I returned the book to its rightful owner.*
give back, restore
4 *Faulty goods may be returned to the shop.*
send back, take back
5 *Please return the money I lent you.*
give back, repay, refund
6 *We hoped that the fever would not return.*
happen again, recur

return noun
1 *She looked forward to her friends' return.*
reappearance, homecoming
2 *Did you get a good return from your investment?*
profit, interest, gain

a
b
c
d
e
f
g
h
i
j
k
l
m
n
o
p
q
r
s
t
u
v
w
x
y
z

A
B
C
D
E
F
G
H
I
J
K
L
M
N
O
P
Q
R
S
T
U
V
W
X
Y
Z

reveal verb
1 *The spy refused to* reveal *his real identity.*
declare, disclose, make known, confess, admit, announce, proclaim, publish, tell
2 *She swept aside the curtain to* reveal *a secret door.*
uncover, unveil, expose
opposite hide

revenge noun
He sought revenge *for the killing of his brother.*
reprisal, vengeance
to take revenge on someone
He declared that he would take revenge on *them all.*
get even with, repay
(informal) get your own back on

revere verb
The painter was greatly revered *by his fellow artists.*
admire, respect, honour, esteem, worship, adore
opposite despise

reverse noun
The letter had a handwritten note on the reverse.
other side, back

reverse verb
1 *You can use tracing paper to* reverse *a drawing.*
turn round, swap round, transpose, invert
2 *The driver tried to* reverse *into the parking space.*
back, drive backwards, go backwards

review noun
1 *They are carrying out a* review *of after-school clubs.*
study, survey, examination, inspection
2 *We had to write* reviews *of our favourite books.*
report, criticism, appraisal, critique

review verb
1 *The judge began to* review *the evidence.*
examine, go over, study, survey, consider, assess, appraise, evaluate, weigh up

2 *He* reviews *the latest films for the Sunday paper.*
criticize, write a review of

revise verb
1 *We* revised *the work we did last term.*
go over, review, study
2 *The new evidence forced me to* revise *my opinion.*
change, modify, alter, reconsider, re-examine
3 *The last chapter has been* revised *by the author.*
correct, amend, edit, rewrite, update

revive verb
1 *The patient* revived *slowly after the operation.*
come round, come to, recover, rally, wake up
2 *A cold drink will* revive *you.*
refresh, restore, invigorate, bring back to life, revitalize

revolt verb
1 *The people* revolted *against the cruel king.*
rebel, riot, rise up
To revolt on a ship is to **mutiny.**
2 *They were* revolted *by the stench in the dungeon.*
disgust, repel, sicken, nauseate, offend, appal

revolting adjective
What is that revolting *smell?*
disgusting, foul, horrible, nasty, loathsome, offensive, obnoxious, repulsive, repugnant, sickening, nauseating, vile, unpleasant
opposites pleasant, attractive

revolution noun
1 *The* revolution *brought in a new government.*
rebellion, revolt, uprising
2 *Computers brought about a* revolution *in the way people work.*
change, transformation, shift
3 *One* revolution *of the earth takes 24 hours.*
rotation, turn, circuit, cycle

revolutionary adjective
The inventor had come up with a revolutionary design.
new, novel, innovative, radical

revolve verb
The earth revolves once every 24 hours.
rotate, turn
To revolve quickly is to **spin** or **whirl**.
To move round something is to **circle** or **orbit** it.

reward noun
There is a reward for finding the missing cat.
prize, bonus, payment, award, decoration
opposite punishment

reward verb
1 *The firefighters were rewarded for their bravery.*
honour, decorate
2 *She was generously rewarded for her work.*
compensate, pay

rewarding adjective
Being a vet must be a rewarding job.
satisfying, pleasing, gratifying, worthwhile
opposite thankless

rhyme noun
The children like listening to nursery rhymes.
poem, verse

rhythm noun
We tapped our feet to the rhythm of the music.
beat, pulse
The speed or type of rhythm of a piece of music is the **tempo**.
The type of rhythm of a piece of poetry is its **metre**.

rich adjective
1 *They must be rich to live in a castle.*
wealthy, affluent, prosperous, well-off, well-to-do
opposite poor

2 *The palace was full of rich furnishings.*
expensive, costly, luxurious, sumptuous, opulent, lavish, splendid, ornate
3 *The dancer wore a dress of a rich red colour.*
deep, strong, vivid, intense
4 *The soil in this area is very rich.*
fertile, productive

riches plural noun
They acquired riches beyond their wildest dreams.
wealth, money, affluence, prosperity, fortune, treasure

rickety adjective
Take care—that ladder looks rickety.
shaky, unsteady, unstable, wobbly, flimsy
opposite solid

rid verb rids, ridding, rid
The new vaccine may rid the world of the disease.
clear, free, empty, strip, purge
to get rid of
He decided to get rid of his old guitar.
dispose of, throw away or out, scrap
(informal) dump

riddle noun
They had to solve the riddle to find the treasure.
puzzle, mystery, question, conundrum, problem

ride verb rides, riding, rode, ridden
My little brother is learning to ride a bike.
control, handle, manage, steer

ride noun
They took us for a ride in their new car.
drive, run, journey, trip
(informal) spin

ridicule verb
The inventor was ridiculed for his wacky ideas.
laugh at, make fun of, mock, scoff at, jeer at, sneer at, taunt, tease, deride

a
b
c
d
e
f
g
h
i
j
k
l
m
n
o
p
q
r
s
t
u
v
w
x
y
z

A
B
C
D
E
F
G
H
I
J
K
L
M
N
O
P
Q
R
S
T
U
V
W
X
Y
Z

ridiculous adjective
1 *My little sister looked* ridiculous *in high-heeled shoes.*
silly, stupid, foolish, daft, absurd, funny, laughable
2 *That is a* ridiculous *price for a jacket!*
ludicrous, senseless, nonsensical, preposterous, outrageous, absurd, unreasonable, crazy
opposite **sensible**

right adjective
1 *The entrance is on the the* right *side of the building.*
The right side of a ship when you face forwards is the **starboard** side.
opposite **left**
2 *Put up your hand if you got the* right *answer.*
correct, accurate, true, exact
opposite **wrong**
3 *She was waiting for the* right *moment to tell him.*
proper, appropriate, fitting, suitable, ideal
opposite **wrong**
4 *It's not* right *to steal.*
fair, honest, decent, just, honourable, lawful, moral, upright, virtuous, ethical
opposite **wrong**

right adverb
1 *Turn* right *at the corner.*
opposite **left**
2 *Turn* right *round.*
all the way, completely
3 *She stood* right *in the middle.*
exactly, precisely
4 *Go* right *ahead.*
directly, straight

right noun
1 *The post office is on the* right *along the High Street.*
opposite **left**
2 *People have the* right *to walk across the common.*
freedom, liberty
3 *You don't have the* right *to tell me what to do.*
authority, power

rigid adjective
1 *The tent was supported by a* rigid *framework.*
solid, stiff, firm, hard
2 *The referee was* rigid *in applying the rules.*
strict, inflexible, harsh, stern, uncompromising
opposite **flexible**

rigorous adjective
The detective carried out a rigorous *investigation.*
thorough, careful, meticulous, painstaking

rim noun
Mrs Sharpe peered at us over the rim *of her glasses.*
brim, edge, lip, brink

ring¹ noun
1 *The children danced around in a* ring.
circle, round, loop, circuit
2 *The wooden barrel had metal* rings *round it.*
band, hoop

ring¹ verb rings, ringing, ringed
The whole area was ringed *by a high fence.*
surround, encircle, enclose, circle

ring² verb rings, ringing, rang, rung
1 *The doorbell* rang.
chime, peal, toll, jangle, tinkle, sound, buzz
See also **bell**
2 *Ring me tomorrow evening.*
phone, call, telephone, ring up
(informal) give a buzz

rinse verb
After shampooing your hair, rinse *it in clean water.*
wash, clean, bathe, swill
To rinse out a toilet is to **flush** it.

riot noun
The police moved in to stop the riot.
commotion, disorder, disturbance, turmoil, uproar, uprising

riot verb
The crowds were rioting in the streets.
run riot, run wild, run amok, rampage, revolt, rise up, rebel

rip verb
She ripped the letter to pieces.
tear

ripe adjective
Some of the plums on the tree are ripe now.
mature, ready to eat
To become ripe is to **ripen**.

ripple verb
The wind rippled the surface of the pond.
ruffle, stir, disturb, make waves on

rise verb rises, rising, rose, risen
1 *The kite rose high into the air.*
climb, mount, fly up, ascend, soar
When a plane rises into the air, it **takes off**.
When a rocket rises into the air, it **lifts off**.
opposite descend
2 *The outer wall of the castle rose before us.*
tower, loom, reach up, stick up
3 *House prices rose again last year.*
go up, increase
opposite fall
4 *The audience rose and applauded wildly.*
stand up, get up
opposite sit

rise noun
1 *There will be a rise in temperature over the next few days.*
increase, jump
opposite fall
2 *At the top of the rise they paused for a break.*
hill, slope, ascent, incline, bank, ramp
(Scottish) **brae**

risk verb
1 *If you place a bet, you risk losing the money.*
chance, dare, gamble, venture
2 *The firefighter risked his life to save them.*
endanger, put at risk, jeopardize, hazard

risk noun
1 *All outdoor activities carry an element of risk.*
danger, hazard, peril
2 *Starting a business involves risk.*
a gamble, uncertainty
3 *The forecast says there's a risk of snow.*
chance, likelihood, possibility

risky adjective
Cycling on icy roads is risky.
dangerous, hazardous, perilous, unsafe
opposite safe

ritual noun
The temple was used for ancient religious rituals.
ceremony, rite, service

rival noun
He has no serious rival for the championship.
competitor, adversary, challenger, opponent, contender, contestant

rival verb
Few countries can rival Scotland for mountainous scenery.
compete with, contend with

rivalry noun
There was fierce rivalry between the two local teams.
competition, competitiveness, opposition
opposite cooperation

river noun
A small river is a **stream** or **rivulet** or (Scottish) **burn**.
A small river which flows into a larger river is a **tributary**.
The place where a river begins is its **source**.
The place where a river goes into the sea is its **mouth**.
A wide river mouth is an **estuary** or (Scottish) **firth**.
The place where the mouth of a river splits before going into the sea is a **delta**.
A river of ice is a **glacier**.

a
b
c
d
e
f
g
h
i
j
k
l
m
n
o
p
q
r
s
t
u
v
w
x
y
z

A
B
C
D
E
F
G
H
I
J
K
L
M
N
O
P
Q
R
S
T
U
V
W
X
Y
Z

WRITING TIPS

You can use these words to describe a river

TO DESCRIBE **HOW A RIVER FLOWS**
cascade, eddy, flood, flow, glide, gush, meander, plunge, rush, snake, sweep, swirl, twist, wind

TO DESCRIBE **HOW A RIVER SOUNDS**
babble, burble, gurgle, murmur, ripple, roar, splash, thunder

road noun

WORD WEB

KINDS OF ROADS
bypass, dual carriageway, highway, main road, motorway, one-way street, ring road, trunk road

A road which is closed at one end is a dead end.
A private road up to a house is a drive.

KINDS OF ROAD IN A TOWN
alley, avenue, boulevard, crescent, cul-de-sac, lane, street, terrace

See also path

roam verb

1 *We roamed about town aimlessly.*
wander, ramble, drift, stroll, amble, meander
2 *Herds of wild deer roamed over the hills.*
range, rove, prowl

roar noun & verb

The dragon lifted its mighty head and roared.
bellow, cry, yell, bawl, howl, thunder

rob verb

The thieves planned to rob several banks in the city.
steal from, break into, burgle, hold up, raid, loot, ransack, rifle

robber noun
see thief

robbery noun
see stealing

robe noun
A kind of robe you might wear in your bedroom is a dressing gown or bathrobe. Robes worn by a priest are vestments. The robe worn by a monk or nun is a habit. A robe an official might wear at a ceremony is a gown.
Robe is also a formal word for a woman's dress.

robot noun
The robot spoke in a metallic voice.
automaton, android
A robot which is part-human is a cyborg.

WORD WEB

PARTS A ROBOT MIGHT HAVE
antenna, buttons, computer brain or chip, control panel, flashing lights, arm or limb, gripper, laser, motor, sensor, wheels

SOME WAYS TO DESCRIBE A ROBOT
bionic, intelligent, machine-like, mechanical, metallic, super-human

Please see illustration on following page.

robust adjective
1 *To be an explorer, you must be robust.*
strong, vigorous, fit, hardy, healthy, rugged
opposite weak
2 *I bought a robust pair of boots for hiking.*
sturdy, tough, durable, hard-wearing
opposite flimsy

rock¹ noun
We clambered over the rocks on the seashore.
boulder, stone
A small rock is a pebble.
A steep face of rock is a cliff or crag.

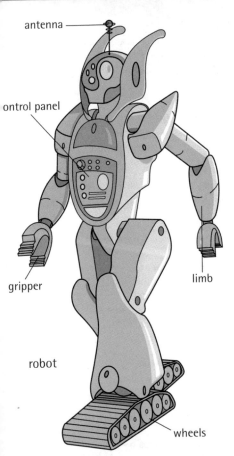

antenna

ontrol panel

gripper

limb

robot

wheels

WORD WEB

SOME KINDS OF ROCK

basalt, chalk, flint, granite, gypsum, lava, limestone, marble, quartz, sandstone, shale, slate

Rock from which metal or valuable minerals can be extracted is **ore**.
A layer of rock is a **stratum**.
A person who studies rocks is a **geologist**.

rock² verb
1 *I rocked the baby's cradle to and fro.*
sway, swing
2 *The ship rocked in the storm.*
roll, toss, lurch, pitch, tilt, reel

rocky adjective
1 *Nothing was growing in the* rocky *ground.*
barren, stony, pebbly
2 *Take care—that chair's a bit* rocky.
rickety, shaky, unsteady, unstable, wobbly

rod noun
The framework is held together by steel rods.
bar, rail, pole, strut, shaft, stick, spoke, staff

rode
past tense see **ride**

rodent noun
For various kinds of animal see **animal**

rogue noun
Don't trust him—he's a rogue.
rascal, scoundrel, villain, cheat, fraud, swindler

role noun
1 *Who is playing the lead* role *in the play?*
character, part
2 *Each player has an important* role *in the team.*
job, task, function, position

roll verb
1 *The wheels of the carriage began to roll.*
move round, turn, revolve, rotate, spin, twirl, whirl
2 Roll *the paper around your finger.*
curl, wind, wrap, twist, coil
To roll up a sail on a yacht is to **furl** it.
3 Roll *the pastry into a large circle.*
flatten, level out, smooth
4 *The ship* rolled *about in the storm.*
pitch, rock, sway, toss, wallow, lurch

romantic adjective
1 *The film had a very* romantic *ending.*
sentimental, emotional, tender
(informal) **soppy, mushy**
2 *The life of an explorer sounds very romantic.*
exotic, glamorous, exciting

a
b
c
d
e
f
g
h
i
j
k
l
m
n
o
p
q
r
s
t
u
v
w
x
y
z

A
B
C
D
E
F
G
H
I
J
K
L
M
N
O
P
Q
R
S
T
U
V
W
X
Y
Z

romp verb

The children romped *around the playground.*

leap about, run about, skip about, caper, frisk, frolic

roof noun

The sloping beams in the framework of a roof are **rafters**.
The overhanging edge of a roof is the **eaves**.
A building without a roof is an **open-air** building.
A vehicle without a roof is an **open-top** vehicle.

room noun

1 *How many* rooms *are there in your house?*
An old word for room is **chamber**.
2 *Is there* room *in the car for another suitcase?*

space, capacity

WORD WEB

ROOMS YOU MIGHT FIND IN A HOUSE OR FLAT
bathroom, bedroom, box room, conservatory, dining room, drawing room, hall, kitchen or kitchenette, landing, lavatory or toilet or (informal) loo, living room, lounge, nursery, pantry, parlour, scullery, sitting room, spare room or guest room, study, utility room

ROOMS YOU MIGHT FIND IN A SCHOOL
assembly hall, classroom, cloakroom, corridor, drama room, laboratory, lavatories or toilets or (informal) loos, library, music room, office, sickroom, staffroom, storeroom
A small room in a monastery or prison is a **cell**.
An underground room is a **basement** or **cellar**. In a church it is a **vault**.
The space in the roof of a house is the **attic** or **loft**.
A room where an artist works is a **studio**.
A room where you wait to see a doctor or dentist is a **waiting room**.

A room in a boarding school where pupils sleep is a **dormitory**.
A room in a hospital for patients is a **ward**.

roomy adjective

The flat is surprisingly roomy *inside.*

big, large, spacious, sizeable

root noun

We need to get to the root *of the problem.*

origin, source, cause, basis, starting point

rope noun

The sailors threw a rope *to the men in the water.*

cable, cord, line
The ropes that support a ship's mast and sails are the **rigging**.
A rope with a loop at one end used for catching cattle is a **lasso**.

rose

past tense see **rise**

rot verb

The wooden fence had begun to rot.

decay, decompose, become rotten, crumble, disintegrate
If metal rots it is said to **corrode**.
If rubber rots it is said to **perish**.
If food rots it is said to **go bad** or **putrefy**.

rotate verb

The globe rotates *on its axis.*

revolve, turn, spin, pivot, wheel, swivel, twirl, twist, whirl

rotten adjective

1 *The window frame is* rotten.

decayed, decaying, decomposed, crumbling, disintegrating
Rotten metal is **corroded** or rusty metal.
opposite **sound**
2 *The fridge smelled of* rotten *eggs.*

bad, mouldy, mouldering, foul, putrid, smelly
opposite **fresh**

3 (informal) *The weather has been* rotten.
bad, unpleasant, disagreeable, awful,
abysmal, dreadful, nasty
(informal) lousy
opposite good

rough adjective
1 *A rough track led to the farm.*
bumpy, uneven, irregular, rocky, stony,
rugged, craggy, jagged
opposites even, smooth
2 *The sea was rough and the boat lurched
from side to side.*
stormy, turbulent, heaving
If the sea is rough with small waves it is said
to be choppy.
opposite calm
3 *The woman wore a rough woollen cloak.*
coarse, harsh, scratchy, bristly
opposite soft
4 *The prisoners had suffered rough
treatment.*
harsh, severe, cruel, hard, tough,
violent
opposites gentle, mild
5 *I had only a rough idea of where we were.*
approximate, vague, inexact, imprecise,
hazy
opposite exact
6 *Our guide made a rough sketch of the
route.*
quick, hasty, crude, basic
opposites detailed, careful

roughly adverb
*The cinema can seat roughly a hundred
people.*
approximately, about, around, close to,
nearly

round adjective
Holly bushes have small round berries.
rounded, spherical
A flat round shape is circular.

round noun
*Our team got through to the second round of
the competition.*
stage, heat, bout, contest, game

round verb
*The motorbike rounded the corner at top
speed.*
go round, travel round, turn
to round something off
*They rounded the evening off with some
songs.*
bring to an end, conclude, end, finish,
complete
to round up people or things
The captain rounded up his players.
assemble, gather, bring together, collect,
muster, rally

roundabout adjective
*We went by a roundabout route to avoid the
traffic.*
indirect, circuitous, long, winding, twisting
opposite direct

rouse verb
1 *We were roused by the sound of birds
singing.*
arouse, awaken, call, wake up
2 *He was a quiet man, not easily roused to
anger.*
provoke, agitate, excite, stimulate, stir up

route noun
We drove home by the quickest route.
path, road, way, course, direction, journey

routine noun
1 *Brushing my teeth is part of my morning
routine.*
pattern, procedure, way, custom, habit,
practice, order
2 *The ice-skaters practised their new routine.*
act, programme, performance, number

row¹ noun (rhymes with go)
The gardener planted the vegetables in rows.
column, line, string, series, sequence
A row of people waiting for something is a
queue.
A row of people walking behind each other
is a file.
A row of soldiers standing side by side on
parade is a rank.

row² noun (rhymes with cow)
1 *The class next door was making a terrible row.*
noise, racket, din, commotion, disturbance, uproar, rumpus
2 *One of the pirates had a row with the captain.*
argument, fight, quarrel, squabble, disagreement, dispute

rowdy adjective
Later in the evening, the party became rowdy.
noisy, unruly, wild, disorderly, boisterous, riotous
opposite **quiet**

royalty noun

WORD WEB
SOME MEMBERS OF A ROYAL FAMILY
king, monarch, prince, princess, queen, queen mother, sovereign
The husband or wife of a royal person is a **consort**.
The way to address a king or queen is **Your Majesty**.
The way to address a prince or princess is **Your Highness**.

See also **ruler**

rub verb
1 *Kathy rubbed her sore elbow.*
stroke, knead, massage
2 *I rubbed some suncream on my arms.*
spread, smooth, smear, apply (to)
3 *These boots are rubbing against my ankles.*
graze, scrape, chafe
4 *She rubbed the mirror until it gleamed.*
polish, wipe, shine, buff
to rub something out
Can you rub out those pencil marks?
erase, wipe out, delete, remove

rubbish noun
1 *Mike took the rubbish out to the bin.*
refuse, waste, trash, garbage, junk, litter, scrap

2 *Don't talk rubbish!*
nonsense, drivel, balderdash, piffle, gibberish, claptrap, gobbledegook
(informal) rot, tripe, twaddle

rude adjective
1 *It's very rude to talk with your mouth full.*
impolite, discourteous, disrespectful, impertinent, impudent, insolent, offensive, insulting, bad-mannered, ill-bred
To be rude to someone is to **insult** or **snub** them.
To be rude about sacred things is to be **blasphemous** or **irreverent**.
opposite **polite**
2 *Some of the jokes in the film are rather rude.*
indecent, improper, offensive, coarse, crude
opposites **decent, clean**

ruffle verb
The peacock shook and ruffled its tail feathers.
stir, ripple, rumple, tousle

ruin verb
The storm had ruined the farmer's crops.
damage, destroy, spoil, wreck, devastate, demolish, lay waste, shatter

ruin noun
When they lost the match, it was the ruin of their dream.
collapse, failure, breakdown
Financial ruin is **bankruptcy**.
ruins
Archaeologists have discovered the ruins of a Roman fort.
remains, remnants, fragments

ruined adjective
Bats flew in and out of the ruined abbey.
wrecked, crumbling, derelict, dilapidated, tumbledown, ramshackle

rule noun
1 *Players must stick to the rules of the game.*
law, regulation, principle
A set of rules is a **code**.

2 *The country was formerly under French* **rule**.
control, authority, command, power, government, reign

rule verb
1 *The Romans* **ruled** *a vast empire*.
command, govern, control, direct, lead, manage, run, administer
2 *Queen Victoria continued to* **rule** *for many years*.
reign, be ruler
3 *The umpire* **ruled** *that the batsman was out*.
judge, decree, pronounce, decide, determine, find

ruler noun

> **WORD WEB**
> SOME KINDS OF RULER
> emir, emperor, empress, governor, head of state, king, lord, monarch, president, prince, princess, queen, sovereign
> A person who rules while a monarch is too young or too ill to rule is a **regent**.
>
> SOME RULERS IN PAST TIMES
> Caesar, pharaoh, raja or rani, sultan or sultana, tsar or tsarina

rummage verb
I **rummaged** *through my bag looking for my purse*.
search, hunt, ransack, scour

rumour noun
There was a **rumour** *that the queen was a witch in disguise*.
gossip, hearsay, talk
(informal) tittle-tattle

run verb runs, running, ran, run
1 *We ran as fast as our legs could carry us*.
race, sprint, dash, tear, bolt, career, speed, hurry, rush, streak, fly, whizz, zoom, scurry, scamper, scoot
To run at a gentle pace is to **jog**.

When a horse runs, it **gallops**, **canters**, or **trots**.
2 *Tears ran down the mermaid's cheeks*.
stream, flow, pour, gush, flood, cascade, spill, trickle, dribble, leak
3 *That old sewing machine still* **runs** *well*.
function, operate, work, go, perform
4 *My uncle* **runs** *a restaurant in Leeds*.
manage, be in charge of, direct, control, supervise, govern, rule
5 *The High Street* **runs** *through the city centre*.
pass, go, extend, stretch, reach
to run away or off
The thieves ran off when they heard footsteps.
bolt, fly, flee, escape, take off, hurry off
(informal) make off, clear off, scarper
to run into
1 *Guess who I ran into the other day?*
meet, come across, encounter
(informal) bump into
2 *A cyclist skidded and ran into a tree*.
hit, collide with

run noun
1 *She goes for a* **run** *in the park every morning*.
A fast run is a **dash**, **gallop**, **race**, or **sprint**.
A gentle run is a **jog**.
2 *We went for a* **run** *in the car*.
drive, journey, ride
3 *They've had a* **run** *of good luck recently*.
sequence, stretch, series
4 *The farmer built a new chicken* **run**.
enclosure, pen, coop

runaway noun
A person who has run away from the army is a **deserter**.
A person who is running away from the law is a **fugitive** or **outlaw**.

runner noun
The **runners** *were ready to start the race*.
athlete, competitor
Someone who runs fast over short distances is a **sprinter**.
Someone who runs to keep fit is a **jogger**.

A
B
C
D
E
F
G
H
I
J
K
L
M
N
O
P
Q
R
S
T
U
V
W
X
Y
Z

runny adjective
This custard is too runny.
watery, thin, liquid, fluid
opposite **thick**

rural adjective
They live in a peaceful rural *area.*
country, rustic, agricultural, pastoral
opposite **urban**

rush verb
I rushed *home with the good news.*
hurry, hasten, race, run, dash, fly, bolt,
charge, shoot, speed, sprint, tear, zoom
When cattle or other animals rush along
together they stampede.

rush noun
1 *We've got plenty of time, so what's the
rush?*
hurry, haste, urgency
2 *There was a sudden* rush *of water.*
flood, gush, spurt, stream, spate

rustic adjective
The village had a rustic *charm.*
country, rural, pastoral, countrified

rut noun
The tractor left ruts *along the track.*
furrow, groove, channel, trough

ruthless adjective
The pirates launched a ruthless *attack.*
cruel, brutal, bloodthirsty, barbaric,
heartless, pitiless, merciless, callous,
ferocious, fierce, savage, vicious, violent
opposite **merciful**

Ss

sack noun
The farmer delivered a large sack *of potatoes.*
bag, pack
sack verb
The manager threatened to sack *the whole
team.*
dismiss, discharge
(informal) fire, give someone the sack

sacred adjective
The Koran is a sacred *book.*
holy, religious, divine, heavenly

sacrifice verb
1 *I* sacrificed *my lunch break to practise
guitar.*
give up, surrender, go without
2 *The ancient Greeks* sacrificed *animals to
please the gods.*
offer up, kill, slaughter

sad adjective

OVERUSED WORD

Try to vary the words you use for **sad**.
Here are some other words you could use.

FOR A SAD MOOD OR SAD PERSON
unhappy, sorrowful, miserable,
depressed, downcast, downhearted,
despondent, crestfallen, dismal, gloomy,
glum, blue, low, dejected, forlorn,
desolate, doleful, wretched, woeful,
woebegone, tearful, heartbroken,
broken-hearted
Mia felt miserable *when her best friend
moved away.*

If you are sad because you are away from
home, you are homesick.
opposite **happy**

FOR A **SAD STORY** OR **SAD TUNE**
depressing, melancholy, mournful,
moving, touching, plaintive, wistful
The pirate related the mournful *tale of
Billy Bones.*
opposite cheering

FOR A **SAD SITUATION** OR **SAD NEWS**
unfortunate, unpleasant, painful,
regrettable, lamentable, grim, serious,
grave, tragic, grievous
The letter contained some painful *news.*
opposites cheerful, pleasant

FOR SOMETHING THAT **MAKES YOU FEEL SAD**
upsetting, distressing, heartbreaking,
heart-rending, pitiful, pathetic
It was heartbreaking *to watch the injured
bird.*

sadden verb
*The news of her friend's illness
saddened her.*
distress, upset, depress, grieve,
disappoint
(informal) break your heart
opposite cheer up

sadness noun
see sorrow

safe adjective
1 *The kitten was found safe and well in a
neighbour's garden.*
unharmed, unhurt, uninjured,
undamaged, sound, intact
(informal) in one piece
opposites hurt, damaged
2 *They felt safe indoors as the storm raged
outside.*
protected, guarded, defended, secure
opposite vulnerable
3 *The secret code is in safe hands.*
reliable, trustworthy, dependable
4 *Is the tap water safe to drink?*
harmless, uncontaminated,
innocuous
opposite dangerous

safety noun
*You must wear a seat belt for your own
safety.*
protection, security, well-being
opposite danger

sag verb
*The settee was old and stained and sagged in
the middle.*
sink, dip, droop, flop, slump

said
past tense see say

sail verb
1 *We sailed to Norway rather than going by
air.*
travel by ship
To have a holiday sailing on a ship is to
cruise or go on a cruise.
To begin a sea voyage is to put to sea or
set sail.
2 *None of the survivors knew how to sail.*
pilot, steer, navigate

sailor noun
The crew comprised three sailors and a cook.
seaman, seafarer, mariner, boatman
A person who sails a yacht is a yachtsman
or yachtswoman.

sake noun
for the sake of
*He put money aside for the sake of his
children.*
for the good of, on behalf of,
in the interests of, to help

salary noun
The job has an annual salary of £30,000.
income, pay, earnings
If your pay is paid week by week, it is called
wages.

sale noun
*They made a lot of money from the sale of
their house.*
selling, marketing, vending
opposite purchase

a
b
c
d
e
f
g
h
i
j
k
l
m
n
o
p
q
r
s
t
u
v
w
x
y
z

salvage verb
The crew tried to salvage some supplies from the wreck.
rescue, save, recover, retrieve, reclaim

same adjective
the same
1 *Each pirate was given the same ration of rum.*
equal, identical, equivalent
2 *Everyone in the choir wore the same outfit.*
matching, similar, alike, uniform
3 *Her feelings have remained the same.*
unaltered, unchanged, constant
Words which mean the same are synonymous with each other.
opposite **different**

sample noun
The detective asked for a sample of her handwriting.
specimen, example, instance, illustration, selection

sample verb
Would you like to sample some home-made jam?
taste, test, try

sand noun
We built a huge castle out of sand and seashells.
Hills of sand along the coast are **dunes**.
sands
They played on the sands until the tide came in.
beach, shore

sane adjective
No sane person would stand out in the pouring rain!
sensible, rational, reasonable
opposite **insane**

sang
past tense see sing

sank
past tense see sink

sarcastic adjective
He made a sarcastic remark about my hat.
mocking, satirical, ironical, sneering, taunting

sat
past tense see sit

satisfaction noun
He gets a lot of satisfaction from growing vegetables.
happiness, pleasure, enjoyment, contentment, fulfilment, sense of achievement, pride
opposite **dissatisfaction**

satisfactory adjective
I'm afraid this work is not satisfactory.
acceptable, adequate, passable, good enough, tolerable, competent
(informal) all right, up to scratch
opposite **unsatisfactory**

satisfy verb
Nothing satisfies him—he's always complaining.
please, content, make someone happy
opposite **dissatisfy**
To satisfy your thirst is to quench or slake it.

savage adjective
1 *The invaders launched a savage attack on the town.*
vicious, cruel, barbaric, brutal, bloodthirsty, pitiless, ruthless, merciless, inhuman
opposite **humane**
2 *A savage beast is said to live in the cave.*
untamed, wild, ferocious, fierce
opposite **domesticated**

save verb
1 *They managed to save most of the books from the fire.*
rescue, recover, retrieve, salvage
2 *The knight pledged to save the princess from the witch's curse.*
protect, defend, guard, shield, preserve

3 *She* saved *him from making a fool of himself.*

stop, prevent, deter

4 *I* saved *you a piece of my birthday cake.*

keep, reserve, set aside, hold on to

5 *If you share a car, then you can* save *petrol.*

be sparing with, conserve, use wisely

savings plural noun

They used all their savings *to go on a cruise.*

reserves, funds, resources, investments

saw¹ noun

For various tools see tool

saw²

past tense see see

say verb says, saying, said

1 *He found it hard to* say *what he meant.*

express, communicate, put into words, convey

2 *I would like to* say *a few words before we start.*

utter, speak, recite, read

OVERUSED WORD

Try to vary the words you use for say, especially with direct speech. Here are some other words you could use.

TO SAY LOUDLY

call, cry, exclaim, bellow, bawl, shout, yell, roar

'Land ahoy!' bellowed *the cabin boy.*

TO SAY QUIETLY

whisper, mumble, mutter

'That woman,' I whispered, *'is a secret agent.'*

TO SAY STRONGLY

state, announce, assert, declare, pronounce, insist, maintain, profess

'I never cut my toenails,' the ogre declared.

TO SAY CASUALLY

remark, comment, observe, note, mention

'It's very warm for this time of year,' Mr Lewis remarked.

TO SAY ANGRILY

snap, snarl, growl, thunder, bark, rasp, rant, rave

'Give me that piece of paper!' snapped *Miss Crabbit.*

TO SAY SUDDENLY

blurt out

'That's just a pretend dinosaur!' Ben blurted out.

TO SAY UNCLEARLY

babble, burble, gabble, stammer, stutter

The stranger kept babbling *about hidden treasure.*

TO SAY IN SURPRISE OR ALARM

gasp, cry, squeal

'The tunnel is sealed! There's no way out!' gasped *Alex.*

TO SAY SOMETHING FUNNY

joke, quip, tease

'Were you singing? I thought it was a cat,' teased *my big sister.*

TO GIVE AN ORDER

command, demand, order

A voice outside demanded, *'Open the door at once!'*

TO ASK A QUESTION

enquire, demand, query

'How do you spell your name?' the judge enquired.

TO GIVE A REPLY

answer, reply, respond, retort

'Certainly not!' retorted *Lady Dimsley.*

TO MAKE A REQUEST

beg, entreat, implore, plead, urge

The mouse pleaded, *'Please let go of my tail!'*

TO MAKE A SUGGESTION

suggest, propose

'Let's make them walk the plank,' suggested *Captain Hook.*

TO SAY AGAIN

repeat, reiterate, echo

The Martians repeated, *'Take us to your leader!'*

A
B
C
D
E
F
G
H
I
J
K
L
M
N
O
P
Q
R
S
T
U
V
W
X
Y
Z

saying noun
'Many hands make light work' is a common saying.
expression, phrase, motto, proverb, catchphrase
An overused saying is a cliché.

scamper verb
The rabbits scampered away to safety.
hurry, dash, run, rush, hasten, scuttle

scan verb
1 *The lookout scanned the horizon, hoping to see land.*
search, study, survey, examine, scrutinize, stare at, eye
2 *I scanned through some magazines in the waiting room.*
skim, glance at, flick through

scandal noun
1 *The waste of food after the party was a scandal.*
disgrace, embarrassment, shame, outrage
2 *Some newspapers like to publish the latest scandal.*
gossip, rumours, dirt

scar noun
The warrior had a scar across his forehead.
mark, blemish, wound

scar verb
The injuries he received scarred him for life.
mark, disfigure, deface

scarce adjective
Water is very scarce in the desert.
hard to find, in short supply, lacking, sparse, scanty, rare, uncommon
(informal) thin on the ground
opposite **plentiful**

scarcely adverb
She was so tired that she could scarcely walk.
barely, hardly, only just

scare noun
The explosion gave them a nasty scare.
fright, shock, alarm

scare verb
My brother tried to scare us by making ghost noises.
frighten, terrify, petrify, alarm, startle, panic
opposite **reassure**

scared adjective
When she heard the footsteps, Lily was too scared to move.
frightened, terrified, petrified, horrified, alarmed, fearful, panicky
See also **afraid**

scary adjective (informal)
I had to close my eyes at the scary bits in the film.
frightening, terrifying, horrifying, alarming, nightmarish, fearsome, chilling, spine-chilling, hair-raising, blood-curdling, chilling, eerie, sinister

scatter verb
1 *She scattered the seeds on the ground.*
spread, sprinkle, sow, strew, throw about, shower
opposite **collect**
2 *The animals scattered when the children ran towards them.*
break up, separate, disperse, disband
opposite **gather**

scene noun
1 *The police arrived quickly at the scene of the crime.*
location, position, site, place, situation, spot
2 *They were rehearsing a scene from the play.*
episode, part, section, act
3 *I gazed out of the window at the moonlit scene.*
landscape, scenery, view, sight, outlook, prospect, spectacle, setting, backdrop
4 *He didn't want to create a scene in the restaurant.*
fuss, commotion, disturbance, quarrel, row

scenery noun
We admired the scenery from the top of the hill.
landscape, outlook, prospect, scene, view, panorama

scent noun
Rowena loves the scent of roses.
smell, fragrance, perfume, aroma
See also **smell**

sceptical adjective
At first, I was sceptical about the legend of the ghost.
disbelieving, doubtful, doubting, unconvinced, dubious, incredulous, suspicious, uncertain, unsure
opposite trustful

schedule noun
The athletes had a rigorous training schedule.
programme, timetable, plan, calendar, diary
A schedule of topics to be discussed at a meeting is an **agenda**.
A schedule of places to be visited on a journey is an **itinerary**.

scheme noun
They worked out a scheme to raise some money.
plan, proposal, project, procedure, method, system

scheme verb
The smugglers were scheming against each other.
plot, conspire, intrigue

school noun

WORD WEB
VARIOUS KINDS OF SCHOOL
academy, boarding school, comprehensive school, faith school, grammar school, high school, independent school, infant school, junior school, kindergarten, nursery school, preparatory or prep school, primary school, private school, public school, secondary school

For rooms in a school see **room**

science noun

WORD WEB
SOME BRANCHES OF SCIENCE
aeronautics, anatomy, astronomy, biology, botany, chemistry, computer science, earth sciences, electronics, engineering, genetics, geology, information technology, mechanics, medicine, meteorology, physics, psychology, veterinary science, zoology

scoff verb
to scoff at
Everyone scoffed at her ideas.
mock, ridicule, sneer at, jeer at, deride, make fun of, poke fun at

scold verb
He scolded the paper boy for being late.
reprimand, reproach, tell off
(informal) **tick off**

scoop verb
We scooped out a moat for our sandcastle.
dig, gouge, scrape, excavate, hollow

scope noun
1 *The park offers plenty of scope for children to play.*
opportunity, room, space, freedom, liberty
2 *These things are outside the scope of the project.*
range, extent, limit, reach, span

scorch verb
The dragon's breath scorched the wizard's beard.
burn, singe, sear, blacken, char

a
b
c
d
e
f
g
h
i
j
k
l
m
n
o
p
q
r
s
t
.
u
v
w
x
y
z

363

score noun
We added up each other's scores.
marks, points, total
The final score is the result.

score verb
1 *How many goals did you score?*
win, get, make, gain, earn
2 *Some lines were scored into the bark of the tree.*
cut, gouge, mark, scrape, scratch

scorn noun
She dismissed my suggestion with scorn.
contempt, derision, disrespect, mockery, ridicule
opposite admiration

scour verb
1 *He scoured the pan until it shone.*
scrape, scrub, rub, clean, polish
2 *Edith scoured the room looking for her glasses.*
search, hunt through, ransack, comb

scowl verb
The witch scowled under her floppy black hat.
frown, glower
For other facial expressions see **expression**

scramble verb
1 *The smugglers escaped by scrambling over the rocks.*
clamber, climb, crawl, scrabble
2 *The children scrambled to get the best seats.*
push, jostle, struggle, fight, scuffle

scrap¹ noun
1 *They fed the scraps of food to the birds.*
bit, piece, fragment, morsel, crumb, speck, particle
2 *He took a pile of scrap to the tip.*
rubbish, waste, junk, refuse, litter
Scraps of cloth are **rags** or **shreds**.

scrap¹ verb
The author scrapped the last paragraph.
discard, throw away, abandon, cancel, drop, give up
(informal) **dump**

scrap² noun
(informal) *There was a scrap between the two gangs.*
fight, brawl, scuffle, tussle, squabble

scrap² verb
(informal) *The cubs enjoy scrapping with each other.*
fight, brawl, tussle, scuffle

scrape verb
1 *She scraped her knee when she fell over.*
graze, scratch, scuff
2 *I tried to scrape the mud off my trainers.*
rub, scour, scrub, clean

scrape noun
My little brother is always getting into scrapes.
trouble, mischief
(informal) **jam, pickle**

scratch verb
1 *Someone scratched the side of the car.*
mark, score, scrape, gouge, graze
2 *The cat tried to scratch me.*
claw

scratch noun
Who made this scratch on the side of the car?
gash, groove, line, mark, scrape

scrawl verb
She scrawled his phone number on a scrap of paper.
jot down, scribble, write

scream noun & verb
A woman ran out of the house screaming.
We heard a woman's scream in the distance.
shriek, screech, shout, yell, cry, bawl, howl, wail, squeal, yelp

screen noun
The room was divided into two by a screen.
curtain, partition, divider

screen verb
1 *Miss Bennett used a parasol to screen her face from the sun.*
shield, protect, shelter, shade, cover, hide, mask, veil

2 *All employees are* **screened** *before being appointed.*
examine, investigate, test, check

scribble verb
He scribbled *his number on a scrap of paper.*
scrawl, jot down, dash off, write
To scribble a rough drawing, especially when you are bored, is to **doodle**.

script noun
The script for a film is a **screenplay**.
A handwritten or typed script is a **manuscript**.

scrub verb
She scrubbed *the floor clean.*
rub, brush, clean, wash, scour

scruffy adjective
I wore an old jumper and scruffy *jeans.*
untidy, messy, ragged, tatty, tattered, worn-out, shabby
opposite smart

scrutinize verb
She scrutinized *the handwriting on the letter.*
examine, inspect, look at, study, investigate, explore

sculpture noun
The temple was full of marble sculptures.
carving, figure, statue

sea noun
The very large seas of the world are called **oceans**.
An area of sea partly enclosed by land is a **bay** or **gulf**.
A wide inlet of the sea is a **sound**.
A wide inlet where a river joins the sea is an **estuary**, or (in Scotland) a **firth**.
A narrow stretch of water linking two seas is a **strait**.
The bottom of the sea is the **seabed**.
The land near the sea is the **coast** or the **seashore**.
Creatures that live in the sea are **marine** creatures.

WORD WEB

THINGS YOU MIGHT SEE ON THE SEA
breaker, iceberg, sea spray, surf, swell, waves; boat, cruise ship, ocean liner, yacht

SOME CREATURES THAT LIVE IN THE SEA
dolphin, eel, fish, killer whale, octopus, porpoise, sea horse, seal, sea lion, shark, squid, stingray, turtle, whale

See also **seashore**

WRITING TIPS

You can use these words to describe the sea

TO DESCRIBE A **CALM SEA**
calm, crystal clear, glassy, sparkling, tranquil, unruffled

TO DESCRIBE A **ROUGH SEA**
choppy, raging, rough, stormy, tempestuous, turbulent, wild

WAVES ON THE SEA MIGHT
billow, break, crash, heave, pound, roll, surge, swell, tumble, wash

seal verb
The entrance to the burial chamber had been sealed.
close, fasten, shut, lock, secure
To seal a leak is to **plug** it or **stop** it.

seam noun
1 *The* seam *on his trousers split.*
join, stitching
2 *Geologists discovered a* seam *of coal.*
layer, stratum

search verb
1 *He was* searching *for the book he had lost.*
hunt, look, seek
To search for gold or some other mineral is to **prospect**.
2 *The police* searched *the house but didn't find anything.*
explore, scour, ransack, rummage through, comb

A
B
C
D
E
F
G
H
I
J
K
L
M
N
O
P
Q
R
S
T
U
V
W
X
Y
Z

3 *Security staff* **searched** *all the passengers.*
check, inspect, examine, scrutinize
(informal) frisk

search noun

After a long search, *she found her keys.*
hunt, look, check
A long journey in search of something is
a quest.

seashore noun

We explored the seashore, *looking for shells
and fossils.*
seaside, beach, shore, coast

WORD WEB

THINGS YOU MIGHT SEE ON THE SEASHORE
cave, cliff, coral reef, driftwood, dunes,
lighthouse, mudflats, pebbles, rock pool,
rocks, sand, seashell, seaweed, shingle

See also seaside

CREATURES THAT LIVE ON THE SEASHORE
barnacle, clam, cockle, coral, crab,
cuttlefish, jellyfish, limpet, mussel,
oyster, prawn, razor shell, sea anemone,
sea bird, seagull, sea urchin, shrimp,
sponge, starfish, whelk

For names of sea birds see bird

For other sea creatures see sea

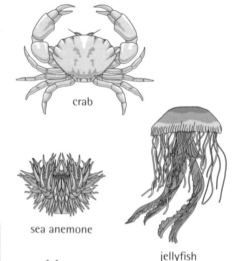

crab

sea anemone

jellyfish

seaside noun

*If it's sunny tomorrow, we might go to the
seaside.*
beach, sands, seashore

WORD WEB

THINGS YOU MIGHT SEE AT THE SEASIDE
beach huts, funfair, harbour,
ice-cream van, jetty, pier, promenade

A town where you go to have fun by the
sea is a seaside resort.

THINGS YOU MIGHT TAKE TO THE SEASIDE
beach ball, bucket and spade, deckchair,
fishing net, snorkel, sunglasses, sunhat,
sunshade, suncream, surfboard, wetsuit,
swimming costume, towel, windbreak

THINGS YOU MIGHT DO AT THE SEASIDE
ball games, beach-combing,
building sandcastles, collecting shells,
fishing, paddling, scuba diving,
snorkelling, sunbathing, surfing,
swimming, waterskiing, windsurfing

seagull

starfish

season noun

The hotels are full during the holiday season.
period, time

seat noun
We found two empty seats at the back of the cinema.
chair, place
A long seat for more than one person is a **bench**.
A long wooden seat in a church is a **pew**.
A seat on a bicycle or horse is a **saddle**.
A special seat for a king or queen is a **throne**.

seat verb
1 *The guests seated themselves around the table.*
place, position, sit down, settle
2 *The theatre can seat two hundred people.*
have seats for, accommodate, hold, take

second adjective
Would anyone like a second helping of pudding?
another, additional, extra, further

second noun
1 *The magic potion only takes a second to work.*
instant, moment, flash
(informal) **jiffy, tick**
2 *Inga was second in the cross-country race.*
runner-up

second verb
We need someone to second the proposal.
back, support

secondary adjective
She loves to run and winning is of secondary importance to her.
lesser, lower, minor, inferior, subordinate

second-hand adjective
The shop sells second-hand computers.
used, pre-owned
opposite new

secret adjective
1 *The spy managed to get hold of a secret document.*
confidential, classified, restricted
(informal) **hush-hush**
2 *The detectives are part of a secret operation.*
undercover, covert
3 *The things I write in my diary are secret.*
private, confidential, personal, intimate
4 *The cook showed us a secret passageway into the castle.*
hidden, concealed, disguised
For secret agents see **spy**

secretive adjective
Why is she being so secretive about her past?
uncommunicative, tight-lipped, reticent, reserved, mysterious, quiet
(informal) **cagey**
opposites communicative, open

section noun
The website has a special section aimed at children.
part, division, sector, portion, segment, bit, fragment
A section of a book is a **chapter**.
A section from a piece of classical music is a **movement**.
A section taken from a book or long piece of music is a **passage**.
A section of a journey is a **stage**.

secure adjective
1 *The ladder was not very secure.*
steady, firm, solid, fixed, fast, immovable
opposites insecure, unsafe
2 *She is still trying to find a secure job.*
permanent, regular, steady
3 *They bolted the doors to make the castle secure.*
safe, guarded, protected, defended

secure verb
1 *The door wasn't properly secured.*
fasten, lock, seal, bolt
2 *He managed to secure two tickets for the match.*
get hold of, acquire, obtain

security noun
You must wear a seat belt for your own security.
protection, safety

a
b
c
d
e
f
g
h
i
j
k
l
m
n
o
p
q
r
s
t
u
v
w
x
y
z

A

B

C

D

E

F

G

H

I

J

K

L

M

N

O

P

Q

R

S

T

U

V

W

X

Y

Z

see verb sees, seeing, saw, seen
1 *If you look closely, you might see a dragonfly.*
catch sight of, spot, notice, observe, make out, distinguish, note, perceive, recognize, sight, spy
To see something briefly is to **glimpse** it.
To see an accident or an unusual event is to **witness** it.
2 *Did you see the news yesterday?*
watch, look at, view
3 *See me in my office after school.*
go to, report to
4 *I didn't expect to see you here!*
meet, run into, encounter
(informal) bump into
5 *Will we have time to see them on the way home?*
visit, call on, drop in on
6 *I see what you mean.*
understand, appreciate, comprehend, follow, grasp, realize, take in
7 *I find it hard to see him in the role of Peter Pan.*
imagine, picture, visualize
8 *Please see that the windows are shut.*
make sure, make certain, ensure
9 *I'll see what I can do.*
think about, consider, ponder, reflect on, weigh up
10 *I'll see you to the door.*
conduct, escort, accompany, guide, lead, take
to see to something
Who's going to see to the refreshments?
deal with, attend to, take care of, sort out

seed noun
The seeds in an orange, lemon, etc., are the pips.
The seed in a date, plum, etc., is the stone.

seek verb seeks, seeking, sought
1 *For many years he sought his long-lost brother.*
search for, hunt for, look for
2 *The king sought only to make his daughter happy.*
try, attempt, strive, want, wish, desire

seem verb
Everything seems to be all right.
She is far more friendly than she seems.
appear, look, give the impression of being

seep verb
Oil began to seep through the crack.
leak, ooze, escape, flow, dribble, trickle, soak

seethe verb
The mixture in the cauldron began to seethe.
boil, bubble, foam, froth up
to be seething
Greg was seething when I crashed his bike.
be angry, be furious, rage, storm

segment noun
Divide the orange into segments.
section, portion, piece, part, bit, wedge, slice

seize verb
1 *The climber stretched out to seize the rope.*
grab, catch, snatch, take hold of, grasp, grip, clutch
2 *The police seized the robbers as they left the bank.*
arrest, capture
(informal) collar, nab
To seize someone's property as a punishment is to **confiscate** it.
To seize someone's power or position is to **usurp** it.
To seize an aircraft or vehicle during a journey is to **hijack** it.

seldom adverb
It seldom rains in the desert.
rarely, infrequently
opposite **often**

select verb
They had to select a new captain.
choose, pick, decide on, opt for, settle on, appoint, elect

select adjective
Only a select few were invited to the party.
privileged, chosen, special, hand-picked

selection noun
The shop has a wide selection of roller skates.
choice, range, variety, assortment

selfish adjective
He's so selfish that he kept all the chocolate to himself.
greedy, mean, miserly, grasping, self-centred, thoughtless
opposites unselfish, generous

sell verb sells, selling, sold
The corner shop sells newspapers and sweets.
deal in, trade in, stock, retail
Uncomplimentary synonyms are peddle and hawk.
opposite buy
For people who sell things see shop

send verb sends, sending, sent
1 *I sent each of my friends a postcard.*
post, mail, dispatch
2 *They plan to send a rocket to Mars.*
launch, propel, direct, fire, shoot
to send for someone
I think we should send for a doctor.
call, summon, fetch
to send something out
The device was sending out weird noises.
emit, issue, give off, discharge

senior adjective
1 *She's one of the senior players in the squad.*
older, long-standing, principal
2 *He is a senior officer in the navy.*
high-ranking, superior
opposite junior

sensation noun
1 *She had a tingling sensation in her fingers.*
feeling, sense
2 *The unexpected news caused a sensation.*
excitement, thrill
A sensation caused by something bad is an outrage or a scandal.

sensational adjective
1 *The newspaper printed a sensational account of the murder.*
shocking, horrifying, startling, lurid
2 (informal) *Did you hear the sensational result of yesterday's match?*
amazing, extraordinary, remarkable, fantastic, spectacular, stupendous

sense noun
1 *A baby learns about the world through its senses.*
Your five senses are hearing, sight, smell, taste, and touch.
2 *A drummer needs to have a good sense of rhythm.*
awareness, consciousness, perception, feeling (for)
3 *If you had any sense you'd stay at home.*
common sense, intelligence, wisdom, wit, brains
4 *The sense of the word is not clear.*
meaning, significance, import
to make sense of something
They couldn't make sense of the garbled message.
understand, make out, interpret, follow

sense verb
1 *He sensed that she didn't like him.*
be aware, realize, perceive, feel, guess, notice, suspect
2 *The device senses any change of temperature.*
detect, respond to

senseless adjective
1 *Smashing the window was a senseless act.*
foolish, stupid, crazy, daft, irrational, mad, illogical, pointless, futile
opposite sensible
2 *The blow on the head left the ogre senseless.*
unconscious, knocked out
opposite conscious

a
b
c
d
e
f
g
h
i
j
k
l
m
n
o
p
q
r
s
t
u
v
w
x
y
z

A
B
C
D
E
F
G
H
I
J
K
L
M
N
O
P
Q
R
S
T
U
V
W
X
Y
Z

sensible adjective

1 *It would be sensible to wait until the weather improves.*
wise, intelligent, shrewd, rational, reasonable, careful, prudent, logical, sane, sound
opposite **stupid**

2 *You will need sensible shoes for the trip.*
comfortable, practical
opposite **impractical**

sensitive adjective

1 *She has sensitive skin.*
delicate, tender, fine, soft

2 *Take care what you say—he's very sensitive.*
easily offended, easily upset, touchy

3 *She's very sensitive towards other people.*
tactful, considerate, thoughtful, sympathetic, understanding
opposite **insensitive**

sentence verb

The judge sentenced him to five years in prison.
pass judgement on, pronounce sentence on, condemn

sentimental adjective

1 *He gets sentimental looking at old photographs.*
emotional, nostalgic, tearful

2 *I hate sentimental messages on birthday cards.*
romantic, tender
(informal) soppy, mushy

sentry noun

He gave the password to the sentry at the gate.
guard, lookout, sentinel, watchman

separate adjective

1 *The zoo kept the male lions separate from the cubs.*
apart, separated, distinct, independent
opposite **together**

2 *They slept in separate rooms.*
different, detached, unattached
opposites **attached, joined**

separate verb

1 *The sheepdog separated the sheep from the lambs.*
cut off, divide, fence off, isolate, keep apart, remove, segregate, set apart, take away
To separate something which is connected to something else is to **detach** or **disconnect** it.
To separate things which are tangled together is to **disentangle** them.
opposites **combine, mix**

2 *They walked along together until their paths separated.*
split, branch, fork
opposite **merge**

3 *Her friend's parents have separated.*
split up, break up, part company
To end a marriage legally is to **divorce**.

sequence noun

The detective tried to piece together the sequence of events.
order, progression, series, succession, string, chain, train

serene adjective

The woman had a serene smile on her face.
calm, contented, untroubled, peaceful, quiet, placid, tranquil
opposite **agitated**

series noun

1 *We had to answer a series of questions in our exam.*
succession, sequence, string, set, chain, train

2 *Are you watching the new series on TV?*
serial

serious adjective

1 *His serious expression told them something was wrong.*
solemn, sombre, unsmiling, grave, grim
opposite **cheerful**

2 *She is writing a serious book about global warming.*
learned, intellectual, scholarly
(informal) heavy
opposite **light**

3 *Are you* **serious** *about wanting to learn to ski?*

sincere, genuine, in earnest

4 *This hospital ward is for people with* **serious** *injuries.*

severe, acute, critical, bad, terrible, appalling, dreadful, major, grave

opposites minor, trivial

servant noun

This part of the house was where the servants *lived.*

attendant, retainer, helper, domestic, manservant, maid

The chief manservant in a private house is a **butler**.

The servant of a medieval knight was a **page** or **squire**.

serve verb

1 *The shopkeeper was busy* **serving** *customers.*

help, assist, aid

2 *When everyone had sat down they* **served** *the first course.*

give out, dish up, pass round, distribute

3 *This room will* **serve** *as a study.*

be suitable, be useful, function

service noun

1 *The genie bowed and said he was glad to be of* service.

help, assistance, aid, use, usefulness, benefit

2 *Their marriage* service *was held in the local church.*

ceremony, ritual, rite

A service in church is a meeting for **worship**.

3 *Mum says her car needs a* service.

check-over, maintenance, servicing

service verb

The garage serviced *her car.*

maintain, check, repair, mend, overhaul

session noun

1 *We have a training* session *on Saturday mornings.*

period, time

2 *The Queen will open the next* session *of Parliament.*

meeting, sitting

set verb sets, setting, set

1 *The removal men* set *the piano on the floor.*

place, put, stand, position

2 *I helped Dad to* set *the table.*

arrange, lay, set out

3 *Have they* set *a date for the wedding yet?*

appoint, specify, name, decide, determine, choose, fix, establish, settle

4 *The jelly will* set *quicker in the fridge.*

become firm, solidify, harden, stiffen

5 *The sun was just beginning to* set.

do down, sink

to set about something

We set about *clearing the table immediately.*

begin, start, commence

to set off

1 *The knights* set off *on their quest.*

depart, get going, leave, set out, start out

2 *The burnt toast* set off *the smoke alarm.*

activate, start, trigger

to set something out

The information is clearly set out *on the page.*

lay out, arrange, display, present

to set something up

They're trying to set up *an after-school club.*

establish, create, start, begin, introduce, organize

set noun

1 *There is a* set *of measuring spoons in the drawer.*

collection, batch, kit

2 *Is there something wrong with the TV* set?

apparatus, receiver

3 *Our class painted the* set *for the play.*

scenery, setting

setting noun

The house stood in a rural setting.

surroundings, location, place, position, site, background

settle verb

1 *The brothers tried to* settle *their differences.*

resolve, sort out, deal with, end

371

2 *The cat had just settled on the sofa.*
sit down, relax, rest
3 *A robin settled on a nearby branch.*
land, alight
4 *The family is planning to settle in Canada.*
emigrate (to), move (to), set up home
5 *You can see lots of fish when the mud settles.*
sink to the bottom, clear, subside
6 *We'll settle the hotel bill in the morning.*
pay, clear, square
to settle on
Have you settled on a date for the wedding?
agree on, decide on, choose, name, fix

settlement noun
There was once a Viking settlement in this area.
community, colony, encampment, village

sever verb
The couple decided to sever their relationship.
break off, end, terminate
To sever a branch of a tree is to cut it off or remove it.
To sever a limb is to amputate it.

several determiner
The spy was able to adopt several disguises.
a number of, some, a few, various

severe adjective
1 *The jailer was very severe with the prisoners.*
harsh, strict, hard, stern
opposite lenient
2 *The traffic warden gave him a severe look.*
unkind, unsympathetic, disapproving, grim
opposite kind
3 *Ruby has a severe case of chickenpox.*
bad, serious, acute, grave
opposite mild
4 *The Arctic has a severe climate.*
extreme, tough, harsh, hostile
A severe frost is a sharp frost.
Severe cold is intense cold.
A severe storm is a violent storm.

sew verb sews, sewing, sewed, sewn or sewed
Mum sewed a name tag on to my coat.
stitch, tack
To sew a picture or design is to embroider it.
See also needlework

sex noun
What sex is the hamster?
gender

shabby adjective
1 *The witch disguised herself in a shabby cloak.*
ragged, scruffy, tattered, worn, worn-out, threadbare, frayed, tatty, seedy, dingy
opposite smart
2 *That was a shabby trick!*
mean, nasty, unfair, unkind, dishonest, shameful, low, cheap

shade noun
1 *They sat in the shade of a chestnut tree.*
shadow
2 *The porch had a shade to keep out the sun.*
screen, blind, canopy
A type of umbrella used as a sun shade is a parasol.
3 *The bathroom walls are a pale shade of blue.*
hue, tinge, tint, tone, colour

shade verb
1 *Wearing a cap will shade your eyes from the sun.*
shield, screen, protect, hide, mask
2 *He shaded the background of the picture with a pencil.*
fill in, make darker, darken

shadow noun
Her face was deep in shadow.
shade, darkness, gloom

shadow verb
The detective was shadowing the suspect.
follow, pursue, tail, stalk, track, trail

A
B
C
D
E
F
G
H
I
J
K
L
M
N
O
P
Q
R
S
T
U
V
W
X
Y
Z

shady adjective
1 *They found a shady spot under a tree.*
shaded, shadowy, sheltered, dark, sunless
opposite sunny
2 *He took part in some shady business deals.*
dishonest, disreputable, suspicious, dubious, suspect, untrustworthy
(informal) fishy, dodgy
opposite honest

shaft noun
1 *Modern arrow shafts are made of wood.*
spine, stick, pole, rod, staff
2 *He nearly fell into an old mine shaft.*
pit, tunnel, hole
3 *A shaft of moonlight shone through the window.*
beam, ray

shaggy adjective
Llamas have long shaggy coats.
bushy, woolly, fleecy, hairy, thick

shake verb shakes, shaking, shook, shaken
1 *The hurricane made the whole house shake.*
quake, shudder, shiver, rock, sway, totter, wobble, quiver, vibrate, rattle
2 *He was so upset that his voice was shaking.*
tremble, quaver
3 *The giant shook his fist and growled.*
wave, brandish, flourish, wag, waggle, joggle
4 *They were shaken by the terrible news.*
shock, startle, distress, upset, disturb, alarm, frighten

shaky adjective
1 *Be careful—the table is rather shaky.*
unsteady, wobbly, insecure, rickety, flimsy, weak
2 *He was so nervous that his hands were shaky.*
shaking, trembling, quivering
3 *He spoke in a shaky voice.*
quavering, faltering, nervous, tremulous
opposite steady

shallow adjective
The children paddled in the shallow water.
opposite deep

sham noun
The story he told about his family was all a sham.
pretence, deception, lie

shame noun
The guilty man hung his head in shame.
disgrace, dishonour, humiliation, embarrassment, guilt
a shame
It's a shame that you can't stay for longer.
a pity, unfortunate

shameful adjective
The player was sent off for his shameful conduct on the pitch.
disgraceful, outrageous, scandalous, contemptible, despicable, wicked
opposite honourable

shape noun
The Halloween cake was in the shape of a bat.
form, figure
A line showing the shape of a thing is the outline.
A dark outline seen against a light background is a silhouette.
A container for making things in a special shape is a mould.

WORD WEB
FLAT SHAPES
circle, diamond, ellipse, heptagon, hexagon, oblong, octagon, oval, parallelogram, pentagon, polygon, quadrilateral, rectangle, rhombus, ring, semicircle, square, trapezium, triangle

THREE-DIMENSIONAL SHAPES
cone, cube, cylinder, hemisphere, polyhedron, prism, pyramid, sphere

Please see illustration on following page.

a
b
c
d
e
f
g
h
i
j
k
l
m
n
o
p
q
r
s
t
u
v
w
x
y
z

A
B
C
D
E
F
G
H
I
J
K
L
M
N
O
P
Q
R
S
T
U
V
W
X
Y
Z

outline

silhouette

hexagon

ellipse

cone

prism

3 *He felt a* **sharp** *pain in his side.*
acute, piercing, stabbing
opposite dull
4 *Eagles have* **sharp** *eyes to see far in the distance.*
keen, keen-sighted, observant, perceptive
opposite unobservant
5 *You need to focus the camera to get a* **sharp** *picture.*
clear, distinct, well defined, crisp
opposite blurred
6 *Sherlock Holmes had a very* **sharp** *intelligence.*
clever, quick, shrewd, perceptive
opposites dull, slow
7 *The bus slowed down before a* **sharp** *bend in the road.*
abrupt, sudden, steep
A bend that doubles back on itself is a **hairpin bend.**
opposite gradual
8 *The* **sharp** *frost killed our geraniums.*
severe, extreme, intense, serious
opposites slight, mild
9 *This salad dressing is a bit* **sharp.**
sour, tart, bitter
opposites mild, sweet

sharpen verb
I need to **sharpen** *these crayons.*
make sharp, grind, whet, hone

shatter verb
1 *The ball* **shattered** *a window.*
break, smash, destroy, wreck
2 *The windscreen* **shattered** *when a stone hit it.*
break, splinter, disintegrate

sheaf noun
She had a **sheaf** *of papers in her hand.*
bunch, bundle

sheath noun
The knight put his sword back in its **sheath.**
casing, covering, sleeve
A **sheath** for a sword or dagger is a **scabbard.**

shape verb
The potter **shaped** *the clay into a tall vase.*
form, mould, fashion
To **shape** something in a mould is to **cast** it.

share noun
Each of the pirates got a **share** *of rum.*
ration, allowance, portion, quota, helping, division, part
(informal) **cut**

share verb
The robbers **shared** *the loot between them.*
divide, split, distribute, allot, allocate, deal out, ration out

sharp adjective
1 *Use a pair of* **sharp** *scissors.*
keen, sharpened, razor-sharp
opposite blunt
2 *Barbed wire has* **sharp** *points all along it.*
pointed, spiky, jagged
opposite smooth

shed¹ noun
They kept their lawnmower in the garden shed.
hut, shack, outhouse

shed² verb sheds, shedding, shed
A lorry shed its load on the motorway.
drop, let fall, spill, scatter

sheen noun
He waxed the table to give it a nice sheen.
shine, polish, gloss, gleam, lustre

sheep noun
A male sheep is a **ram**.
A female sheep is a **ewe**.
A young sheep is a **lamb**.
Meat from sheep is **mutton** or **lamb**.
The woolly coat of a sheep is its **fleece**.

sheer adjective
1 *The story he told was sheer nonsense.*
complete, total, utter, absolute, pure
2 *Don't try to climb that sheer cliff.*
vertical, perpendicular
3 *The ballgown was made of sheer silk.*
fine, thin, transparent, see-through

sheet noun
1 *She started her diary on a fresh sheet of paper.*
page, leaf, piece
2 *The pond was covered with a thin sheet of ice.*
layer, film, covering, surface
3 *The glazier came to fit a new sheet of glass.*
panel, pane, plate

shelf noun
She put the books back on the shelf.
ledge, rack
A shelf above a fireplace is a **mantelpiece**.

shell noun
Tortoises have hard shells.
covering, case, casing, outside, exterior

shellfish noun

> **WORD WEB**
> SOME TYPES OF SHELLFISH
> **barnacle, clam, cockle, conch, crab, crayfish, cuttlefish, limpet, lobster, mussel, oyster, prawn, razor shell, scallop, shrimp, whelk, winkle**
>
> Shellfish with legs such as crabs, lobsters, and shrimps are **crustaceans**.

shelter noun
They reached shelter just before the storm broke.
cover, protection, safety, refuge, sanctuary

shelter verb
1 *The hedge shelters the garden from the wind.*
protect, screen, shield, guard, defend, safeguard
2 *We sheltered from the rain under the trees.*
hide, take refuge

shelve verb
They had to shelve their plans for a summer holiday.
postpone, put off, defer, suspend
(informal) **put on ice**

shield noun
The trees act as an effective wind shield.
screen, barrier, defence, guard, protection
The part of a helmet that shields your face is the **visor**.

shield verb
The mother bear shielded her cubs from danger.
protect, defend, guard, safeguard, keep safe, shelter

shift verb
1 *I need some help to shift the furniture.*
move, rearrange, reposition
2 *It was hard work shifting the mud off the tyres.*
remove, dislodge, budge

a
b
c
d
e
f
g
h
i
j
k
l
m
n
o
p
q
r
s
t
u
v
w
x
y
z

shine verb shines, shining, shone or, in sense 2, shined

1 *A light* shone *from an upstairs window.*
beam, glow, blaze, glare, gleam
For other ways to describe light see light[1]

2 *He* shines *his shoes every morning.*
polish, rub, brush

3 *She's good at all sports, but she* shines *at tennis.*
be outstanding, excel, stand out

shiny adjective

She polished the mirror until it was shiny.
shining, bright, gleaming, glistening, glossy, polished, burnished, lustrous
opposite dull

ship noun

Ships that travel long distances at sea are **ocean-going** or **sea-going** ships.
People who work on ships at sea are **nautical** or **seafaring** people.
For types of boat or ship see boat

ship verb

The firm ships *goods all over the world.*
transport, send, post, mail

shirk verb

He always shirks *the unpleasant tasks.*
avoid, evade, get out of, dodge, duck

shiver verb

Ali waited outside, shivering *with cold.*
tremble, quiver, shake, shudder, quake

shock noun

1 *The news of his death came as a great shock.*
blow, surprise, fright, upset

2 *People felt the* shock *of the explosion miles away.*
bang, impact, jolt

3 *The driver involved in the accident was in a state of* shock.
distress, trauma

shock verb

The whole town was shocked *by the news.*
horrify, appal, startle, alarm, stun, stagger, shake, astonish, astound, surprise, dismay, upset
A formal synonym is traumatize.

shoe noun

WORD WEB

SOME TYPES OF SHOE OR BOOT
ankle boot, ballet shoe, baseball boot, boot, brogue, clog, court shoe, espadrille, flip-flop, football boot, gym shoe, high-heel shoe, moccasin, mule, platform shoe, plimsoll, pump, sandal, slip-on, slipper, sneaker, stiletto, tap shoe, tennis shoe, trainer, wader, wellington or (informal) wellie

trainers

football boots

flip-flops

wellington boots

shone
past tense see **shine**

shook
past tense see **shake**

shoot verb shoots, shooting, shot
1 *Robin Hood* shot *an arrow into the air.*
fire, discharge, launch, aim
2 *It is now illegal to hunt and* shoot *tigers.*
fire at, hit, open fire on, gun down
3 *They watched the racing cars* shoot *past.*
race, speed, dash, rush, streak, hurtle, fly, whizz, zoom
4 *Part of the film was* shot *in Canada.*
film, photograph

shoot noun
Young shoots *grow in the spring.*
bud, sprout

shop noun

🕸 WORD WEB

VARIOUS TYPES OF SHOP
boutique, corner shop, department store, hypermarket, market, shopping arcade, shopping centre, shopping mall, supermarket

SPECIALIST SHOPS
antique shop, baker, bookshop, butcher, cheesemonger, chemist, clothes shop, confectioner, delicatessen, DIY or **do-it-yourself shop, fishmonger, florist, garden centre, greengrocer, grocer, haberdasher, health-food shop, ironmonger, jeweller, music shop, newsagent, off-licence, pharmacy, post office, shoe shop** or **shoemaker, stationer, toyshop, watchmaker**

PEOPLE WHO WORK IN SHOPS
cashier, salesman or **saleswoman, shop assistant, shopkeeper** or **storekeeper**

shopping noun
Just put the shopping *in the boot of the car.*
goods, purchases

shore noun
see **seashore**

short adjective
1 *They live a* short *distance from the shops.*
little, small
opposite **long**
2 *It was a very* short *visit.*
brief, quick, fleeting, hasty, temporary
opposite **long**
3 *The troll was very* short *and fat.*
small, tiny, little, squat, dumpy, diminutive, petite
opposite **tall**
4 *The supply of water was getting* short.
low, meagre, scant, limited, inadequate, insufficient
opposite **plentiful**
5 *There is no need to be* short *with me!*
abrupt, rude, sharp, curt, impolite, snappy
opposites **patient, polite**

shortage noun
The shortage *of water is worrying.*
scarcity, deficiency, lack, want, dearth
A shortage *of water is a* **drought.**
A shortage *of food is a* **famine.**

shortcoming noun
As an actor, he has some shortcomings.
defect, failing, fault, weakness, limitation, drawback

shorten verb
She had to shorten *the essay because it was too long.*
cut down, reduce, cut, trim, abbreviate, abridge, condense, compress, curtail
opposite **lengthen**

shortly adverb
The post should arrive shortly.
soon, before long, presently

shot¹ noun
1 *I heard a noise like the* shot *of a pistol.*
bang, blast, crack
2 *The archer was an excellent* shot.

a
b
c
d
e
f
g
h
i
j
k
l
m
n
o
p
q
r
s
t
u
v
w
x
y
z

A
B
C
D
E
F
G
H
I
J
K
L
M
N
O
P
Q
R
S
T
U
V
W
X
Y
Z

A person who is good at shooting with a gun is a **marksman**.
3 *The striker had an easy* shot *at the goal.*
hit, strike, kick
4 *The photographer took some unusual* shots.
photograph, picture, snap, snapshot
5 (informal) *We each had a* shot *at solving the riddle.*
try, go, attempt
(informal) **bash**

shot²
past tense see **shoot**

shout verb
The ogre was shouting *and stamping with rage.*
call, cry out, bawl, yell, bellow, roar, howl, yelp, scream, screech, shriek
opposite **whisper**

shove verb
A man ran past and shoved *me to the side.*
push, thrust, force, barge, elbow, jostle, shoulder

shovel verb
We shovelled *the snow into a huge heap.*
dig, scoop, shift, clear, move

show verb shows, showing, showed, shown
1 *My uncle* showed *us his coin collection.*
present, reveal, display, exhibit
2 *The photo* shows *my grandparents on holiday.*
portray, picture, depict, illustrate, represent
3 *The dance tutor* showed *them what to do.*
explain to, make clear to, instruct, teach, tell
4 *The evidence* shows *that he was right.*
prove, demonstrate
5 *A nurse* showed *them into the waiting room.*
direct, guide, conduct, escort, usher
6 *The signpost* shows *the way.*
indicate, point out
7 *His vest* showed *through his shirt.*
be seen, be visible, appear

to show off
Walter is always showing off.
boast, brag, crow, gloat, swagger
(informal) **blow your own trumpet**
A person who shows off is a **show-off**.

show noun
1 *There is a* show *of artwork at the end of term.*
display, exhibition, presentation
2 *There's a good* show *on at the theatre.*
performance, production, entertainment

shower noun
For various types of rain see **weather**

shower verb
A passing bus showered *mud over them.*
spray, splash, spatter, sprinkle

showy adjective
She was wearing very showy *earrings.*
gaudy, flashy, bright, loud, garish, conspicuous
opposite **plain**

shred noun
The police couldn't find a shred *of evidence.*
bit, piece, scrap, trace
shreds
The gale ripped the tent to shreds.
tatters, ribbons, rags, strips

shrewd adjective
The spy was too shrewd *to be caught.*
clever, quick-witted, intelligent, sharp, cunning, crafty, artful, ingenious, wily, canny
opposite **stupid**

shriek noun & verb
'Quick!' shrieked *Alice. 'Open the door!'*
cry, scream, screech, shout, howl, bawl, squeal, wail, yell

shrill adjective
They heard the shrill *sound of a whistle.*
high, high-pitched, piercing, sharp, screechy
opposites **low, soft**

shrink verb
My jeans have shrunk in the wash.
become smaller, contract
opposite **expand**

shrivel verb
The plants shrivelled in the heat.
wilt, wither, droop, dry up, wrinkle, shrink

shroud verb
The mountain was shrouded in mist.
cover, envelop, wrap, blanket, hide,
conceal, mask, screen, veil

shrub noun
She bought some shrubs at the garden centre.
bush

shudder verb
*They shuddered with fear when they heard
the creature roar.*
tremble, quake, quiver, shake, shiver

shuffle verb
1 *She shuffled along the corridor in her
slippers.*
shamble, scuffle, hobble, scrape
2 *Did you remember to shuffle the cards?*
mix, mix up, jumble

shut verb shuts, shutting, shut
Please shut the door behind you.
close, fasten, seal, secure, lock, bolt, latch
To shut a door with a bang is to **slam** it.
to shut down
The restaurant may have to shut down.
close down
to shut someone up
*He had been shut up in a dungeon for five
years.*
imprison, confine, detain
to shut up (informal)
I wish those people behind us would shut up!
be quiet, be silent, stop talking,
hold your tongue

shy adjective
The little girl was too shy to say anything.
bashful, timid, coy, reserved, hesitant,
self-conscious, inhibited, modest
opposite **bold**

sick adjective
1 *Katie is off school because she's sick.*
ill, unwell, poorly, sickly, ailing,
indisposed, off colour, peaky
opposite **healthy**
2 *The sea was rough and the cabin boy felt
sick.*
nauseous, queasy
to be sick of
I'm sick of this miserable weather!
be fed up with, be tired of,
have had enough of

sicken verb
*They were sickened by the smell in the
dungeon.*
disgust, revolt, repel, offend
(informal) **turn your stomach**

sickly adjective
He has always been a sickly child.
unhealthy, weak, delicate, frail
opposites **healthy, strong**

sickness noun
see illness

side noun
1 *A cube has six sides.*
face, surface
2 *The path runs along the side of the field.*
edge, border, boundary, fringe, perimeter
The side of a page is the **margin**.
The side of a road is the **verge**.
3 *I could see both sides of the argument.*
point of view, view, angle, aspect
4 *The football club has a strong side
this year.*
team

side verb
to side with someone
*Some of the townspeople sided with the
enemy.*
support, favour, take the side of,
agree with, back

a
b
c
d
e
f
g
h
i
j
k
l
m
n
o
p
q
r
s
t
u
v
w
x
y
z

siege noun
The town held out against the siege for months.
blockade

sift verb
Sift the flour to get rid of any lumps.
sieve, strain, filter
to sift through something
The detective began to sift through the evidence.
examine, inspect, sort out, analyse, scrutinize, review

sigh noun & verb
'I'll never be good at tennis,' sighed Libby.
moan, lament, grumble, complain

sight noun
1 Weasels have sharp sight and excellent hearing.
eyesight, vision
2 The woods in autumn are a lovely sight.
spectacle, display, show, scene
3 By the third day, the ship was in sight of land.
view, range
4 We went to London to see the sights.
attraction, landmark
sight verb
The lookout sighted a ship on the horizon.
see, spot, spy, make out, observe, notice, distinguish, recognize, glimpse

sign noun
1 A sign pointed to the exit.
notice, placard, poster, signpost
The sign belonging to a particular business or organization is its logo.
The sign on a particular brand of goods is a trademark.
2 The witch gave no sign that she was angry.
indication, clue, hint, warning
3 The guard gave us a sign to pass through the gates.
signal, gesture, cue, reminder
sign verb
1 Please sign your name on the form.
write, inscribe

2 The club signed a new player last week.
take on, engage, recruit, enrol

signal noun
The spy waited for the signal that all was clear.
sign, indication, prompt, cue
A signal that tells you not to do something is a warning.
signal verb
The pilot signalled that he was going to descend.
give a sign or signal, gesture, indicate, motion

significance noun
What's the significance of that symbol?
importance, meaning, message, point, relevance

significant adjective
1 The book describes the significant events of last century.
important, major, noteworthy, influential
2 Global warming is having a significant effect on wildlife.
noticeable, considerable, perceptible, striking
opposite **insignificant**

signify verb
1 A red light signifies danger.
represent, stand for, symbolize, indicate, denote, mean
2 The crew signified their agreement by raising their hands.
show, express, communicate, convey

silence noun
There was silence while we sat the exam.
quiet, quietness, hush, stillness, calm, peace
opposite **noise**
silence verb
He silenced the audience by ringing a gong.
deaden, muffle, quieten, suppress
To silence someone by putting something over their mouth is to gag them.

silent adjective
1 *At night, the desert was cold and* silent.
quiet, noiseless, soundless, still, hushed
Something you can't hear is **inaudible**.
A common simile is **as silent as the grave**.
opposite noisy
2 *Morris kept* silent *throughout the meeting.*
quiet, speechless, mute
(informal) **mum**
To be too shy to speak is to be **tongue-tied**.
opposite talkative

silky adjective
Some types of rabbit have long, silky *fur.*
smooth, soft, fine, sleek, velvety

silly adjective
It was silly *of me to lock myself out of the house.*
foolish, stupid, idiotic, senseless,
thoughtless, brainless, unwise,
unintelligent, half-witted, hare-brained,
scatterbrained
(informal) **daft**
opposite sensible

similar adjective
The puppies are similar *in appearance.*
alike, identical, indistinguishable,
matching, the same
opposites dissimilar, different
similar to
The new book is similar to *the previous one.*
like, close to, comparable to
opposites unlike, different from

similarity noun
It's easy to see the similarity *between the twins.*
likeness, resemblance
opposite difference

simple adjective
1 *Can you answer this* simple *question?*
easy, elementary, straightforward
opposite difficult
2 *The help file is written in* simple *language.*
clear, plain, uncomplicated,
understandable, intelligible
opposite complicated

3 *The girl wore a* simple *cotton dress.*
plain, undecorated
opposite elaborate
4 *He enjoys* simple *pleasures like walking and gardening.*
ordinary, unsophisticated, humble, modest,
homely
opposite sophisticated

simply adverb
1 *I found his story* simply *unbelievable.*
absolutely, wholly, completely, totally,
utterly
2 *He won't eat peas* simply *because they're green!*
just, merely, purely, only, solely

sin noun
Some people believe that lying is a sin.
wrong, evil, wickedness, wrongdoing

sincere adjective
Please accept my sincere *apologies.*
genuine, honest, true, truthful, real,
earnest, wholehearted, frank
opposite insincere

sing verb sings, singing, sang, sung

WORD WEB
SOME WAYS TO SING
chant, chirp, croon, hum, trill, warble,
yodel

TYPES OF SINGING VOICE
alto, baritone, bass, contralto, soprano,
tenor, treble

For kinds of music for singing see **song**

singe verb
The iron was too hot and singed *my T-shirt.*
burn, scorch, sear, blacken, char

singer noun
The band comprises two guitarists and a singer.
vocalist
A group of singers is a **choir** or **chorus**.
A member of a choir is a **chorister**.

a
b
c
d
e
f
g
h
i
j
k
l
m
n
o
p
q
r
s
t
u
v
w
x
y
z

A B C D E F G H I J K L M N O P Q R **S** T U V W X Y Z

single adjective
1 *We saw a single house high on the moors.*
solitary, isolated
When only a single example of something exists, it is unique.
2 *Miss Dempster was quite content to stay single.*
unmarried
An unmarried man is a bachelor.
An unmarried woman is a spinster.

single verb
to single someone out
They singled her out as the best player in the team.
pick out, select, choose, identify

sinister adjective
He looked up with a sinister smile on his face.
menacing, threatening, malevolent, evil, disturbing, unsettling, eerie
(informal) creepy

sink verb sinks, sinking, sank, sunk
1 *The ship hit the rocks and sank.*
go down, become submerged, founder, capsize
To let water into a ship to sink it deliberately is to scuttle it.
2 *The sun began to sink below the horizon.*
drop, fall, descend, subside, dip
When the sun sinks to the horizon it sets.

sit verb sits, sitting, sat
1 *Rachel sat on the sofa reading a magazine.*
have a seat, settle down, rest, perch
To sit on your heels is to squat.
To sit to have your portrait painted is to pose.
2 *My brother is sitting his driving test next week.*
take
(informal) go in for

site noun
This is the site of an ancient burial ground.
location, place, position, situation, setting, plot

site verb
The new cinema will be sited in the middle of the town.
locate, place, position, situate

situation noun
1 *The house is in a pleasant situation.*
location, locality, place, position, setting, site, spot
2 *I found myself in an awkward situation.*
position, circumstances, condition, state of affairs
A bad situation is a plight or predicament.
3 *She applied for a situation in the bank.*
job, post, position, appointment

size noun
1 *What size is the garden?*
dimensions, proportions, area, extent
2 *They were amazed by the sheer size of the pyramids.*
scale, magnitude, immensity

skeleton noun
1 *Inside the crypt, they found several human skeletons.*
bones
2 *So far they've only put up the skeleton of the building.*
frame, framework, shell

sketch noun
1 *She drew a quick sketch of her cat.*
drawing, picture, outline
A sketch you do while you think of other things is a doodle.
2 *The actors performed a comic sketch.*
scene, turn, routine

sketch verb
He sketched a rough design for the poster.
draw, draft, outline, rough out

skid verb
The postman skidded on the icy pavement.
slide, slip

skilful adjective
Dickens was a skilful writer.
expert, skilled, accomplished, able, capable,

talented, brilliant, clever, masterly, deft
If you are skilful at a lot of things, you are versatile.
opposite incompetent

skill noun
It takes a lot of skill to build a boat.
expertise, ability, aptitude, capability, competence, accomplishment, talent, proficiency, deftness

skim verb
The stone skimmed across the surface of the pond.
glide, slide, skid, slip
to skim through
Luke skimmed through the newspaper.
scan, look through, skip through, flick through

skin noun
The cave people were dressed in animal skins.
coat, fur, hide, pelt
The type of skin you have on your face is your complexion.
Skin on fruit or vegetables is peel or rind.
Skin that might form on top of a liquid is a coating, film, or membrane.

skinny adjective
A skinny girl in bare feet answered the door.
thin, lean, bony, gaunt, lanky, scrawny, scraggy
opposite plump

skip verb
1 *The children skipped along the pavement.*
hop, jump, leap, bound, caper, dance, prance
2 *I skipped the boring bits in the book.*
pass over, miss out, ignore, omit, leave out

skirt verb
The path skirts the playing field.
circle, go round, pass round

sky noun
Clouds drifted slowly across the sky.
air, heavens

WRITING TIPS
Use these words to describe **the sky**

TO DESCRIBE **THE SKY BY DAY**
blue, clear, cloudless, cloudy, grey, overcast, stormy, sunless, sunny, thundery
The sky was overcast and still. Thin wisps of mist clung to the tops of the pine trees, and the oak and wild cherry were bare-leaved, waiting for spring.
— Gill Lewis, *Sky Hawk*

See also **weather**

TO DESCRIBE **THE SKY AT NIGHT**
moonless, moonlit, pitch-black, starless, starlit, starry, star-studded

slab noun
The words were engraved on a slab of marble.
block, piece, tablet, slice, chunk, hunk, lump

slack adjective
1 *One of the ropes on the tent was slack.*
loose, limp
opposite tight
2 *The team looked very slack in defence.*
lazy, lax, negligent, casual, relaxed, easy-going
opposite alert

slacken verb
1 *The climber slackened the rope around his waist.*
loosen, relax, release, ease off
opposite tighten
2 *The pace of the game slackened after half-time.*
lessen, reduce, decrease, slow down
opposite increase

slam verb
Don't slam the door!
bang, shut loudly

slant verb
1 *Her handwriting slants backwards.*
lean, slope, tilt, incline, be at an angle

a
b
c
d
e
f
g
h
i
j
k
l
m
n
o
p
q
r
s
t
u
v
w
x
y
z

A B C D E F G H I J K L M N O P Q R S T U V W X Y Z

2 *He slanted his story to make it more dramatic.*
distort, twist, warp

slant noun
1 *The floor of the caravan was at a slant.*
slope, angle, tilt, incline, gradient
A slant on a damaged ship is a **list**.
A slanting line joining opposite corners of a square, etc., is a **diagonal**.
A surface slanting up to a higher level is a **ramp**.
2 *The film brings a new slant to an old story.*
point of view, angle, emphasis, bias

slap verb
He slapped his hand against his thigh and laughed.
smack, strike, spank, hit, clout
(informal) whack

slash verb
For various ways to cut things see **cut**

slaughter verb
They had to slaughter the diseased cattle.
kill, butcher, massacre

slaughter noun
The battle ended in terrible slaughter.
bloodshed, killing, massacre, butchery

slave verb
They slaved all day to get the job done.
work hard, labour, toil, grind, sweat

slavery noun
The prisoners were sold into slavery.
captivity, bondage
opposite **freedom**

sledge noun
We pulled our sledges up the snowy slope.
sled, toboggan
A large sledge pulled by horses is a **sleigh**.
A sledge used in winter sports is a **bobsleigh**.

sleek adjective
Otters have sleek coats.
smooth, glossy, shiny, silky, soft, velvety
opposite **coarse**

sleep verb sleeps, sleeping, slept
The baby is sleeping in the next room.
be asleep, take a nap, doze
(informal) snooze
To go to sleep is to **drop off** or **nod off**.

sleep noun
Mr Khan had a short sleep after lunch.
nap, rest, doze, catnap
(informal) snooze, forty winks, shut-eye
An afternoon sleep is a **siesta**.
The long sleep some animals have through the winter is **hibernation**.

sleepless adjective
The wanderers spent a sleepless night.
restless, wide awake
The formal name for sleeplessness is **insomnia**.

sleepy adjective
The giant was usually sleepy after dinner.
drowsy, tired, weary, heavy-eyed, lethargic, ready to sleep
(informal) dopey
opposite **wide awake**

slender adjective
1 *The ballerina had a slender figure.*
slim, lean, slight, graceful, trim, svelte
opposite **fat**
2 *The spider dangled on a slender thread.*
thin, fine, fragile, delicate
opposite **thick**
3 *They only had a slender chance of winning.*
poor, slight, slim, faint, negligible, remote
opposite **good**
4 *The team won by a slender margin.*
narrow, small, slim
opposite **wide**

slice verb
To slice meat is to **carve** it.
See also **cut**

slick adjective
He was very slick at shuffling cards.
skilful, artful, clever, cunning, deft, quick
opposite **clumsy**

slide verb
I like sliding down the chute in the playground.
glide, skid, slip, slither

slight adjective
1 *There's a slight problem with the computer.*
minor, unimportant, insignificant, negligible, superficial, trifling, trivial
opposite important
2 *The fairy was a slight creature, barely two inches tall.*
delicate, fragile, frail, slender, slim, small, spare, thin, tiny
opposites stout, tall

slightly adverb
She was slightly hurt in the accident.
a little, a bit, somewhat, rather
opposites very, seriously

slim adjective
1 *A tall, slim figure appeared out of the fog.*
graceful, lean, slender, spare, thin, trim
opposite fat
2 *Their chances of winning are slim.*
faint, poor, slight, slender, negligible, remote
opposite good
3 *They won by a slim margin.*
narrow, small, slender
opposite wide

slimy adjective
The floor of the tunnel was covered with slimy mud.
slippery, slithery, sticky, oozy
(informal) gooey, icky

sling verb slings, slinging, slung
Robin Hood slung his quiver over his shoulder.
throw, cast, fling, hurl, pitch, heave, toss, lob
(informal) chuck

slink verb slinks, slinking, slunk
The spy slunk away without being seen.
slip, sneak, steal, creep, edge, sidle

slip verb
1 *The paper boy slipped on the ice.*
skid, slither, skate
2 *The lifeboat slipped into the water.*
glide, slide
3 *Marion slipped out while everyone was talking.*
sneak, steal, slink, tiptoe, creep, edge, sidle

slip noun
1 *She wrote her phone number on a slip of paper.*
piece, scrap
2 *The pianist made a tiny slip at the start of the concert.*
mistake, error, fault, blunder, gaffe, lapse
to give someone the slip
The robber gave them all the slip.
escape, get away, run away

slippery adjective
Take care—the floor is slippery.
slithery, slippy, smooth, glassy
A surface slippery with frost is **icy**.
A surface slippery with grease is **greasy** or **oily**.
A common simile is as **slippery as an eel**.

slit noun
The archers shot arrows through the slits in the castle wall.
opening, chink, gap, slot, split, tear, cut

slit
For various ways to cut things see **cut**

slither verb
The rattlesnake slithered through the long grass.
slide, slip, glide, slink, snake

slope verb
The beach slopes gently down to the sea.
fall or rise, incline, bank, shelve

a b c d e f g h i j k l m n o p q r s t u v w x y z

A
B
C
D
E
F
G
H
I
J
K
L
M
N
O
P
Q
R
S
T
U
V
W
X
Y
Z

slope noun
1 *It was hard work pushing my bike up the slope.*
hill, rise, bank, ramp
An upward slope is an **ascent**.
A downward slope is a **descent**.
2 *Rain runs down the roof because of the slope.*
incline, slant, tilt, gradient

sloppy adjective
1 *For breakfast, there was a bowl of steaming, sloppy porridge.*
runny, slushy, watery, liquid, wet
(informal) **gloopy**
2 *His handwriting is very sloppy.*
untidy, messy, careless, slovenly, slapdash, slipshod

slot noun
1 *To use the locker, put a pound coin into the slot.*
slit, chink, hole, opening
2 *The programme has been moved from its usual slot.*
time, spot, space, place

slouch verb
Enid sat at her desk, slouched over the computer.
hunch, stoop, slump, droop, flop

slow adjective
1 *Tortoises move at a slow but steady pace.*
unhurried, leisurely, gradual, plodding, dawdling, sluggish
2 *They took the train to London, followed by a slow bus journey.*
lengthy, prolonged, drawn-out, tedious
3 *The prisoner was slow to answer.*
hesitant, reluctant, tardy
opposite quick

slow verb
to slow down
Slow down—you're driving too fast!
go slower, brake, reduce speed, decelerate
opposite accelerate

sludge noun
They cleared a lot of sludge out of the pond.
muck, mud, ooze, slime
(informal) **gunk**

slump verb
1 *Sales of music CDs have slumped recently.*
decline, fall, drop, plummet, plunge, crash, collapse
2 *The professor slumped into an armchair.*
flop, collapse, sink, sag, slouch

slump noun
There was a slump in trade after Christmas.
collapse, drop, fall, decline
A general slump in trade is a **depression** or **recession**.
opposite boom

sly adjective
The chess player knew several sly moves.
crafty, cunning, artful, clever, wily, tricky, sneaky, devious, furtive, secretive, stealthy, underhand
A common simile is as **sly as a fox**.
opposite straightforward

smack verb
He smacked the other player on the head by accident.
slap, strike, hit, cuff
(informal) **whack**
For other ways of hitting see **hit**

small adjective

OVERUSED WORD
Try to vary the words you use for **small**. Here are some other words you could use.

FOR A **SMALL OBJECT**
little, tiny, minute, compact, miniature, microscopic, minuscule, mini, baby
(informal) **teeny, titchy, dinky**
(Scottish) **wee**
Moles have incredibly tiny eyes and ears.
opposites big, large

FOR A **SMALL PERSON**
little, short, petite, slight, dainty,

diminutive
(informal) **pint-sized**
A petite little elf was standing on a toadstool.
opposites **big, tall, large**

FOR A SMALL HELPING OR SMALL PORTION
meagre, inadequate, insufficient, paltry, scanty, stingy, skimpy
(informal) **measly**
For breakfast there was stale bread with a meagre scraping of butter.
opposites **large, generous, ample**

FOR A SMALL CHANGE OR SMALL PROBLEM
minor, unimportant, insignificant, trivial, trifling, negligible
The writers made some trivial changes to the script.
opposites **major, substantial**

smart adjective
1 *Everyone looked smart at the wedding.*
elegant, well-dressed, well-groomed, stylish, spruce, fashionable, chic, neat, trim
To make yourself smart is to **smarten up.**
opposite **scruffy**
2 *They booked a table in a very smart restaurant.*
fashionable, high-class, exclusive, fancy
(informal) **posh**
3 *The detective made a very smart move.*
clever, ingenious, intelligent, shrewd, crafty
opposite **stupid**
4 *The cyclists set off at a smart pace.*
fast, quick, rapid, speedy, swift, brisk
opposite **slow**

smart verb
The smoke from the barbecue made our eyes smart.
hurt, sting, prick, prickle, tingle

smash verb
A vase fell off the table and smashed to pieces on the floor.
break, crush, shatter, crack
When wood smashes it **splinters.**
To smash something completely is to **demolish, destroy,** or **wreck** it.
to smash into
A lorry had smashed into the side of a bus.
crash into, collide with, bang into, bump into

smear verb
The chef smeared butter over the cooking dish.
spread, wipe, plaster, rub, dab, smudge, daub

smear noun
There were smears of paint all over the carpet.
streak, smudge, blotch, splodge, splotch, daub, mark

smell noun
1 *The air was filled with the smell of roses.*
scent, aroma, perfume, fragrance
2 *The smell of mouldy cheese was unbearable.*
odour, stench, stink, reek, whiff
(informal) **pong, niff**

smell verb smells, smelling, smelt or smelled
1 *I could smell something baking in the oven.*
scent, sniff
(informal) **get a whiff of**
2 *After walking all day, my feet were beginning to smell.*
stink, reek
(informal) **pong**

> **WRITING TIPS**
> You can use these words to describe how something smells
>
> TO DESCRIBE SOMETHING WHICH SMELLS GOOD
> **fragrant, aromatic, perfumed, scented, sweet, sweet-smelling**

a
b
c
d
e
f
g
h
i
j
k
l
m
n
o
p
q
r
s
t
u
v
w
x
y
z

In the garden below were lilac-trees purple with flowers, and their dizzily sweet fragrance drifted up to the window on the morning wind.
– L. M. Montgomery, Anne of Green Gables

TO DESCRIBE SOMETHING WHICH **SMELLS BAD**
smelly, stinking, evil-smelling, foul-smelling, musty, odorous, reeking, rotten, fetid, foul
(informal) **stinky, pongy, whiffy**
The witch stirred the evil-smelling brew.

smile verb & noun
The stranger smiled and introduced himself.
grin, beam
To smile in a silly way is to **simper**.
To smile in a self-satisfied way is to **smirk**.
To smile in an insulting way is to **sneer**.

smoke noun
Puffs of green smoke came from the dragon's nostrils.
fumes, gas, steam, vapour
The smoke given out by a car is **exhaust**.
A mixture of smoke and fog is **smog**.

smoke verb
1 *The bonfire was still smoking next morning.*
smoulder
2 *A man stood silently smoking a cigar.*
puff at

smooth adjective
1 *This part of the road is smooth and good for cycling.*
flat, even, level
opposite **uneven**
2 *In the early morning, the lake was perfectly smooth.*
calm, still, unruffled, undisturbed, glassy
opposite **rough**
3 *Otters have smooth and shiny coats.*
silky, sleek, velvety
opposite **coarse**

4 *The journey by train is very quick and smooth.*
comfortable, steady
opposite **bumpy**
5 *Stir the cake mixture until it is smooth.*
creamy, flowing, runny
opposite **lumpy**

smooth verb
Charlotte stood up and smoothed her dress.
flatten, level, even out
To smooth cloth you can **iron** or **press** it.
To smooth wood you can **plane** or **sand** it.

smother verb
1 *Pythons smother their prey to death.*
suffocate, choke, stifle
2 *The pudding was smothered with cream.*
cover, coat

smoulder verb
see **burn**

smudge noun
There were smudges of ink all over the page.
smear, blot, streak, stain, mark

smudge verb
Don't smudge the icing on the cake!
smear, blur, streak

snack noun
I usually bring an apple or banana for a snack.
bite, refreshments
(informal) **nibble**
A snack in the middle of the morning is sometimes called **elevenses**.

snag noun
We've hit a snag with our holiday plans.
problem, difficulty, obstacle, hitch, complication, setback

A
B
C
D
E
F
G
H
I
J
K
L
M
N
O
P
Q
R
S
T
U
V
W
X
Y
Z

soft adjective
1 *The kittens can only eat* soft *food.*
pulpy, spongy, squashy
(informal) squidgy
opposites hard, dry
2 *My head sank into the* soft *pillow.*
supple, pliable, springy, yielding, flexible
opposites firm, rigid
3 *The rabbit's fur felt very* soft.
smooth, silky, sleek, velvety, downy,
feathery
opposite coarse
4 *A* soft *breeze stirred the leaves.*
gentle, light, mild, delicate
opposites rough, strong
5 *The smugglers spoke in* soft *whispers.*
quiet, low, faint
opposite loud
6 *It was hard to see clearly in the* soft *light.*
subdued, muted, pale, dim, low
opposites bright, dazzling
7 *You are being too* soft *with that puppy.*
lenient, easy-going, tolerant, indulgent
opposites strict, tough

soggy adjective
1 *The pitch was* soggy *after all the rain.*
wet, drenched, soaked, saturated, sodden,
waterlogged
2 *The bread in my sandwich had become*
soggy.
moist, soft, pulpy, squelchy
(informal) squidgy
opposite dry

soil[1] noun
The plants grow best in well-drained soil.
earth, ground, land
Good fertile soil is loam.
The fertile top layer of ~~and grass~~
~~...n, muddy,~~

soil[2]
~~...st tense see sell~~

soldier noun
Three soldiers *stood guard outside the*
building.
serviceman or servicewoman
A soldier paid to fight for a foreign country
is a mercenary.
An old word for a soldier is warrior.
Soldiers who use big guns are the artillery.
Soldiers who fight on horseback are the
cavalry.
Soldiers who fight on foot are the infantry.
See also armed services.

sole adjective
The castaway was the sole *inhabitant of the*
island.
only, single, one, solitary, lone, unique

solemn adjective
1 *The butler always had a* solemn *expression*
on his face.
serious, grave, sober, sombre, unsmiling,
glum
opposite cheerful
2 *The coronation was a* solemn *occasion.*
formal, dignified, grand, stately, majestic,
pompous
opposite frivolous

solid adjective
1 *A cricket ball is* solid.
opposite hollow
2 *The water turned into* solid *ice.*
hard, firm, dense, compact, rigid,
unyielding
A common ~~...~~ ~~...~~s solid as a rock.
A common ~~...~~
~~...~~s of the climbing frame are quite
firm, robust, sound, strong, stable,
sturdy
opposites weak, unstable
4 *The crown was made of* solid *gold.*
pure, genuine
5 *He got* solid *support from his te* ~~...~~
mates.
firm, reliable, dependable
unanimous
opposites weak, di ~~...~~

a
b
c
d
e
f
g
h
i
j
k
l
m
n
o
p
q
r
s
t
u
v
w
z

392

A
B
C
D
E
F
G
H
I
J
K
L
M
N
O
P
Q
R
S
T
U
V
W
X

solidify verb
The lava from the volcano solidifies as it cools.
harden, become solid, set, stiffen
opposites soften, liquify

solitary adjective
1 *He was a solitary man and rarely spoke to others.*
isolated, secluded, lonely, unsociable
To be solitary is to be alone.
opposite sociable.
2 *There was a solitary tree in the middle of the field.*
single, sole, one, only

solitude noun
On the island, there was total peace and solitude.
privacy, seclusion, isolation, loneliness

solve verb
The professor was trying to solve an ancient riddle.
interpret, explain, answer, work out, find the solution to, unravel, decipher

sombre adjective
1 *The hall was decorated in sombre shades of grey.*
dark, dull, dim, dismal, dingy, drab, cheerless
opposite bright
2 *A messenger arrived with a sombre look on his face.*
gloomy, serious, grave, sober, sad, melancholy, mournful
opposite cheerful

song noun

> **WORD WEB**
> SOME KINDS OF SONG
> anthem, aria, ballad, calypso, carol,
> chant, ditty, folk song, hymn, jingle,
> lament, lay, love song, lullaby, madrigal,
> nursery rhyme, pop song, psalm, rap,
> round, shanty, spiritual

A play or film that includes many songs is a musical.
A song from a musical is a number.
The words for a song are the lyrics.

For other musical terms see **music**

soon adverb
Dinner will be ready soon.
before long, in a minute, shortly, presently, quickly

soothe verb
1 *The quiet music soothed her nerves.*
calm, comfort, relax, pacify
2 *This cream will soothe the pain.*
ease, lessen, relieve

soothing adjective
They played soothing music.
calming, relaxing, restful, peaceful, gentle, pleasant

sophisticated adjective
1 *Diana looked very sophisticated in her ballgown.*
grown-up, mature, cultivated, cultured, refined
opposite naive
2 *She has a sophisticated digital camera.*
advanced, complex, complicated, intricate, elaborate
opposites primitive, simple

sorcerer and **sorceress** noun
see **magic**

sore adjective
My feet are still sore from the walk.
aching, hurting, smarting, tender, wound, inflamed, raw, red

sorrow noun
1 *He felt great sorrow .....*
sadness, unhappiness, ...

THINGS A SPACESHIP MIGHT DO
blast off, burn up, drift off-course, land, lift off, malfunction, orbit, re-enter the earth's atmosphere, splash down, touch down

spacious adjective
The living room is spacious and bright.
big, large, roomy, sizeable
opposites small, cramped

span noun
The bridge has a span of 200 metres.
breadth, extent, length, width, distance, reach
A span of time is a period or stretch.

span verb
A rickety footbridge spanned the river.
cross, stretch over, extend across, straddle, bridge, traverse

spare verb
1 *Can you spare any money for a good cause?*
afford, part with, give, provide, do without
2 *Gretel begged the witch to spare her brother.*
show mercy to, pardon, reprieve, let off, release, free

spare adjective
1 *The spare tyre is in the boot.*
additional, extra, reserve, standby
2 *Have you any spare change?*
leftover, surplus, odd, remaining, unused, unwanted
3 *The ghostly figure was tall and spare.*
lean, thin, slender, slim, trim

spark noun
There was a spark of light as he struck the match.
flash, gleam, glint, flicker, sparkle

sparkle verb
The diamond ring sparkled in the sunlight.
glitter, glisten, glint, twinkle

sparse adjective
In the desert, vegetation is very sparse.
scarce, scanty, scattered, inadequate, infrequent
opposite plentiful

spatter verb
The bus spattered mud all over us.
splash, spray, sprinkle, scatter, shower

speak verb speaks, speaking, spoke, spoken
The robot opened its mouth and began to speak.
communicate, express yourself, say something, talk, utter

speaker noun
A person who gives a talk is a lecturer.
A person who makes formal speeches is an orator.
A person who speaks on behalf of an organization is a spokesperson.

spear noun
A spear used in whaling is a harpoon.
A spear thrown as a sport is a javelin.
A spear carried by a medieval knight on horseback was a lance.

special adjective
1 *Are you keeping the champagne for a special occasion?*
important, significant, memorable, noteworthy, momentous, exceptional, extraordinary, out-of-the-ordinary
opposite ordinary
2 *My granny has her own special way of making porridge.*
unique, individual, characteristic, distinctive, different, peculiar
3 *You need a special camera to film underwater.*
particular, specific, proper, specialized

speciality noun
The chef's speciality is sticky toffee pudding.
strength, strong point, expertise, forte

A B C D E F G H I J K L M N O P Q R **S** T U V W X Y Z

specific adjective
The treasure map gave specific directions.
detailed, precise, exact, definite, particular, clear-cut
opposites general, vague

specify verb
Please specify your shoe size.
be specific about, identify, name, define

specimen noun
The police asked for a specimen of his handwriting.
sample, example, illustration, instance

speck noun
She brushed a speck of dust from her shoes.
bit, dot, spot, fleck, grain, particle, trace, mark
See also bit

speckled adjective
A brown, speckled egg lay on the nest.
flecked, spotted, spotty, mottled
If you have a lot of brown spots on your skin you are freckled.
Something with patches of colour is dappled or patchy.

spectacle noun
The fireworks for Diwali will be a great spectacle.
display, show, performance, exhibition, extravaganza

spectacles plural noun
see glasses

spectacular adjective
1 *The acrobats gave a spectacular performance.*
dramatic, exciting, impressive, thrilling, magnificent, sensational
2 *The tulips are spectacular at this time of year.*
eye-catching, showy, splendid, breathtaking, colourful

spectator noun
The spectators at a show are the audience.

The spectators at a football match are the crowd.
A person watching TV is a viewer.
If you see an accident or a crime you are an eyewitness or witness.
If you just happen to see something going on you are a bystander or onlooker.

speech noun
1 *His speech was slurred and he looked tired.*
speaking, talking, articulation, pronunciation
2 *She was invited to give a speech.*
talk, address, lecture, oration
A talk in church is a sermon.
Speech between actors in a play is dialogue.
A speech delivered by a single actor is a monologue.

speechless adjective
She was speechless with surprise.
dumbstruck, dumbfounded, tongue-tied

speed noun
1 *Could a spaceship travel faster than the speed of light?*
pace, rate
A formal synonym is velocity.
The speed of a piece of music is its tempo.
To increase speed is to accelerate.
To reduce speed is to decelerate.
2 *They finished clearing up with amazing speed.*
quickness, rapidity, swiftness
opposite slowness

speed verb speeds, speeding, sped
The skiers sped down the mountain.
race, rush, dash, dart, hurry, hurtle, career, fly, streak, tear, shoot, zoom, zip

speedy adjective
They sent their best wishes for a speedy recovery.
fast, quick, swift, rapid, prompt, brisk
opposite slow

spell¹ noun
We're hoping for a spell of dry weather.
period, interval, time, stretch, run

spell² noun
A magic spell had turned the knight into a toad.
charm, incantation
Making magic spells is **sorcery, witchcraft,** or **wizardry.**
For other words to do with magic see **magic**

spend verb spends, spending, spent
1 *Have you spent all your pocket money already?*
pay out, use up, get through, exhaust (informal) **fork out, shell out**
To spend money unwisely is to **fritter** or **squander** it.
2 *She spends a lot of time working in the garden.*
pass, occupy, fill
To spend time doing something useless is to **waste** it.

sphere noun
1 *The earth has the shape of a sphere.*
ball, globe, orb
2 *He's an expert in the sphere of photography.*
subject, area, field

spherical adjective
The earth is spherical.
round, ball-shaped

spice noun

WORD WEB
SOME SPICES USED IN COOKING
allspice, aniseed, bay leaf, capsicum, cardamom, cayenne, chilli, cinnamon, cloves, coriander, cumin, curry powder, ginger, juniper, mace, nutmeg, paprika, pepper, pimento, saffron, sesame, turmeric

spicy adjective
The meat was cooked in a spicy chilli sauce.
hot, peppery, fiery

spike noun
His shirt got caught on a metal spike.
point, prong, spear, stake, barb

spill verb
1 *Katie spilled her juice all over the table.*
overturn, upset, tip over
2 *Milk spilled onto the floor.*
overflow, pour, slop, slosh, splash
3 *The treasure chest fell open, spilling gold coins everywhere.*
shed, tip, scatter, drop

spin verb spins, spinning, spun
The rear wheels of the jeep spun round.
turn, rotate, revolve, whirl, twirl

spine noun
1 *Your spine runs down the middle of your back.*
backbone, spinal column
The bones in your spine are your **vertebrae.**
2 *A porcupine has sharp spines.*
needle, quill, point, spike, bristle

spiral noun
The staircase wound upwards in a long spiral.
coil, twist, corkscrew, whorl
A tight spiral of swirling air or water is a **vortex.**

spirit noun
1 *He carried a charm to keep evil spirits away.*
ghost, ghoul, phantom, spectre, demon
See also **ghost**
2 *The orchestra played the piece with great spirit.*
energy, liveliness, enthusiasm, vigour, zest, zeal, fire
3 *There is a real spirit of cooperation in the team.*
feeling, mood, atmosphere

spiritual adjective
The Dalai Lama is the spiritual leader of Tibet.
religious, holy, sacred
opposite **worldly**

a
b
c
d
e
f
g
h
i
j
k
l
m
n
o
p
q
r
s
t
u
v
w
x
y
z

A B C D E F G H I J K L M N O P Q R **S** T U V W X Y Z

spite noun
I believe that she ripped my book out of spite.
malice, spitefulness, ill will, ill feeling, hostility, bitterness, resentment, venom

spiteful adjective
He made some really spiteful *comments.*
malicious, malevolent, ill-natured, hostile, venomous, vicious, nasty, unkind
opposite kind

splash verb
1 *The bus* splashed *water over us.*
shower, spray, spatter, sprinkle, squirt, slop, slosh, spill, splatter
(informal) **splosh**
2 *The children* splashed *about in the playing pool.*
paddle, wade, dabble, bathe

splendid adjective
1 *There was a* splendid *banquet on the eve of the wedding.*
magnificent, lavish, luxurious, impressive, imposing, grand, great, dazzling, glorious, gorgeous, elegant, rich, stately, majestic
2 *That's a* splendid *idea!*
excellent, first-class, admirable, superb, wonderful, marvellous

splendour noun
They admired the splendour *of the cathedral.*
magnificence, glory, grandeur, majesty, richness, brilliance, spectacle

splinter noun
There were splinters *of glass all over the floor.*
fragment, sliver, chip, flake

splinter verb
The glass splintered *into pieces.*
shatter, smash, fracture, chip, crack, split

split verb
1 *He* split *the log in two.*
chop, cut up, crack open, splinter
2 *He* split *his trousers climbing over the fence.*
rip open, tear
3 *The pirates* split *the gold between them.*
distribute, share out

4 *The path* splits *here.*
branch, fork, separate
to split up
The search party decided to split up.
break up, part, separate, divide
If a married couple splits up, *they may* divorce.

split noun
He had a split *in the seat of his trousers.*
rip, tear, slash, slit

spoil verb
1 *Bad weather* spoiled *the holiday.*
ruin, wreck, upset, mess up, mar, scupper
2 *The graffiti* spoils *the look of the new building.*
damage, harm, hurt, disfigure, deface
3 *His parents have* spoiled *him since he was a baby.*
indulge, pamper, make a fuss of

spoke
past tense see **speak**

spoken adjective
Her spoken *French is excellent.*
oral, verbal
opposite written

spongy adjective
The mossy ground felt spongy *to walk on.*
soft, springy, squashy, absorbent, porous

spoon noun
see **cutlery**

sport noun
I enjoy playing sport *at the weekend.*
exercise, games

WORD WEB
TEAM SPORTS INCLUDE
American football, baseball, basketball, bowls, cricket, football or soccer, hockey, lacrosse, netball, polo, rounders, rugby, volleyball, water polo

INDIVIDUAL SPORTS INCLUDE
angling, archery, athletics, badminton, billiards, boxing, bowling, canoeing, climbing, croquet, cross-country running, cycling, darts, diving, fencing, golf, gymnastics, horse racing, jogging, judo, karate, motor racing, mountaineering, orienteering, pool, rowing, sailing, showjumping, snooker, squash, surfing, swimming, table tennis, tae kwon do, tennis, waterskiing, weightlifting, windsurfing, wrestling

For individual athletic events see **athletics**

WINTER SPORTS INCLUDE
bobsleigh, curling, ice hockey, ice skating, skiing, snowboarding, speed skating, tobogganing

PEOPLE WHO TAKE PART IN SPORT
athlete, coach, competitor, Olympian, Paralympian, player, sportsman or **sportswoman**

PLACES WHERE SPORT TAKES PLACE
arena, field, ground, park, pitch, pool, ring, rink, run, slope, stadium, track

sporting adjective
It was sporting of him to admit defeat.
sportsmanlike, fair, generous, honourable
opposite **unsporting**

spot noun
1 *There were several spots of paint on the carpet.*
mark, stain, blot, blotch, smudge, dot, fleck, speck
Small brown spots on your skin are **freckles**.
A small dark spot on your skin is a **mole**.
A mark you have had on your skin since you were born is a **birthmark**.
A small round swelling on your skin is a **pimple**.
A lot of spots is a **rash**.
2 *We felt a few spots of rain.*
drop, blob, bead

3 *Here's a nice spot for a picnic.*
place, position, location, site, situation, locality

spot verb
1 *Nina spotted her friend in the crowd.*
see, sight, spy, catch sight of, notice, observe, make out, recognize, detect
2 *The tyres were spotted with mud.*
mark, stain, blot, spatter, fleck, speckle, mottle

spotless adjective
Mr Travis washed his car until it was spotless.
clean, unmarked, immaculate, gleaming
opposite **dirty**

spout verb
Molten lava and ash spouted from the volcano.
gush, spew, pour, stream, spurt, squirt, jet

sprawl verb
1 *We sprawled on the lawn.*
flop, lean back, lie, loll, lounge, recline, relax, slouch, slump, spread out, stretch out
2 *New houses have started to sprawl across the countryside.*
spread, stretch

spray verb
A passing bus sprayed mud over us.
shower, spatter, splash, sprinkle, scatter

spray noun
1 *We gave the plants a spray of water with the hose.*
shower, sprinkling, fountain, mist
2 *She picked a spray of snowdrops from the garden.*
bunch, posy

spread verb
1 *I spread the map on the table.*
lay out, open out, fan out, unfold, unfurl, unroll
2 *The milk spilled and spread all over the floor.*
expand, extend, stretch, broaden, enlarge, swell

a
b
c
d
e
f
g
h
i
j
k
l
m
n
o
p
q
r
s
t
u
v
w
x
y
z

3 *The school website is a good way of spreading news.*
communicate, circulate, distribute, transmit, make known, pass on, pass round
4 *She spread jam on a piece of toast.*
smear
5 *He spread the seeds evenly over the ground.*
scatter, strew

sprightly adjective
My granny is quite sprightly for her age.
lively, energetic, active, agile, nimble, frisky, spry
opposite **inactive**

spring verb springs, springing, sprang, sprung
Suddenly a rabbit sprang over the fence.
jump, leap, bound, hop, vault
When a cat springs at a mouse, it **pounces**.
to **spring up**
Weeds spring up quickly in damp weather.
appear, develop, emerge, shoot up, sprout

springy adjective
The bed felt soft and springy.
bouncy, elastic, stretchy, flexible, pliable
opposite **rigid**

sprinkle verb
She sprinkled flakes of chocolate over the cake.
scatter, shower, spray, dust, powder

sprout verb
The seeds will sprout if they are warm and damp.
grow, germinate, shoot up, spring up, develop, emerge

spruce adjective
He looked very spruce in a clean white shirt.
smart, well-dressed, well-groomed, elegant, neat, trim
opposite **scruffy**

spun
past tense see spin

spur verb
to **spur someone on**
The cheers of the crowd spurred on the athletes.
egg on, encourage, inspire, prompt, stimulate, urge

spurt verb
Water spurted from the hole in the pipe.
gush, spout, shoot out, stream, squirt, jet

spy noun
The spy was on a top-secret mission.
agent, secret agent
The work of a spy is **spying** or **espionage**.
A spy who works for two rival countries or organizations is a **double agent**.
An informal name for a spy who works undercover is a **mole**.

WORD WEB

THINGS A SPY MIGHT DO
adopt a disguise or cover,
assume a secret identity,
carry out a secret mission,
crack or decipher a code,
gather intelligence,
keep someone under surveillance,
report to headquarters,
uncover an enemy agent,
work undercover

See also **code**

THINGS A SPY MIGHT USE OR CARRY
coded message, false passport,
hidden camera or microphone,
listening device, motion detector,
night-vision goggles, password, torch,
walkie-talkie

A SPY'S MISSION MIGHT BE
clandestine, covert, secret, stealthy,
surreptitious, top-secret, undercover,
(informal) cloak-and-dagger,
hush-hush

spy verb
The lookout spied a ship on the horizon.
see, sight, spot, catch sight of, notice, observe, make out, detect

squabble verb
The twins are always squabbling in the car.
argue, fight, quarrel, bicker, wrangle

squalid adjective
The prisoners were kept in a squalid underground cell.
degrading, dingy, dirty, filthy, foul, mucky, nasty, unpleasant
opposite clean

squander verb
He squandered his money on an expensive watch.
waste, fritter away, misuse
(informal) blow
opposite save

square adjective
All the tiles have square corners.
right-angled
A pattern of squares is a chequered pattern.

squarely adverb
The ball hit him squarely in the face.
directly, straight, head on
opposite obliquely

squash verb
1 *My sandwich got squashed at the bottom of my school bag.*
crush, flatten, press, compress, mangle
To squash food deliberately is to mash or pulp or purée it.
2 *We squashed our sleeping bags into our rucksacks.*
squeeze, stuff, force, cram, pack, ram

squat verb
We squatted on the ground to watch the puppet show.
crouch, sit

squat adjective
The alien had a squat little body on three short legs.
dumpy, stocky, plump, podgy, portly

squeak and squeal noun & verb
For various sounds see sound[1]

squeeze verb
1 *She squeezed the water out of the sponge.*
press, wring, compress, crush
2 *Five of us squeezed into the back of the car.*
squash, cram, crowd, stuff, push, ram, shove, wedge
3 *Holly squeezed her sister affectionately.*
clasp, hug, embrace, cuddle
To squeeze something between your thumb and finger is to pinch it.

squirm verb
The guinea pig squirmed out of the vet's grasp.
wriggle, writhe, twist

squirt verb
My little brother made the tap water squirt all over me.
spurt, spray, gush, spout, shoot, jet

stab verb
1 *He stabbed the sausage with his fork.*
spear, jab, pierce, impale
2 *She stabbed a finger at him.*
stick, thrust, push, jab

stab noun
Jake felt a sudden stab of pain in his chest.
pang, prick, sting

stable adjective
1 *The ladder doesn't look very stable.*
steady, secure, firm, fixed, solid, balanced
opposites wobbly, shaky
2 *He's been in a stable relationship for years.*
steady, established, lasting, durable, strong
opposite temporary

stack noun
There were stacks of books all over the floor.
pile, heap, mound, tower

a
b
c
d
e
f
g
h
i
j
k
l
m
n
o
p
q
r
s
t
u
v
w
x
y
z

Another word for a stack of hay is a **rick** or **hayrick**.

stack verb
Stack the papers on the desk.
gather, assemble, collect, heap up, pile up

staff noun
There was a party at the hospital for all the staff.
workers, employees, personnel, workforce, team
The staff on a ship or aircraft are the **crew**.

stage noun
1 *They went up on the stage to collect their prizes.*
platform
2 *The final stage of the journey was made by coach.*
leg, step, phase, portion, stretch
3 *At this stage in her life, she wants to try something new.*
period, point, time, juncture

stagger verb
1 *The wounded knight staggered and fell.*
reel, stumble, lurch, totter, sway, falter, waver, wobble
2 *We were staggered at the size of the pyramid.*
amaze, astonish, astound, surprise, flabbergast, stupefy, startle, stun

stagnant adjective
Mosquitoes swarmed around the pool of stagnant water.
still, motionless, static
opposites flowing, fresh

stain noun
There were several coffee stains on the tablecloth.
mark, spot, blot, blotch, blemish, smear, smudge

stain verb
1 *Her trainers were stained with mud.*
discolour, mark, soil, dirty, blacken, tarnish
2 *The wood can be stained a darker shade.*
dye, colour, paint, tint, tinge

stairs plural noun
The stairs up to the front door were worn with age.
steps
A set of stairs taking you from one floor to another is a **flight** of stairs, or a **staircase** or **stairway**.
A moving staircase is an **escalator**.
A handrail at the side of a staircase is a **banister**.

stake noun
The fence was made from sharp wooden stakes.
pole, post, stick, spike, stave, pile

stale adjective
The bread had gone stale.
dry, hard, old, mouldy, musty
opposite fresh

stalk¹ noun
The recipe requires half a stalk of celery.
stem, shoot, twig

stalk² verb
1 *The cheetah stalked its prey.*
hunt, pursue, track, trail, follow, shadow, tail
2 *Miss Foster turned and stalked out of the room.*
stride, strut
For other ways to walk see **walk**

stall verb
The man was stalling to give his friends time to escape.
play for time, delay, hesitate, hedge

stammer verb
Angela went red and started stammering.
stutter, falter, stumble, splutter

stamp verb
1 *He stamped on the flower by mistake.*
step, tread, trample
2 *The librarian stamped my library book.*
mark, print
To stamp a postmark on a letter is to **frank** it.

A B C D E F G H I J K L M N O P Q R **S** T U V W X Y Z

To stamp a mark on cattle with a hot iron is to **brand** them.

stamp noun
I put a first-class **stamp** *on the letter.*
A person who studies or collects stamps is a **philatelist**.

stand verb stands, standing, stood
1 *The newborn pup was too weak to* **stand**.
get to your feet, get up, rise
2 *They* **stood** *the ladder against the wall.*
put, place, set, position, station, erect
3 *The offer still* **stands**.
remain valid, be unchanged, continue
4 *I can't* **stand** *the smell any longer.*
bear, abide, endure, put up with, tolerate, suffer
to stand for something
1 *She won't* **stand for** *any nonsense.*
put up with, tolerate, accept, allow, permit
2 *What do these initials* **stand for**?
mean, indicate, signify, represent
to stand out
Among all the photographs, this one really **stood out**.
catch your eye, stick out, be prominent
to stand up for someone
He always **stands up for** *his friends.*
support, defend, side with, speak up for
(informal) **stick up for**

stand noun
A three-legged stand for a camera or telescope is a **tripod**.
A stand for a Bible or other large book is a **lectern**.
A stand to put a statue on is a **pedestal** or **plinth**.

standard noun
1 *Their writing is of a very high* **standard**.
grade, level, quality
2 *He considered the book good by any* **standard**.
guidelines, ideal, measurement, model
3 *The soldiers carried their* **standard** *proudly.*
colours, flag, banner

standard adjective
The teacher showed us the **standard** *way to write a letter.*
normal, usual, common, conventional, typical, customary, accepted, approved, established, orthodox, regular, traditional
opposite abnormal

standby noun
We need a **standby** *in case someone drops out.*
reserve, substitute, replacement

standstill noun
to come to a standstill
The traffic had **come to a standstill.**
stop moving, draw up, halt, stop

staple adjective
Rice is the **staple** *food in many countries.*
chief, main, principal, standard, basic

star noun
1 *Astronomers study the* **stars**.
For objects found in space see **space**
For signs of the zodiac see **zodiac**
A word meaning 'to do with stars' is **stellar**.
A night sky in which you can see stars is **starry** or **star-studded**.
A mark in the shape of a star in a piece of writing is an **asterisk**.
2 *Several Hollywood* **stars** *attended the premiere of the film.*
celebrity, idol, superstar

stare verb
The guard **stared** *straight ahead, not blinking.*
gaze, gape, peer, look
to stare at someone
The wolf was **staring** *hungrily at us.*
gaze at, gawp at, goggle at, eye, ogle, scrutinize, watch
To stare angrily at someone is to **glare** at them.

start verb
1 *The new course will* **start** *in the autumn.*
begin, commence, (informal) **get going,**

a
b
c
d
e
f
g
h
i
j
k
l
m
n
o
p
q
r
s
t
u
v
w
x
y
z

A B C D E F G H I J K L M N O P Q R **S** T U V W X Y Z

get cracking, kick off
opposites finish, end
2 *We are planning to* start *a book club.*
create, set up, establish, found, institute,
originate, introduce, initiate, open, launch
opposite close
3 *The horses* started *when the gun went off.*
jump, flinch, jerk, twitch, recoil, wince

start noun
1 *Try not to miss the* start *of the film.*
beginning, opening, introduction,
commencement
opposites end, close, finish
2 *She has been with the theatre company
right from the* start.
beginning, outset, creation, inception,
birth, dawn, launch
3 *The explosion gave us all a nasty* start.
jump, jolt, shock, surprise

startle verb
The sudden noise startled *the deer.*
alarm, panic, frighten, scare,
make you start, make you jump, surprise,
take you by surprise

starve verb
Many animals will starve *if the drought
continues.*
die of starvation, go hungry
To choose to go without food is to **fast**.

starving adjective (informal)
What's for dinner? I'm starving!
hungry, famished, ravenous
To be slightly hungry is to be **peckish**.

state noun
1 *The roof of the cottage is in a bad*
state.
condition, shape
The state of a person or animal is their
fitness or health.
2 *He gets into a terrible* state *before
an exam.*
panic, fluster
(informal) flap
3 *The Queen is the head of* state.
country, nation

state verb
Her passport states *that she is an Australian
citizen.*
declare, announce, report, say, proclaim,
pronounce, communicate

stately adjective
The royal banquet will be a stately *occasion.*
grand, dignified, formal, imposing,
majestic, noble, splendid

statement noun
The prime minister made a statement *to the
press.*
announcement, declaration,
communication, report, testimony

station noun
1 *Does the train stop at the next* station?
The station at the end of a line is the
terminus.
For other words to do with trains see
railway.
2 *He was taken to the police* station *for
questioning.*
depot, headquarters
3 *There are two local radio* stations.
channel

station verb
A lookout was stationed *on the roof of the
building.*
place, position, put, stand, situate, locate

stationary adjective
The bus was stuck behind a stationary
vehicle.
still, static, unmoving, immobile,
motionless, standing, at rest
opposite moving

statue noun
There is a statue *of Lord Nelson in Trafalgar
Square.*
figure, sculpture, carving
A small statue is a **statuette**.

status noun
Slaves had a very low status *in Ancient Rome.*
rank, level, position, grade, importance,
prestige

staunch adjective
The Black Knight was a staunch ally of the prince.
firm, strong, faithful, loyal, true, reliable, dependable, steadfast, trusty
opposite unreliable

stay verb
1 *Can you stay there while I park the car?*
wait, hang about, remain
opposites leave, depart
2 *We tried to stay warm by stamping our feet.*
keep, carry on being, continue
3 *Do you plan to stay in America for long?*
live, reside, dwell, lodge, settle, stop

stay noun
Our friends came for a short stay.
visit, stopover, holiday, break

steady adjective
1 *You need a steady hand to be a surgeon.*
stable, balanced, settled, secure, fixed, firm, fast, solid
A common simile is as steady as a rock.
opposites unsteady, shaky
2 *The plants need a steady supply of water.*
continuous, uninterrupted, non-stop, consistent
opposite intermittent
3 *The runners kept up a steady pace.*
regular, constant, even, smooth, rhythmic, unvarying
opposite irregular

steady verb
The crew managed to steady the yacht.
balance, stabilize

steal verb steals, stealing, stole, stolen
1 *The thieves stole several valuable paintings.*
rob, thieve, take, lift, make off with
(informal) pinch, nick, swipe, snaffle
2 *The children stole quietly upstairs.*
creep, sneak, tiptoe, slip, slink

stealing noun
The police have accused him of stealing.
robbery, theft

Stealing from someone's home is burglary or housebreaking.
Stealing from a shop is shoplifting.
Stealing small things is pilfering.

stealthy adjective
We heard stealthy footsteps going upstairs.
furtive, secretive, surreptitious, sly, sneaky, underhand
opposites conspicuous, open

steam noun
Clouds of steam were coming from the cauldron.
vapour, mist, haze
Steam on a cold window is condensation.

steamy adjective
1 *The climate in a jungle is hot and steamy.*
humid, muggy, close, damp, moist
2 *She wiped the steamy mirror.*
misty, hazy, cloudy

steep adjective
The bus inched its way slowly up the steep slope.
abrupt, sudden, sharp
A cliff or drop which is straight up and down is sheer or vertical.
opposites gradual, gentle

steer verb
She steered the car into the parking space.
direct, guide
To steer a vehicle is to drive it.
To steer a boat is to navigate or pilot it.

stem noun
The gardener pulled out the dead stems.
stalk, shoot, twig, branch
The main stem of a tree is its trunk.

stem verb
Chloe blinked, trying to stem the flow of her tears.
stop, check, hold back, restrain, curb

step noun
1 *The baby took her first steps yesterday.*
footstep, pace, stride

a
b
c
d
e
f
g
h
i
j
k
l
m
n
o
p
q
r
s
t
u
v
w
x
y
z

2 *Be careful not to trip on the* step.
doorstep, stair
A set of steps going from one floor of a
building to another is a **staircase**.
A folding set of steps is a **stepladder**.
The steps of a ladder are the **rungs**.
3 *The first* step *in making a cake is to weigh
the ingredients.*
stage, phase, action

step verb
Don't step in the puddle!
put your foot, tread, walk, stamp, trample
to step something up
They have stepped up *security at the
airport.*
increase, intensify, strengthen, boost

sterile adjective
1 *Very little grows in the* sterile *soil of the
desert.*
barren, dry, arid, infertile, lifeless
opposite **fertile**
2 *The nurse put a* sterile *bandage on the
wound.*
sterilized, disinfected, germ-free,
antiseptic, hygienic, clean,
opposite **infected**

stern adjective
The coach gave each of the players a stern
look.
disapproving, unsmiling, severe, strict,
hard, harsh, grim
opposite **lenient**

stew verb
For ways to cook food see **cook**

stick¹ noun
1 *They collected* sticks *to make a fire.*
twig, branch, stalk
2 *The elderly patient walked with a* stick.
cane, rod, staff, pole
A stick used by a conductor is a **baton**.
A stick carried by a police officer is a
truncheon.
A magic stick used by a witch or fairy is
a **wand**.

stick² verb sticks, sticking, stuck
1 *He* stuck *his fork into the potato.*
poke, prod, stab, thrust, dig, jab
2 *She tried to* stick *the broken pieces of china
together.*
glue, paste, cement, bond, join, fasten
3 *The stamp wouldn't* stick *to the envelope.*
adhere, attach, cling
4 *The wheels of the caravan* stuck *fast in
the mud.*
jam, wedge, become trapped
5 (informal) *I can't* stick *people who're
always complaining.*
put up with, stand, tolerate, bear, abide,
endure
to stick out
The shelf sticks out *too far.*
jut out, poke out, project, protrude
to stick up for someone (informal)
She stuck up for *him when he was in
trouble.*
support, defend, side with, stand up for,
speak up for

sticky adjective
1 *Someone had left a blob of* sticky *toffee on
the chair.*
tacky, gummy, gluey
(informal) gooey, icky
2 *I don't like hot* sticky *weather.*
humid, muggy, clammy, close, steamy,
sultry
opposite **dry**
3 (informal) *The pirates came to a* sticky *end.*
grisly, gruesome, horrible, nasty,
unpleasant

stiff adjective
1 *Stir the flour and water to a* stiff *paste.*
firm, hard, solid
A common simile is **as stiff as a poker**.
opposite **soft**
2 *He mounted the picture on* stiff *card.*
rigid, inflexible, thick
opposite **pliable**
3 *Her muscles were* stiff *after the long walk.*
aching, achy, painful, taut, tight
opposite **supple**

A
B
C
D
E
F
G
H
I
J
K
L
M
N
O
P
Q
R
S
T
U
V
W
X
Y
Z

4 *The team face* stiff *competition in the final.*
strong, powerful, tough, difficult
opposite **easy**
5 *His* stiff *manner made him hard to talk to.*
unfriendly, cold, formal, awkward, wooden
opposite **relaxed**
6 *The judge imposed a* stiff *penalty.*
harsh, severe, strict, hard
opposite **lenient**
7 *A* stiff *breeze was blowing.*
strong, brisk, fresh
opposite **gentle**

stifle verb
1 *We were almost* stifled *by the fumes from the exhaust pipe.*
choke, suffocate, smother
To kill someone by stopping their breathing is to **strangle** or **throttle** them.
2 *She tried to* stifle *a yawn.*
suppress, muffle, hold back, repress, restrain

still adjective
1 *The prisoner sat* still *and said nothing.*
motionless, unmoving, stationary, static, inert
2 *It was a beautiful* still *evening.*
calm, peaceful, quiet, tranquil, serene, hushed, silent, noiseless, windless

still verb
I breathed deeply to try to still *my nerves.*
calm, quieten, soothe, lull
opposite **agitate**

stimulate verb
1 *Her travels* stimulated *her to write a book.*
encourage, inspire, spur
2 *The exhibition* stimulated *my interest in painting.*
arouse, rouse, stir up, kindle, excite, provoke, trigger
opposite **discourage**

sting verb stings, stinging, stung
1 *One of the campers was* stung *by a wasp.*
bite, nip
2 *The smoke made our eyes* sting.
smart, hurt, prick, prickle, tingle

stingy adjective (informal)
He's too stingy *to give anyone a birthday card.*
mean, miserly, selfish, uncharitable
(informal) **tight-fisted, penny-pinching**
opposite **generous**

stink verb
The dungeon stank *of unwashed bodies.*
reek, smell
See also **smell**

stink noun
The mouldy cheese gave off a dreadful stink.
odour, stench, reek, bad smell

stir verb
1 Stir *the mixture until it is smooth.*
mix, beat, blend, whisk
2 *The giant* stirred *in his sleep.*
move slightly, shift, toss, turn
to stir something up
The bandits were always stirring up *trouble.*
arouse, encourage, provoke, set off, trigger, whip up

stir noun
The news caused quite a stir.
fuss, commotion, excitement, hullabaloo

stock noun
1 Stocks *of food were running low.*
supply, store, reserve, hoard, stockpile
2 *The shopkeeper arranged his new* stock.
goods, merchandise, wares
3 *The duke is descended from royal* stock.
descent, ancestry, family, line

stock verb
Most supermarkets now stock *organic food.*
sell, carry, trade in, deal in, keep in stock

stocky adjective
The wrestler had a strong stocky *body.*
dumpy, squat, thickset, solid, sturdy
opposite **thin**

stodgy adjective
1 *The pudding was rich and* stodgy.
heavy, solid, starchy, filling
opposite **light**

a
b
c
d
e
f
g
h
i
j
k
l
m
n
o
p
q
r
s
t
u
v
w
x
y
z

2 *I'm finding the book a bit* stodgy.
boring, dull, uninteresting, slow, tedious
opposite **lively**

stole
past tense see **steal**

stomach noun
He rolled over and lay on his stomach.
belly, gut, paunch
(informal) tummy
The part of the body that contains the stomach is the abdomen.

stomach verb
I can't stomach *watching horror films.*
stand, bear, put up with, tolerate, take

stone noun
The columns of the temple were carved from stone.
A large lump of stone is a rock.
A large rounded stone is a boulder.
Small rounded stones are pebbles.
A mixture of sand and small stones is gravel.
Pebbles on the beach are shingle.
Round stones used to pave a path are cobbles.
For precious stones see **jewel**

stony adjective
1 *The waves broke over the* stony *beach.*
pebbly, rocky, shingly
opposite **sandy**
2 *There was a* stony *silence in the room.*
unfriendly, cold, hostile, frosty, icy
opposites **warm, friendly**

stood
past tense see **stand**

stoop verb
We had to stoop *to go through the tunnel.*
bend, duck, bow, crouch

stop verb
1 *I'll go into town when the rain* stops.
end, finish, cease, conclude, terminate
opposite **start**

2 *Can you* stop *talking for a minute?*
give up, cease, suspend, quit, leave off, break off
(informal) knock off, pack in
opposites **continue, resume**
3 *Guards,* stop *that man!*
hold, detain, seize, catch, capture, restrain
4 *You can't* stop *me from going.*
prevent, obstruct, bar, hinder
5 *How do you* stop *this machine?*
turn off, immobilize
6 *The bus will* stop *at the school gates.*
come to a stop, halt, pull up, draw up
7 *If you tighten the valve, it will* stop *the leak.*
close, plug, seal, block up, bung up

stop noun
1 *Everything suddenly came to a* stop.
end, finish, conclusion, halt, standstill
2 *They drove down through France, with a short* stop *in Paris.*
break, pause, stopover, rest

store verb
Squirrels need to store *food for the winter.*
save, set aside, stow away, hoard, reserve, stockpile
(informal) stash

store noun
1 *The building is now used as a grain* store.
storeroom, storehouse, repository, vault
A store for food is a larder or pantry.
A store for weapons is an armoury or arsenal.
2 *He kept a large* store *of wine in the cellar.*
hoard, supply, quantity, stock, stockpile, reserve
3 *He's the manager of the local grocery* store.
See also **shop**

storey noun
The new building has six storeys.
floor, level, tier

storm noun
1 *Crops were damaged in the heavy* storms.
squall, blizzard, gale, thunderstorm, hurricane, typhoon

A
B
C
D
E
F
G
H
I
J
K
L
M
N
O
P
Q
R
S
T
U
V
W
X
Y
Z

An old word for storm is **tempest**.
When a storm begins to develop it is **brewing**.
See also **weather**

2 *Plans to close the library caused a* storm *of protest.*
outburst, outcry, uproar, clamour

storm verb
The soldiers stormed *the castle.*
charge at, rush at, attack

stormy adjective
1 *It was a dark,* stormy *night.*
blustery, squally, tempestuous, wild, windy, rough, choppy, gusty, raging
opposite **calm**
2 *Fighting broke out at the end of a* stormy *meeting.*
bad-tempered, quarrelsome, turbulent, violent

story noun
Peter Pan is a story *about a boy who never grew up.*
tale
(informal) yarn

WORD WEB
VARIOUS KINDS OF STORY
adventure story, bedtime story, crime story, detective story, fable, fairy tale, fantasy, folk tale, ghost story, horror story, legend, love story, mystery, myth, narrative poem, novel, parable, romance, saga, science fiction or SF, short story, spy story, thriller

Invented stories are **fiction**.

For other types of writing see **writing**
The book tells the story *of her childhood in New York.*
account, history, narrative

A story of a person's life is a **biography**.
The story of your life, told by you, is your **autobiography**.

It was the front-page story *in all the papers.*
article, item, feature, report, piece
(informal) lie, fib
Have you been telling stories *again?*

stout adjective
1 *The doctor was a* stout *man with grey hair.*
fat, plump, chubby, dumpy, tubby, portly, stocky, beefy, burly
opposite **thin**
2 *You will need a pair of* stout *walking boots.*
strong, sturdy, tough, robust, sound, substantial
opposite **weak**
3 *The enemy put up a* stout *resistance.*
brave, courageous, spirited, plucky, determined, staunch, resolute, firm
opposite **cowardly**

stow verb
They stowed *the boxes in the attic.*
store, put away, pack, pile, load

straight adjective
1 *They walked in a* straight *line.*
direct, unswerving
A common simile is as straight as an arrow.
opposite **crooked**
2 *It took a long time to get the room* straight.
neat, orderly, tidy
opposite **untidy**
3 *She found it difficult to get a* straight *answer from him.*
honest, plain, frank, straightforward
opposites **indirect, evasive**

straightforward adjective
The cake recipe is fairly straightforward.
simple, plain, uncomplicated, easy, clear, direct
opposite **complicated**

strain verb
1 *The dog was* straining *at its lead.*
pull, tug, stretch, haul

a
b
c
d
e
f
g
h
i
j
k
l
m
n
o
p
q
r
s
t
u
v
w
x
y
z

A
B
C
D
E
F
G
H
I
J
K
L
M
N
O
P
Q
R

S

T
U
V
W
X
Y
Z

2 *People were straining to see what was going on.*
struggle, strive, make an effort, try, attempt
3 *Take it easy and don't strain yourself.*
weaken, exhaust, wear out, tire out, tax

strain noun
The strain of her job was making her ill.
stress, tension, worry, anxiety, pressure

strand noun
The strands of the wool began to unravel.
fibre, filament, thread

stranded adjective
1 *A whale lay stranded on the beach.*
run aground, beached, marooned
2 *He was stranded in London without any money.*
abandoned, deserted, helpless, lost, stuck
(informal) high and dry

strange adjective
1 *A strange thing happened this morning.*
funny, odd, peculiar, unusual, abnormal, curious, extraordinary, remarkable, singular, uncommon
opposites ordinary, everyday
2 *Did you hear strange noises in the night?*
mysterious, puzzling, baffling, mystifying, perplexing, bewildering, inexplicable
3 *The professor showed us his strange inventions.*
weird, eccentric, peculiar, bizarre
(informal) oddball, wacky
4 *I find it hard to get to sleep in a strange bed.*
unfamiliar, unknown, new, alien
opposite familiar

stranger noun
A stranger stopped us and asked for directions to the castle.
newcomer, outsider, visitor, foreigner

strangle verb
The victim had been strangled.
throttle

strap noun
The trunk was fastened with a leather strap.
belt, band

strategy noun
The school has a strategy to deal with bullying.
plan, policy, procedure, approach, scheme, programme

stray verb
Some sheep had strayed onto the road.
wander, drift, roam, rove, straggle, meander, ramble

streak noun
1 *The horse had a white streak on his muzzle.*
band, line, stripe, strip, smear, stain
2 *There is a streak of meanness in his character.*
element, trace

streak verb
1 *Rain had begun to streak the window.*
smear, smudge, stain, line
2 *A group of motorbikes streaked past.*
rush, speed, dash, fly, hurtle, flash, tear, zoom

stream noun
1 *The climbers dipped their feet in the cool mountain stream.*
brook, rivulet
(Scottish) burn
2 *The raft was carried along with the stream.*
current, flow, tide
3 *A stream of water poured through the hole.*
cataract, flood, gush, jet, rush, torrent
4 *The museum had a steady stream of visitors.*
series, string, line, succession

stream verb
Warm sunlight streamed through the window.
pour, flow, flood, issue, gush, spill

street noun
see road

strength noun

1 *Hercules was said to have enormous strength.*
power, might, muscle, brawn, toughness, force, vigour
2 *The main strength of the team is in scoring goals.*
strong point, asset, advantage
opposite weakness

strengthen verb

1 *Regular exercise strengthens your muscles.*
make stronger, build up, toughen, harden
2 *Concrete was used to strengthen the tunnel.*
fortify, reinforce, bolster, prop up
opposite weaken

strenuous adjective

1 *We are making strenuous efforts to recycle our rubbish.*
determined, strong, vigorous, energetic, resolute
opposite feeble
2 *The doctor told him to avoid strenuous exercise.*
hard, tough, difficult, demanding, tiring, exhausting
opposite easy

stress noun

1 *The hospital staff were working under a lot of stress.*
strain, pressure, tension, worry, anxiety
2 *My piano teacher puts great stress on the need to practise.*
emphasis, importance, weight

stress verb

She stressed the need for absolute secrecy.
emphasize, draw attention to, highlight, underline

stretch verb

1 *He stretched the rubber band until it snapped.*
expand, extend, draw out, pull out, elongate, lengthen
2 *She stretched her arms wide.*
extend, open out, spread out

3 *The road stretched into the distance.*
continue, extend

stretch noun

1 *He had a two-year stretch in the army.*
spell, period, time, stint
2 *There are often accidents on this stretch of road.*
section, length, piece
3 *It's a beautiful stretch of countryside.*
area, tract, expanse, sweep

strict adjective

1 *The club has strict rules about who can join.*
rigid, inflexible
(informal) **hard and fast**
opposite flexible
2 *The sergeant was known for being strict with his men.*
harsh, severe, stern, firm
opposite lenient
3 *He used the word in its strict scientific sense.*
exact, precise, correct
opposite loose

stride noun

The robot took two strides forward.
pace, step

strike verb strikes, striking, struck

1 *Roy struck his head on the low ceiling.*
bang, bump, hit, knock, thump, collide with
(informal) **wallop, whack**
2 *The enemy could strike again at any time.*
attack
3 *The clock struck one.*
chime, ring

striking adjective

The most striking feature of the mermaid was her iridescent tail.
conspicuous, noticeable, prominent, remarkable, memorable, extraordinary, outstanding, impressive
opposite inconspicuous

a
b
c
d
e
f
g
h
i
j
k
l
m
n
o
p
q
r
s
t
u
v
w
x
y
z

string noun

1 *She tied some* string *round the parcel.*
rope, cord, twine
For musical instruments with strings see
music
2 *They have received a* string *of complaints.*
series, succession, chain, sequence

string verb strings, stringing, strung

We strung the lights on the Christmas tree.
hang, arrange, thread

stringy adjective

This meat is very stringy.
chewy, fibrous, tough
opposite **tender**

strip¹ verb

1 *Lottie* stripped *the paper off her present.*
peel, remove
opposites **cover, wrap**
2 *He* stripped *and got into the bath.*
get undressed, undress
opposite **dress**

strip² noun

In front of the house was a strip *of grass.*
band, length, ribbon, piece, bit

stripe noun

The tablecloth was white with blue stripes.
line, strip, band, bar

strive verb strives, striving, strove, striven

Each athlete strives *to do his or her best.*
try hard, aim, attempt, endeavour

stroke¹ noun

1 *He split the log with a single* stroke.
blow, hit, action, movement, effort
2 *She added a few quick pencil* strokes *to her drawing.*
line, mark

stroke² verb

Jess was curled up on the sofa, stroking *the cat.*
pat, caress, rub, touch, fondle, pet

stroll verb

The children strolled *quietly home.*
walk slowly, amble, saunter

strong adjective

OVERUSED WORD

Try to vary the words you use for **strong**.
Here are some other words you could use.

FOR A **STRONG PERSON** OR **STRONG BODY**
powerful, muscular, mighty, well-built,
beefy, brawny, burly, strapping
Crocodiles have powerful *jaws.*
opposites **weak, puny**

A common simile is as **strong** as an ox.

FOR **STRONG MATERIAL**
robust, sturdy, tough, hard-wearing,
durable, stout, substantial
The tent is made from hard-wearing
material.
opposites **thin, flimsy**

FOR A **STRONG LIGHT** OR **STRONG COLOUR**
bright, brilliant, dazzling, glaring
The fugitive was caught in the glaring
beam of a searchlight.
opposites **weak, pale**

FOR A **STRONG FLAVOUR** OR **STRONG SMELL**
overpowering, pronounced, pungent,
piquant
I smelt the pungent *aroma of coffee.*
opposites **faint, slight**

FOR A **STRONG ARGUMENT** OR **STRONG CASE**
convincing, persuasive, effective, sound,
solid, valid
The police have solid *evidence of his guilt.*
opposites **weak, feeble, flimsy**

FOR A **STRONG INTEREST** OR **STRONG SUPPORTER**
enthusiastic, keen, passionate, fervent,
avid, zealous
Zelda takes a keen *interest in fashion.*
opposite **slight**

A B C D E F G H I J K L M N O P Q R **S** T U V W X Y Z

struck
past tense see **strike**

structure noun
1 *The pagoda is a magnificent* structure.
building, construction, framework
2 *Can you explain the* structure *of the poem?*
design, plan, shape, arrangement,
organization

struggle verb
1 *The captives* struggled *to get free.*
strain, strive, wrestle, writhe about, tussle,
fight, battle
2 *The expedition had to* struggle *through a
snowstorm.*
stagger, stumble, flounder, labour

struggle noun
1 *The rebels surrendered without a* struggle.
fight, battle, combat, clash, contest
2 *It was a* struggle *to keep going in the
blazing heat.*
effort, exertion, problem, difficulty

stubborn adjective
She's too stubborn *to admit that she was
wrong.*
obstinate, pig-headed, strong-willed,
uncooperative, inflexible, wilful
A common simile is as stubborn as a mule.
opposite **compliant**

stuck
past tense see **stick²**

stud verb
studded with
The lid of the chest was studded *with jewels.*
inlaid with, encrusted with

student noun
A student *at school is a* pupil.
An old word for a pupil is scholar.

studious adjective
Sadiq is a quiet, studious *boy.*
hard-working, diligent, scholarly,
academic, bookish

study verb
1 *He went to university to* study *medicine.*
learn about, read, research into
2 *The spy* studied *the document carefully.*
examine, inspect, analyse, investigate,
look closely at, scrutinize, survey
3 *She has to* study *for her exams.*
revise, cram
(informal) swot

stuff noun
1 *What's that sticky* stuff *on the carpet?*
matter, substance
2 *You can put your* stuff *in one of the lockers.*
belongings, possessions, things, gear

stuff verb
1 *We managed to* stuff *everything into the
boot of the car.*
pack, push, shove, squeeze, ram, compress,
force, cram, jam
2 *The cushions are* stuffed *with foam
rubber.*
fill, pad

stuffy adjective
1 *Open a window—it's* stuffy *in here.*
airless, close, muggy, humid, stifling,
musty, unventilated
opposite **airy**
2 *I found the book a bit* stuffy.
boring, dull, dreary, pompous, stodgy
opposite **lively**

stumble verb
1 *He* stumbled *on a tree root and twisted his
ankle.*
trip, stagger, totter, flounder, lurch
2 *The actress* stumbled *over her words.*
stammer, stutter, falter, hesitate
to stumble across something
I stumbled across *some old photos.*
come across, encounter, find, unearth,
discover

stump verb
The detective was stumped *by the case.*
baffle, bewilder, perplex, puzzle, fox,
mystify, outwit, defeat
(informal) flummox

a
b
c
d
e
f
g
h
i
j
k
l
m
n
o
p
q
r
s
t
u
v
w
x
y
z

A
B
C
D
E
F
G
H
I
J
K
L
M
N
O
P
Q
R
S
T
U
V
W
X
Y
Z

stun verb
1 *The pilot was alive but* stunned.
daze, knock out, knock senseless, make unconscious
2 *The whole town was* stunned *by the news.*
amaze, astonish, astound, shock, stagger, stupefy, bewilder, dumbfound

stunt noun
The acrobats performed breathtaking stunts.
feat, exploit, act, deed, trick

stupid adjective
1 *Trolls are often very* stupid.
foolish, unintelligent, dense, dim, dim-witted, brainless, dumb, slow, thick, feeble-minded, half-witted, simple, simple-minded, dopey, dull
2 *It would be* stupid *to go snowboarding without a helmet.*
senseless, mindless, idiotic, unwise, foolhardy, silly, daft, crazy, mad
opposite **intelligent**

sturdy adjective
1 *Shetland ponies are short and* sturdy.
stocky, strong, robust, athletic, brawny, burly, healthy, hefty, husky, muscular, powerful, vigorous, well-built
opposite **weak**
2 *She bought some* sturdy *walking boots.*
durable, solid, sound, substantial, tough, well made
opposite **flimsy**

stutter verb
He tends to stutter *when he's nervous.*
stammer, stumble, falter

style noun
1 *I don't like that* style *of jeans.*
design, pattern, fashion
2 *The book is written in an informal* style.
manner, tone, way, wording
3 *The actress always dresses with great* style.
elegance, stylishness, taste, sophistication

stylish adjective
Jacqueline always wears stylish *clothes.*
fashionable, elegant, chic, smart, sophisticated, tasteful
(informal) trendy, snazzy
opposite **unfashionable**

subdue verb
1 *The army managed to* subdue *the rebels.*
beat, conquer, defeat, overcome, overpower, crush, vanquish
2 *Jason tried hard to* subdue *his anger.*
suppress, restrain, repress, check, hold back, curb, control

subject noun
1 *Do you have any strong views on the* subject?
matter, issue, question, point, theme, topic
2 *Her passport shows that she is a British* subject.
citizen, national

subject verb
The press subjected *him to a string of questions.*
expose, submit, lay open

submerge verb
1 *The submarine* submerged *slowly.*
dive, go down, go under
opposite **surface**
2 *The tsunami* submerged *several coastal villages.*
engulf, flood, drown, immerse, inundate, swallow up

submit verb
1 *The swordsman finally* submitted *to his opponent.*
give in, surrender, yield
2 *You need to* submit *a membership form to join the club.*
give in, hand in, present

subordinate adjective
He began as a police officer of subordinate *rank.*
junior, lesser, lower, inferior
opposites **superior, higher**

subscribe verb
to subscribe to
She subscribes to *several good causes.*
contribute to, donate to, give to, support

subsequent adjective
I missed the first episode and two subsequent ones.
later, succeeding, following, ensuing, next
opposite previous

subside verb
1 *One side of the old cottage has started to subside.*
sink, settle
2 *After three days, the flood waters began to subside.*
go down, fall, recede, decline, ebb
3 *The pain will eventually subside.*
decrease, diminish, lessen, die down, dwindle

substance noun
1 *The spaceship was made from an alien substance.*
material, matter, stuff
2 *What was the substance of the book?*
theme, essence, gist, subject matter

substantial adjective
1 *They have made substantial improvements to the city.*
considerable, significant, sizeable, worthwhile, big, large, generous
opposite small
2 *There is a substantial fence to keep out wild animals.*
strong, sturdy, solid, robust, hefty, durable, sound, well-built
opposite flimsy

substitute verb
You can substitute margarine for butter in the recipe.
exchange, swap, switch

> You can also say: *'Margarine can take the place of butter.'* or: *'You can replace butter with margarine.'*

to substitute for someone
He substituted for the injured goalkeeper.
stand in for, take the place of, deputize for

substitute noun
The manager brought on a substitute during extra time.
replacement, reserve, standby, stand-in
A substitute for a sick actor is an understudy.

subtle adjective
1 *There was a subtle smell of roses in the air.*
faint, slight, mild, delicate
2 *His jokes are too subtle for most people.*
ingenious, sophisticated
3 *I tried to give her a subtle hint.*
gentle, tactful, indirect
opposite obvious

subtract verb
If you subtract 5 from 20, you will have 15.
take away, deduct, remove
opposite add

succeed verb
1 *You have to work hard if you want to succeed.*
be successful, do well, prosper, flourish, thrive
(informal) **make it**
2 *Everyone hoped that the plan would succeed.*
be effective, produce results, work
(informal) **catch on**
opposite fail
3 *Edward VII succeeded Queen Victoria.*
come after, follow, take over from, replace

success noun
1 *She talked about her success as an actress.*
achievement, attainment, fame
2 *They congratulated the team on their success.*
victory, win, triumph

a
b
c
d
e
f
g
h
i
j
k
l
m
n
o
p
q
r
s
t
u
v
w
x
y
z

A B C D E F G H I J K L M N O P Q R **S** T U V W X Y Z

3 *The group's last CD was a great* success.
hit, bestseller
(informal) winner
4 *The* success *of the mission depends on the astronauts.*
effectiveness, successfulness, successful outcome, completion
opposite failure

successful adjective
1 *She owns a very* successful *chain of restaurants.*
thriving, flourishing, booming, prosperous, profitable, popular
2 *The supporters cheered the* successful *team.*
winning, victorious, triumphant
opposite unsuccessful

succession noun
Arthur received a succession *of mysterious emails.*
series, sequence, run, string, chain

successive adjective
It rained on seven successive *days.*
consecutive, uninterrupted

You can also say: *it rained on several days in succession.*

suck verb
to suck something up
A sponge will suck up *water.*
soak up, draw up, absorb

sudden adjective
1 *Maria felt a* sudden *urge to burst into song.*
unexpected, unforeseen, impulsive, rash, quick
opposite expected
2 *The bus came to a* sudden *halt.*
abrupt, sharp, swift
opposite gradual

suffer verb
1 *He* suffers *terribly with his back.*
feel pain, hurt

2 *He will* suffer *for his crime.*
be punished, pay
3 *The home team* suffered *a humiliating defeat.*
experience, undergo, go through, endure, withstand, bear, tolerate

suffering noun
The people endured great suffering *during the war.*
hardship, deprivation, misery, anguish, pain, distress

sufficient adjective
The castaways had sufficient *food for a few days.*
enough, adequate, satisfactory
opposite insufficient

suffix noun
opposite prefix

suffocate verb
The firefighters were nearly suffocated *by the fumes.*
choke, stifle
To stop someone's breathing by squeezing their throat is to strangle or throttle them. To stop someone's breathing by covering their nose and mouth is to smother them.

suggest verb
1 *Mum* suggested *going to the zoo.*
propose, advise, advocate, recommend
2 *Her comments* suggest *that she's not happy.*
imply, hint, indicate, signal

suggestion noun
They didn't like his suggestion.
proposal, plan, idea, proposition, recommendation

suit verb
1 *Would it* suit *you to stay here overnight?*
be convenient for, be suitable for, please, satisfy
opposite displease

2 *His new haircut doesn't* **suit** *him.*
look good on, become, flatter

suitable adjective

1 *Please wear clothes* **suitable** *for wet weather.*
appropriate, apt, fitting, suited (to), proper, right
opposite unsuitable
2 *Is this a* **suitable** *time to have a chat?*
convenient, acceptable, satisfactory
opposite inconvenient

sulk verb

I was **sulking** *because I wasn't allowed to play outside.*
be sullen, mope, brood, pout

sulky adjective

Ron had turned into a **sulky** *teenager.*
moody, sullen, brooding, moping, mopey

sullen adjective

Beth slouched on the sofa, looking **sullen.**
sulky, moody, bad-tempered, mopey, morose, surly, sour
opposites cheerful, good-tempered

sum noun

1 *The* **sum** *of 2 and 2 is 4.*
total, result
2 *They lost a large* **sum** *of money.*
amount, quantity
sums
Desmond is good at doing **sums.**
adding up, arithmetic
(informal) maths
For other mathematical terms see
mathematics

sum verb

to sum up
see **summarize**

summarize verb

Can you **summarize** *the main points of the story?*
sum up, outline, review
(informal) recap

summary noun

We each wrote a **summary** *of the poem.*
synopsis, precis, outline

summit noun

The **summit** *of the mountain was shrouded in mist.*
top, cap, peak, tip
opposite base

summon verb

The king **summoned** *his knights from far and wide.*
call, send for, order to come, bid to come
To ask someone politely to come is to **invite** them.

sun noun

They went out into the garden to sit in the sun.
sunshine, sunlight
To sit or lie in the sun is to **sunbathe.**

sunlight noun

Most plants can only grow in **sunlight.**
daylight, sun, sunshine
Rays of light from the sun are **sunbeams.**

sunny adjective

1 *It was a beautiful* **sunny** *day.*
fine, clear, cloudless
opposite cloudy
2 *The flat has a large,* **sunny** *living room.*
bright, sunlit, cheerful
opposite gloomy
A place that gets a lot of sunshine is **sunbaked.**
See also **weather**

sunrise noun

The magic spell wears off at **sunrise.**
dawn, daybreak
opposite sunset

sunset noun

They arranged to meet in the churchyard at **sunset.**
sundown, dusk, twilight, evening, nightfall
opposite sunrise

A B C D E F G H I J K L M N O P Q R **S** T U V W X Y Z

superb adjective
Brazil scored another superb goal.
excellent, outstanding, exceptional, remarkable, impressive, magnificent, marvellous, splendid, tremendous, wonderful
(informal) brilliant, fantastic, terrific, fabulous, sensational, super
For other ways to describe something good see good

superficial adjective
1 *The scratch on his leg was only superficial.*
on the surface, shallow, slight
opposite deep
2 *The book gives a very superficial view of history.*
simple, trivial, lightweight, shallow, frivolous, casual
opposites thorough, profound

superior adjective
1 *A colonel is superior in rank to a captain.*
senior, higher, greater
2 *They only sell chocolate of superior quality.*
first-class, first-rate, top, top-notch, choice, select, better
3 *I don't like her superior attitude.*
arrogant, haughty, snobbish, stuck-up, self-important
(informal) snooty
opposite inferior

supernatural adjective
The fortune-teller claimed to have supernatural powers.
magic, magical, miraculous
opposite natural

supervise verb
Children must be supervised by an adult in the park.
oversee, superintend, watch over, be in charge of, be responsible for, direct, manage
To supervise candidates in an exam is to invigilate.

supple adjective
The moccasins are made of supple leather.
flexible, pliable, soft
opposites stiff, rigid

supplementary adjective
There is a supplementary charge for postage.
additional, extra

supply verb
The art shop can supply you with paints.
provide, equip, furnish

supply noun
They had a good supply of fuel for the winter.
quantity, stock, store, reserve
supplies
We bought supplies for the camping trip.
provisions, stores, rations, food, necessities

support noun
1 *She thanked them for their support.*
assistance, backing, aid, cooperation, encouragement, help
2 *The cinema was reopened with support from local businesses.*
donations, contributions, sponsorship
3 *The supports prevented the wall from collapsing.*
prop, brace
A support for a shelf is a bracket.
A support built against a wall is a buttress.
A support for someone with an injured leg is a crutch.
A bar of wood or metal supporting a framework is a strut.
A support put under a board to make a table is a trestle.

support verb
1 *The rope couldn't support his weight.*
bear, carry, stand, hold up
2 *The beams support the roof.*
prop up, strengthen, reinforce
3 *His friends supported him when he was in trouble.*
aid, assist, help, back, encourage, stand by, stand up for, rally round
4 *She had to work to support her family.*
maintain, keep, provide for

5 *He supports several local charities.*
donate to, contribute to, give to
6 *Which team did you support in the World Cup?*
be a supporter of, follow

supporter noun
1 *The home supporters cheered their team.*
fan, follower
2 *She is a well-known supporter of animal rights.*
champion, advocate, backer, defender

suppose verb
1 *I suppose you want to borrow some money.*
expect, presume, assume, guess, believe, think
2 *Suppose a spaceship landed in your garden!*
imagine, pretend, fancy
to be supposed to do something
The bus is supposed to leave at 9 o'clock.
be meant to, be due to, be expected to, ought to

suppress verb
1 *He managed to suppress his anger.*
check, hold back, contain, control, repress, restrain, curb, bottle up, stifle
To suppress ideas for political or moral reasons is to **censor** them.
2 *The army suppressed the rebellion.*
crush, quash, quell, put down, stamp out, stop, subdue

supreme adjective
Her supreme achievement was winning a medal.
greatest, highest, best, outstanding, top

sure adjective
1 *I'm sure that I'm right.*
certain, convinced, confident, definite, positive
opposites unsure, uncertain
2 *He's sure to phone tonight.*
bound, certain
opposite unlikely
3 *A high temperature is a sure sign of illness.*
clear, definite, true, undoubted, undeniable
opposites unclear, doubtful

surface noun
1 *The surface of Mars is barren and rocky.*
exterior, outside
The surface of something may be covered with a **crust** or **shell** or **skin**.
A thin surface of expensive wood on furniture is a **veneer**.
opposite centre
2 *A dice has dots on each surface.*
face, side
opposite inside
3 *Oil floated on the surface of the water.*
top
opposite bottom

surface verb
1 *The road is surfaced with cobbles.*
cover, coat
2 *The head of an alligator surfaced in the river.*
rise to the surface, come up, emerge, appear
(informal) **pop up**

surge verb
1 *Massive waves surged around the tiny raft.*
rise, roll, swirl, heave, billow
2 *The crowd surged forward.*
rush, push, sweep

surpass verb
It will be hard to surpass last year's performance.
beat, exceed, do better than, outdo

surplus noun
Farmers have produced a surplus of apples this year.
excess, glut, surfeit, oversupply
opposites shortage, lack

surprise noun
The news that Sara was married came as a surprise.
shock, revelation
(informal) **bombshell; amazement, astonishment, wonder**

a
b
c
d
e
f
g
h
i
j
k
l
m
n
o
p
q
r
s
t
u
v
w
x
y
z

A
B
C
D
E
F
G
H
I
J
K
L
M
N
O
P
Q
R
S
T
U
V
W
X
Y
Z

surprise verb

1 *I was surprised by how well she could sing.*
amaze, astonish, astound, stagger,
startle, stun, take aback, take by surprise,
dumbfound
(informal) bowl over, flabbergast
2 *He surprised the burglars as they came
through the window.*
discover, come upon, catch unawares,
catch off guard, catch red-handed

surprised adjective

WRITING TIPS

SOMEONE WHO **FEELS SURPRISED** MIGHT
**have eyes bulging out of their head,
have eyes on the end of stalks,
jump out of their skin, stare wide-eyed**

SOMETHING WHICH **SURPRISES YOU** MIGHT
**knock you for six, knock your socks off,
knock you sideways,
make your eyes pop**

For things you might say when surprised
see **exclamation**

surprising adjective

*There are a surprising number of errors in the
book.*
amazing, astonishing, astounding,
extraordinary, remarkable, incredible,
staggering, startling, stunning, unexpected
opposite predictable

surrender verb

1 *The band of outlaws refused to surrender.*
admit defeat, give in, yield, submit,
capitulate
2 *Please surrender your ticket to the driver.*
give, hand over

surround verb

1 *The garden was surrounded by a stone
wall.*
enclose, fence in, wall in
2 *The pack of wolves surrounded its prey.*
encircle, ring, hem in, besiege

surroundings plural noun

The hotel is set in very pleasant surroundings.
setting, location, environment

survey noun

1 *They did a survey of local leisure facilities.*
review, investigation, study
A survey to count the population of an area
is a **census**.
2 *The builders did a survey of the house.*
inspection, examination

survey verb

1 *You can survey the whole valley from the
top of the tower.*
view, look over, look at, observe
2 *They surveyed the damage done by the
storm.*
inspect, examine, scrutinize, study
3 *The builders will need to survey the area.*
map out, plan out, measure

survive verb

1 *He managed to survive alone on the island
for six months.*
stay alive, last, live, keep going, carry on,
continue
opposite die
2 *Ada survived her husband by twenty years.*
outlast
3 *Will the birds survive this cold weather?*
endure, withstand, live through, weather

suspect verb

1 *The police suspected his motives.*
doubt, mistrust, have suspicions about
2 *I suspect that the shop will be closed on
Sundays.*
expect, imagine, presume, guess, sense,
fancy

suspend verb

1 *The meeting was suspended until the next
day.*
adjourn, break off, discontinue,
interrupt
2 *For the party, we suspended balloons from
the ceiling.*
hang, dangle, swing

suspense noun
The film was a thriller, full of action and suspense.
tension, uncertainty, anticipation, expectancy, drama, excitement

suspicion noun
I have a suspicion that he is lying.
feeling, hunch, inkling, intuition, impression

suspicious adjective
1 *There is something about him which makes me suspicious.*
doubtful, distrustful, mistrustful, unsure, uneasy, wary
opposite trusting
2 *What do you make of his suspicious behaviour?*
questionable, suspect, dubious, shady (informal) fishy

sustain verb
1 *Squirrels store nuts to sustain them through the winter.*
keep going, nurture, provide for
2 *The runners couldn't sustain the high speed.*
keep up, maintain
3 *Will the bridge sustain his weight?*
support, bear, carry, stand

swagger verb
The lead actor swaggered about on stage.
strut, parade

swallow verb
The bread was so dry that it was hard to swallow.
gulp down
For other ways to eat and drink see **eat, drink**
to swallow something up
As it climbed higher, the rocket was swallowed up by the clouds.
envelop, engulf, cover over, absorb

swam
past tense see **swim**

swamp verb
A huge wave threatened to swamp the ship.
overwhelm, engulf, inundate, flood, submerge

swamp noun
Much of the land near the coast is swamp.
marsh, bog, mire, fen, quicksand, quagmire

swan noun
A female swan is a **pen**.
A male swan is a **cob**.
A young swan is a **cygnet**.

swap or swop verb
We swapped seats so I could sit in the aisle.
change, exchange, switch, substitute

swarm verb
Hundreds of people swarmed around the film star.
crowd, flock
to swarm with
The garden is swarming with ants.
be overrun by, be crawling with, be infested with, teem with

sway verb
The tall grass swayed in the breeze.
wave, swing, rock, bend, lean

swear verb swears, swearing, swore, sworn
1 *The knight swore that he would protect the unicorn.*
pledge, promise, vow, give your word, take an oath
2 *The player swore when he bashed his knee.*
curse

sweat verb
He sweats a lot in hot weather.
perspire

sweaty adjective
When I'm nervous, my palms get sweaty.
sweating, perspiring, clammy, sticky, moist

a
b
c
d
e
f
g
h
i
j
k
l
m
n
o
p
q
r
s
t
u
v
w
x
y
z

sweep verb
1 *She swept the floor with an old broom.*
brush, clean, dust
2 *The bus swept past.*
shoot, speed, zoom
to sweep something away
1 *He tried to sweep away the rubbish.*
clear away, get rid of, remove
2 *The flood swept away several houses.*
destroy, flatten, level

sweet adjective
1 *The pudding is too sweet for me.*
sickly, sugary, sweetened, syrupy
opposite **acid** or **bitter** or **savoury**
2 *The sweet smell of roses filled the room.*
fragrant, pleasant
opposite **foul**
3 *Fergus heard the sweet sound of a harp.*
melodious, pleasant, soothing, tuneful
opposite **ugly**
4 *What a sweet little cottage!*
attractive, charming, dear, lovely, pretty, quaint
opposite **unattractive**

sweet noun
1 *The bag contained a mixture of sweets.*
An American word is candy.
A formal word for sweets is confectionery.
2 *We had rhubarb crumble as our sweet.*
dessert, pudding

sweet noun

WORD WEB
SOME KINDS OF SWEET
barley sugar, boiled sweet, bull's-eye, butterscotch, candyfloss, caramel, chewing gum, chocolate, fruit pastille, fudge, humbug, liquorice, lollipop, marshmallow, marzipan, mint or peppermint, nougat, rock, tablet, toffee, Turkish delight

swell verb swells, swelling, swelled, swollen or swelled
The balloon swelled as it filled with hot air.
expand, inflate, bulge, grow, enlarge, puff up, billow
opposite **shrink**

swelling noun
He had a painful swelling on his foot.
inflammation, lump, bump, growth
A **tumour** is a serious swelling on the body.

swerve verb
The car swerved to avoid a hedgehog.
turn aside, veer, dodge, swing

swift adjective
1 *They set off at a swift pace.*
fast, quick, rapid, speedy, brisk, lively
2 *She received a swift reply to her email.*
quick, fast, immediate, instant, prompt, speedy, snappy
opposite **slow**

swim verb swims, swimming, swam, swum
We swam in the sea on our holiday.
go swimming, bathe, take a dip

WORD WEB
VARIOUS SWIMMING STROKES
backstroke, breaststroke, butterfly, crawl, doggy-paddle

PLACES WHERE YOU CAN SWIM
baths, leisure pool, lido, paddling pool, swimming bath or swimming pool

CLOTHING FOR SWIMMING
bathing costume, bathing suit, bikini, swimming cap, swimming costume, swimsuit, trunks

OTHER EQUIPMENT FOR SWIMMING
armbands, flippers, float, goggles, nose-clip, rubber ring, snorkel

swindle verb
He swindled them out of a lot of money.
cheat, trick, dupe, fleece
(informal) con, diddle

A B C D E F G H I J K L M N O P Q R **S** T U V W X Y Z

swing verb swings, swinging, swung
1 *A glass chandelier swung from the ceiling.*
hang, dangle, sway, flap, wave about
2 *She swung round when I called her name.*
turn, twist, veer, swerve

swipe verb
The polar bear swiped the seal with its paw.
swing at, hit, strike, slash
For other ways to hit things see **hit**

swirl verb
Clouds of dust swirled up in the desert wind.
spin, twirl, whirl, churn

switch verb
1 *Please remember to switch off the light.*
turn
2 *The teams will switch ends at half-time.*
change, swap, exchange, shift

swivel verb
The dentist swivelled round in her chair.
spin, turn, twirl, pivot, revolve, rotate

swollen adjective
My feet were swollen from walking all day.
inflamed, bloated, puffed up, puffy

swoop verb
The owl swooped and caught the mouse.
dive, drop, plunge, plummet, descend, pounce

sword noun
Athena raised her shield and drew her sword.
blade

WORD WEB
SOME TYPES OF SWORD
broadsword, cutlass, foil, rapier, sabre, scimitar

Fighting with swords is **fencing** or **swordsmanship**.
A person who fences with a sword is a **swordsman** or **swordswoman**.

For other weapons see **weapon**

swore
past tense see **swear**

symbol noun
The dove is a symbol of peace.
sign, emblem, image
The symbols we use in writing are **characters** or **letters**.
The symbols used in ancient Egyptian writing were **hieroglyphics**.
The symbol of a club or school is their **badge**.
The symbol of a firm or organization is their **logo**.

symbolize verb
The dove symbolizes peace.
represent, stand for, signify, indicate, mean, denote

sympathetic adjective
They were sympathetic when my mother was ill.
understanding, compassionate, concerned, caring, comforting, kind, supportive
opposite **unsympathetic**

sympathize verb
to sympathize with
We sympathized with those who had lost their homes.
be sympathetic towards, be sorry for, feel for, commiserate with

sympathy noun
Did you feel any sympathy for the characters in the story?
understanding, compassion, pity, fellow-feeling, tenderness

synonym noun
'Cheerful' is a synonym of 'happy'.
opposite **antonym**

synthetic adjective
Nylon is a synthetic material.
artificial, man-made, manufactured, imitation
opposite **natural**

a
b
c
d
e
f
g
h
i
j
k
l
m
n
o
p
q
r
s
t
u
v
w
x
y
z

system noun
1 *The city has an archaic transport* system.
organization, structure, network,
framework
(informal) set-up
2 *Do you understand the new cataloguing
system?*
procedure, process, scheme, arrangement,
method, routine

systematic adjective
Inspector Giles works in a systematic way.
methodical, logical, orderly, organized,
scientific
opposite **unsystematic**

Tt

table noun
For items of furniture see **furniture**

tablet noun
1 *The doctor prescribed some tablets for the
pain.*
pill, capsule, pellet
2 *There was a stone tablet above the
entrance to the tomb.*
slab, plaque
3 *He put a tablet of powder in the washing
machine.*
block, piece, bar, chunk

tack verb
1 *The carpet needs to be tacked down.*
nail, pin
2 *She tacked up the hem of her skirt.*
sew, stitch

tackle verb
1 *They left him to tackle the washing-up.*
cope with, deal with, attend to, handle,
manage, grapple with
2 *Another player tackled her and got the ball.*
challenge, intercept, take on

tackle noun
1 *The referee said it was a fair tackle.*
challenge, interception
2 *He kept his fishing tackle in a special case.*
gear, equipment, apparatus, kit

tactful adjective
*She gave him a tactful reminder about her
birthday.*
subtle, discreet, diplomatic, sensitive,
thoughtful
opposite **tactless**

tactics plural noun
*They discussed their tactics for the next
game.*
moves, manoeuvres, plan of action
An overall plan for a game or battle is a
strategy.

tag noun
The price is marked on the tag.
label, sticker, ticket

tag verb
Every item is tagged with a price label.
identify, label, mark
to tag along with someone
She tagged along with them when they left.
accompany, follow, go with, join
to tag something on
He tagged on a PS at the end of his letter.
add, attach, tack on

tail noun
He joined the tail of the queue.
end, back, rear

tail verb
*The detective tailed the suspect to this
address.*
follow, pursue, track, trail, shadow, stalk
to tail off
The number of tourists tails off in October.
decrease, decline, lessen, diminish,
dwindle, wane

take verb takes, taking, took, taken
1 *Naomi took her sister's hand.*
clutch, clasp, take hold of, grasp, grip,
seize, snatch, grab

2 *The soldiers* took *many prisoners.*
catch, capture, seize, detain
3 *Someone has* taken *my pen.*
steal, remove, make off with
(informal) **swipe, pinch**
4 *The guide will* take *you to the edge of
the forest.*
conduct, escort, lead, accompany
5 *The bus* took *us right to the station.*
bring, carry, convey, transport
6 *It'll* take *two people to lift that table.*
need, require
7 *The caravan can* take *six people.*
**hold, contain, accommodate,
have room for**
8 *He couldn't* take *the heat of the sun.*
**bear, put up with, stand, endure, tolerate,
suffer, stomach**
9 *He* took *their names and addresses.*
make a note of, record, write down
10 *The magician asked me to* take *a card.*
pick, choose, select
11 Take *2 from 8 and you get 6.*
subtract, take away, deduct
to take someone in
Everyone was taken in *by his disguise.*
**fool, deceive, trick, cheat, dupe,
hoodwink**
to take off
Our flight took off *on time.*
depart, lift off
to take something off
Please take off *your coat.*
remove, strip off, peel off
to take part in something
Would you like to take part in *the show?*
participate in, be involved in, join in
to take place
When did the accident take place?
happen, occur, come about
to take something up
She has recently taken up *tap dancing.*
begin to do, start learning

tale noun
Pinocchio is a tale *about a boy made of wood.*
story, narrative, account
(informal) **yarn**
For various kinds of story see **story**

talent noun
She has a great talent *for music.*
gift, ability, aptitude, skill, flair, knack
Unusually great talent is **genius**.

talented adjective
He's a very talented *dancer.*
**gifted, able, accomplished, capable, skilled,
skilful, clever, brilliant**
If you are talented in several ways, you are
versatile.

talk verb
1 *Doug was trying to teach his parrot to
talk.*
**speak, say things, communicate,
express yourself**
2 *The two old friends had a lot to* talk *about.*
discuss, converse, chat, chatter, gossip
(informal) **natter**
3 *The prisoner refused to* talk.
give information, confess
For other ways to say things see **say**

talk noun
1 *I need to have a* talk *with you soon.*
conversation, discussion, chat
The talk between characters in a story is the
dialogue.
2 *There is a* talk *about Egyptian art at
lunchtime.*
lecture, presentation, speech, address
A talk in church is a **sermon**.

talkative adjective
You're not very talkative *this morning.*
**chatty, communicative, vocal, forthcoming,
articulate**
An informal name for a talkative person
is a **chatterbox**.

tall adjective
1 *Jasmine is* tall *for her age.*
big
opposite short
2 *Singapore has many* tall *buildings.*
high, lofty, towering, soaring, giant
Buildings with many floors are **high-rise** or
multi-storey buildings.
opposite low

a
b
c
d
e
f
g
h
i
j
k
l
m
n
o
p
q
r
s
t
u
v
w
x
y
z

A B C D E F G H I J K L M N O P Q R S **T** U V W X Y Z

tally verb
to tally with
Her story didn't tally with her husband's.
agree with, correspond with, match

tame adjective
1 *The guinea pigs are tame and used to people.*
domesticated, broken in, docile, gentle, obedient, manageable
opposite wild
2 *The film seems very tame nowadays.*
dull, boring, tedious, bland, unexciting, uninteresting
opposite exciting

tame verb
They were trying to tame a wild horse.
break in, subdue, master, control

tamper verb
to tamper with something
Someone has been tampering with the lock.
meddle with, tinker with, fiddle about with, interfere with

tan verb
Do you tan easily in the sun?
get a tan, go brown
If your skin goes red in the sun, you get sunburn.

tang noun
You can taste the tang of oranges in the soup.
sharpness, zest, zing

tangle verb
1 *Her sewing threads were all tangled together.*
entangle, twist, knot, jumble, muddle
Tangled hair is dishevelled or matted hair.
2 *Dolphins can get tangled in fishing nets.*
catch, trap, ensnare, entangle

tangle noun
The computer cables have got into a tangle.
muddle, jumble, knot, twist, confusion

tap verb
Someone tapped three times on the door.
knock, rap, strike

tape noun
The stack of old letters was tied up with tape.
ribbon, braid, binding

target noun
1 *Her target was to swim thirty lengths.*
goal, aim, objective, intention, purpose, hope, ambition
2 *She was the target of his jokes.*
object, victim, butt

tarnish verb
1 *The sculptures had tarnished with age.*
discolour, corrode
When iron corrodes it rusts.
2 *The scandal tarnished his reputation.*
stain, taint, blot, spoil, mar

tart adjective
Lemons have a tart taste.
sharp, sour, acid, tangy
opposite sweet

task noun
1 *The robot was given a set of tasks to do.*
job, chore, exercise, errand
2 *The soldiers' task was to capture the hill.*
assignment, mission, duty, undertaking

taste verb
1 *Taste the soup to see if it needs salt.*
sample, try, test, sip
2 *The curry tastes quite mild.*
For ways to describe how food tastes
see food

taste noun
1 *I love the taste of ginger.*
flavour
2 *May I have a taste of the cheese?*
mouthful, bite, morsel, nibble, bit, piece, sample
3 *Her taste in clothes is a bit odd.*
choice, preference, discrimination, judgement

tasteful adjective
The room was decorated in tasteful colours.
refined, cultivated, smart, stylish, artistic, elegant, attractive
opposite tasteless

tasteless adjective
1 *He apologized for making a tasteless remark.*
crude, tactless, indelicate, inappropriate
opposite **tasteful**
2 *The sprouts were overcooked and tasteless.*
flavourless, bland, insipid
opposite **flavourful**

tasty adjective
That pie was very tasty.
delicious, appetizing
See also **food**
opposite **unappetizing**

tattered adjective
Some of the blankets were worn and tattered.
ragged, ripped, torn, frayed, tatty, threadbare
opposite **smart**

taught
past tense see **teach**

taunt verb
The gladiator taunted his opponent.
barrack, insult, jeer at, laugh at, make fun of, mock, ridicule, sneer at

taut adjective
Make sure the rope is taut.
tight, tense, stretched
opposite **slack**

teach verb teaches, teaching, taught
My dad is teaching me to play the guitar.
educate, inform, instruct
To teach people to play a sport is to **coach** or **train** them.
To teach one person at a time or a small group is to **tutor** them.

teacher noun
We have a new ballet teacher.
tutor, instructor, trainer
Someone who teaches you to play a sport is a **coach**.
In the past, a woman who taught children in a private household was a **governess**.

team noun
She's been picked for the junior hockey team.
side

tear verb tears, tearing, tore, torn
1 *The tree branch tore a hole in our kite.*
rip, snag, gash, shred, split, slit
2 *He tore home to watch his favourite TV programme.*
run, rush, dash, hurry, race, sprint, speed
See also **run**

tear noun
There was a tear in one of the sails.
cut, rip, rent, split, gash, hole, opening, slit, gap

tease verb
They teased him about his new haircut.
taunt, make fun of, poke fun at, mock, ridicule, laugh at

technical adjective
The computer manual uses technical language.
specialized, scientific, advanced

technique noun
1 *The archaeologists use modern techniques.*
method, procedure, approach
2 *The pianist's technique was flawless.*
skill, expertise, art, craft

tedious adjective
It was a tedious journey by bus.
boring, dreary, dull, tiresome, monotonous, unexciting, uninteresting
opposite **exciting**

teem verb
to teem with
The pond teemed with tadpoles.
be overrun by, be crawling with, be infested with, swarm with

teenager noun
The film is designed to appeal to teenagers.
adolescent, youth

a
b
c
d
e
f
g
h
i
j
k
l
m
n
o
p
q
r
s
t
u
v
w
x
y
z

427

A B C D E F G H I J K L M N O P Q R S **T** U V W X Y Z

telephone verb
He telephoned to say that he'd be late.
phone, call, ring, dial

tell verb **tells, telling, told**
1 *Tell us what you can see.*
describe, explain, reveal, report, say, state
2 *Tell me when you are ready.*
let you know, inform, notify, announce, communicate
3 *He told them to stop making so much noise.*
order, command, direct, instruct
4 *We told each other scary ghost stories.*
narrate, relate
5 *He told me he would buy the tickets.*
assure, promise
6 *She couldn't tell where she was in the dark.*
make out, recognize, identify, perceive
7 *Can you tell one twin from the other?*
distinguish, separate
to tell someone off
She told them off for being late.
scold, reprimand, reproach
(informal) tick off

temper noun
1 *Mr Black had been in a bad temper all morning.*
mood, humour, state of mind
2 *The chef is always flying into a temper.*
rage, fury, fit of anger, tantrum
to lose your temper
When she loses her temper, her cheeks go red.
get angry, get annoyed, fly into a rage
See also **angry**

temperature noun
For units for measuring temperature see
measurement

tempestuous adjective
There was a tempestuous storm at sea.
stormy, squally, rough, raging, turbulent, wild
opposite calm

temple noun
For places where people worship see
building

temporary adjective
They made a temporary shelter for the night.
makeshift, provisional
opposite permanent

tempt verb
Can I tempt you to have more pudding?
coax, entice, persuade, attract
To tempt someone by offering them money is to **bribe** them.
To tempt an animal into a trap is to **lure** it.

tend¹ verb
to tend to do something
She tends to worry too much.
be inclined to, be liable to, be apt to

tend² verb
1 *One of the campers was left to tend the fire.*
mind, watch over, maintain
2 *Ned spends a lot of time tending his garden.*
take care of, cultivate, manage
3 *Nurses tended those who were injured.*
care for, attend to, look after, nurse, treat

tendency noun
He has a tendency to be lazy.
inclination, leaning, predisposition

tender adjective
1 *Frost may damage tender plants.*
delicate, fragile
opposites hardy, strong

2 *Cook the meat slowly until it is tender.*
soft, succulent, juicy
opposite tough
3 *The bruise is still tender.*
painful, sensitive, sore
4 *She gave him a tender smile.*
affectionate, kind, loving, caring, warm-hearted, compassionate, sympathetic, fond
opposite uncaring

tennis noun

WORD WEB

WAYS TO HIT A TENNIS BALL
lob, serve, slice, smash, volley; drop shot, backhand, forehand

SCORING USED IN A TENNIS MATCH
love, deuce, advantage, break point, match point, tiebreak; game, set

OTHER TERMS USED IN TENNIS
ace, ballboy or ballgirl, court, doubles, net, racket or racquet, service, singles, umpire

tense adjective
1 *The muscles in her shoulders were tense.*
taut, tight, strained, stretched
2 *The crowd were tense as they waited to hear the results.*
anxious, nervous, apprehensive, edgy, on edge, fidgety, jumpy, jittery
(informal) uptight
3 *It was a tense moment for all of us.*
nerve-racking, stressful, worrying
opposite relaxed

tension noun
1 *Can you check the tension on the guy-ropes?*
tightness, tautness
2 *The tension of waiting was almost unbearable.*
stress, strain, anxiety, nervousness, suspense, worry

tent noun

WORD WEB

SOME KINDS OF TENT
big top or **circus tent, dome tent, frame tent, marquee, pop-up tent, tipi** or **teepee, tunnel tent, wigwam, yurt**

The ropes which hold down a tent are the **guys** or **guy-ropes**.

term noun
1 *He was sentenced to a term in prison.*
period, time, spell, stretch, session
2 *The book has a glossary of technical terms.*
word, name, expression

terrible adjective
We heard there had been a terrible accident.
awful, dreadful, horrible, appalling, shocking, ghastly, horrific, frightful
For other ways to describe something bad see **bad**

terrific adjective (informal)
1 *The footprint of the yeti was a terrific size.*
big, huge, immense, enormous, giant, gigantic, colossal, massive
See also **big**
2 *She's a terrific tennis player.*
excellent, first-class, first-rate, superb, marvellous, wonderful
(informal) brilliant, fantastic, fabulous

terrify verb
The dogs were terrified by the thunder.
frighten, scare, startle, alarm, panic, horrify, petrify

territory noun
We had now entered uncharted territory.
land, area, ground, terrain, country, district, region, sector, zone
A territory which is part of a country is a **province**.

A
B
C
D
E
F
G
H
I
J
K
L
M
N
O
P
Q
R
S
T
U
V
W
X
Y
Z

terror noun
Her eyes filled with terror as she described the ghost.
fear, fright, horror, panic, alarm, dread

test noun
How did you do in the maths test?
exam, examination, assessment, appraisal, evaluation
A set of questions you answer for fun is a **quiz.**
A test for a job as an actor or singer is an **audition.**
A test to find the truth about something is an **experiment** or **trial.**

test verb
1 *I made an appointment to have my eyes tested.*
examine, check, evaluate, assess, screen
2 *He is testing a new formula for invisible ink.*
experiment with, try out, trial

text noun
1 *The lawyer studied the text of the document.*
wording, words, content
2 *She quoted a text from Shakespeare.*
passage, extract, quotation

textiles plural noun
see **cloth**

texture noun
Silk has a smooth texture.
feel, touch, quality, consistency
For ways to describe texture see **feel**

thankful adjective
to be thankful for something
The travellers were thankful for our help.
grateful for, appreciative of, pleased about, relieved about
opposite ungrateful

thanks plural noun
She sent them a card to show her thanks.
gratitude, appreciation

thaw verb
1 *The snowman gradually began to thaw.*
melt, dissolve
2 *Leave frozen food to thaw before cooking it.*
defrost, unfreeze
opposite freeze

theatre noun

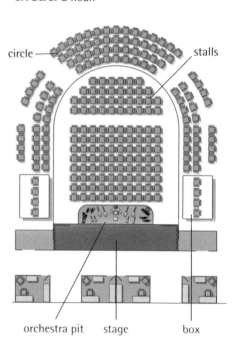

circle — stalls

orchestra pit   stage   box

A person who writes plays for the theatre is a **dramatist** or **playwright**.

PERFORMANCES YOU MIGHT SEE AT A THEATRE
ballet, comedy, dance, drama, farce, mime, musical, opera, pantomime, play, puppet show

theft noun
He was found guilty of theft.
robbery, stealing
For various kinds of theft see **stealing**

theme noun
What is the theme *of the poem?*
subject, topic, idea, gist, argument

theory noun
1 *The detective has a* theory *about the case.*
explanation, hypothesis, view, belief, idea, notion, suggestion
2 *She bought a book about musical* theory.
laws, principles, rules

therapy noun
She tried several therapies *to cure her headaches.*
treatment, remedy

thick adjective
1 *The Roman wall was about 2 metres* thick.
wide, broad
2 *The cabin was made from* thick *logs.*
stout, chunky, heavy, solid, substantial
opposites thin, slender
3 *The explorers hacked their way through the* thick *jungle.*
dense, close, compact
4 *His boots got stuck in a* thick *layer of mud.*
deep, heavy
opposites thin, shallow
5 *The guide spoke with a* thick *Polish accent.*
heavy, noticeable
opposite slight
6 (informal) *Fortunately, the giant was rather* thick.
stupid, brainless, foolish
opposite intelligent

thief noun
The police managed to catch the thief.
robber
Someone who steals from people's homes is a **burglar** or **housebreaker**.
Someone who steals from people in the street is a **pickpocket**.
Someone who steals from shops is a **shoplifter**.
Someone who used to steal from travellers was a **highwayman**.

thin adjective
1 *The prisoners were dreadfully* thin.
lean, skinny, bony, gaunt, spare, slight, underweight
Someone who is thin and tall is **lanky**.
Someone who is thin but strong is **wiry**.
Someone who is thin but attractive is **slim** or **slender**.
Thin arms or legs are **spindly**.
A common simile is **as thin as a rake**.
opposite fat
2 *The fairy wore a* thin *cloak of spider's silk.*
fine, light, delicate, flimsy, sheer, wispy
A thin line is a **fine** or **narrow** line.
A thin book is a **slim** book.
opposite thick
3 *The icing should be* thin *enough to spread.*
runny, watery
opposite thick

thin verb
You can thin *the paint with a little water.*
dilute, water down, weaken
to thin out
The crowd thinned out *later in the day.*
diminish, disperse

thing noun
1 *What's that green* thing *on the floor?*
item, object, article
2 *We had a lot of* things *to talk about.*
matter, affair, detail, point, factor
3 *A lot of* things *had happened since we spoke.*
event, happening, occurrence, incident

a
b
c
d
e
f
g
h
i
j
k
l
m
n
o
p
q
r
s
t
u
v
w
x
y
z

4 *I have only one thing left to do.*
job, task, act, action
things
Put your things in one of the lockers.
belongings, possessions, stuff, equipment, gear

think verb thinks, thinking, thought
1 Think *before you do anything rash.*
consider, contemplate, reflect, deliberate, reason
To think hard about something is to **concentrate** on it.
To think quietly and deeply about something is to **meditate**.
To keep thinking anxiously about something is to **brood** on it.
2 *Do you think this is a good idea?*
believe, feel, consider, judge, conclude
3 *What do you think this ring is worth?*
reckon, suppose, imagine, estimate, guess, expect
to think about something
I need some more time to think about it.
consider, reflect on, ponder, muse on, mull over
to think something up
They thought up a good plan.
invent, make up, conceive, concoct, devise

thirsty adjective
They were thirsty after their long walk.
dry, parched
If someone is ill through lack of fluids, they are **dehydrated**.

thorn noun
The florist cut the thorns off the rose stems.
prickle, spike, needle, barb

thorny adjective
1 *He scratched his arm on a thorny rose bush.*
prickly, spiky, spiny, sharp, bristly, scratchy
2 *They discussed the thorny problem for hours.*
tricky, difficult, complicated, hard, perplexing, ticklish

thorough adjective
1 *The doctor gave him a thorough examination.*
comprehensive, full, rigorous, careful, methodical, systematic, meticulous, painstaking, conscientious
opposite superficial
2 *He's made a thorough mess of things!*
complete, total, utter, absolute, downright

thought¹ noun
1 *She gave a lot of thought to the problem.*
consideration, deliberation, study
2 *The detective spent some time in thought.*
thinking, contemplation, reflection, meditation
3 *What are your thoughts on modern art?*
opinion, belief, idea, notion, conclusion

thought²
past tense see **think**

thoughtful adjective
1 *He had a thoughtful expression on his face.*
pensive, reflective, absorbed, preoccupied
opposites blank, vacant
2 *She added some thoughtful comments in the margin.*
well-thought-out, careful, conscientious, thorough
opposite careless
3 *It was very thoughtful of you to visit me in hospital.*
caring, considerate, kind, friendly, good-natured, unselfish
opposite thoughtless

thoughtless adjective
It was thoughtless of him to mention her dead husband.
inconsiderate, insensitive, uncaring, unthinking, negligent, ill-considered, rash
opposite thoughtful

thrash verb
1 *The rider thrashed and spurred his horse to go faster.*
hit, beat, whip, flog
(informal) **whack, wallop**

2 *The crocodile* thrashed *its tail in the mud.*
swish, flail, jerk, toss
3 (informal) *The visitors* thrashed *the home side 6–0.*
beat, defeat, trounce

thread noun
1 *There was a loose* thread *hanging from her dress.*
strand, fibre
2 *Do you sell embroidery* thread*?*
cotton, yarn, wool, silk
Sewing thread is wound onto a **reel** *or* **spool**.

threat noun
1 *She made a* threat *about phoning the police.*
warning
2 *Earthquakes are a constant* threat *in California.*
danger, menace, hazard, risk

threaten verb
1 *The bandits* threatened *him when he tried to escape.*
make threats against, menace, intimidate, terrorize, bully, browbeat
2 *The forecast* threatened *rain.*
warn of
3 *Wild tigers are* threatened *with extinction.*
endanger, put at risk

three noun
A group of three musicians is a **trio**.
Three babies born at the same time are **triplets**.
A shape with three sides is a **triangle**.
To multiply a number by three is to **triple** *it.*

threw
past tense see **throw**

thrifty adjective
Wendy had been thrifty *and saved her pocket money.*
careful, economical, frugal, prudent, sparing
opposite extravagant

thrill noun
Kim loves the thrill *of rock climbing.*
adventure, excitement, sensation, tingle
(informal) **buzz, kick**

thrill verb
The thought of seeing a real shark thrilled *him no end.*
excite, exhilarate, electrify, rouse, stir, stimulate
opposite bore

thrilled adjective
I was thrilled *to be invited to the wedding.*
delighted, pleased, excited, overjoyed, ecstatic

thrive verb thrives, thriving, thrived or throve, thrived or thriven
Tomato plants thrive *in greenhouses.*
do well, flourish, grow, prosper, succeed

throb verb
She could feel the blood throbbing *through her veins.*
beat, pound, pulse, pulsate

throng noun
There were throngs *of people on the street.*
crowd, swarm, horde

throttle verb
My tie was so tight that it nearly throttled *me!*
strangle, choke

throw verb throws, throwing, threw, thrown
1 *I* threw *some bread into the pond for the ducks.*
fling, cast, pitch, sling, toss
(informal) **bung, chuck**
To deliver the ball in cricket or rounders is to **bowl**.
To throw the shot in athletics is to **put** *the shot.*
To throw something high in the air is to **lob** *it.*
To throw something heavy is to **heave** *it.*

a
b
c
d
e
f
g
h
i
j
k
l
m
n
o
p
q
r
s
t
u
v
w
x
y
z

A
To throw something with great force is to **hurl** it.

B
If someone throws a lot of things at you, they **pelt** you.

C
2 *The horse threw its rider.*
throw off, shake off, dislodge

D
to throw away
We threw away *a pile of old junk.*

E
get rid of, dispose of, discard, scrap
(informal) **dump, ditch**

F

thrust verb

G
1 *Drew* thrust *his hands into his pockets.*
push, force, shove

H
2 *The bandit* thrust *at him with a dagger.*

I
lunge, jab, prod, stab, poke

J
thump verb

K
'Silence!' he rasped, thumping *his fist on the table.*

L
bang, bash, pound, hit, strike, knock, rap
(informal) **whack, wham**

M
thunder noun & verb

N
We could hear thunder *in the distance.*
A burst of thunder is a **clap, crack, peal,** or roll of thunder.

O
See also **weather**

P
tick verb

Q
A clock was ticking *in the background.*
For various ways to make sounds see **sound¹**

R
to tick someone off (informal)

S
She ticked him off *for talking in class.*
tell off, reprimand, reproach, scold

T
ticket noun

U
1 *They got free* tickets *for the concert.*
pass, permit, token, voucher, coupon

V
2 *What does it say on the price* ticket?
label, tag, tab

W
tide noun

X
The beach is completely covered at high tide.
When the tide is coming in it is **flowing** or **incoming.**

Y
When the tide is going out it is **ebbing** or **outgoing.**

Z

The tide is fully in at **high tide** and fully out at **low tide.**

tidy adjective
Mr Rackham likes to keep his office tidy.
neat, orderly, uncluttered, trim, smart, spruce, straight
opposite **untidy**

tie verb
1 *Zoe* tied *a pink ribbon round the parcel.*
bind, fasten, hitch, knot, loop, secure
To tie up a boat is to **moor** it.
To tie up an animal is to **tether** it.
opposite **untie**
2 *The two teams are still* tied.
be equal, be level, draw

tight adjective
1 *The lid was too* tight *for him to unscrew.*
firm, fast, secure
If something is so tight that air cannot get through, it is **airtight.**
If something is so tight that water cannot get through, it is **watertight.**
opposite **loose**
2 *They squeezed into the* tight *space.*
cramped, compact, small, narrow, poky, snug
opposite **spacious**
3 *Make sure that the ropes are* tight.
taut, tense, stretched, rigid
A common simile is as **tight as a drum.**
opposite **slack**
4 *He can be very* tight *with his money.*
mean, miserly, stingy
opposite **generous**

tighten verb
1 *She* tightened *her grip on his hand.*
increase, strengthen, tense, stiffen
2 *You need to* tighten *the guy-ropes.*
make taut, pull tighter, stretch
3 *He tried to* tighten *the screw.*
make tighter, screw up
opposite **loosen**

till verb
Farmers use tractors to till *the land.*
cultivate, farm, plough, dig

tilt verb
The caravan tilted to one side.
lean, incline, tip, slant, slope, angle
When a ship tilts to one side, it **lists**.

timber noun
He bought some timber to build a shed.
wood, lumber, logs, planks

time noun
1 *Is this a convenient time to talk?*
moment, occasion, opportunity
2 *Autumn is my favourite time of the year.*
phase, season
3 *He spent a short time living in China.*
period, while, term, spell, stretch
4 *Shakespeare lived in the time of Elizabeth I.*
era, age, days, epoch, period
5 *Please try to keep time with the music.*
tempo, beat, rhythm
on time
Please try to be on time.
punctual, prompt

🕸 WORD WEB
UNITS FOR MEASURING TIME
second, minute, hour, day, week, fortnight, month, year, decade, century, millennium
INSTRUMENTS USED TO MEASURE TIME
clock, egg timer, hourglass, pocket watch, stopwatch, sundial, timer, watch, wristwatch

alarm clock

stopwatch

hourglass

sundial

watch

mobile phone

timid adjective
At first, the mermaid was too timid to say anything.
shy, bashful, modest, nervous, fearful, shrinking, retiring, sheepish
A common simile is **as timid as a mouse**.
opposites brave, confident

tingle verb
My ears were tingling with the cold.
prickle, sting, tickle

tingle noun
1 *She felt a tingle in her foot.*
prickling, stinging, tickle, tickling, pins and needles
2 *He felt a tingle of excitement.*
thrill, sensation, quiver, shiver

tinker verb
He tinkered with the computer to get it to work.
fiddle, play about, dabble, meddle, tamper

tint noun
The paint was white with a faint tint of blue.
colour, hue, shade, tone
For names of colours see **colour**

tiny adjective
The ladybird was so tiny that you could hardly see it.
little, minute, miniature, microscopic, minuscule
(informal) **teeny, titchy**
opposites big, large

tip¹ noun
1 *The tip of his nose felt cold.*
end, point
The tip of an ink pen is the **nib**.

a
b
c
d
e
f
g
h
i
j
k
l
m
n
o
p
q
r
s
t
u
v
w
x
y
z

A

B

C

D

E

F

G

H

I

J

K

L

M

N

O

P

Q

R

S

T

U

V

W

X

Y

Z

2 *The tip of the mountain was covered in snow.*
cap, peak, top, summit, pinnacle, crown

tip² noun
He gave them some useful tips on first aid.
hint, piece of advice, suggestion, clue, pointer

tip verb
Have you tipped the waiter?
give a tip to, reward

tip³ noun
They took a load of rubbish to the tip.
dump, rubbish heap

tip verb
1 *The caravan tipped to one side.*
lean, tilt, incline, slope, slant
When a ship tips slightly to one side, it **lists**.
When a ship tips right over, it **capsizes**.
2 *Sophie tipped the box of crayons onto the table.*
empty, turn out, dump, unload
to tip over
He tipped the milk jug over by accident.
knock over, overturn, topple, upset

tiptoe verb
For various ways to walk see **walk**

tire verb
to tire someone out
Running in the playground had tired us all out.
exhaust, wear out
opposites **refresh, invigorate**

tired adjective
Have a lie down if you're tired.
exhausted, fatigued, weary, worn out, listless, sleepy, drowsy
(informal) all in
to be tired of something
I'm tired of watching TV.
bored with, fed up with, sick of
If you are not interested in anything, you are **apathetic**.

tiring adjective
Digging the garden is tiring work.
exhausting, fatiguing, demanding, difficult, hard, laborious, tough
opposite **refreshing**

title noun
1 *She couldn't think of a title for the story.*
name, heading
The title above a newspaper story is a headline.
A title or brief description next to a picture is a **caption**.
2 *The form asks you to fill in your name and title.*
form of address, designation, rank
The ordinary title used before a man's name is Mr.
The ordinary title used before a woman's name is Miss or Mrs or Ms.
A polite way to address someone whose name you don't know is **sir** or **madam**.
For royal titles see **royalty**

together adverb
1 *They walked to school together.*
side by side, hand in hand
2 *The choir sang the first verse together.*
all at once, at the same time, simultaneously, in chorus, in unison
opposites **independently, separately**

toil verb
They had been toiling all day in the fields.
work hard, labour, sweat, slave
(informal) **grind, slog**

toilet noun
Can you tell me where the toilet is?
lavatory, WC, bathroom
(informal) **loo**

token noun
1 *You can exchange this token for a free drink.*
voucher, coupon, ticket, counter

2 *They gave her a card as a **token** of their thanks.*
sign, symbol, mark, expression, indication, proof, reminder

told
past tense see **tell**

tolerant adjective
*Molly was very **tolerant** towards other people.*
understanding, easy-going, open-minded, sympathetic, charitable, forgiving, lenient, indulgent, long-suffering
opposite **intolerant**

tolerate verb
1 *He won't **tolerate** sloppy writing.*
accept, permit, put up with
2 *Cactus plants can **tolerate** extreme heat.*
bear, endure, stand, abide, suffer, stomach
(informal) stick

tomb noun
*Inside the **tomb** were several ancient skeletons.*
burial chamber, crypt, grave, mausoleum, sepulchre, vault
An underground passage containing several tombs is a **catacomb**.
A tomb is often marked by a **tombstone**, **gravestone**, or **headstone**.
See also **pyramid**

tone noun
1 *There was an angry **tone** to her voice.*
note, sound, quality, intonation, manner
2 *The room is painted in subtle **tones**.*
colour, hue, shade, tint
3 *Eerie music created the right **tone** for the film.*
feeling, mood, atmosphere, spirit, effect

took
past tense see **take**

tool noun
*There's a box of **tools** in the garage.*
implement, utensil, device, gadget, instrument

WORD WEB

TOOLS THAT ARE USED FOR WOODWORK
awl, chisel, clamp, drill, gimlet, hammer, jigsaw, plane, rasp, sander, saw, set square, T-square, vice

TOOLS THAT ARE USED IN THE HOME
broom, brush, ladder, mop, needle, pliers, scissors, screwdriver, tape measure, tweezers

For cooking utensils see **cook**

TOOLS THAT ARE USED FOR GARDENING OR FARMING
dibber or dibble, fork, hoe, lawnmower, pitchfork, rake, roller, scythe, secateurs, shears, shovel, sickle, spade, strimmer, trowel

TOOLS YOU MIGHT USE ON A BIKE OR CAR
(trademark) Allen key, jack, lever, pump, spanner, wrench

OTHER TOOLS
axe, chainsaw, crowbar, file, hacksaw, hatchet, mallet, paintbrush, pallet knife, penknife, pick, pickaxe, punch, sledgehammer, stapler

tooth noun

WORD WEB

TEETH IN A PERSON'S MOUTH
canine tooth, eye tooth, incisor, molar, wisdom tooth

A dog's or wolf's canine tooth is a **fang**.
A long tooth that sticks out of an animal's mouth is a **tusk**.

THINGS A DENTIST MIGHT FIT TO YOUR TEETH
braces, bridge or bridgework, crown, dentures, plate

SOME PROBLEMS PEOPLE HAVE WITH THEIR TEETH
cavity, decay, plaque, tartar, toothache

See also **dentist**

a
b
c
d
e
f
g
h
i
j
k
l
m
n
o
p
q
r
s
t
u
v
w
x
y
z

top noun
1 *They climbed to the top of the hill.*
peak, summit, tip, crown, crest, head
opposites **bottom, base**
2 *The desk top was covered with newspapers.*
surface
3 *The top of the jar was screwed on tightly.*
lid, cap, cover, covering

top adjective
1 *Their office is on the top floor.*
highest, topmost, uppermost, upper
opposites **bottom, lowest**
2 *She got top marks in her exam.*
most, best, highest
3 *The skiers set off at top speed.*
greatest, maximum
4 *He is one of Europe's top chefs.*
best, leading, finest, foremost, principal, superior
opposite **junior**

top verb
1 *Mum topped the cake with fudge icing.*
cover, decorate, garnish, crown
2 *The athlete is hoping to top her personal best.*
beat, better, exceed, outdo, surpass

topic noun
What was the topic of the conversation?
subject, talking point, issue, matter, question

topical adjective
The website often discusses topical issues.
current, recent, up-to-date

topple verb
1 *The books were piled too high and toppled over.*
fall, tumble, overbalance, collapse
2 *The gale toppled their TV aerial.*
knock down, overturn, upset
3 *The rebels plotted to topple the king.*
overthrow, bring down, remove from office

tore
past tense see **tear**

torment verb
1 *He was tormented by bad dreams.*
afflict, torture, plague, distress
2 *He told them to stop tormenting the other children.*
annoy, bother, harass, pester, tease, bully
To torment someone continually is to persecute or victimize them.

torrent noun
A torrent of water flowed down the hill.
flood, gush, rush, stream, cascade

toss verb
1 *He tossed a coin into the wishing-well.*
throw, cast, hurl, fling, pitch, sling
(informal) chuck
2 *Let's toss a coin to see who'll go first.*
flip, spin
3 *The little boat tossed about in the storm.*
lurch, pitch, roll, heave, rock, bob
4 *She tossed and turned, unable to get to sleep.*
thrash about, flail, writhe, wriggle

total noun
You need a total of fifty points to win.
sum, whole, entirety, amount

total adjective
1 *The bill shows the total amount due.*
full, complete, whole, entire
2 *The party was a total disaster.*
complete, utter, absolute, thorough, downright, sheer

total verb
The donations total almost 300 euros.
add up to, amount to, come to, make

totter verb
The child tottered across the floor.
stagger, stumble, reel, wobble
For various ways to walk see **walk**

touch verb
1 *Some animals don't like to be touched.*
feel, handle, stroke, fondle, caress, pat, pet
2 *The car just touched the gatepost.*
brush, graze, contact
3 *The speed of the racing car touched 200 miles per hour.*
reach, rise to
4 *I was touched by the poem that she wrote.*
move, affect, stir
to touch on something
Your letter touched on the issue of payment.
refer to, mention, raise

touch noun
1 *I felt a light touch on my arm.*
pat, stroke, tap, caress, contact
2 *Working with animals requires a special touch.*
sensitivity, understanding, feel, knack, manner
3 *There's a touch of frost in the air.*
hint, trace, suggestion

touchy adjective
Be careful what you say—he's very touchy.
easily offended, sensitive, irritable, quick-tempered

tough adjective
1 *You'll need tough shoes for hiking.*
strong, sturdy, robust, durable, stout, hard-wearing, substantial
Common similes are **as tough as nails** and **as tough as old boots**.
opposite flimsy

2 *The meat was very tough.*
chewy, leathery, rubbery
opposite tender
3 *They played against tough opposition.*
strong, stiff, powerful, resistant, determined, stubborn
opposites weak, feeble
4 *The police deal with some tough criminals.*
rough, violent, vicious, hardened
5 *It was a tough job to clean the oven.*
demanding, laborious, strenuous, gruelling, tiring, exhausting
opposite easy
6 *The crossword puzzle was too tough for him.*
difficult, hard, puzzling, baffling, knotty, thorny
opposite easy

tour noun
They went on a sightseeing tour.
journey, trip, excursion, expedition, outing, drive, ride

tourist noun
The cathedral was full of tourists.
sightseer, holidaymaker, traveller, visitor

tournament noun
She reached the semi-final of the chess tournament.
championship, competition, contest, series

tow verb
Horses used to tow barges up and down the river.
pull, tug along, drag, haul, draw

tower noun
A small tower on a castle or other building is a **turret**.
A church tower is a **steeple**.
The pointed structure on a steeple is a **spire**.
The part of a tower with a bell is a **belfry**.
The tall tower of a mosque is a **minaret**.

a
b
c
d
e
f
g
h
i
j
k
l
m
n
o
p
q
r
s
t
u
v
w
x
y
z

A
B
C
D
E
F
G
H
I
J
K
L
M
N
O
P
Q
R
S
T
U
V
W
X
Y
Z

tower verb
to tower above something
The castle towers above the village.
rise above, stand above, dominate,
loom over

town noun
A town with its own local council is a
borough.
A large and important town is a **city.**
Several towns that merge into each other
are a **conurbation.**
A word meaning 'to do with a town or city'
is **urban.**
The people who live in a town are the
townspeople.
See also **city**

toxic adjective
The flask contained a toxic gas.
poisonous, deadly, lethal, harmful
opposite harmless

toy noun

WORD WEB
SOME TOYS YOU MIGHT PLAY WITH
**ball, balloon, bicycle,
board game, building bricks,
computer** or **video game,
construction kit, doll, doll's house,
frisbee, hoop, jigsaw, kaleidoscope,
kite, marbles, model, playing cards,
puppet, puzzle, rattle, rocking horse,
(trademark) Rollerblades, roller skates,
skateboard, skipping rope, teddy bear,
top, train set, yo-yo**

See also **game**

trace noun
1 *The burglar left no trace of his presence.*
evidence, sign, mark, indication, hint, clue,
track, trail
A trace left by an animal might be its
footprint or **scent** or **spoor.**
2 *They found traces of blood on the carpet.*
tiny amount, drop, spot

trace verb
She is trying to trace her distant ancestors.
track down, discover, find, uncover,
unearth

track noun
1 *A rough track leads past the farm.*
path, pathway, footpath, trail
2 *They followed the deer's tracks for miles.*
footprint, footmark, trail, scent
3 *They are laying the track for a new railway.*
line, rails
4 *The athletes are warming up on the track.*
racetrack, circuit, course

track verb
*Astronomers are tracking the path of the
comet.*
follow, trace, pursue, chase, tail, trail,
hunt, stalk
to track someone or something down
They tracked down the owner of the car.
find, discover, trace, hunt down, sniff out,
run to ground

tract noun
They had to cross a tract of desert.
area, expanse, stretch

trade noun
1 *The trade in antiques has been booming
recently.*
business, dealing, buying and selling,
commerce, market
2 *He is still learning his trade as a
plumber.*
craft, skill, occupation, profession,
business

trade verb
to trade in something
*The company trades in second-hand
computers.*
deal in, do business in, buy and sell
For people who sell things see **shop**

tradition noun
*It's a tradition to sing 'Auld Lang Syne' on
New Year's Eve.*
custom, convention, habit, routine, fashion

traditional adjective
1 *The African drummers wore traditional costumes.*
national, regional, historical
2 *They chose to have a traditional wedding.*
conventional, customary, established, time-honoured, habitual, typical, usual

traffic noun
For types of traffic see **vehicle**

tragedy noun
1 *'Romeo and Juliet' is a tragedy.*
opposite **comedy**
2 *The accident at sea was a terrible tragedy.*
disaster, catastrophe, calamity, misfortune

tragic adjective
1 *He died in a tragic accident.*
catastrophic, disastrous, calamitous, terrible, appalling, dreadful, unfortunate, unlucky
2 *She had a tragic expression on her face.*
sad, sorrowful, mournful, grief-stricken, pitiful, woeful, wretched, pathetic
opposites **comic, happy**

trail noun
1 *We walked along a trail through the woods.*
path, pathway, track, route
2 *The police were on the trail of the bank robbers.*
track, chase, hunt, pursuit
The trail left in the water by a ship is its **wake**.

trail verb
1 *The detective trailed the suspect all day.*
follow, chase, tail, track, pursue, shadow, stalk, hunt
2 *She trailed her suitcase behind her.*
pull, tow, drag, draw, haul
3 *He is already trailing behind the front runners.*
fall behind, lag, straggle, dawdle

train noun
1 *They travelled to Johannesburg by train.*
For words to do with trains see **railway**
2 *It was a strange train of events.*
sequence, series, string, chain, succession

train verb
1 *He trains the football team every Saturday.*
coach, instruct, teach, tutor
2 *They are training hard for the race.*
practise, exercise, prepare yourself
(informal) work out
3 *The archer trained his arrow on the target.*
aim (at), point (at), level (at)

trainer noun
1 *Their trainer makes them work hard.*
coach, instructor, teacher, tutor
2 *These trainers are for indoor use.*
For types of shoe or boot see **shoe**

tramp verb
They tramped across the muddy fields.
march, hike, trek, trudge, plod, stride
For other ways to walk see **walk**

trample verb
Don't trample the flowers!
crush, flatten, squash, tread on, walk over, stamp on

trance noun
The fortune-teller was lost in a trance.
daydream, daze, dream
One way to be in a trance is to be **hypnotized**.
Unconsciousness caused by an illness or accident is a **coma**.

tranquil adjective
1 *They led a tranquil life in the country.*
calm, peaceful, quiet, restful, serene, sedate
(informal) laid-back
opposites **eventful, busy**
2 *The sea was tranquil after the storm.*
calm, placid, still, undisturbed, unruffled

transfer verb
Some paintings have been transferred to the new gallery.
move, remove, shift, relocate, convey, hand over

a
b
c
d
e
f
g
h
i
j
k
l
m
n
o
p
q
r
s
t
u
v
w
x
y
z

A
B
C
D
E
F
G
H
I
J
K
L
M
N
O
P
Q
R
S
T
U
V
W
X
Y
Z

transform verb
They transformed the attic into an office.
change, alter, turn, convert, adapt, modify

translate verb
She translates Russian poetry into English.
interpret, convert
A person who translates a foreign language
is an interpreter or translator.
An expert in languages is a linguist.

transmit verb
1 *The spy transmitted her messages in code.*
send, communicate, relay, emit
To transmit a programme on radio or TV is to
broadcast it.
opposite receive
2 *Can the disease be transmitted to humans?*
pass on, spread, carry

transparent adjective
The box had a transparent lid.
clear
(informal) see-through
Something which is not fully transparent,
but allows light to shine through, is
translucent.

transport verb
*The goods are transported to Europe
by sea.*
take, carry, convey, ship, transfer, move,
bring, fetch, haul, shift
transport noun

WORD WEB
METHODS OF TRANSPORT

TRANSPORT BY AIR
aeroplane, airship, helicopter,
hot-air balloon

See also aircraft

TRANSPORT BY ROAD
bicycle, bus, car, coach, horse, jeep,
lorry, minibus, taxi, van

See also vehicle

TRANSPORT BY RAIL
monorail, train, tram, underground

See also railway

TRANSPORT BY WATER
barge, boat, canoe, ferry, punt, raft,
ship, yacht

See also boat

For various ways to travel see travel

train

helicopter

bicycle

trap noun
1 *The animal was caught in a* **trap.**
snare, net, noose, booby trap
2 *The police set up a* **trap** *to catch the robbers.*
ambush

trap verb
They tried to **trap** *the mouse.*
capture, catch, snare, corner

trash noun
1 *He put the* **trash** *into the bin.*
rubbish, waste, garbage, junk, litter, refuse
2 *Don't listen to that* **trash***!*
nonsense

travel verb
She prefers to **travel** *to work by bus.*
go, journey, move along, proceed, progress

WORD WEB

VARIOUS WAYS TO TRAVEL
cruise, cycle, drive, fly, go by rail, hike, hitch-hike, motor, pedal, ramble, ride, roam, row, sail, tour, trek, voyage, walk, wander

When birds travel from one country to another they **migrate**.
When people travel to another country to live there they **emigrate**.

For methods of transport see **transport**

PEOPLE WHO TRAVEL AS A WAY OF LIFE
itinerant, nomad, traveller

OTHER PEOPLE WHO TRAVEL
astronaut, commuter, cyclist, driver or motorist, explorer, hitch-hiker, holidaymaker, motorcyclist, passenger, pedestrian, pilot or aviator, rambler or walker, sailor, tourist

A person who travels to a religious place is a **pilgrim**.
A person who travels illegally on a ship or plane is a **stowaway**.
A person who likes travelling round the world is a **globetrotter**.

treacherous adjective
1 *His* **treacherous** *plan was to ambush them as they escaped.*
disloyal, traitorous, deceitful, double-crossing, faithless, false, unfaithful, untrustworthy
A treacherous person is a **traitor**.
opposite **loyal**
2 *The roads are often* **treacherous** *in winter.*
dangerous, hazardous, perilous, unsafe, risky
opposite **safe**

tread verb
Please **tread** *carefully.*
step, walk, proceed
to tread on
Don't **tread on** *the wet cement!*
walk on, step on, stamp on, trample, crush, squash

treasure noun
The **treasure** *was buried somewhere on the island.*
hoard, riches, wealth, fortune
A hidden store of treasure is a **cache**.
For things you might find as treasure see **coin**, **jewel**

treasure verb
She **treasures** *the photograph of her grandmother.*
cherish, prize, value

treat verb
1 *The old woman had always* **treated** *him kindly.*
behave towards, deal with
2 *She is being* **treated** *for minor injuries.*
give treatment to
To treat a wound is to **dress** it.
To treat an illness or wound successfully is to **cure** or **heal** it.
3 *Let me* **treat** *you by buying you dinner.*
give you a treat, pay for

treatment noun
1 *The hospital is for the* **treatment** *of sick animals.*
care, nursing, healing

a
b
c
d
e
f
g
h
i
j
k
l
m
n
o
p
q
r
s
t
u
v
w
x
y
z

A
B
C
D
E
F
G
H
I
J
K
L
M
N
O
P
Q
R
S
T
U
V
W
X
Y
Z

2 *He is trying a new* treatment *for back pain.*
remedy, therapy, medication
Emergency treatment at the scene of an accident is **first aid**.
For kinds of medical treatment see **medicine**
3 *The sculpture has been damaged by careless* treatment.
handling, use, care, management

treaty noun
The two sides signed a peace treaty.
agreement, pact, contract

tree noun

> ### WORD WEB
>
> Trees which lose their leaves in winter are **deciduous**.
> Trees which have leaves all year round are **evergreen**.
> Trees which grow cones are **conifers**.
> A young tree is a **sapling**.
> Small, low trees are **bushes** or **shrubs**.
> Miniature trees grown in very small containers are **bonsai** trees.
>
> SOME VARIETIES OF TREE
> alder, ash, aspen, baobab, banyan, bay, beech, birch, cedar, chestnut, cypress, elder, elm, eucalyptus, fir, flame tree, hawthorn, hazel, holly, jujube, juniper, larch, lime, maple, oak, olive, palm, pine, plane, poplar, redwood, rowan, spruce, sycamore, tamarind, willow, yew
>
> For names of fruit trees see **fruit**
>
> PLACES WHERE TREES GROW
> forest, grove, jungle, plantation, spinney, thicket, wood, woodland
>
> An area covered with trees is a **wooded** area.
> A small group of trees is a **copse** or **coppice**.
> An area planted with fruit trees is an **orchard**.

tremble verb
The little fairy was trembling *with cold.*
shake, shiver, quake, quiver, shudder

tremendous adjective
1 *They heard a* tremendous *roar issuing from the cave.*
big, enormous, great, huge, immense, massive, mighty, fearful
2 *Winning the cup was a* tremendous *achievement.*
marvellous, magnificent, wonderful, superb, terrific, sensational, spectacular, stupendous, extraordinary, outstanding

tremor noun
A tremor *in her voice showed she was nervous.*
trembling, shaking, quavering, quivering, vibration, wobble

trend noun
1 *There is a general* trend *towards healthier eating.*
tendency, movement, shift, leaning
2 *This type of computer game is the latest* trend.
fashion, style, craze, fad, vogue

trial noun
1 *Scientists are conducting* trials *on a new space probe.*
test, experiment
2 *The* trial *will be heard in a crown court.*
case, hearing
A military trial is a **court martial**.

triangular adjective
A triangular shape is **three-cornered** or **three-sided**.

tribe noun
see **family**

trick noun
1 *Stephie played a* trick *on her brother.*
joke, practical joke, prank
Tricks which a magician performs are **conjuring tricks**.

2 *The Trojans never guessed that the wooden horse was a trick.*
deception, pretence, fraud, cheat, hoax
(informal) con

trick verb
He tricked them into believing he was a police officer.
deceive, dupe, fool, hoodwink, cheat, swindle
(informal) con

trickle verb
Water trickled from the tap.
dribble, drip, leak, seep, ooze
opposite **gush**

tricky adjective
1 *There were a couple of tricky questions in the exam.*
difficult, complicated, awkward, intricate, involved, ticklish
opposites **straightforward, easy**
2 *Redbeard is a tricky person to deal with.*
crafty, cunning, sly, wily

trigger verb
The burnt toast triggered the smoke alarm.
activate, set off, switch on, start

trim adjective
Mr Stanley always keeps his garden trim.
neat, orderly, tidy, well-kept, smart, spruce
opposite **untidy**

trim verb
1 *He asked the barber to trim his beard.*
cut, clip, shorten, crop, neaten, tidy
2 *The blouse is trimmed with lace.*
edge, decorate, adorn

trip noun
They went on a trip to the seaside.
journey, visit, outing, excursion, jaunt, expedition

trip verb
1 *He tripped on the loose carpet.*
catch your foot, stumble, fall, slip, stagger
2 *Little Red Riding Hood was tripping happily along.*
run, skip

triumph noun
The team celebrated their triumph at the Olympic Games.
victory, win, success, conquest

triumphant adjective
1 *They cheered the triumphant team.*
winning, victorious, conquering, successful
opposite **unsuccessful**
2 *'I've solved the riddle!' said Nat with a triumphant smile.*
elated, exultant, joyful, gleeful, jubilant

trivial adjective
Don't bother me with trivial details.
unimportant, minor, insignificant, trifling, negligible, petty, silly, slight, frivolous
opposite **important**

troop noun
A troop of horse riders crossed the river.
group, band, party, body, company

troop verb
The children trooped along the road.
march, parade, walk, proceed
To walk one behind the other is to **file** along.

troops plural noun
see **armed services**

trophy noun
My friend, Marnie, won a trophy for gymnastics.
award, prize, cup, medal

trouble noun
1 *The family has had a lot of trouble recently.*
difficulty, hardship, suffering, unhappiness, distress, misfortune, pain, sadness, sorrow, worry
2 *The police dealt with trouble in the crowd.*
disorder, unrest, disturbance, commotion, fighting, violence
3 *The trouble with this computer is that it's very slow.*
problem, difficulty, disadvantage, drawback
to take trouble
He took trouble to remember all our names.
bother, make an effort, take pains

a
b
c
d
e
f
g
h
i
j
k
l
m
n
o
p
q
r
s
t
u
v
w
x
y
z

trouble verb
1 *What's* troubling *you?*
distress, upset, bother, worry, concern, pain, torment, vex
2 *I don't want to* trouble *her if she's busy.*
disturb, interrupt, bother, pester
3 *Nobody* troubled *to tidy up the room.*
bother, make an effort, take trouble

troublesome adjective
1 *Do you find the heat* troublesome?
annoying, irritating, trying, tiresome, bothersome, distressing, inconvenient, upsetting
2 *There are two* troublesome *teenagers in the family.*
badly behaved, disorderly, rowdy, unruly, disobedient

trousers plural noun
For items of clothing see clothes

truce noun
The two sides agreed on a truce.
ceasefire, armistice, peace

true adjective
1 *Do you think the newspaper report is* true?
accurate, correct, right, factual, authentic, undeniable
opposites **untrue, false**
2 *This is a* true *copy of my birth certificate.*
genuine, real, actual, faithful, exact
opposite **false**
3 *Esther has always been a* true *friend.*
faithful, loyal, constant, devoted, sincere, steady, trustworthy, dependable, reliable
opposite **unreliable**

trunk noun
1 *The* trunk *of a palm tree can bend in the wind.*
stem, stock
2 *Push up from the ground, keeping your* trunk *straight.*
torso, body, frame
3 *The magician kept his things in a huge travelling* trunk.
chest, case, box, crate, suitcase, coffer

trust verb
1 *I* trusted *her to keep my identity a secret.*
rely on, depend on, count on, bank on, believe in, be sure of, have confidence in, have faith in
2 *I* trust *you are well.*
hope

trust noun
1 *The director has* trust *in her acting ability.*
belief, confidence, faith
2 *They put their lives in the* trust *of the pilot.*
responsibility, safe-keeping, hands

trustworthy adjective
Sir Boldwood was a trustworthy *ally of the king.*
reliable, dependable, loyal, trusty, true, honourable, responsible
opposite **untrustworthy**

truth noun
1 *The detective doubted the* truth *of her story.*
accuracy, authenticity, correctness, genuineness, reliability, truthfulness, validity
opposites **inaccuracy, falseness**
2 *Are you sure you're telling the* truth?
facts
opposite **lies**

truthful adjective
1 *She is normally a* truthful *person.*
honest, frank, sincere, straight, straightforward, reliable, trustworthy
2 *He gave a* truthful *answer.*
accurate, correct, proper, right, true, valid
opposite **dishonest**

try verb
1 *I'm going to* try *to beat my dad at chess.*
aim, attempt, endeavour, make an effort, strive, struggle
2 *Would you like to* try *a larger size?*
test, try out, evaluate, experiment with

try noun
1 *We may not succeed, but it's worth a* try!
attempt, effort, go, shot

A
B
C
D
E
F
G
H
I
J
K
L
M
N
O
P
Q
R
S
T
U
V
W
X
Y
Z

2 *Would you like a try of my mango smoothie?*
trial, test, taste

trying adjective
The way he keeps asking questions is very trying.
tiresome, irritating, annoying, wearing, wearisome

tub noun
We shared a large tub of popcorn between us.
pot, drum, barrel, cask, vat

tube noun
Roll the paper into a tube.
cylinder, pipe
A flexible tube is a **hose**.
A tube which liquid pours out of is a **spout**.

tuck verb
He tucked his t-shirt into his jeans.
push, insert, stuff

tuft noun
The goat stood munching on a tuft of grass.
clump, bunch

tug verb
1 *It annoys me when my brother tugs my hair.*
pull, yank, jerk, pluck, wrench
2 *We tugged the sledge up the hill.*
drag, pull, tow, haul, lug, draw, heave

tumble verb
The boy slipped and tumbled into the water.
topple, drop, fall, pitch, flop, stumble, plummet

tumult noun
He had to shout to be heard above the tumult.
noise, uproar, commotion, clamour, din, racket, rumpus, hubbub

tune noun
Can you play the tune to 'Happy Birthday'?
melody, song, air, theme

tunnel noun
A tunnel dug by rabbits is a **burrow**.
A system of burrows is a **warren**.
A tunnel in a mine is a **gallery**.
A tunnel beneath a road is a **subway** or **underpass**.

tunnel verb
Badgers use their strong front paws to tunnel for food.
burrow, dig, excavate

turmoil noun
The whole country was in turmoil.
chaos, upheaval, uproar, disorder, unrest, commotion, disturbance, ferment, pandemonium
opposites **calm, peace**

turn verb
1 *A wheel turns on its axle.*
go round, revolve, rotate, roll, spin, swivel, pivot, twirl, whirl
2 *The van turned into a side street.*
change direction, corner
To turn unexpectedly is to **swerve** or **veer** off course.
If you turn to go back in the direction you came from, you **do a U-turn**.
If marching soldiers change direction, they **wheel**.
3 *He turned a curious shade of green.*
become, go, grow
4 *They turned the attic into a spare bedroom.*
convert, adapt, change, alter, modify, transform, develop
to turn something down
She turned down the offer of a part in the play.
decline, refuse, reject
to turn something on or off
He turned on the radio.
switch on or off
to turn out
Everything turned out well in the end.
end up, come out, happen, result

a
b
c
d
e
f
g
h
i
j
k
l
m
n
o
p
q
r
s
t
u
v
w
x
y
z

A B C D E F G H I J K L M N O P Q R S **T** U V W X Y Z

to turn over
The boat turned over.
capsize, overturn, turn upside down, flip over, keel over

to turn up
A friend turned up unexpectedly.
arrive, appear, drop in

turn noun
1 *She gave the handle a turn.*
twist, spin, whirl, twirl
A single turn of a wheel is a **revolution**.
The process of turning is **rotation**.
2 *The house is just past the next turn in the road.*
bend, corner, curve, angle, junction
A sharp turn in a country road is a **hairpin bend**.
3 *It's your turn to do the washing up.*
chance, opportunity, occasion, time, slot, go
4 *Everyone had to do a turn in the show.*
act, performance, scene, sketch
5 (informal) *Seeing the skeleton gave her quite a turn.*
fright, scare, shock, start, surprise

turret noun
see **tower**

twig noun
They gathered twigs to make a fire.
stick, branch, stalk, stem, shoot

twin noun
This vase is a twin of the one in the museum.
double, duplicate, lookalike, match, clone

twinkle verb
The stars twinkled in the sky.
sparkle, shine, glitter, glisten, glimmer, glint

twirl verb
1 *The dancers twirled faster and faster.*
spin, turn, whirl, revolve, rotate, pirouette
2 *He paced up and down, twirling his umbrella.*
twiddle, twist

twist verb
1 *She twisted a bandage round her wrist.*
wind, loop, coil, curl, entwine
2 *Twist the handle to open the door.*
turn, rotate, revolve, swivel
3 *The road twists through the hills.*
wind, weave, curve, zigzag
4 *He twisted and turned in his sleep.*
toss, writhe, wriggle
5 *I tried to twist the cap off the bottle.*
unscrew
6 *Heat can twist metal out of shape.*
bend, buckle, warp, crumple, distort

twisted adjective
The trunk of the olive tree was twisted with age.
warped, gnarled, buckled, misshapen, deformed

twitch verb
The dog twitched in his sleep.
jerk, jump, start, tremble

two noun
Two musicians playing or singing together are a **duet** or a **duo**.
Two people or things which belong together are a **couple** or a **pair**.
To multiply a number by two is to **double** it.

type noun
1 *What type of films do you like to watch?*
kind, sort, variety, category, class, genre
2 *The book was printed in large type.*
print, lettering, letters, characters

typical adjective
1 *The weather is typical for this time of year.*
normal, usual, standard, ordinary, average, predictable, unsurprising
opposite **unusual**
2 *The pointed arch is typical of Gothic architecture.*
characteristic, representative
opposite **uncharacteristic**

Uu

ugly adjective

1 *The princess had to kiss a fat, ugly toad.*
grotesque, hideous, unattractive, repulsive,
revolting, monstrous
opposite beautiful

2 *The room was filled with ugly furniture.*
unattractive, unsightly, displeasing,
tasteless, horrid, nasty
opposite beautiful

3 *The crowd was in an ugly mood.*
unfriendly, hostile, menacing, threatening,
angry, dangerous
opposite friendly

ultimate adjective

Her ultimate goal is to be a writer.
eventual, final
opposite initial

umpire noun

see **referee**

un- prefix

WRITING TIPS

To find synonyms for words beginning
with **un-** which are not listed below, try
the following. Look up the word to which
un- has been added, then add **un-** or the
word NOT to its synonyms. For example,
to find synonyms for UNABLE, you would
look up ABLE and then work out the
synonyms NOT ALLOWED, UNWILLING, etc.

unanimous adjective

It was a unanimous decision.
collective, joint, united
A decision where most, but not all, people
agree is a **majority** decision.

unattractive adjective

see **ugly**

unavoidable adjective

The accident was unavoidable.
inevitable, bound to happen, certain,
destined

unaware adjective

unaware of
*They were unaware of the dangers that lay
ahead.*
ignorant of, oblivious to, unconscious of

unbearable adjective

The stench in the cave was unbearable.
unendurable, intolerable,
impossible to bear

unbelievable adjective

1 *The account of the UFO sighting was
unbelievable.*
unconvincing, unlikely, far-fetched,
improbable, incredible

2 *She scored an unbelievable goal.*
amazing, astonishing, extraordinary,
remarkable, sensational, phenomenal

uncertain adjective

1 *I was uncertain what to do next.*
unsure, doubtful, in two minds, unclear

2 *They are facing an uncertain future.*
indefinite, unknown, undecided,
unpredictable

unclean adjective

see **dirty**

unclear adjective

see **uncertain**

uncomfortable adjective

1 *She complained that her shoes were
uncomfortable.*
restrictive, cramped, hard, stiff, tight,
tight-fitting

2 *He spent an uncomfortable night sleeping
on the floor.*
restless, troubled, disagreeable, uneasy
opposite comfortable

uncommon adjective

see **unusual**

a
b
c
d
e
f
g
h
i
j
k
l
m
n
o
p
q
r
s
t
u
v
w
x
y
z

A
B
C
D
E
F
G
H
I
J
K
L
M
N
O
P
Q
R
S
T
U
V
W
X
Y
Z

unconscious adjective
1 *The patient had been* unconscious *for two days.*
If you are unconscious because of a hit on the head, you are **knocked out**.
If you are unconscious for an operation, you are **anaesthetized**.
If you are unconscious because of an accident or illness, you are **in a coma**.
2 *They laughed at her* unconscious *slip of the tongue.*
accidental, unintended, unintentional
opposite conscious
unconscious of
He's unconscious *of all the trouble he's caused.*
unaware of, ignorant of, oblivious to

uncover verb
1 *Archaeologists have* uncovered *two more skeletons.*
dig up, unearth, expose, reveal, show, disclose
To uncover your body is to **strip** or **undress**.
2 *He* uncovered *the truth about his family's past.*
detect, discover, come across
opposites cover up, hide

undergo verb
Wizards have to undergo *rigorous training.*
go through, be subjected to, experience, put up with, endure

undermine verb
Losing the race could undermine *her confidence.*
weaken, lessen, reduce, destroy, ruin
opposites support, boost

understand verb *understands, understanding, understood*
1 *I don't* understand *what you mean.*
comprehend, grasp, follow, see, take in, realize, appreciate, recognize, work out, fathom
2 *Can you* understand *this writing?*
read, interpret, make out, make sense of

To understand something in code is to **decode** or **decipher** it.
3 *I* understand *they're moving to Sydney.*
believe, hear

understanding noun
1 *The robot has limited powers of* understanding.
intelligence, intellect, sense, judgement
2 *The book will increase your* understanding *of science.*
appreciation, awareness, knowledge, comprehension, grasp
3 *The two sides reached an* understanding.
agreement, deal, settlement, arrangement, accord
4 *She treats her patients with* understanding.
sympathy, compassion, consideration

understanding adjective
Martha is an understanding *person.*
sympathetic, caring, friendly, kind, helpful, open-minded, tolerant

undertake verb
1 *She was asked to* undertake *a secret mission.*
take on, accept, tackle, handle
2 *He* undertook *to pay all the costs.*
agree, consent, promise, guarantee, commit yourself

underwear noun
underclothes, underclothing, undergarments
(informal) **undies**
Women's underclothes are **lingerie**.
For items of underwear see **clothes**

undo verb *undoes, undoing, undid, undone*
1 *I'll have to* undo *this row of knitting.*
unfasten, untie, unravel, loosen, release
To undo stitching is to **unpick** it.
2 *Sue* undid *the wrapping on the parcel.*
open, unwrap, unfold, unwind, unroll, unfurl
3 *The good witch tried to* undo *the spell.*
reverse, cancel out, wipe out

undoubtedly adverb
She is undoubtedly our best player.
definitely, certainly, surely, doubtless, of course

undress verb
He undressed quickly and got into bed.
get undressed, take off your clothes, strip
opposite dress

unearth verb
1 *The dog unearthed an old bone.*
dig up, uncover
2 *She unearthed some old diaries in the attic.*
find, discover, come across, stumble upon, track down

uneasy adjective
1 *I had an uneasy feeling that something was wrong.*
anxious, nervous, apprehensive, tense, troubling, upsetting, worrying
opposite confident
2 *Our guest passed an uneasy night.*
restless, unsettled, uncomfortable, disturbed
opposite comfortable

unemployed adjective
Since the factory closed, he has been unemployed.
out of work, jobless
(informal) on the dole
To be unemployed because there is not enough work to do is to be redundant.
opposites employed, working

uneven adjective
1 *The ground was very uneven in places.*
rough, bumpy, rutted
opposite smooth
2 *Their performance has been uneven this season.*
erratic, inconsistent, irregular, variable, unpredictable
opposite consistent
3 *It was a very uneven contest.*
one-sided, unbalanced, unequal, unfair
opposite balanced

unexpected adjective
Her reaction was totally unexpected.
surprising, unforeseen, unpredictable, unplanned
opposite expected

unfair adjective
1 *Do you think that the umpire's decision was unfair?*
unjust, unreasonable, wrong, one-sided, unbalanced, impartial, biased
opposites fair, just
2 *I felt that her criticism of my work was unfair.*
undeserved, unmerited, uncalled for, unjustified
opposites fair, deserved

unfaithful adjective
see disloyal

unfamiliar adjective
The astronauts looked on an unfamiliar landscape.
strange, unusual, curious, novel, alien
unfamiliar with
They were unfamiliar with the local customs.
unaccustomed to, unused to, unaware of

unfit adjective
1 *She used to be unfit before she took up swimming.*
out of condition, unhealthy
opposite fit
2 *He is unfit to be left in charge of the house.*
unsatisfactory, unsuitable, incompetent, inadequate

unfortunate adjective
1 *The unfortunate couple had lost all their possessions.*
unlucky, poor, unhappy, hapless, wretched, ill-fated
2 *The goalkeeper made one unfortunate error.*
disastrous, calamitous, unwelcome
opposites fortunate, lucky

a
b
c
d
e
f
g
h
i
j
k
l
m
n
o
p
q
r
s
t
u
v
w
x
y
z

3 *He made an* unfortunate *remark about her cooking.*

regrettable, inappropriate, tactless, unsuitable, untimely

unfriendly adjective
The housekeeper greeted us with an unfriendly glare.

unwelcoming, inhospitable, unsympathetic, unkind, impolite, uncivil, unhelpful, hostile, cold, cool, distant, stand-offish, aloof, unsociable, unneighbourly
opposites **friendly, amiable**

ungrateful adjective
Don't be so ungrateful.

unappreciative, unthankful
opposite **grateful**

unhappy adjective
1 *You look* unhappy—*what's the matter?*
sad, miserable, depressed, downhearted, despondent, gloomy, glum, downcast, dejected, forlorn, woeful, crestfallen
(informal) down in the dumps, down in the mouth
opposites **happy, cheerful**
2 *I'm still* unhappy *with my score.*
dissatisfied, disappointed, displeased, discontented
opposites **satisfied, pleased**

unhealthy adjective
1 *One of the calves has been* unhealthy *since birth.*
unwell, ill, sick, diseased, infirm, sickly, poorly, weak, delicate, feeble, frail
opposites **healthy, strong**
2 *He eats an* unhealthy *diet of junk food.*
unwholesome, unnatural, harmful, unhygienic
opposites **healthy, wholesome**

unhelpful adjective
The shop assistant was most unhelpful.
uncooperative, unfriendly, inconsiderate, reluctant to help
opposite **helpful**

unidentified adjective
An unidentified *aircraft was spotted at night.*
unknown, unrecognized, unspecified, unnamed, anonymous, nameless
opposite **named**

uniform noun
The guards at the Tower of London wear fancy uniforms.
costume, outfit, regalia, livery

uniform adjective
The greenhouse is kept at a uniform *temperature.*
consistent, regular, even, unvarying, identical, similar, the same
opposites **different, varying**

unify verb
The new president tried to unify *the country.*
unite, bring together, harmonize, combine, integrate, join, merge, amalgamate
opposite **separate**

unimportant adjective
Don't worry about unimportant *details.*
insignificant, minor, trivial, trifling, irrelevant, secondary, slight, small, negligible, worthless, petty
opposite **important**

uninhabited adjective
The island had been uninhabited *for centuries.*
unoccupied, empty, deserted, abandoned
opposites **inhabited, populated**

uninteresting adjective
see **boring**

union noun
The city was formed by the union *of two neighbouring towns.*
uniting, joining, integration, combination, merger, amalgamation, fusion
A union of two rivers is a **confluence**.
A union of two countries is their **unification**.
A union of two people is a **marriage** or **partnership**.

unique adjective
Each person's fingerprints are unique.
distinctive, different, individual, special, peculiar
(informal) one-off

unit noun
The bookcase is built up from separate units.
piece, part, bit, section, segment, element, component, module
For units of measurement see
measurement

unite verb
1 *King Bluetooth united the kingdoms of Denmark and Norway.*
combine, join, merge, link, integrate, unify, amalgamate, bring together
opposite separate
2 *People of all ages united to celebrate Chinese New Year.*
collaborate, cooperate, join forces
opposite compete
To unite to do something bad is to **conspire**.

universal adjective
Scientists have made a discovery of universal importance.
general, widespread, global, worldwide

unjust adjective
see **unfair**

unkind adjective
It was a thoughtless and unkind remark.
callous, hard-hearted, cruel, thoughtless, heartless, uncaring, unfeeling, inconsiderate, unsympathetic, unfriendly, uncharitable, harsh, mean, nasty, selfish, spiteful, vicious, malicious
opposite kind

unknown adjective
1 *The letter was in an unknown hand.*
unidentified, unrecognized
opposite known
2 *The author of the story is unknown.*
anonymous, nameless, unnamed, unspecified
opposite named

3 *The explorers entered unknown territory.*
unfamiliar, alien, foreign, undiscovered, unexplored, uncharted
opposite familiar
4 *The part was played by an unknown actor.*
little known, unheard of, obscure
opposite famous

unlike adjective
The food was unlike anything I had tasted before.
different from, distinct from
opposite similar (to)

unlikely adjective
No-one believed her unlikely excuse.
unbelievable, unconvincing, improbable, implausible, incredible, far-fetched
opposite likely

unlucky adjective
1 *Some people think that 13 is an unlucky number.*
unfavourable, ill-omened, ill-starred, jinxed
2 *By an unlucky chance, their plan was discovered.*
unfortunate, unwelcome, untimely
opposite lucky

unmarried adjective
If you are unmarried, you are **single**.
If your marriage has been legally ended, you are **divorced**.
An unmarried man is a **bachelor**.
An unmarried woman is a **spinster**.

unmistakable adjective
There was an unmistakable smell of burnt toast.
distinct, distinctive, clear, obvious, plain, telltale

unnatural adjective
1 *It's unnatural for it to snow in April.*
unusual, abnormal, odd, strange, weird, bizarre

a
b
c
d
e
f
g
h
i
j
k
l
m
n
o
p
q
r
s
t
u
v
w
x
y
z

2 *Some of the acting in the film was a bit unnatural.*
stiff, stilted, unrealistic, forced, self-conscious
3 *Her hair was an unnatural orange colour.*
artificial, synthetic, man-made, manufactured
opposite **natural**

unnecessary adjective
I'm deleting any unnecessary files from my computer.
inessential, non-essential, uncalled for, unwanted, excessive, superfluous, surplus, extra, redundant
opposite **necessary**

unoccupied adjective
1 *Since the fire, the flats have been unoccupied.*
empty, uninhabited, deserted, unused, vacant
opposite **occupied**
2 *The bathroom is unoccupied.*
available, vacant
opposite **engaged**

unpleasant adjective
1 *Mr Smallweed was a thoroughly unpleasant man.*
disagreeable, unfriendly, unkind, bad-tempered, nasty, malicious, spiteful, hateful
2 *Being lost in the jungle had been an unpleasant experience.*
uncomfortable, disagreeable, awful
3 *The smell from the drain was very unpleasant.*
disgusting, foul, repulsive, revolting, horrible, horrid, repellent, offensive, objectionable
See also **bad**
opposite **pleasant**

unpopular adjective
The new manager was unpopular at first.
disliked, hated, despised, unloved
opposite **popular**

unreal adjective
Everything seemed unreal, as if in a dream.
imaginary, made-up, fictitious, false, pretend
opposite **real**

unsafe adjective
see **dangerous**

unsatisfactory adjective
The repairs to the roof were unsatisfactory.
unacceptable, inadequate, disappointing, displeasing, poor, incompetent, insufficient
opposite **satisfactory**

unseen adjective
see **invisible**

unsteady adjective
The table was a bit unsteady.
unstable, shaky, wobbly, insecure, unbalanced, rickety
opposites **stable, steady**

unsure adjective
see **uncertain**

untidy adjective
1 *Our house is the one with the untidy garden.*
messy, disorderly, cluttered, jumbled, tangled, littered, chaotic
(informal) higgledy-piggledy, topsy-turvy
2 *His work was untidy and full of mistakes.*
careless, disorganized, slapdash
(informal) sloppy
3 *She arrived looking untidy and flustered.*
dishevelled, bedraggled, rumpled, unkempt, scruffy, slovenly

untrue adjective
see **false**

unusual adjective
1 *The weather was unusual for the time of year.*
abnormal, out of the ordinary, exceptional, remarkable, extraordinary, odd, peculiar,

A
B
C
D
E
F
G
H
I
J
K
L
M
N
O
P
Q
R
S
T
U
V
W
X
Y
Z

singular, strange, unexpected, irregular, unconventional, unheard of
opposite **ordinary**
2 *Ebenezer is an unusual name.*
uncommon, rare, unfamiliar
opposite **common**

unwell adjective
see **ill**

unwilling adjective
see **reluctant**

unwise adjective
see **foolish**

upheaval noun
Moving to a new house causes such an upheaval.
disruption, disturbance, upset, commotion, fuss

uphill adjective
1 *The last part of the road is uphill.*
upward, ascending, rising
2 *Finding a job proved to be an uphill struggle.*
hard, difficult, tough, strenuous, laborious, arduous, exhausting, gruelling, taxing

upkeep noun
The upkeep of a car can be expensive.
care, maintenance, running

upper adjective
My bedroom is on the upper floor.
higher, upstairs
opposite **lower**

upright adjective
1 *The car seat should be in an upright position.*
erect, perpendicular, vertical
opposite **horizontal**
2 *He is an upright member of the local community.*
honest, honourable, respectable, reputable, moral, virtuous, upstanding, principled, trustworthy
opposite **corrupt**

uproar noun
The meeting ended in uproar.
chaos, confusion, disorder, commotion, turmoil, pandemonium, mayhem, rumpus, furore

upset verb
1 *Something in the letter had upset her.*
distress, trouble, disturb, displease, unsettle, offend, dismay, grieve, fluster, perturb
2 *Bad weather upset the train timetable.*
disrupt, interfere with, interrupt, affect, throw out
3 *The baby upset a whole bowl of cereal.*
knock over, spill, tip over, topple
4 *A fallen tree branch upset the canoe.*
overturn, capsize

upset noun
1 *He is off school with a stomach upset.*
illness, ailment
(informal) bug
2 *They caused a major upset by winning 7–0.*
shock, surprise, upheaval

upside-down adjective
1 *I can't read the writing if it's upside-down.*
wrong way up, inverted
(informal) topsy-turvy
2 (informal) *Everything in her life seemed to be upside-down.*
in a mess, chaotic, disorderly, jumbled
(informal) higgledy-piggledy
opposite **orderly**

up to date adjective

Note that you write **up-to-date** immediately before a noun.

1 *The spacecraft uses up-to-date technology.*
new, modern, present-day, recent, current, the latest, advanced, cutting-edge
opposite **out of date**
2 *Her clothes are always up to date.*
fashionable, stylish, contemporary
(informal) trendy, hip
opposite **old-fashioned**

a
b
c
d
e
f
g
h
i
j
k
l
m
n
o
p
q
r
s
t
u
v
w
x
y
z

455

A

upward adjective
He started on the steep, upward climb.
uphill, ascending, rising
opposite **downward**

urban adjective
Most of the population live in urban areas.
built-up, densely populated
opposite **rural**

urge verb
He urged her to reconsider her decision.
advise, counsel, appeal to, beg, implore, plead with, press
To urge someone to do something is to **advocate** or **recommend** it.
to urge someone on
The fans tried to urge on their team.
encourage, spur on, egg on
opposite **discourage**

urge noun
I had a sudden urge to burst into song.
impulse, compulsion, longing, wish, yearning, desire, itch
(informal) **yen**

urgent adjective
1 *She had urgent business in New York.*
pressing, immediate, essential, important, top-priority
opposite **unimportant**
2 *He spoke in an urgent whisper.*
anxious, insistent, earnest

usable adjective
1 *The lift is not usable today.*
operating, working, functioning, functional
opposite **unusable**
2 *This ticket is usable only on certain trains.*
valid, acceptable
opposite **invalid**

use verb
1 *She used a calculator to add up the figures.*
make use of, employ, utilize
To use your knowledge is to **apply** it.
To use your muscles is to **exercise** them.
To use a musical instrument is to **play** it.

To use an axe or sword is to **wield** it.
To use people or things selfishly is to **exploit** them.
2 *Can you show me how to use the photocopier?*
operate, work, handle, manage
3 *You've used all the hot water.*
use up, go through, consume, exhaust, spend

use noun
1 *Would these books be any use to you?*
help, benefit, advantage, profit, value
2 *A sonic screwdriver has many uses.*
function, purpose, point

useful adjective
1 *A flask is useful for keeping food warm.*
convenient, handy, effective, efficient, practical
2 *The website offers some useful advice.*
good, helpful, valuable, worthwhile, constructive, invaluable
opposite **useless**

useless adjective
1 *This old vacuum cleaner is useless.*
ineffective, inefficient, impractical, unusable
opposites **useful, effective**
2 *Her advice was completely useless.*
worthless, unhelpful, pointless, futile, unprofitable, fruitless
opposite **useful**
3 (informal) *I'm useless at drawing.*
bad, poor, incompetent
(informal) **rubbish, hopeless**
opposite **good**

user-friendly adjective
The computer manual isn't very user-friendly.
easy to use, straightforward, uncomplicated, understandable

usual adjective
1 *I'll meet you at the usual time.*
normal, customary, familiar, habitual, regular, standard

A B C D E F G H I J K L M N O P Q R S T U V W X Y Z

2 *It's usual to knock before entering.*
common, accepted, conventional, traditional
opposite **unusual**

utensil noun
A row of cooking utensils hung on the wall.
tool, implement, device, gadget, instrument, appliance
For various tools see **tool**

utter¹ verb
The robot could only utter a few phrases.
say, speak, express, pronounce, put into words

utter² adjective
They stared at the unicorn in utter amazement.
complete, total, absolute, sheer, downright, out-and-out

vacancy noun
They have a vacancy for a trainee journalist.
job, opening, post, position, situation

vacant adjective
1 *The house over the road is still vacant.*
unoccupied, uninhabited, deserted, empty
opposite **occupied**
2 *The receptionist gave me a vacant stare.*
blank, expressionless, mindless, absent-minded, deadpan
opposite **alert**

vague adjective
1 *The directions she gave me were rather vague.*
indefinite, imprecise, broad, general, ill-defined, unclear, woolly
opposites **exact, detailed**

2 *A vague shape could be seen in the mist.*
blurred, indistinct, obscure, dim, hazy, shadowy
opposite **definite**

vain adjective
1 *The duchess was vain about her appearance.*
arrogant, proud, conceited, haughty, self-satisfied
opposite **modest**
2 *He made a vain attempt to tidy the room.*
unsuccessful, ineffective, useless, worthless, fruitless, futile, pointless
opposite **successful**

valid adjective
1 *The ticket is valid for three months.*
current, legal, approved, authorized, official, permitted, suitable, usable
2 *She made several valid points.*
acceptable, reasonable, sound, convincing, genuine, legitimate
opposite **invalid**

valley noun
A rocky path meandered through the valley.
vale, dale, dell, gorge, gully, hollow, pass, ravine, canyon
(Scottish) glen

valuable adjective
1 *Apparently the painting is very valuable.*
expensive, costly, dear, precious, priceless
2 *He gave her some valuable advice.*
useful, helpful, constructive, good, worthwhile, invaluable
opposite **worthless**

Notice that *invaluable* is not the opposite of **valuable.**

value noun
1 *The house has recently increased in value.*
price, cost, worth
2 *He stressed the value of taking regular exercise.*
advantage, benefit, merit, use, usefulness, importance

a
b
c
d
e
f
g
h
i
j
k
l
m
n
o
p
q
r
s
t
u
v
w
x
y
z

A
B
C
D
E
F
G
H
I
J
K
L
M
N
O
P
Q
R
S
T
U
V
W
X
Y
Z

value verb
1 *He had always valued her advice.*
appreciate, respect, esteem,
have a high opinion of, set great store by
To value something highly is to prize or
treasure it.
2 *A surveyor was sent to value the house.*
price, cost, rate, evaluate, assess

van noun
For various vehicles see vehicle

vanish verb
*With a flick of his wand, the wizard vanished
into thin air.*
disappear, go away, fade, dissolve,
disperse
opposite appear

vanity noun
*His vanity is such that he never admits he's
wrong.*
arrogance, pride, conceit, self-esteem,
self-importance

vapour noun
*Thick clouds of vapour poured from the
volcano.*
smoke, fumes, steam, gas
Vapour hanging in the air is haze, fog, mist,
or smog.
When something turns to vapour it
vaporizes.

variable adjective
*The temperature is variable at this time of
year.*
changeable, varying, fluctuating, erratic,
inconsistent, uncertain, unpredictable,
unsteady, unstable
If your loyalty to friends is variable,
you are fickle.
opposite constant

variation noun
*There are huge variations in age within the
group.*
difference, alteration, change,
fluctuation, shift

variety noun
1 *The centre offers a variety of leisure
activities.*
assortment, mixture, array
2 *The supermarket has over thirty varieties
of pasta.*
kind, sort, type, make, brand
A variety of animal is a breed or species.
3 *There is not much variety in her choice of
words.*
variation, change, difference, diversity

various adjective & determiner
The hats are available in various colours.
different, assorted, several, varying,
differing, a variety of, diverse

vary verb
1 *The length of daylight varies with the
seasons.*
change, alter, differ, fluctuate
2 *They vary the menu from week to week.*
change, modify, adjust, alter

vast adjective
1 *The miser accumulated a vast fortune.*
large, huge, enormous, great, immense,
massive
2 *A vast stretch of water lay between them
and dry land.*
broad, wide, extensive, sweeping
opposites small, tiny

vault verb
to vault over something
He vaulted over the fence.
jump over, leap over, bound over,
spring over, clear, hurdle

vault noun
*The gold was stored in the vaults of
the bank.*
strongroom, treasury
An underground part of a house is a cellar.
A room underneath a church is a crypt.

veer verb
The car suddenly veered to the left.
change direction, swerve, turn

vegetable noun

WORD WEB

GREEN VEGETABLES
broccoli, Brussels sprout, cabbage, cauliflower, Chinese cabbage, kale, spinach

ROOT VEGETABLES
beetroot, carrot, parsnip, radish, swede, sweet potato, turnip

LEGUMES OR PULSES
broad bean, butter bean, chickpea, French bean, kidney bean, lentil, mangetout, sugar-snap, pea, runner bean, soya bean

OTHER VEGETABLES
artichoke, asparagus, aubergine, celeriac, celery, courgette, garlic, leek, marrow, mushroom, okra, onion, pepper, potato, pumpkin, shallot, squash, sweetcorn, water chestnut, yam

vegetarian noun
A person who doesn't eat any animal products is a **vegan**.
An animal that feeds only on plants is a **herbivore**.
The opposite—a person or animal that eats flesh—is a **carnivore**.

vegetation noun
The rainforest is filled with lush vegetation.
foliage, greenery, growth, plants, undergrowth

vehicle noun

WORD WEB

VEHICLES WHICH CARRY PEOPLE
bus, cab, camper, car or motor car, caravan, coach, jeep, minibus, minicab, people carrier, rickshaw, taxi, train, tram, trolleybus

See also **aircraft, bicycle, boat, car, railway**

VEHICLES USED FOR WORK
ambulance, bulldozer, dustcart, fire-engine, hearse, HGV or heavy goods vehicle, horsebox, lorry, milk float, removal van, pick-up truck, police car, steamroller, tank, tanker, tractor, truck, van

VEHICLES WHICH TRAVEL ON SNOW OR ICE
sled, sledge, sleigh, skidoo, snowplough, toboggan

OLD HORSE-DRAWN VEHICLES
carriage, cart, chariot, coach, gig, stagecoach, trap, wagon

veil verb
Her face was partly veiled by a scarf.
cover, conceal, hide, mask, shroud

vein noun
A tube in the body that carries blood away from the heart is an **artery**.
Veins and arteries are **blood vessels**.
Delicate hair-like blood vessels are **capillaries**.

vengeance noun
The knight swore vengeance on his enemies.
revenge, retribution, retaliation
opposite **forgiveness**

venomous adjective
The adder is Britain's only venomous snake.
poisonous
opposite **harmless**

vent noun
A vent in the roof lets the smoke out.
gap, hole, opening, outlet, slit
to give vent to
She gave vent to her anger.
express, let go, release

venture noun
His first business venture was a disaster.
enterprise, undertaking, project, scheme

a
b
c
d
e
f
g
h
i
j
k
l
m
n
o
p
q
r
s
t
u
v
w
x
y
z

A B C D E F G H I J K L M N O P Q R S T U **V** W X Y Z

venture verb
They ventured out into the snow.
journey, set forth, dare to go

verdict noun
What was the jury's verdict?
conclusion, decision, judgement, opinion

verge noun
Don't park on the verge of the road.
side, edge, margin
A stone or concrete edging beside a road is a kerb.
The flat strip of road beside a motorway is the hard shoulder.

verify verb
Several witnesses verified his statement.
confirm, prove, support
(informal) check out

versatile adjective
He's a very versatile musician.
adaptable, resourceful, many-sided, all-round, flexible

verse noun
1 *Most of the play is written in verse.*
rhyme
The rhythm of a line of verse is its metre.
Something written in verse is poetry or a poem.
See also poem
2 *We need to learn the first two verses of the poem by heart.*
stanza

version noun
1 *The two newspapers gave different versions of the accident.*
account, description, story, report
2 *It's an English version of a French play.*
adaptation, interpretation
A version of something which was originally in another language is a translation.
3 *A new version of the computer game will be released in May.*
design, model, form, variation

vertical adjective
The fence posts must be vertical.
erect, perpendicular, upright
A vertical drop is a sheer drop.
opposite horizontal

very adverb
Carl is a very talented juggler.
extremely, highly, enormously, exceedingly, truly, intensely, especially, particularly, remarkably, unusually, uncommonly, outstandingly, really
(informal) terribly
opposite slightly

vessel noun
1 *A fishing vessel has gone missing in the North Sea.*
boat, ship, craft
For types of boat or ship see boat
2 *Archaeologists found clay vessels at the site.*
pot, dish, bowl, jar, bottle, container
blood vessels
Blood vessels are your arteries, capillaries, and veins.

vex verb
It vexed her that he'd forgotten her birthday.
annoy, irritate, make you cross, upset, anger, exasperate

vibrate verb
I pulled a lever and the whole engine began to vibrate.
shake, shudder, tremble, throb, judder, quake, quiver, rattle

vicious adjective
1 *This was once the scene of a vicious murder.*
brutal, barbaric, violent, bloodthirsty, cruel, merciless, pitiless, ruthless, callous, inhuman, malicious, sadistic, atrocious, barbarous, murderous, villainous, wicked
2 *Male baboons can be vicious if provoked.*
fierce, ferocious, violent, savage, wild

victim noun
1 *Ambulances took the victims to hospital.*
casualty
Victims of an accident are also **the injured** or **the wounded**.
A person who dies in an accident is a **fatality**.
2 *The hawk carried its victim in its talons.*
prey

victor noun
Who were the victors in the battle?
winner, conqueror, champion

victorious adjective
A trophy was presented to the victorious team.
winning, triumphant, conquering, successful, top, first
opposite defeated

victory noun
Hannibal won several victories over the Romans.
win, success, triumph
opposite defeat

view noun
1 *There's a good view from the top of the hill.*
outlook, prospect, scene, panorama, scenery
2 *What are your views on animal testing?*
opinion, thought, attitude, belief, conviction, idea, notion
in view of something
In view of the circumstances, they gave her a refund.
because of, as a result of, considering, taking account of

view verb
1 *Thousand of tourists come to view Niagara Falls each year.*
look at, see, watch, observe, regard, contemplate, gaze at, inspect, survey, examine, eye
2 *Wanda viewed her cousin with extreme dislike.*
think of, consider, regard

viewer noun
People who view a performance are the **audience** or **spectators**.
People who view something as they happen to pass by are **bystanders**, **onlookers**, or **witnesses**.

vigilant adjective
A lookout has to be vigilant at all times.
alert, watchful, attentive, wary, careful, observant, on the lookout, on your guard
opposite negligent

vigorous adjective
1 *She does an hour of vigorous exercise every week.*
active, brisk, energetic, enthusiastic, lively, strenuous
2 *I gave the door a vigorous push.*
forceful, powerful, mighty
3 *He was a vigorous man in the prime of life.*
healthy, strong
opposite feeble

vigour noun
When they sighted land, they began to row with vigour.
energy, force, spirit, vitality, gusto, verve, enthusiasm, liveliness, zeal, zest

vile adjective
1 *The professor gave us a vile concoction to drink.*
disgusting, repulsive, revolting, foul, horrible, loathsome, offensive, repellent, sickening, nauseating
opposite pleasant
2 *Murder is a vile crime.*
dreadful, despicable, appalling, contemptible, wicked, evil

villain noun
Detectives are on the trail of an infamous villain.
criminal, offender, rogue, wrongdoer
An informal word for the villain in a story is **baddy**.
opposite hero
See also **criminal**

A B C D E F G H I J K L M N O P Q R S T U V W X Y Z

violate verb
He was penalized for violating the rules.
break, disobey, infringe, flout, disregard, ignore

violation noun
He's guilty of a violation of the rules.
breach, breaking, offence (against)
A violation of the rules of a game is a foul or an infringement.

violence noun
1 *The marchers protested against the use of violence.*
fighting, might, war, brute force, barbarity, brutality, cruelty, savagery
opposites non-violence, pacifism
2 *The violence of the storm uprooted trees.*
force, power, strength, severity, intensity, ferocity, fierceness, fury, rage
opposites gentleness, mildness

violent adjective
1 *There were violent clashes in the streets..*
aggressive, forceful, rough, fierce, frenzied, vicious, brutal
opposites gentle, mild
2 *The bridge was washed away in a violent storm.*
severe, strong, powerful, forceful, raging, tempestuous, turbulent, wild
opposites weak, feeble

virtually adverb
It's virtually impossible to tell if the letter is genuine.
almost, nearly, practically, as good as, in effect

virtue noun
1 *She has the virtue of a saint!*
goodness, decency, honesty, integrity, righteousness, uprightness, worthiness, morality
opposite vice
2 *One virtue of living in the country is that it's quiet.*
advantage, benefit, asset, good point, merit, strength

virtuous adjective
She had always tried to lead a virtuous life.
good, honest, honourable, innocent, just, law-abiding, moral, praiseworthy, pure, righteous, trustworthy, upright, worthy
opposite wicked

visible adjective
There were no visible signs that the door had been forced.
noticeable, obvious, conspicuous, clear, distinct, evident, apparent, perceptible, recognizable, detectable
opposite invisible

vision noun
1 *He began to have problems with his vision.*
eyesight, sight
2 *The soothsayer saw a vision of the future.*
apparition, dream, hallucination
Something travellers in the desert think they see is a mirage.
3 *As an artist, she has great vision.*
foresight, imagination, insight

visit verb
They're visiting friends in Toronto for a few days.
call on, come to see, drop in on, go to see, pay a call on, stay with

visit noun
1 *My grandmother is coming for a visit.*
call, stay
2 *We are planning a short visit to Paris.*
trip, excursion, outing

visitor noun
1 *They've got some Polish visitors staying with them.*
guest, caller
2 *Rome welcomes millions of visitors every year.*
tourist, holidaymaker, sightseer, traveller

visualize verb
I can't visualize her with curly hair.
imagine, picture, envisage, see

vital adjective
It is vital *that you remember the secret password.*
essential, crucial, imperative, important, necessary, indispensable
opposite **unimportant**

vitality noun
That painting of sunflowers bursts with vitality.
energy, life, liveliness, spirit, animation, exuberance, vigour, zest

vivid adjective
1 *Gauguin often painted in* vivid *colours.*
bright, colourful, strong, intense, vibrant, dazzling, brilliant, glowing, striking, showy
2 *He gave a* vivid *description of his travels in Mexico.*
lively, clear, powerful, evocative, imaginative, dramatic, lifelike, realistic, graphic
opposite **dull**

voice noun
The robot spoke with a slow, metallic voice.
speech, tone, way of speaking
For types of singing voice see **sing**

WRITING TIPS
You can use these words to describe a voice
croaky, droning, gruff, high-pitched, husky, low, shrill, soft-spoken, squeaky, throaty
It was a low, soft voice, plush as velvet, with sibilants as swashing as the sea.
— Geraldine McCaughrean, *Peter Pan in Scarlet*

voice verb
He voiced *several objections to the plan.*
express, communicate, put into words, speak

volcano noun
Molten rock that builds up inside a volcano is **magma**.
Molten rock that pours from a volcano is **lava**.
Lava and ash pouring from a volcano is an **eruption**.
A volcano that often erupts is an **active** volcano.
A volcano that can no longer erupt is an **extinct** volcano.
A scientist who studies volcanoes is a **vulcanologist**.

volume noun
1 *We had to measure the* volume *of the jug.*
capacity, size, dimensions
2 *They struggle to cope with the* volume *of fan mail they receive.*
amount, quantity, bulk, mass
3 *The full encyclopedia consists of twenty* volumes.
book, tome

voluntary adjective
She does voluntary *work for a charity.*
optional, unpaid
opposite **compulsory**

volunteer verb
No-one volunteered *to do the washing-up.*
offer, put yourself forward, be willing

vomit verb
The seasickness made him want to vomit.
be sick, heave, retch
(informal) **throw up**

vortex noun
see **spiral**

vote verb
Everyone has a right to vote *in the election.*
cast your vote
to vote for someone or something
I haven't decided who to vote *for.*
choose, opt for, nominate, elect

A
B
C
D
E
F
G
H
I
J
K
L
M
N
O
P
Q
R
S
T
U
V
W
X
Y
Z

vote noun
The results of the vote will be known tomorrow.
ballot, election, poll, referendum

voucher noun
You can exchange this voucher for a free drink.
coupon, ticket, token

vow verb
He vowed never to reveal the genie's name.
pledge, promise, guarantee, swear, give your word, take an oath
vow noun
The mermaid took a vow to leave the sea forever.
pledge, promise, oath, word

voyage noun
A holiday voyage is a cruise.
A voyage across a channel or sea is a crossing.
A long voyage is a sea passage.
For other ways to travel see travel

vulgar adjective
1 *The new colour scheme just looks vulgar to me.*
tasteless, unsophisticated, cheap, tawdry
(informal) tacky
opposite tasteful
2 *The book sometimes uses vulgar language.*
indecent, offensive, rude, coarse
opposite decent

vulnerable adjective
As night fell, the outlaws were in a vulnerable position.
defenceless, exposed, unguarded, unprotected, at risk
opposite safe

waddle verb
A pair of geese waddled along the path.
toddle, totter, shuffle, shamble, wobble

wade verb
1 *Is it safe to wade in the river?*
paddle, wallow
2 *She had piles of paperwork to wade through.*
toil, labour, work, plough

wag verb
The dog was eagerly wagging its tail.
move to and fro, shake, swing, wave, waggle, wiggle

wage noun
How much is your weekly wage?
earnings, income, pay, pay packet
A fixed regular amount you are paid for work is a salary.

wage verb
The Greeks waged a long war against Troy.
carry on, conduct, fight

wail verb
Upstairs, the baby began to wail.
cry, howl, bawl, cry, moan, shriek

wait verb
Please wait here until I get back.
remain where you are, stay, stop, rest, pause, linger
(informal) hang about or around, hold on
wait noun
There was a long wait before the show began.
interval, pause, delay, hold-up

wake or **waken** verb
1 *Hagor the giant woke from a deep sleep.*
awake, awaken, become conscious, come round, rise, arise, stir, wake up
2 *The alarm clock woke me at 6 a.m.*
rouse, arouse, awaken, disturb

walk verb

OVERUSED WORD

Try to vary the words you use for walk.
Here are some other words you could use.

TO **WALK SLOWLY**
amble, crawl, creep, dodder, pace, plod,
saunter, step, stroll, wander
*I sauntered down the lane, humming a
tune.*

TO **WALK UNSTEADILY**
hobble, limp, lope, lurch, shamble,
shuffle, stagger, stumble, toddle, totter,
waddle
*A squat little troll shuffled towards the
forest.*

TO **WALK HEAVILY OR LOUDLY**
clump, pound, stamp, traipse, tramp,
trudge, wade
The robot clumped its way up the stairs.

TO **WALK QUIETLY**
pad, patter, prowl, slink, stalk, steal,
tiptoe
The burglar slunk away into the shadows.

TO **WALK SMARTLY OR PROUDLY**
march, parade, stride, strut, swagger,
trot
*Captain Flint swaggered on board the
ship.*

TO **WALK A LONG DISTANCE**
hike, trek, ramble
*They are planning to trek across the
Himalayas.*

TO **WALK IN A GROUP**
file, troop
The children trooped into the classroom.

walk noun

1 *We went for a walk in the country.*
stroll, saunter, ramble, hike, trek, tramp,
trudge
2 *There are some lovely walks through the
forest.*
path, route

walker noun

When you walk along the street, you are a
pedestrian.
If you go for long walks, you are a **hiker** or
rambler.

wall noun

*A crumbling stone wall surrounded the
cottage.*
barricade, barrier, fortification,
embankment
A wall to hold back water is a **dam** or **dyke.**
A low wall along the edge of a roof is a
parapet.
A wall built on top of a bank of earth is a
rampart.
A wall or fence made of sticks is a **stockade.**

wallow verb

1 *Hippos like to wallow in mud.*
roll about, flounder, wade, lie, loll
2 *He is wallowing in all the attention.*
revel, take delight, bask

wand noun

The fairy gave a flick of her magic wand.
stick, rod, baton, staff
For other words to do with magic see **magic**

wander verb

1 *Sheep wandered about the hills.*
stray, roam, rove, range, ramble, meander,
travel, walk
2 *We must have wandered off the path.*
stray, turn, veer, swerve

wane verb

1 *At sunset, the light began to wane.*
fade, fail, dim
opposite **brighten**
2 *Her enthusiasm waned after a while.*
decline, decrease, lessen, diminish, subside,
weaken, dwindle
opposite **strengthen**

want verb

1 *He desperately wants to win a medal.*
wish, desire, long, hope

a
b
c
d
e
f
g
h
i
j
k
l
m
n
o
p
q
r
s
t
u
v
w
x
y
z

465

2 *Gayle had always* wanted *a pony.*
wish for, desire, fancy, crave, long for,
yearn for, hanker after, pine for,
set your heart on, hunger for, thirst for
3 *That floor* wants *a good scrub.*
need, require

want noun

1 *The hotel staff saw to all their* wants.
demand, desire, wish, need, requirement
2 *The plants died for* want *of water.*
lack, need, absence

war noun

The war *between the two countries lasted
many years.*
fighting, warfare, conflict, strife, hostilities
See also **fight**

ward verb

to ward off someone or something
1 *He put up his shield to* ward off *the blow.*
avert, block, check, deflect, turn aside,
parry
2 *The charm was meant to* ward off *bad luck.*
fend off, drive away, repel, keep away,
push away

wares plural noun

The market traders displayed their wares.
goods, merchandise, produce, stock,
commodities

warlike adjective

The Picts were said to be a warlike *people.*
aggressive, fierce, violent, hostile,
quarrelsome, militant
opposite **peaceful**

warm adjective

1 *It was a* warm *September evening.*
Weather which is unpleasantly warm is **close**
or **sultry**.
Water or food which is only just warm is
lukewarm or **tepid**.
A common simile is **as warm as toast**.
opposite **cold**
2 *Sandy put on a* warm *jumper.*
cosy, thick, woolly
opposite **thin**

3 *The fans gave the singer a* warm *welcome.*
friendly, warm-hearted, welcoming, kind,
affectionate, genial, amiable, loving,
sympathetic
opposite **unfriendly**

warm verb

She sat by the fire, warming *her hands and
feet.*
heat, make warmer, thaw out
opposite **chill**

warn verb

The guide warned *us to keep to the path.*
advise, caution, alert, remind
To warn people of danger is to
raise the alarm.

warning noun

1 *There was no* warning *of the danger ahead.*
sign, signal, indication, advance notice
2 *The traffic warden let him off with a
warning.*
caution, reprimand

warp verb

The wheel had slightly warped *with age.*
bend, buckle, twist, curl,
bend out of shape, distort

warrior noun

see **fighter**

wary adjective

The cat is always wary *when strangers are
around.*
cautious, distrustful, suspicious, careful,
watchful, attentive, vigilant, on your guard
opposite **reckless**

wash verb

1 *It took Rapunzel a long time to* wash *her
hair.*
clean
To wash something with a cloth is to **mop,
sponge,** or **wipe** it.
To wash something with a brush is to
scrub it.
To wash something in clean water is to
rinse, sluice, or **swill** it.

To wash yourself all over is to **bath** or
shower.
2 *Waves washed over the beach.*
flow, splash

waste verb
Let's not waste any more time.
squander, misuse, throw away,
fritter away
opposite save

waste noun
A lot of household waste can be recycled.
rubbish, refuse, trash, garbage, junk,
litter
Waste food is **leftovers**.
Waste metal is **scrap**.

wasteful adjective
*It's wasteful to cook more food than
you need.*
extravagant, uneconomical, prodigal,
lavish, spendthrift
opposites economical, thrifty

watch verb
1 *I could sit and watch the sea for hours.*
gaze at, look at, stare at, view,
contemplate
2 *Watch how the batsman holds the bat.*
observe, take notice of, keep your eyes on,
pay attention to, attend to, heed, note
3 *Could you watch my bag for a minute?*
keep an eye on, keep watch over, guard,
mind, look after, safeguard, supervise,
tend
to watch out
Watch out—there's a car coming!
be careful, pay attention, beware,
take care, take heed

watch noun
For instruments used to measure time
see **time**

watchful adjective
She kept a watchful eye on the baby.
alert, attentive, observant, vigilant, careful,
sharp-eyed, keen

water noun

WORD WEB
SOME AREAS OF WATER
brook, (Scottish) burn, canal, lake,
lido, (Scottish) loch, ocean, pond, pool,
reservoir, river, rivulet, sea, stream

Animals and plants which live in water
are **aquatic**.

SPORTS PLAYED IN OR NEAR WATER
angling, canoeing, deep-sea diving,
diving, kayaking, rafting, rowing,
sailing, snorkelling, swimming, surfing,
water polo, waterskiing, windsurfing

WRITING TIPS
You can use these words to describe
how water moves

bubble, cascade, dribble, drip, flood,
flow, froth, gurgle, gush, jet, ooze,
overflow, ripple, roll, run, seep, shower,
spill, spatter, splash, spout, spray,
sprinkle, spurt, squirt, stream, surge,
sweep, swirl, swish, trickle, well up
*The water cascaded over the lip of the
basin and dropped, in a miniature Niagara
Falls, onto the kitchen floor.*
— Ian Ogilvy, *Measle and the Slitherghoul*

See also **flow**

water verb
Please remember to water the plants.
wet, irrigate, sprinkle, dampen, moisten,
soak, drench

watery adjective
1 *The soup was watery and tasteless.*
weak, thin, runny, diluted, watered down
2 *Chopping onions makes my eyes watery.*
tearful, wet, damp, moist

wave verb
1 *The tall grass waved in the breeze.*
move to and fro, sway, swing, flap, flutter

A
B
C
D
E
F
G
H
I
J
K
L
M
N
O
P
Q
R
S
T
U
V
W
X
Y
Z

2 *I got their attention by* **waving** *a newspaper.*
shake, brandish, flourish, twirl, wag,
waggle, wiggle

wave noun

1 *We watched the* **waves** *break on the shore.*
breaker, roller, billow
A very small wave is a **ripple**.
A huge wave caused by an earthquake is a
tidal wave or **tsunami**.
A number of white waves following each
other is **surf**.
The top of a wave is the **crest** or **ridge**.
2 *A* **wave** *of anger spread through*
the crowd.
surge, outbreak

waver verb

1 *She* **wavered** *about whether to send the*
letter.
hesitate, dither, falter, be uncertain,
think twice
2 *The candle flame* **wavered** *in the draught.*
flicker, quiver, tremble, shake, shiver

wavy adjective

The mermaid combed her long **wavy** *hair.*
curly, curling, rippling, winding, zigzag
opposite **straight**

way noun

1 *Which* **way** *is it to the bus station?*
direction, route, road, path
2 *Is your house a long* **way** *from here?*
distance, journey
3 *This is the best* **way** *to make porridge.*
method, procedure, process, system,
technique
4 *What a childish* **way** *to behave!*
manner, fashion, style
5 *In some* **ways**, *the brothers are very alike.*
respect, particular, feature, detail,
aspect
6 *Things are in a bad* **way**.
state, condition

weak adjective

1 *The footbridge was old and* **weak** *in places.*
fragile, flimsy, rickety, shaky, unsound,
unsteady, unsafe, decrepit

2 *The patient was too* **weak** *to walk very far.*
feeble, frail, ill, sickly, infirm, delicate,
puny
3 *The nobles plotted against the* **weak** *king.*
timid, spineless, ineffective, powerless,
useless
4 *The film was fun, but the plot was a bit*
weak.
feeble, lame, unsatisfactory,
unconvincing
5 *He asked for a mug of* **weak** *tea.*
watery, diluted, tasteless, thin
(informal) wishy-washy
opposite **strong**

weaken verb

1 *Too much water will* **weaken** *the flavour.*
reduce, lessen, diminish, sap, undermine
2 *The storm had* **weakened** *overnight.*
decrease, decline, die down, fade, dwindle,
ebb away, wane
opposite **strengthen**

weakness noun

1 *He pointed out the* **weakness** *in their plan.*
fault, flaw, defect, imperfection,
weak point
2 *Eve has a* **weakness** *for toffee apples.*
liking, fondness
(informal) soft spot

wealth noun

The family had acquired its **wealth** *from coal.*
fortune, money, riches, affluence,
prosperity
opposite **poverty**
a wealth of
There's a **wealth of** *information on the*
Internet.
lots of, plenty of, an abundance of,
a profusion of

wealthy adjective

They say that he comes from a very **wealthy**
family.
rich, well-off, affluent, prosperous,
moneyed, well-to-do
(informal) flush, loaded
opposite **poor**

weapon noun
Weapons in general are **weaponry**
or **arms**.
A collection or store of weapons is an
armoury or **arsenal**.

WORD WEB

VARIOUS WEAPONS
bayonet, blowpipe, bomb, dagger,
gun, hand-grenade, harpoon,
machine-gun, missile, mortar, pistol,
revolver, rifle, shell, sword, torpedo,
truncheon
See also **sword**

SOME WEAPONS USED IN THE PAST
battering ram, battleaxe, blunderbuss,
bow and arrow, cannon, catapult,
crossbow, javelin, lance, longbow,
musket, pike, spear, staff, tomahawk,
trident

wear verb wears, wearing, wore, worn
1 *Can I* wear *my new dress to the
party?*
dress in, be dressed in, have on
2 *The rug in the hallway is starting
to* wear.
fray, wear away, wear out
3 *Those tyres have* worn *well.*
last, endure, survive
to wear off
The pain will wear off *soon.*
die down, disappear, ease, fade, lessen,
subside, weaken

weary adjective
The children were weary *after the long
walk.*
tired, worn out, exhausted, fatigued,
flagging
(informal) all in

weather noun
The typical weather in a particular area is
the **climate**.
A person who studies and forecasts the
weather is a **meteorologist**.

WORD WEB

SOME TYPES OF WEATHER
fog: mist, (Scottish) haar, haze,
smog; ice and snow: blizzard,
frost, hail, ice, sleet, snowstorm;
light rain: drizzle, shower;
heavy rain: cloudburst, deluge,
downpour, monsoon, torrent;
sun: drought, heatwave,
sunshine; storm: squall, tempest;
light wind: breeze, gust;
strong wind: cyclone, gale, hurricane,
tornado, typhoon, whirlwind

See also **sky**, **wind**[1]

WRITING TIPS
You can use these words to describe
weather

TO DESCRIBE **CLOUDY WEATHER**
dull, grey, overcast, sunless

TO DESCRIBE **COLD WEATHER**
arctic, bitter, chilly, frosty, icy, nippy,
perishing, raw, snowy, wintry

TO DESCRIBE **SNOW**
crisp, powdery, slushy

TO DESCRIBE **HOT WEATHER**
baking, humid, melting, roasting,
sizzling, sticky, sultry, sweltering

TO DESCRIBE **STORMY WEATHER**
rough, squally, tempestuous, turbulent,
violent, wild

THUNDER MAY
boom, crash, resound, roar, rumble

TO DESCRIBE **SUNNY WEATHER**
bright, cloudless, fair, fine, springlike,
summery, sunny, sunshiny

TO DESCRIBE **WET WEATHER**
damp, drizzly, raining cats and dogs,
showery, spitting, torrential

RAIN MAY
lash or pelt down, pour, pour down,
teem
(informal) bucket, tip down

The sky rumbled loudly above them and the rain continued to pour down, bouncing on the lane and running into little streams.
— Michelle Magorian, *Goodnight Mister Tom*

TO DESCRIBE **WINDY WEATHER**
biting, blowy, blustery, breezy, gusty
WIND MAY
batter, blast, buffet, howl, moan, wail

weather verb
The tiny ship weathered the storm.
survive, withstand, endure, come through

weave verb
He weaved his way through the crowd.
wind, zigzag, twist and turn

web noun
A web of tunnels lay under the castle.
net, network, mesh

wedding noun
She was a bridesmaid at the wedding.
marriage
A formal word for a wedding is **nuptials**.

WORD WEB

PEOPLE WHO MAY BE INVOLVED IN A WEDDING
best man, bride, bridegroom, bridesmaid, groom, maid or **matron of honour, page, registrar, usher, wedding guests**

See also **marry**

wedge verb
The door was wedged open with an old shoe.
jam, stick

weep verb weeps, weeping, wept
Deirdre began to weep.
cry, sob, shed tears
To weep noisily is to **bawl** or **blubber**.
To weep in an annoying way is to **snivel** or **whimper**.

weigh verb
to weigh someone down
1 *Many troubles* weighed *him* down.
bother, worry, trouble, distress, burden
2 *She was* weighed down *with shopping.*
load, burden, lumber
to weigh something up
The detective weighed up *the evidence.*
consider, assess, evaluate, examine, study, ponder

weight noun
Take care when lifting heavy weights.
load, mass, burden
For units for measuring weight see **measurement**

weighty adjective
1 *He lifted a* weighty *volume off the shelf.*
heavy, bulky, cumbersome
opposite light
2 *They had* weighty *matters to discuss.*
important, serious, grave, significant
opposites unimportant, trivial

weird adjective
1 *Weird noises have been heard in the tower at midnight.*
eerie, ghostly, unearthly, mysterious, uncanny, unnatural
(informal) **spooky, creepy**
opposites ordinary, natural
2 *My big sister has a* weird *taste in music.*
strange, odd, peculiar, bizarre, curious, quirky, eccentric, outlandish, unconventional, unusual
(informal) **wacky, way-out**
opposite conventional

welcome noun
The landlady gave us a friendly welcome.
greeting, reception
welcome adjective
1 *A cup of tea would be very* welcome.
pleasant, pleasing, agreeable, appreciated, desirable, acceptable
opposites unwelcome, unacceptable

2 *You're* welcome *to use my bike.*
allowed, permitted, free
opposite **forbidden**

welcome verb
1 *An elderly butler* welcomed *us at the door.*
greet, receive, meet, hail
2 *We* welcome *suggestions from the public.*
appreciate, accept, like, want

welfare noun
Her only concern was the welfare *of her children.*
well-being, good, benefit, interests

well adverb
1 *The whole team played* well *on Saturday.*
ably, skilfully, expertly, effectively, efficiently, admirably, marvellously, wonderfully
opposite **badly**
2 *It's cold outside, so you'd better wrap up* well.
properly, suitably, correctly, thoroughly, carefully
3 *I know her brother* well.
closely, intimately, personally

well adjective
Mrs Orr looks surprisingly well *for her age.*
healthy, fit, strong, sound, robust, vigorous, lively, hearty
opposite **ill**

well-known adjective
A well-known *athlete will open the new sports shop.*
famous, celebrated, prominent, notable, renowned, distinguished, eminent
opposites **unknown, obscure**

went
past tense see **go**

west noun, adjective, & adverb
The parts of a continent or country in the west are the **western** parts.
To travel towards the west is to travel **westward** or **westwards**.
A wind from the west is a **westerly** wind.

wet adjective
1 *Archie took off his* wet *clothes and had a hot bath.*
damp, soaked, soaking, drenched, dripping, sopping, wringing wet
2 *The pitch was too* wet *to play on.*
waterlogged, saturated, sodden, soggy, dewy, muddy, boggy
3 *Take care—the paint is still* wet.
runny, sticky, tacky
4 *It was cold and* wet *all afternoon.*
rainy, showery, pouring, drizzly, misty
See also **weather**
opposite **dry**

wet verb wets, wetting, wet or wetted
Wet the clay before you start to mould it.
dampen, moisten, soak, water
opposite **dry**

wheel noun
A small wheel under a piece of furniture is a **caster**.
The centre of a wheel is the **hub**.
The outer edge of a wheel is the **rim**.

wheel verb
1 *A pair of seagulls* wheeled *overhead.*
circle, orbit
2 *The column of soldiers* wheeled *to the right.*
swing round, turn, veer, swerve

whiff noun
I caught a whiff *of coffee as I walked past the café.*
smell, scent, aroma

while noun
You may need to wait a while *for the next train.*
period, time, spell

whimper or whine verb
A dog whimpered *in the corner of the room.*
cry, moan

whip verb
1 *The jockey* whipped *his horse to make it go faster.*
beat, hit, lash, flog, thrash

A
B
C
D
E
F
G
H
I
J
K
L
M
N
O
P
Q
R
S
T
U
V
W
X
Y
Z

2 Whip *the cream until it is thick.*
beat, whisk

whirl verb
The snowflakes whirled in the icy wind.
turn, twirl, spin, twist, circle, spiral, reel,
pirouette, revolve, rotate

whisk verb
Whisk the egg yolks together in a bowl.
beat, whip, mix, stir

whisper verb
What are you two whispering about?
murmur, mutter, mumble
opposite **shout**

whistle noun & verb
For various sounds see **sound**¹

white adjective & noun

WORD WEB
SOME SHADES OF WHITE
**cream, ivory, off-white, platinum,
silvery, snow-white**

When coloured things become whiter
they become **bleached** or **faded**.
When someone turns white with fear
they **blanch** or **turn pale**.
Hair that is **hoary** is white with age.
Something which is rather white is
whitish.
Common similes are **as white as a sheet**,
as white as chalk, and **as white as snow**.

whole adjective
1 *I haven't read the whole book yet.*
complete, entire, full, total,
unabbreviated
opposite **incomplete**
2 *The dinosaur skeleton appears to
be whole.*
in one piece, intact, unbroken,
undamaged, perfect
opposites **broken, in pieces**

wholesome adjective
Pets should be fed a wholesome diet.
healthy, nutritious, nourishing
opposite **unhealthy**

wholly adverb
I'm not wholly convinced by his story.
completely, totally, fully, entirely, utterly,
thoroughly
opposite **partly**

wicked adjective
1 *Cinderella had a wicked stepmother.*
evil, cruel, vicious, villainous, detestable,
mean, corrupt, immoral, sinful, foul,
vile
opposites **good, virtuous**
2 *They hatched a wicked scheme to take over
the world.*
evil, fiendish, malicious, malevolent,
diabolical, monstrous, deplorable, dreadful,
shameful
3 *The goblin had a wicked grin on his face.*
mischievous, playful, impish, naughty

wide adjective
1 *The hotel is close to a wide sandy beach.*
broad, expansive, extensive, large,
spacious
opposite **narrow**
2 *She has a wide knowledge of classical
music.*
comprehensive, vast, wide-ranging,
encyclopedic
opposite **limited**

widely adverb
The story of Cinderella is widely known.
commonly, everywhere, far and wide

widespread adjective
*There is widespread interest in the new
engine design.*
general, extensive, universal, wholesale
Something which spreads over the whole
world is **global** or **worldwide**.
opposite **uncommon**

width noun
The room is about eight feet in width.
breadth
The distance across a circle is its diameter.

wield verb
The lumberjack was wielding his axe.
brandish, flourish, hold, use

wife noun
Katherine is Mr Gray's second wife.
Another word for a person's wife or husband is spouse.

wild adjective
1 *I don't like seeing wild animals in captivity.*
undomesticated, untamed
opposite tame
2 *The hedgerow was full of wild flowers.*
natural, uncultivated
opposite cultivated
3 *To the west is a wild and mountainous region.*
rough, rugged, uncultivated, uninhabited, desolate
opposite cultivated
4 *The crowd was wild with excitement.*
riotous, rowdy, disorderly, unruly, boisterous, excited, noisy, uncontrollable, hysterical
opposites calm, restrained
5 *The weather looked wild outside.*
blustery, windy, gusty, stormy, turbulent, tempestuous
opposite calm

wilful adjective
1 *He was very wilful as a child.*
obstinate, stubborn, strong-willed, pig-headed
2 *There is a fine for wilful damage to trees.*
deliberate, intentional, planned, conscious

will noun
They seem to have lost the will to win.
desire, wish, determination, resolution, will-power, resolve, purpose

willing adjective
1 *She is always willing to help.*
eager, happy, pleased, ready, prepared
opposite unwilling
2 *I need a couple of willing volunteers.*
enthusiastic, helpful, cooperative, obliging

wilt verb
The flowers wilted in the heat.
become limp, droop, flop, sag, fade, shrivel, wither
opposite flourish

wily adjective
The player was outwitted by his wily opponent.
clever, crafty, cunning, shrewd, scheming, artful, sly, devious

win verb wins, winning, won
1 *Who do you think will win?*
come first, be victorious, succeed, triumph, prevail
To win against someone is also to beat, conquer, defeat or overcome them.
opposite lose
2 *She won first prize in the poetry competition.*
get, receive, gain, obtain, secure
(informal) pick up, walk away with

wind¹ noun
A gentle wind is a breath, breeze, or draught.
A violent wind is a cyclone, gale, hurricane, or tornado.
A sudden unexpected wind is a blast, gust, puff, or squall.
See also weather
For wind instruments see music

wind² verb (rhymes with find) winds, winding, wound
1 *She wound the wool into a ball.*
coil, loop, roll, turn, curl
2 *The road winds up the hill.*
bend, curve, twist and turn, zigzag, meander

a
b
c
d
e
f
g
h
i
j
k
l
m
n
o
p
q
r
s
t
u
v
w
x
y
z

window noun

The glass in a window is a **pane**.
A semicircular window above a door is a **fanlight**.
A window in a roof is a **skylight**.
A decorative window with panels of coloured glass is a **stained-glass window**.
A person whose job is to fit glass in windows is a **glazier**.

windy adjective

1 *It was a cold,* windy *day.*
breezy, blustery, gusty, squally, stormy
opposite **calm**
2 *This spot is too* windy *for a picnic.*
windswept, exposed, draughty
opposite **sheltered**

wink verb

1 *My friend* winked *at me and smiled.*
To shut and open both eyes quickly is to **blink**.
2 *The lights* winked *on and off.*
flash, flicker, sparkle, twinkle

winner noun

The winner *was presented with a silver cup.*
victor, prizewinner, champion, conqueror
opposite **loser**

winning adjective

The winning *team went up to receive their medals.*
victorious, triumphant, conquering, successful, top-scoring, champion
opposite **losing**

wintry adjective

It was a grey, wintry *day.*
cold, frosty, freezing, bitter, icy, snowy

wipe verb

I wiped *the table with a cloth.*
rub, clean, polish, mop, swab, sponge
to wipe something out
Pompeii was wiped *out by the eruption of Mount Vesuvius.*
destroy, annihilate, exterminate, get rid of

wire noun

Several wires *protruded from the robot's head.*
cable, lead, flex
A system of wires is **wiring**.

wisdom noun

She's a woman of great wisdom.
sense, judgement, understanding, intelligence, common sense, good sense, insight, reason

wise adjective

1 *The soothsayer was very old and* wise.
sensible, reasonable, intelligent, perceptive, knowledgeable, rational, thoughtful
2 *I think you made a* wise *decision.*
good, right, proper, sound, fair, just, appropriate
opposite **foolish**

wish noun

Her dearest wish *was to travel to the Amazon.*
desire, want, longing, yearning, hankering, craving, urge, fancy, hope, ambition
(informal) **yen**

wish verb

I wish *that everyone would sit still for a minute!*
If you wish something would happen, you can say that you **want** or **would like** it to happen.
to wish for
If you had three wishes, what would you wish *for?*
desire, want, crave, fancy, long for, yearn for, hanker after

wisp noun

She blew a wisp *of hair away from her face.*
shred, strand

wistful adjective

She gave a wistful *sigh as she read the letter.*
sad, melancholy, thoughtful, pensive

wit noun

1 *Ogres are creatures with very little* wit.
intelligence, cleverness, brains, sharpness, understanding

A
B
C
D
E
F
G
H
I
J
K
L
M
N
O
P
Q
R
S
T
U
V
W
X
Y
Z

2 *The film script sparkled with* wit.
humour, comedy, jokes
3 *Charlie is regarded as the class* wit.
joker, comedian, comic

witch and witchcraft noun
see **magic**

withdraw verb withdraws, withdrawing, withdrew, withdrawn
1 *The general* withdrew *his troops.*
call back, recall
opposite send in
2 *She* withdrew *her offer of help.*
take back, cancel, retract
opposites make, present
3 *The wolves* withdrew *into the forest.*
retire, retreat, draw back, fall back, back away
opposite advance
4 *He* withdrew *his hands from his pockets.*
draw back, pull back, take away, remove
opposites put out, extend
5 *Some competitors* withdrew *at the last minute.*
pull out, back out, drop out
opposite enter

wither verb
The flowers had withered *and died.*
shrivel, dry up, shrink, wilt, droop, sag, flop
opposite flourish

withhold verb withholds, withholding, withheld
We believe he is withholding *information.*
hold back, keep back, refuse
opposite grant

withstand verb withstands, withstanding, withstood
Penguins can withstand *extreme cold.*
bear, endure, stand up to, tolerate, cope with, survive, resist, weather

witness noun
A witness *said that the car was going too fast.*
bystander, observer, onlooker, eyewitness, spectator

witty adjective
He gave a witty *account of his schooldays.*
humorous, amusing, comic, funny
opposite dull

wizard noun
1 *The* wizard *cast a spell over the whole palace.*
magician, sorcerer, enchanter
See also **magic**
2 *My sister is a* wizard *with computers.*
expert, specialist, genius
(informal) **whizz**

wobble verb
1 *The cyclist* wobbled *all over the road.*
sway, totter, teeter, waver, rock
2 *The jelly* wobbled *as I carried the plate.*
shake, tremble, quake, quiver, vibrate

wobbly adjective
1 *The baby giraffe was a bit* wobbly *on its legs.*
shaky, tottering, unsteady
2 *This chair is a bit* wobbly.
loose, rickety, rocky, unstable, unsafe
opposite steady

woman noun
A polite word for a woman is **lady**.
A married woman is a **wife**.
A woman who has children is a **mother**.
An unmarried woman is a **spinster**.
A woman whose husband has died is a **widow**.
A woman on her wedding day is a **bride**.
A woman who is engaged to be married is a **fiancée**.
Words for a young woman are **girl** and **lass**.
Old words for a young woman are **maid** and **maiden**.

won
past tense see **win**

a
b
c
d
e
f
g
h
i
j
k
l
m
n
o
p
q
r
s
t
u
v
w
x
y
z

A
B
C
D
E
F
G
H
I
J
K
L
M
N
O
P
Q
R
S
T
U
V
W
X
Y
Z

wonder noun

1 *The sight of the Taj Mahal filled them with wonder.*
admiration, awe, reverence, amazement, astonishment
2 *It's a wonder that he is still alive.*
marvel, miracle

wonder verb

I wonder why she left in such a hurry.
be curious about, ask yourself, ponder, think about
to wonder at
People wondered at the skill of the acrobats.
marvel at, admire, be amazed by, be astonished by

wonderful adjective

1 *It's wonderful what computers can do these days.*
amazing, astonishing, astounding, incredible, remarkable, extraordinary, marvellous, miraculous, phenomenal
2 *We had a wonderful time at the party.*
excellent, splendid, superb, delightful
(informal) brilliant, fantastic, terrific, fabulous, super, great
opposite ordinary

wood noun

1 *All the furniture in the room was made of wood.*
timber, lumber, planks, logs
2 *We followed a nature trail through the wood.*
woodland, woods, forest, trees
See also **tree**

wood noun

WORD WEB

KINDS OF WOOD OFTEN USED TO MAKE THINGS
ash, balsa, beech, cedar, chestnut, ebony, elm, lime, mahogany, oak, pine, rosewood, sandalwood, spruce, teak, walnut
A person who makes things from wood is a **carpenter** or **wood-carver**.

A person whose job is to cut down trees for wood is a **lumberjack** or a **woodcutter**.

wooden adjective

1 *They sat down on a wooden bench.*
wood, timber
2 *The acting was a bit wooden at times.*
stiff, lifeless, awkward, unnatural, unemotional, expressionless

woolly adjective

1 *He wore a woolly hat with a bobble on top.*
wool, woollen
Clothes made of wool, such as hats and scarves, are **woollens**.
2 *Mammoths were like elephants with woolly coats.*
thick, fleecy, furry, downy, fuzzy, hairy, shaggy, soft, cuddly
3 *Some parts of the plot were rather woolly.*
vague, confused, unclear, unfocused, hazy, indefinite, uncertain

word noun

1 *What's the French word for 'birthday'?*
expression, term
All the words you know are your **vocabulary**.
2 *You gave me your word.*
promise, assurance, guarantee, pledge, vow
3 *There has been no word from him for several weeks.*
news, message, information

word verb

I spent ages trying to word the letter correctly.
express, phrase, put into words
The way that you word something is the **wording** or **phrasing**.

wore

past tense see **wear**

work noun

1 *Digging the garden involves a lot of hard work.*
effort, labour, toil, exertion

2 *Do you have any* work *to do today?*
task, assignment, chore, job, homework,
housework
3 *What kind of* work *does she do?*
occupation, employment, job, profession,
business, trade, vocation
For various kinds of work see **job**

work verb
1 *She's been* working *in the garden
all day.*
be busy, exert yourself, labour, toil, slave
2 *He* works *in the bookshop on Saturdays.*
be employed, have a job, go to work
3 *My watch isn't* working.
function, go, operate
4 *Is the DVD player easy to* work?
operate, run, use, control, handle
to work out
Things didn't quite work out *as planned.*
turn out, happen, emerge, develop
to work something out
Can anyone work out *this sum?*
answer, calculate, solve, explain, figure out

worker noun
The factory employs around 200 workers.
employee
All the workers in a business or factory are
the **staff** or **workforce**.
For people who do specific jobs see **job**

world noun
1 *Antarctica is a remote part of the* world.
earth, globe
2 *Scientists are searching for life on other*
worlds.
planet

worried adjective
You look worried. *Is something the matter?*
anxious, troubled, uneasy, distressed,
disturbed, upset, apprehensive, concerned,
bothered, tense, strained, nervous
opposite **relaxed**

worry verb
1 *There's no need to* worry.
be anxious, be troubled, be disturbed,
brood, fret

2 *It* worried *her that he hadn't replied to
her letter.*
trouble, distress, upset, concern, disturb
3 *Don't* worry *her now—she's busy.*
bother, annoy, disturb, pester, harass
(informal) badger, bug

worry noun
1 *He's been a constant source of* worry
to her.
anxiety, distress, uneasiness, vexation
2 *I don't want to add to your* worries.
trouble, concern, burden, care, problem

worsen verb
1 *Moving the patient may* worsen *the pain.*
make worse, aggravate
2 *The weather had* worsened *overnight.*
get worse, deteriorate, degenerate
opposite **improve**

worship verb
1 *Ancient Egyptians* worshipped *the
sun god, Ra.*
pray to, glorify, praise
For places where people worship see
building
2 *She adores her sons and they* worship *her.*
adore, be devoted to, look up to, love,
revere, idolize

worth noun
*This ring was once an object of great
worth.*
value, merit, quality, significance,
importance

worthless adjective
It's nothing but a worthless *piece
of junk.*
useless, unusable, valueless
(informal) trashy
opposite **valuable**

worthwhile adjective
It may be worthwhile *to get a second
opinion.*
helpful, useful, valuable, beneficial,
profitable
opposite **useless**

a
b
c
d
e
f
g
h
i
j
k
l
m
n
o
p
q
r
s
t
u
v
w
x
y
z

A
B
C
D
E
F
G
H
I
J
K
L
M
N
O
P
Q
R
S
T
U
V
W
X
Y
Z

worthy adjective
They gave the money to a worthy cause.
good, worthwhile, deserving,
praiseworthy, admirable,
commendable, respectable
opposite **unworthy**

wound[1] noun
He is being treated in hospital for a head wound.
injury, cut, gash, graze, scratch, sore
For other types of wound see injury

wound[1] verb
The fox was wounded in the leg and bleeding.
injure, hurt, harm

wound[2] (say wownd)
past tense see wind[2]

wrap verb
1 *She wrapped the presents in shiny gold paper.*
cover, pack, enclose, enfold, swathe
To wrap water pipes is to insulate or lag them.
2 *The mountain was wrapped in mist.*
cloak, envelop, shroud, surround, hide,
conceal, wreathe

wreathe verb
The tree was wreathed in fairy lights.
encircle, festoon, surround, adorn, decorate

wreck verb
1 *His bicycle was wrecked in the accident.*
demolish, destroy, crush, smash, shatter,
crumple
2 *The injury wrecked her chances becoming a dancer.*
ruin, spoil

wreckage noun
Divers have discovered the wreckage of an old ship.
debris, fragments, pieces, remains
The wreckage of a building is rubble or ruins.

wrench verb
The giant wrenched the door off its hinges.
pull, tug, prise, jerk, twist, force
(informal) yank

wrestle verb
He wrestled with the thief as he tried to escape.
struggle, tussle, grapple

wretched adjective
1 *I lay in bed with flu feeling wretched.*
miserable, unhappy, woeful, pitiful,
unfortunate
2 *The wretched computer has frozen again!*
annoying, maddening, exasperating,
useless

wriggle verb
The prisoner managed to wriggle out of his bonds.
twist, writhe, squirm, worm your way

wring verb wrings, wringing, wrung
1 *She wrung the water out of her skirt.*
press, squeeze, twist
2 *He wrung her hand enthusiastically.*
shake, clasp, grip, wrench
wringing wet
Your socks are wringing wet!
soaked, drenched, dripping, sopping,
saturated

wrinkle noun
The old hag's face was covered in wrinkles.
crease, fold, furrow, line, ridge, crinkle,
pucker, pleat
A small hollow on someone's skin is a dimple.

wrinkle verb
The creature wrinkled its nose and sniffed.
pucker up, crease, crinkle, crumple,
fold
opposite **smooth**

write verb writes, writing, wrote, written

1 *My granny wrote a diary when she was a girl.*

compile, compose, draw up, set down, pen

To write letters or emails to people is to **correspond** with them.

To write a rough version of a story is to **draft** it.

2 *He wrote his address on the back of an envelope.*

jot down, note, print, scrawl, scribble

To write on a document or surface is to **inscribe** it.

To write your signature on something is to **autograph** it.

writer noun

A person who writes books is an **author**.
A person who writes novels is a **novelist**.
A person who writes plays is a **dramatist** or **playwright**.
A person who writes scripts for films or television is a **scriptwriter** or **screenwriter**.
A person who writes poetry is a **poet**.
A person who writes about someone else's life is a **biographer**.
A person who writes for newspapers is a **correspondent**, **journalist**, or **reporter**.
A person who writes music is a **composer**.
A person who writes a blog is a **blogger**.

writhe verb

The wounded man was writhing in agony.

thrash about, twist, squirm, wriggle

writing noun

1 *Can you read the writing on the envelope?*

handwriting

Untidy writing is a **scrawl** or **scribble**.
The art of beautiful handwriting is **calligraphy**.

2 *The writing on the stone was very faint.*

inscription

3 (often plural) *She introduced me to the writings of Roald Dahl.*

literature, works

WORD WEB

VARIOUS FORMS OF WRITING AND LITERATURE
autobiography, biography, blog, children's literature, classic, comedy, crime or **detective story, diary, drama** or **play, essay, fable, fairy story** or **fairy tale, fantasy, fiction, film** or **TV script, folk tale, ghost story, historical fiction, history, journalism, legend, letters** or **correspondence, lyrics, myth, newspaper article, non-fiction, novel, parody, philosophy, poetry** or **verse, prose, romance, satire, science fiction** or (informal) **sci-fi, spy story, thriller, tragedy, travel writing, western**

I'm not really sure what makes a book a 'classic' to begin with, but I think it has to be at least fifty years old and some person or animal has to die at the end.
— Jeff Kinney, *Diary of a Wimpy Kid: Dog Days*

WRITING TIPS

You can use these words to describe **a piece of writing**

TO DESCRIBE THE **LANGUAGE** OR **STYLE** IN A POSITIVE WAY
elegant, literary, ornate, poetic; colloquial, informal, slangy; formal, old-fashioned; hard-boiled, sparse

TO DESCRIBE THE **LANGUAGE** OR **STYLE** IN A NEGATIVE WAY
banal, dry, insipid, lacklustre, monotonous, plodding, prosaic
The author uses poetic words, like cornucopia.'

TO DESCRIBE A **CHARACTER**
hero, heroine, protagonist, narrator, villain; believable, convincing, lifelike, realistic, strong, well-drawn; feeble, thin, unbelievable, unconvincing, weak
Mr Scruggs is a thoroughly convincing villain.

a
b
c
d
e
f
g
h
i
j
k
l
m
n
o
p
q
r
s
t
u
v
w
x
y
z

A
B
C
D
E
F
G
H
I
J
K
L
M
N
O
P
Q
R
S
T
U
V
W
X
Y
Z

TO DESCRIBE THE **SETTING**
atmospheric, moody; alien, exotic, fanciful, fantastic, fictitious, made-up, imaginary, strange, unfamiliar; eerie, spooky, weird; accurate, authentic, familiar, recognizable, true to life
The story is set on an imaginary *planet.*

TO DESCRIBE THE **STORYLINE** OR **PLOT** IN A POSITIVE WAY
action-packed, dramatic, dynamic, engrossing, entertaining, eventful, fast-paced, gripping, hair-raising, intruiguing, mind-boggling, page-turning, rip-roaring, spellbinding, thrilling; creative, imaginative, intriguing, moving, thought-provoking, well-crafted; amusing, diverting, entertaining, hilarious, humorous; romantic, sentimental

TO DESCRIBE THE **STORYLINE** OR **PLOT** IN A NEGATIVE WAY
dull, insipid, uneventful, unimaginative; absurd, far-fetched, ludicrous, ridiculous, unbelievable, unlikely
Finn's adventures are dramatic *and at times* moving.

TO DESCRIBE THE **ENDING** IN A POSITIVE WAY
cliffhanger, climax, conclusion, finale; electrifying, nail-biting, sensational, spectacular, surprising, unexpected

TO DESCRIBE THE **ENDING** IN A NEGATIVE WAY
abrupt, banal, clichéd, predicable, trite, unsatisfying
The book keeps you guessing until the sensational *finale.*

wrong adjective
1 *It was* wrong *to take the book without asking.*
bad, dishonest, irresponsible, immoral, sinful, wicked, criminal, unfair, unjust
2 *His calculations were all* wrong.
incorrect, mistaken, inaccurate
3 *Did I say the* wrong *thing?*
inappropriate, unsuitable, improper
4 *There's something* wrong *with the TV.*
faulty, defective, not working, out of order
opposite **right**
to go wrong
The professor's plan began to go wrong.
fail, backfire
(informal) flop, go pear-shaped
opposite **succeed**

wrote
past tense see **write**

Yy

yacht noun
For types of boat or ship see **boat**

yard noun
A solitary tree stood in the middle of the yard.
court, courtyard, enclosure

yearly adjective
I'm due for my yearly dental check-up.
annual

yearn verb
to yearn for something
She yearned for some peace and quiet.
want, wish for, desire, long for, pine for
(informal) be dying for

yell verb
I yelled to attract their attention.
call out, cry out, shout, bawl, bellow

yellow adjective & noun

WORD WEB

SOME SHADES OF YELLOW
amber, chrome yellow, cream, gold, golden, lemon, tawny

Something which is rather yellow is yellowish.

yelp verb
For sounds made by animals see **animal**

yield verb
1 *In the end, her parents yielded and let her go out.*
give in, give way, concede, surrender, admit defeat, submit, comply
2 *The apple trees yielded a good crop of fruit.*
bear, grow, produce, supply, generate

yield noun
They got a good yield from the orchard this year.
crop, harvest, produce, return

young adjective
1 *A lot of young people went to the concert.*
youthful, juvenile
opposites **older, mature**
2 *I think this book is a bit young for you.*
childish, babyish, immature, infantile
opposites **adult, grown-up**
A young person is a **child** or **youngster**.
A young adult is an **adolescent** or **youth**.
A very young child is a **baby** or **infant**.
A young bird is a **chick**, **fledgling**, or **nestling**.
Young fish are **fry**.
A young plant is a **cutting** or **seedling**.
A young tree is a **sapling**.
For other young animals and birds see **animal, bird**

young plural noun
The mother bird returned to feed her young.
offspring, children, young ones, family
A family of young birds is a **brood**.
A family of young cats or dogs is a **litter**.

youth noun
1 *In her youth, she had been a keen tennis player.*
childhood, boyhood or girlhood, adolescence, teens
2 *The fight was started by a group of youths.*
adolescent, youngster, juvenile, teenager, young adult

youthful adjective
The magic potion will keep you eternally youthful.
young, youngish, vigorous, sprightly, young-looking

a
b
c
d
e
f
g
h
i
j
k
l
m
n
o
p
q
r
s
t
u
v
w
x
y
z

A
B
C
D
E
F
G
H
I
J
K
L
M
N
O
P
Q
R
S
T
U
V
W
X
Y
Z

Zz

zero noun
Four minus four makes zero.
nothing, nought
A score of zero in football is nil; in cricket it is a duck, and in tennis it is love.

zest noun
Uncle Arthur has a great zest *for life.*
enthusiasm, eagerness, enjoyment

zigzag verb
The road zigzags *up the hill.*
wind, twist, meander

zodiac noun

WORD WEB

THE SIGNS OF THE ZODIAC ARE
Aquarius (or the Water-Carrier),
Aries (or the Ram), Cancer (or the Crab),
Capricorn (or the Goat),
Gemini (or the Twins), Leo (or the Lion),
Libra (or the Scales), Pisces (or the Fish),
Sagittarius (or the Archer),
Scorpio (or the Scorpion),
Taurus (or the Bull),
Virgo (or the Virgin)

zone noun
No-one may enter the forbidden zone.
area, district, region, sector, locality,
neighbourhood, territory, vicinity

zoo noun
Which is your favourite animal in the zoo?
menagerie, safari park, wildlife reserve,
nature reserve, zoological gardens
For animals you might see in a zoo see
animal

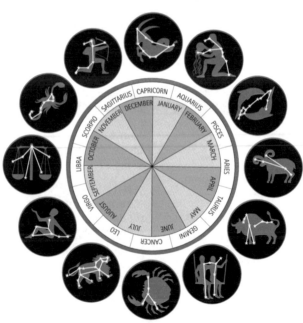

Become a Word Explorer

You don't need a map and a compass to be an explorer. You can explore the world of **words** equipped with your thesaurus.

For example, you can:

- explore the differences between **synonyms**
- explore effects like **simile** and **alliteration**
- explore ways to **build words**
- explore ideas to improve your **story writing** and other writing

Use the following pages to help you.

Contents

Explore:	Basic writing skills	484
	Synonyms	485
	Overused words	486
	Similies	487
	Idioms	488
	Special effects	488
	Word building	489
	Writing stories	490
	Writing non-fiction	496
	Writing letters	498

Explore: Basic writing skills

Punctuation

Punctuation makes writing easier to read and understand. You should use these basic punctuation marks in your writing:

- a full stop (.) comes at the end of a sentence
- a comma (,) separates items in a list, or parts of a sentence:

  Hedgehogs eat slugs, snails, and worms.

  After four days at sea, we sighted land.
- an apostrophe (') shows that a letter is missing, or tells you who something belongs to:

  Don't enter the dragon's lair! = Do not enter the lair of the dragon!

These punctuation marks are especially useful for writing dialogue in a story:

- quotation marks (' ' " ") come before and after words that a character says:

  'My name,' said the knight, 'is Sir Joustalot.'
- a question mark (?) comes at the end of a question:

  'How old are you?' I asked the wizard.

  Note that you don't need a question mark if the question is reported, not spoken:

  I asked the wizard how old he was.
- an exclamation mark (!) comes after a shout, or shows that a character is excited:

  'Wow! Look at the size of that crater!'

Explorer tip:

The Word web panel for **punctuation** lists various punctuation marks that you might use or come across. You will find more tips on writing **dialogue** and using **exclamations** in the Explore: Writing stories section too.

Confusable words

Take extra care when you use any of these confusable words in your writing. Although the words in each group sound alike, they each have a different *spelling* (some with an apostrophe) and a different *meaning*. If you choose the wrong one, your writing will not make sense.

its		The crocodile snapped its jaws.
it's	[= it is]	It's a blustery day.
your		When is your birthday?
you're	[= you are]	You're all invited to my party.
their		The pirates rattled their swords.
there		There are only two chocolates left.
they're	[= they are]	They're coming for tea tomorrow.

Note the three different spellings in this example:

'Where are the penguins?'

'They're over there, feeding their chicks.'

Explore: Synonyms

The main job of a thesaurus is to list synonyms. Synonyms are words which mean the same—or nearly the same—as each other, like *big* and *huge*, or *horrible* and *nasty*.

Sometimes, you can choose between a few synonyms. A giant's nose might be *huge* or *immense* or *colossal* or *mammoth*: you can swop the words around and it makes no difference to the meaning.

Other synonyms are more limited and only fit in certain contexts. For example:

* formal or informal synonyms (*yummy* is an informal synonym of *delicious*)
* synonyms which are special cases (*trunk* and *casket* are special types of box).

Examples

- In a piece of schoolwork, you might write:

  The cake was delicious / tasty.

- But in your diary or an email, you could write instead:

  The cake was scrumptious / yummy!

- In a story, you might write:

  The magician carried his things in a trunk.

  The treasure was sealed in a wooden casket.

Explorer tip:

You can easily spot special **synonyms** in the thesaurus. Look for the labels *formal*, *informal*, or *old use*. Synonyms which are special cases are listed and defined in a separate paragraph.

Explore: Overused words

Words like *bad*, *big*, and *nice* are very useful, but they can make your writing boring if you use them too often. If you choose a synonym which is more unusual, it will make your writing more interesting.

Examples

- Instead of making a fairy simply *beautiful*, try describing her as *radiant* or *resplendent*.

- Is a *big ogre* scary enough? If not, transform it into a *hulking* or *monstrous ogre*.

Explorer tip:

You can easily spot **overused words** in the thesaurus.

There is a complete list of **overused words** at the front of the thesaurus.

Explore: Similies

This thesaurus notes common **similes** like *as fit as a fiddle*.
But you can also make up your own, using your thesaurus for ideas.
Similes are useful for describing how a character looks or sounds,
or how a landscape appears.

Examples

- *Miss Mullins had a face* like a soggy sponge.
- *The dragon's eyes were* as dark as a moonless night.
- *The waves crashed* like cymbals *on the shore.*

Similes allow you to mix and match: you can describe a person like an animal
(*Mr Scruggs scuttled off like a spider*), or an animal like a thing (*the snake
sprang up like a jack-in-the-box*).

Similes can also make your writing individual. Lots of people may describe a
road as *bumpy*, but you may be the only person to say it is *as bumpy as the
back of a crocodile.*

Explorer tip:
The **animal** and **bird** panels list ways to describe animals and birds.
But you can also use these words in similes to describe **people**.

Explore: Idioms

An idiom is a phrase that doesn't mean exactly the same as the words in it. For example, *to be in hot water* is an idiom which means 'to be in trouble' (not to be in actual hot water).

Idioms can make your writing more lively. But be careful: your writing can look clichéd if you use too many!

Examples

A character in your story has just seen a ghost. How do you describe their reaction?

- Anita *blanched* and stood *rooted to the spot*.
- She *had goosebumps* all over and began to *tremble like a leaf*.

Explorer tip:
You will find suggestions for idioms and other words to use in the **writing tips** panels for **afraid**, **angry**, and **surprised**.

Explore: Special effects

Some words come with their own sound effects. These are called onomatopoeic words, and they sound like the thing they are describing. Using a sound-effect word can give an extra zing to your writing.

Examples

You are describing footsteps on a path.

- On a dry, stony path, the footsteps might *crunch*, but on a muddy path, they would *squelch*.
- A child's feet might *patter* on the path, whereas a giant's feet would *thud*.

Explorer tip:
You will find lots of sound-effect words at the **word web** for **sound**.

A sound effect that you can create yourself is alliteration, which means using two or more words which start with the same sound. This is especially useful in poetry, but can also be effective in story writing.

Examples

You are writing a poem about food. Use alliteration to make it *crispy and crumbly*, or maybe *sweet and sticky*.

If the food is disgusting, you might describe it as *slimy and sloppy*, or even *mouldy and mushy*!

Explorer tip:

You will find words to describe both **delicious** *and* **disgusting** food in the **writing tips** panel for **food**.

Explore: Word building

Have you ever thought about making up a word? You can add to the words in your thesaurus by creating your own.

Try building a new word by starting with a word you know, or a word you have found in the thesaurus, and adding one of these suffixes (endings) to it:

–ish	*purplish, shortish, hairyish*
–less or –free	a *flowerless* garden, a *chocolate-free* chin
–like	a *ghost-like* shadow, a *swan-like* neck
–proof	a *sword-proof* shield, a *magic-proof* castle
–y	a *lemony* pudding, a *herby* flavour

You can also build compounds by joining two whole words together. Here are a few suggestions for words to use, but you can also try out your own:

–feeling	*rough-feeling* skin
–looking	*scary-looking* teeth
–smelling	a *musty-smelling* room
–sounding	an *eerie-sounding* wail

Examples

You are describing a dragon. You could give it: *lidless* eyes   *bat-like* wings   *sour-smelling* breath   *fire-emitting* nostrils

Explore: Writing stories

Before you write:

1. Plan your story. Think about setting, the characters, and the action.

2. Share the story with a friend before you write. Would you want to read this story? Would your friend? Change your plan if necessary.

While you are writing:

3. Keep to your plan.

4. Write in sentences and think about punctuation.

5. Don't forget paragraphs. If you need to begin a sentence with an adverbial clause of time (e.g. Later that day...When it was all over...) or place (e.g. Outside...In the woods) you probably need to start a new paragraph.

After you have written the first draft:

6. Use a dictionary to check your spelling.

7. Use a thesaurus to make sure you have chosen the best words.

8. Look at the overused words list. Try to use other words.

9. Can you add in some details about your characters to increase your reader's interest in them?

10. Can you add more information about your setting to help your reader 'see' it in their mind?

Creating a setting: Place

The first thing to decide is *where* your story takes place.

- Does the action happen at sea or on a *desert island*?
- Is it set in an *ancient castle* or in *outer space*?

Once you have a general setting, you can draw attention to details such as trees or buildings, animals or birds, or even mythological creatures.

Explorer tip:

Entries and panels to use: **cave   desert   island   jungle   landscape   mountain   planet   polar   river   sea   seashore   seaside   space**

Look up more specific panels, such as **boat, castle, ice,** and **tree,** for more *features* to include in your setting.

Creating a setting: Time

You also need to tell your readers *when* your story takes place.

- Does it take place in *late spring* or in *early autumn*?
- Does it begin at *dusk* or at *dawn*?
- Is it set in the *present* day, in *ancient* times, or even in the *future*?

Explorer tip:
Entries and panels to use: **season   day   night   time**

Creating a setting: Atmosphere and weather

Once you've settled on the place and time, you can start to think about the atmosphere. What is the weather like?

- Is the *sky cloudy* or *cloudless*?
- Is the wind *blustery* or *breezy*?
- Is a storm *brewing*?

Explorer tip:

Entries and panels to use: **ice   rain   sky   snow   sun   wind**

You can look up **hot** and **cold** for more ways to describe temperature.

Describing a character

Describing how your characters look, sound (and even smell!) will make them more believable and vivid. Think about the details which make people different from each other.

- Are your characters *lean* and *lanky*, or *short* and *squat*?
- Is their hair *straight* and *stringy*, or *fine* and *frizzy*?
- Are they more likely to *scowl* and *grimace*, or to *beam*?

Explorer tip:

Entries and panels to use: **body, expression, eye, face, hair, nose, and voice**

Look at the **clothes** panel for things that your characters might wear.

Typical characters

Some types of story require certain characters. For example, a detective story needs a detective, and a pirate story needs at least one pirate. A number of the word web panels focus on typical story characters like these. They are rather like dressing-up boxes with words (rather than costumes) with which to dress up your characters.

- **detective** lists things a detective might look for (*fingerprints, suspect*)
- **astronaut** lists places an astronaut might visit (*moonbase, spacelab*)

These **word web** panels don't list *everything* a detective or astronaut might do, but they do list *typical* things and can give you ideas for writing your own mystery story or space story.

Explorer tip:

Entries and panels to use: **astronaut   criminal   detective   explorer fairy   ghost   knight   pirate   robot   spy**

The **magic** panel also has suggestions for **witches** and **wizards**.

Imaginary creatures

If your characters are not human, it is even more important to let your readers know how they look and sound. Not all aliens and ogres are alike, so be sure to describe your imaginary creatures in detail. You can make an imaginary monster vivid by giving it body parts of real animals, for example the head of a snake, the wings of a bat, and the legs of a beetle.

Examples

You are writing a space story. How do you describe your alien creatures?

- *The aliens had insect-like bodies, with spindly legs and spiky antennae.*
- *Their scaly backs were patterned with purple blotches.*
- *They spoke to each other in high-pitched screeches.*

Describing action

When you describe what your characters do, try to be specific.

- How do your characters move? Do they scurry quickly, glide gracefully, or slink stealthily?
- Do they tap gently on a door, or pound it insistently?
- Do they nibble their food politely, or gobble it greedily?

There is nothing wrong with using simple words like *move*, *hit*, and *eat*. But your writing will be more interesting if you use more colourful verbs at times.

Examples

You are writing a detective story. How does your main character act?

- *Inspector Giles paced slowly round the room, twitching his moustache. He inspected the broken window and peered closely at the stains on the carpet.*

Explorer tip:

Look at the word webs at **eat drink look move walk**

You will find even more action words in the entries for **hit** and **run**.

Look up the **animal** or **bird** panels for ways that creatures might move.

Writing dialogue

The words that your characters say in the story is the *dialogue*.
When you are writing dialogue, try not to use the verb **say** each time.
Your story will be more interesting if you vary the words which report what each character says.

Examples

- *'Stop that racket!' snapped Miss Grump* and *'Don't look now, but there's a ghost behind us', whispered Evie.*

This sounds far more interesting than simply *said Miss Grump* and *said Evie.*

Exclamations

Lively dialogue can bring the characters in your story to life.

Try using *exclamations* at exciting moments in your story.

Examples

A character in your story suddenly gets angry or annoyed.

What should he or she say?

- *'Blast that parrot!' said Captain Cutlass with an evil leer.*
- *'Bother! The magic potion is wearing off!' said Megan, frowning.*

Explorer tip:

Look up **say** and **exclamation**.

Explore: Writing non–fiction

Your thesaurus can help you with non–fiction writing, too.

- How can you describe a *book* you have read, or a *place* you have visited?
- What words can you use to report a *sports match*?
- What words can you use in a *recipe* for cooking?

Examples

You are writing a book review. How do you describe the way that the book ends?

- *'Smugglers Cove' hurtles towards a gripping finale. The final chapter is a nail-biting description of a sea chase.*

You are writing a report of a football match. How do you describe the winning goal?

- *Martinez dribbled the ball past two defenders, then chipped it across to the captain who blasted it into the back of the net.*

Explorer tip:
You will find useful words and phrases to describe a book in the **writing tips** panel for **writing**.

Explorer tip:
You will find words that are used in various sports in the **word web** panels for **football, tennis**, etc. You can also get ideas for how a player might hit or throw a ball in the **writing tips** panel for **ball**.

The **word web** panels in the thesaurus include lists of related words which can give you ideas or information for a project on that topic.

Examples

You are writing a project on animals. Look up the **animal** panel to find:

- animals that live on land (*aardvark, zebra*) or in the sea (*dolphin, whale*)
- names of young animals (*cub, pup*)
- names of animal body parts (*claw, snout*)
- names of wild animal homes (*earth, warren*)

Explorer tip:

You can easily spot **word webs** in the thesaurus. They are treated in special panels and have this symbol next to them: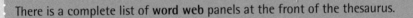

There is a complete list of **word web** panels at the front of the thesaurus.

explore further . . .

Like a good explorer, be prepared to follow a trail. **Cross references** in the word webs will help you to find other panels with related information. For example, the panel for **dinosaur** points you also to **prehistoric**, where you will find a list of other prehistoric animals.

You may want to explore your topic further by looking up the listed words in a dictionary or an encyclopedia.

Explore: Writing letters

When you are writing a letter or email, think about *who* you are writing to, and *why*. This will help you decide what type of letter to write.

- You might write a formal letter to a teacher, but an informal email to a friend.
- You might send informal invitations to your birthday party, but receive a formal invitation to a wedding.

If a character in your story writes a letter, it should also fit with the person and situation you are describing.

- A medieval knight would write an elaborate, formal letter to a king.
- A spy might send a hasty, informal email to headquarters.

Here are some tips for writing both formal and informal types of letter.

Formal letters

In a **formal letter**, you should:

- write in complete sentences
- avoid short forms like *don't* and *I'm* (use *do not* and *I am*)
- avoid informal words and phrases, such as *thanks* (use *thank you* instead)
- begin with *Dear*, and end with *Yours sincerely* or *Yours truly*
- call the person you are writing to by their family name or title (if you don't know their name, call them *Sir* or *Madam*)

> *Dear Prince Charming,*
>
> *Thank you for your invitation to the Palace Ball on Saturday.*
> *Unfortunately I am unable to come, as I must stay at home all*
> *evening to sweep the floors. Please accept my apologies.*
> *Yours sincerely,*
> *Cinderella*

Informal letters

Informal letters and emails are often chatty in tone, as if you were speaking rather than writing the words.

- use incomplete sentences
- use short forms like *don't* and *I'm*
- use informal words and phrases, such as *terrific* or *thanks*
- use exclamation marks when you (or your characters) are excited
- begin with *Dear* or *Hello* or *Hi* (or just a name), and end with *Yours* or *Best wishes*
- call the person you are writing to by their first or given name, or by a nickname

> *Dear Cinders*
> *Just had a terrific idea! Meet me at the kitchen door at 6pm on Sat.*
> *Bring a pumpkin and a few mice.*
> *Yours*
> *Fairy Godmother*

Explorer tip:

Use the **word web** panel at **communication** to help you look for ways to address people you are speaking to or writing to.

Praise for *Libertie*:

'In this singular novel, Kaitlyn Greenidge confronts the anonymising forces of history with her formidable gifts. *Libertie* is a glorious, piercing song for the ages – fierce, brilliant and utterly free' Brandon Taylor, author of *Real Life*

'I want to say that Kaitlyn Greenidge's *Libertie* is a glorious diasporic literary song, but the novel is so much more than that. A book so deeply invested in the politics and place of silence is one of the most melodious books I've read in decades. The ambition in *Libertie* is only exceeded by Greenidge's skill. This is it' Kiese Laymon, author of *Heavy*

'This is a historical novel, a magical novel, a familial novel, a Bildungsroman – a work that defies simple categorisation. The complexities herein signify an important writer throwing all her talents and brilliance on the page, offering us more than we deserve. Reading *Libertie* can feel like reading Toni Morrison. Such a comparison, however, is a disservice to Kaitlyn Greenidge, who is an original light, a writer to emulate, a master of the craft, and a mind we're fortunate to have living among us' Gabriel Bump, author of *Everywhere You Don't Belong*

'*Libertie* is a Bildungsroman for America in the twenty-first century, providing us with a spiritual education we sorely need. What is care and what is poison? Where does life end? Where does liberty begin? By creating Libertie – a nineteenth-century "black gal", a modern existential heroine – Greenidge has resurrected more than an ancestor – she has revived the anger and the love, the grief and the pride, and, above all, the fierce need for freedom that still drive our nation today' C. Morgan Babst, author of *The Floating World*

'Wielding both her knowledge of our history and her incredible sense of story, Kaitlyn Greenidge further establishes herself as one of the sharpest minds working today. *Libertie* is a novel of epic power and endless grace' Nana Kwame Adjei-Brenyah, author of *Friday Black*

'From the first page, Greenidge catapults us into a masterfully crafted story in which the possibilities, limitations and shifting contours of freedom for Black people take centre stage ... She conjures a fiercely gorgeous, complex portrait of life for Black women during the Reconstruction era. It is a story that's at once politically weighted and intimately resonant ... Greenidge perfectly weds the precision of historical details and context with fantastical elements of myth and magic to illuminate the enduring questions: What does freedom mean for Black girls and women? What does it look, smell, feel, sound and taste like? *Libertie* is a beautifully written meditation on Black liberation and imagination. It is exquisite historical fiction that lovingly reminds us to reassess our own present-day commitments to fighting for, and practising, freedom' *Ms.*

'Few novels have as strong a sense of place as this fascinating blend of magical realism and African American historical fiction ... Greenidge succeeds beautifully at presenting the complexities of an intense mother–daughter bond ... Greenidge creates a richly layered tapestry of Black communal life, notably Black female life, and the inevitable contradictions and compromises of "freedom"' *Booklist*, starred review

'Greenidge (*We Love You, Charlie Freeman*) delivers another genius work of radical historical fiction ... This pièce de résistance is so immaculately orchestrated that each character, each setting and each sentence sings' *Publishers Weekly*, starred and boxed review

LIBERTIE

a novel by

KAITLYN GREENIDGE

First published in Great Britain in 2021 by
Serpent's Tail,
an imprint of Profile Books Ltd
29 Cloth Fair
London
EC1A 7JQ
www.serpentstail.com

First published in the US by Algonquin Books of Chapel Hill,
a division of Workman Publishing, 2021

Design by Steve Godwin.

1 3 5 7 9 10 8 6 4 2

Printed and bound in Great Britain by
Clays Ltd, Elcograf S.p.A.

The moral right of the author has been asserted.

A CIP catalogue record for this book is available from the British Library.

ISBN 978 1 78816 900 4
Export ISBN 978 1 78816 901 1
eISBN 978 1 78283 895 1

FSC
www.fsc.org
MIX
Paper from
responsible sources
FSC® C018072

For Ariel and Ariel and M. Ariel

ALSO BY KAITLYN GREENIDGE

We Love You, Charlie Freeman

LIBERTIE

Se pa tout blesi ki geri

Not all wounds heal

1860

I saw my mother raise a man from the dead. "It still didn't help him much, my love," she told me. But I saw her do it all the same. That's how I knew she was magic.

The time I saw Mama raise a man from the dead, it was close to dusk. Mama and her nurse, Lenore, were in her office—Mama with her little greasy glasses on the tip of her nose, balancing the books, and Lenore banking the fire. That was the rule in Mama's office—the fire was kept burning from dawn till after dinner, and we never let it go out completely. Even on the hottest days, when my linen collar stuck to the back of my neck and the belly of Lenore's apron was stained with sweat, a mess of logs and twigs was lit up down there, waiting.

When the dead man came, it was spring. I was playing on the stoop. I'd broken a stick off the mulberry bush, so young it had resisted the pull of my fist. I'd had to work for it. Once I'd wrenched it off, I stripped the bark and rubbed the wet wood underneath on the flag-stone, pressing the green into rock.

I heard a rumbling come close and looked up, and I could see, down the road, a mule plodding slow and steady with a covered wagon, a ribbon of dust trailing behind it.

In those days, the road to our house was narrow and only just cut through the brush. Our house was set back—Grandfather, my mother's father, had made his money raising pigs and kept the house and pens away from everyone else to protect his neighbors, and his reputation, from the undermining smell of swine. No one respects a man, no matter how rich and distinguished-looking, who stinks of pig scat. The house was set up on a rise, so we could always see who was coming. Usually, it was Mama's patients, walking or limping or running to her office. Wagons were rare.

When it first turned onto our road, the cart was moving slowly. But once it passed the bowed-over walnut tree, the woman at the seat snapped her whip, and the mule began to move a little faster, until it was upon us.

"Where's your mother?"

I opened my mouth, but before I could call for her, my mother rushed to the door, Lenore behind her.

"Quick," was all Mama said, and the woman came down off the seat. A boy, about twelve or thirteen, followed. They were both dressed in mourning clothes. The woman's skirt was full. Embroidered on the bodice of her dress were a dozen black lilies, done in cord. The boy's mourning suit was dusty but perfectly fit to his form. At his neck was a velvet bow tie, come undone on the journey. The woman carried an enormous beaded handbag—it, too, was dusty but looked rich. It was covered in a thousand little eyes of jet that winked at me in the last bit of sun.

"Go, Lenore," my mother said, and Lenore and the woman and the boy all went to the back of the wagon, the boy hopping up in the bed and pushing something that lay there, Lenore and the woman standing, arms ready to catch it. Finally, after much scraping, a coffin heaved out of the wagon bed. It was crudely made, a white, bright wood, heavy enough that Lenore and the woman stumbled as they carried it. When the coffin passed me, I could smell the sawdust still on it.

My mother stepped down off the stoop then, and the four of them lifted it up and managed it into the office. As soon as they got it inside, they set it on the ground and pushed it home. I could hear the rough pine shuffling across the floor.

"You're early." Mama struggled with the box.

"Don't start with me, Cathy," the woman said, and Lenore looked up, and so did I. No one, except Grandfather before he died, dared call Mama "Cathy." To everyone except for me, she was always "Doctor." But Mama did not bristle and did not correct, as she would have with anyone else.

"Word was you'd be here at midnight."

"We couldn't leave," the woman said. "He wasn't ready."

The woman knelt down in her dusty skirts and drew a long, skinny claw hammer from the handbag. She turned it on its head and began to pull at the nails on the coffin's face. She grunted. "Here, Lucien." She signaled to the boy. "Put some grease into it." He fell down beside her, took the hammer from her hands, and began to pull at the nails she'd left behind.

Mama watched, eagerly. We all did. I crossed the room to stand beside her, slipped my hand into hers.

Mama started at my touch. "If you'd only come later."

The woman's head jerked up, her expression sharp, and then she looked at my hand in Mama's, and her frown softened.

"I know we've done it differently. This time we really tried," she said. "Besides, my Lucien sees all this and more. If you do this work, Cathy, your children will know sooner or later."

Mama did not take advice from anyone, certainly not advice on me, but she said nothing at this softest of rebukes, only watched the woman and her son.

The boy, Lucien, pulled hard, and when the final nail was out, he and Lenore pulled at the splintering plank until it gave a terrible yawn. And then I saw:

a man curled in on himself like a dried mulberry leaf,

his skin gray, his eyes open and staring,

his pants damp. He smelled sharp,

like the spirits Lenore used to cut Mama's medicines.

The woman gasped and reached for the boy and held him close. Lenore gasped, too. Mama let go of my hand and knelt down at the side of the coffin. She held her ear over the man's open mouth, and her eyes went blank, that look she always got when she left this world and entered the one of her mind.

She stood up suddenly. "The arnica, please," she said to Lenore, who hurried to the shelf over Mama's worktable.

Lenore held the big glass jar close to her chest, then set it down beside the coffin. Without looking at her, never taking her eyes off the dead man, Mama held out her right hand.

"Thirty grains," she said. "Exactly. Don't skimp me, girl."

Lenore counted them out.

One . . . two . . . three . . .

I watched the yellow pellets move from the jar to Mama's open palm. Mama wet the fingers of her free hand with her spit, the better to gain purchase, and then pinched each grain, one by one, from her right palm and fed them into the dead man's mouth.

fifteen sixteen seventeen

"He wasn't like that when we put him in, Cathy," the woman said.

Lucien turned his face into her side, and I felt a flash of pride, that a boy bigger than me couldn't watch what I could.

twenty-one twenty-two twenty-three

Thirty seeds passed between his lips.

The last five left them yellow.

Mama stood up. The man lay still in his coffin. Mama put her hands on her hips, frowned. Then she knelt down suddenly and whacked his back. The man sputtered and coughed and made the lowest moaning sound. His eyes blinked, and he rolled them up to look at all of us, from his resting place.

"There," Mama said.

The woman sighed. "Cathy, I don't know what we would have done—"

"Well, we don't have to wonder." Mama wiped her hands on her skirt. The man in the coffin was still groaning.

"He was so eager to keep going," the woman said. "He and his sister came to us three days ago. He said he should leave before his sister. That he was strong enough to make it first. But when he saw how he had to come, he got scared. He was shaking something fierce."

"I told him, 'Me and Manman took a girl not but ten years old this way, and she was brave and didn't cry the whole time,'" Lucien said. He was much recovered now and had stepped away from his mother's side. "I said, 'Be brave, Mr. Ben.'"

"Last night, he disappeared," the woman said. "That's why we left at the wrong time. He went missing and almost killed us all. He was down in Market Square, begging for whiskey to help him through. I said, 'You fool,' but he was already drunk by the time he got back. Pierre told me to wait till he sobered up, but if we'd done that, he would have kept yelling, drawing even more attention to us. It took Pierre and

Lucien both to get him in the box, and the whole time he was hollering that we were trying to kill him. He kept saying 'Damn, nigger, what'd I ever do to you?'"

Mama started to laugh but caught herself. Instead, she said, "How did you get him to be quiet?"

"I soaked that rag in some laudanum and stuffed it in his mouth, and then he fell right still. When we nailed the top on, I swear he was still breathing."

Mama shook her head. "You always overdo it, Elizabeth," she said, and then we all heard a great whoosh as Mr. Ben sat up in his coffin and began to cry.

"That black bitch right there promised to get me out. They all said she can get you out. No one ever said it was like this. In a goddamn coffin." Mr. Ben was upright, and I could see him clearly. The color came back to him—his skin was a dark brown. I liked his face. It was soft and, I thought, handsome, made more so by his cheeks and chin. They rounded in to the pout of a spoiled and much-loved baby. I could not tell how old he was—his skin was smooth, but his hair, what was left of it, was turning gray and clipped close to his skull. He wore a graying shirt and britches and no hat. His hands were enormous and calloused. He was crying, loud, racking sobs that I did not think a grown person could make. He made no move to leave his coffin, and my mother and the woman made no move to comfort him.

The woman said, "Behave yourself, Mr. Ben."

Mama pursed her lips. "Is this his final destination?"

"We take his sister to Manhattan next month."

"Then perhaps Mr. Ben can wait for her there. Mr. Ben," Mama said, "you will have to stay the night here, but I trust we can count on you to be quiet?"

Mr. Ben did not look at her; instead, he gazed up at the ceiling. "As long as I don't ever have to sleep in any coffin."

Mama laughed. "Only the good Lord can promise that."

MAMA HAD LENORE set up a bed for Mr. Ben by the fire, and she and the woman—Madame Elizabeth, she'd said to call her—took Mr. Ben by both elbows and helped him stand for the first time in twelve hours and walk around the room before settling down.

Mr. Ben went easily enough to sleep, and Mama and Madame Elizabeth fell to talking.

I was too cowed to say anything to our visitors. With the other people who came to see Mama at the house—her patients, and the runners from the pharmacy closer to town, and all the women in the committees and societies and church groups Mama headed—I had been trained to make polite conversation and ask, "How do you do?" But Madame Elizabeth was different. She spoke to Mama as if we had not all just seen her raise a man from the dead. As if Mama was the same as she.

"Cathy," she said when Mama stood over Lenore as she made up Mr. Ben's cot, "you work this poor woman to death."

As they talked, I did not dare to interrupt them. I did not want to be sent away to bed. Mama brewed strong sassafras tea for both of them—they had seemed to agree, without ever speaking it aloud, that they would both stay up the night to make sure Mr. Ben made it. I sat very still and close to Mama, and the only way I was sure she had not forgotten me was when, after she finished her mug, she silently handed it to me, because she knew that I believed that the sweetest drink in the world came from the dregs of a cup she had drunk from.

From their talking, I learned that Madame Elizabeth was a child-hood friend of Mama's. She had a husband, whom she called Monsieur Pierre. "A Haitian Negro, so you know he's unruly," Madame Elizabeth said, and Mama laughed.

"Oh hush," she said.

He and Madame Elizabeth owned a storefront down in Philadelphia—Madame Elizabeth ran a dressmaker's shop on one side of the house, and Monsieur Pierre ran an undertaker's on the other.

"You are doing well?" Mama asked, and Madame Elizabeth stood up, stamping her feet so her skirt hung down straight.

"Well? Well? Look at this dress, Madame Doctor." She turned. It was, indeed, a very fine dress. The lilies embroidered on the bod-ice stretched tendrils down to the skirt—a queer embellishment on a mourning dress that she had clearly worn over many travels.

"You play too much," Mama said. "A dress like that draws attention, and that's the last thing any of us need."

"We're doing the Lord's work in a cruel world, but that doesn't mean we can't do it with style," Madame Elizabeth said.

Mama looked at the fire. "If we are found out because you insist on introducing yourself with an ostrich feather, I don't know that I, or the Lord, can forgive you."

"Well, ostrich feathers are déclassé." Madame Elizabeth took the hem of her dress in her hand and artfully shook it. "Pierre always hated them, and lo and behold, the ladies say they're no longer in fashion. So nothing to worry about on that account."

They fell into a practiced quarrel, one that must have been older than me, centered on Mama's bad dress sense. Mama did not care for beauty; this was true. Like all the women in our town, she dressed for work—in heavy dark-colored gowns that could bear the mark of other people's sweat and tears and spit and vomit, and never show the stain.

But where others took care to tie a scarf at an angle or thread sweetgrass through a shirt cuff, Mama did not care. She was not scraggly. She was always neat, and on Sundays she allowed for the vanity of a hat with a big sweeping brim, which was decorated with the same set of silk flowers she'd won in a church raffle before I was born. But when one of the ladies' groups she belonged to would occasionally fall into giddy talk about the newest bolt of fabric or a new way of tying a head scarf, she would always quickly steer the conversation back to what was at hand. She would have been mortified to know it, but I had heard some of the women point to those same silk flowers on her hat that had not changed position for many seasons and call them "more reliable than springtime."

Madame Elizabeth teased Mama about the cramped practicalities of their youth until finally she turned to me, the first she had acknowledged me since she came in.

"Do you think she was always this way?" She glanced sideways at my mother.

"You turn my own daughter against me?" Mama said, but she was laughing, really laughing, in a way I had not heard before.

"When we were girls at the Colored School"—Madame Elizabeth leaned in, her voice low, as if I was as old as she and Mama—"I used to be so terrible at arithmetic. But not her. She was the best at it. Oh, so quick! You'd think the devil was giving her notes."

"Elizabeth!"

"But he wasn't of course. She was just so smart, your mother. Smarter than the devil, but good. But not all the way good. Can I tell you? Can I tell you a secret, my dear?"

"Don't listen to her." Mama went to cover my ears, but Madame Elizabeth drew me to her and held me close to her lap, and mock whispered, loud enough for Mama to hear: "Do you know what your clever mama would do? She'd ask me to dye her ribbons purple for her. Yes, even your good and smart mama wanted a bit of purple ribbon. And me, being her bestest friend, being her kind Elizabeth, mashed up all the blackberries I could find and dyed those ribbons the prettiest purple anyone in Kings County had ever seen."

"And extorted me and forced me to agree to do your arithmetic for you in exchange," Mama said.

"But can you blame me?" Madame Elizabeth's breath was so soft on my ear I shivered. "Your mama has always been the brightest."

Madame Elizabeth stroked the plaits in my hair and ran her fingers over my brow. "Lord," she said, "your girl may be dark, Cathy, but isn't she pretty."

"Libertie is beautiful," Mama said, gazing happily at me, and I flushed warm, because Mama did not often comment on anyone's appearance, unless it was to note that their skin had gone jaundiced or developed a rash.

"It's a shame she got her father's color," Madame Elizabeth said absently, and Mama stopped smiling.

"It's a blessing," she said, very distinctly, and Madame Elizabeth's hand paused.

"You aren't scared?" she said. She was stroking my face again. I did not want her to stop, but I could see from Mama's face that she wished that she would. "This work grows more dangerous, you know. You are all right. You're bright enough they hassle you less, maybe. But she's too dark."

Mama stood up abruptly. "It's less dangerous work if your help-meets come to you at midnight, as promised, not dusk," she said. She bent over Mr. Ben's cot.

Madame Elizabeth let go of my face.

"I told you why we missed our time."

But Mama didn't answer. She held her palm over Mr. Ben's open mouth.

"How is he?" Madame Elizabeth called.

"If he makes it through the next hour without any upset, he should be recovered."

Madame Elizabeth looked over at her son, who had fallen asleep in Mama's leather examination chair. Lucien, like Madame Elizabeth, had brassy velvet skin, and it was blushing now, in the last heat of the fire.

"Lucien's good-looking as well." Madame Elizabeth glanced sideways at Mama. "Perhaps one day, he and Libertie will make us proud and marry."

Mama was still watching Mr. Ben, but she smiled. "And move my Libertie all the way to Philadelphia, away from me? I couldn't bear that," she said. But she was pleased, I could see, that Madame Elizabeth, even in jest, considered me worthy of her son.

"What did Mama do with the purple ribbons?" I asked before I could stop. I cursed myself. Surely, now they would send me to bed. But Madame Elizabeth pulled me onto her lap.

"She wore them every day, because she knew they looked so fine. She was wearing them the day she met your good and kind father. She only let me borrow them once, when I asked her because I was going to a lecture at the lyceum. And, wouldn't you know, it was there where I met my own good man, Monsieur Pierre. He was fresh from Haiti, and I do believe meeting him is because of those lucky purple ribbons. Maybe she'll let you wear them one day, too, and you will tell us of finding your love with them."

"Tall tales," Mama said.

The rope on the cot whinnied as Mr. Ben turned over in his sleep. He began to cry. He was saying something, a word gargled by the bend of his neck. Mama gently lifted his head, and he sighed. Then he shouted, "Daisy."

"He certainly is giving us work," Madame Elizabeth said.

"We grow too bold. You should not have taken him."

"He insisted. In his state, it's safer to keep him moving. Once his sister comes, she can take him on to Troy or Syracuse. Or Canada."

"He won't be safe till he's out of this country. Even then, he will probably still be in danger," Mama said.

"Daisy," Mr. Ben cried again.

"His sister said that was his girl," Madame Elizabeth said. "He took up with her, and then she ran. They got word last spring she died. That's what finally made him despair enough to leave, his sister said. She'd been trying to get him to work up the courage for forever. Their mother gone, brother gone, and then the girl he'd started to love, for just a little bit of comfort, gone, too. That's why he's here."

"He's running away, not running towards. They're the most dangerous kind," Mama said. "They have nothing to lose, and so they grow reckless."

"He won't harm us, though."

"Let us hope," Mama said. She did not sound convinced.

My mother named me Libertie for a dead man's dream, the dream of my father—the only other dead man I knew before Mama resurrected Mr. Ben.

My father died when I was still in Mama's womb. He was a traveling preacher, and on one of his trips west, he fell ill. By the time he made it back to her, it was too late. Even Mama, who I believed could heal everyone, could not heal him. In his final moments, as he lay sweating his life away in her arms, he told her to name me Libertie, in honor of the bright, shining future he was sure was coming.

Father was one of those who'd stolen themselves away and come up north. Did he come in one of Madame Elizabeth's coffins? I do not know. Mama did not like to talk about him. His name was Robert. I know it only from tracing it on his gravestone with my finger. He is buried in my mother's family's plot—he, of course, did not have his people up here. His gravestone reads ROBERT SAMPSON, and then, underneath it, instead of his time on this Earth, only one word: FREEDOM.

Although Mama did not like to talk about my father, she did like me to take care of his grave. Every other Sunday, after church, we stopped in the burial place and washed down his stone and pulled up the weeds. One of the first presents she made me, when I was four or five, was a small pair of scissors to wear at my waist, so that I could trim the grass that grew over him. "It's his home now," was how she'd explained it to me. "We have to make it comfortable for him."

While Father was the one dead man I knew, I knew of a dead little girl, too: my mama's sister. She was also buried in the family plot, but her stone had no name, and Mama wouldn't tell it to me. Mama did not like to speak of her, either. She was not a name, not a memory—just a white stone that only Mama was allowed to tend and a glass jar on the parlor's mantelpiece, where Mama kept three braids clipped from her sister's head right after she passed. The dead girl's braids sat gathering dust in the bottom of the jar, curled in on one another like the newborn milk snakes we'd sometimes find asleep in the barn. I only learned how the little girl passed from Lenore, who told me one day, plain, while Mama was on a house call and had left me to help wash the sheets.

As she beat the linen clean, Lenore said, "Pneumonia." The dry cough racking the small, sweaty body, the muffled air: it was a painful way for a child to go. "Back then, there was no colored doctor, man or woman, in the county. If you wanted to go to see a doctor, you had to find a white person willing to accompany you—white doctors did not treat colored people if we came alone. Your grandfather was light enough. He could get by. But the little girl who passed, she couldn't. She was too dark. They would have known her to be colored. They would not have taken her for white, as they would have if it was your grandfather or your mama who fell ill."

"Your grandfather had a white friend," she continued. "A Mr. Hobson, who he sometimes chewed tobacco with. So he ran to him to see if he would accompany his daughter to the hospital. But when he reached Mr. Hobson, the man was playing cards and did not want to get up from the table—not yet. Mr. Hobson waited a hand, and then another, just to make sure he was losing, and by the time he had gotten up and gotten back to the house, your mother's sister was gone."

Lenore ended the story matter-of-factly. "Your mama became a doctor because she watched her sister die."

I think it is also why, even though Mama could have gotten by, she always made it clear she was a colored woman. They let her into the medical school alongside two white women before they realized their mistake, though she was quick to point out she'd never deceived anyone, never claimed she wasn't a Negro, always signed her real name and address. And then, of course, she married my father, who must have been dark, because I could never get by the way she could. But Mama saw that as a mark of honor, a point of pride for her Libertie. Almost as if she'd planned it.

I know that they met at a lecture. Maybe one where Madame Elizabeth met her Haitian? I never had the courage to ask. Mama only told me that the lecture was about the country being founded for us in

Africa. It was a lecture about whether or not American Negroes should go. Should free men leave? Mama did not want to—I know that. And I know that my father always did. So I am named for his longing. As a girl, I did not realize what a great burden this was to bear. I was only grateful.

Where did Father go? Where was he now, since he was not here on Earth with me and Mama? Every other Sunday, I lay on my father's grave and imagined that new place he'd journeyed to in death: Freedom. In the muggy summertime, in the hot July sun, I imagined Freedom was a cool, dark cave with water dripping down the walls—like the one where Jesus slept for three days. And in November, when the wind bit the tips of my fingers and turned them red, I imagined Freedom was a wide, grassy field on a warm and cloudy day.

What did Father do, now that he was dead? He went to more lectures. Since it was the only thing I knew about him, about how they met, I imagined that was Freedom to him. In Freedom, he sat in the cool cave or in the wide field in a pew like we had at church, but comfortable, and he closed his eyes and listened to learned men and women make the world anew with words. And at his side were two seats: one for Mama at his left and one for me at his right. I imagined that when I died and made it to Freedom, whenever that would be, I would have to spend eternity very politely pretending to like these lectures as much as Mama and Father did. It would be hard to do that forever, but Mama would be happy, at least, and I would have my father's hand in mine, while I sat, slightly bored but loved, in Freedom.

WE ALL SLEPT in the examination room that night—me curled on Mama's lap, and Madame Elizabeth and Lucien collapsed on each other, and Mr. Ben still in his cot.

I woke up first, a little before dawn. It was strange to be awake without Mama, but it gave me time to very carefully crawl down off her lap and creep across the floor and sit, hugging my knees, right by Mr. Ben's pillow, so I could get a better look at him. Mr. Ben was the first person I'd ever met who had been brought back from death, and I watched him avidly for signs of what Freedom had been like.

I saw where his lips were damp with spittle, and I smelled, on his breath, the dried flowers that my mother had made him eat. And then I had the shock of watching him open his eyes, very slowly, to stare back at me.

"I been awake for hours," he said.

I nodded.

"You her girl?"

"She's my mama."

He whistled. "She must've liked her niggers black to get a girl like you."

I had heard worse. It was the refrain of so many when Mama and I walked in the street.

"Mama says I'm like a mulberry."

"Yeah, you a pretty little girl—no denying it. Just dark. Where your daddy at?"

"He's dead."

"So who else live here?"

"It's just me and Mama—and her nurse, Lenore, who comes every morning to help with the patients."

He propped himself up on his elbow and winced. "Lord, I'm dizzy." He contemplated the ceiling for what felt like a long time. Then he looked to the window that was just beginning to turn white with the rising sun. "She own all of this? From doctoring? Just from doctoring?"

"Mama grew up in this house. Her daddy owned it. He was a pig

farmer. We still have some of his hogs, but we don't raise 'em to sell
anymore. You don't know about his hogs?" I warmed to the telling.
What a change, what a delight to have a stranger in the house, someone who did not already know everything about me, as was usually the
way with Mama's visitors. "His hogs used to be famous. Grandfather
was very religious, and he taught every hog born under his care to
bow its head in prayer before it ate at the trough. He'd say the Lord's
Prayer with 'em, Mama says. A few of the pigs here are old enough to
still do it. Sometimes . . ." I leaned forward to share this secret with
my new friend. "Sometimes, I say the Lord's Prayer really loud when
I'm feeding 'em to see which ones will bow. But they don't listen to me
like that."

This confidence was lost on Mr. Ben, though, because he wasn't
paying attention. He was looking up, over my shoulder, and I turned
to see that he was looking at Mama, who had stirred in her chair, and
who was watching Mr. Ben back.

"That's enough, Libertie."

She stood up and stood over Mr. Ben. On her face now was a familiar expression, one I had seen often enough in the examination room,
and when I accompanied her on her house calls.

When Mama was diagnosing someone, when she was calculating
how best to heal them, she got this look. Her eyes emptied out and
turned dark, and her brow went completely smooth, and she stared for
a good three or four minutes. She did not respond to anything—not
a patient's babbling, not the sound of the wind at the door, not the
distraught mother saying, "Please, please, please," not the cries of the
baby who was too young to understand the failings of its own small
body. Certainly not to me, the girl at her side holding her bag, watching her disappear from me and go deep into her mind, where the right
answer nearly always was. She'd leave me behind, leave us all behind, to

commune with the perfection of her intellect. And when she returned, it was with a resolve that was almost frightening to see.

It was sad and cold to be outside her caring. It had scared me as a smaller child, made me cry.

As consolation, Mama had explained that one day I would join her when she left for her mind like that, that one day I would be a doctor, too, standing beside her, both our minds flying free while our bodies did the work. And we'd have a horse and carriage, and a sign with gold letters on it that said DR. SAMPSON AND DAUGHTER. "Wouldn't that be nice, Libertie?" she'd said.

And that had been a kind of hollow comfort when she left me behind for her calculations.

Mr. Ben was watching her now. "It feels like I'm dying. Am I gonna die?"

Mama's eyes filled up again, and she was back. "Not yet," she said.

He propped himself up on his elbows. "This the worst pain I ever felt. I was whupped till my back was ribbons when I was a younger man, and I thought that was dying, but this is different. It feels like there's a hole in me, in the very center of me, and the wind's running through it."

Mama sat back. "That's a problem of the spirit."

"So medicine women are supposed to fix that."

"I'm a trained doctor," Mama said, straightening up. "I fix the body. The spirit can tell me what's wrong with the body sometimes. But what you are describing—you can talk to Reverend Harland at the church about the spirit."

"Seems you should be able to do it all."

I did not think, then, that Mama was even listening. If she had heard it, I was sure she had discounted it, because all she said was, "You will stay here to rest."

The next morning, it took Mama and Madame Elizabeth and Lucien, struggling, to lift the empty coffin back onto the wagon bed it was so unwieldly. Finally, they slid it home.

Madame Elizabeth was just taking up the whip to prod the mule when Mama seized her friend's hand and kissed the knuckles where they wrapped around the switch.

Madame Elizabeth looked startled. Lucien smirked—oh, how I hated him for that.

For Mama looked genuinely pained. "If you should run into any trouble—"

"We won't," Madame Elizabeth said.

"But if you should . . ." She held her friend's hand for a beat more, then flung it away from her. "Be safe."

Mr. Ben had come outside for this last bit. He bent his head slightly in the wagon's direction. "Thanks, mamselle," he said with slight mockery, to which Madame Elizabeth rolled her eyes.

Then she called to the mule, and they were on their way.

Mama stayed to watch them go. Mr. Ben stood beside her.

"Y'all ain't afraid of getting caught?" he said.

"She's very good at what she does."

Mr. Ben sniffed. "When she's not trying to murder a man."

Mama glanced at me, then looked back to the road, where the wagon moved slowly away from us. "You made it here well enough."

"Back in Maryland," Mr. Ben said, "where I was before . . ." He looked down at his hands. "Before I was sold the first time, there was a group of niggers like you gals. They did what you doing. They got fifteen out. And then they was caught. You don't want to hear what happened."

Mama glanced again at me, then back at Mr. Ben. "We most certainly do not," she said.

"What happened?" I asked.

"Blood—"

"That's enough," Mama said. "Mr. Ben, if you're well enough to stand and well enough to talk, do you think you're well enough to help us today?"

He sniffed again. "I suppose so."

"Good," Mama said. "The best way to help is to stay quiet and stay out of the way, then. Don't let anybody who comes to the house see you yet."

"Your neighbors don't know you in this business? Mamselle Elizabeth told me she was bringing me to an all-colored town."

"We are," Mama said. "You'll settle well here. But it's best if we allow people to truthfully say they thought you came here on your own. Generally, we take care of each other here. But I don't want to put anyone into a position of lying for us. It's too dangerous. Besides, you know as well as I do, Mr. Ben. Even with our own, you can't trust everybody."

He looked out over the yard again, to the barn and the squat crabapple tree, to the hog pen with the two pigs just now rising from the mud to wander, to Mama's medicine garden and the small field that lay just beyond it, where we grew the vegetables for the kitchen, to all the things that I'd just told him she owned.

"I suppose that's right," he said. "Just because a person's a nigger doesn't mean they know the life you do." Then he looked at Mama and stalked back into the house.

I slipped my hand into hers.

"What does he mean, Mama?"

"He has just suffered a great shock to his system and won't make much sense for a while."

"Because you and Madame Elizabeth got him free?"

She took her hand out of mine and knelt so that we could look each other in the eye. I did not like this at all. I preferred looking up at her, tilting my head back till all I saw was her chin. Eye to eye was more frightening.

People said Mama was a beautiful woman, but I think what they really meant was she was light enough to pass. She had large eyes, true, set deep in her skull, but they were more owl-like than anything else. She had a heavy brow, hooded, that made it look as though she was about to scowl, even when she was laughing. Her skin, of course, was pale but it was sallow. It was her one vanity, the only one she allowed me to witness anyways—she dried lily petals in the spring and ate them year-round, to make the tone of her cheeks even. It was, up until this moment, my favorite secret we shared between us. I was the only one who saw her do it. Her nose was straight—I think this is what people meant when they called her beautiful—but it was severe. Her lips were the only pretty thing about her, the same as mine, full and always resolving themselves into the shape of a rose. When I looked at her, I never saw my own face, and maybe that is why I found it so disturbing, these times when she'd kneel down to look me in the eye.

I preferred, at that age, to think of us as the same person. I was still young enough for that.

She looked me in the eye and said, "What did you say?"

"You got him free. You and Madame Elizabeth. You got him here to be free."

She looked me steadily in the eye. Finally. "This is true."

I expected her to stand again, but she did not. "You cannot repeat to anyone what you just said to me—"

"But why?"

"This is not a game, Libertie. What we did, what we are doing, is very dangerous. If you tell somebody, it would not end well for us. We would go to jail, Mr. Ben would go back to bondage, and you and I would never see each other again. Do you understand?"

I did not, entirely. But to admit this would not please her, so I nodded.

She stood up and put her hand on her hip. The sun was finally out, and we could see, in the new light, Lenore coming up the road. Lenore was not a big woman, but she still managed to roll her hips when she walked, and she liked to ball her skirts in her two fists and switch them this way and that, to keep the dust off her. Mama was insistent that no dust be brought into the examination room, except by her patients themselves, and made Lenore wipe herself down with damp cloth and beat her skirt with a straw brush before she could join her each day, so Lenore had devised this method to make it a bit easier.

She made her way to us, where we stood, glanced at me.

"The girl up?"

"I woke up before anyone," I said proudly.

Lenore gave Mama a look.

"I told her," Mama said. "She says she can keep a secret."

"She a child," Lenore said.

"I can do it," I said again.

Lenore looked steadily at my mother, and my mother looked back for a bit, then lowered her eyes.

"It's not safe for the baby to be up," Lenore said.

"I'm not a baby," I insisted.

Lenore sighed. "Grown folks know when to keep quiet. Babies run they mouths every which way. Y'all can't help it." Her voice was drained of malice. She was merely stating a fact. This wounded my pride even more. Worse, she was not even looking at me when she said it; she was looking at Mama.

"Dr. Sampson, I won't get sold to a slavecatcher because a child can't stop talking."

"Nobody's saying that's going to happen," Mama said.

"Still"—Lenore moved past her, to the house, to start the fire burning for the day—"you can't trust babies with the ways of the world."

We were alone together again.

"I am not a baby, Mama."

She looked at me skeptically.

"I can help. I can do what you do. Let me help."

"You cannot, Libertie."

"Mama," I said, "you always say that when I am big, you and I will have a horse and carriage together, with 'Dr. Sampson and Daughter' written in gold on the side. You promised me, when I am big. You said that. You did. So let me help you now."

She sighed.

"I am eleven, nearly twelve in July. Let me do it, too, Mama."

She was not looking at me anymore, but at the dusty road that Madame Elizabeth had left on and Lenore had returned to us on. "I suppose it was inevitable," she said.

"What does 'inevitable' mean?"

"If you're to join us in this work, Libertie, the first lesson is the one Lenore said. Don't ask so many questions. Only listen and learn."

THIS LESSON DID not appear to apply to Mr. Ben.

The whole day, all he did was question.

"What's that you've got going there, Miss Doctor?"

"Lord, why does the house smell like greens gone bad?"

"Y'all don't stop at noon to eat?"

"But I still don't understand who pays you for all this work, because you know niggers ain't got no money."

Mama tried, politely, to answer his questions at first while Lenore flat-out ignored him from the start. It was not so bad in the morning, before patients, and before John Culver, the pharmacist's son, came running for more supplies. Usually, in those hours, Mama and Lenore worked in a silent dance, the only sound being the fire crackling and the glass tops of the medicine jars shifting as they reached for this or that to make or measure.

But the silence of their work seemed to unnerve Mr. Ben, and any time the house began to quiet down, to start the rhythms of women working, he was compelled to speak and break it.

"Does every woman in New York make a biscuit as dry as this?" he said as he reached for his third one that morning.

Mama was only half listening.

"If my woman, Daisy, was still here," Mr. Ben said, "she'd learn you. Even you, Miss Doctor. Whoever heard of a woman knowing how to make a pill but not a biscuit? It's not natural. Daisy would learn you, though, if she was still with us. She was sweet like that. She was the type to learn you if you asked."

Lenore looked up sharply. "Mr. Ben, you're bothering the doctor."

And Mr. Ben said, "She can nurse and listen at the same time, can't she?"

A few moments' silence. Then.

"Miss Doctor, this tea is weak," he said.

No answer this time from Mama or Lenore, who had pointedly decided to ignore him.

"Miss Doctor," he tried again, "why don't you ever put on new ribbons? My Daisy always tried to make herself pretty, and she wasn't half as rich or important as you. But she knew how to make herself look nice. If you thought of looking nice, then maybe you'd find a man to come here and live with you. You're not too old for all that, Miss Doctor."

At that point, Lenore moved as if she would show him the door, but Mama held up her hand to stay her. She took a deep breath, and then she turned, a tight smile on her face.

"Mr. Ben, I do believe you have not seen the rest of our town. Libertie, take Mr. Ben for a walk."

"Mama . . ."

"You said you wanted to be of service in our work. Well, be of service," Mama said.

So I took Mr. Ben's hand in my own and led him out into the afternoon sun. When I went back for my cloak, I overheard Mama and Lenore.

"Honestly, it's a wonder how that Daisy woman got with him in the first place," Lenore said, and Mama laughed outright. "When will he leave?"

"His sister will be here soon."

"It's too much, Doctor."

"We can bear it," Mama said.

I took my coat and left.

WE WERE THE sole house on the way to town—Grandfather had cleared the brush himself and tried to sell the lots along it to other colored men, but most men, if they were buying, wanted to live closer to the school and the church. Because we were the only family on that road, and had the privilege of naming it after ourselves.

"Sampson Lane," I told Mr. Ben proudly.

He nodded. He looked above us, where the tree canopy stretched, through which we could see the white sky of spring.

"It's colder up here in New York," he said. "I didn't think a place could be colder than Philadelphia, but Kings County has it beat."

I did not feel right talking badly about our town, but I also felt my cheeks stinging in the bitter air. I nodded politely, not committing to my guest's belief but trying to be neighborly, which is what we learned in Sunday school.

Our house, and the road that led to it, were all on higher ground than the rest of our settlement, and as the path sloped down, as our feet began to angle to the earth, the ground became wetter. My boots were spotted in mud, and Mr. Ben's began to squelch.

"I'm sorry," I said. "We will tell Mama, and she will find better shoes for you."

"She will, will she?" he said.

"You don't like Mama," I said. It had not occurred to me, up until then, that anybody, anyone colored anyways, could dislike my mother. I always saw people speak to her with respect, and even the sick children, who knew to be afraid when they saw a doctor, did not have dislike in their fear, only a kind of awe. So it was a revelation to meet someone who disliked her, and it was so strange that I did not understand it as a threat.

Mr. Ben did not deny it. He only kept walking until finally he said, "You always been free?"

"Yeah," I said.

"You ain't never been a slave? Your mama neither?"

"No," I said.

He sighed. "They tell us over and over again what's not possible. White folks say this ain't possible, this place ain't possible. But it's real.

It's a glory, but it's . . . it's . . . I wish my Daisy was still here to see it with me. She told me there was places like this. She said if she was ever free, she'd spend all day in silk and she'd paint her face pretty. I wish she was still alive to see it. She knew what she would do with freedom. It wasn't man's work she'd do with freedom. Not like your mama. She knew better than that."

Then he stopped, and was silent, and seemed to have gone away to another world, too. Not the one where Mama went to figure out how to make a body work right, but somewhere else, probably with his Daisy in her silks. But in the moment, I decided to apply Mama's new lesson for me and not ask questions.

"This it?" Mr. Ben said.

Sampson Lane had reached the crossroads, where the main road stretched to downtown and the waterfront—the journey most people who lived here made every dawn and dusk for their livelihood. In the other direction, the road stretched deeper into Kings County, to the farms some of us worked. The final fork spread south. Around us was some of the land cleared for fields, the cabins and houses built close together so that neighbors could share gardens and animals and conversation.

There was the schoolhouse, which was empty now, because it was spring and most children were working. It would start up classes again in a few weeks, when they returned, and I would sit there, too, away from Mama.

There was the low, rambling building that was Mr. Culver's pharmacy. His son, John, was regularly running from Mama's to here, passing messages between the two of them. Out front sat six glass vials, filled to the brim with blue and green and red liquid remedies—the sign to all, even those of us who did not know our letters, that Culver's was a place for medicine. I knew the front room well. Culver's also was our general store, where we could buy seed and burlap and thread from a welcoming face, not the begrudging white ones downtown who sold the same, at two times the price for colored people.

And finally, there was the church, the building everyone was proudest of. It had been the first one built, after our grandfathers bought land here, and it stood back, next to a little glen of trees we took turns pruning to keep pretty, and the graveyard shaded lower on the hill, protected from any passerby.

Mr. Ben looked around. "This it, then?" he repeated.

"We play over there," I said, pointing to the other side of the churchyard, where in the summertime a meadow always sprang up, which I and the other children liked to run through. In this new spring, it was bare, but I tried to explain it to him, what the future glory would look like. "We run so hard there you feel like you're bursting."

His face was unmoved.

"But I guess it's all just mud now," I said, trailing off.

A crow called above us, wheeled in the sky, and settled on the branch of the nearest tree, shaking a too-new blossom loose.

Mr. Ben said, "I couldn't see what this place looked like on the way in. I could only hear what this town was like, when I was in that box."

"What was it like?" I said. "In there."

"Awful, gal. What kind of a question is that? What you think it like, to be shut up in the dark with nothing but yourself all around you?"

He made another turn, looked up at the sky again, which seemed too white and was closing in around us.

I was seized with the wild desire for him to love our home as much as I did. He had said he was lonely for his Daisy, but maybe he was lonely because of being in the box, of having been so close to her in death but then being snatched away to rise up. I knew part of making a guest feel comfortable was to introduce them to those they might have something in common with. That is what they taught us girls in deportment at the Sunday school, anyways. And he seemed to enjoy talking about the dead. I pointed to the churchyard again.

"That's where my daddy is," I said. "Mama's sister, too. They're dead like your Daisy. Like you were. 'Cept Mama couldn't bring them back. She did that for you, though."

He looked at me from the corner of his eye and smiled slightly. "They all in there, then?" he said.

"Yeah." I thought about it for a minute. "Not all of 'em, though. Mama's sister's hair, it lives in the glass jar in the parlor. But all of my daddy's in there."

Mr. Ben nodded. He was quiet for a moment, and then he spit in disgust on the ground. "I don't even know Daisy's resting place."

He limped to the middle of the crossroads, turning first in one direction, then the other. He looked up above him again, at the sky. Then he said, "Let's go back to your mother's." And so we did.

He allowed me, though, the kindness of slipping my hand in his as we walked back home.

Dinner was eaten in near silence. Mr. Ben seemed to be thinking still of our trip to town, and Mama, she ate not for pleasure but for utility. She often said that if it was not for Lenore, I would not know good cookery at all. She seemed to notice that there was a sadness around Mr. Ben, because she said, at the end of a meal where the sole talk was between our tin spoons scraping our plates, "Is everything all right, then?"

He looked up at her, hard, for a minute. So hard Mama startled.

Then he looked back down at his plate and said, "Yes, ma'am."

It was my job to clear the table, to take everything to the basin of water Lenore always left, her last duty before the end of the day. So I did not hear how it started between them, only how it ended.

I had taken our plates and come back for the pitcher when I saw Mr. Ben by the parlor mantelpiece, running his hand along it. Mama was still at the table. She had taken out her accounting ledger for the day. She was back in the world of her mind.

Mr. Ben ran his fingers along the family Bible that sat there, then over the little mirror in a gold frame that Mama displayed and the bowl where Lenore put cut blossoms from the tulip tree outside. He skipped over the jar with the braids in it. His fingers next ran over a pile of newsprint.

"What's this?" he said.

Mama glanced up over the greasy spectacles on her nose, narrowed her eyes. "Ah, that? That is our newspaper. They print it once a month. It has lots for sale, and news of the church. And here . . ." Mama got up to stand beside Mr. Ben.

"I can't cipher," he said.

"Of course," Mama said. "But, you see, there's a primer in the back."

She rustled the pages to the very end. She held her hand over the paper and read aloud the print there. "See? This part are words to learn. 'Free.' 'Life.' 'Live.' 'Took.' 'Love.' 'Loves.' 'Man.' 'Now.' 'Will.' 'Thank.' 'God.' 'Work.' 'Hard.' 'House.' 'Land.' 'Made.' 'Slaves.'"

With each word she spoke, I saw him wince, as if the words had pricked his finger.

"And these," Mama said, "are the sentences to learn. 'I am free and well.' 'I will love God and thank Him for it.' 'And I must work hard and be good and get me a house and lot.'"

"'Work hard,'" he said.

"Yes."

It was quiet between them for a bit, only the fire crackling.

Then Mr. Ben panted out, as if it was taking him great effort to do so, "There was a nigger back in Maryland who learned how to cipher. You wanna know how he learned, Miss Doctor?"

"How?"

"He took pot liquor fat and dipped pages of the Bible in 'em. Dipped 'em in till the pages was clear through. Greased the Word and hid it underneath his hat, and that clever, pretty nigger walked around with the Bible fat on his head, and if any white man saw it, he wouldn't know it as the word of God. He'd only see some greasy, dirty papers on a nigger's head and leave 'im be."

"Well, that's marvelous," Mama said gravely. "That's quite beautiful."

"You think?" Mr. Ben sucked in a gulp of air, cleared his throat loudly. "I always thought it was a whole lot of work. But"—he pointed at the newspaper held between them—"we must work hard and be good even in freedom. That's what you telling me. With rules like that, don't it make you wonder what freedom's for?"

He let his fingers run along the mantel again, from the Bible, to the mirror, to the flowers and back again, skipping over the newsprint.

"You got so many pretty things, Miss Doctor," he said. "Such pretty things. My Daisy was the same way. She kept three stones she'd found: pink ones, and a white one, too. And a shell she'd found down by the wharf. She even had a mirror like this," he held up the mirror and set it down again. "She wanted one something fierce. 'Course, she didn't need one. My eyes were enough of a mirror for her, I told her. But she said no, she needed a mirror. To see herself. First thing she bought with the money from her market garden, even before she tried to save for freedom. She loved looking at herself in that thing. Sometimes, I'd have to beg her to put it down so my Daisy would talk to me."

He picked up the mirror at last, cradled it in his palm. "Do you think someone like that belongs in freedom?" Mr. Ben said. "I mean, if she'd lived to make it here. Do you think she would have been able to work hard and have her lot of land to earn her freedom, like that paper says?"

"We all work hard," Mama said. "I do not follow what you mean, Mr. Ben."

"I told you about my Daisy, didn't I?" He still would not look at her. He carefully set down the mirror. "She was almost as fair as you. No, fairer. And big brown eyes. And hair down her back in curls, when she let it out. Almost like . . ." He let his fingers run again along the mantelpiece once more, until they lit on the last thing he hadn't touched. The jar with the braids coiled at the bottom.

His back was still toward Mama. When he picked up the jar, he didn't see her flinch. But I did.

I moved to remind him. "Oh, you know what that is, Mr. Ben," I began, but Mama shot me a look so pained I stopped my explanation.

"Her hair was almost like this then," he said. He held the jar up to better catch the dusty braids in the light.

"Nah," he said, turning the jar around in his hands. "Daisy's hair was finer."

He set the jar back down and turned around. He was watching Mama's face carefully, as if tracking which way it might turn. "Who'd all that belong to, then?" he said.

Mama took her glasses off her nose so that she could see him more clearly. "My youngest sister," she said. She cleared her throat. "It is a keepsake."

"And what happened to her?" Mr. Ben said. "You lose her to the body or the spirit?"

Mama took in a sharp breath. She made a low, guttural sound, as if something was wrenched from her throat. And then she looked quickly down at the newsprint in her hand. I could see her eyes moving back and forth, making some kind of calculation. I could see, in the fever of it, one eye wet and watery. She looked up.

"I think," Mama said, her voice entirely steady but her eyes wet, "that we have come to an end with our time together, Mr. Ben. I think perhaps this is your last night here and you should wait for your sister in town. The back room at Culver's will have you. He takes in many of our new arrivals, and—"

"So that's it, then," he said.

"Yes," Mama said. "I believe it is."

She turned to me, still crying, her voice deadly level. "Libertie, please make up Mr. Ben's cot for him. Make sure it's comfortable for his last night here with us. I will be working in the examination room. Be quick, girl. We have a long day tomorrow."

And then she gathered up her ledger in her arms and walked out of the room. Mr. Ben watched her go.

He would not look at me, only at the fire, as I made his bed for him.

"Why did you go and do that?" I said as I pulled the cot closer to the fire for him.

"Leave it alone, girl."

When the bed was done, I stood beside it. I did not know exactly what I was waiting for, what I hoped I or he would say. I knew I should say something in defense of Mama. If Lenore was here, she would have loudly cursed Mr. Ben the whole time. But he looked at me with a sadness so deep it startled me. I could not say anything to reprimand him. Instead, I stepped forward and hugged him fiercely.

He smelled of fresh-cut grass, up close. I had not expected that. He was still in my arms for a moment, and then he put his own arms around me once, a quick, tight squeeze, the tightest I'd ever known, the air squeezed out of my lungs. And then he let me go.

"I'll be all right, girl," he said. "You go on now."

I WAS OF an age then when I had just left Mama's bed for one of my own, and even though I wished to comfort her, I did not wish to give up my hard-won independence of a cot to myself, under the eaves.

I stood by her examination room door while she sat with her back toward me, bent over her books.

"Mama," I began.

"Go to bed, Libertie."

So I did.

I did not see Mr. Ben to Culver's back room. Mama decided to take him there herself after Lenore came. She said, "You stay here, Libertie. You asked for your education to begin, and so it begins today."

As Mama walked down the road with Mr. Ben, neither of them speaking or looking at each other, I imagined what secrets I was about to be initiated into. What big-woman ways I was about to learn. What I would be able to chart about hearts and spleens and tongues. But Lenore only turned to me and said, "You can start with the cats in the barn."

We had a band of stray cats that had lived in the hay there since Mama was a girl. Big nature-raised hooligans with gnarled and matted fur, and sometimes sores on their sides. Whole generations that Mama and Lenore took care of, nursing their battle scars and birthing their litters. They terrified me. Even from far away, I knew them as too rough to be pets.

"Not them," I said.

Lenore smirked. "Your mama said it's how you'll learn to care."

So I took the bucket that Lenore usually did, and filled it with what she fed the cats—guts and bits from the kitchen, ground up for them. In the dim light of the barn, I could hear them all around me, and soon a few came closer and rubbed up against me. I felt panicked. Not because of their sharp teeth or their hissing, but because of their need. They wanted so much from me. The smell of their food made me ill, not because it was putrefying but because of how much it made them want me, made them mimic the action of love to get it, swirling around me, their softness hiding a deep, yawning hunger inside of them, just below their skin. I could feel it humming when they got too close. Their need was monstrous.

I fed them quick and ran from the barn, and when Mama came back, I wanted to tell her all of that, that their need was too much of a burden to carry. How could she do it? How could she see them so naked and yearning, and not want to turn away?

But Mama looked so tired, her face was so worn, that all I could say when I saw it was, "I don't like the cats, Mama."

Lenore sucked her teeth. "You bother her with that?"

But Mama was too tired, even, to hold my silliness against me. She did look disappointed, though.

But now that the idea of my taking on her work had gripped her, had become something she favored, Mama would not let me give up.

"You have to learn," she told me. "Care does not come natural to me, either."

What a lie, I thought. I could still see her, in my mind's eye, walking slow and steady beside Mr. Ben, who had picked up her dead sister's braids and tossed them aside, but who, I could tell, she understood had not meant it.

"But care, it is our lot now," Mama was saying. "It is our service to others that defines us. We are doers of the Word."

She sighed. "If you cannot keep the cats, you'll learn how to keep the garden."

The garden is no small thing to a homeopath. Mama kept a huge one to grow the most common things she needed: elderflower, ginger, mint, aloe. She was so orderly in everything, and the garden was no exception. The herbs were close by the door, and everything else was in neat rows, labeled clearly on posts made from scraps of wood. Up until now, the garden had been mostly Lenore's domain. But Lenore was so busy with everything else she'd been paying it less attention, and the garden had begun to be unruly. When they needed something from it, Mama would question Lenore, and Lenore would think for a minute, and they would argue back and forth about where it should be.

"You will keep it in the correct order, Libertie," Mama said. By which she meant the order of her imagination.

How was I to learn her mind? Before I could take over the garden, I would have to make a more diligent study of homeopathy, Mama's discipline of medicine. "The guiding principle," Mama had told me, many times as I grew, "is that like cures like." But it was, as all things Mama insisted were straightforward, more complicated than that.

I was allowed a rest from my regular chores, and Mama had me sit in her examination room with her materia medica, the big black leather-bound book that listed every remedy and the diseases they belonged to.

Yarrow	*is for*	*Anemia and Colic and Bed-Wetting and Hysteria and Nosebleeds and Hemorrhages and Varicose Veins and When Women's Wombs Lose Children*
Bitterwood	*is for*	*Indigestion and Fever and Heartburn*
Datura	*is for*	*Drunkards and Stammering and Ecstasy*
Belladonna	*is for*	*Nymphomania and Gout and Hemorrhoids and Delirium and Depression*
Calendula	*is for*	*Burns and Knife Cuts and Flesh Wounds*
Daisies	*are for*	*Acne and Boils and Giddiness and Railway Spine*

Milkweed	*is for*	*Syphilis and Leprosy and Swelling of the Hands and Feet*
Chamomile	*is for*	*Restlessness and Waspishness and Bleeding Wombs*

I had to transcribe what I read into notes, to remember which substance was for which symptom. And then, the next morning, I took my scrap of paper and searched for each plant in its proper place, and recorded if it lived and flourished, or if it had become overgrown or invaded the space of another.

I did not have an eye for recognizing plants on sight, and I spent many frantic minutes comparing the description of a leaf pattern or a petal to what was flowering before me. The only things I could recognize with any ease were pansies. Not very impressive, as pansies grow everywhere and are known even to fools. But when I saw a thatch of them in my mama's lanes, they cheered me—panting yellows and purples and blues.

Pansies	*are for*	*Obstinate Skin*

In my new life of study, I thought often of Mr. Ben. He lived in the back room of Culver's now, a place I had never seen, only heard about. Culver himself had found him so waspish that he'd offered to pay Mr. Ben's way across the river to Manhattan.

"To Mr. Ruggles's place in Manhattan, on Golden Hill. Ruggles and his friends would help him." This was Lenore, gossiping with Mama in the mornings while she banked the fire and I sat, head propped in my hands, reading the materia medica.

"And Mr. Ben refused?" Mama said.

Lenore nodded. "He said he'd die if he crossed the water. He said he'll drown. Said he's seen it in a dream. Says the water's full of dead niggers calling his name, and he'd rather stay here, on land."

"His sister can't come soon enough," Mama said.

But she did not come for another month, perhaps two. When I went into town sometimes, to bring a note to Culver or his son, I would see Mr. Ben wandering the crossroads, turning one way or another. He always had a smile for me. Weak, but he gave it. He never called me Libertie, though. Instead, he called me Black Gal.

"Hey there, Black Gal, and good morning to you."

"What you doing for your mama, Black Gal?"

And it was with a sense of pity, which we both could feel between us, that I would return his greeting, show him what was in my bag, raise my hand back to him.

What I wanted to say each time was, *How could you do that to Mama?*

What I wanted to say each time was, *Mama can be your friend.*

What I wanted to say each time was, *I wish I could be your friend, but this is too sad a start for friendship.*

I was that age when I was not young enough to speak that frankly, yet I was not so old that I could pretend the sadness did not exist. So I raised my hand and smiled at him and then went home, to read the remedies and wonder what it meant to care. I had been so cavalier in my request to Mama, to be inducted into her world of secrets. It was overwhelming enough to care for bodies that had turned against themselves, that had sickened and soured on miasmas and disease, that had collapsed under the burden of fevers and chills.

It was still another thing to care for someone like Mr. Ben, who was of whole body, I knew, but of broken spirit.

But Mama said when the spirit broke like his had, it was not our realm.

I was not so sure.

Sometimes, I tried to talk to her about it. I would venture to her, as we sat side by side in her examination room, "What do you do with someone like a Mr. Ben?"

To which she would say quickly, "I do not know what you mean, Libertie."

And we would be left in silence again.

Once, bored by the rows of flower names stretched out before me on a long night of study, I went out at night into the garden, to walk along the rows.

I absently rubbed my fingers along a yarrow bush's leaves. After a few minutes, they began to swell and my tongue thickened. I looked down at my fattened fingertips in the moonlight and looked up and saw Mama through the window, sitting at her desk behind the muslin curtain, working through her ledger. As I watched her, I reached for the yarrow leaves and ripped five of them off the branch, stuffed them into my mouth, and chewed them. It did not take long before my cheeks and mouth began to itch. I ate three more leaves. Two more. And then I ran into the office, and finally Mama looked up from her ledger.

I had the satisfaction of seeing her startled, but she was not scared. She treated me as she would any other of her patients. I could not speak at that point, could barely breathe. I only held up the last few yarrow leaves that I clutched in my hand, and then she nodded and went to work.

She laid me down away from the fire. She went over to her shelves of medicine and reached for one glass jar—she didn't even have to look at the label. She called for Lenore, her voice clear and strong, and when Lenore came in and saw my swollen face, she gasped.

"Keep her mouth open," Mama said. "The danger here is losing air."

Mama made my remedy and then came over and placed it under my tongue herself.

It was a kind of heaven, made dreamier because of my sick state—the room all hazy and warm, my mother's face steady above me. I watched it as closely as I could, and saw her disappear again into her mind. But it was all right, because I knew, this time, when she went there she was thinking only of me. Of how to keep me alive. Of where my lungs and tongue connected, and how deeply I was taking in air, and what to do next to bring my body back. To be at the center of my mother's work was a wonderful place to be. Mr. Ben had had that experience, and as I lay there, sick, I allowed myself to feel the full envy of it. I craved her care, even though I knew I should not.

I fell into a restless sleep. One of the times, when I surfaced from oblivion, I heard Mama whisper to Lenore as she gazed at my face, looking for signs of progress, "She looks just like . . ." And then there was nothing. She was gone again, into her mind.

I realize, now, where she was going. And I know, now, how cruel this all was. I should have known then. I'd seen her face stricken when Mr. Ben held up her dead sister's hair. With the same unconscious cunning all young children possess around their mothers, I had devised the best way to get her attention—make her relive one of her most painful memories—the sick little-girl body, limp in bed, the small gasps for breath, the throat closing, the skin flushing from brown to a deep velvet and then emptying out into gray. What kind of daughter who loves her mother does something like that?

She worked on me all evening, and I would have been brought close to death all over again, from the sheer joy of that attention, if Lenore had not leaned over me while Mama was distracted and shook her head.

"Your mama is a saint," she said, and the way she said it, I knew she knew what I had done. Lenore, who knew and saw all, saw all that Mama, with her big heart and big brain, could not see. I had acted so small. Lenore, God bless her, could see petty a mile away.

I could not meet her eye.

Saints have big enough hearts that they can care for the whole world. Their hearts are so large they dwarf normal people's—and their hearts aren't dumb like human hearts. It is stupid and selfish to ask a saint to use such an extraordinary organ solely on you, even if you are the saint's daughter.

I did not get away with anything like the yarrow trick again for a long time. Even though, in shame at my audacity, it still occurred to me, many times, to try.

ANOTHER WEEK PASSED. It was a too-warm spring that year. So hot we wished for the cold and gray of March. Our settlement was in a valley, not the fine, cooler tracts of land that the white people had reserved for themselves, and so it was always warmer in our town, we imagined, than elsewhere. Culver's shop was even busier, with its pump out back, where we children liked to play at catching the final dribbles of cool, rusty water to rub on our tongues and splash behind our necks.

Mr. Ben liked the pump, too. He liked to sit out there, as the sun went down, before heading into Culver's back room. By the pump, he was always mumbling that name, Daisy, turning it over and over in his mouth, a kind of lullaby he said to soothe himself, to encourage him to keep lifting one foot in front of another, without his woman by his side.

The boldest children used her name to rechristen him. I took this as a sign of hope—you knew a newcomer belonged to the town when they got a nickname. The children called the new name after him at dawn, as he made his way to the wharves downtown, as he left all of us at Culver's. They called it to him as he stood on Front Street, palming a penny before passing it to the woman with a rush basket full of eels and taking the slinking black coil down beneath the wharves, to cook over an open fire, because, as he loudly cried to anyone who would listen, he had no Daisy to cook it for him. They called it to him as he emerged from under the docks in the dusk, to venture out along the board, and look out across the angry gray river to Manhattan and softly whisper to his love across the stinking, cold, and unforgiving waves.

So by the time his sister Hannah came at the end of May, no one bothered to call him Mr. Ben anymore. Everyone called him Ben Daisy.

Miss Hannah came to us in the same coffin Ben Daisy did. The first time I saw her was when Lucien and Madame Elizabeth performed the same sleight of hand they had with him—set down the coffin, pried off the lid. But instead of a lifeless body, there was Miss Hannah, eyes shining bright, looking avidly up at us, her hands clutching a small, irregular yarn handkerchief to her chest. She sat up in the light immediately, put her free hand to her back and winced, and stretched out her other hand to Madame Elizabeth, handing her the piece of cloth.

"How I passed the time on the journey," she said. "Took a line of yarn with me and weaved it the whole way."

Mama looked very pleased at that, and Madame Elizabeth beamed. Miss Hannah was a steadier hand than Ben Daisy could ever hope to be.

Miss Hannah was impatient to see her brother, but Mama asked her to stay for a moment, to drink a cup of tea. "You'll see him soon enough," she said.

"But my brother," she kept saying, even as she clung to Lucien's arm, her legs still soft from lying down for so long. "He made it all right? He doin' fine?"

Mama would only say, "I'll take you to him." Her voice was even, but she would not look Miss Hannah in the eye. I had never seen my mama ashamed of anything before, so I did not know to recognize it. I stayed close, eager to hear what Mama would say to Miss Hannah.

"Ben Daisy is—"

"Ben what?" Miss Hannah said.

Mama reddened. "It is what the children sometimes call him here."

"Why would they say that?"

"He, well—"

"He has a good Christian name." Miss Hannah kept talking. "We was gonna choose ours together, when we got free. We was gonna be the Smiths, on account of our mama saying our daddy always wanted a smithy someday. Why you call him by that woman's name?"

"Then you know her?"

Miss Hannah sniffed, in distaste. "Before we agreed to run, he fell hard in love with that woman. I thought it would be good for him. He was just beat something awful for trying to run, and after that I thought he was lost to us. He only stared at the wall. But then he found Daisy, and she liked him enough. I hoped it was a good thing. Have a little fun, remember what sweetness this world can hold, so he'd want to stay here in it. He was talkin' 'bout drowning before he met Daisy. But he met her and he was happy. For a while. He turned sick with love. That Daisy, he'd do anything for her. She didn't deserve him. You know, he'd save up what little money he could and buy her butter to lick.

"And you know how that little girl repaid him? Three springs ago she ran away without him, even though she knew me and him was fixing to run, too. That little girl didn't even warn him or nothing, just up and disappeared. They found her body a few miles away, with the man she run with, both of 'em torn apart by the paddyroller's dogs.

"And every spring like this, he pines for her worse and worse. I thought he'd do better when we made our escape. That's why I had him go first, even though it was risky. He didn't even want freedom anymore. He says she's his love. Says she's all he's ever had. Easier to love a haint than this broken world. For him, anyways. And if I have to hear that Daisy's name one more time, I'll scream."

Miss Hannah set down her mug and glared, back and forth, at Mama and Madame Elizabeth, her chest heaving.

"We'll take you to him, then," Mama said, her voice low.

And the five of us—me, Lucien, Madame Elizabeth, Mama, and Miss Hannah—put our cloaks on to walk through the dusk to Culver's back room.

I did not understand then. Can a child, who has so few memories, no history of her own, know what it is to be haunted? To understand a ghost is to have an understanding of time that is not possible for a child. Children can feel spirits, but they do not discriminate between the living and the dead the way adults do. For them, it is all the living. And so I did not understand the look of anguish on Mama's face as we got closer to the reunion, and I did not understand why Miss Hannah was so angry at a dead woman, and I still did not understand why I felt so sad around Mr. Ben.

But I was about to learn.

THE ONLY PEOPLE allowed in Culver's back room were new-comers. More and more often, new people were appearing—not just the ones brought by Madame Elizabeth, but those who found us on their own. If you saw an unrecognizable face in town, someone new walking down the roads, who tried to stay close to the underbrush so that they could run, we all knew to send that person first to Culver's. In those days, you did not ask about the past of the newly arrived.

They'd stay for a few nights, and then they would find a room or take a lot from one of the deacons of our church and put together a home of their own.

It was not families who arrived like this. It was mostly men. We welcomed them, of course, and most of them eventually settled in. But a few of them, maybe four or five, never fully joined us. Even after they'd found places to live and women to love, they still returned to the back of Culver's pharmacy to meet up with those most like themselves.

The back-room visitors would sit and watch Culver work. It was where Culver mixed up the different-colored remedies of his shop. He poured each one into the saltmouth and tincture glass bottles, as tall as a child.

Culver sold the back-room people beer and rum, even though we were a dry town. But the deacons and Reverend Harland pretended not to know Culver's back room, only obliquely mentioning it in their sermons, and Culver was careful that only colored people drank there. The few times white men tried to come and sit, they just saw Culver painstakingly measuring out the granules and liquids that turned the remedies their necessary hue.

Like every child in our village, I knew the people of the back room well. All had been christened with their own nicknames, which we sang to them. The people of Culver's back room had all lost themselves. They had returned in their minds back to the places they'd run from, the places they didn't name, even to their fellow travelers. So maybe when the boys yelled at them and the girls braided their names into song, we were trying to call them back to us. At least, that's what I tell myself now. The alternative hurts too much to bear.

There was Otto Green Leaf. Otto lived only four houses down from Culver's. It was a straight line home for him. But one night, he didn't return home, and when his wife called for him the next day, the three or four men in Culver's back room searched for him for hours. They found him in a field, two miles away. He said he'd gotten lost. His wife brought him home, but he kept wandering out, to sleep among the cabbages. He could only sleep in dirt, it seemed, from then on. After he'd found his way out of Culver's room, you'd see him every morning rising from the fields, his shirt covered in mud and dew, blinking at the dawn.

There was Birdie Delilah, the only woman who regularly went to Culver's. She became certain that her daughter, whom she'd lost in some way she never told any of us, had returned to her in the form of the woodpecker who lived under Culver's eaves. All night, she sat in Culver's back room, drinking corn whiskey until her eyes shone, waiting for the woodpecker to start her pestering when the moon was high. At the sound of the first knock, Birdie Delilah's whole face, which before had been dour and cold and slick with sweat from the burn of her drink, would light up, and she would begin to suck her teeth in response to the bird, steady in her conversation.

And there was Pete Back Back, who came to us still covered in sores from the whipping that drove him to run. No matter what Mama did, what compresses or dilutions she tried, his back wouldn't heal and his wounds remained as fresh as the day he first got them.

They were all there when we arrived with Mr. Ben's sister. The room was warm and small and dark, lit only by a few lamps up high. It smelled sharp and too sweet. When my eyes adjusted and I saw all the regulars, I was not so afraid. Mama and I had seen the people of Culver's back room out and about in town so often they no longer scared us.

But when Madame Elizabeth stepped in behind us, she drew her shawl over her mouth, and Miss Hannah, coming in right behind her, poor Miss Hannah began to cry.

Ben Daisy was sitting up, talking to Pete Back Back, who was steadfastly ignoring every word out of his mouth, in favor of the drink in his hand.

"She smelled like the ocean," Ben Daisy was saying. "I only smelled the ocean once, back when I was in Maryland, but that's what she smelled like. Good, clean salt. I told you 'bout her hair, didn't I? And her eyes? I'd tell you about the rest, but a lady's present . . ." Here, he looked sideways at Birdie Delilah, and then he looked up and saw his sister and he stopped talking.

Miss Hannah stepped a little more forward. "Ben?"

"So they got you here, too, did they?" He peered past Miss Hannah and caught Madame Elizabeth's eye. "So you managed not to kill my sister this time, like y'all did me?"

Madame Elizabeth did not respond. On her face was a look of the utmost pity, which seemed to annoy Mr. Ben even further.

"She got you good, Hannah."

"Ben, you look a mess."

"You would, too, if you'd been through what I have," Mr. Ben said. "Drug here in a coffin all by myself."

Miss Hannah knelt down beside him and touched his arm. "I came that way, too."

He wouldn't look at her. Looked down at the floor instead. Took another sip of his drink.

"They tell you the food here is horrible?" he said.

Miss Hannah gasped, laughed, then finally allowed herself to fully sob.

She turned to Mama. "You let my brother live like this?" she said, her voice breaking. "You let 'em all live like this? These people are not well."

Mama put her hand up to her mouth and only nodded.

"You said you was a doctor. She said . . ." Miss Hannah turned and looked at Madame Elizabeth. "She said you knew how to help people and make 'em safe."

"I tried," Mama said, but then stopped herself. Her words sounded so lost, in this small, hot room.

"He can't stay here," Miss Hannah said. "None of 'em can stay here."

Culver looked up from his bench. "No one's forcing anyone to stay. We stay together because we like it."

Miss Hannah ignored him, pulled at her brother's arm. "Come on," she said. "Come with me."

He did not move at first. He did not move for a long time. We all stood, and watched, while she pulled at his arm and said, "Come with me," until it became almost unbearable—her ask, his refusal.

But finally, he stood up and put his arm through hers, and Miss Hannah guided him from the room.

I think it was that—more than Miss Hannah's shaming, more than Ben Daisy's glassy eyes and his lips muttering nonsense, it was the fact that he would follow his sister out of the room, because of Miss Hannah's patience, that convinced Mama of how badly she had failed. And I saw her, standing right there beside me, disappear again, into the world of her ambition.

She was going to make him right.

I DO NOT know when, exactly, she started it. The letter she sent to begin it all, she wrote alone—she took the rare step of not dictating it to me. She must have written it that same night, when she realized she had lost Ben Daisy, because it was only a week or so later that I stood beside her in Culver's shop as she looked at the mail that had come for her and she turned to me, the envelope still in her hand, and bent down, and she hugged me, hard—she never hugged hard—and told me excitedly, "We can begin."

That afternoon, she gathered me and Lenore in her examination room and told us that she had decided to run a proving.

A proving is when you bring together a small group of volunteers to take a new dose, a new remedy. It is a way to test what can be a cure. Everyone tracks their reactions to the substance, minutely, and then you compare notes. With enough provings, you begin to understand the cures that are available to you, what will produce those reactions in the body, that push and pull that homeopathy rests on.

Since Mama was a colored woman, other homeopaths did not invite her to partake in their provings. She had to read the medical journals carefully, comparing articles and footnotes, making her own notations. She was looking for their mistakes. She had been doing this for years— it was what she often did late at night, when the books were done and committee work put away.

For this, her first proving, she told us that she wrote away to a man out west, a scientist like her. A colored naturalist who had recently come back from West Africa, where he had taken an all-black group of explorers. A wondrous thing. I remembered reading aloud an article to her about it a few months earlier. It had appeared in the *Mystery*—a newspaper Madame Elizabeth sometimes brought us with one of her emptied coffins. There, on the front page, was an account of his tour. I noticed the article because it had the place I had been named for, my father's dream, in the title: "Martin Delany's Exploration of Liberia."

At first, when I'd read it aloud, Mama, as always, was skeptical of any talk of homelands and empires—"It is futile to imagine, Libertie," she said. But she made me stop and read one line, three times, to make sure she understood:

*The Emigration Board of Commissioners has asked Mr. Delany
to make a scientific inquiry into the topographical, geological and
geographic qualities of the Niger Valley to determine whether it
can host a colony of American Negroes.*

So Mama had remembered him, and had sent him her secret letter,
and now, in the palm of her hand, she had the results.

Delany had sent a small package, passed hand to hand, through
every African Methodist Episcopal preacher in the North. All the way
from Ohio, to us, in Kings County. Reverend Harland himself had
delivered it to Culver's counter, though he'd felt a need to write, underneath Delany's hand, the admonishment *For good, Doctor.*

Mama bristled at that. "As if it would be for anything else."

Now, in her examination room, Mama had me unwrap the package
for her. I pulled at the twine and the paper—"Gentle now, Libertie,
gentle with your hands"— until it fell open. Wrapped in the brown
paper were ten dried seahorses, curled over one another. Their skin was
a low, dusky yellow, the same color as the oranges we studded with
cloves every Christmas and left to desiccate in our linen trunk to keep
our good cloth smelling sweet. I looked up at Mama. "Just as Delany
promised," she said. "He's a good man."

The very first task was to grind the dried seahorses into a gray powder, which smelled like the bottom of a privy and clung to the palms of
your hands in a fine, damp silt.

"'The male seahorse can be found in the estuary of the Niger River,'"
Mama read from Delany's letter, as Lenore ground and I was instructed
to transcribe into a notebook, what was to be the experiment's log. "'He
is a solitary creature. He does not swim in packs. He only interacts
with his female counterpart to mate. He floats through the dark, temperate in-between world of brackish water alone, with only his secret

for creation.'" Here, Mama broke off. "Delany believes he is some sort of poet, I suppose," she said, and frowned. She did not like flights of fancy. She especially resented them when people tried to mix them up with science.

When Lenore had finished grinding, we moved on to dilution. Mama had told us she would begin this trial with a 2C dilution, which meant we added one hundred grams of water to one gram of seahorse, and then another hundred grams, until we had our solution.

Finally, Lenore passed the vial over to me for the succussion. I took the vial and slapped it against the special board of leather and horsehair Mama had in her office for the purpose.

As I pumped my arms up and down, shaking the cure, Mama read some more. "'The male seahorse is a virtuous beast, romantic and loyal, steadfast in his heart and in his affections, the moral light of the animal kingdom. The male seahorse is not a profligate; he is frugal with his affections. When he mates, he mates for life. Every morning, he wakes and performs a dance with his partner—it is not a mating dance, but a dance that reaffirms their commitment to each other and the deep affection and love between the two. If he loses his mate, he will remain alone for the rest of his short life, unable to replace her with another.'"

Here, Mama stopped. "That's it," she said. "Make sure to get that part when you write the notes, Libertie."

When the solution was done, Mama told me to put it on her highest shelf. And then she sat down and wrote a letter of apology to Ben Daisy.

It did not seem to be a great burden for her to apologize, and I remember thinking this strange. I had never seen my mother do it before, but she wrote this letter with ease, as if she was sending off a note to Madame Elizabeth. When she was done, she handed it to me, to bring to Mr. Culver and ask him to read it to Ben Daisy or Miss Hannah the next time they came in.

On the way to town, I carefully ripped the edges of the letter open to see what she had written there, but it was only pleasantries, a single sentence with "profound apologies," and an invitation to Ben Daisy, and Ben Daisy alone, for tea in a few days' time.

He came. I was surprised he came, but he did. It was the end of the workday, and he had clearly had a good one downtown—he smelled of clean sweat, and he was smiling when he walked in. "What's this?" he said, laughing. "You sure you happy to see me?"

Mama smiled and nodded. She had asked Lenore to make a cake. She placed the cake in the middle of her examination room table and led him there. She took her place on the small wooden seat.

"Now," Mama said as she spread her skirts out about her, "how are you, Mr. Ben?"

He looked taken aback, but he answered. "Fine, Miss Doctor, just fine," he replied. "Figure I may as well pass the time with you ladies, and now that I've got such a warm welcome, you'll be hard pressed to get me to leave." He laughed again.

Mama laughed, too. They talked for a bit more. Mama reached over to cut Ben Daisy a slice of cake, and when he caught that, he smiled, a little meaner. She placed the slice in a square of cloth, put it in the palm of his hand. He hunched over to eat it, looking at her sideways.

I sat on a stool in the corner. Mama had told me beforehand to only begin when she gave me the signal. At last, Mama lifted one finger, and I picked up my pen.

"I wish to talk to you a bit about Daisy."

I watched his shoulders slump forward, ever so slightly, and then back upright, as if he had remembered something. "So that's what you want," he said.

"You miss her," Mama said.

It was quiet for a bit. But then Ben Daisy trusted himself enough to say "She was a fine gal. I miss her something terrible."

"What if I could give you something," Mama said. "Something to help with the pain."

"I've already got that down at Culver's." Ben Daisy laughed sadly.

"But Culver's whiskey doesn't help you," Mama said.

"It'll do what it'll do."

"But it makes you listless and miss your work. It makes you quarrel with your sister."

Ben Daisy was quiet. Then he said, "What does Hannah want from me?"

"Nothing," Mama said.

"That's right. It's all nothing." Ben Daisy lifted his head off the back of the chair and put his hands on the arms, ready to push himself off the big leather seat and out our door.

That's when Mama said, "You wouldn't want Daisy, if she were here, to know you like this, though, would you? If she were able to see you. Are you the man she'd wish you to be in freedom?"

Ben Daisy lowered himself back into the chair. "So, what are you proposing?"

Mama stood up and told me to fetch the solution. She measured some out, very carefully, into a smaller vial and handed it to him.

"You take this," she said. "One swallow, and one swallow only each night. It's night, isn't it, that the pain's the worst?"

Ben Daisy sighed. "Night is when it all catches up with me," he said.

Mama instructed him to return the following afternoon, and for every afternoon after that for five days. "You see how you feel," she told him. "And if it seems to help, tell your friends down at Culver's. It may help them, too."

When he'd left, she sat and began to dictate to me again.

"We have in our midst," she said, "a group of men, and a few women, who, upon discovering our community and life here in freedom, find their souls still oppressed. Their bodies are here with us in emancipation, but their minds are not free. Their spirits have not recovered from the degradation of enslavement, despite the many hardships and privations they have suffered to come here.

"Indeed, I argue that it is precisely because of these hardships and privations that when they arrive here, with us, some part of them does not return. When they arrive, I can treat the physical effects of their enslavement—the yaws in their limbs, and the scars on their backs and heads, and the bones that broke and were never set. But I have, up until now, not been able to treat what would be called the mental effects, the spiritual effects, which do not respond to prayer or clean living or even the embrace of friends.

"I believe the root cause for this is an intense solitude and loneliness, even in their freedom. At least, that is how some of them have described it to me. We have seen this illness before," she said. "In the cases of those we love, like Mr. Ruggles and Miss Sojourner Truth. They were afflicted by this deep and abiding loneliness even in freedom and took to drink, and then the water cure, lying in bathtubs and wrapped in cold, wet sheets to try and soak it out. And it has not done much for them. If all these good and kind warriors are felled by this disease of feeling, what hope is there for any of us?

"And what is at the root cause of loneliness? It is a lack of love. I believe if we can treat this deficit of affection, we can begin to see an improvement in those new to freedom. We can make them whole in both body and in spirit and see a real change in their condition. They will ingest this substance, which is made of the solitude and longing for love of the ocean, and it will rebalance what has been made unsteady inside them. Take Mr. Ben, who is lost in amorousness, who is able to do nothing but pine. We will realign his affections, so that he no longer loves what is dead but loves us here, the living. He will be filled with agape. He will love his fellow man. It is what I attempt to test, in my proving. He will be my first patient."

Then she raised her hand again, her sign that we were done for the day. She gathered the pages I had written, so that she could read what I'd taken from her own voice and correct it.

Ben Daisy took the solution faithfully. During that time, he did not appear any different—he still walked with one shoulder up high, and the other men still walked a little bit ahead so that they did not have to be in conversation with him. No one else from Culver's came to Mama's door. Either Ben Daisy didn't tell them to come or they were unimpressed with his progress.

The only time we saw his sister was at church on Sundays. Miss Hannah sat in the back pews, near the door, and her brother never came with her. We sat in the pews in the front, because Mama's father had been one of the men to build that church. When Mama was a girl, she and her brothers and sisters took up two whole pews. But now, of the old family, it was just me and her left sitting up front—the rest of the seats given away to friends. When we passed Miss Hannah on the way to our pew every Sunday, she would stiffly nod in Mama's direction, but she didn't smile. If Culver had read the apology aloud to her, it had not impressed her at all.

When Ben Daisy came back to our house two weeks later, it was in the last bit of light. His shirt was wet from work, and when we let him in, he sat sideways in his chair and we could smell the drink on him.

"I can't give it to you if you've been to Culver's already," Mama said. "Tell me the truth."

"No, ma'am," he said. "This is from one of the other men. They knocked a ladleful of cider on me, and that's why I smell like this. I'm as sober as a judge." Ben Daisy gave her a glassy smile.

Mama looked at him, and she came to some sort of decision.

"Libertie, my record book," she said, and I went and fetched it for her.

She took the book and looked at the columns of numbers. Then she licked her thumb, very carefully, and smudged out one. She dipped her pen in ink and wrote something else over it. Then she sprinkled some sand to let the ink dry.

As she rubbed the grains from her fingers, she said, very steadily, "A dose and a half today for Ben Daisy, I think."

Lenore sucked her teeth.

"Yes," Mama said.

Lenore took the little steel file she used, and measured a few more grains onto the slip of paper she'd set on the scale.

By the time the dose was prepared, Ben Daisy's head had begun to loll, and Mama had to hold his chin steady as she placed it in his mouth.

The other times he'd taken it, Ben Daisy had only grimaced at the taste—"Golly, Doctor, you can't cut this with nothing?" This time, he truly gagged. His knees rose up to his chest and he coughed, and Mama stepped back, surprised, then called for water.

She poured it in a slow trickle in his mouth until he was swallowing good and steady, and then she let him go. He slumped back in the chair, breathing heavily. Another cough. A third. He swallowed. And then he vomited something green and awful-smelling, all down the front of his shirt.

I jumped forward, Lenore cursed—"Oh damn"—and Mama stepped back again.

"Get it off," she said to Lenore. She grabbed one sleeve. "We've got to get it off."

Between the two of them, they managed to get the shirt over his head.

Ben Daisy lay in the chair bare-chested, his belly soft in his breeches, his eyes still closed, his breath in shuffles. Then his eyes flickered open, and he slowly sat up straight.

"You all right?" Lenore asked.

He put his hands on his knees, shook his head gently.

"Sit still, sit still," Lenore insisted. But Ben Daisy stood up, creaking, and made his way toward the door. By now it was dark; the sun was gone, and the fireflies of Kings County were out.

At the door, he looked out over the fields and watched the lights scatter across the long grass, as if everything was new to him. Then he gave a deep sigh, like the sound the water makes when the ocean turns over. And he lurched out into the night, still bare-chested.

"Well," Mama said. "Well," she half laughed. She was nervous.

"Should I run after him?" Lenore asked.

"No," Mama said. "I am sure he will be fine." But she did not look certain.

The next evening, just as Lenore was to leave for the day, the office door swung open and Ben Daisy stood in the frame.

"What did you give me?" he said.

"Why?" Mama asked. She snapped her fingers for my attention, and then pointed to the ledger book. I reached for a pen to transcribe their conversation.

"All day long," he said. "All day long, it's felt like this."

"Like what?"

"I hear it lapping at my ear, you know. I hear it crashing."

"Sit down," Mama said, guiding him to the leather chair. "Tell me what you mean."

"I hear it, in my ear. Lapping, lapping. It's been lapping all damn day, Doctor."

"Were you able to work?"

"I had to stop a turn and box my own ears, I did. Nothing came out."

"Lie back," Mama said. "Let me see."

She snapped her fingers again, and I put down the record book, took one of the slim white candles she used for close examination, and lit its wick in the fire. I placed it in the small glass lantern and came and stood at Mama's side.

"Steady, there, Libertie," she said as she lifted my arm herself, so I could get the angle of the light right.

She settled down into the little chair and leaned forward. She took his ear in her hand, as gently as a lover, and stretched the lobe very carefully, so that she could see inside.

"And it's so damn cold!" Ben Daisy said suddenly, rising up.

Mama sat back.

"So cold all the time. And my mouth, I tell you, it tastes like salt. Ever since yesterday. It just tastes like salt in my mouth. And Hannah, she says my breath stinks like the wharves. What do I care," he said. "That sister of mine finds every way to tell me I'm wrong. But the foreman said it, too, this morning."

He sat back down. As he spoke, indeed, a deeply salty smell filled the room. It was not necessarily unpleasant. Just very strong.

"I feel," he said. "I feel . . ." He slumped back down. "I feel like I'm falling underwater."

Mama lifted her chin. "Note that down, Libertie." She was trying, very hard, to conceal her excitement.

"Well," she said after a moment, "there is not much I can do for the smell of the breath. But chew these, twice a day." She handed him a bundle of mint leaves. "And come back again next week—"

"Like hell I will," Ben Daisy said.

"Just to talk," Mama said quickly, and Ben Daisy grumbled and then moved toward the door.

Mama watched him go and then turned to me.

"Is he cured?" I asked. I was excited.

"We shall see," she said. She was not going to play her hand.

All week long, I asked Mama if she thought Ben Daisy would come back to us, and she said, "It's not for me to decide, Libertie. It's up to him." But I could see by Saturday she was as nervous as I was, even though she would not say it.

Sunday morning, we headed to church and walked past the stony-faced Miss Hannah to our pew, as always.

Reverend Harland began the sermon—about Belshazzar's feast and the disembodied hand that had appeared to him and had begun to write on the wall the thoughts of God. Reverend Harland was talking about rulers dishonoring God and the calamity that would follow, but while he talked, I tried to think of that hand, floating in the air. Were its fingers long or stubby? Its palms jaundiced? What color was its skin— deep black or warm brown or the same pink as Mama's cheeks? Did that hand also float above a pyramid, or in a distant desert, shimmering in the heat? And did Belshazzar, who saw the wonder, ever think in the moment of astonishment to keep the marvel to himself, to keep a secret, to not reveal it, to revel in the mystery of words untranslatable?

The sermon ended, and so did my speculations. The singing was about to begin. The choir assembled, and then, as they were about to start, we heard a loud, off-tune voice, too straw-like to be called a tenor, rise from the back of the church.

Oh Lord,

        Oh Lord,

Oh Lord,

        I'm saved again.

We all turned to see who it could be, and it was Ben Daisy, his shirt now cleaned and pressed, his hat back on his head, singing as loud as he could while his sister stood beside him, crying tears of joy and sharp embarrassment.

After that, Mama was revered. Everyone could see Ben Daisy was cured. He was the first man down the road at dawn, heading to the fields. He helped out the reverend at church. He stopped drinking altogether. He only went to Culver's to pay the few cents he could, to settle his debt for all the corn whiskey he'd drunk in the past.

The others came out of Culver's back room and began to take the cure with Mama, too—Otto Green Leaf and Birdie Delilah, and even Pete Back Back, whose shirt was still wet from his never-closing wounds.

Ben Daisy was truly a new man, anyone could see, and Reverend Harland dedicated a special sermon to it that next week.

"The psalms tell us that the Lord heals the brokenhearted and binds up their wounds," Reverend Harland said. "He determines the number of the stars and calls them each by name. Great is our Lord, and mighty in power; his understanding has no limit. The psalms tell us to sing to the Lord, as Ben Daisy has done, with grateful praise and make music to our God. For the Lord delights in those who fear him and who put their hope in his unfailing love. And he sends his word to melt the snow; he stirs up the breezes, and the waters flow."

Afterward, when everyone had surrounded Mama to congratulate her, Ben Daisy pushed through the scrum of people, and hooked his little finger into Mama's and shook it—a queer offer of thanks, I remember thinking.

"You done it," he said with a wink. And then he sighed, "I can't wait to tell Daisy all about this."

Mama looked taken aback, but then she smiled and said, "I'm happy for you." She did not ask me to note that exchange in her little book, not yet.

Ben Daisy was cured right before Pinkster. Pinkster was what the old ones celebrated, the ones who had been alive for slave days here in Kings County—so ancient they seemed to me then, as old as the hills all around us. They all spoke in that strange singsong accent of old New York. They had celebrated Pinkster when they were young, and their hips still moved, and it was a queer kind of pleasure we all took, to make sure they could still celebrate it in their old age.

Every Pentecost, we young ones were instructed to make the old ones gingerbread and gather bunches of azaleas. In Sunday school, we worked to make the paper crowns that would sit on top of their graying heads. A few men Mama's age practiced the old songs on the drums, but they did not teach them to us children. They were the rhythms of the past, and only the old ones remembered them for sure, lifting their walking sticks to pound in time, sucking their teeth in disapproval when the beat was off.

At Pinkster, we crowned a King Charles, who was in charge of the festivities. We built him a grass hut, and he teased the children and paraded for the old. Usually, it was one of the church ushers, who would dance and twirl around town. But that year, because of his miraculous recovery, it was unanimously decided that Ben Daisy should lead the celebrations.

On Pinkster morning, I and the other girls in Sunday school woke up early, when the day was still cold. All week, we had been gathering rushes from the fields, setting them out to dry, and pounding them flat. We had been weaving the strands into thick walls, the green of the grass fading to a fragile brown. And now, we pieced them together, finishing the huts we were to celebrate in.

When we were done with the largest hut, the girls sent me to find Ben Daisy and lead him to it. He was standing in the crowd with the others, our neighbors and friends, waiting for the celebration to begin. I took his warm hand in mine and brought him into the enclosure.

The day was one of those sharply cold sunny ones, where you panted in the light but any bit of shade chilled you. It was even cooler in the largest hut, under all the grass. Ben Daisy stood peering out onto the churchyard. The old ones, already gathered in the hut, sat in a corner, skeptical of a newcomer having the place of honor.

The drums pounded, and everyone started dancing. I ran out of the hut as soon as I could, to spin in a circle with the other girls, their hands soft and slipping through mine as we tried to hold close, and to run up and down the yard. Pinkster was the only holiday when everyone tried a little cider—every other celebration we kept temperate. But on Pinkster, because the old ones celebrated it, a beer or two was allowed. Which is to say that someone may or may not have slipped Ben Daisy a sip of something that afternoon.

At the height of the day, when all our bodies were still humming from the dance, Ben Daisy stood in the doorway of the hut, paper crown pushed back on his head.

"A yup, a yup!" he called. He was getting into the spirit of it. Some others began to clap, a syncopated rhythm, to his name.

Ben

   Day

     Zee

Ben

   Day

Zee

"That's me," he called over the din. "That there's my name. And soon you will meet my Daisy, too."

One of the children laughed. "Truly?" the child said.

"Truly," he said. "Daisy came to me just the other day. I wish y'all could have seen her. She's here right now, in fact. But she's shy."

Some people laughed louder, thinking he was playing.

"I tell you, she looks marvelous now. She's got long curly hair all the way down her back, and she's got a pink silk gown."

"Oh really? Where'd she get that from?"

"She's got a silk gown," Ben Daisy continued. "It's pink and white, like nothing you've ever seen. And on her finger, one diamond ring so bright. Oh, I can't wait for y'all to see her."

"So where is she now?" someone else called, giggling.

"She's on her way. She came to visit me just last week, but she couldn't stay. But she's coming back, to live with me and mine. You hear that, Hannah?" Ben Daisy called. "You gonna have to make room for my Daisy."

I turned to look for Miss Hannah in the crowd. She was listening, her face stricken.

"To Daisy," he cried, holding up his hand in benediction, and the children chanted it back to him. I myself joined in, chanting and laughing till my voice was hoarse, even though I knew I should be scared.

So I made sure to whirl myself harder, dance faster, the rest of the night.

As night came, the old ones remembered Pinksters past: who was known for the freshest oysters and the sweetest bread, who could be counted on to stay awake the longest, who was the best dancer. They did not, of course, mention that they had celebrated all these feats while enslaved, that the whites had banished Pinkster and stopped observing it with them once they gained their freedom. The old ones spoke of it as its own day of release, as if it existed outside of time, and none of them mentioned how it used to end—with the men and women and children tearing down the grass huts and returning to their masters, saying goodbye to their loved ones owned by other men, with sometimes nothing but a blade of grass tucked away to remember them by, until they met again the following year, if they were lucky.

Miss Hannah came to Mama the next day, crying in her reception room. "You didn't fix him," she said. "He's as bad as ever. He really thinks that dead heifer is coming to live with us."

"He can't believe that," Mama said.

"He does. He really does," Miss Hannah sobbed. "You've only made it worse."

The next week, at church, Mama called to Ben Daisy, "How about you come and see me again."

"I haven't got time for that, Doctor," he said. "I need to buy some things for Daisy, to make her comfortable."

And he left Mama to go ask Miss Annie, who headed the church's auxiliary club, to bake him some cakes. "Little ones," he said. "Dainty ones, because Daisy eats like a bird, you know? But they've got to be pink and white. That's what she told me. Have to be pink and white." Miss Annie grumbled about it, but she agreed to make him three cakes, because he was willing to pay for them.

A few days later, he saw me again on the road to Culver's.

"Hey there, Black Gal."

"Hey, yourself," I said, wary. I could smell on him that he was unwell.

"I've heard," he said, "you grow pansies nice."

I paused. "I do."

"I'll give you a penny for five of them, for my Daisy."

I knew I should not agree to give him anything for her. "But how are they going to stay fresh?" I asked.

"Won't need to stay fresh long, because she's here," he said. But his voice was uncertain.

I felt a spasm of conscience. "I could," I said carefully, "press them for you. If you'd like."

"All right. But don't cheat me, girl," he said, smiling again.

"I can give them to you," I said finally. "Find me after church."

I did not tell my mother. By then, Miss Hannah had enlisted the reverend, and the three of them spent evenings talking about how best to fix his strange behavior. "Give it time," Mama kept assuring. "It takes a while for the dose to even out." She seemed to believe it, even though the reverend and Miss Hannah perhaps did not.

I do not know what I believed at that point. I thought my mother infallible. But I had also been up close to Ben Daisy, smelled the salt water of his breath and seen the dullness of his eyes. I trusted my mother, but I knew that Ben Daisy had no hope of becoming a steady man.

Still, I was a craven little thing. I wanted the penny he promised for myself. While I was tending the garden, I snipped off the heads of five pansies, big and wide. That was the least I could do for him—give him the hardiest ones. I dropped them into the pocket of my apron, and then, at night, when Mama was bent over her books, I bent over my own and placed each flower's head between the pages of my ledger, right in the corner, up close to the spine. Then I shut the book and did not open it again until later that week, when they had dried and turned crisp and thin, their color only dimming slightly.

The Sunday morning I was to give them over to Mr. Ben, I wrapped them up in a piece of fine paper pinched from Mama's writing desk.

Ben Daisy and I were to meet in the little copse by the graveyard. When I saw Mama and Lenore were caught up in the talk of the other women in the churchyard, I went closer to the trees, calling for him underneath my breath.

"Ben Daisy," I hissed. I stepped past the stones of my father and Mama's sister with no name, past where the land dipped and sank over their final resting place, into the cold shadow of the fir trees. "I have your pansies for you."

There he was. I could see his back was straight. He was the sweetest I had ever smelled him. But when he turned to me, his face was broken. "Forget them."

"But why?"

"She's already here. Saw her last night. On her finger was three wedding bands—one, two, three—all real gold, too. I said, 'What's the meaning of this Daisy?' And she only laughed."

He began to cry, great shaking sobs, while I stood beside him with the dried flowers on their sheet of paper, wishing he would stop.

"She betrayed me," he said. "She betrayed me all over again."

"At least take your flowers, Mr. Ben," I said. But he was sobbing so hard, his hands shaking, that he couldn't hold them.

"Here." I looked over at the crowd of parishioners. My mother stood in the middle, searching for me, I knew. "Kneel down."

He sat at my feet while I peeled each papery flower off the page and stuck them, carefully, into the band of his hat.

The church bell rang. The crowd began to move into the chapel. I had to take my place at my mother's side.

"Black Gal, your penny," he called.

"You can keep it," I said, and hurried toward the church.

I had expected him to follow me and join his sister in service, but he didn't. As I rushed to the doors, I looked back to the graveyard. Ben sat on the ground in the green and brown, his head still low. As the door swung shut, I swore I saw, through a flash in the trees, the figure of a woman rushing toward him, the long trail of her pink silk skirt fluttering in her haste. The church door closed, I walked to my pew, and when I craned my head to try and see him out the window, no one was there. I thought it must have been a shadow, that my pity for Ben Daisy had led me to yearn to see what he did, to bring the dead woman back for him and me—as if that would have healed anything at all.

During the service, I kept seeing that penny in Ben Daisy's hand, and I thought about the woman who he'd claimed had come to him at night, who wore the rings of other lovers on her fingers, who could not even manage to be faithful as a spirit. Was this what caring for another did? Resurrect them, even in death, to only become your worst fears? Did Ben Daisy suffer from too much care? Mama thought he did not have enough of it. But it seemed to me as though Ben Daisy had too much.

In the following weeks, he did not go to work with the other men anymore. He did not leave his bed in the room he shared with Miss Hannah. He even stopped saying that name. He became a ghost. When Mama tried to talk to Miss Hannah about it, she would only shake her head and say, "I don't know, Miss Doctor," before walking away.

One Saturday night, Pete Back Back came to Mama's door. He would not sit in her big leather chair, only stood in the middle of her examination room.

"Ben finally left his bed last night. Agreed to have a tipple with me," Pete said. "We drunk from Friday night into this morning. Culver threw us out at dawn. Said we was unruly. So we walked to the waterfront downtown.

"We stood on the wharves. We looked at the ferries. I got paid Friday, so I still had a few coins in my pocket. The wind was blowing the stink of the river into our faces, but we was happy. We was the closest thing to free any nigger's ever been," Peter told us. He stopped for a minute, his eyes wet.

"We went to go sit down by the water, to rest awhile. We was going to sit on the bank, near the wharves, when suddenly Ben Daisy lifted his head. All around us, we could smell flowers. I swear to you, Doctor, the air changed. The wind coming off the river was so soft and warm. Ben, he caught a whiff of that water, and he looked up and out across the dark river. He smiled. And then he bolted.

"Before I could stop him, he ran to the end of the wharf, calling 'Daisy!' He leapt into the river, and the water closed around him. And he was gone."

"What do you mean, gone?" Mama said.

"I tried to call someone to help me get him out." Peter rubbed at his shoulder. "Some of the kids who live by the wharf, they dived into the water to try and find him. Dived in right after him, they did, but when one of the boys came back up, he only said Ben Daisy was gone, and then they all scrambled out of the water, as if they'd took a fright. That boy wouldn't tell me what he saw down there, but none of them would go back in, even when I begged them to."

Pete Back Back took something out from underneath his shirt. "Only this was still there, floating on top of the waves."

It was Ben Daisy's hat, the pink-and-white pansies I'd pressed for him still tucked into the band, the whole thing dry as bone.

"I can't bring myself to tell Miss Hannah. So I stopped here first," Pete Back Back said. He still would not meet Mama's eye.

That night, after Peter left, Mama said three prayers: one for Ben Daisy and one for his sister, and the final one for Daisy herself. "May her spirit finally rest." And then I watched as she took her ledger down, the one she'd been keeping her notes in about the experiment, and, with her pen, scratch something out, write something new on the page. Then she tore the whole page out of the book altogether and took it with her to her bedroom, and I never saw it again.

The proving was over. Mama wrote the conclusion for it herself, so I do not know how she explained it. She would not let me read it, and she never published anything about this study. In a few years' time, this failure would be overshadowed by the hospital for women and children that would make her name, and the consulting room downtown, and my eventual life of ladyhood. But that particular night, she bundled up the last little bit of seahorses in a brown envelope and carefully placed it on the highest shelf.

Nobody in our village would say that Ben Daisy had died. Miss Hannah, in her grief would not allow it. She stayed on with us, her eyes hollow. Ben Daisy's hat with the dried pansies she took to wearing on her own head. And when we spoke to her of him, if we ever spoke to her of him, we only said the river had him.

That first night when we'd learned of Ben Daisy, I asked Mama, "What happens to the dead?" We had cleaned the examination room, put everything in its rightful place, and we stood side by side, washing our faces and hands before bed.

"Why, they go to heaven with our Lord and Savior. You know this."

"But what happens to their thoughts and minds?"

"What do you mean?"

"Where does their will go?"

Mama looked as if she was about to cry. "It has been a long day. Hush, please, Libertie."

"But what happens? Where is Ben Daisy? Is he in the same place Father is and . . . and . . . everyone else?"

"Libertie, you ask too much of your mama sometimes."

And so I understood. Mama did not have an answer. Mama did not know. That great big brain of hers could not tell me where Ben Daisy was. And because Mama didn't know, the dead were not to be spoken of. They were all of them in another country.

Eventually, we learned, from whispers, what the boys said they saw when they jumped in the river to rescue him. That underneath the water, the boy swimmer had seen Ben, had tried to pull him up, but he was stopped. Ben was wrapped in the arms of a woman, her skin glowing golden in the waves, the pink of her dress flashing through the murk of the river, her hair long. She had looked at the boy as he swam close and reached for Ben Daisy's hand. He said she was the most beautiful woman he had ever seen, and she'd beckoned to him, as if to welcome him into her arms, too. He said he was overcome with the desire to swim into them until she smiled at him—with a mouth full of thousands of pointed teeth. Then Ben had tugged his hand out of the swimmer's, had waved softly and turned his whole body inward, like a baby's, to be cradled in the arms of the woman in the water. And the boy kicked away, up to the surface, before he could be tempted to join them.

> *Ben Daisy and his woman sleep in the river*
> *Sleep in the river*
> *Sleep in the river*
> *Ben Daisy and his woman sleep in the river*
> *Even past Judgment Day*

That was the song, I am ashamed to say, that I made up after hearing this story, and the other children sang it, too. It became the anthem of our schoolyard for a year, and children still sing it today, I am told. I sang it because of all that I did not know and could not know about what happened. But even at that age, I knew curiosity could be heartless and I made sure not to sing it around Miss Hannah or my mother.

My heart hurt, and I was full of disgust, though for who or for what I did not know. I only knew I did not ever want to care for another if it made me act like Mr. Ben. If it made me wander the fields of Brooklyn, pressing flowers for someone who would never come. If it made me speak another's name until it became my own, even when I was guaranteed no answer. If it made me try to heal my people and fail so disastrously. If it made me put my brother in a coffin to get him free and still have him die anyways.

Care, I decided, was monstrous.

It was as clear as Ben Daisy's hat, floating on the waters. I would not be a doctor, no matter what Mama wished. I could not deceive others, and I could not deceive myself, as she did.

Sa ki bon avèk yon kè, sè ke li pa pote jijman

What's good about the heart is that it does not reason

W as freedom worth it if you still ached like that? If you were still bound on this Earth by desire?

It was a blasphemous thing to think, and I could not speak it to anyone, except to the plants in Mama's garden. I whispered it into the open blossoms' faces in the mornings, and then I carefully ran my thumb over each velvety petal. I knew my words were poison, and I was certain they could kill whatever good lived there.

Who was the woman Ben Daisy loved enough to die for? I looked for her where we'd all last seen her—in the water. I looked at the bottom of our well, in the muddy pools that collected in the ditches by the path to downtown. I looked for her in the pond, just past our settlement, where we took our laundry to wash. I looked for her in the wetlands, where the turtles and frogs and dragonflies swept through, where the men sometimes fished on Saturday afternoons. I stood, the tongues of my leather boots stiffening with mud, my feet sinking into the ground, and breathed in that murky smell of lake beds, and knew, in an instant, she wasn't there. Despite what Ben Daisy had said about her love of cakes and sugar, I did not think a woman who could drown a man in her arms lived in anything as sweet as fresh water. Her domain was brackish. She would live in salt.

The few times we went close to the waterfront, when Mama had to travel downtown and take the cart, I would lift my head to try and catch the smell of it over all the other scents—the rotted fruit in the gutters, the sweet blossoms of the trees planted in front of the nicer houses, the warm breath of horse manure, the sweat of all the bodies teeming around us. At the very top, maybe, when the wind was right, I could smell that other woman's home. Mostly, though, I listened.

If you listen closely, water, when it laps against the sides of a bucket, when it mouths a riverbed, sounds like hands clapping. It sounds like a congregation when prayers are done. But what is its message? It is not deliverance, I don't think. It is not salvation. It is something just underneath that, something that even Mama couldn't reach with her mind. So what hope was there for me of finding it?

A few times, riding beside her in our cart or walking beside her through our town, the rhymes I'd started myself about women and water ringing in our ears, I asked Mama, "Is the woman in the water real?" but she would only say, "I've taught you too well to fall for nonsense." It was a flash of her old assurance, which had gone somewhere underground, inside her, after Ben Daisy was gone.

After he left us, whenever new people came to us, whether by Madame Elizabeth's coffins or, when that route became too dangerous, by secret means of their own, Mama looked at them with sadness. She did not try to feed them ground seahorses. Instead, when they came, when she encountered them at church, she touched their shoulders and told them to come speak to her about what ailed them.

She still saw patients. She still gave aid. But she no longer imagined new cures, and when the people came with something strange, she looked at the remedies already written and did not offer her own.

People distrusted her. They did not always stop at our pew, first, after services to say hello. Reverend Harland was sympathetic, Mama was sure, but sometimes I caught him watching her, his eyes clouded over. Miss Hannah said, to anyone who would listen, "You can't trust a woman without a man to fix anything in a man's heart. How she know what wrong if she never even live with a man up close? You can't trust a woman without a man to ever understand what's needed," and though most people ignored Miss Hannah, you could feel the air shift around Mama when she entered a room, as if people were deciding something about her.

At night, she no longer disappeared into the trees of her mind but, instead, had me sit across from her while she drilled me on the habits of all the plants in the garden, of the uses of the parts of tongues and ears, of the mechanics of a stomach and a lung. It was as if she had become scared that all bodies would sink, as Ben's had, and that my voice, naming the parts of anatomy, singing of bile and blood, could somehow keep them on the surface. While I recited, her brow creased and worried, and she would mouth the words as I said them. When I was able to finish a list without error, she breathed so heavily it was as if she'd just run a race.

Mama and I were still haunted by Daisy and Ben, so when the war began, it was easy to ignore it, at first. And we did not know how long it would last, or who, exactly, was our enemy, when it started.

Some men in our town talked about joining right away, about convincing the white people to let us fight, convincing the white people that we were worthy enough to die. Or that's how Mama talked about it when no one else could hear, when it was just me and Lenore listening. "They think that will fix it," she said. "That white people will finally respect us when we're dead." And then she sighed and shot a glance to Lenore, who rolled her eyes and sighed, too.

I think, those first few months of war, I learned a whole new language from just their sighs.

BUT THEN IT was at our door. That spring, two years into the war, some of the men had left us to join the armies fighting two states over, maybe marching near.

The other ones, they came to us in July, by rowboat, deep in the dark. They found Mama's by midnight.

It was a family who came first. A mother and father, the mother's dress torn, her children balling the cloth of her skirts in their fists. They would not let go for anything—that's what I remember most—their tiny fists tight on muddied homespun, the mother holding the top of her dress to her chest, to keep herself decent. The father had a hat clamped to his head, the brim sticky with blood from his own brow. He wouldn't take it off while his children were in the room. Mama had to wait while the mother distracted them.

When Mama took off the hat, the father closed his eyes. He did not cry out, because he did not want to scare his children. Then he said, "They've gone crazy. The whites in Manhattan have gone crazy. They took Gold Street and Pearl Street, and then they made it all the way to Forty-Second. They're burning our churches. They are shouting that they won't fight for niggers, not ever. They surrounded our orphanage, so we were told.

"We were hiding in the house, till we heard that. That's when we picked up the babies and ran. One of 'em threw a bottle at my head, but we kept running.

"The white men were looking for anyone colored they could find. The white women were reaching out, trying to catch any colored child who ran by. When they caught one, they'd dash 'em against the stones in the street and cheer.

"On our way to the dock, we saw three men hanging from lamp-posts. The whites were hoisting up a fourth when we reached the wharf.

"We paid all we have in the world to an oysterman for his boat to take us across. We knew not to stay downtown, because there were too many whites there, and we were not sure who was friendly and who would attack. We slept under some pilings, or tried to, and when night fell, we walked to you. We knew it would be safe. Mr. Culver told us to come to you for our wounds. Said this one too deep for him."

Mama only nodded. She had learned, since Ben Daisy, you let them talk. She called me over after the man's head was bandaged.

"With luck, there should be more coming," Mama said. I looked at the man, blood drying on his closed eyelids. *So this is luck*, I thought. Mama said, "We have to be ready."

She told me to run to the houses of as many women as I could think of. To find as many of them as I could. I did. I ran down our dirt road and to the main drag, past the church. To Miss Annie, the schoolteacher, and to the choir director and her sister, Miss Nora and Miss Greene, and to Reverend Harland's daughter, Miss Dinah, to the women who lived on the other side of the churchyard, and even to Miss Hannah. To her door I ran, and said, "Come with me, sister, if you can."

I brought them all to the crossroads, where Mama and Lenore were waiting with the cart. Mama had her doctor's bag, and Lenore had lined the cart bed with blankets. Together, we made the long trip to the waterfront. Mama had Miss Hannah sit with her on the driver's bench. I walked steadily beside them, and I saw Mama, every so often, lean over and whisper in Miss Hannah's ear that it would be all right. We all knew Miss Hannah hadn't been downtown since Ben was lost, but she was determined now. Miss Hannah gripped Mama's arm, and Mama said, "There will be so many of them. You'll only have their want to think about." Mama had Miss Hannah hold a blanket over her other arm, to keep her hands from shaking.

But when we got to the waterfront, the whole stretch was empty. There were no boats. "Where are they all?" Miss Dinah said, and only the waves slapping the bottom of the wharf answered her. By then, it was just after dawn. The water before us was first a long line of silver and then a sudden wall of cloud and fog. The smoke from all the fires the whites had set was rolling over to us, across that wide expanse of river, and it mixed with the muggy July dawn until one swirling mass of white and gray sat on top of the water.

I had never seen smoke mix with fog like that before, how it hovered like a curtain between this world and maybe the next, from light to dark, from heaven to hell, from sleep to consciousness. That was where the woman in the water lived even now—I knew it. I knew it in my bones. And I felt how foolishly I had spent the last year, looking for her in common well water, when she was here all along. While I stood with the women on the dock as they tried to see what was coming to them through the veil, I prayed to her, that woman,

Let 'em through, let 'em through, LET 'EM THROUGH.

I heard the tiniest drop of a wave, the sound a fish makes when it turns over on the surface of the water and falls back to its home. Was that her? Was that her byword? I thought it was. I knew it was, because the next thing I saw, finally, was something nosing its way through the clouds.

It was a long boat, with four rowers—two at the bow, two at the stern—followed by two more. As they got closer, I could see that the rowers had kerchiefs wrapped around their mouths, to keep from breathing in the smoke as they worked, and their hats pulled down over their eyes, to keep them from stinging in the wind. Between the rowers, on the boats, were tens of children. What was most eerie about it all was that the only sound was the water slapping the oars. Even the babies were silent.

But then the first boat docked, and the women all around me took in a deep breath, and they began to sing.

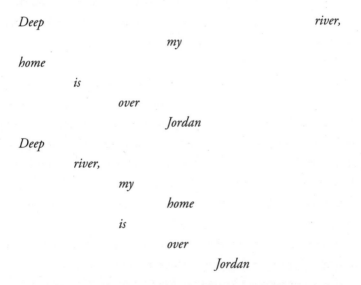

Deep   river,

                                     my

home

       is

             over

                 Jordan

Deep

          river,

              my

                 home

             is

                 over

                       Jordan

By the time we got to the chorus, a baby in one of the boats began to cry, a big robust yell, as if he was trying to harmonize with us. And the women all around me broke out in whoops. "That's it," Miss Annie called out. "Keep it up." And then the other babies began to cry, as well, and I have never seen a group of women happier to hear a bunch of infants bawling at five in the morning.

We got the children out of the boats. A girl my age, her face streaked with soot, her arms covered in scratches, her skirts dark with something damp, held a fat baby in her arms. When she clambered off the boat and up onto the dock, she looked at me, looked in my eyes, came straight toward me, and handed the baby off before crouching down to sit, lowering her head to enter the peace of the fabric stretched between her knees. Mama saw her, saw the stain on her skirt, and went to her first, shielding her with her body so the others couldn't see or hear what she was asking.

I carried that baby all the way back to our house. She was not yet a year old, by the look of her. Still too young to walk. She lay against my chest. I could feel her spittle pool on the front of my dress. She was so heavy, and with every step, I could feel her chest rise and fall. It unnerved me. I tried to match her rhythm, to breathe along with her, but her heart was beating too fast. Still, despite all this, she would look around, keep her eyes wide open, staring at something in the tree branches above us—part of the past, or the present, or maybe the future, that I could not see. I kept praying to the woman in the water, even as every step took me farther from her. *Don't take this one with you. Keep her here with us. Let her spirit leave the water and come with me to land.*

The baby was still in my arms at noon, when we had gotten some of the survivors to our houses, some of them to the church.

"You can put the baby down," Mama told me.

I looked up at her. "I can't," I said. By which I meant if I gave up the weight of that baby, the whole weight of what had happened across the river—the fire and the hangings and the beatings and the white women dashing babies' brains and whatever had been done to that girl from the boat who had handed me the baby, that had made her hold her dress between her thighs—all of that weight would take the baby's place, and I knew I was not strong enough to hold it. Not yet.

Not then. Even if I made a million prayers to the woman in the water, I knew it wouldn't help.

And Mama, my mama, she looked at me and she understood. She said, "This is the hardest part of our work." She said, "Keep the baby close if you need to. But you can't carry her all the time." And she had me sit in the nicer armchair in the parlor while the women of our town crowded into the room.

They had gathered there, all sweating in the full heat of the day, their apron fronts and pinafores damp, their voices merging together into a new song, this one made up of just the question they asked one another in the room over and over again:

What to do?

"Look at that baby's skin," Miss Dinah said, gazing at the girl in my arms. "Covered in rashes, even worse than the singe from the burns."

"And that little boy who rode with me in the cart, his feet were too tore up to walk." Miss Hannah said this, in a hollow voice, looking straight ahead, back to being stuck in between this world and the one with her brother in the water.

"That one," Miss Clara said, pointing to the baby still slumped in my arms, "her father left her with the orphanage when he went to go and try to join the war. They told him she'd be well cared for. What's he going to come back to now?" Miss Clara was the youngest member of the women's club at church. There, she was given to making righteous statements that made the other women shuffle and shift, embarrassed by her blunt holiness.

"One of the girls said the white people went around and marked every colored person's home in Manhattan," Miss Annie said. "With red chalk, they marked it. They marked the homes of our white friends, too. So they knew who to burn." As she spoke, she fanned herself with her hand in quick, sharp strokes, trying to shift the weight of humidity with the palm of a hand.

"What terrors," Miss Dinah said. "Can you imagine? I mean, can you imagine, your very own neighbor marking your house to attack? Can you imagine all those people you pass in the street every day, planning for your demise?" Miss Dinah leaned forward and said, in a gruff, low voice that I suppose was meant to be that of a terror, "Mark 'em all and burn 'em down." I'd heard Miss Dinah try on this voice before, at church meetings when she was describing certain devils, and it had always raised a laugh. But not now. The accent only curdled in the hot air.

"Surely, the governor can stop it," Miss Clara said uncertainly. "He'll send troops to make it stop."

Mama looked at Miss Clara, with her high, smooth neck and clear brown skin. "You understand less than I thought you did if you think he'd lift a finger."

Miss Clara blinked, and her cheeks darkened.

"One of the men says"—Miss Annie leaned forward, eager to stop the sadness and share what she knew—"the mayor begged the governor for help, but the governor plans to come and cheer the rioters on."

"He'd do it," Mama murmured.

"How can you be so hopeless?" Miss Clara said.

Miss Annie sat back in her chair again. "It is not being hopeless. We have to plan for the worst of what white folks do. Because they always choose the worst. They do what they do, and—"

"We do what we can," Mama said. She took a sip of water from her tin cup.

"I hope the governor burns," I said, from my seat at the corner.

I had thought Mama would nod in agreement. Some of the other women did. I saw Miss Clara and Miss Annie smile when I said it. But Mama looked at me sharply. "It's a sin to wish such a thing on another person," she said. "Even on him."

I thought of the woman under the water, who I was sure had the vengeance in her to do something horrible like that, and I directed my thoughts to her. *Burn him up. Drowning's too good for him.*

Mama stood up. "To work," she said. Even then, our household had more than the households of the other women—more jars of preserves, more salt pork, more cloth, more firewood. And so we spent the afternoon taking stock of the pantry and of the root cellar, dividing what we had to feed everyone, which household should take from the extra barrel of salted cod and which needed more blankets.

We did not know it then, but this is how we would spend the rest of the war. All of us in that room there became a sisterhood. We called ourselves the Ladies' Intelligence Society—it had started as a kind of joke, when the few men in town asked the women where they were going, why they spent so much time at Dr. Sampson's house. I was a mascot of sorts—the doctor's girl, who was always in the room.

We were hell-bent on plotting. How could we get information from Kings County to Ohio, to Maryland, to Virginia, to the West, about the children left in the destroyed orphanage? How could we find their parents? It was from hours of those meetings that we found the father of the baby I'd carried off the boat, got word to him, were able to send her to relatives in Massachusetts. She was no longer in my arms, but I could still feel the weight of her there, pressing. Whenever I did, I'd fold my arms over my chest and pray again, to the woman in the water. *Keep her safe. Keep them safe. Keep us safe.*

"After the war" became everyone's refrain. We read of men dying every day, even as a few of those made their way off the battlefield, their eyes wide with horror. Whenever the war ended, if it ended, whoever won, we knew there would be colored people in need of aid. And what could we do, from the safety and comfort of our town that the whites had overlooked? What would help them best?

"A school," Miss Annie said. The women all nodded; that was a given. "Homes," Miss Dinah added. But it was Mama who cleared her throat and said, "A hospital." She looked around the room. "For colored people," she said. "We cannot live in freedom if we are not well."

There was a moment of silence as the women turned the idea around, and Mama, very carefully would not look at Miss Hannah, who was crying now. But Miss Annie, Miss Clara, and Miss Dinah nodded, and it was decided then that this was what their efforts would go toward. A hospital, for whoever made it out alive, to become whole again.

It was hard planning, oftentimes hours of talking with no clear answers. But when the women got going, the whole room began to vibrate. Sometimes, it seemed that the white walls themselves flushed when the women raised their voices. How strange it was to sit around them, at their feet or in the corner, and hear them shout, these same women who all week long told me and the other colored girls in town to speak softly, to keep our heads down and our backs straight, to train our eyes to overlook the insults the world outside of town heaped at our feet. Those women told girls like me to ignore the present-day horrors around us, to look only toward the future, toward another place that did not exist yet.

But here, in the room, I could imagine that I was already there. The women would begin the meeting sitting upright, but by the end, they would be sprawled. Leaning against seats, arms crossed over stools, sipping water, laughing, shouting back and forth.

You knew a meeting was getting work done when Miss Dinah

began her sharp, piercing giggle. It was uncontrollable, a little hysterical, and did not necessarily prompt the other women to join in. It
was more like the whistle of a teakettle; it told you pressure was high,
waters were rolling to a boil, that something was happening, and that
whatever it was, it was as wondrous and yet as deceptively common as
water transforming into air.

I have never in my life felt anything as powerful as whatever force
was in that room while those women talked, and I began to believe that
it was the talking itself that did it, that perhaps women's voices in harmony were like some sort of flintstone sparking, or like the hot burst of
air that comes through a window, billowing the curtains, before rain.
Sometimes, I imagined the whole room lifting up from their talk—
lifting up and spinning out, out, into the future times to come, when
everyone would be truly free. The time I thought we were all planning
for.

To bring them back down, when a workday was done, they would
turn to some sort of amusement. It had to be something calming,
something sober. "We need to rest a little in order to keep going," was
what Miss Annie always said.

They decided on trading compliments. They'd write them down on
slips of paper, unsigned but addressed to the lady they wished to compliment, and then put them in an old flour tin Mama had. At the end
of the meeting, they'd draw the slips out one at a time and read the ode,
and then the fun began in guessing the author.

Everyone saved their praise by pasting the compliments into little books they stitched together and then passing them around to
be signed by every lady present—a record of attendance. They made
bindings out of the rags they had around, stuffed into the bottom of
their sewing baskets. 'Friendship albums,' they called them. Everyone's

album started neat and clean and pretty, of course, but it was every woman's goal to have a ruined one, a book with worn pages and extra leaves stuffed in, one bursting at the seams, because that showed how loved you were.

Mama was jealous of the other women. Sometimes, at the end of a meeting, I caught her fingering the pages of her own album, looking from hers to theirs. Hers were always a bit neater, a bit cleaner, and much thinner. Even after all she'd done for the orphans, even as the group conspired about how to make her a hospital, even after all that work, Mama would lift the other women's heavier books and sign them, smiling, while only a few of them signed hers. Ben Daisy still stood dripping over her, a rebuke.

I suppose I should have been angry at the other women on behalf of Mama. If I was a loyal daughter, I would have felt that. But at the end of every meeting, I looked at Mama's thin book and only felt sorry for her, not mad at them. *Is everything at least forgiven underwater?* is what I would have asked the woman in the water if I could have, but I did not really want to know the answer.

I did not know what to do with a vanquished Mama. I saw her hurt, but I still thought she could overcome it. She never spoke of it, so to me, it was another thing to add to the load she carried. "Everyone has their own burden, Libertie," she was fond of telling me whenever I complained about my inability to do arithmetic or when another girl was mean or petty. So I thought she could solve this setback, that it was temporary, that it was something Mama could fix with her cleverness.

Once, in her office, I found the discards of her attempts at praise for the other women, written on the backs of notes to the pharmacist and on the discarded labels of old medicine bottles.

You've done fine work, and I look forward to your work improving
even more.
Although at first I was not sure, I see now you are a true Christian
woman.

It was as if she could not, in spite of herself, break her reserve and
warmly compliment any of these women, who'd discarded her from
their care.

"You see, I am not very talented at this."

I started. Mama was standing beside me, watching me read her
weak words. I think it was the first time she admitted a failing to me.

I felt a little flush of embarrassment for her.

"Libertie," she said, "write something for me. Kind, but not too
kind. Nothing that would inspire envy."

"You cannot do it?"

"I do not have a way with words, like you do." She sighed. Then
she said, very quietly, "The only good poem I've ever written is you. A
daughter is a poem. A daughter is a kind of psalm. You, in the world,
responding to me, is the song I made. I cannot make another."

My heart filled but quickly sank, because what freeborn thing can
bear to be loved as much as that?

The least I could do was write a poem for her.

They were supposed to be anonymous. That was the whole point. It
was my job at the meeting to take the unsigned works out of the box
and read them to the room, with no bias. At the next meeting, when I
took out the paper written in my own hand but elongated to look like
Mama's, I stood up before them all and sang the love my mama had
for the women there. The love she would have sung, if she'd had the
voice for it.

True women friends are fine and rare
You search for them, here and there
The bonds between us bloom like a rose
For we are companions true affection has chose
Within our hearts lie trust and faith
Our true friendship, bonds will never break

Mama was not a good poet. Neither, at fourteen, was I.

But those women heard that awful poetry and smiled and clapped, and when I revealed it was my mama who wrote it, they said, "Very fine, Dr. Sampson. Very fine indeed." It was as if she had proven that she was one of them again, because she could praise them so warmly, even if the praise was clumsy. Maybe because of that. It was what they had been waiting for, and there was a kind of thawing in their relations.

Even rude love is better than no show of love at all. That must be why you took Ben Daisy, I thought to the woman in the water.

That is how I remember the rest of the war: my hands covered in the flour dust from long-baked biscuits at the bottom of the tin of love poems, the tips of my fingers stained with black ink, and Mama searching for every opportunity to be useful. I learned during the war how to scheme for the best way to set the world right, to change it. And I knew that this change was wrapped up in the love notes these women wrote to one another and dropped into a box, even as the world around us burnt.

Which world was burning, anyways? I wrote this question out to her, the woman in the water. After each meeting of the Ladies' Intelligence Society, I took what little bits were left of the poems and made a book of my own.

What did Ben Daisy say she liked? Pink and white and gold. Cakes

and candy. Scent bottles and silk. I left pansies alone, but I collected
everything else I could for her.

These things were hard to come by in our hamlet. We did not eat
or buy sugar, because slaves made it—Mama was one of the few who
were righteous enough to observe this boycott. But then, with the war,
it wasn't to be had anyways. So I took to dripping honey in the pages
of the book, underlining each question to the lady with a thick golden
smear. Into the honey, I pressed flower petals, and then I let the page
dry and started another one.

The songs I wrote in my book were made for the woman under the
water, the one who offered something other than this world.

> *Is the water really better?*
> *Should we all just try to drown?*
> *Is your love better than this world?*
> *Which world is burning, anyways?*

I thought it was the world that drove Ben Daisy under the water,
that kept Pete Back Back pocked with sores, that conspired to steal and
beat and kill the children of the women around as soon as they left
their wombs. So, what was there, really, to mourn? In annihilation, I
saw a celebration. My book to the lady became a place to celebrate the
destruction of all the devices of this world that had tried to snare my
people and snap us in two, that had sworn to kill every last one of us
one way or another.

And even as the wider world did not agree, did not even care what
the women around me thought or believed, discounted colored women
as entirely irrelevant—the thing to remember, I learned, was that these
women, here, loved one another and cared for one another as no other.

Even for my shifty, jumpy, defeated Mama, they cared. And from that care grew a steady foundation.

WHEN THE WAR ended, I ran through the streets with everyone else, crying and saying my hosannas. Finally, the world I had dreamt of, had prayed for, was on its way.

A bunch of us colored girls and boys ran all the way down to the waterfront. We danced on the boards of the wharf, and I even leaned over the side to whisper into the waves of the water a "Thank you." I half believed, even though I knew I was fooling myself, that this was all her doing.

We left the riverbank at dawn, headed for home, and I walked backward the whole way, while the other girls laughed and the boys called me silly. I looked toward the river. I watched the sky for fires and probed the earth for blood.

Now, the newspapers were full of longing, not battles. White people longing for their sons' bodies, hoping they were whole. If their bodies did not come back intact, then what would happen to these good white Christian boys on Judgment Day? They would stand up in their graves and topple back down, as on some overgrown battlefield their errant leg or lost foot would rise without the rest of them. They made it sound like a horror. But I read each notice as the reports rolled in during that jostling year after the war, and prayed to the woman who had taken Ben Daisy under *Keep their arms scattered and their legs separated. Keep them without integrity when Judgment Day comes.*

It was a small price to pay, in my opinion. The war had broken bodies apart, and that seemed to be what caused so much terror among the whites, what made them shoot their own president. But I had stood in Culver's back room and seen the people broken from slavery, I had held that orphan girl in my arms, I had seen so many die from those same white people's hatred that I could not muster any sympathy for their terror, and I could definitely not feel it on my own.

They did not care for us. I would not care for them. I would only care for the women around me, the woman in the water, and Mama, of course.

It was the closest I'd come, at that point in my life, to a state of jubilee. Something that people had told us was impossible for two hundred years was here—colored people were free, the slaveholders were defeated, and everything around me led me to believe that it would be this way forever.

It was finally time for the Ladies' Intelligence Society to show their care for the world, which they did with a building they bought for Mama's hospital downtown. They decided that a location near the wharfs could serve more of the colored women in Kings County, and maybe some others adventurous or rich enough to take a boat from lower Manhattan. A COLORED WOMEN'S HOSPITAL was painted carefully on the sign there, and we all cheered when it was finally raised up and nailed above the door.

The women of the LIS painted the walls of Mama's hospital waiting room a deep red and raised money for the padded leather benches there. Walking into it was like walking into some expensive womb. It was dark and warm and designed to calm the patient, while she sat, scared, shocked by the betrayals of her own body.

When patients climbed the stairs to the examination rooms, they were called to a kind of rebirth. They passed through a hallway painted a deep, peaceful white and emerged onto a floor with wide windows and the white muslin curtains Mama put such stock in. They rose to a world of light. In the bright light, their bodies were not a shame, not a secret, and they were examined by the light of the sun "as the good Lord intended," as Mama would say. For some of the women, it was the first time they had ever exposed as much as their stomach to the sun, and sometimes they would break into tears, overwhelmed by the light. But even the most conservative of them, the ones who insisted there must be something indecent about all that brightness, came back to Mama and the hospital, to be tended.

As Mama and Lenore examined them, and I stood back, ready to assist, Mama named each part of a woman as she touched it. "This is your sternum. This is your rib. Here is your navel, but you knew that. Here, what I push on here, is your womb and your ovaries. This is your mons pubis. These are is your labia, minora and major. This is your prepuce. Pardon."

I stood in those examination rooms, and I heard her say this every day, to every woman, like a kind of benediction. And when I was not with her in the hospital, when she had me stay at the house to tend the garden or look after the land, sometimes in the middle of the day, I lay in the garden, felt the hot earth on my skin, and contemplated how my own limbs joined together. I traced for myself my sternum, my ribs, my navel, my womb, which I imagined as empty and small as a coin purse, my ovaries, which I could palpate with my own hand, my own mons pubis, my own labia, which I touched and thought the thrill I felt was merely the daring of touching something private in the light of the sun.

It was so quiet at the house without Mama and Lenore that I listened to my own pulse, could track my own breath, could maybe even hear my own body growing.

My mother was giving me the great gift that no other Negro girl my age, anywhere on Earth, I am sure, had experienced before. What other Negro girl had the freedom to lie in a garden on a workday afternoon?

Because of this, I was not scared or disgusted by my body changing, as I knew other girls were.

I'm sweating jewels, was how I explained it in my book to the woman in the water. Red rubies in my drawers, yellow pearls at the seams of my blouse, black diamonds across the bridge of my nose. I eagerly wrote to her about the wonderful rude shock that came when I woke up one day and realized that I now smelled like a woman. *I will be what Mama knows, what Miss Annie and the LIS know, what we study all day in her hospital, I wrote.*

One day at the house in a planning meeting, as the women talked about how to raise just a hundred more dollars, two hundred, to keep the hospital open, Miss Annie sniffed loudly while I walked by and said, "Womanhood is nothing but tears and sorrow." Then she looked at me. "I can smell it on you, Black Gal."

I was not offended, because I knew Mama saw honor in my changing body—how my measurements grew millimeter by millimeter, how the numbers that described me shifted. She told me she was proud. It was as if the change in my body was one she had willed herself, not the same cycle every other girl went through.

I think Mama thought if she gave me that space, I would reproduce her spirit and her will in exact measure. Like a cell dividing itself.

This new world of adult busyness and abundance that Mama was building at the hospital seemed as robust as my own body. I saw them as one and the same—that Mama's fortunes were changing right when my body was felt like a kind of omen, one I thanked the woman in the water for. I thought she had heard my cries for blood and revenge and was making them real for me, in the sweetest way possible: in Mama's prosperity.

I did not even realize that what I had grown into was a different person than my mother until she had COLORED painted off the hospital sign. She sent for a boy to do it maybe a year and a half after the hospital was open, after the fourth or fifth charity bazaar the LIS had run that came back with diminishing funds. All over the country, colored people were building things that seemed bigger than Mama's hospital for women, that the colored men and white people preferred to fund.

The possibilities for colored people seemed so many, so varied, each more fantastic than the last, but which one was right and which one should they choose? If I could have, I would have chosen all of them— every idea, one after the other, seemed correct. A school for freedmen; a letter service to reunite those separated by the auction block; a caravan to Canada; another one to Kansas; Mama's hospital. *Why can't we have all of it, all of it?* I wanted to say.

The Ladies' Intelligence Society told Mama they could not raise the money solely for her hospital, in the way that they could during the war. And certainly not solely for a hospital just for colored women, when colored men were back and needed healing more. "We do not like it," Miss Annie said, "but we think people will be more amenable to your cause if we raise money for you and other things."

Mama did not even bat an eye. She only nodded, once, and said, "Well, then."

And so Mama decided to change the hospital name. "It's a sign of the reconciliation, of the harmony of the times we now live in," Mama said to me and Lenore as we stood beside her, looking up at the boy on his ladder in the street. "Here it is, only two years after the end of the war, and white women will sit side by side colored women in our hospital waiting room, willing to be treated because they know, deep down, their organs are the same."

But I knew, and she knew, this was not true. Because after the boy came down off his ladder, she had him put a rod up on the waiting room ceiling, and then she instructed Lenore to hang a scrap of red velvet on it, to make a little curtain, so that the new patients she admitted, the white women, could pull the curtain shut and avoid the sight of colored women beside them.

The white women came because Mama was colored but not too colored. In fact, her color worked in her favor. She would never be invited to a dinner party, or a lecture, or sit across from them in a private club. They would never run into her in their worlds and be reminded of their most embarrassing ailments: a stubborn and treacherous womb, smelly fluids, bodies insisting on being rude and offensive. Mama could restore these women's bodies back to what they wished them to be, make them well enough to join this world again—and they would never encounter her in their real lives, this woman who knew exactly what was beneath their skirts.

The first time I touched one of these new white-woman patients, she flinched. I remember, she was only a few years older than me, a young bride who'd come in with thrush between her legs, too embarrassed to see her own doctor and be found out. *Found out of what?* I wrote to my woman in the water.

I grasped the white woman's elbow to help her to the examination table, which she did not mind, and then I began to feel at her middle, as Mama had instructed at the start of the appointment, and she batted my hands away. "Off me," she said. And when Mama looked up, from where she was standing in the corner, preparing for the examination, the woman said, "Your girl is molesting me."

And Mama, my brave mama, did not come to my aid. She only narrowed her eyes slightly, and then she said, "Come take notes, Libertie," and she herself went to touch the woman's middle.

And so I understood. Mama was light enough that the white women did not feel awkward when her hands touched them. Mama, to them, was not all the way black. When the black women they knew outside the hospital touched the white women, they touched them with what they told themselves to be dumb hands. They did not have to imagine those hands as belonging to anyone, least of all someone thinking and feeling. But I'd touched that white woman with a knowing of what was deepest inside her, and she'd recoiled—it was beyond her imagination.

After that, I noticed how the white-woman patients watched me while I assisted Mama. They stared at where my dress tightened on my chest, at the roundness of my arms, at where my skirt darted at my hips—stared openly, because they knew I would not rebuke them—and then they would sigh, exasperated, and look away.

The older ones, I could understand their jealousy—the jealousy of age for youth, I thought it was. *Dried up corncobs*, I wrote of them in my never-ending letter to the woman in the water. But the patients about my age, I did not understand. I had grown up free, only around colored people, and I could not fathom their scrutiny.

And Mama chose them over me, every time.

When the women flinched, when they scowled at my body, Mama ignored them. Sometimes, she said, "Come stand here, Libertie," so that I was out of their eyesight. But Mama, dear Mama, my fierce Mama, never told them to stop.

Mama acted as though the white women's pain was the same as ours. As if when they cried, they grieved for the same things lost that we did. Mama did not seem to mind that a woman who came to our waiting room and sat on the other side of the velvet curtain could not be comfortable. Even when she came at her most vulnerable, when she had to be vigilant for some sort of abuse, she had to stare at that velvet curtain and wonder if on the other side of it was the very white woman who had caused her pain to begin with.

How, when the world was splitting wide open for colored women, could Mama choose to yoke herself to the very white ones who often were trying to sew it all up for us? "There's prudence and practicality, and then there is a complete failure of imagination," Miss Annie said shortly after Mama took COLORED off her sign, and that was all any self-respecting member of the LIS allowed themselves to say in front of me.

There was no drawn-out fight. The women in the group did not argue that way. Instead, one Sunday at church, our pew was empty, except for us. No one gathered around Mama's seat as soon as the sermon was over, as they had when we were plotting. We were back to the same loneliness we'd lived in after Ben Daisy. Mama had squandered every good feeling those women had ever mustered for her.

I saw Mama raise her hand to Miss Annie, and Miss Annie raise hers back limply and then turn to one of the other women she was talking to. I saw Mama register this, set back her shoulders, turn, and say, "Home, Libertie. I'm too tired for socializing today."

She gave up co-conspirators for customers, I wrote to my woman.

"What does it feel like?" I asked Mama one Sunday as we walked back home from church.

She looked at me, startled. "What do you mean?"

What does it feel like to lose your friends? is what I wanted to ask, but I knew it was an impossibly cruel question. So I only said, "What does it feel like to heal someone?"

But this, too, was a mistake, because my mother looked ahead and said, "I've never thought about it, Libertie. I don't know that I can answer."

How could she?

How could she?

It was the rhythm I walked to all the way to our house, up the steps of our porch to the front door.

I stood in the parlor and watched Mama unpin her bonnet until I could not take it anymore. "How can you treat those white women," I said, "after what you've seen them and their husbands do to the people who came to us? They marked our houses for destruction not three years ago, and you welcome them as if it was nothing. All the blood and sweat you mopped up for years, the bones we set right. All the people we lost—"

"You are so young, Libertie," she said. It infuriated me. "The world is bigger than you think." She was still watching her reflection in the parlor mirror.

I tried to meet her eyes, but I couldn't. I looked at the glass jar with her sister's braids in it, untouched since Ben Daisy—no one brave enough to touch it since he left us.

No, Mama, I wanted to say. *The world can live in the palm of my hand. The world is in the burning between the thighs of the colored women who seek you out for comfort. The world is in the wounds on the heads of the fathers, and in the eyes we treated, burnt by smoke from the fires the white mobs set.*

I can measure the world. Can you?

But I didn't have the courage to say that. I lowered my eyes. For a time.

"I've raised you wrong," Mama said to her reflection. "I've raised you all wrong if some white folks being cruel is a surprise to you."

I felt my face go hot with anger again. "I am not surprised by the cruelty, Mama," I said. "I am surprised we are expected to ignore it, to never mention it, to swim in it as if it's the oily, smelly harbor water the boys dive into by the wharves."

Mama finally took off her bonnet and set it down. She turned to me, her eyes exacting. "You want to write poetry?" she said. "Or do you want to get things done?"

"I want a clean pool to swim in."

She snorted. "Always with the flowery talk. You're spoiled."

"Call me spoiled," I said. "I won't rot if I swim in clean water, though."

She picked up her bonnet and folded it tighter in her hands, her only sign of distress.

She said with a sigh, "You are becoming too old for these scenes, Libertie. You can keep asking me your questions, your accusations full of God knows what. But the answer is never going to change. And I am tired." She set the bonnet down again, crossed the room as if to leave.

"But I am tired," I called after her, wanting to make her feel something, wanting to make her react, feel the same slippery sense of unease I'd felt when I saw that our pews were empty and that our friends had left us. "I am very, very tired, Mama. I am tired of bending over women's stomachs, and I am tired of feeling for babies' limbs under skin, and I am tired of smelling the sickroom breath of women who won't even look me in the eye."

Mama stopped at the door and turned. "If you are tired at sixteen years old, you understand how tired I am of having this argument with you. You can do as you please. But I won't have this discussion anymore."

And she left, calling over her shoulder, "Put the kettle on will you? A cup of tea would be nice."

I sat down in the parlor, in the seat in the corner where I'd watched my mother plan and plot and scheme and heal. Where I'd loved her and wanted only her understanding. I sat there for a long time, as the room darkened around me, as I heard her move about upstairs in her regular ambulations. I had my little book in my lap, full of notes to my woman in the water, but I could not write now. I saw my own handwriting, childish and looping large, and I thought of what she would think if she saw it, and I imagined she would feel only disgust with me, what I imagined was the same disgust my mother felt now, walking about her office, setting things right for the work-day tomorrow. Mama had fled into her mind, away from me—and I should be used to the cold by now, I should, but I still could not bear it.

It was a question of good. I had never doubted before that Mama was good. But here she was, discounting everything I asked in exchange for the money of these women, for the sake of the gold lettering on her building downtown. I could not, in all conscientiousness, call that righteous or good.

I am a fool, and maybe you are, too, I wrote in the book, and then I closed it, and sat back, and cried.

The next morning, we rode into downtown as if nothing had happened—Mama telling me the tasks ahead. Indeed, it felt worse to know that our reckoning had not even been a reckoning for her, it seemed, just a slight annoyance at the end of the day. Here was another break between us. She could not even see when we were at odds with each other.

I thought it had not affected her at all, until a few weeks later when she looked up from her books as I brought her a cup of tea one night and said, her voice cool but her face blushing slightly, "Cunningham College in Ohio has accepted you for further studies. I think it's for the best, don't you? I have taught you all I can here." She took off her glasses and smiled wanly at me. "I think I cannot teach you anymore."

I did not even protest. I said nothing and understood I was to leave her, had been banished, for wishing her to ask more of the world around us.

Se lè yon sous seche, moun konn valè dlo

*It's when the spring goes dry that people appreciate the
value of water*

She sent me away, so I'd send her away, too, I resolved. I would banish her from the very recesses of my heart, from my consciousness, to forge a new self that had not ever been touched by my mother.

In the weeks leading up to my departure, she did not speak to me of it at all. It was Lenore who directed how to pack my trunk, told me what route I should travel, reminded me to never look a strange man in the eye. Mama went about her work as if I would be there with her forever.

So she wants silence, I wrote to the lady. *I'll give her the silence of the grave.*

On the morning I left, she told Lenore to take me to the ferry to Manhattan. "I should stay at the hospital," she said. But as I climbed into the cart, she stopped and held my hand and kissed it, in that same desperate way I'd seen her do to Madame Elizabeth.

"You write to me, you hear?" she said, her voice strangled. "You write to me everything that happens to you so I can know it."

I kept my hand in hers for as long as I could. *Let me stay with you, and I wouldn't have to write anything at all*, is what I wished to say. But I only said, "Yes, Mama."

And then she threw my hand away, and the silence rose up between us again, as inevitable and heavy as an ocean's wave.

Dear Mama,

The train was tolerable. The stagecoach was not. I had to sit on the top, at the back, because at first I was the only Negro traveling and there was a white family, moving to Ohio. The wife did not want me to sit beside her or her children. But after the first stop, a Negro man and his son joined me. The man was named Mr. Jonathan, and he taught me how to press my body forward into the wind. He said it was the best way to endure the ride. He told me I have a habit of looking back over my shoulder at the road behind us, and that is no good when you are traveling through open country.

The land here is strange. I find it all too flat. Not like the hills in Kings County. The air, though—that, I can concede, is better. The first few days out of New York, my nose dripped a thin black liquid that made the coachman laugh. He told me it was all the soot of the city, fleeing my nostrils. I must confess, I bunched my cloak into the balls of my hands and rubbed my nose at his rudeness.

The stagecoach left me in a town called Butterfield, and the college is five miles farther than that. There was one cart waiting to make a mill run, luckily, that agreed to take us—otherwise I would have walked the five miles, pulling the twenty pounds of clothing and quilts and books in my trunk behind me.

On the ride into school, I sat beside two other girls, one plump, one stout, both with skin the color of damp sand. The thin one leaned in to all three of us and said, "At night, you can't see nothing

*in these fields. You, for instance, out in those fields you'd be nothing
but eyes and teeth."*

*I knew it was a joke, but when I heard it, it shot through me and
I spent the rest of the ride turning suddenly, trying to catch, out of
the corner of my eye, glimmers of teeth and eyes from the fields. Or
maybe just another girl as dark as me who folded down into molars
and corneas as soon as the sun set.*

*I will stop myself from speculating further. I know you do not
like poetry. I will write another letter to you when I've gathered
enough facts, not just impressions, for your liking.*

Your

Libertie

I had resolved to wash her influence off me like dust from the road.
But everything in that place she'd banished me to looked to me exactly
like Mama. The gray sky that arched above me was the same color as
her front tooth, and the fields smelled like the inside of her shawl, and
the wind in the trees, I thought, sounded just like the whisper of her
voice when she was being urgent.

The cart stopped a quarter of a mile before it reached campus, in
front of a wide, low log cabin, set back a little, with a short, rough-hewn
fence in the front.

As I headed up the path in the dusk, my trunk trailing behind me,
the door opened. A woman stood there. When I reached her, I realized
she was shorter than me—the top of her kerchief only came up to my
shoulder. She was almost as dark as me, too. She looked up at me,
laughed at my dirt-smeared face. "You look like you walked here from
Brooklyn," she said.

She came out behind me and pushed me inside. "Leave the trunk,"
she said. "One of the boys will get it."

This was where I was to board—the home of an old friend of Mama's, Franklin Grady. He was from Kings County, too, and had moved out west to study law at Cunningham College, run for over twenty years by abolitionists, an experiment in Negro education. The woman who greeted me was Grady's wife, Madeline.

Grady had been there since before the war, since the days of spiriting away, and now that war was over and there were so many ways for a Negro to get ahead, he had chosen to stay at the college, to become its first Negro dean of law. Indeed, as Mama had told me, all the teachers were Negroes—drawn out to these fields to grow the teachers and doctors and farmers and lawyers our race would need in freedom.

I realized that Mama had sent me to a place that was the antithesis of her hospital. There would be no white students behind a velvet curtain in the classrooms of Cunningham College, claiming reconciliation. But Mama also knew, as did I, that I couldn't get away with the trick she'd pulled so many years ago—register at a white medical school and be taken for merely a white woman, not a colored one, until first semester marks came through.

The Grady household was not like mine. There were three rooms—the big front one, with the hearth, the back room, where Grady, Madeline, and the three children slept, and then a smaller room, where Mr. Grady's books were kept and where he went to work on the cases that came his way. The main room was hot. Hanging from the ceiling, draped over every beam and surface, were skirts and shirts and pants. Enough clothing for a regiment. "Keep looking," Madeline Grady said as I craned my neck up to stare at the ceiling beams through the leg hole of a pair of bloomers. "They'll be here till Wednesday."

Then she moved off, out the door to the yard, where more clothing hung out to dry.

She did not ask me to follow her, and I was at a loss as to what to do, so I sat down on my trunk and waited, while the two boys who were supposed to help me drag it in stood in front of me and stared. "Hello," I said, and they both ran off with a start to hold on to their mother.

Mrs. Grady came back in to the room and began to pull down some of the skirts and shirts and throw them over her arm. I moved to help, but she held up her hand. "There'll be time enough for that once you're properly settled in. Sit still. Play at being a lady," she said, and then laughed again.

I stayed on the trunk, awkwardly. When she came back in again, she pushed one of the boys forward, who held out a branch he'd broken off from the oak tree out front.

"Well, take it, then. Beat the dust out you, at least," Mrs. Grady said.

When Grady came home, that's what I was doing—hitting my knees and ankles until the dust from the road danced in the air. I was the only one to greet him, because Mrs. Grady and the boys were back outside, wringing the last of the gray water out of strangers' shirts.

Grady blinked at me once, twice. His cheeks flushed pink in the heat of the room—he was, perhaps, a little bit darker than Mama, and much, much lighter than his wife. But he was also clearly a Negro—he would not have been able to get by. He was short, too, with a round, pleasant face decorated with freckles and a broad, friendly nose, across the bridge of which perched the same small spectacles that Mama always wore.

When he saw me, though, he frowned as if I was a misplaced book.

"That's the girl, Libertie," Mrs. Grady called from the yard, and Grady grunted in response.

Later, at dinner, I told him, "Mama says thank you for your hospitality, and I do, as well," but he only managed to mumble a reply into his soup.

"She's asked me to give you this," I said, and I handed him the small pamphlet on prayer by Reverend Harland that our church had commissioned to be printed to celebrate the end of the war.

"Well, go on. Thank her," Mrs. Grady said. Let your own pickaninnies learn good grace." That made him smile, slightly.

He glanced at the title, then read it aloud. THE GLORY OF TOMORROW it said in proud, correct letters.

"Mama doesn't like that," I said. "She says it assumes too much."

"Huh," Grady said. "Well, Cathy never did put too much stock in forecasting."

"I, for one, agree with her on that," Mrs. Grady said to her bowl of soup.

"But you know Reverend Harland," I said. "He just refuses to respond to any of Mama's hints about unseemliness."

I blushed then, unsure if I had offended Grady with my irreverence.

He said nothing, only picked up the pamphlet carefully and carried it back to the room the rest of the family respected as his study.

It was to always be like that. He rarely stayed in a room when I entered. At first, I was sure the awkwardness would dissipate. Before I'd left home, the gossips at church had told me that Grady had been my mother's sweetheart before she met my father. So I was curious to meet him, to see if he could explain her to me, tell me what she had been like when she was young and gay, before she'd become this woman I could not understand. But it was perhaps this past connection that made Grady wary of me.

And so, to learn about him, I was forced to watch his wife.

I could not determine what about her made her the reason Grady had never come back to Kings County but instead had chosen a place with fields full of eyes and teeth. Madeline Grady was nothing like my mother. She liked to gossip and she liked to sing loudly, off-tune. She told me once, sighing, that if she had to spend another night at the college listening to lectures about the Negro condition, she would maybe yawn so wide she'd swallow her own nose.

That first night, she watched me as I put my Bible and my anatomy book—the two books I had managed to pack—under the pillow next to the mess of blankets she'd set up for me by the hearth. "Lord," she said, fanning the pages with her thumb, "imagine reading all of this. Sometimes I wonder."

"Oh," I said, understanding what she meant. And then I decided to be brave. "I could teach you," I told her shyly.

She shook her head. "I said 'sometimes,' girl. Not all the time." She laughed. "Grady reads enough for both of us."

I lay on the cooling hearthstones and wondered. Just that night, before we all retired to bed, Grady had read from their family Bible and Mrs. Grady had sat beside him, a child on her knee, patting in time to the cadence of the words. *But she does not wish to read them for herself?* I thought. It was even more strange to me because at the college, though I had yet to meet them, I knew there were women who had scrimped and saved and walked a thousand miles to be able to read a book. There were women Madeline Grady's age who stayed up late each night to learn the alphabet. And here she slept beside a man who not only read books but wrote them. And she'd never rolled over in bed and said, "Teach me."

I stopped myself from thinking further then—it was bad enough that I could hear, in the dark, the whole family shifting and sighing and passing gas in the next room. I did not have to imagine the Gradys' marital bed. But still, it was as if Grady and his wife lived in a kind of willed blindness.

I thought, *I have never seen a more incurious woman*. I thought, *My mother is better than Madeline Grady, at least*. I thought I was better, too.

Grady and his wife had married late, and their children were much younger than I was. They had a girl and two boys still in short pants. Grady, in contrast to his gruff indifference to my presence, doted on the boys and girl. He was always reaching for them—running his hand over the clipped scalps of the boys or suddenly squeezing the fat of the little girl's knees. I had never seen, up close, a family with a father, and whenever Grady made one of his sudden attacks of affection, I felt my cheeks burn and I had to turn my eyes away because they stung, as if a glare from the sun had suddenly caught them. I could not shake the feeling that I was seeing something I was not supposed to see.

Being in Grady and Madeline's house, I remembered the silence of my mother's. All those evenings spent where the only sound was her breath as she sighed over her reading, and sometimes the surprise of a log breaking into fire in the hearth, and here, at the Gradys', there was noise always around and within us. I realized that I had been raised up in something like a shroud, the muffling shroud of my mother's grief—for my father and maybe for life. To be at the Gradys' meant I was faced with life, and sometimes it felt like too much for my ears and my heart.

I would have written to my woman, if I could. But the Gradys' house did not have the long stretches of privacy that living with Mama did. There was no place to hide away and write verses. No ground to lie on and build myself anew. Those first few days, overwhelmed by the thunder of Madeline Grady pouring water into tin tubs, I found a corner of the front room and sat, facing the wall, the shroud of other people's laundry providing a cover. I had my book in my lap, my pen in my hand, when the youngest Grady toddled over and placed her chubby hands on my knees over and over again, until I put the paper aside to play with her.

The little girl tumbled away, satisfied. Through the piles of dirty petticoats, as I sat alone in the corner, I could hear Madeline Grady teaching her children her trade.

"Grady says a boy isn't ready for a proper education till he's seven," she'd told me that first day, "but it's never too early to learn to press."

"You've got to press the memory out of 'em," she told the children, who stood back in a circle, frightened of the heat, as she laid out each shirt and pulled the wrinkles out of the cloth. I heard the thud of the iron, the creak of the cotton, and I closed my eyes. When classes started, I told myself, I would be pressed clean at Cunningham—the wrinkles of my mother's passivity and stunted ideas smoothed out of me.

As Mrs. Grady worked, the room filled with the smell of other people's sweat, and she said, "Lord, it'd wake the dead."

She said this constantly about her work and did not wait to hear a laugh in response, but I provided one, because I wasn't sure what else to do. She teased Grady all the time, and he seemed to enjoy it. But for me . . . should I laugh at each one? Should I stay serious and ignore her? Should I add my own? She had a freedom I had never seen before. The freedom to laugh. Mama would have dismissed her for that. I felt myself doing the same, but then stopped.

The point of an education was to learn to do better, wasn't it?

Dear Libertie,

I trust you are finding the Gradys' home comfortable. I do not know what you mean when you say I do not approve of poetry. I am eager to hear of where you live now.

You did not ask about the hospital. It is doing very well. We are busier than ever, and Lenore has asked me to hire a girl to help her, now that you are gone. We have so many patients I fear we may have to turn some away. I have written to Madame Elizabeth for advice.

Reverend Harland has suggested that we stop serving unmarried women, and that we cannot do, as you know.

Miss Annie put on a wonderful concert last Sunday, all the children singing truly beautifully. I went downtown to hear the most interesting lecture on botany—I have included a clip, describing what was said, from the Eagle. I have also been twice to the theater the past few weeks—a very good Macbeth and then something very silly that a patient told me all the girls go to see. I enjoyed both— even the sillier show, I think. I suspect you would have, as well.

Please write as soon as classes begin.

Your

Mother

My anger had retreated in the face of my confusion at this new place, but now it came back, in such a rush that it made the letter tremble in my hand. I read it and read again—astonished. I read only for her cruelty then, not her longing. Her longing, I thought in a blaze of fury, was irrelevant and probably false.

There was no theater that admitted colored patrons downtown, so she had passed, as easily as that, to see her *Macbeth* and her silly play, in order to be able to talk more directly with her patients. A feat she would not have dared if I had been home and at her side. I crumpled the page up, tore it into smaller and smaller pieces, threw them into the wind as I walked to the Gradys' door.

I cannot not share myself with her, I told myself. My hand trembled again, slightly, at the memory of the strength of her hand holding mine. Write me so I know where you are.

But if she did not want my rage, which part of me did she wish to know the location of?

Dear Mama,

The college has remarkably progressed in the twenty years since its founding. I know you would be very proud of what the race has been able to accomplish here, what Negro men and women have been able to build when we take care of our own.

When the college began, classes were held in an abandoned barn on a stretch of land that the ten founders saved and schemed to buy. Over the years, they have saved to erect, one by one, additional buildings, so that today there is a lecture hall as fine as anything in Brooklyn, complete with old logs set up as columns. Beside each log is a chisel, and the male students, when they have an idle moment, drive the chisels into the wood, to flute the columns and make them truly Ionic. They are already half done.

There is a small chapel, used in shifts on Sundays, since it is the only colored church for many miles. People come from all over, not only the students, to worship there. There is a full brick building set up as the main hall, and another building where some of the students and teachers eat and sleep. It is all arranged around a bald square of dirt that will soon sprout grass and be the campus common. The agriculture students tend to it each day. Past the square and four buildings is the road into town, and then only the fields. At night, the lanterns in the windows of the college are the only light for many miles.

The college is run under the strict belief that silence is a sign of great intellect. Work begins at 5 a.m.—the boarders are expected to wake and wash, and then most of the students are assigned duties to keep the campus running. The young men clear brush, chop wood, construct outbuildings, and grow the small field of wheat and the market plots down near the river. The girls clean the campus, launder, and cook the food for all faculty and students. I am exempt, as a day student. But every day, as I walk from the Gradys' to class, I pass my classmates bent over in the fields.

The oddest thing is that we are expected to even do hard labor in silence. No one is allowed to sing any of the songs we all know to make work go faster. If anyone starts the melody to make work not so weary, he is dismissed from his post and sent to work alone in the woodshed.

It is a very queer custom, one that makes the campus dreary, in my opinion, though everyone else does not seem to think so. When chores are over, the campus erupts into chatter, and people laugh and talk again, as if nothing had happened.

Love

Dear

Libertie,

Silence is a virtue, and it is good that you learn this now. I am so glad to hear the college is thriving and that you are finding a home there.

You did not send back any notes on the botany lecture I sent. I suspect they have perhaps passed this letter in the mail, or maybe you are so deep in study you have forgotten to send. Make sure you do when you have a moment. I am curious of your opinion.

You must also make sure that you are avoiding any strong spices. Does Mrs. Grady cook with onions? It is not healthful for you. Be sure to continue your exercises twice daily—rotate the ankles, flex the wrists—to stay flexible.

You also must send me your list of classes, the names of your professors, and which books they have asked you to read. I am enclosing three articles from the latest Journal of Homeopathy, and I ask that

you write back your analysis of the arguments and your rebuttal, if
any, and send to me as soon as you are able.

    Your

    Mother

I would send her nothing. I had nothing to give her except petty
rebellions like this.

The other girl students were all assigned to the courses for teaching.
They were taking the ladies' course of study, which was concerned with
how to best direct a class. I was the only woman in the men's course,
the only girl taking biology and chemistry and rhetoric.

In lecture, I sat at the front, a bit to the side, at a separate desk. The
men all sat on rows of benches. I could not pay attention to lectures
and take my notes and see them at the same time, but I was aware of
them there, behind me. When I'd first walked into the lecture room,
I had wrinkled my nose—I had not smelled anything like that before.
Not a bad smell, just the heavy murk of young men that was caught
up in that hall. It was so overpowering I was not sure if I could even
differentiate one man from the other. They were just a cloud of scent,
pressing at my back as I tried to sketch the shape of a fibula. I smelled
it everywhere on campus, and it made me long for the company of
women even more.

The boys were polite enough—they waved to me at the end of class
sometimes. But that was not enough company for me, and I was lonely.
I would have tried to befriend the girls as we sat in the dining hall. In
that room, though, we spoke only in whispers.

I learned there was a kind of hierarchy. There were some girls who
had stolen themselves away before the war. They were a kind of aristoc-
racy, and they tended to stick together. At meals, they bent their heads

and spoke without even looking at one another—they had perfected a
way to speak even below whispers, even beyond glances. Sometimes, in
their silent language, one of them would communicate something to
make another laugh, and it was in those moments that I felt it keenest
that they were better than me. Not a single one of them would ever, I
guessed, be as wasteful with their time here as I was, sitting at the front
of a classroom of men and wondering what they thought of me. Those
girls knew something about the world that I did not know, could never
know.

Then there were the freeborn girls like me, from places like
Philadelphia and Manhattan and Washington, DC. I should have
naturally made friends with them. I heard them tell their histories to
one another—their mothers were all, they claimed, "at home"; their
fathers were clerks or tobacconists or preachers. No one would claim
a mother or father who was a servant. It was strange since we all knew
that each of us must have scrimped and saved to sit at that table. My
own mother, in the weeks before I left, set the clinic's books in front
of me and showed me the column she had added for her calculations:
Libertie's Education. But not one girl would admit this fact. Something
stopped me from telling them my mother was a doctor. I was not sure
how they would respond—eagerness and solicitation seemed somehow
worse than scorn. I did not want to still, hundreds of miles away, be
relying on Mama for my position. So I chose to keep my distance from
them until I could understand any of this better.

But the truth soon came out, and I began to catch them watching
me. I only smiled at them and bowed my head and hurried on. My boldness had burnt away, and the strangeness of the place had engulfed me.

"You know, every last one of them up there at that college are colorstruck," Madeline Grady said to me finally, after many nights at home
beside her and her children.

"You've never heard of love of copper?" she said. "They'll love us black ones if we make a lot of noise, but when we keep to ourselves, like you do, they don't know what to do. But don't worry. They're young. You're a pretty enough girl. One of the boys up there will peel away for you, like my Grady did for me, and leave those yellow girls behind. You just have to let him take his time."

And that was another kind of humiliation. That she thought my solitude was a symptom of wanting love.

So that was it. The perimeter of this world, the one I had tried to escape to, was color. I recalled, with bitterness, that Mrs. Grady did not know how to read, but she sure knew how to count. In this world, the lighter girls were unsure what to make of me—by birth, I should have been their peer. But I was not, somehow, and I was studying to become something closer to a man, not what they understood as ambition.

I spent a lot of time in the outbuilding that had been newly designated as a library, books piled all around me, not reading a word. Instead, I read the books' frontpieces. Many had been donated by churches from across the East. There was an entire lot from one congregation in Philadelphia; another from a congregation in Albany, a stack that had the *x*'s and handprints of a flock in Virginia. I would trace all the names of all these people who believed that I could be part of a bright shining future, but I couldn't bear to turn the page and begin to read.

It had been very easy to denounce Mama to her face and call her a traitor in my heart. I'd thought it was painful, but it was the easiest thing in the world compared with sitting here, feeling the weight of my mother's expectations and the world's indifference to my failure and my self. Mrs. Grady had taken to calling to me, as I left for class, "Go on, Black Gal, make me proud," and though I smiled at her each time she said it, knew she meant it with love, I could only hear a lie in her voice.

My rage at the world returned whenever I sat in that library. I knew what a stronger girl would do—sip her wrath like corn liquor, have it drench her ambition, sweat the rage out her pores as she worked harder and better, be smarter. But instead I suckled my anger like Lenore did the abandoned offspring of the barn cats, and it was about as effective as one of those little animals, doing nothing but mewling and flipping over in distress.

I knew I was not strong enough to touch a hundred white abdomens while feeling their contempt, while Mama stood beside me saying nothing. I did not think I was strong enough to pretend, even ten years on now, that the sons and husbands and fathers of the white women who sat behind our clinic's velvet curtain hadn't marked our houses with red chalk for destruction. And I knew, like the ache of a broken bone that hadn't been set right, that I was not strong enough to be faced with another Mr. Ben, and to fail him, and to have to live with that failure for the rest of my days.

I was not strong enough for this world, is what I meant, and it was a low-down, worming thing to discover about yourself when all around you, men and women who had been beaten, scorned, burnt, drowned, still found a way to come to this silence and sit within it and answer questions about what a lung was good for.

I began to think there must be something wrong with me: that I was slow or stupid, or merely ungrateful. Most of all, I felt a deep, burning shame in the center of my chest, that I could not work my rage better. When Mama was my same age, she had already finished her studies and was submitting herself to examination after examination, to try to enter medical school. She was working, in the evenings, with the local pharmacist, to learn how pills were made, and she was conducting her own experiments, and writing to friends to send the latest medical books to her to study.

But here I was, with an entire library open to me at midday, and I couldn't read a word.

I was only dull, hidden Libertie.

Dear Libertie,

You must make sure to ask that the latest anatomy books be found for you. The following is a comprehensive list of authors to trust:

Dear Mama,

The college's library is tolerable. The books have been donated by many kind churches. I've read the frontpieces of each and seen books from

Drs. Henshaw, Borley, Crawley and Madison and Fredricks (the older)

Ohio, Delaware, Virginia (of course), Connecticut, and even Maine.

For your review, I present you the following case: A girl came with Adipsia.

I must say that I miss you, and even Lenore (tell her she's a busybody), and if I

She had neither appetite nor thirst, and the thought of food was disgusting.

could but see you & stand beside you two & hear your voices,

So, in your professional opinion (ha), my good girl, what would you give

I would perhaps not be so lonely here, with you, but that's a silly thing

as remedy?

to wish, I know.

This impotent anger was another kind of grave. I thought I would be buried in it on campus, until one day when Madeline Grady chased me out of her house and told me to stay at the college for the evening "with the youth your own age." So one evening, when the dark came sooner, I did not hurry home to the Gradys' but wandered around campus until a few girls told me to follow them. And that is when I heard it. It was the queerest thing to hear the sound of a piano at night, outside, but I could hear it—the deep tones of the notes and then after it, the whisper of the hammer hitting the strings, because it was an older piano and someone was tuning it.

Music at night, music after dark, music finding its way to you across sweetgrass, can feel almost like magic.

A bunch of students, men and women, had gathered in one of the music classrooms, where a slanting upright piano had been pushed against a wall. Standing at it were two women, pushing the keys. It was a student-run affair—the room was decorated with holly and ivy, and there was hot cider, donated by one of the farms, and roasted apples and sugared biscuits. It was so hot that the windows were open to the cold night air, and from where I stood, pressed against one of them, my back stung with cold and the full front of me steamed with discomfort.

The first to perform was a sleek and chubby boy who had memorized his own dreary poetry—rhyming couplets intended to celebrate the beauty of the seasons but that thumped along forever. Then there was a girl who read a monologue, in the voice of Theda—a scandalous thing. And finally, for wholesomeness' sake, the Graces.

And then the two women who had been at the piano stood. Louisa Habit and Experience Northmoor. Louisa sang alto and Experience sang soprano. The two of them singing together, that first night I went out, made a kind of joyful noise—sweeter than what it sounded like when the LIS sang together at home or when the choir sang on Sunday. I watched them as they sang—I could see, under the cloth of their bodices, where their lungs expanded for more air, where they were holding in their stomachs to force out the lighter sound. To watch Experience and Louisa sing was the same as seeing a fast, small boy run or a man swing an ax and break up a tree. It was the same singularity of form and muscle, the same pushing of a body toward a single point on the horizon. I wanted, right then and there, to be as close to them as I possibly could.

Experience was tall and thin, with sharp elbows, and skin like a bruised peach. When she stood up to sing, she slumped her shoulders, as if she was afraid of her own height. Louisa, in contrast, was short, and as dark as me, and fat, with a flare of a burn scar down her forehead, which draped dramatically over her left eye. Whoever had tended to it when she'd gotten it had done well—it was nearly perfectly healed, only a dark flush color and, of course, raised above the rest of her smooth skin. She made up for it with pretty, round cheeks that flushed with red undertones whenever she took in breath to sing more loudly, and when she opened her mouth, I could see she had perfect pearls for teeth.

Mama had taught me long ago—the first tell of good health is the mouth. *Louisa has probably never had a toothache*, I thought, longingly. Experience, on the other hand, most definitely had. When she wasn't singing, she kept her fist curled at the bottom of her chin, at the ready to cover her mouth whenever she was called upon to speak, because her bottom teeth were rotten.

I imagined a whole life for them there, while I watched. I thought they would never be what Madeline Grady said everyone at the college was: colorstruck. They moved together as they sang, and I thought they had found an escape from this world. I thought if I got as close as possible, I could maybe escape, too.

When the evening was over, I stood beside them.

"You are wonderful," I said to Experience. Her eyes widened, and her shoulders shot back. I had startled her. I regretted it immediately.

"Well, thank you," she said.

"You and Louisa, you are both really marvelous."

"Mm-hmm," she said uneasily. She was looking through the crowd, for her companion.

"Are you first-years here? I haven't seen you yet."

"This is our second year here. We are close to graduation. We are the only two women in the music department," Experience said. "We wish, I wish, to be music teachers." She had spotted Louisa, and made to move toward her. I followed, determined to keep speaking.

"If you wish to practice teaching," I said, "then I would make an excellent practice pupil."

"Who's this?" Experience had reached Louisa, with me trailing behind, and now they both were looking at me, Louisa expectant, Experience as if she wanted to flee.

"Libertie Sampson," I said. I held out my hand for a strong hand-shake—a gesture my mother had taught, which the proctors here, at least, discouraged.

Louisa took it, and I started to speak again.

"I was saying to Miss Experience—"

Louisa snorted at that.

"Experience," I corrected myself, uncertain, "that if you needed to practice teaching a pupil, I am happy to do that with you."

"Do you sing, then?"

"A little. In church, of course."

"Well, come to where we practice. Near the market plots, by the river. It's easier there," Louisa said. And then she carefully pulled her hand out of mine and linked arms with Experience.

It was easy enough to convince them to let me listen to them practice. It was harder to learn their histories. Louisa was the more personable of the two. She was witty and liked to flirt with the boys, and even the lightest ones flirted back with her, because of the mark and her height and her chins. It was clear, everyone knew, that this was only in fun. She could imitate any animal sound with a whistle or a fold of her tongue—the call of a loon, the cluck of a turkey, the growl of a cat in the bush. She would use this menagerie to give a running commentary on the affairs of everyone at college. The handsomest boy, she referred to with the lurch of a katydid, and the prettiest, stubbornest girl, with a billy goat's whinny. Everybody liked Louisa.

Experience was harder to know—she seemed to walk about in a kind of mist, the only thing dispelling it the sound of an instrument or Louisa's voice. She was terribly serious about music. She could play any instrument you put in front of her. Her most prized possession was a small, battered metal pitch pipe. When I and the other students would gather to sing with her, she liked to mournfully blow it to call us to attention.

She would sit in the bare square of the future green, her skirts spread out before her, working on her scores, making notations, following the scrip of music.

I learned that Louisa and Experience were not from the same place.

Louisa was from Virginia, and Experience was from South Carolina. That's all they would tell me when I accosted them, giddy with the sound of their breath, after the first practice. The way they said it, quietly, with no more elaboration, I understood that they had been born enslaved, and that they were not prepared to tell me who or what they'd fought with to end up here, singing beauty in a cabin in the fields.

Willkommen,
   lieber
      schöner Mai,
   Dir tönt der Vögel
Lobgesang

was what they sang in a round that first afternoon by the river.

And then, when they combined their voices, it was another thing altogether. I believed that to attempt to sing with them in harmony would be like pouring bacon grease into a vat of water.

But Louisa said, "I cannot trust you if you do not sing. Why are you around the two of us? Just to listen?"

"I'm not very good," I said.

Experience shrugged impatiently. "That's not possible."

"Not as good as you," I said.

Louisa sighed. "False modesty wins you no friends, you know."

So I took a breath in. And I did it.

When I sang with Experience and Louisa, it was as if my very self merged with them. I was, I learned, a mezzo-soprano, and they each took pains to teach me how to make my voice stronger.

"You draw in air here," Louisa said, pointing.

When I sang with them, my whole history fell away. There was no past, no promised future, only the present of one sustained note.

When we sang together, we three stood in a round so that we could see one another's faces—and it was almost unbearable, to sing a song and watch Louisa's face change slightly and Experience's voice respond, and then my own, struggling for just a minute to reach theirs.

When I sang with them, I entered something greater than my sorry, bitter self.

I thought that anyone with a voice as powerful as that could teach me how to bend my anger to my will. I sat on that riverbank, and I thought that I had finally found my ambition. It was not to set bones right or to become my mother's double. It was to befriend the both of them, to make them love me and sing to me for the rest of my life. I knew this was a silly wish, but in my discombobulation at Cunningham College, I did not stop to question it. I knew enough to keep it quiet, to not speak it outright—not to Experience or Louisa, whom I did not wish to scare away, and not to Mrs. Grady, and certainly not to Mama. I spent the rest of the semester doing the bare minimum of work so I would not fail out of class and so I could keep meeting the two girls and have them sing to me.

Mama had told me freedom would come by following her, and I had known it was not true for a long time. Now I had someone else to follow, I was sure, and the thrill of having a new direction filled me up, blushed my cheeks, almost made me like the place. I put away my sticky journal to my imagined woman in the water and delighted in these real women, in front of me, made flesh.

"I wish my mama could hear you," I said one afternoon. "I wish she could hear how fine you are."

"I bet you wish your mama could do it," Experience said, and though she was smiling slightly when she said it, I felt the sting in her words and I saw the bitterness in her eyes. I turned away, ashamed. I had said something wrong again.

Louisa took my arm in hers and walked with me a little farther down the riverbank. "You sure do talk about your mama a lot," she said.

"Do I?"

"Yes."

I looked down at my shoes. "I'm sorry," I said.

"It's not something you should mind," Louisa said. "It is hard for Experience because she lost hers. She doesn't know where she is."

"Oh."

My rage burnt for an affront that was far less than hers. And here were the two of them not even hot, not even warm, just righteously cool in their voices. I had hoped that there would be a place where I found other burning bushes like me, willing to make the world anew with riotous anger. The fact that they had none unnerved me.

"But you do talk about your mother a lot, you do know?" Louisa gently chided. "It is always what your mama would think or what she would say or what she would like to say. Sometimes, I think your mama's here with us on this riverbank."

I walked on, in silence, ashamed again, until we heard a loud, rude croak from a frog ahead of us, more like a belch.

"See," Louisa said. "There she go," and I swatted her arm in laughter.

Dear Mama,
I have met the two most extraordinary girls, whose voices

Dear Libertie,
Today we had an interesting case: a young Hebrew serving girl

I believe can lead us to a kind of promised land. I know that
sounds like a

*with inflammation of the uvula and palate and an inclination to
swallow*

*fancy and like a dream, but that's what their singing is like to
me. Together,*

during the night.

they could be the greatest singers our world has yet heard.

What would you prescribe, Libertie?

Dear Mama,

*Do you remember, Mama, when there was the bad fever a few
years ago? And the churches took to pealing bells to count the dead?
Two tolls for a man, three tolls for a woman, one for a child. And
how at night you would hear each ring of the bell, and wait, wait,
wait for the next ring—whose life were you hearing called out?
Whose life was coming to you through the dark? The Graces' singing
is like that. Except you're waiting to hear about life beginning, not
ending. And it is marvelous.*

PS. I would prescribe, I think, Cimicifuga.

Dear Libertie,

*I remember that, of course, Libertie, but I'm not sure what you
mean by the rest. I am glad you are finding amusement there, but
please do not forget your purpose.*

*Yesterday, a woman came to me with a toothache, caused by the
damp night air. What would you prescribe?*

Mama—

Nux m., cepa, rhus. Wind: aeon., puis., rhus, sil. Draught: bell.,
calc, chin., sulph.
Libertie

I would go to the barrels of water Madeline Grady kept in her yard
and take off the cover and try to catch my reflection in the black-silver
surface there. She once found me like this, and I said, by way of explanation, "I am not a good daughter."

"Well, that's just pure nonsense if I ever heard it."

"I don't think I can be what she wishes me to be," I said. "I feel too
much, and she's never felt like this at all."

Madeline Grady fixed me with a hard stare. "I've never met a girl
as hard-pressed on making life difficult for herself as you, Libertie,"
she said. "Usually, it's men get caught in that current. I always thought
women had more sense. But I suppose you live long enough, you see
everything." And she sucked her teeth and looked for her wooden ladle,
and I hated her, a little bit, for seeing me so well.

I'd rather have had my mother and her obliviousness. There
is a greater comfort in being unseen than being understood and
dismissed.

Sometimes, I thought Madeline Grady was wiser than any of us,
but Experience and Louisa were not admirers of her. When they found
out where I lived, they exchanged a look that I eagerly asked them to
explain.

"What? What is it?"

"Well," Louisa said, "Mr. Grady is a sad man."

"Why? What's the matter with him?" I said, alarmed.

"He is very brilliant," Experience said hesitantly.

"Yes, very learned," Louisa said.

"And why should that cause you to feel sorry for him?" I said.

They looked at each other, and then they gave me the same pitying look.

"Well, you have seen his wife?"

"Yes, you have seen his wife?"

"Yes," I said slowly. I did not want to hear all the unkind things I'd thought of Madeline Grady said aloud by these two girls.

But they were subtler than me. "It's a study of what can happen when you do not let pure romantic love lead you," Experience said.

"When lust takes over," Louisa said theatrically.

Then they both laughed. I smiled, as well. I wished, perhaps, they were joking.

"Madeline Grady was a laundress when they met," Experience said.

"Well, that's respectable."

"Yes, but she was not just a laundress. She sold beer and spirits from her home."

"That's how her first husband died," Louisa said. "The father of her two boys. He mistook a barrel of lime for beer one night and drank a whole draught before he realized, and then he died in agony."

"I didn't know," I said.

"And then, she went to see Grady, to help her claim her husband's pension, and in a matter of course, the two have their little girl, and are married right before she was delivered."

"And Grady, the best colored legal mind of his generation is interrupted before he even gets a chance to leave here."

"She has thrift and grift to support him," Louisa said. "She's got the constitution for it."

"Yes," Experience said. "Those shoulders." And they both glanced at my own, as if judging how broad they were, to see if they were as broad as Madeline Grady's.

"But it really is a study in what can go wrong when a brilliant colored man makes the wrong choice for a wife," Louisa said.

In the women's dining room at Cunningham College, there was a big panel of fabric, with green velvet leaves bordering a list stitched out in red thread, three meters high.

MAN IS STRONG—WOMAN, BEAUTIFUL

MAN IS DARING AND CONFIDENT—WOMAN, DEFERENT AND UNASSUMING

MAN IS GREAT IN ACTION—WOMAN, IN SUFFERING

MAN SHINES ABROAD—WOMAN, AT HOME

MAN TALKS TO CONVINCE—WOMAN, TO PERSUADE AND PLEASE

MAN HAS A RUGGED HEART—WOMAN, A SOFT AND TENDER ONE

MAN PREVENTS MISERY—WOMAN, RELIEVES IT

MAN HAS SCIENCE—WOMAN, TASTE

MAN HAS JUDGMENT—WOMAN, SENSIBILITY

MAN IS A BEING OF JUSTICE—WOMAN, AN ANGEL OF MERCY

The first time I read it, I thought, *Then what is a man?* I thought of my mother, of course, and myself. I tried to parcel out where she lay on the fabric, but she was somewhere in between. Men then, for me, were still too terrifying to contemplate directly. They were an abstract. The only man I had seen up close was Mr. Ben, and he was not described by any of the words on that quilt. The left side of the quilt may as well have been stitched in gold thread; that was how fanciful a man's character was to me. And I had never known anyone who would claim Mama had taste and not science, who would call her deferent and unassuming.

I regarded that quilt as a kind of private joke, something no one who had eyes could believe. I saw its falseness again when I came home to find Mrs. Grady sitting, skirt spread out in front of her, on the kitchen floor.

"It's the last of it," she said, turning out the flour sack. "The school is behind on paying for the laundry, and we'll be short by next week."

I flushed. "Mama sent you my share, didn't she?"

Mrs. Grady nodded. "It's already spent, girl."

"But why don't you tell Mr. Grady? I'm sure he will give you more for the household accounts."

And at this, Mrs. Grady laughed for a long time, rolling the sack into a tighter and tighter ball as she did so.

"It's me give him his money. Do you think we'd be eating our dinner under other women's drawers if Grady had anything for a 'household account'?" And then she laughed again.

But that night, at dinner, she said nothing, and when Grady looked up from his plate and asked if there was any more tea for that evening, Mrs. Grady just smiled and said she had forgotten it. And then a cloud passed over his face, a recognition, and Grady stood up and went to his study.

The Gradys may have followed the rules of that quilt, but only by a kind of willed fiction between the two of them.

Mama and Madeline Grady and Lenore insisted that men were to be babied and entertained, but not obeyed. The Graces seemed to revere obedience, at least in the abstract. Louisa and Experience, these girls I loved, who I thought held providence on their tongues, were so sure of themselves. I began to doubt myself. Perhaps the rules Mama and Lenore and Madeline Grady lived by were wrong. Or not wrong, but they seemed only to apply in the velvet waiting room and white-washed examination room of Mama's practice or in the humid air of Mrs. Grady's laundry. And how good was a rule, how strong, how sensible was it to obey, if it lost all meaning as soon as you left your front door?

I wondered who Experience and Louisa would pick if they could pick their mate, since it was so important. Both were ignored by the men of Cunningham College, though they did not seem bothered by this.

"The other ones here, they call us the Graces because they think they're clever," Louisa told me. "Look at Experience. She's bright, but gawky."

I tried very hard not to look at Experience. "No, she is not," I said.

Louisa laughed. "Yes, she is. Not naming it isn't gonna change it."

"I'm gawky," Experience said, and that set Louisa to laughing.

"And I'm like you, Libertie," Louisa said. "Pretty but dark. And fat. And this scar. Altogether helpless. They called us the Graces, and maybe it's meant to be an insult or a tease or a joke, but I think it's a love note."

"It makes it easier to sing for them," Experience said, "when you think of it that way."

"My mama made it a point to never comment on another woman's beauty, or lack thereof," I said, and this made them both laugh, though I wasn't sure why.

It was the same way when they sang. They looked each other in the eye, and it seemed like they always kept their gaze like that. Nothing broke it. It was deeper than whatever was stitched across that musty quilt in the dining room. It was the same connection that exists between a flower and a bee, between a river and its bank, between a muscle and a bone.

And it was because of that I thought perhaps they were right and Mama and Mrs. Grady were wrong, and something turned over again inside me, some resolve that pushed me away from Mama a little bit more.

I DID NOT go home for winter term, so my grades were given to me directly to mail to my mother, which I did not do. I was close to failing—not quite, but close, and I took the letter with this message and pressed it into my old anatomy book and put it at the bottom of my trunk, resolved to think about it when I could get the sound of the Graces out of my head.

Over the Christmas break, the snow was so high we did not have mail for many weeks, so that when my mother's letters came, there were five of them to read in a row, and each one, every single one, was filled with the addition of a new name: Emmanuel.

He is a student of homeopathy, recently graduated from a medical school in Philadelphia. He is eager to study under anyone, including, he says, myself, "though you are a woman" (ha).

It was only one pair of parentheses, but Mama may as well have written me in dried berry juice. What did this "ha" mean, from a woman who I knew would bristle at a dismissal like that? A woman who had never been fond of parentheses.

Madame Elizabeth has sent him to me—he is lately of the city of Jacmel, Haiti, before he came to America to study medicine. He was not able to find a doctor who suited his interests in that city. So Madame Elizabeth and the church who sponsored him have sent him here, and he has been a welcome addition to the practice.

He sleeps in your bedroom—he has found it most comfortable. He has also suggested a new way to organize the garden—we will try it come this spring.

He recently saw one of our most persistent cases, Mrs. Cookstone, the judge's wife, who lives on Pineapple Street. She was resistant that a colored man should treat her, but Emmanuel is able to get by. He is a high yellow homme de couleur (as Emmanuel is known back home in Haiti, he tells us). She relented once she saw him. She agreed that he should consult with her from behind a sheet. Lenore conducted the actual physical exam, and Emmanuel asked questions.

As you remember, Mrs. Cookstone is a bit of a nervous case, but she has written already to tell me that under Emmanuel's care, she already is quite recovered from the pain in her chest and is even able to walk in her garden now, for a few hundred paces without needing to sit down and rest.

And here, the letter continued, enumerating all the ways this Emmanuel was a wonder.

Emmanuel has brought with him an album . . . He is collecting all of the plants and wildlife of Haiti, and we spend evenings comparing the plant life of his homeland to that of Kings County.

Emmanuel has created a tea that sweetens the breath, which we are now able to offer our wealthier patients. Sales have boosted clinic revenues by 2 percent alone this month.

Emmanuel is an especial favorite of our child patients and has a
light touch with even the most fearful ones.

I counted each time she wrote that name. I knew enough that it
was ridiculous to be jealous of a name on paper, but I could not help
it, though I dared not mention it to Madeline Grady—or Experience
and Louisa.

Mrs. Cookstone is now complaining of a pain in her calf muscle,
which she says she also feels in her left shoulder. Emmanuel has
already prescribed something that has done wonders, but I'm won-
dering if you can guess what it was.

This was even worse, to be set against a rival I could not even see, in
a race I was no longer particularly interested in but, because of pride, I
could not abandon. She wrote of Emmanuel with the voice of a proud
mother. She praised him in a way she had never praised me—except for
that one time, so long ago, when Mr. Ben first came to us and she had
stroked my cheek and said, "Libertie is beautiful."

But she had never called me clever, or smart, or good with patients,
or even particularly hardworking.

Now when she sent me problems to solve, she would write, *Emmanuel*
has already found the answer, but I wonder if you can.

She did not send me cutouts from journals anymore, because
Emmanuel has asked to study them and add to his own collection. She
would send them to me when he was done.

Can you feel brotherly jealousy for a man you have never met? A
figment of your imagination, a ghost of your mother's convictions? I
did. I could not even store her letters in my chest, beside my list of

grades—I felt that somehow the letters would whisper to one another, and my mother would instinctively know, back home in Brooklyn, how close I was to failing.

I SPENT THAT spring more in the music room than the library again, until, as the days began to lengthen, Louisa and Experience fell into a bitter disagreement.

A dean had suggested to the two of them that perhaps they should sing spirituals, that they should add these songs to their repertoire and then make a show of performing them.

Louisa and Experience had already brought in a little money for the fundraising efforts of the school with their singing. The songs they sang were German and Italian pieces—they prided themselves on this. They did not sing hymns, and they did not sing the songs we knew from church, or those our parents and grandparents and lost ones sang to keep from crying. The songs we'd all once sung in the fields. The songs that our parents sang at night or with one another, that we still sang now, even in freedom. No, in public, Louisa and Experience only sang in a foreign tongue, about springtime and love and offering apples to your beloved. But the college suggested they could raise more money if they sang the slave songs.

"There's that college out in Tennessee that's done it," Louisa said, worrying the cloth of her skirt. "And they've sung to the Queen of England."

Indeed, we'd heard of those singers and even tried to see them when it was reported that they were playing in Cincinnati. We'd even started out to make the long journey to hear them, but we'd turned around after half a day when the stationmaster told us it was not the real Jubilee Singers but a fraudulent group—four men and a girl who couldn't harmonize and made a mockery of not knowing the words.

"The group from Tennessee sang pain for the Queen," Experience said, in that strange hollow way she had, and this stopped both me and Louisa from speaking further as we tried to understand what she meant.

"They say the Queen gave them an ovation," Louisa countered. "She invited them to her palace, and they dined with lords and ladies." Even when she was impassioned, Louisa made everything she was saying sound like a joke, so I laughed at this.

But Experience shook her head. "I won't sing my sorrow for anyone," she said.

And then she blew her pitch pipe, to bring Louisa back to the music.

"She's stubborn, is all," Louisa explained to me, later. "She's thinking of herself and not of what can be done with what we have."

She took my arm in hers. We were crossing the square of dirt. The college president spoke to us all the time of the grass to go there— bright and healthy and cut short and orderly. Every Sunday sermon ended with his invocation of this future time, when the college and the men and women there would be so prosperous, so abundant, they would have a whole mess of earth that grew grass solely for strolling in, which no animal would eat from.

In the meantime, a few of the women students had sprinkled sunflower seeds around the grounds the previous summer, and now, in the spring, we could see the battered stalks poking up still here and there through the muddy snow.

"She's not thinking of all that singing could do for us," Louisa said, kicking at the flower roots.

"That's what you would do if the Queen said she'd give you a stack of coins to sing your pain?"

I was teasing, but Louisa stopped and looked at me gravely—one of the few times I ever saw her stop joking.

"Before I came here, I slept in the corncrib and I saw my mother and brothers sold. I sang for each one when they left me, but that's my own song, and I wouldn't sing it for a queen of anything. But this is the only home I have had or will ever have on this Earth. You can't just throw away a home. You do whatever you can to keep it." And then she took my arm again and walked me the rest of the road to the Gradys'.

There was a coldness between Louisa and Experience after that, and I saw them once, from afar, Experience loping a few feet in front of Louisa across the field, Louisa trotting to keep up. They sang together, but had stopped speaking, and it was awful to feel the silence returning, the silence coming back in, and I tried to think of something to make it stop.

I was not sure how to convince Experience. I knew my own mother didn't sing those songs. Her father did not pass them on to her. I only learned them from the women at the LIS, who sang them before, during, and after each meeting, who sang them to keep time as we did some tedious task, like piecing together the stitching in a quilt or rolling bandages. Sometimes, I sang the songs to myself with the words changed, to help me remember all the parts of a body—the names of bones and muscles and organs. I took a certain satisfaction in fitting those phrases into the loop of songs, the songs of work, the songs that made an art out of burden. But to say that to either Louisa or Experience, I knew, was a kind of insult.

IT WAS A few weeks later when the women's dean, Alma Curtis, asked to meet with me. She tapped on my shoulder as I sat and ate in the whispered companionability of the dining hall.

"Stay behind, Miss Sampson, if you will."

Alma Curtis was a broad-shouldered woman of forty-five or fifty— back then, I thought of her as old. She was the only married woman who taught at the college. Just the year before, before I had come, she had married the college president, Thomas Curtis. After they had said their vows in the campus chapel and pressed their hands in front of the minister, Alma Curtis had dropped to one knee and bent her head, and requested, in front of the entire college, her husband's permission to continue her career. And President Curtis had raised her up, cupped his hands underneath her elbows, standing her steady, and said, "Of course."

Louisa and Experience had repeated this story often—it was always whispered when Alma Curtis walked by.

I had asked, "But how long did he wait to say yes?"

Louisa had blinked. "What do you mean?"

"Did he agree right away? Or did he make her wait?" I thought of a long silence in the hall, Alma Curtis holding her breath while her husband decided her fate, the flowers on the wedding bower shivering around them. And then I laughed. "It sure was clever of her, to ask for permission in front of a crowd like that."

I had meant it in an admiring way. I had thought, *What a slick woman!* in the same way that, back home, Lenore applauded the barn cats when one of them swiped the biggest fish head.

But Louisa had looked at me coolly. "What a cynic you are," she had said. "I happen to find it romantic."

So I had learned another rule I had gotten wrong, and every time I looked at Alma Curtis, I tried to imagine her as an agent of romance— invisible cherubs and steadfast ivy curling around her everywhere she went. Which was difficult to think of, because Alma Curtis's broad, jaundiced, straightforward face seemed to discourage anything like that.

I thought of this as I sat at the table, watching the other girls work together to clear the plates and food. When the room was nearly empty, when it had gone from quiet to silent, Alma Curtis sat on the bench across from me.

"We must discuss your performance, Libertie," she said with unbearable kindness. "The other deans, they were hesitant to take on a young lady in the men's course. They were not sure if she would be able to keep up. But your mother assured us, we were all assured, that you were capable. I personally intervened with President Curtis and asked that you be placed in the men's course. And your work, when you turn it in, is passable. So, then, what is distracting you?"

I could not exactly answer. I could only swallow and say, "I am unsure. If you would give me more time. Perhaps it is being so far from home."

She said, "You spend an awful lot of time in the music room."

We let this sit between us for a moment.

"Yes. Yes. You see . . ." I licked my lips, readying for the lie. "You see, I've come to a sort of conclusion."

Alma Curtis looked at me skeptically.

"The Graces—that is, Louisa and Experience—they mentioned that President Curtis wished for them to found a chorale. In the mode of the Jubilee Singers in Tennessee."

"Yes," she said. "I am aware."

"And Miss Experience," I said. I figured the formal address would help my cause. "Miss Experience was uncertain about performing the slave songs for a different audience. For our white friends."

Alma Curtis looked unconvinced.

"She says she would feel distressed," I said, "to sing the slave songs in front of them."

Alma Curtis sighed again and under her breath said, "These young people."

"So . . ." I wet my lip. "So I have been formulating an idea. A compromise of sorts. That they could perform in Brooklyn, for the colored people there. I know that the women's groups are planning many celebrations for the summer. We could raise some good money. I could organize it. My mother has friends in Philadelphia and Boston who would gladly support. It would be a kind of jubilee."

Alma Curtis blew out a breath.

"If anything," I said, "it would help convince them that performing is possible. And then, perhaps, they would not be so shy of mixed company."

The dean sat back for a moment. "This is what's been distracting you?"

"I very much love this college," I said, "and wish to aid in any way that I can."

Alma Curtis shook her head. "You may love it," she said, "but I have come to tell you that you cannot return next year. We do not have a place for you."

I searched her face to see if she might regret it, if she might leave me an opening to argue. But there was nothing, not even pity, not even sympathy. Just resolve.

She patted my hand, and then she stood up, shook out her skirts, and walked away.

"FOR COLORED PEOPLE," I said to Louisa and Experience later that day. "The women's club my mother founded will organize a benefit, and you two will be the stars. Louisa, we can raise the money for your home. And, Experience, you will not have to sing your pain for anyone else but people who already know it."

"If these colored ladies are so rich," Experience said, "why can they not just give the money to the college? Why do we have to sing for them?"

Louisa snorted. "Can't get nothing without giving nothing. Anyone knows that."

"They'll raise more if it's a celebration," I said. "A talented duet all the way from Ohio? If it is new people in town, we can get our friends from Jersey and from outside the city to come. It will be a whole celebration. You'll see."

I talked so much and promised so much that I found, by the end of the night, that I had made myself out to be some sort of impresario and not a failure. I spoke and felt my mouth form these lies, my tongue wet with them. I could hear the desperation in my voice. I was certain they would doubt me.

But Louisa was smiling again, and Experience had allowed Louisa to hold her hand, and so it seemed they believed me, after all.

There was no time to feel shame. There was only the beat of blood in my ears as I spoke faster and faster.

At the Gradys' that night, when Madeline Grady had pulled herself and her children and her husband into their bed a few feet from me, I lay on the stones that had been my resting place for nearly a year and pulled a stranger's cotton stocking up to my mouth and screamed the song I had been trying to sing, falsely, all these months. The song of my anger and my sadness, the song that I knew I could never sing in front of the Graces—I did not want them to disown me. I sang it for myself only: a thin, high thing, ugly and satisfying. I sang till my throat was raw and dry, and white flashed before my eyes, till I was panting. And then I lay back on my stones and told myself I felt lighter.

Dear Libertie,

You have only written me of music and nothing of your studies. Miss Annie tells me that you are planning, with the ladies of the old LIS, a concert in the summer—I would wish to know about it. I hope you will tell me of it when you come to stay.

Emmanuel is eager to hear of it, as well. I fear he grows bored here, out in the country, as it is. But he does not wish to go downtown and he rarely travels to Manhattan.

I am most excited for you two to meet. I think you will find him an excellent brother in study. He is so levelheaded, so calm, so persevering, that it is impossible not to wish to work as he does.

It is strange to have someone in the house who is not you, who is not my daughter.

I am eager to welcome you here, to your home, to where you belong, before you leave me again for your studies.

I hope this is not a sign that my Libertie is leaving me behind.

Your

Mother

Di m' sa ou renmen, epi m'ava di ou ki moun ou ye

Tell me what you love and I will tell you who you are

I had not counted on the Graces' fear of death. By the time we reached Philadelphia on our journey back east, we had slept in the barns and sheds and church pews of smaller towns, and I'd thought they would be happy for real beds in the city, which Madame Elizabeth had promised we would find in her home.

Louisa saw the coffins first, and she reached for Experience's hand. I think Experience would have spit at me if she could have.

Madame Elizabeth stood in the center of her shop and watched them. "I did not take you girls for being superstitious. I know you are good Christians and you know the only haint is the Holy Spirit."

She had three coffins stacked alongside the shop's dusty brick wall—a large one, for men, a slightly smaller one, for women, and then the smallest one, for children, stacked at the very top. The room was divided between coffins and dresses—on the left, the stacked coffins, on the right, a headless, armless torso in a long muslin skirt, horsehair blooming out of its stitched shoulders, and a table scattered with bolts of cloth.

Madame Elizabeth had us sit at the hearth that straddled both sides, to recover.

"Lord, but you must be busy," she said to me.

"Yes, I suppose," I said.

"A full year of studies done. I am sure you are tired." She smiled and held my gaze.

I shook my head and looked into the fire. "But is Mama well?" I said. And then, "She seems to have aid in her new pupil—"

"Emmanuel, yes." Madame Elizabeth nodded. "A fine boy, from a good family. He and Lucien were the best of friends, before they left for Haiti. He is very handsome, too." She directed this to Experience, the lightest of us. I had forgotten how color-conscious Madame Elizabeth was. Experience, realizing she was the intended recipient of this information, blushed and cleared her throat.

"Yes, Emmanuel's all right," Lucien said. He had been sitting by the coffins, wiping one of them down with a rag, and had been watching the Graces with a smile that was not altogether kind. "I wish Emmanuel'd stayed down here with us. It would have made my life less dull."

Madame Elizabeth laughed. "More like you would have gotten into more trouble than you already do."

"So you see," I said, "Mama has no need of word from me."

"Oh, Libertie," Madame Elizabeth said, "you're a smart girl. You know you'd whip him in any contest. Especially after a full year at school. You do not ever have to worry of being crowded out of her affections. You are too old to be jealous of a person you've not even met."

I glanced over at Louisa, who was following the whole conversation with interest. Only Experience had the thoughtfulness to look away, embarrassed. She stared at the fire, working to suppress one more yawn, then stood up suddenly. "I fear, Madame Elizabeth, that we must retire," she said very carefully, in a low tone she used when she was speaking to older people.

They stood and embraced Madame Elizabeth, who stayed in her chair, and waved to Lucien. Then they were gone.

I turned in my chair and made a show of asking Lucien about himself.

He had remained as pleasant-looking as he had been ten years earlier, and I realized, with a start, that he was lightly flirting with me, though it seemed to be more for the amusement of his mother, I realized, then any sort of genuine interest. He made his jokes and verbal flips loud enough for her to hear and when one was finished, looked sideways for her approval. Madame Elizabeth would sally him on with a tap of her fan or a pull at her shawl.

In one of his moments of joking, he called me "Black Gal," and I shivered.

"Do you remember?" I said. "Do you remember Mr. Ben?"

"Oh, Daisy!" Lucien cried in a nasal falsetto, and then fluttered his hands. "But of course."

Madame Elizabeth narrowed her eyes. "That poor man."

"Do you ever wonder what happened to Daisy?"

"If there's any justice in the world," Madame Elizabeth said, "her soul's repented for all the pain she caused that man."

"But how is it Daisy's fault," I said, "if Ben Daisy was the one who chose to die for her?"

"Well, listen to you, Miss Libertie," Lucien said. His eyes shifted between me and his mother, sizing each of us up.

Madame Elizabeth tilted her head and held her finger to her chin, a practiced pose of concentration. Then she said, "Love is a mysterious thing, and a gift. A woman is a keeper of love, and when she does not take that duty as sacred, then things like that happen."

Lucien sighed. "You lose your mind and end up trying to make love to a river."

"You are terrible," I said.

"Glug, glug, glug," Lucien replied, and I saw, from the way his mother held in her laugh, that the joke was not a gamble.

I stood up. "I should go to bed, as well, Madame Elizabeth."

"Ah," Lucien said, "we've made you mad."

"Lucien, stop it." Madame Elizabeth held up her arms, and I stepped awkwardly toward her. "Good night. And say your prayers for your mama and me." Her breath was murky with the smell of tea and sugar.

Madame Elizabeth and her family lived above the shop. The stairway to get to their rooms was clammy, built into the brick of the house. At the top of the stairs was a short hallway, dim, with only one cramped window at the end, which faced out onto the street. I hadn't taken a light with me upstairs, and Madame Elizabeth had not offered one, so I moved along the hallway, my fingers running along the doors. I counted, one, two, three—Madame Elizabeth had said the third room was where we should sleep. I reached for the doorknob and turned it and pushed, but the door would not move.

I tried again, turning the knob back and forth, the iron becoming sweaty in the heat of my hand. I thought for sure Experience or Louisa would rise to let me in, but there was nothing. I scratched at the panel. "Louisa," I called. "Experience." Still no reply.

I held my ear to the door and heard the faintest shuffle, as if someone in bare feet was moving carefully. Then I bent down to the keyhole to look through. There was no candle, only the very faint moonlight from the window in the room. I could see nothing, really. But suddenly I heard someone on the other side of the door gasp, as if she had been holding her breath for a long time. I blinked once, twice. And then, again, nothing.

I stood up from the keyhole. And I think, then, that I knew. I looked at the doorknob in my hand, shook it idly, almost forlornly, one more time, and then felt my hand along the hallway wall until I was back at the cold staircase, and then down to Madame Elizabeth and Lucien at the fire. The two of them had resumed work on a cape, spread out before them at the table. Madame Elizabeth looked up, six pins between her lips, while Lucien stood beside her with a line to measure stretched between his hands.

"They were already asleep," I said, not sure how else to explain myself. "And I shouldn't wake them. It's been so long since they've slept in a bed. They need as much rest as possible before their performance."

Madame Elizabeth looked back at her work. "Well," she said, her voice muffled by the pins, "sit by the fire for a bit, and then you may sleep here if you wish."

And so that was where I fell asleep that night, listening to the hum of heavy scissors cutting through damask.

That sigh behind a closed door in the dark was a song I had never heard either of them sing before. It was the same song I heard, sometimes, while lying on the hearth of the Gradys' home, many hours after everyone in the house had gone to bed. When I'd heard it there, I had instinctively pulled my blanket tighter around my head, hummed what songs I could remember from rehearsal, and, sometimes, resorted to clearing my throat loudly, to make it stop.

But I had not wanted to make whatever was behind that door quit. I had only felt a pang of longing. I had never wanted to know something so badly in my life. Not even when I saw Mama make a dead man walk, not even when I stared at the river for a lost lady, had I ever wanted to know something as much as I wanted the knowledge of what, exactly, Louisa and Experience were doing—no, not what they were doing, but what they were feeling—behind that locked door. Longing to know what had caused that smallest, sweetest of sighs made me shut my eyes tight as Lucien and his mother lazily quarreled about the best way to attack the fabric before them.

When Louisa had said that home was in Experience's arms, and when she had defended Experience from every call questioning her coldness . . . they had been traveling to another country, I realized. They had lived there all along, while I stayed a citizen of this one, a land without sighs.

Mama, before I had left for college, had made oblique mention of what could happen to girls in school—"Girls, when they are left on their own, they become each other's sweethearts sometimes"—but she had told it to me as something her white-lady patients sometimes fretted about, and for me, she made it clear, it was only another possible distraction to avoid on my way toward greatness. She had not suggested it could be like this. A closed door with a mystery behind it that I could never know.

Up until then, I had told myself that my disgrace at Cunningham College was a blessing. I'd thought I could endeavor to make this trip with the Graces into a permanent state of being—I could become their manager, writing to the respectable colored ladies of the North and finding drawing rooms and church floors and forest clearings where the Graces could sing. The three of us would never have to return to the place of my shame—we could indefinitely live in the admiration of colored women who would otherwise have scorned me for the failure I had become.

I did not see how that was possible now. Because in my fantasy, Louisa and Experience would stay with me always, would never leave me—we would travel together; there would be no secrets between us. And eventually, with a long enough proximity, I would understand the covenant between them and enter into it on my own.

But there was no room for me there. Perhaps that was what I had been responding to in their voices all along—their desire. As wide as their desire was, it could not make room for me. I knew that. It was a bride song, a song for twin souls, for one mate to call to another. And I, a fool, had mistaken it for a song of federation.

And so I was alone again. On the wrong side of a locked door. An interloper in what I had been so certain would someday be my country.

WE WERE TO take the train to New York for the last part of our journey—Lucien and Madame Elizabeth accompanying us. We left early the next morning—Experience's cheeks flushing red at the sight of me, cramped in the same chair, by the fire, but Louisa looked up at me through her lashes and said, "You should have knocked louder, for us to hear you."

She was so bold that, for a moment, I thought that I was mistaken, but I noticed that as she said this, her fingers trembled, and so I only nodded and looked away.

The train used to have mixed seating, but at the station we discovered it had a newly implemented car solely for colored passengers. Lucien wanted to contest it—"I'll speak to the porter," he said, but Madame Elizabeth waved her fan.

"I am tired," she said, and Lucien fell back beside her, willing himself to swallow all of it.

Experience and Louisa tried to smooth over the ride by telling Madame Elizabeth how comfortable a train was, compared to a stagecoach—even Experience made an effort to say something merry, though all four of us were watching as something slowly ate Lucien up from the inside. He would not look at any of us, only at the country that rushed by the open window.

He seemed to recover by the time we reached New York. I had not
written to my mother directly, had arranged for the LIS to welcome
Experience and Louisa at the church. But when we arrived, there was my
mother, standing among the group of women, looking almost hopeful.

A year and a half away, I had not forgotten her face, but I was shocked
by the changes to it. Her hair was not as bright—it was fainter— not
yet given over to gray but closer to it than when I had left. And when
I stepped close to her, I saw that her face was threaded with a thousand little lines of worry. As I embraced her, I heard Madeline Grady's
instruction: *You've got to press the memory out.*

Even her embrace felt different—my mother's arms were not a place
I knew well, but in my recollections of them, her arms had always been
heavy and strong. They felt lighter now, and her skin, where it touched
mine, felt soft.

Is Mama ill? I remember thinking for one terrible moment, but then
realized, with a shock, the truth was more awful. I had not noticed her
age when we were together. But seeing her, after we were apart, all her
years on this Earth came down between us.

I pulled away.

"We have missed you," she said. And then she looked over my shoulder expectantly. "Is this your great cause, then?"

"Miss Louisa and Miss Experience," I said. I saw Louisa quickly
reach for Experience's hand and then drop it as they moved forward to
greet my mother.

"Libertie speaks so much about you," Louisa said.

"And this," my mother said, "is Monsieur Emmanuel Chase."

He was only a little bit taller than Mama. This is the first thing
I remember noticing about him. He had been there this whole time
while I embraced her, just back behind her elbow, but I had not noticed
him in the excitement of reunion.

He held out his hand, the other tucked behind his back, the model of a gentleman.

I took it.

He was most nearly white—Mama had been modest when she said he could get by. He was even lighter than she was. His hair was fine, but balding at the temples, narrowing back into a widow's peak, the rest of it slicked back with oil, though curling at the bottoms. His eyes were deep and wide-set and black, and his mouth was thin. This was because he sucked his lips in whenever his mouth was relaxed, a habit his mother had switched into him. When his mouth was allowed to fully rest, as it did in sleep, his lips were as full as any of ours, fuller even than my own. His mother beat him because his lips were, in her imagination, the only sign that he was a Negro. Holding them in or letting them loose was a choice between life and death, she believed. But I would only learn this from him later, when I lay close enough to trace his mouth's outline for myself, with my little finger.

"It's a pleasure to meet you," he said, and then he turned and said the same to Experience and Louisa. He had a trace of an accent, I assumed it was French, and this made him sound even more distinguished. I felt a pang of acknowledgment, that this was the person my mother had chosen to relish instead of me. And, of course, shame with myself, that I had proven my mother's doubts correct, that she was right to bring him in when she thought I might not see my schooling through. And underneath it, running as high and bright as a mountain stream, a longing that Emmanuel Chase should think well of me, which I hated myself for even wishing.

Lucien rushed forward to embrace him and slap him on the back. It was the masculine version of the hundred little flatteries he had directed my way to make his mother laugh, though now he seemed to have forgotten her entirely, focused only on Emmanuel Chase.

"Long time, old boy. Too long, old boy. What a sight, old boy," Lucien said, his voice curving up into an approximation of a gentleman—different from the voice he'd used on me and Experience and Louisa.

To which Emmanuel Chase only said, "Yes."

And for that, I felt another pang, that Emmanuel Chase was very politely making a fool out of Lucien in public, a pastime I had liked to do myself as a child. But my jibes had never landed, because Lucien had never cared what I thought of him.

At the house, Lenore played much cooler than my mother had. She said, "Oh, look, a ghost," when she saw me, forcing me to accost her with apologies and swears of devotion until she grudgingly accepted my embrace.

The house was full then, for once, in the evening, with Mama, Lenore, myself, the Graces, Madame Elizabeth, Lucien, and Emmanuel Chase, who, I noticed as we all sat down to dinner together, had taken the head of the table. Mama sat to his right.

"There won't be much time to rest," Mama said, "before you must begin preparations for the performance."

"The Graces can rest here during the day," I said. "I've already volunteered for the LIS." I waved my hands, a flourish, in front of me. "Behold, a mule."

This made Mama laugh, at least. Lucien, too, though Emmanuel Chase only smiled and kept his face close to his plate.

"And you must tell us," Mama said, "how your studies are faring and what the college is like and, oh, how are Mr. Grady and his wife doing?"

I had expected this, and I had a dodge—what I had learned from so many years as a doctor's daughter. That nobody wished to speak of any greater subject than themselves. So I turned to Emmanuel Chase and said, trying to keep the envy and the fear of him from my voice, "My studies are boring, but a doctor all the way from Haiti, that is much more fascinating. Mama has spoken of your talents, but she has not mentioned much of your history."

Emmanuel Chase laid down his knife and fork, as if he was about to make a speech. I thought, *At least I have guessed right about you. You are vainglorious.*

"My father was born free here, in Maryland, and my mother was a slave. She escaped twice, to join him—the first time, she and my three brothers were recaptured; the second time, she made it away, but with only one of them. In Maryland, she and my father had five more children—I am the youngest. My father joined the Church of England. They do not have much of a presence in Maryland, but their faith is strong.

"Even before war broke out, he wished to leave this country, but my mother would not hear of it—she wished to stay, in case my two brothers ever found a way to return to her. But my father could not see how colored people could make anything of ourselves here. He petitioned the church to send him to Haiti—the president there had promised land to any American Negro who could come. And my father was determined.

"Right before the diocese agreed to send him, we got word that my two other brothers had died—one of a whipping, from an overseer in Mississippi, and the other drowned while trying to cross the Delaware River. So we left, certain we would miss nothing back here. We left the same day war broke out at Fort Sumter, though we did not learn of it until we arrived in Haiti."

Emmanuel Chase spoke as if he had practiced this speech many times in his head and had warmed to telling it. He paused for breath, for gasps, for admiring sighs, and Madame Elizabeth and the Graces humored him. I noticed, though, that he seemed to take their noises as genuine—he was not so savvy as to realize that these were the sounds women learn to make to keep men talking. I thought, again, *I know you*. And I widened my eyes as he spoke, made my smile slightly bigger. Then an extraordinary thing: as he finished his first speech, as he said "arrived in Haiti," he raised his eyes to look in mine, as if to say *I know you, too*.

He paused to take a sip from his cup of water, and I lowered my eyes and kept them down as he continued.

"So it seemed my father had gambled well, and he was very proud. But, as you can imagine, it was quite a shock for a young boy such as myself to be spirited away from Baltimore to Haiti. The first year there was very hard—my brothers died, as did two of my sisters. Before the year was over, my mother died, too. That left only myself and my sister Ella. And my father, of course."

"I'm sorry," I said, but he just blinked and continued.

"The second year, my father was able to begin to raise funds for his ministry, and our farm there, and so life became a bit easier. My father remains there. I plan to return, as I hope all freeborn men do one day. Perhaps even Lucien will come, if we can tempt him."

Lucien looked up, momentarily shocked at this, but he recovered. "Leave Philadelphia for Haiti and the rule of Negroes?" he said, and rolled his eyes.

Madame Elizabeth laughed and slapped his arm, and I saw Emmanuel Chase's gaze harden, his lips grow even thinner.

"It's where our people's ambition lies," he said.

But Lucien shook his head. "My father's Haitian, it's true," he said, "but I am an American by birth, and I'll stay here in her land, if I please."

"You'd stay here even as they kill us for trying to vote? You'd stay here even as they cut us down in Colfax and in Hamburg?"

"We'll fight them back," Lucien said. "We'll win in the end. The white men will learn that colored people mean business."

"You have too much faith in white folks," Emmanuel Chase said.

Lucien said, "You have not enough faith in colored people."

"Do you know a story my father used to tell me?" Emmanuel said. "He used to work with a white family just past Baltimore. He would send people their way, when they were escaping. But he had to stop when one of them told them what the white people were doing—inviting slave owners over for dinner and then asking everyone to debate the slave question, together, at the table. Black men, scared and tired and just trying to run, forced to sit and prove how worthy they were to the very men who should have been apologizing to them—"

"Emmanuel," Mama said. If it had been me getting angry, Mama would have stopped the whole conversation. She would have tried to drown my rage. But here was only a very quiet "Emmanuel," which he ignored.

"You can't ever be free in a place like that," he said. "In a house that runs by those rules. I can tell you, no one in Haiti has ever asked for such an indignity. It is our own republic. It's for colored men such as us."

"But they are not Christians," Experience said. "They are papists."

"And cannibals," Lucien said.

Emmanuel looked pained, as if Lucien had reached across the table and slapped him. "Your father would let you speak of his country like that?"

"He is who told me this of his country!" Lucien said. "Colored people are a cursed lot, but at least in our good fortune, we are cursed in the good Christian nation of America, where good government and understanding of God prevail—"

"You say that as they riot any time we try to sit in a railway car," Emmanuel said.

"Those are only potholes on the road to progress. We will prevail. We have the tradition of good Anglo-Saxon law and fairness to guide us. Haiti has none of that. We could go there, I suppose, to raise them up—now, I agree with you on that. As good Christian Negroes, we should act as a mother to our race, to bring it up to manhood."

"But there's still so much to be done here," Mama said.

Emmanuel had that pained look again, the one that had creased his face when Lucien called his countrymen cannibals. It momentarily flashed across his face, and then it was gone, suppressed. He looked at Mama with polite interest, though I was beginning to think that underneath, he was burning the same way I did.

He turned back to Lucien. "None of us will ever triumph," he said, "until we are completely free." Emmanuel may have sat at the head of the table, but he would not have dared to say this directly to Mama.

"But what does freedom mean?" I said. I could not help myself. I had heard something in his voice then that I thought—that I believed, that I flattered myself, that I hoped—was only for me.

The table stopped to look at me. My mother, I saw, looked the hardest. It was as if she was seeing me for the first time. But all I could think was, *I have embarrassed her again. She wishes I was not her daughter, that clever Emmanuel was her son.*

I closed my eyes, wishing I had not spoken.

"It means," Emmanuel said, his voice shaking, either from excitement or dread, I could not tell yet, "that we are wholly in charge of our own destiny."

"And we seize it, apparently, with violence and blood," Lucien said, "if we are to follow the Haitian model. That does not sound like freedom to me. Freedom goes hand in hand with peace and harmony and prosperity. But did you ever notice"—he leaned over to Louisa—"how the lightest ones burn brightest for revolution? Why is that?"

"They're closest to freedom and can taste it, so they'll do anything for it," Louisa said, laughing. She had begun to relax and regain her playfulness.

Emmanuel Chase laughed along, but he wouldn't look at her. He only said to Lucien, "Revolution already happened there."

"Here, too. Twice," Lucien replied. "It's hard work, but we'll prevail. Colored men will be free. And in the meantime, I don't have to speak French."

"It would give your father great pleasure if you did," Madame Elizabeth said.

Lucien slapped his hand on the table. "Mwen se yon American."

"I did not know you were such a patriot," Louisa said.

"Oh, but I am." Lucien leaned back in his chair and began to sing the first few verses of "Yankee Doodle Dandy" in the nasal tones of a northerner. "Please join me," he said.

Louisa scoffed. "I have a voice to preserve," she said, which made the whole table laugh, except for Emmanuel, who sat back, quiet.

It was hard to get a look at him, because every time I glanced at his face he stared back at me.

My mother declared that the Graces should sleep in my room, with me, and Madame Elizabeth should sleep in her room, with her, leaving Lucien to sleep with Emmanuel in Mama's old examination room, which Emmanuel would take, now that I was home. As the sleeping arrangements were announced, I watched Louisa and Experience's faces, closely, but neither one gave anything away. I imagined that they held hands underneath the table, and I felt a rush of sadness. I cupped my own hand, under the lace tablecloth, around empty air, and imagined what it would feel like for another hand to rest there.

I did not want to be in the room alone with them while we all undressed and pretended that none of us knew what had happened. I didn't think I could bear to hear any of the excuses they would give for why they had not opened the door at Madame Elizabeth's. It felt, perhaps, even more lonely-making to know they had not trusted me with the truth. So I made a show of announcing I would sit on the porch for a bit before bed.

"I missed the garden," I told my mother.

Lenore tilted her head. "Leaving home really does change a person," she said.

But Mama gave an approving smile and kissed my head before taking her candle and leading Madame Elizabeth off, so that they could gossip in peace in her room.

I sat on the porch for a bit, listening to the saw of flies all around the house in the night. It felt like the world was still drowsy from the winter, nothing alive out there in the dark was at its full pitch yet. I counted one Mississippi after another, trying to leave enough time for Experience and Louisa. I grew uncertain, though, if I had waited long enough, and so I stood up from the porch and walked out into the yard, trying to see if the candle was still burning in my room upstairs.

I tilted my head back. I could see the flare of light, where the flame sat on the windowsill of my room. I sighed, waiting for when the two of them would feign sleep and I could return to lie in my own bed, a stranger among friends.

"You hold yourself like that and you could swallow the moon."

I jerked my head back, and there was Emmanuel Chase, coming down the porch steps to stand with me.

I think I'd known that it would be this way. I think, if I was being honest, I'd hoped that it would.

He smiled, pleased with himself for the bit of poetry. "My nurse used to say that to me, when I was little."

"A nurse?"

But he was not flustered. He nodded and drew a very short, fat cigar out of his jacket pocket. He sucked on the end but did not move to light it. Not yet.

"It is like that in Haiti," he said. "The better families have servants."

"Other Negroes?"

"The people who live in the country, yes. They're used to work like that."

I blinked.

"I sound hinkty," he said.

"You haven't forgotten that word, at least, with all the French you speak."

"No," he said. "I haven't forgotten. Wherever there's niggers in this world, you need to have a word for uppity."

I laughed at that, and he smiled wide again. It was a kind of agreement between us.

I stepped back to look up at the window again, to hide my excitement. The candle still burnt.

Emmanuel came to stand beside me and tilted his head back, as well. Then he said, his voice lower, so that no one in the house could hear him,

"My nurse, we learned to call her Ti Me. It means Little Mother. She would tell me stories about the gods. Haiti has different gods than here. They came from Africa, on the ships with the Negro slaves, and stayed—they did not forsake the Negroes there, like they did the Negroes here. They are always around us there."

"You weren't scared?"

"No," he said, still looking up at the window. "My sister was scared and thought it was all heathen nonsense. But I loved them. Ti Me told me a story about the god who has the moon. The goddess. 'Yon lwa' is what Ti Me would say. She is called La Sirèn—"

"Haiti has sirens then? Mermaids, like here?"

"She lives under the water, yes. She rules the oceans—she is as changeable as a wave."

I shivered. "I knew someone once, who used to speak nonsense like that."

He sucked on the end of the cigar again, a sound almost like a kiss, which made my stomach lurch.

"Really?" he said. "So you've already heard of La Sirèn, who is so beautiful she takes men underwater with her, who possesses her subjects and makes them walk as though they had fins for legs. And they gasp—oh, they gasp—because they cannot breathe air anymore, and the only way to get them to stop is to douse them with water. I have seen it myself, as a boy, in the temples Ti Me took me to.

"Sometimes, La Sirèn gets jealous and she'll drown a man and take him down under and teach him her magic. When he comes back to the surface, his skin is light, as bright as mine, and his hair is straight, and he knows all about the world."

"Is that why you look like that, then?"

He laughed. "But you told me you already knew all about her. That another man has already told you this tale. And who was he?"

I felt the grass, insistent, on the bottom of my shoes. I felt the calm cold of the night air. "There was a man my mother tried to help. Madame Elizabeth tried to help him, too. He was a funny sort of man—he stole away here before the war. But he couldn't abide freedom. It was almost as if he couldn't understand it. That sounds wrong, but that's how he acted. He said his sweetheart, who had long died, was here with him, that she wore pink and white and loved sweet cakes and that he only wanted to be with her. He became upset when he caught her with three wedding rings on her finger, so he claimed, and he drowned himself in the river. All because he was sick with love and freedom."

Even as I said it, I felt a roll in my stomach. I had never given Ben Daisy's history like that to anyone so plain. To do so felt like a betrayal of Mama, and I half expected her to throw open the house's front door and stare me down. But the door stayed shut.

"Ah," Emmanuel said. "That was not La Sirèn. That was Erzulie Freda. She is the goddess of love, and she is married to the god of the sky, the god of the ocean, and the god of iron. She loves hard and loves beautifully, but she is never satisfied. She ends every day crying for what she has not done, what she cannot have. Your poor man had no chance against her."

He hadn't heard me, I thought. Or he thought my story was part of our dance. Or maybe what I had said about Mr. Ben was too monstrous. Imagine telling a revolutionary like him that freedom made a man sick. I felt a burn of shame at my perversity. I wanted to be better for him. So I did not say, "You misunderstood." Instead, I said, "I suppose you are correct."

The window was still illuminated. As I remembered Ben Daisy, the song I had made up for him came back to me, as loud as the flies drowsing in Mama's garden.

When I looked back at Emmanuel, I saw he was watching me, in the light of the moon, with those wide-set, watery eyes. He was still sucking on the end of the cigar.

"Why haven't you lit it yet?"

"You have to taste it first, before you can light it. I brought ten of them from home, and have been trying to ration them." Then, still looking at me with interest, he said, "I save them for special occasions."

I thought, with a flash, of how he had watched my face as he gave his speech at dinner, that silly remark about the moon.

"There is nothing special about tonight," I said, despite knowing what he meant.

"But there is," he said. "It is very rare that I can meet a devotee of Erzulie herself, this far north, near the waters of a river as cold and muddy as one in Kings County."

"So I am a goddess of love, then."

"If you insist," he said.

It was a game I was no longer sure how to play. To be earnest seemed wrong. I thought of Mrs. Grady's hectoring. I was not quite up to that, either. Louisa and Experience, they were true with each other. *Quick, Libertie, quick*, I told myself. *Something clever.* But all I could say was, "Why are you interested, then?"

"My father thinks the Haitian gods are demons. He thinks it is his life mission to get every Haitian to Christ and to forget the blasphemies. But I think those gods are our genius. The genius of the Negro people. Our best invention. And Erzulie, the goddess of love, she's called with honey and flowers and sweet things, and she speaks to the longing, the desire for perfection in this world, and our sorrow that we will never achieve it. And I try to stay close to people who know her."

"But none of it is real," I said. "It was a thing Ben Daisy made up when he couldn't stand to be here. And I was just a child. That's why I believed him."

Emmanuel Chase finally struck a match and lit his cigar, and the heavy smoke rolled over both of us. "It was real enough to drown the man. I think it is remarkable."

It was my turn to speak, my turn to say something fascinating to him, but I could think of nothing. My bedroom window was dark now.

I only pointed up above, at the moon, just a sliver of white behind a black ribbon of clouds. He followed my gaze. He breathed heavily, and another gust of too-sweet smoke came over us.

"Good night," I said.

"Good night, then, Libertie."

Upstairs, at the entrance to my own room, I stood at the door for a minute, my hand on the knob, afraid it wouldn't turn. But it did, easily enough, and in the dark I could just make out the two rounded forms of the Graces, on opposite sides of the bed, a clear space between them.

I crawled into the space. Louisa turned and breathed in, then coughed.

"You smell like a bad man," she murmured.

Experience sneezed.

"It was Dr. Chase's cigar," I said, even though I knew she spoke in her sleep. "He smokes in the garden at night. Cigars he has to work up to taste."

"Hmm," Louisa said. Then she turned on her back, away from me. Experience turned in the other direction.

For a long time, I lay between my two friends' love, my eyes open in the dark, breathing in the smell of the night curdled with the stink of cigar through the open window, where Emmanuel Chase, I guessed, still stood below, smoking at the moon.

In those days, in Brooklyn, Tom Thumb weddings were all the rage.

The prettiest boy and the most docile girl of any Sunday school class would be chosen as the groom and bride. Churchwomen would spend weeks sewing a morning suit for the boy—silk and velvet cut down for a child's shoulder span. For the girl, a veil and train made comically long, so that she would look even smaller and slighter when she walked to the altar. To act as the reverend, they would ask the child who loved to play the most—one who could ignore his classmates' tears and keep the gag going with his comical sermon. People paid good money to see them, and to laugh at the children weeping at the altar, unsure if they'd just been yoked to their schoolyard nemesis for life.

This passion for children's marriages came on us quick after the war. It was a celebration and an act of defiance and a joke—we could marry legally now, even though we knew our marriages were always real, whether the Constitution said it or not. So real a child could know it, too.

Louisa had insisted we add one to our benefit.

"It makes the children cry every time," I said.

"We'll sing 'Ave Maria' to drown out their tears," Louisa said.

I looked to Experience, who shrugged. "They get to keep their costumes when it's over, don't they? Tears are a small price to pay for a new dress."

I'd laughed. "You are both hard women."

But I was not laughing while Louisa and Experience stayed at my mother's house, preparing their voices for the performance, and I stood in the church, six little girls lined up in front of me, four of them already weeping.

I grabbed the hot hand of the girl closest to me. "That's Caroline," Miss Annie called as I pulled the girl out of the church, past the graveyard, to the copse of trees where Ben Daisy used to wait for his love.

Now the little girl Caroline stood before me in tears. "Stay here," I ordered. I tried to be stern, but this only made her cry harder.

I knelt down and touched her shoulder. "You must know it's just for play? You won't really marry anyone. You just have to wear a pretty dress and walk down the aisle." Then, "Look, look here." I squeezed her hand once, then dropped it quickly and stepped ten paces away from her, until I was out of the trees, nearly to the graveyard's gate.

"Watch me, Caroline," I called. "This is all you have to do."

And then I counted to myself—one, two, three—and took the

exaggerated steps of a march to where Caroline, skeptical, stood in the shade. I held my head up and twisted my face into a grin, which, I realized, probably frightened her more.

"You walk and smile," I said through clenched teeth. "Walk and smile, and then you get to the front and bow your head and wait, and when everyone claps, it's over, and we give you sweets and flowers."

"That is precisely how marriage works," I heard from the set of trees, and there was Emmanuel Chase.

"Yes," I said. "Exactly that. Flowers and sweets. So what is the point of carrying on?"

"I don't want to marry Daniel," Caroline said. She had stopped crying and was watching us both with interest.

"It's the same as when you play with your sister or your friends," I said. "It's not real."

"That's not very kind to Daniel," Emmanuel said. "His heart will be broken."

Caroline looked at me uncertainly, her eyes threatening more tears.

"You confuse her for the sake of a joke," I said.

It had been all well and good to try to flirt with Emmanuel at night, while looking up at my window, my mother a few feet away. But it was less appealing here, in the woods, with only a six-year-old as witness.

Emmanuel Chase knelt down and said with great ceremony, for my benefit, "Listen closely to Miss Libertie." Then he stood up and smiled at me.

It was strange, to see the way Caroline looked at Emmanuel Chase— it was pure adoration, mixed with a little bit of fear. "Go on," he said to her, and Caroline closed her eyes and began to march, her knees raised to her chest, her arms stretched out in front of her, lurching toward me where I stood at the edge of the circle of trees.

When she reached me, she opened her eyes, her arms still held out as if she was balancing a great weight, and whispered, in a voice loud enough for him to hear, though she didn't wish it, "Is the white man still watching us?"

I lightly slapped her arms down. "Dr. Chase is a Negro, just like you," I said.

She looked at him over her shoulder again, to make sure, which he laughed at.

"Now walk back," I said, "slower. You do not have to lift your knees as high. March on my clap. And go slow."

When she reached Emmanuel Chase, he looked at her awkwardly, then reached out, turned her around by the shoulders, and sent her back to me.

So we did this a few times, sending Caroline back and forth between us, sometimes watching each other, until she grew tired. "I know it," she insisted. "I know it now. Let me be."

She did her slow, lurching march all the way back to the church, and then Emmanuel and I were alone together. By then, the shadows of the trees had grown long enough to reach me where I stood. I allowed myself to feel the cold for a moment, then stepped back into the sun. He followed.

We stood there, both looking at the church. Today, there were no props for him to play with. He looked almost nervous. It pleased me to imagine that I made him nervous. He raised one hand to his temple and then dropped it just as suddenly.

"I have thought a lot about what you told me," I said, to break the silence. He looked relieved.

"It really is remarkable," he said.

"This is where I used to play with Ben Daisy when I was a girl. But still, I don't know anything about the gods you talked about."

"Well," he said, "not many of us here do. But in Haiti, everyone knows them."

"Even the Christians?"

"Everyone's a good Christian in Haiti."

"I don't believe you."

"It's possible to be many things at once, Libertie."

I walked a little farther into the warmer part of the grass.

"You like riddles," I said.

"It's not a riddle. It's like the marriage you'll officiate."

"Another riddle," I said. "You aren't doing much to convince me."

"But it is," he said. It had caught his imagination now, and he turned toward me, eager to talk. "When a man and woman marry, they become one, correct? One being bound together, but two very separate people. They remain separate, but act and work as one, for the better of all."

"You are very modern," I said, laughing. "A woman remains separate from a man? She's not swallowed in him, whole, to replace that missing rib?"

I had found my rhythm with him now, I thought. I understood now why Madeline Grady teased so much. It made it easier to talk to a man if you pretended everything they said to you was false.

But Emmanuel Chase was hard to understand, because sometimes he became very earnest. As now. He reached out to catch at the tallest cattail and broke it off, then tossed it away, impatient. "I believe in companionate marriage," he said, rather proudly.

"So you are very modern."

"It is only logical that a man and wife should share friendship and charity and understanding. They should be friends for life."

This embarrassed me, and so I looked away. "That's where my father is buried," I said, pointing at the grave. FREEDOM stood out on it, as stark as ever, but his name had worn down, no longer deep in the stone but risen faint to the surface. "I do not know if it was that way between my mother and father, though it makes me sad to think she lost not only her husband but her closest friend."

"It is a pity. A house needs a man and a woman to function."

"I don't know about that," I said. "We did just fine."

He smiled, as if he disagreed but was too polite to say, and I felt a rush of sympathy for my mother, a wish to defend her.

"Was it like that with your parents?" I asked. "Were they companions?"

He didn't turn from my father's grave. "No," he said. "They were nothing of the sort."

And then he was silent, and we listened to the wind move over the grass and, behind us, an exasperated Miss Annie telling the children to quiet.

I was too embarrassed to ask him more. And he did not seem to want to relieve the silence; he stood in it as if it was the most comfortable place to be. Finally, I could not stop myself.

"Is it strange," I said, "being here in America, after so long away?"

"Everything is grayer. I had forgotten that. The trees, the clothing, the people's faces. Even the sun is grayer here than it is there."

"Is it so beautiful there?"

"It's a better world there," he said. "Or it will be. Very soon."

"You're not a patriot anymore."

"I am not as optimistic as Lucien or your mother," he said.

I looked up finally. He was staring at me again. "I never thought of my mother as an optimist."

"She is only that," he said. "What other word would you use to describe a colored woman who has so thoroughly decided to work with whites, who trusts the white women who come into her office telling tales about hurt spleens, but won't trust me to touch those same women with my bare hands?"

"They used to ask me to turn to the wall," I said, "when she was examining them. Mama said it was because they were jealous, that I was young and they were not any longer."

"I could understand that," he said.

He said, "When you blush, your skin glows darker somehow. It's remarkable."

"It should not be."

"You don't find this place changed, since you've been away?"

"I don't know," I said. "I missed it, I thought. It was mostly just—different. But now I am not sure I can call it home."

"Is that why you are now an impresario?"

"You can make fun if you'd like. I've never found anything truer in this world than Louisa and Experience singing. And the one thing my mother taught me, above all, is to fight for truth when you find it."

"That's very pretty."

"You are making fun again."

"No, it is very pretty. But also not true."

It was a thrill to hear someone outwardly doubt my mother. I had never heard it before, and a part of me leapt to him as he said it.

"She's taught you so many good things, though," he continued. "You probably got a better medical education as a child than I have now."

"I am not a very good student," I ventured. I almost told him right then, that I was disgraced. But then he said, "Oh, I find that very hard to believe," and I thought perhaps we were back in the language of flirtation, with no place for truth.

I wished I could be whatever it was that he saw when I stood before him. It was clearly not the same person that the Graces saw, or Alma Curtis or Madeline Grady, or even who Mama saw, when she looked at me. He looked at me as if I was a wondrous being, as if my voice was a song, as if I was magic. And I did not want to disappoint him.

By then, the sun had shifted, and we were on the cold side of the field again. He held out his arm to me, and I took it, and he walked me back toward the road, toward my mother's house.

"You are not at the hospital," I said. "Why?"

"It's too nice a day to be indoors." And then glanced at me. "Good, you don't believe me. I told your mother I wished to work on some notes back at the house, and when I was on the way there, I was lucky enough to see you and the little girl in the field. A happy coincidence."

"My mother lets you come and go."

"I'm not a servant here," he said, sounding offended, which seemed strange to me.

"She never did with me," I said. "I could only leave the clinic for errands. She said if I got too used to wandering off on my own, it would break my concentration. She knew it took me so long to work it up."

"So you were a servant then. The little scullery maid, forced to become a doctor."

"It was not so bad," I said. "If you were a girl given to that work."

We walked on a bit longer in silence. Then I took a breath. "Has my mother told you how she taught herself anatomy? When she was a girl my age, there was a cholera outbreak downtown. She followed the gravediggers for a day, until she found a baby's body, asked for it, and took it to her father's barn to dissect. She did it because they wouldn't let her work with the cadavers."

I am not sure why I told him this, this secret my mother kept. It was a story she did not even trust to Lenore, and only told me when my dedication waned, when she suspected I would not work hard enough, to shock me into diligence. It had worked, but I had told no one since.

Now I looked over at Emmanuel Chase. I had told him, too, to shock him, to see if it could shake that look off his face. But he was saying nothing, only looking back at me, as if what I had said was perfectly normal, as if he'd expected no less from me or from her. So I took an even deeper breath, and told him my greatest secret.

"I am not so passionate as my mother," I said. "I could not do something like that."

He nodded, and then he let his hand brush against mine and took it in his. We kept going like that, hand in hand, not speaking, only looking at the road laid out before us until we could see the turn for my mother's house. Then he squeezed my hand once and tossed it away from him. I thought, in this new language we were building together, that maybe it meant he believed I was passionate after all.

"Good afternoon, then, Libertie," he said. And he turned to go back the way we'd come.

I was at the front door again, but I could not bring myself to go in.

I had admired my mother, in her ability to use the people around her for greater good: the baby in the bush; Mr. Ben and his delusions; the matrons who funded her hospital. I had thought myself a coward that I could not do the same. I had burnt in anger at a physics of the world that my mother took as given. And even in that anger, I had failed to do anything, had been disgraced as a student. I was no one's promise.

But Dr. Emmanuel Chase still thought me good. Or, at least, thought of me as someone to admire. Mama had made it clear my anger was useless, unbecoming, superfluous in this world. But anger looked marvelous on Dr. Chase. It gave him a conviction, a heaviness, that he would not have had if he was sweet, if he was asked to be as polite as I was. He would be my avatar.

Through him, I could taste righteousness.

And he understood me. I thought.

To choose him would be to hurt my mother in a way I was not even sure of yet. I knew it would make a wound. I did not know then how deep, or how lasting.

I HAD BEEN a success in something after all, and there were too many people to fit into the church alone. The children would marry in the copse of trees, which we hung with garlands of flowers. Colored people came from Manhattan, from Jersey, from Long Island. Some even came up from Philadelphia, on the word of Lucien and Madame Elizabeth. The whole thing had turned into a kind of homecoming for the older people, some of whom had not seen one another since the war ended, who cried as they embraced, who walked together arm in arm, who stopped to whisper to one another or sometimes draw back to laugh at some change in fortune.

Sometimes, when I looked up from wiping a child's nose, I saw my mother in the crowd. She was on the arm of Madame Elizabeth, and the two of them were always in the midst of at least five other ladies. None of the former members of the LIS—that was not to be. But a few women stood gravely beside her as she spoke, and only allowed themselves to smile when Madame Elizabeth broke in and interrupted her.

Suddenly, Mama looked up and caught my eye, and I looked away. I crushed the purse at my side, just to hear the crinkle of a piece of paper there. It was a note, slipped under my door that morning in the small span of time between the Graces leaving the bed and when I turned over in sleep. The note was addressed to Erzulie, and it had been written in a hand I had not seen before but had known immediately who it belonged to.

"You need to say 'dearly beloved,'" I told Chester, the boy we had picked to play minister.

He looked up at me and twisted his face into a scowl.

"You need to at least try raising your hand at them," Emmanuel Chase called.

I raised my hand half-heartedly, but the boy had already jerked his arm free, and now he ran.

"You showed him your bluff," Emmanuel Chase said as he came closer. "You're too kind."

"You would not call me kind if you knew me."

"But I do know you, or at least the most important part of you," he said. "You are my Erzulie. You're the lover, never the fighter."

"You are very presumptuous."

"I know you," he repeated, still smiling. I wished he would repeat it forever.

I looked away from him, back out to the crowd. My mother still stood with her group of ladies, but she was turned toward us, watching.

"You cannot send notes like you wrote to me this morning," I said. I knew she couldn't hear us from where she stood—no one could have—but I dropped my voice anyways.

"I only write the truth."

"You should understand, I am not as sophisticated as you. I've only been from my mother's garden to her waiting room and back again. The only other place I know is the inside of an anatomy hall. I do not know the world like you do. You won't find a very satisfying game with me."

"You think I'm false."

"I think you are not hearing what I am saying."

"You've mistaken me if you think I only tease you. I wrote it to you, but I'd say it out loud to anyone here who'd ask. I'd say it even without their asking. You wish me to ask your mother now?" he said, and he turned as if to walk toward her.

I knew enough, at least, that in the next beat of the game I was supposed to grab his arm and stop him and laugh. But I stood with my arms at my sides and did nothing.

He turned on his heel and smiled wider. "You called my bluff."

"I do not understand you," I said. "You write declarations of love and marriage on the back of a scrap of paper I may not even see, and slip it under my door like an assassin, and then tell me your intentions are pure."

"So you read it," he said, "and it's true. I love and adore you, and wish you would be my wife. And you want to know if my intentions are good. I think that tells me all that I was hoping."

"I do not like games like this," I said.

Then I raised my voice to its normal tone. "We are about to begin. Excuse me."

It is a strange thing, to see something you have imagined over and over again finally acted out in front of you. It is almost like a kind of death, a loss of something, that the thing is not as you had thought it would be. I myself had laid out a path of pine needles, brown and dry in the July heat, from the end of the copse of trees to the stump of the altar. I watched Caroline shuffle down it, almost tripping over the hem of her too-long dress, to the little boy we'd chosen for her groom, who was looking not at Caroline or at the spectators who laughed and called out encouragement, but above him, at a cardinal in a branch of a tree.

When the child minister called out, "You may kiss the bride," the crowd began to laugh and jeer, but Caroline stepped forward, grasped her boy groom's head in her hands, and brought his face to hers in a cruel smack, which everyone cheered.

The Graces were to sing in the church, we had decided. But after the wedding was done, Louisa came to me. "We'll sing here, under the trees, where God and everyone else can hear us."

So Louisa and Experience stood side by side in front of a crowd of three hundred colored people. They did not look at each other, but before they began, Experience grabbed Louisa's hand and held it, and did not let go until the songs were over.

The sound they made, with just their two voices marrying in the air, filled the whole clearing.

My Lord,
        what a morning
My Lord,
        what a morning
Oh, my Lord,
        what a morning
When
        the
                stars
        be gin
             to
                  fall
You'll hear the trumpet sound
        To wake the nations underground
Looking to my God's right hand
        When the stars
        be gin
             to
             fall
You'll hear the sinner moan
        To wake the nations underground

Looking to my God's right hand
        When the stars
                be gin

                        to

                                fall

You'll hear the Christian shout
        To wake the nations underground
Looking to my God's right hand
        When the stars
                be gin

                        to

                                fall

You read in the Bible about the voice of God shaking leaves and commanding bushes to burst into flame, about trumpets making walls fall, about the songs that can sweep waves across the planet's face, but it is quite a different thing to stand in the heat of July, the smell of damp lace and pine sap and other people's bodies all around you, and know those words to be true.

By the time they got to "What Ya Gonna Do When Ya Lamp Burn Down," the crowd joined in—men, women, and children, singing and slapping hands and the bark of the trees—Experience and Louisa in the middle, still hand in hand, their voices rising above it all. I think it is the closest I have ever come in my life to seeing true love, and for a moment my sadness and anger were gone. I only felt the warmth of something fulfilled, and I closed my eyes to make it stop, because it felt too much.

The rest of the afternoon was the bazaar and the feast—long tables brought out and set with cake. Plates of oysters, too, which Experience and Louisa had never seen before.

"You tip them back, like this." I showed them, and when I held one up to Louisa's lips, she began to giggle. "That smell!" she cried. Experience pinched her elbow and then blushed hard, and they would not tell me anymore what it was about, so I drifted away from them, alone again.

Emmanuel Chase kept his distance from me, walking among the crowd, talking to the prettiest women and girls, laughing with the men. I thought, *Had we really stood under those trees and talked of marriage?* I could not believe, would not have believed it, to look at him.

"You are in-fat-u-a-ted." It was Lucien who sang this. There was a slight weave in his step as he moved toward me, slapping the rhythm on his thigh. When he reached me, he smelled the same as Madeline Grady's barrels of beer.

"You know this place is temperate," I said.

"Not over there it's not." He pointed behind the trees, where a man was making his way gingerly out of the underbrush, passing another who was stepping in. "They have one barrel there, not too much, just enough to keep us all toasty."

"You disrespect our mothers."

"You keep acting so sour, Dr. Chase will never look your way," he said, and then began to laugh.

"You should leave, Lucien, before your mother discovers you."

"You never leave their skirts."

"You do not seem too interested in that either."

"You shouldn't run after the first man who makes your blood roll like a river, Libertie."

"I will see you this evening, when you've sobered up a bit," I said.

I did not like to admit it, but Lucien had troubled me. I walked through the rest of the bazaar, stopping to look at the tables with things for sale. Some of the younger girls had knitted a set of fingerless gloves, and I spent time pulling them on and off my hands, becoming angrier and angrier at Lucien's presumption. My feelings toward Emmanuel could not be so obvious as he wished to imply. I was not anything that a person like that could easily know—a man who looked to make his mother laugh first, a man who couldn't hold his own after one mug of beer drunk under the trees.

I opened my purse and took the piece of paper out of it again. There was my own hand, writing out the events of this day. And on the back, the other script, the one I'd seen that morning.

To My Libertie

   This is a note to declare my undying affection for you. I wish, above all, for you to become my wife. I think, if you are being honest with yourself, you would wish it, too.

   Yours,

   Emmanuel Chase

Not even a bit of poetry, I thought. I admired him for that. For speaking plainly. For avoiding some terrible simile about my eyes, as someone as low as Lucien would have done.

"You are back," I heard, and then I turned and saw it was Miss Hannah, standing with Miss Annie, both of them looking at me with a friendly weariness.

"Yes," was all I could say.

In the years since her brother left us for the water, Miss Hannah had grown smaller, so that now she stood at Miss Annie's shoulder, Her back was still straight, but her eyes were nearly colorless. I had thought her old when I was a girl, but more or less the same age as my mother. Now, I saw she was much older.

"Studies suit you well," Miss Hannah said, and I reached out to grab her hand.

"I have thought of you and Mr. Ben often," I said.

It was the wrong thing. Miss Hannah's face broke, and she lowered her eyes, and Miss Annie looked at me, exasperated. But Miss Hannah held my hand in hers so tight that my fingers tingled, and she would not let go.

"Have you seen?" she said. "He's here, with us."

She would not let go. I put my other hand on top of hers, and she clasped her other hand over that, so that we were bound together. She led me away from the table before I could snatch up again my slip of paper from where I'd stuffed it, underneath the pile of empty gloves.

"Here," she said.

It was a wooden marker. It was painted with the name BENJAMIN SMITH—the name Miss Hannah had chosen for him and herself. Someone had painted wings on either side, but they were so clumsy they looked like crescent moons.

The church, at least, had given him a prized space, in the middle of the yard between two larger stones. Miss Hannah gazed at the plot as if her brother's body was really underneath it, as if he could rise up through the grass to be with us.

"I am saving up for stone," she said. "I had this put up last year."

She still held my hands in hers. "You are a good sister," was all I could manage to say, but she did not seem to wish for more. She only wanted me to stand in her fifteen years of grief, beside the play grave of her brother.

It was colder and almost dusk by the time Miss Hannah let my hand go and I could leave the graveyard. By then, the celebration had quieted. Some men and women lingered, eating the last of strawberries that had been set out. A few children, waiting for their parents, slept in a pile underneath one of the tables.

There was no sign of Emmanuel Chase. When I went back to the table to try and find his letter, it was gone. I told myself, even though I knew it wasn't true, that maybe someone had swept it away with the dirty rushes or packed it with their extra pairs of gloves. I tried to find Louisa or Experience to help, but I was told they had already headed back to my mother's house. So I started the walk from the church alone, my hands still pressed from Miss Hannah's grip.

The lightning bugs were out already. They darted all around me, sometimes deep into the fields, sometimes just a few steps ahead. The light was almost purple, and it made me wish that Emmanuel was beside me—if only to be able to remark on how strange and beautiful it was, if only to have a testimony. I slowed, as if I was walking arm in arm with a companion. It did not seem fair that this whole night was stretched before me and I was its lone witness.

I was thinking about this, about the ghost of Emmanuel beside me, when I came to my mother's house and I saw her, standing in the open doorway, the light from inside blazing behind her.

"Hello," I said, startled.

And she said, "You're lying to me, Libertie."

"It's not enough," she said, "that my only daughter has not spoken a word to me since she has come home. That she has hidden behind friends and acquaintances. That she has not even given me a report of her year—"

"I wasn't—"

"It is not enough that she has not come to visit our clinic, has

ignored my letters for months. But above all of that, I find she has kept
her worst secret from her own mother."

How could she know? I thought. *Who could have told her that I had
failed, that I was cast out of Cunningham College?* Briefly, I flashed in
anger upon Experience and Louisa. But I had not shared my disgrace
even with them. Who could have told my mother?

"You've lied to me. How long have you been lying to me?"

"I don't know what you mean, Mama."

"Stop! It makes me sick to hear it."

She had not moved from the door. She would not let me pass, I
realized with terror. I stood out in that night air that had seemed so
beautiful, so magical, just a minute ago. If only she would let me into
the house.

I started up the stairs, but she moved from the door to meet me at
the top step.

"How long? That's all I ask. I put the blame on you. How long?"

"Please, Mama, let me inside."

"I cannot trust you in this house anymore. How can I trust you
even to sleep under this roof?"

I began to cry. "I am sorry, Mama. Please forgive me."

"I can't even trust those," she said, her voice thick. I realized, with a
start, she was crying herself. "Your tears are lies, too."

"Please, Mama, just let me inside, and I will explain. I will explain
everything."

"You cannot sleep here," she said.

"Please!"

"I cannot trust you underneath this roof."

I do not know how I managed to be on the ground, but I was. I had
sunk all the way down into the earth, and could only double over and

cry. I knelt like that until I heard the swing of her skirts as she came down off the porch, as she stood over me. I could smell her perfume, the smell of the lemon juice she used to bathe her lily petals and keep her skin soft and bright, the hot cotton of her waistcoat—my mother's good graces in the air around me.

And then she thrust something small and crumpled up underneath my nose.

In that queer purple light of the evening, I could just make out *my wife . . . you would wish it, too . . . Emmanuel Chase.*

"What is this?" I said.

"I am not a fool, Libertie. So do not treat me as one."

I took the paper from her hand and turned it over in my own.

"This is what's upset you?"

"You've compromised your honor with a man who lives in my house. Of course this has upset me! Have you lost your mind?"

She did not know. She did not know that I had failed. I heard myself give a short, hoarse laugh. And then she slapped me.

My mother had never hit me before. Even as a small child, she had not swatted me—only Lenore, on rare occasions, had done something like that. I cannot say it even hurt very much—her blow landed soft, like a brush of silk, as if she had changed her mind between raising her arm and swinging it down.

When it was done, we both could only look at each other in surprise.

She recovered first. "I cannot believe you could be so foolish."

"I haven't done anything."

"You have ruined your future. You have spoiled our plans."

I laughed again at that, in the same hoarse voice, which sounded foreign, even to me. "They're already spoiled."

She raised her hand again. "Don't! Don't tell me if you've sunk that low! Don't say it!"

I should have said, *I am a failure, but not in the way you think.* I should have said, *I cannot pass a simple anatomy class, and even if I raise all the money in the world from Tom Thumb weddings and girls singing, Cunningham College will probably not want me back.*

Instead, I said, to the dirt beneath me, "I will never be a doctor."

She sank down beside me. She was there on the road beside me, in front of our house, and her face now was merely her own, the moonlight masking the changes that had shocked me when I first saw her that day. My mother.

"You've given up your dream."

"It wasn't mine," I said. "You dreamt it for me."

"It was ours."

"I cannot join you," I said. "I am sick of the smell of other women's blood, Mama. Please."

"So you'll leave me," she said. "So you chose your body over your mind. So you were weak."

"I am weak. But I did not fail you like that. Dr. Chase has been nothing but a gentleman. I have conducted myself with honor with him—"

"I have no reason to believe you," she said. "You've already proven yourself a liar."

She sat back in the dirt. Then she lay all the way down in the dust until she was looking at the night sky. We sat like that: Mama seeing stars, and me not daring to raise my eyes from the dirt, until she sighed heavily and settled even deeper into her skirts.

"I gave you too much freedom," she said. "So much freedom and you gave it up for the first bright man who smiled at you."

"I don't want him, Mama."

She took my hand in hers, still staring into the sky. Her voice was smaller now. "I know these tricks, Libertie. I hear them every day from the girls and women who come into my clinic, all big with child from a man who's left them. They tell me, even then, 'I don't want him,' but it's only to save their dignity. You think he will do this to you, too? I should know that, at least."

"He hasn't done a single thing to me," I said. "And I assure you, I don't want him to."

"You think it's love," she said. "Maybe it is love. But it is quite a thing, to be a wife. It is not the same as a lover. It is not the same as a doctor—"

"I know that, at least, Mama."

"It is definitely not the same as being a free woman." She turned to me, her eyes shining. "This is your ambition? You could be so much more, Libertie."

"No," I said, my voice thick with tears. "I can't."

She gave a ragged cry, the most terrible sound I have ever heard in the world, and if you would have told me as a little girl that I would have been the one to cause my mother to make that sound, I would have called you a liar. But here I was, beside her, as she sobbed.

"Come, Mama." I pushed myself up, to stand above her. She looked so small in her circle of skirts, her head bent. I leaned down and pulled her up by her elbows. "Come, Mama. I am not lost to you yet. I will not marry him, if it makes you cry," I said. I would have said anything to get her to stop making that sound. I got her to her feet. I put my arm through hers. I walked with her slowly, through the yard, up the steps, through the still-open door.

It took a moment to realize we were not alone in the room. There was Lenore, and our houseguests—the Graces, Madame Elizabeth, Lucien, and Emmanuel Chase himself, who stood at the mantel, a look of nervous expectation on his face.

He stepped forward. "You told her?" he said. I realized he was speaking to me.

"She discovered on her own," I said.

Mama stepped forward and held out her hand. "Congratulations," she said.

As Emmanuel reached to take it, she doubled over, a stream of sick splattering the hem of her skirts.

And that was how we announced we were to be married.

EMMANUEL SAID WE could always elope. "We do not need to stand up before your mother and family. We could be married by a judge and leave for Haiti as soon as possible." But I knew if the mere mention of marriage had made my mother sick, it would possibly kill her if we brought more humiliation through an elopement.

So we planned for our wedding. Quickly, because in my harried scheming, I'd figured it would be another two months before Cunningham College's letter informing my mother that I was not welcome back would reach the house. If I was safely married by then, and on a ship to Haiti, I could spare myself the exquisite pain of seeing her further disappointment. I was a coward in that way.

It seemed to me marriage was as good a plan as any other. I would not be a doctor, but I could perhaps be a wife. This optimism sprang from the fact that I was still not sure what a wife would be, but I knew what a doctor was and that I couldn't be one.

We were to be wed quickly. Madame Elizabeth announced she would make my wedding dress and wrote to Monsieur Pierre to tell him she would not be home for another month. She installed herself in Mama's front parlor, with a ream of white cotton and one long panel of lace that we had managed to buy, which she assured me she would drape across my shoulders.

All of the preparations I had made for the play wedding just a few weeks before suddenly became real. We were to be married in the same circle of trees, as close to my father's grave as possible. I had insisted on that for Mama's sake, but my mother had looked at me blankly when I'd told her, then nodded. She was not speaking to me. She nodded or shook her head, but she did not share any words with me. She continued to speak to Emmanuel—with him, she kept everything the same—issuing him orders for the clinic, conferring with him on patients, showing him the books. It was only I who was enveloped in silence.

Madame Elizabeth tried to talk with her. Emmanuel himself asked her to please stop. But she would only say, "I'll speak to my daughter again on her wedding day."

The Graces had left by then. They were committed to two more dates in the North—one in Hartford, Connecticut, and one in Florence, Massachusetts. We'd watched them leave for Manhattan, and as the boat pulled away to cross the East River, I tried to remember that I had never fully belonged to them at all. I had always been left out. Emmanuel took my hand as he stood beside me. I told myself, *Soon, you will belong to him*, and the thought was both thrilling and made me sad. If you would have asked me then what my heart's desire was, it would have been to be with the Graces on a ferry or in a coach, maybe thinking pleasantly about Emmanuel Chase but not anywhere close to him in reality.

When we could no longer see the ship, we walked back downtown to Mama's hospital, to where Emmanuel now slept, in the red velvet waiting room of the clinic. He had agreed to leave my mother's house the night our engagement was announced. "Believe me," he had said to her as he held his bags before him, "I meant no disrespect to your household, Madame Doctor. You have been nothing but—"

And Mama had cut him off. "I believe you," she'd said, and he had been so relieved he did not hear what I had heard, the words unsaid, which were that she believed him—but not me, her own daughter.

Emmanuel and I allowed ourselves a half hour visit each day in the waiting room, when it had closed for the afternoon, while Mama and Lenore, on the floors above us, set the clinic right for the night. We would sit in that parlor, and Emmanuel would tell me what would come to pass in Haiti.

"In Haiti, you will meet my sister and Ti Me."

"In Haiti, Papa will be the first to greet you."

"You'll learn how to say that word, once we are in Haiti."

And I could almost believe him, I desperately wished to believe him, that the future was a promise. But then I would leave him and go back home.

Madame Elizabeth did not, of course, have her dressmaker's dummy in Kings County, and so instead she laid out the pieces of my dress on the parlor floor. Every night, there was a bit more to my bridal costume, and I would come back from my talk with Emmanuel and see it where it lay, deflated, on the floorboards, a kind of skinny ghost of my life to come. It made me sick to see it all flat like that. A bad omen.

"Put it on me," I told Miss Elizabeth, and she laughed. "I've never seen a girl so eager to be a bride."

The night before the wedding, Emmanuel Chase came for dinner, and it was almost as it had been when we had first met. Mama stood at the top of the table and raised her cup and toasted both of us. "A happy marriage to my Libertie," she said, and I felt the tears run down my face in gratitude that she had seemed to forgive me.

But when I went to embrace her later that evening and held her close, she whispered in my ear, "Don't do it," and I realized that she would never bring herself to forgive me, and I went up to bed cold.

Emmanuel Chase stayed the night, since he did not wish to travel back to the clinic so late. I lay in my room, feeling the heat creep back up my bones, imagining that I heard him crawling up the stairs to scratch at my door and beg for . . . what, I was not sure. I knew what happened in the marriage bed. I had known since a young age—Mama had not been shy about that. I thought of what would happen the next night and kicked the sheets off—they suddenly felt too heavy.

In the last week, our time together in the parlor had become something else. It was no longer a telling of what would happen once we got to that country I still could not quite imagine. Our time had become a kind of war between ourselves—or rather, a war of both of us against desire. I did not think a man could make the sounds that Emmanuel Chase made, as he reached first to grab my shoulders, then my arms, then my forearms, then my hands, where they rested in my lap—too daring, that. Then back to my shoulders and then my neck, which he pulled close to his, forcing me to bend my head toward his, as he desperately moved his mouth. I would watch him do all this and realize, with amazement, that I was doing the same to him, holding with the same urgency to his neck, mirroring the movement of his lips with my own.

And then we would hear a step above us, or Lenore or Mama drop a scalpel, or the sound of a canister rolling across the floor, and we would separate—those last few days, I'd heard him gasp as we did so—and pull apart, and sit in the velvet again, to quiet our breathing.

So I lay awake and waited to hear his fingernails draw across my door. But all night long, there was nothing.

At dawn, I rose. I could not stand lying there anymore. I crept down to the parlor and knelt on the floor, running my thumb up and down the seams of the wedding gown. Madame Elizabeth had stitched them with such care I wasn't even sure where they were. I discovered one stray tuft of a thread, and I almost pulled it loose.

That's how Madame Elizabeth found me when she came down an hour later. "You waste time in fancies," she said. "You only have so many hours in your wedding day." And she had helped me stand, directed me to the bowl of water she'd set out for my bath.

When I put on the final dress, the armpits and the neck immediately darkened, sweat leaking into tight cotton.

I was standing in the parlor, my arms above my head, as Madame Elizabeth dabbed underneath them with bicarbonate of soda, oohing and aahing about her progress, when Lenore rushed in.

"It is Miss Hannah," she said. "She's breathing heavy and almost gone."

So Mama and Emmanuel both left the house—Mama in her nicest shawl, and Emmanuel half-shaved. "I can come, too," I said, but neither stopped to tell me no; they were both already on their way.

Madame Elizabeth looked at me, full of pity. "It's probably best for you to stay here."

The house was suddenly quiet again, without them. It was almost like the old days. I lifted the hem of my skirt and headed toward the garden. "You'll spoil it!" Madame Elizabeth called.

I turned my head to look at her. "I won't."

Lenore had taken good care of the garden while I was away. I saw my mother's hand on the little pieces of wood she'd stuck by each row, and below it, sometimes, in Lenore's, a drawing of the leaves in question. I squatted, just enough, over the grass. I closed my eyes. I breathed in.

Mama still grew pansies. I picked the pinkest one, pulled it from its stem, and rolled the petals between my fingers till they tore apart. They left a stinging stickiness, made the palms of my hands dry and thirsty.

I held my palm to my nose, smelling my skin and the petals. I lifted my open palm to my mouth and licked it clean, each finger carefully, the bitter taste of flowers on my tongue. I reached out, with both fists, for the heads of more flowers and crammed them into my mouth. Did not the Bible say, *My beloved is mine, and I am his: he feedeth among the lilies?* I rolled petals over my lips and between my teeth until my mouth was sour with them. I'd read so many poems comparing beauty and love to flowers, but no one talked of how much they actually stung your tongue.

My haunches ached, from squatting. Finally, I stood up, placed my hand on the small of my back, and stretched backward to keep the hem of my gown out of the dirt. Then I left the garden and went back up the stairs, to wait for my groom and my mother.

Our wedding, I do not remember well. I only remember the sadness and shock from the loss of Miss Hannah. Madame Elizabeth and I cut the hem of one of Mama's old cloaks and tore it up into black arm-bands. Mama wore hers on her right arm, and I wore mine on my left, as she walked me down the aisle.

"A wife truly is a helpmate and a pillar," Reverend Harland said as Emmanuel and I knelt before him. "She is obedient to her Lord, her husband. We cannot raise up a great nation of man without a loyal and obedient wife and mother—as she stands, as she decides, so stands and decides the fate of the Negro people. The redemption and the triumph of the Negro race will come from the hearth, will come from the home, and will spread from there to the ballot box, to the pulpit, to the world. A wife holds the world in her lap and hands it to her husband."

While he spoke, Emmanuel and I looked straight ahead. I could see, from the corner of my eye, Emmanuel bend his head at the word "lord" and not raise it again till Reverend Harland pronounced us married. Then I turned to him. He kissed my cheek, and there was a smattering of subdued applause. He helped me to my feet, and we walked down the aisle, arm in arm, the whole church watching us.

The heat did not break. We stood out in the sun while the men shook Emmanuel's hand and the women looked from him to me and back again and then at the waist of my dress, trying to determine if it was thicker than it had been a month before, trying to find a reason we had married so hastily or even, I saw in the petty flash of a few eyes, why he had married me at all.

Our wedding night, we slept the same we had the day before—myself in my own bedroom, my husband down below. There was a moment when Lucien had leered and Madame Elizabeth had nudged Mama—"Perhaps we should leave the house to the newlyweds"—but Mama had looked so stern the joke had died, and so no one had tried to test her.

I lay as I had only a few hours ago, restless in bed, even the thinnest of sheets oppressive. Except now, there was the scratch at the door I had waited for. I opened it, and Emmanuel stood before me. In the dark of the hallway, his skin gleamed, so pale.

"We will wait," he said. "It is enough to wait." And then he leaned over and kissed me, this time full on the mouth. "You taste of flowers," he said.

"Flowers taste awful, you know."

He smiled at me, until I returned his smile, and then he left my door.

We were to leave in three days for Haiti, accommodations Emmanuel had worked so hard to secure as soon as I'd accepted him.

Vrè lanmou pa konn danje

Real love knows no danger

Because our ship was headed to Haiti, there was no embarrassment about our berth. On Haitian ships—at least this one—colored people were allowed cabins. Already, this world was better. The ship's captain knew Emmanuel's father, and so we had a private cabin, given over to us with much winking and nodding, so much that I could not look anyone on board in the eye.

Mama did not come to see me off—she took her leave at her own front door. Lenore was the one who stood on the pier below us and waved the white handkerchief for us, the last little bit of home I would see for a long time, maybe until I died. That thought brought a sharp taste to my tongue, a tightness to my throat. Not tears, because I had promised myself I would not cry about saying goodbye to that world, Mama's world; I had promised myself I would celebrate. I saw Lenore's handkerchief flash once more, and I turned my head to spit into the ocean, to get rid of that acid within me.

I spent the rest of the afternoon in the cabin. I was seasick. I did not know this about myself, as I had never traveled for so long on a boat before. It made me hate water and curse waves as we were rolled around over and over again. My head had a dull ache. Sometimes, Emmanuel would bring me cups of musty water, flat beer, sour cider. I could not eat the biscuits and dried fish that everyone else did. Even the sight of the curled tails, studded in salt, made me turn and be sick. I was miserable.

The only relief came at night. That first one, Emmanuel lay beside me, stinking of petrified fish, and told me to lie down on my stomach. "Take off your nightgown," he said.

I should have felt scared or shy. If I was a good woman, I would have felt trepidation at the first person besides Mama to see me whole. But all I felt was the roll of the waves, and relief that I could get the muslin off my sweaty skin.

I shut my eyes tight while he traced a botany lesson on my skin with a single finger

"Dorstenia," he said. "It looks like a tiny tree, crowned with a shooting star. You do not have trees like this, in America. It is a cousin of the fig. Its flower isn't soft and inviting . . ." Here, his finger traced all the way down to my hips, where they met my thighs, lingered there, then made its way back up. "Its flower is hard and standoffish. It is called a 'shield flower.' Its face looks like a wall of stone. But when you look more closely, you see the flower is made up of a hundred little blossoms, all closed off tight." He had reached my shoulders again, spread out his hands, felt the strength of my back.

"Why do you tell me these things now?" I asked. "You do not speak like a lover." I at least felt calm enough to tease.

"Because as my wife," he said, "there will be a whole new knowledge to learn, to aid me, and we may as well begin now."

His voice was light, so I opened my eyes and saw the shape of him roll above me, before I closed them again, still cowed by the waves.

"But what if I am too sick to remember?"

"I'm not speaking to you. The lessons are not for you. They're for your body. She will remember." And then I felt his hand again, in the middle of my back, drawing, I suppose, the flowers that made up the shield of a Dorstenia.

He touched me until his fingers trembled. I shut my eyes even tighter, pressed myself into the hay mattress of the berth. His fingers lifted, and then I felt him turn over, onto his own back. He breathed hard and heavy, as if he was at a gallop, and the sheet that covered us began to shake.

I opened my eyes, sat up on my elbows, and watched him.

A man touching himself is a peculiar thing. My mother had told me about women's bodies but not men's. I'd seen male members on barnyard cats before, and sometimes rude and red on a stray dog. I remembered, once, glimpsing one, folded over on itself in a nest of gray hair, between the legs of an old man whom Mama helped to dying. I'd been six or seven then, and Mama had had to ask me three times to hand her her bag, before she'd looked up and followed my gaze. She'd pursed her lips, pulled the man's cloak over him, and said, "You shouldn't make patients uncomfortable with staring, Libertie."

At Cunningham, in anatomy class, they had asked me to leave the room during the lessons on glands. I'd leaned against the side of the building, staring out into the unfinished green, listening to the muffled voice of the professor calling out the body parts. When the class was done, the men had left and I returned to the room, alone, to the lesson written on the chalkboard, to name the parts to myself. Since no one was in the room with me, I'd practiced saying them in different voices—high-pitched, like a superior lady's, or low and growly, like a cat's.

I watched my husband's hand move faster. In the dark of the cabin, his skin was so dim—like a gray stone glimpsed at the bottom of a well. His breath shuddered. The whole cabin, so close, became nearly unbearably hot. And then he groaned—like a body taking its last breath—and shuddered one more time and was quiet.

I looked at him. He was staring glassily at the beams of the ship. "I'm sorry, my love," he said. When he reached to touch my cheek, his hand was damp.

I did not leave my bed the next day. I tried to stand in the cabin, but the roll of the ship nearly forced me to my knees, so I crawled back into the berth and shut my eyes.

Emmanuel left me to walk on the deck. Above the groan of the ship as it moved through the water, I heard his high shout or some of his laughter.

The ship was a trading one that sold only a few berths to travelers. In the morning, he pulled me out of our bed to walk the deck with him. He said, "You cannot lie down forever. It will make everything worse." My legs did not feel like my own. I was scared, and I took just a few steps before going back down. I did not know if there were any other women on board, or if there were, if those women were colored. And in my sickness, I did not have the will to ask him.

That night, he did not even have to ask me to lie down. I did so gladly, eager to feel something besides the waves.

"Plumeria," he said, "are beautiful flowers. Long and thin and white. They look almost like stars, or maybe the legs of jellyfish. They could be as at home beneath the water as on land. They smell strongest at night." Here, he leaned over and smelled my lap.

"The smell is beautiful," he said. "So beautiful that three hundred years ago an Italian count stole it from the isles and made it into a perfume. The flowers make it to lure in sphinx moths, to do their pollinating for them. The moths are driven mad by the scent, looking everywhere for nectar, but the flowers are a flirt. Like my Libertie sometimes is. They have no nectar, but they've convinced the moths to do their propagating for them."

And here, his fingers stopped trailing on my spine and swept down, and his whole hand grabbed my behind.

He was already touching himself. I turned over, and he knew I would watch him, so he looked into my eyes, his face looking first furious, then frightened, and then so melancholy I worried he would weep. He finally closed his eyes. His shoulders shuddered, he groaned again, like the ship in the ocean, and then he was still.

I was determined to walk the whole ship the next morning. I did so on my husband's arm—he took me to the front and the other end. He made a show of calling me his "dear wife." He said, "We are to live in Haiti." I realized that the white men on board were mostly Northerners. It probably had not occurred to them, until that moment, that Emmanuel was colored. A few of them looked at him as if he had played some sort of trick. They, perhaps, had taken me for some sort of concubine. The crew was mostly Negroes—some American, but most from Haiti. They said, "Trè bèl" when they saw me, and tipped their hat if they had one.

There was one other woman on board, a white one, the captain's daughter. She looked to be my age, maybe a few years younger. She looked straight through me when we passed, made a show of looking straight ahead.

"How much longer is the trip?" I asked Emmanuel.

"We have been on this journey for five days," he said. "We have eight or nine more."

Before us, the sea stretched in all directions, the water a deep green. "Do you see there?" he said, leaning in to point, his cheek on mine. "Look over there. Dolphins jumping in the waves."

It only looked like flashes of light, and I told him so.

"No," he said. "They're dolphins."

"Or maybe they are sirens," I said "come to lure all these men to their deaths."

"La Sirèn has a song," he said solemnly. "They say her home is at the back of the mirror. In the other world."

He did not move his mouth from my ear. Instead, he chanted into it,

La Sirèn, la balèn,
　　Chapo m' tonbe nan lanmè.
　　　　　　　　M' t'ap fè yon ti karès ak La Sirèn,
　　Chapo m' tonbe nan lanmè.
　　　　　　　M' kouche ak La Sirèn,
　　　　　　　　Chapo m' tonbe nan lanmè.

"What does it mean?"

"You have to guess."

"I do not know your language well enough yet."

"And you'll never learn it with that attitude."

"Tell me what it means."

He leaned in close again. He had been waiting for this. I had played the game he wished, without even knowing it. "You'll learn tonight."

That night, he told me to lie on my back this time. As he pushed my nightgown down past my shoulders, I covered my face with my hands. He said:

"*The mermaid, the whale,*
"*My hat falls into the sea.*
"*I caress the mermaid,*
"*My hat falls into the sea.*
"*I lie down with the mermaid,*
"*My hat falls into the sea.*"

I saw Ben Daisy's hat, covered in pansies, held to my mother's chest. I pressed my fingertips into my eyelids until the image was washed over in an explosion of stars.

"Take your hands from your face, Libertie."

I did what Emmanuel asked. We stared at each other for a minute, listening to the water move beneath us.

"Take off your shirt," I said to him finally. He did not break my gaze as he obeyed me.

His skin looked so smooth in the dark. I reached for it, to run my hands along it, and he drew his breath in, sharp, as if I had burnt him. And then he caught my hand in his and firmly placed it back at my side.

"What we do together, the word for it in Kreyòl is 'kouche.' It means to make love, but it also means to be born and to die, and to lie down, too."

"All those things at once?"

"All those things happen when we lie together. You must have felt that."

I looked at him. I twitched my hips, impatient. "So begin, then."

"Dogs' bloodberries." He reached for my breasts and began to softly touch them.

"What are those?" My voice was faint.

"They are little red berries—peppers, really—that grow at home. Women take them for their wombs—with the plant you have, vervain. It waters them. They become fertile."

"You are very poetic," I said. "For a doctor."

I disobeyed him. I touched the skin on his chest as he knelt above me, until he doubled over himself and shuddered, the wet of him falling across my thighs.

It was strange, to stand with him in the mornings, in daylight, in the middle of the ocean, and act as though what had happened between us at night had not happened. I could see, in the glances of the crew members, in the eyes of the white men on board, that they had guessed what we did at night, had imagined something even more. But here was Emmanuel, walking me carefully up and down the deck, as if he hadn't wiped his seed on my skin at dawn.

We were four days from landfall when it happened. He had drawn every one of the plants in his knowledge, some of them twice, and the sheets in our cabin were stiff and scratchy with his work.

"There is only one more," he said, "that I have not told you."

"What is it?" I said.

By now, when he shuddered, I held him. Sometimes, he pressed his face into my neck. When he touched himself, I allowed myself to look everywhere—his face, his chest, his arm moving ridiculously quickly. Even his member I knew now, like some other specimen to understand. It was still strange, but it had become expected.

"Persimmon," he said. "They are yellow, and you wait until they are so ripe they are swollen, almost bursting, and when you finally taste them, they taste like the gods."

And then he did what he had not done before. He pushed my legs apart and bent his head there, and moved his tongue until I was moving my legs apart farther for him, without shame, only urgency. Then he was in me and above me, moving with the same rapidity as he did his own hand, so that it was over quickly enough—the groan again, and then the collapse, though this time I could feel him as he grew softer, soft enough to slip from between my legs.

I had thought, from Mama, that all love was fair. That's the way Mama practiced it. Love was doling out the right amount of care to each patient and spending the right amount of time at each bedside. No more, no less. Mama's love was democratic. But Emmanuel was a despot in his love. He grasped at me—at my legs and my arms and my belly and back—as if, if he held on tight enough, he could claim it all.

Our final nights before we reached Haiti, I told him to be quiet. I looked at his body and saw a psalm. Mama had told me a daughter is like a poem, and so a mate's body, as made for me as mine was made for him, was like a psalm from God, I thought.

I am black but comely, I sang to him to make him laugh. He did, though he blushed, and it was another point of wonder, that about this my husband could be pious.

"You sing to me the poetry of nature, and I sing to you the poetry of God," I said to him. Again, he looked shocked, and that was a pleasure, too, maybe the deepest one, after all these nights.

> *Behold, thou art fair, my love;*
> *behold, thou art fair;*
> *thou hast doves' eyes.*
> *Behold, thou art fair, my beloved, yea, pleasant:*   *also our bed*
> *is green . . .*
> *A bundle of myrrh is my well-beloved unto me;*
> *he shall lie all night betwixt my breasts . . .*
> *As the apple tree among the trees of the wood,*
> *so is my beloved among the sons.*
> *I sat down under his shadow with great delight,*
> *and his fruit was sweet to my taste.*

This is what I sang to him, the word of God all jumbled up, as I held the back of him in my hands, as I tasted his skin and flesh and muscle and bone.

My beloved put in his hand by the hole of the door, and my very self, my inside, opened up to him. *I rose up to open to my beloved,* is what I sang when I saw Emmanuel's brow at my thigh, his head between my legs, his eyes closed, the only movement the ship and him.

He told me about all the plants discovered by man, and I sang back to him the fruits from God. I panted in his ear, "We are one, we are together, as you promised," and I did not think of who I belonged to (my mother) before I belonged to him.

I spoke to him God's poetry while he lay in me, the holy words which seemed to have spoken of us before all creation, all nature, all wrath.

BEFORE I HAD left, Mama had given me a satchel with five bags of powders she had ground herself. "You do not have to be a slave to him in that way, at least," she'd said. I had seen enough of her books, copied her columns of writings, to know that she gave this remedy to most of the women who passed through her clinic. The richer ones, she asked for payment; the poorer ones, she did not. And sometimes, a woman had had the course but came to Mama anyways, a few months later, her monthlies stopped and her middle thickening, and then Mama would shut the office door and I would hear the woman sob that Mama was fallible in this.

That would never be me, I thought giddily. My freedom with Emmanuel would come from children. We would build a nation out of each other. That was what we were traveling toward. And our new country needed citizens—babies, so many babies, so many beautiful brown babies, all fat and ready to fill a house.

So I took the medicine she gave me and, one day before we spotted land at Jacmel, I scattered it all over the rail. I told Emmanuel what I was doing, too, and he was delighted.

We were sure that where we were headed, we wouldn't need it. We were free to be abundant.

EMMANUEL HAD TOLD me, "Jacmel is the most beautiful city in the world."

It is a difficult thing, to be told something is beautiful by someone who already loves it best. As we approached, he watched my face avidly for my approval, and I tried to look expectant, to look amazed by what I saw. But it looked, at first, like any other town. I smiled and gasped, for his sake, and I did not think it bad, this first falsehood that stood between me, Emmanuel, and this land. I thought it was another sign of love.

The town hugged the base of the mountains—you could see them rolling up, as the ship approached. They were a deep, inviting green, and the buildings that came up to the shore were variations of white and pink and yellow.

We had come only with two trunks—one packed with our clothes, intermingled, the other full of Emmanuel's supplies: his doctor's bag, the plant specimens he had managed to collect in New York, and the homeopathic literature he was eager to bring back to Haiti. The rest of what we would need for our life together, he said, would be in his father's house. Since we did not have many possessions, we hired a man and a mule to take us to Emmanuel's home, which we reached by steadily climbing the road from the wharves, up through town. We passed the Rue de Commerce, where the traders and businessmen had their shops and then, farther, up the steep city streets, until we got to the quarter where Emmanuel lived, where the wealthiest lived and looked down at the harbor below. All around me, people spoke and called and laughed in a language I did not understand, and it struck me, finally, what I had done. The sun was high above us, my skin was warm and sweating, I was in a heat I did not recognize, climbing a hill a thousand miles away from my mother's face, and I had not heard her voice for longer than a moment in nearly a year. I could not help it: I began to cry.

"What is the matter?" he asked.

All I could say to him was, "I am a foolish girl."

The road got steeper. The dust rose to my eyes, making them even wetter. By the time we reached the house, Emmanuel had begun to walk many feet ahead of me, overwhelmed by the tears on my face.

When Emmanuel had whispered to me in my mother's waiting room about his father's house, I admit I had not paid much attention to his actual words. It was from his tone, the urgency of how he described it, that I had imagined it as something much grander than what was before me. He had spoken lovingly of the large shuttered windows that faced the street. Of the front veranda his father had built, with the iron railings. Of the oak front door that was always kept shut and, cut into it, the smaller door that the family used to pass in and out of the house. "We only open the doors proper," Emmanuel had told me, "when someone in our family dies."

The actual house that was before me was shorter than what I had pictured, but still impressive. The wood was painted a pale pink, and the black iron railings were winking in the sun. Emmanuel's father had been given the land when he came to Haiti ten years before—the promise to American Negro settlers fulfilled. He had traveled up and down the island, writing to the mother church back home, until they gave him the money to build a house worthy of the bishop that he was. At the very top of the house's flat roof was a weather vane with the imprint of an iron rooster. It was strange to have on a house in a place that felt as if wind had not been born yet, I thought, as I looked above and felt the sweat trickle down my neck.

At the front door, the mule driver untied our two trunks from the back of the animal and said something to Emmanuel. A joke—because Emmanuel threw back his head and laughed, and tipped him an extra coin.

"What was it?" I asked, wiping the sleeve of my dress across my face, trying to rub it clean of dirt and tears.

"He only noticed you crying," Emmanuel said. "And teased me about it."

"What did he say?"

"You have to learn the language sometime, Libertie," he said.

I thought at first he had arranged for the household to greet us; inside the hall, three people stood in a straight line. His father broke form first—a man a few inches shorter than Emmanuel, so just about level with my height. He was the same complexion as Emmanuel. He reached out to shake his son's hand. But he did not extend one to me, only blinked.

Beside him was Ti Me. She, too, was not quite how Emmanuel had described her. In Kings County, he had told me that Ti Me had been young once but had dedicated her youth to raising him, after his mother and siblings had died. I had pictured a woman old and bent, with gray hair. But the woman who stepped forward to greet me was probably at most thirty. Her skin was smooth. And she had bright, intelligent eyes, which darted over Emmanuel's face, then my own. She embraced him, as his father had, and pulled at his cheeks—scolding him, I guessed, for not eating enough. She was the only person in the house as dark as me.

Beside her was a woman Emmanuel's height. Ti Me was dressed in white, in this heat. But this woman was dressed in a rusty-red skirt and a black jacket. Her skin was as pale as Emmanuel's and his father's, but it had a bright-pink undertone, as if she was about to burn. Her hair hung in great stiff sections around her cheeks. Each section had been ironed once and then again, to get rid of the kink, and then violently curled. Her face was Emmanuel's, but leaner. His twin, Ella, I realized, with a start.

"And who is this?" she said as I stood beside Emmanuel.

"My wife," he said.

"You're married?" She raised one pale hand to her mouth.

I turned to Emmanuel. "You did not tell them?"

His father looked as if he was going to shout, and his sister was holding her stiff hair back from her face, her lips beginning to part—in a smile or a scream, I could not tell.

"You did not get my letters?" Emmanuel stepped back.

"You've married without my permission?" his father said. "And to whom?" He looked at me again, the whole length of me. I was, I could tell, in some way, lacking.

"Libertie Sampson. She is Dr. Sampson's very own daughter. A physician in her own right. A graduate of Cunningham College."

I pulled on Emmanuel's arm to stop him, but he would not. "A true scholar," he said.

"You married without my blessing," his father said.

"I wrote to you to tell you. I sent three letters to you to tell you of it."

"Who married you?" This was from his sister.

"The reverend of my church in Kings County," I said. "Reverend Harland, whom I believe you know, Bishop Chase."

Emmanuel's father looked from me to his son. "You are always too rash," he said.

I could feel myself begin to cry again. But I could see, from the corner of my eye, Emmanuel's sister watching me. So I stepped forward and unknotted the bonnet from under my chin. Once I had gotten it off, I moved toward Ella and took her in my arms. I held her there, though I could feel her body stiffen. I felt her tortured curls scratch against my cheeks, made harsh by whatever hot comb she'd lain on them. She smelled of dried perspiration and burnt hair.

"I am sorry," I said. "But I hope we can be sisters now."

I let her go and hurried over to her father, avoiding whatever look was on her face. "I am sorry, sir," I said, holding him in the same way. "I hope you can forgive your daughter."

I held him longer than I had Ella. He, too, was resistant, but I sensed that I should not let him go as soon, or this whole scene would be made even more ridiculous. As I held him, I could hear Emmanuel speaking in Kreyòl to Ti Me, who then shrieked—he must have told her I was his wife—and gave a short laugh.

"It is not funny," I heard Ella scold.

"Sorry, mum," Ti Me said.

I held on for a few moments more, for good measure, and then I let the bishop go. I stepped back to stand beside Emmanuel and watched his face, warily.

"It is not how I wished it would happen," Bishop Chase said finally.

"But we are here with you now, Father."

"Ti Me," the bishop said, "show them to Emmanuel's room," and then he left the foyer.

Ella had composed herself by then.

"Will you show Libertie the house?" Emmanuel asked her.

"We will have four for dinner, not three," she called to Ti Me.

Ella kissed her brother on the cheek. "We are happy you are here," she said. And then she left us.

Emmanuel and I still stood in the foyer of the house, which was so dim all I could see of that murky room with high ceilings was a flash of silver from a mirror hung on the farthest wall. All the shutters were closed against the afternoon sun.

To the right of the foyer, I could see a small room—with a table and chair, and a few books stacked on the end of the table—what must have been Bishop Chase's library. It, too, was dimly lit—its large window opening out onto the street also shuttered. There was a flutter in that room, and I realized that was where Emmanuel's father must have retreated.

To my left was a staircase, leading to the bedrooms. Directly in front of us was a dining room, its heavy oak table set for a formal dinner with six places, a single silver candelabra in the middle. The windows were unshuttered in the dining room, so that you could look out onto the back courtyard. It was full of a few flowering bushes and some clay pots growing herbs. The ground had been overlaid with stone. At the back of the courtyard was a small shed—the cookhouse, I realized—and farther away from everything, the latrine. Through the window, I saw Ella reappear, stalking toward the cookhouse.

"Come," Emmanuel said, taking my hand. He led me up the stairs, Ti Me behind us, carrying one of the trunks on her back.

"Oh," I said when I saw her struggle, and Emmanuel looked over his shoulder, then to me.

"She will carry it," he said carefully.

Upstairs were five rooms—more than I had expected. But then I remembered the mother and brothers and babies long dead. This house had been built for a much-larger family.

The doors for each room were shut. Our room was the first by the staircase. Its windows, at least, faced the backyard, so the shutters were open and the light was not as dim. There was a single double bed, the mattress dipped in the middle, a mirror, this one smaller than the one downstairs in the foyer, a chest of drawers, with a metal owl and a pitcher standing on it, and a wooden cross, above the bed.

Ti Me letting the trunk fall to the floor with a bang. She looked at me, pointedly, and said, "Ti fi sa a twò cho." Then she left us.

"What did she say?"

"You have to learn, Libertie."

"You won't even tell me this once?"

"She said you are a pretty mistress," he said.

I sat on the mattress and felt it dip further beneath me. "You and Ella do look a lot alike," I said.

"She was born three minutes ahead of me, my father tells me, but I've been playing catch-up ever since."

He sat down beside me and put his arms around me. I would have been happy to begin, but as we moved together, I leaned my head back and saw that the walls of the room did not reach the ceiling. The top of the room was open, and if I listened, I could hear Bishop Chase and his daughter and Ti Me talking downstairs, almost as if they were in the room beside us.

"Stop," I said. I pointed.

Emmanuel looked up. "Ah, all the rooms are like that in this house," he said. "If the gap was closed, no air could circulate. It keeps the room cool. So that we may do things like this." And then he pressed himself closer.

To live in a house where we all heard one another—I had not expected this. I thought, again, of my mother, and I wanted to cry. But I did not.

Instead, I pushed him away.

"They are waiting," I said.

THE CHASE HOUSEHOLD seemed to exist in some other country. It was situated not quite in Haiti, not quite in America. Outside the house, the business of the world pulled Emmanuel and his father to different parts of town. Bishop Chase rose early in the morning and refused to take a midday break, even when the rest of Jacmel fell quiet at the hottest part of the day. During that time, he would come back to the house to sit in his office and go over his papers—letters to his diocese back in the United States, to other bishops on other islands, to the deacons and priests in churches he had yet to even see. His progress in building his own church had been quick at first but had slowed in the last few years. The wave of American Negroes he had expected to come and bolster his original outpost, after the war was over, had not arrived. I suspected that they were of the same mind as Lucien, not willing to give up their bets on life in America just yet. But it was the bishop's belief that they would still come, in time.

I was to learn that Bishop Chase's favorite subject was how foolish American Negroes were. It was clear he considered himself as not quite one, which was strange, because he most definitely did not consider himself Haitian. He was a citizen of the imaginary country where his household was based, one of hardworking and disciplined colored people—though he was convinced that these were very rare. Haitians were lazy and kept too many scores. American Negroes were too shortsighted and did not understand history.

"If he hates both, who does he expect to join him in the new world?" I'd asked Emmanuel once, and he had looked at me, wounded.

"No one loves the colored race as much as my father," he'd said.

Well, he has a funny way of showing it, I wished to say. But I did not. I still thought it was love to say nothing.

At dinner that first night, I sat beside Emmanuel, my plate with two fewer potatoes than everyone else's. Bishop Chase leaned over his own plate, heavy with potatoes and topped with the leg of a chicken, and explained himself to his son.

"I have backed the wrong horse," he said.

Since they had arrived in the country, Bishop Chase and his fellow émigrés had rallied around the politician Geffrard, who had managed to become president for a time. Geffrard had given over lands at his own palace to the American émigrés when they'd first arrived, and when their initial crops had failed after the first growing season, he had given them food from his own provisions. He had also taken land from Haitians to give to the Americans. And the Americans were there because the poorer Haitians had refused to return to the sugar plantations that made Haiti such a jewel and a prize. Geffrard had looked for the Americans to take the land and force the smaller Haitian farmers into the type of destitution that would lead them to agree to the awful work of making sugar for no pay. But Bishop Chase did not mention this part of the deal they had entered into with Geffrard and his government. He only spoke of past and future glories.

Bishop Chase sighed. "No truer friend to the American Negro than Geffrard."

"He has not been in power for nearly ten years," Emmanuel said.

"Do not insult Father." This was Ella.

"How is the truth an insult?"

"It is disrespectful," she said.

"A listing of history is disrespectful?"

"You would know. You understand disobedience better than I do," she said.

And then she turned to me. "Do you enjoy the food?"

I had never been looked at with such open hostility, but her mouth was fixed into a very sweet smile.

"I like it very much," I said.

"You do not have to lie for politeness' sake. Haitian food is not like what we have in America."

"This meal is very good."

"In America, you know, our meals are so much better for digestion," she said. "Here, it is always the plantain, the potato, and sometimes the goat. What I would not give for a gooseberry."

"Ah, but they are so sour," I said. "You were lucky to have a good one. There have not been good crops the last few seasons. When were you last in America?"

I had thought this would flatter her, but she narrowed her eyes and turned back to her plate, and the table was quiet for a moment.

"Ella has not lived in America since she was nine years old," Emmanuel said, laughing. I had pleased him with my unintended insult, I realized with dismay.

"If this is supposed to be proof of filial piety," Ella said, "it is not a very good one."

"Again, you are angered by facts."

"Ella has missed your arguments," Bishop Chase said, "though she won't ever admit it."

Perhaps, I thought, this was how siblings behaved. It was strange to see Emmanuel reduced to participating in someone else's game.

"You worry about Boisrond-Canal?" Emmanuel asked his father.

"He is a good man, I think. And he is friendly to the Americans. But he does not understand what we could build here, for the black man. For all black men. He is thinking of his nation, to be sure, but he does not understand cultivating allies with American Negroes. And then the Negroes I introduce to him, their heads are turned by white Americans, by the crumbs they are finding here and there . . ."

"Not crumbs," I said quietly, to my lap. Bishop Chase, at the pulpit in his mind now, did not hear me.

"They do not understand the future," he said. "And Boisrond-Canal . . . he does not understand our mission like Geffrard did."

"Father, Geffrard is not even in the country anymore."

"Good times will come again," the bishop said. "It is just hard to know when."

I ate in silence until I remembered. *At least I may have discovered something to charm them,* I thought.

"Emmanuel," I said, "have you shown your father your gift?"

"Not yet."

"I will go and get it now. I think he would enjoy it."

I stood up from the table before he could stop me, went to the foyer where Ti Me had left the second trunk by the stairs. In the dim light, I fumbled with the latches. The gift had been packed under Emmanuel's instruments and the dried cuttings wrapped in paper.

"Be careful, Libertie," he called.

But I would not be deterred. I called back, "I know how to unpack a trunk."

I gingerly laid each piece, each glass vial and book, on the ground until I found it, folded at the bottom of the trunk. I pulled it out, set it beside me, and repacked the pieces. When I came back to the dining room, the three of them were eating in silence. Ella did not even look up but kept her head bowed over her plate.

It was strange to have a bit of power over the two of them. To know something they did not. It had been so long since I felt this feeling that I relished it for a minute, holding the package behind my back.

"Well," Emmanuel said, smiling, "show it to him."

I shook the paper until it unfolded. It was a full print of all our colored heroes—there was Hiram Revels and Fredrick Douglass and John Mercer Langston, and even Martin Delany, my mother's old friend.

"*The Mystery*, out of Pittsburgh, made prints for Independence Day," I said. "Emmanuel bought it special for you, so that you could add it to your collection."

"Ah." Bishop Chase sighed. He looked at it from over his glasses but did not move to take it from my hands. "Yes. A thoughtful gift." Then he turned his attention back to his plate.

I was left to stand there, all that power in my hands on that print, while Ella smiled in satisfaction at her plate and Emmanuel looked at his father, exasperated. He seemed about to open his mouth, to complain again, but I did not think I could bear it.

"I'll leave it in the hall," I said, "to hang."

Back in the darkness of the foyer, I carefully folded the print and leaned it against the banister. I heard a rustling behind me and turned to see Ti Me. At her hip was a wicker basket, loaded down with linens. She stared steadily at me, holding my gaze. I smiled back at her. She did not move, did not blink, only looked into my eyes with a kind of curiosity.

I did not know what to do. But the way she stared at me, I began to think I understood. I bowed my head to her and made a short curtsy. When I raised my head, she looked at me a moment longer, then turned on her heel and was gone.

"You should touch it," he whispered.

"I can't," I whispered back.

"You did on the ship, without asking."

His voice whistled in my ear.

"We were alone then."

"We were not alone. All around us were tens of men who watched my pretty wife walk up and down the deck—"

"Emmanuel!"

"And still I had her all for my own. But in my own house, she won't touch it."

"I would," I hissed, "but they can hear every word."

He rolled his head back on the pillow, looked at the gap in the ceiling above us.

"They are asleep."

"I can hear them breathing."

"I did not take you for a nervous one, Libertie."

"I am not nervous."

"Nerves will not do well in our life here."

"I am not nervous."

"I thought you had a strong temperament."

"I do."

"Then prove it on me. Kouche."

He took my hand in his, guided it between his legs, where he wished it to go. I did not think I would ever get used to that. The wonder of it—rigid in my hand, not like any other organ. It was a curiosity. I had seen between the legs of more women than I could count, but this, this was strange. It was almost as if it did not belong on a body. As if it was some kind of a prank. I pulled my hand away from his, pressed hard on the end of it to see what he would do. He groaned. Why Mama hadn't told me of this, in all her anatomy lessons, the little bit of power here, I did not know. I wished that I could discuss it with her, or with someone. I could not even write it in a letter to the Graces, I thought. They would not understand.

Beneath my hand, Emmanuel was very slowly thrashing his legs under the sheet, as if the fit itself was luxurious. He was whispering something, too, low and deep: "Bon lanmou, bon lanmou, bon jan love."

"Emmanuel!" It was another hiss, higher than Emmanuel's voice, that seemed to fill the whole room.

His legs immediately stilled, but he could not calm his breathing.

"Emmanuel!" That hiss again, so shrill.

He put his mouth close to my ear.

"Go to the door," he gasped. "If you do not, she will try the lock. She won't leave till you answer."

"Who?"

"Just go! Hurry!"

When I opened the door, Ella was before me. In the light of the candle she held, her face was haggard and overly pale, as if the muscle beneath her skin was inlaid with lime. She did not tie her hair up for bed, like any other Negro woman would. Instead, she had set on top of the mass of it a yellowed nightcap, which threatened to slide off of it all.

She jumped back slightly when it was I who opened the door. Then she recovered.

"Is Emmanuel all right?"

"Of course, he is," I said. "Why would you think he was not?"

"I heard strange noises. As if he was in distress."

"He is not."

She sighed, exasperated, then strained her neck, as if to see around me.

"Emmanuel, did the food not agree with you? You have been so long away—"

"I am fine, Ella," he called back.

"Are you sure?"

"He is fine," I said, and made to close the door.

"You do not know him as I do. He has a sensitive stomach. Anyone making noises like that cannot be well."

"You could not know what those noises meant. You are not married," I said without thinking.

She breathed in heavily at that, so much so that her candle flame shook. I looked at her, aghast at what I had said.

"Ella, I apologize . . ."

But she turned and made her way back down the hall. I watched the back of her, the nightshirt and the wobble of the flame as she walked. I did not want to face Emmanuel.

When I turned back around, he was still in bed but sitting up on his elbows. He was grinning.

"I knew you were the right one," he said. "I knew you were not nervous."

"Your sister now hates me."

"It does her good."

"It doesn't do me any good to have her hate me."

"Ignore her. She doesn't matter."

"What does that mean?"

"Nothing. Only we are twins, but we have not shared the same life for a very long time. Not since we were children."

"What does that mean?"

"Come back," he said, "and I will whisper it to you."

I returned to bed. I pulled my knees up to my chin and turned away from him. He pressed at me for a few minutes, pleading. "It is not so bad, Libertie. She will understand in the morning."

But I stayed tucked into myself, even after I heard him turn over onto his own side, his hands moving fast, before he thrust one arm over to grab at my shoulder and then fell asleep.

I DREAMT THAT night that a million tiny white feathers broke through the skin of the palms of my hands, and when I waved, I felt the breeze flow through them. When I awoke, Emmanuel was gone and his side of the bed was already cold. From the looks of the sun, it was still early in the morning. I had not been so derelict as to sleep in. I dressed as quickly as I could and opened the door, and tiptoed down the hallway and to the stairs. There was no sound of Ella or Bishop Chase. Or even Emmanuel.

The foyer was empty. Bishop Chase's office was empty. I went to stand in the dining room, to look through the windows at the back courtyard. A group of children played there—a few in burlap shirts, another few completely naked, none in pants or shoes. They were slapping their hands together and shouting. I could just hear a bit of their song.

> *Li se yon esklav ki damou*
> *Li se yon esklav ki damou*
> *Li se yon esklav ki damou*
> *Libète moun Nwa!*

They sang it a few more times before I recognized, with a start, my own name. I turned away from the window, my cheeks burning, and moved through the rest of the house.

In the sitting room, Ella was already composed on the lone divan—a battered wooden structure with the horsehair falling from the bottom. Emmanuel sat at the table, writing. Ella was bent over some sewing in her lap.

"There she is!" Emmanuel called, and put down his pen to come and press my hands into his. Ella would not look up.

"Good morning," I said, to both of them.

"My love, I must go see Monsieur Colon, my mentor here in Jacmel. I have not seen him in so many years, and he would be offended if I did not see him first."

"I will come with you."

"It is not necessary," he said.

I looked from his face to Ella's bent head and back again. I narrowed my eyes.

"You will go with Ella and Ti Me to market. When I return, we can begin to unpack the things for my office," Emmanuel said. "Monsieur Colon is a very intelligent man. But he is suspicious of women, especially a woman as beautiful as my wife. I will have to be gentle with the news of our marriage."

"He, at least, warrants that consideration," Ella said to the sewing in her lap.

"You will be happier here, Libertie, than coming with me."

I said nothing, only glared at him.

"You will have time enough to meet the rest of the neighborhood. Half of them know you are here already. Did you not hear the song the children have already made up in your honor?"

I shook my head.

Emmanuel smiled and began to snap his fingers, slightly out of time. "Li se yon esklav ki damou, li se yon esklav ki damou, li se yon esklav ki damou, Libète moun Nwa! Which means, of course, that I am a slave of love to my black Libertie."

My eyes shot through with pain as I felt tears form, but I forced myself not to cry. He looked at me expectantly.

"Very clever," I murmured.

"Ha! You will learn. Anything here that happens at midnight is known by dawn. And by morning, the neighborhood has turned it into a song."

He bent his head to kiss my fingers. I bent my own to meet his.

"Please don't leave me with her," I whispered.

"I thought you were brave," he murmured back.

And then he was gone.

I turned to Ella, who had not moved from the divan. I sat down, primly, on Emmanuel's chair.

"What are you sewing?" I said.

She unbent her head and looked at me. She held up a lady's jacket—black fabric with red thread she was embroidering. The embroidery was so thick and close together in some places that the jacket looked crimson. In others, it was nearly black, with only a bit of red curled over.

"Very nice," I said.

"You cannot possibly understand it."

"It is a jacket."

"Yes, but you can't know it."

I frowned. "I do not understand," I said.

"Exactly," she said. She set aside the jacket, as if in a rush. "We must get to market."

"Ti Me!" she called suddenly. "Ti Me!"

Ella and I sat there in the quiet. She glared at me, her nostrils flaring slightly. Today, her hair was pinned up, but two tendrils framed her face. One still held the paper curler she must have put in last night, after she left our bedroom. The other was valiantly trying to hold on to a curl but was losing in the humidity of Haiti.

Ti Me was slow to come, but she finally appeared in the doorway.

"Mademoiselle," she said.

"We must get to market, Ti Me. Honestly. Fwi a ap gate. We will be left with nothing. Papa must not be made sick paske nou parese."

"Wi, mademoiselle." Ti Me looked from me to Ella. "Just let me get my basket first," she said.

THE MARKET WAS a kingdom of women. All around me, old women were bent with produce loaded onto their backs, baskets topped with the green fringe of sweetgrass. Some of the old women had gray skirts; others, blue and yellow ones. There were younger women, too, who walked faster, hips rolling, legs spread wide, hurrying past. And children. There were children everywhere—some clothed, some naked, all barefoot. I had thought, back home, with my mother and Madame Elizabeth and Lenore all around, that I was dark. But here, shining in the sun, I saw women with skin the color of the night sky.

The sound of the market so loud it was nearly unbearable, but it was sweeter than the silence in the Chase household. It was the hum of a hundred women talking and laughing and trading and gossiping, to make the day run. Every woman, it seemed, was calling out to the others, "Maren, maren!" It was the one word I knew, the one I had learned from weeks on the boat. *Sailor, sailor,* the women were shouting. But when I asked Ti Me and Ella about it, Ti Me opened her mouth to answer and Ella cut her off.

"You'll notice, the Haitian women are not very chaste," she said. "And it all stems from that. All of this does. All of this chaos around us."

Ti Me closed her mouth and drew ahead of us, the basket balanced on her head. She had left this conversation.

Ella followed my gaze. "Oh, Ti Me would agree with me," she said. "It is part of Papa's work, to bring a civilizing force to this great country. Look." Ella pointed one pale finger. Behind us, the mountains rose, impressive and lush and green. "This country could be rich. But a country is only as wealthy as its wives and mothers. You will see."

I was not sure how the same home could produce an Ella, so full of spite her fingers shook at the mountains around us, and an Emmanuel, for whom the very same mountains brought tears to his eyes. I could not make sense of it, and I knew asking Ella directly would not get any response I could understand. It was a question for the night, for the space of time held between two bodies in bed—the one place in this country, I was learning, where I could speak the truth. Emmanuel, too.

I smiled at Ella in response.

To see her out in the market was strange. She walked like a very proud duck—both ankles turned nearly out, toes pointed slantwise. Every few feet, she swept the hem of her skirt up. I think it was to protect it, but it seemed to swirl up more dust and muck from the road. Ahead of us, Ti Me walked steadily, her own skirts tucked up into her apron to keep them from dragging in the mud. This practicality, perhaps, was what Ella thought of as so unchaste. It was what a man would think, not a woman, who knew how heavy skirts could get with dirt.

Watching Ella, I tried to see where Emmanuel was reflected in her movements. It relieved me that I could not. How could I love a man so much and detest the person closest to him? I thought again of what he had said. That they had not shared a life in a long time. I looked around me at the streets, the women bent over, Ti Me now stopping at a market stall, talking with another woman, a fruit I did not recognize in the palm of each of her hands. She was weighing them. Then she leaned over, spat on the ground. The two women began to argue furiously.

Ella stood watching, her arms crossed over her chest. The little boy at the stall watched, too, occasionally looking up at Ella, trying to read her expression. I caught his eye, and he grinned at me—a genuine smile. I smiled back.

Suddenly the argument stopped. Ti Me shouted, "Madame Sara!" and the other woman began to laugh. She held up her hands, as if in surrender.

Ti Me looked back at me slyly over her shoulder. "Madame Sara," she said, and then she looked pointedly at Ella to translate. She did not want me to miss the joke.

"It is a type of bird," Ella said. "It's very small and yellowish and black and green, and it's always chirping. You see it around Marchand Dessalines. She called the market woman that because she, too, is small and always chirping, and she goes from one town to another to sell, always talking, talking. The Madame Sara can build its nest anywhere, and this woman can sell anywhere, too."

"It is a kind of compliment, then?"

"Ti Me is too soft," Ella said.

"She seems to do well."

"Yes, but you must understand. No one here respects you if you're soft. You must be hard and righteous to gain respect. Look, there." She pointed to the other end of the market, where a drawing of the Virgin Mary, sketched on a piece of spare wood in charcoal and mud, hung on a pole over a communal pump. "Popish nonsense like this, everywhere. A whole country that glorifies suffering and not sacrifice. It is a big job, to be here. I hope Emmanuel has made that clear to you."

"He loves Haiti. He says it is where the future of the Negro race lies."

"He is not wrong. If we can ensure the right kind of Negro is here, he is not wrong."

"No one born here is the right kind?"

"Not without education and hard work. We must make them, too. That's what you're here for, I suppose. Why he brought you. Though why he thinks you are good for that, I do not know."

"I beg your pardon," I said. But Ella was not so brave as to meet my eye.

Ti Me stopped her bargaining to toss her head over her shoulder and call to us, "Bon manman, bon pitit." She turned back, picking up the rhythm skillfully, as if there was no interruption.

"What does that mean?" I said.

"It is an old Haitian saying. 'If the mother is good, the child will be good.'"

I looked away from Ella, back to Ti Me, who was grinning at me now. She winked.

"Mèsi," I said to her.

"The people here are very fond of proverbs," Ella said, staring straight ahead. "None of them make sense to me, though. The best proverbs, of course, are in the Bible."

"But these ones sound very agreeable," I said.

Ella said nothing, only kept watching the haggle.

When the deal was finally struck, Ti Me looked from Ella to me expectantly. I smiled back, uncertain.

"What is it?" I said.

Ella wouldn't meet either of our eyes. She looked down at her skirts, and then she stuck one hand to her side and fumbled for her purse there. She unhooked it from her belt and handed it to me.

It was soft and heavy in my hands, the coins inside it spreading over my palms. It was like holding an animal and feeling about on its belly for its organs.

"I suppose," Ella said, still without looking at me, "that you should hold this now. Since you are now the first lady of the house. The purse and keys are yours."

Her voice was halting, and strangely high-pitched, as if someone else was forcing the words out of her with a pair of bellows.

"It is not necessary," I began, thinking that if I could spare her this humiliation, perhaps I could win her favor.

But her eyes flashed at me, and I understood it at once. *Don't you dare pity me. The likes of you could never pity me.*

What had Ella herself said? *You must be strong, in a place like this?*

I took the purse and stepped in front of her and counted out the coins, one by one, to Ti Me's hand, and when we reached the house, it was I who drew the big iron key from my waist and turned it in the door and let the other women inside.

I THOUGHT THE keys at my waist would change things. Emmanuel led me to believe it was so. When he saw them there at dinner, his eyes became bright, and later, alone in our room, he held each one in his hand, one by one, only the length of the key between us as he worked them off their ring.

"The keys used to fascinate me as a boy," he told me. "Ti Me wore them until Ella was old enough, and the sound of them, when Ti Me walked, the sound of their clanking, meant that we were safe. I was scared of this country then. I had not learned to love it yet. I wanted to lock it out all day and all night, and hearing the keys hit Ti Me's hip made me feel safe.

"I learned," he said as he let one key fall against my thigh and picked up another, to work off the ring. "I learned, as I learned to love this place, that the keys were an illusion. Why would you live in a place as beautiful as this and lock out the night sky? I promised myself that if they were ever given to me, I would exorcise their power. When we were sixteen and I found out that Ella got the keys because she was now the woman of the house, I was heartbroken. And she would never let me touch them, because she knew I meant to strip them of their power."

He picked up the last key, began to work it off the ring. "But I have something even sweeter. I have this day, where I see the keys at the waist of my wife," he said, "and you are mine, and I am yours, and it makes the fact of that even more real to my family."

He led me to our bed, where he gently pushed my shoulders till I lay on my back, and lifted my skirt. He placed each key, warm from his shaking hand, across my bare stomach, while I whispered that he should stop moaning—his father and sister could clearly hear him.

But his ecstasy over those keys did not keep him close to me. The next morning, Emmanuel left at dawn, as he had taken to doing. He spent his days on an endless round of visits. To his mentor, the one other doctor in town. To his father's friends and associates—the men who made up the American Negro colony in Jacmel. Sometimes, he came back to the house very late at night, even after his father had eaten and retired to bed.

I was left to spend my days with Ella and Ti Me and the bishop. I say "days," but it may as well have been the same day, over and over again, so little did it change. Ella was always awake before I was, even if, in the dark, Emmanuel and the rooster crowing outside woke me. She spent her mornings working at her embroidery in the parlor—her incomprehensible jacket. Around ten, she would stow it away in a basket she kept underneath the battered divan, and we would all go to the market.

Ti Me went to the same stalls each day and made the same bargains. I realized on the fourth day, from the rhythm of their voices, that this was not so much an argument but a friendly conversation. Sometimes, Ti Me said something quick and low that made the woman laugh and made Ella blush and sniff about morals. I wished then, more than anything, that I could understand. Always, at the end of it, both women turned to me—Ella sullenly, Ti Me with clear amusement at the awkwardness it was causing her—for the coins in the purse at my side.

We returned to the house for the hottest part of the day. Ella took to her room. She said she could not withstand the heat of the tropics, despite having lived there from childhood. Sometimes, I went upstairs, too, but I grew restless lying beneath the sheet, the shutters closed against the heat, listening to the world outside slow down.

When the world began moving again in the late afternoon, it brought the American women of the colony over to the house. There were about ten of them in total—wives of the men who had followed Bishop Chase, the helpmeets of traders and farmers—all of them with the same pale skin as Ella, not a black one among them. The darkest was a very thin woman with yellow skin and no husband, who taught the Haitian women in a kind of domestic academy.

They would all arrange themselves around Ella, who would lead the conversation, usually begun by relating an imagined indignity suffered in the market. The untrustworthiness and the untapped potential of Haitian women was the main topic of conversation. How great the country could be, it was agreed, if only those women understood their place in a chaste home. Instead, they wandered to market and upset the order of the world.

Like Ella, none of these women had been to America for a very long time. The America they described was a kind of dream, where Negro people lived in perfect harmony, with kind and just laws, and every Negro woman stayed home to stitch counterpanes while her husband entered the world. I could not tell if they had been so long gone that they really believed this fantasy to be true, or if it was a collective fiction they engaged in together to pass the time, but to hear it made me wish to scream.

I attempted, once, very early on, to set them right. I told them of the red marks the whites had left on our doors. I said, "There are men following the law right now whom white men string up on trees for exercising their rights."

There was a pause in the room. One woman covered her mouth. Another murmured, "Mercy."

Ella did not even look up from the sewing work in her lap. Her hands moved the needle in and out of the fabric, humming like a cicada. "But there is justice in America," she said. "It will be set right. Here, Negroes cut down other Negroes for politics, too. It is our own against our own. In America, we are not so uncivilized as that."

I very nearly rushed across the room and ripped the embroidery from her hands. Instead, I stood and left, and I made it a habit to do so every afternoon, when I had sat long enough to be deemed polite. The only thing that saved me was the knowledge that the world my husband was building, that I was sure I would soon join him in building, was bigger than what Ella or those women could possibly imagine. I held this knowledge close to me and it cooled me in the middle of these endless, turgid afternoons, as if I had pressed a wet cloth to the back of my neck.

At some point during each discussion, a woman would excuse herself to go to Bishop Chase's door, by prearrangement. "I forgot," she would say, "the bishop asked to see me," and she would get up, and none of the other women in the room would meet her eye, and Ella, especially, would double down in her viciousness as soon as the woman took her leave.

It was always the darker women, or, I should say, the less pale ones who went, and I thought that was what made Ella rage. She had the worst case of colorstruck I'd ever seen, and I figured it was so bad she was even begrudging these women the chance to talk a little salvation with her father in his library. I pitied her for it, and it made me even more wary of her.

The bishop himself avoided both Ella and me, and Ti Me, though he was home when we were, more often than not. He still did not say a word to me directly. Sometimes, he let his eye rest on the fold of my skirt or my apron and he frowned in disapproval, but he never spoke. It was strange to live in a man's house and serve his son and not speak to him, but I thought of Mr. Grady—how shy he had been, how he had avoided speaking to me then—and I thought it must be the same with the bishop. But I did not respect the bishop or yearn to know him half as much as I had Mr. Grady. I thought of him more as an example of the worst parts of Emmanuel, and it was a relief that he did not try to talk to me. Seeing him made me scared of the kind of man my husband could possibly become. And I did not want that for him. For no one was loved in that neighborhood more than he, and it was through this love that everyone else—that is, our Haitian neighbors, not the sour-faced American women who followed Ella's whims—said my new name with respect and pride.

"Madam Chase, se madanm mesye Emmanuel!"

I had always thought titles were silly. Or rather, the only one to be respected was "Doctor." But I took an inordinate, stubborn pride in my new name, in the name I was now called in the streets when I walked to market with Ti Me and Ella. *Madame Chase, Madame Chase, Madame Chase.*

"Call me that, please," I said, teasing Emmanuel at night, and this delighted him almost as much as the iron keys on my naked body.

"You know, Madame Chase," he said, "it is a kind of work, to call things by their true names. To change their names."

"A kind of work?"

"That is what we call the practice of Vodoun when it is done. A work. It is an industry for the spirit. It is a task of repair. And it can be as simple as giving something its rightful name. As I have and as the streets have done for you. And, look, you embrace it. And so we will be right."

I wanted, so badly, to believe him.

Dear Libertie,

I feel it is time to speak plainly. There is no reason not to anymore. I have tried, as your mother, to only speak to you the truth, to remain impartial, to have you grow up with a love as pure as justice. But what good has that done? You've still chosen the flesh, anyways. So let me be fleshy, here, with you, since it makes no difference.

I miss you more than I thought possible. It was different when you were gone to school, and I was sure you would be returned to me. But you have passed over into a divide where I do not believe you can ever come back fully. And I mourn your passing.

When your father died, I spent three weeks in bed. Nearly in bed. I was alone in the house—my own father had passed a year before. Reverend Harland came to see me only once. But when he came, I was sitting up in bed, my mouth open wide in a scream with no sound coming out. I scared him in my grief. The Reverend has never been a brave man. The only other person to come see me was Lenore, who came every few days to hold her hand over my open mouth, to make sure I was still breathing, and to bring biscuits, hard as stone, from some of the women at church.

I spoke to no one except you. I placed both hands on my stomach, and in the quiet of the house I cried to you about your father. How much I missed him. You'd quickened before he passed. I'd held his hand myself over you, where you tossed inside me and rippled the skin on my stomach like a wave.

So after he was gone, I lay in bed and watched you move inside me, even though I wished the whole world had stopped. In that house made still by death, I knew you would continue, at least. At least I would have Libertie.

Elizabeth would write to me of her great political awakening. I liked those letters because they burnt with the same passion your father had, for the world to be set right. Elizabeth was learning so much then—about how slaves really lived, about what our own lives would be like if we had not been born free. I am ashamed to say I had not thought of it before. Even with your father whispering revolution in my ear, I only thought of colored people as the most cursed race in the world. I thought we were merely unlucky. I thought it was a matter of luck. I had read the stories of daring escapes, heard the old ones speak, seen the haunted eyes of our newcomers, and was only glad it wasn't me.

Your father did not talk of his life before he was free. He would not tell me even what town he ran from, only that he had lived for a spell in Maryland, and for some time in Virginia. Who his people were—his mother, his father, his sisters and brothers—he would not tell me, and in the flush of love I did not press him. I saw how asking made his eyes sad. Besides, I told myself, our life together shared a different fate. He had found me, with my bright skin and farm and money and profession, and he would be safe always, because I loved him. That's how young I was then. I really believed that.

After your father died, Elizabeth's letters told me of the women who came to her, the front of their dresses wet with milk, their daughters snatched from their hands, and I feared that would be me. It would be me. You would be taken from me, and it did not matter that I was freeborn, and it did not matter that I could see the blue veins at my wrist. None of that would keep you safe. That's what drove me to give aid. And I decided when you were born that I would hide my heart from you, because I worried I would love you into nervous oblivion.

When you were born, when Lenore raised you up from where she'd placed you on my thigh, the first thing I did was check behind your ears for your true color. And I rejoiced for what I saw there.

Because a part of him would live on in the world. That beautiful color. His skin glowed in the sun, like yours did as a girl, as it does now. I could not look at you in your wedding dress—that black black skin against that field of white—because of the glow of it. I had to turn away, you were so overpoweringly beautiful.

When I saw the color behind your ears, I could no longer deny all the ways you could be taken from me.

Even I was not secure, and my papa was not secure, in our color, because we were known to be colored and we could have been taken at any time. And if you were taken from me, no white person would believe you were mine—they did not think it was possible that I would prefer your black skin to my faint yellow, that I could give birth to something as wondrous as you.

The whole world told me you weren't mine, whenever I held you in my arms outside of our home. And so I grew frightened for you. And I knew what I owed you was very great. I must raise you up to be strong enough for this world. I must teach you how to heal the people in it. Maybe that could save you, I thought. Again, I was still very young then.

You would not believe me now, but you were a happy baby. Your joy brought something back for me. You will see, when you have your own children—it is as if they are your new eyes and your new heart, and you feel sometimes you can live for a hundred years more, even after all the trouble you've seen. You actually want to live for a hundred years more, even knowing how cruel the world is.

Before you came, I stayed in this world out of a sense of duty only. It was my trust to fix it. I would get weary sometimes. I would think of what your father wanted—Liberia. I would think of what would happen if I had followed his desire to be there. Only a heavy sense of duty screwed my ankles down into Kings Country dirt.

But through you, I learned to love our land. I saw you learn to walk, first on the floors my own father had cut and sanded, then on the land that he owned. I saw you learn to talk by calling back to the birds in our trees. I saw when you cried, and I held you close. You would look over my shoulder at the hills around us to soothe yourself. I saw the land, my land, through your eyes, and I learned to love it again. And it was not a burden. None of it was a burden. You told me once, in anger, that you must be such a burden to me, and I tell you, Libertie, caring for you has been the greatest honor of my life.

But I think even now I have failed you, and I am full of sorrow.

Love

Your

Mama

Ti Me had handed me the letter without any expression. I was sitting with Ella in the parlor, and I'd made the mistake of reading it in front of her. I felt her eyes on me, avidly watching, and I felt my skin become hot.

"Good news?" she said when I was done.

"My mother is well," I said.

And then I crushed the letter into a ball and held my hand in a fist until I could go to my room, my husband's and mine, and stuff it in the desk drawer there.

As if that could save me from it.

I will write her back tomorrow, I told myself.

But then I thought of what I would tell her.

The children here have made up a mocking song about me. Emmanuel's father did not even know we were married. His sister hates the sight of me. I spend my days surrounded by people, alone. This is what I have chosen, instead of speaking honestly, "fleshly," as you say, to you, Mama, and fighting to stay by your side.

"Emmanuel," I whispered in his ear that night. "Take me away from here tomorrow."

He was in my hand, his eyes were closed, he nodded his head back into the pillow, I thought that we still had this, at least, despite everything else, and I felt a little stab of pride.

But how do you list that triumph in a letter to your mother?

WE RODE ON his father's horse, across a wide, flat expanse of no-man's-land that was full of puddles of water as large as very shallow lakes, that women and children and men walked and ran across and trod across on donkeys, going back and forth from their homes in the mountains to town.

I could feel the horse breathe beneath me. Every step up the mountain, he took in larger gulps of air. I could feel the ends of his lungs swell. The horse wheezed louder the higher we went. I felt my ears pop as we ascended.

A wife is like a horse. Laboring uphill with the weight of two people's love on her back. My skirts were beginning to get damp with sweat. I thought of Madeline Grady, who had looked at me and said with confidence, "Grady reads for both of us." Where did that surety come from? *I should have watched her better,* I thought.

It was one thing to fail as a student. I had told myself I simply did not have the aptitude to be a doctor. That I did not possess that piece of flint that existed in my mother's soul, which was struck and made light when she had a patient before her. My anatomy was different. I was not built to alleviate the suffering of others.

But I was surely built to be a wife. Wasn't every woman? Even

Louisa and Experience were built for love. And I felt it for Emmanuel, sometimes so strongly it made me dizzy. I did not realize, though, that I could at the same time be so lonely.

I pressed my forehead into my husband's back. "I wish the Graces were here."

"Why? So they could make you laugh?"

"They would at least sing us love songs to cheer us, yes."

"They do not sing love songs," he said.

"But they do," I said. "Every song the Graces sang was a love song."

"No," he said.

"They are. Love is freedom."

His ribs shuddered beneath my arms. He was laughing. "You don't know anything," he said.

We got off the horse for the last bit. "Wouldn't it be kinder to tie him to a tree and come back for him?" I said.

Emmanuel looked ahead, farther up the mountain, then back at me. "If you wish."

We left the horse by a bush. I could hear him, even as we walked, behind me, eating leaves.

Every few twists in the road, we passed a house of one of the families that lived on the mountain. They were set back from the road and made of wood and stone. We could usually hear the family's rooster as we approached, sometimes a goat in the yard. At each house, a person, usually a woman, would come to the door to watch us pass. If she saw me first, she would frown. If she saw Emmanuel first, she would smile and bow her head.

Emmanuel called to each, "Bonjou, madam." Sometimes, a woman would call back, "Monsieur Emmanuel." But every single one recognized me and called me by my new name, though I had never seen any of them before: *Madame Chase, yon fanm ameriken.*

"They know us here," I said.

"I come here nearly every day. I have bragged about you so often they know you by my words." He laughed. "Before I left for America, I used to come here to study."

"You would bring your books here?"

"Sometimes I was studying books. But mostly, I was studying the plants."

"You will get used to this walk," Emmanuel said, taking my hand in his. "You will make it every day with me, once my office is set up again. We will learn this mountain together."

"You have a lot of faith in me."

"It is not faith," he said. "I know you."

We then walked in silence, and I could pretend for a moment that I was the person he imagined. To get to the water, you had to climb uphill till the backs of your legs began to burn and your knees felt as if they would shake, and your skirts, as they moved around your ankles, felt like a burden. I tucked the ends into the waist of my dress, running them through my legs, which delighted Emmanuel. But I felt annoyance at the walk and the heat that he had not prepared me for. We had left in the afternoon, because he had wished to talk with his father first and we had wanted to miss the highest heat of the day. But the heat had lingered, and even the woods all around us felt oppressive.

I did not trust his admiration for me. The only person who had ever watched my movements as closely as he did was my mother. And she had watched not with pride, but with a kind of patient assessing. She was waiting for me to make a mistake, and he did not believe a mistake was possible. Yet.

My mother's scrutiny was a burden. But this other way of looking, this besottedness, was just as damning. My mother expected great things and constant improvement. He seemed to believe in a perfection that existed apart from my actual self.

I watched my husband's slim back as he moved up the mountain. His skin did not brown in the sun, only turned yellow and pink. For this trip, he wore a straw hat with a large brim and a veil of gauze. Ti Me had brought it to him, and they had both laughed about it, a shared joke. *His back is muscled, but he is a little man,* I thought as he walked ahead of me. It was easy to forget this as we wrestled in bed, as I watched him leave me so many mornings. I thought, *I still do not know him, but I think about him at all times, so I suppose it makes no difference if I do or not. It is the same.*

"This is where the women come to wash," he said. Before us was a small pool, the water shallow. "This is where I learned to swim as a boy."

"You swim?"

"You will, too."

He stopped before the bank of the pool and began to take off the ridiculous hat, his shirt.

"Emmanuel—"

"The washing day is done. It will be dusk soon. No one will come."

He rolled his trousers up and waded into the water. Then he turned to me and held out his hands.

"There are two other pools above us. The water for this one comes from a waterfall at the top of the mountain. The pool just above us is about seventy-five feet deep. We will move to that one when you are ready. The best pool is at the top, near the fall. It is maybe a hundred feet deep, but the water is so blue you can almost see to the bottom. We will move to that one together. You'll see."

"You are very confident."

"Of course."

"If I refuse?"

He smiled. "I will demand it."

Following his commands seemed an easier way forward to whatever version of myself he imagined. So I put one foot into the water, then another. I stepped very carefully over to him. I could hear the water as it moved around my feet. If I was quiet, I could hear the clap of the waterfall above us. A deeper sound than the one I had listened for in the puddles and barrels of water back home, when I was a girl and believed in Ben Daisy's lady. Emmanuel held out his hands for me. I put both of mine in his.

And then he threw me down.

The water was not deep enough for me to lose my ground. I went under, onto my knees, but when I raised my head, I broke the surface again.

He was laughing, truly laughing. I thought, *I have misjudged him.* I thought, *I have made a mistake.*

"This is how my father taught me," he kept saying.

I tucked my legs underneath me, sat back in the water. I could feel my skirts filling with the damp, beginning to weigh me down. Emmanuel danced around me, whooping and laughing and splashing. When he got close enough, I held out my hand and pulled his arm, until he was in the water with me.

He rolled happily in the mud of the pool. But if I could have gotten ahold of him, if I had not been scared of the water myself, I would have held him under. If only for a moment, for him to feel what I felt. How could you be bound to someone, for life, to the grave, and fundamentally not feel the same things?

I pushed myself up out of the water, but I felt it still dragging at my skirts, nearly pulling me down again. Emmanuel was still sitting in the water, laughing. I slogged to the shore, one heavy step after another. When I got there, I tried to sit first on the ground, then lean against a tree. I could feel my skirts becoming clammy against my legs. I looked up at the sky. The sun was beginning to set somewhere. You could not see the horizon from this pool, just a pink streak across the sky above us. I was a thousand miles away from my mother because I was too much of a coward to tell her the truth.

In front of me, Emmanuel leaned until he floated on his back. He held his palms out. "This is the first step," he called. "You must make friends with the water."

Around us, it was getting darker. In the dimming light, the dirt road we'd taken to the pool glowed against the shadows of the trees, as if it was lit up from below. I could hear the sounds of birds from far away.

"Libertie, are you listening to me?"

"No," I said. "I am listening to the jungle."

"You are angry?"

"Shh," I said. "I want to hear the trees."

I heard a splash as he sat up. "You don't understand," he said. "That's the way you learn. That's how my father taught me."

"Your father is always right?"

"In this he is."

"You will ignore your father when he tells you how to be a doctor, but if it is about drowning your wife, he is correct."

"You're being dramatic."

"Half drowning your wife."

"You've never wanted me to feel something in the same way you do?" he said quietly, to the water. "That's all I wish for here."

I thought then that maybe we could try to understand each other again. I stood up. I unbuttoned the blouse that stuck to me, stepped out of the skirts that clung to my legs. When I was bare, I walked back into the pool and sat down beside him.

"Like this?" I set my arms on the surface of the water.

"Now lean back."

If you follow his commands, I told myself, *you can become the woman he believes you are.*

I felt the water creep up my spine, around my shoulders, and lick into my ears. Everything within me wanted to hold tight against it. My head dipped further below the surface, and all sound was gone now—except the sound of my own breath. My mouth and nose were still above the surface, and I took in one more bit of air, which felt warm now, when the rest of me was in cold water. And then I let go and trusted the water, and I was free. I opened my eyes a little bit. I could see the moon above us, and its light reflected, white and shimmering, on the water that surrounded me.

"Do you think," I said to Emmanuel, "it's the same moon over Mama right now? Do you think she is looking at it as I look at it, as I lie on top of water? Do you think she can know me right now?"

But he was tired of games by then. Or games that did not involve him. He sat up and crashed out of the water.

He took me to the water every Sunday afternoon. But first, we had to endure the mornings. Those we spent in sweaty prayer with his father's congregation: the bishop sitting behind the pulpit in his heavy robes, the priest standing up to lead the service, Ella's sewing circle sitting in the front pews with some of the Haitians who had joined the church early on, and the newest converts always standing in the back of the church.

No one seemed to question this arrangement, not even Emmanuel, when I asked him about it. "It has always been that way," he told me. But Ella was more blunt. "They are our brothers in Christ, but they aren't of our sort," she said. "The Haitians of our station are lovely, but they remain papists. The ambitious workers here join our church because they know we have schools and aid and help, and they want that for their families. We love them very much and they love us, and we worship together, but we like to be with our sort. Don't pretend you don't understand."

In our pew sat myself, at the farthest end, closest to the church window; Emmanuel, seated beside me; his sister, beside him; and Ti Me, at the aisle. Once, when we were all supposed to have bowed in prayer, I glanced up to see her neck straight, the only head unbent in all the church.

The church was Emmanuel's father's greatest pride. A stone building with rough windows dug out of the walls and a high ceiling. There was only one cross in the whole place, he liked to point out. No idolatry here.

We sang hymns in English first, then the Kreyòl translations. Bishop Chase strongly discouraged any hand clapping. "Americans can take it," he said, "but it excites the Haitians too much." So the songs swelled, but there was always some large piece missing.

It was nothing like when the Graces sang. It was nothing like when we sang at home in Kings County. It did not look like any fellowship I had known, but the bishop was proud of it, and much of the time spent in church was giving thanks for his intelligence, his humanity, and his hard work here.

Ella did not approve of our swimming lessons. She said it was an affront to the Lord's day. But Bishop Chase said it was up to a man to decide how he and his wife would spend the rest of the Sabbath, and so Ella only complained once. When we left for the mountains, though, she'd make it a point to get on her knees in the parlor and continue her prayers.

The bishop continued to say nothing. But after the third swimming lesson, the priest began to preach from Ecclesiastes, about the wife cleaving to her husband's family, about the obedience of marriage. Bishop Chase sat behind him the whole time, in his heavy robes in the heat, not even succumbing to it by fanning himself, as the others did. He was silent, looking straight ahead at some life that none of us could see.

I would reach for Emmanuel's hand while the priest spoke, if only to show some little sign of defiance, and he would take mine, but just for a moment. Then he would set it back down on the pew between us. Even that small rebellion was too much in his father's church, though when I would ask him about it, in our bed at night, he would say, "It was hot, Libertie. Too hot to hold hands."

Libertie,

I have received the notice from Cunningham College. And I understand, now, why you married that silly boy in haste.

I am so angry with you. And you are not even here to rage at! What a clever trick you played on me, my girl. What a lesson you learned at mine and Elizabeth's knee . . . the lesson of escape! You turned something so good and righteous against me. You've used it to your own earthly ends. I cannot think of a more wicked girl than you, and you know I've known my share. You are a deceiver. You are an escape artist. You are a liar.

You chose that man over doing the hard and right thing.

You chose indolence and lust over hard work and humility.

I have no doubt that Emmanuel Chase believes that he loves you. I think you have convinced yourself that you love him. But you know and I know that what you have done is wrong and you have ruined our dreams, your dreams, for what you think is love.

It is not love, Libertie.

Love would not make you think you had to flee your only mother.

You will probably never answer me now. You will probably continue to ignore my letters to you. So be it! So be it! So be it! Know that I hold this against you, though, Libertie. Know how you've made your mother rage.

You sat in my waiting room and looked down your nose at me and told me I was not trying hard enough. That I did not understand how to change the world.

You sneered at the white women I courted to keep you in nice dresses and pay for your classes. You stopped only short of calling me a traitor, and it is you who have betrayed me! Who has broken me. Who has deceived me. Who stood before me in a wedding gown and said, "I love you, Mama." Who gave up your virtue to a silly man so that you would not have to face the truth with me. I see it now.

So all is lost. So you have chosen that life, irrevocably. Do you know a part of me still held out hope you would find your way back to this path? That if I let you go, you would return? But you were already gone, long gone, and did not even bother to tell your mother of it.

You are a fool, and so am I.

Your

Mama

This letter came on a Sunday, after church, and when I read it, it went with the others in the back of the drawer, and I almost cried, I did, that she knew the worst part of me.

But Emmanuel called me down to dinner, and he put his hands on my shoulder and he said, "What is wrong?"

And I was still good to him, in his eyes, so I said, "Nothing," and I resolved I would not answer my mother again. Not for a long time.

When you learn to swim, your body is no longer your own. It becomes enthralled to another dimension, that of the water. Your limbs are weightless, but you can feel your hair and clothes becoming heavy.

"Do you open your eyes underwater?" I asked.

"Of course," he said.

So while I practiced floating, I imagined him just under the surface, eyes open and staring up at me. I was not sure, in that moment, which one of us possessed the other.

This will always be our life together, I told myself as I followed him back down the mountain. I truly believed, then, that this was the start of the world he had promised me. I thought of our time in the pool as his gift to me. During the week, he still would not permit me to join him in his medical work. He said he was not ready yet. Monday mornings in the empty house became easier, though. Ella and I sat side by side or walked to the market together, but my spirit was still on the water.

"You are not so different from me," Ella said after a few weeks of this. She sat in the parlor, with her embroidery still on her lap.

"I do not think I am so different," I lied.

"You do. You think you are better than me," Ella said. "Pride is not attractive on a woman."

"I assure you, I am humbled."

"Fanm pale nan tou de bò bouch yo."

"What does that mean?" I said.

"Three months, and you still have less of a grasp on the language than a baby." Ella still had her head bent over her sewing.

I closed my eyes. Willed myself to remember floating on the water.

"What is it that you've worked on for so many weeks?" I said finally. "Surely you are done?"

She lifted her head. She slit her eyes at me. Then she held up what was in her lap. A jacket, which she held by the shoulders and gave a good shake so that it uncrumpled.

I got up from my seat and went to sit beside her. "May I?" I said.

She nodded.

I took the garment in my hands and turned it over. Close embroidery in that bright red thread. I held it nearer to my eyes. It was words. An incantation. Maybe even a history. I could only make out a few of the words, but I realized she had embroidered a whole story on this jacket in Kreyòl.

"What does it mean?" I said.

"You are like a child, always asking that."

I stuck my thumb into my mouth and hummed, like a baby would. I had the satisfaction of startling her into a laugh.

"Your estimations are always correct, Ella."

"Stop."

"I am an infant and, as such, would be delighted if you schooled me in this."

She looked at me. I raised my thumb back to my mouth. "All right," she said. "He hasn't told you, has he, yet, of the bad year we had here?"

"When your mother and brothers passed. Yes."

"He has not told you, though, what else happened?"

"No," I said.

"We were thirteen," she said. "We had been here three years. We knew the language so well by then. There was a great crime, in Port-au-Prince. We lived there then—we had not yet come here to build the church in Jacmel. A man had sold his niece to the Vodoun priests, and they had slit her throat and drained her blood and drank it and ate her flesh. The government investigated and brought the bad people to justice. We watched them burn in the capital square. Ti Me, my brother, and I. We saw God's law that day. It was extraordinary. Emmanuel fainted, and Ti Me kept saying, "It is not right." She stayed at the square till the last of the embers died down. I think she was waiting for something. I do not know what. My brother was very upset. He said it was a tragedy. That they should never have burnt those terrible people. He still says it was a tragedy. He wrote to me about it, even when he was with you, in New York. So I began to make this for him. To remind him of the true history. I wrote it—see, I stitched it in thread. So he will always remember."

As she spoke, she'd taken the jacket from me and fanned it over her lap. She ran her fingers over the stitches, again and again, as if she was mesmerizing herself. The thread was red and ragged, from her touching it over and over, and the jacket itself, which had started out white, I think, was a dun gray. It was like a child's rag doll, pulled apart by the child's own desire. But Ella treated it like a prize.

I was not sure what to do, until Ti Me came to the door to say "Market." And then Ella tucked the jacket up and put it underneath the divan, as if it was the most natural thing in the world.

Oh, I thought. *Oh.* I saw now her stiff, irregular hair, her rigid dress. That she should know something of Emmanuel that I did not, even now. That he should hold this in him and only share it with her, and not with me, his wife. That he would not tell me this. I felt furious.

WHEN EMMANUEL AND I made it back to the water, I was ready.

"I did not think there was anything to tell," he said. By now, in our lessons, I had learned to wear a pair of old bloomers and one of Emmanuel's undershirts. He swam in the nude. I had become afraid that someone—a woman coming to wash her laundry in the dusk, a child looking for frogs in the mud—would find us, but Emmanuel seemed to almost relish the thought.

"You would not tell me about seeing those people burn?"

"You can't . . . She doesn't . . . You cannot always trust what Ella says."

"She told me she longs to burn heretics at the stake."

"She took our family lessons in differently."

"What does that mean?"

"She is different than me. She has been for a long time. I did not want to tell you at first. It is painful, and then I worried you would treat her poorly."

I was standing in the pool, just at the depth where the water reached my calves. Emmanuel, kneeling in the water, lay back. He said, to the darkening sky above us, "She was not always this way. Papa says she is mad, but I don't believe it is so."

I sank down into the water beside him. "I don't understand why you did not tell me there was something wrong with your sister."

"We made a pact, when she began to . . . began to . . ." I had never seen Emmanuel halt for words, except when we were together in the dark, but he did so now. "When Ella began to . . . talk like that. Father and I agreed. There is no one here to treat her. They do not have mad-houses in Haiti. And I would not put her in one anyways—because she is not mad, I do not think. And if we were to bring her back to America, where would she live? She is best here. She is best at home. I convinced Papa of that. And if I can find something to ease her burden, then I will have done my duty by her."

"So you expect me to live beside her?"

"She is harmless."

"She spends all day dreaming of seeing men burn at the stake."

"She is. She seems to have taken a disliking to you, but she would never outright hurt you."

"You choose her over me," I said. "Every time."

Emmanuel had not stopped looking at the sky. He said now, "I cannot believe you would believe that. When I've shown and said so many times to you that you are my life."

I heard him turn in the water. "Do you want to know what she really is to me? Ti Me says she is like this because our family did not serve us well. The very first words Ti Me said to Ella and me when she saw us were 'Marasa yo rayisab.' Twins don't get along. Especially if they are a boy and a girl. The boy will always prosper, while the girl will suffer. Ti Me is a fatalist, like everybody here. But she believed she could help us a little. She wanted to take us to a houngan, to meet lwa yo, to set it right. Ella refused to do any of it. Even at thirteen, she called it 'popish magic.' Ti Me says that that is when we lost her, and that Ella will not return to us as long as she is so stubborn."

"Do you believe that?"

"Ella has always been like that," Emmanuel said carefully. "When we were children, she was given to fits of weeping. But then, I was, too. And we had so much to cry over—leaving America and coming here, and being hungry the first year while Father set up his ministry. We thought we hated Father then. And then Ma was gone. And then everyone else.

"Ti Me, when she came to us, she would make sure the colors of our clothes were identical, that our plates always had the same number of yams. Sometimes, if I was in the kitchen with her, I would see her switch our plates around, so that I was given Ella's portion and Ella was given mine. I did not understand it. I said, 'Why do you do this?' And Ti Me said that was how you handled twins. She said because we were twins, we were very powerful and prone to resentment. That we must be satisfied and watched for jealousy. That our mother had not known to do so, and look what misfortune had befallen the family. Our poor mother had refused to learn the laws that govern the spirit here. She did not do her duty, and that is why she and our brothers died when they set foot on this land. And Ti Me said she would try to make it right.

"When Ella heard all that, it only made her cry harder. We used to cry together, Ella and I, spend whole afternoons crying over the books Father made us study. But I was young enough that I thought maybe Ti Me could be right. Our first Christmas here was spent with Father and the other mission families, on our knees in the sun, praying to God. That afternoon, Ti Me told us she knew what would make us feel better, and that if we wished to feel happy again, we would come with her when she called us. And she did, later that night—Father was asleep, and Ti Me came to our room and called for both of us. I went right away. Ella only followed because I went first. I remember her in her nightshirt, her eyes wide in the dark, staring straight ahead in fear.

"Ti Me took us out of the city—we walked in the dark for what felt like hours. Ti Me was like our mother, but she was only a few years older than the two of us. So we were all children and able to walk far. I remember the moon was so bright and high above us—it looked like a rib bone, curved into the sky. I would look up at it when my feet were tired. We walked on the road out of Port-au-Prince, and then Ti Me turned down a path into the forest, away from the shoreline. We walked again there, in the dark, with the leaves pressing up on my skin. Ti Me is like my mother, I've told you so many times, but she is not a very affectionate girl, and when I began to cry at the brush of leaves, she only sighed and told me to walk faster. Ella kept whispering to me, 'We will be sacrificed, and it will be your fault.'

"We walked and walked until we made it to a small house, made out of woven grass, and a clearing. There was a pole in the middle, and tens of people sitting and standing, laughing, talking, greeting one another. There were maybe five or six children younger than me, awake that late, on their mothers' laps or riding their older sisters' hips. There were old people and young. A few women and men in white shirts, and white scarfs tied to their heads. Torches all around to illuminate their faces. It did not look like any kind of solemn ceremony. It looked more like what a picnic did back in America, except it was happening in the middle of the night in a clearing, with someone's dog running happily back and forth and in among the people. Someone was even passing around slices of fruit. When we got there, Ti Me had us squat down on the ground alongside some other children our age. It was only as I looked at them more closely in the light from the torches that I saw how many pairs of twins were there. Boy twins. Girl twins. A few that were boys and girls, I guessed, like me and Ella. We sat and waited.

"We had left the house probably at midnight. By the moon in the sky, I would guess we sat and waited for another hour or so. I began to yawn, and Ti Me reached out her arm, so I could lie against her shoulder.

"Then the music began—you haven't heard it yet. It's like the drums of heaven."

"There are no drums in heaven," I said.

"You're wrong, Libertie." Emmanuel still was not looking at me. He still was speaking to the sky.

"I saw the men and women in white walk in a circle around the pole, swaying in time, the women each holding a lighted candle. Sometimes, in their march, they would stop to twirl. Sometimes, a man would come up to them and press his forehead to theirs, and then both, man and woman, would twist around each other, only their brows touching.

"I watched it all," he said, "but Ella hid her face."

"They had a brown-skinned kid goat and a speckled hen. They slit the throats of both and then cooked them, and then put them in a jug with three mouths and offered it to the Marasa. These are the spirits of twins.

"When the spirits had eaten, a woman came and gathered up the meal and put it in a wooden basin. She balanced the basin on the top of her head and walked around the pole three times. Then she took the basin off her head and showed it to each of us, to all the children sitting around. She kept asking us, 'Èske li bon?' When she got to me and Ella, I nodded.

"When she'd showed the food to all the twins present, she took the basin off her head, cast it down, and commanded us to eat. Ti Me told us to eat as much as we liked, until we were satisfied, but just to be sure we did not break any bird or goat bones with our teeth.

"It was a mass of all us children, pulling the food up with our hands, pushing it into our mouths. Ella, though, refused to eat. She was too scared to defy the adults outright, but she spit the food into her hands when they weren't looking. In the frenzy, I ate double her portion, to help her out.

"'Èske ou te manje ase?' they kept asking. *Have you eaten enough?* There were many children, but the kid goat had been fat, the hen, too, and the juice ran down my chin. Every other twin's face shone with grease in the moonlight.

"All during this, they sang a song. It is the song of the twins," Emmanuel said. "Should I sing it for you now?"

The only sound was the two of us, shifting slightly in the water.

"Yes," I said.

He took a deep breath and began.

>   *Mwen kite manman m' nan peyi*
>
>   *Gelefre*
>
>   *Marasa elou*
>
>   *Mwen kite fanmi m' nan peyi Gelefre*
>   *M' pa gen fanmi ki pou pale pou mwen*
>
>   *Marasa elou*
>
>   *Mwen pa gen paran ki pou pale pou mwen*
>
>   *Marasa elou*

I walked through the water where Emmanuel still lay, churning up swells with each step. When I reached him, I sank down onto my knees in the cold.

"Do you understand it?" he said.

"I think so." I closed my eyes and began, haltingly.

"I have left my mother in Africa.

                              "I have left my family in Africa.

"I have no family to speak for me.

                        "I have no relations to speak for me."

"Marasa elou," he said.

I lay back in the water beside him. I began to shiver.

"That's when I started to believe," Emmanuel said. "That's when I understood what this land had for me. Ella is unstable. She has never adjusted to life here. But I have, and I've thrived because of what I have taken in. Because of what Ti Me did for us, for me, on that night. That was my introduction to the work, and it is my most cherished act here. Do you understand? Ti Me saved me. The work saved me."

"You believe it all then? About twins and home and songs," I said. "And you call your sister mad?"

"Of course I believe it. The new ways here, it's where the people are free. We cannot be a nation if we don't have gods in our own image. They made these gods—do you understand? Just as your mother made her place and you made your own. They go further, where we need to. We will never be free until we do as they do."

"You would believe in magic?"

"I would have us serve the spirits." He dipped back in the water then, almost gone under, but then I saw he was pulling himself out, to look at me.

"I had thought you would understand," he said. "I wish my father would understand. I think Ella, in her own way, does understand. It's why she is so frightened of it all. She knows there's power there, but she isn't sure what kind. I believe we will not become a people until we have gods that understand us."

"You speak in riddles."

"I have told you from the beginning. This is my ambition. I can bring what I have learned in America and help the people here, with what they already have. I am building a new world. In the new world"—he curled his hand around my wrist, under the water—"we will be equals, you and I. We will be who we wish to be. There will be no limits on what we can dream or what we can do. You believed it when we married, and nothing has changed. Do not let this business with Ella make you think it is not possible.

"I was not forthcoming about Ella, this is true. I worried she would mean you wouldn't marry me, that you wouldn't marry into a family with people who were unwell. But everything else I've told you about myself should let you know I love you enough to chart new gods for you."

When we left the rock pool, I was still shivering. Emmanuel walked ahead of me, his back strong and straight, his shirt soaked through. I could just make him out as the night reached up to hold us.

Manman Poul grate, grate jouk li jwenn zo grann li

*Mother Hen scratched and scratched till she reached her
grandmother's bones*

Libertie,

I was too angry to write again for a long time. I wrote you many letters and burnt each one, because Lenore said they were too harsh.

I am still angry, to think what I have lost and what has been ruined.

This is the life I had imagined for you. That we would have that coach with the gold lettering. That you would carry on my good deeds. That you would be my great act of love in the world and my redemption. My apology to your father for not understanding where he came from. My atonement to our people for failing them over and over and over again, when I couldn't set them right.

You would be brilliant and set them right. But you are not even right within yourself, I think. And you cannot even understand what I had given you, all I had given you, to prepare you to fight.

They say the Negroes now are a different breed than in my day. The colored people are different. Bolder. And maybe that's what you are. Not my daughter but a daughter of a different age. Maybe your boldness serves better for these times than my fidelity. Maybe my Libertie is really the clever one, and it is Mama who is the betrayer.

Write to me, Libertie dear, and set your mama straight. Give me your words, please. I cannot take your silence.

Love

Your

Mama

I NEVER WROTE her back, because I discovered on Fet Gede that I'd fallen pregnant. That morning, I woke up to the sound of the drums. The drumming was something I had grown used to—it came from the temples that dotted the road to the water basins, and often-times, as Emmanuel and I rode back in the dark, we could hear it echo around us, off the trees.

After Emmanuel told me his life's work, I tried to do my best to make it my own. I had thought it was all poetry—though better poetry than what I'd written for Mama or the woman in the water, because it was inspired by love for me. But it wasn't just poetry; it was the logic by which he governed his actions and his mind, and I told myself I must learn it if I belonged to him now.

I thought that it explained the long silences between him and his father. I looked at Ella and tried to see her with the compassion that Emmanuel did. Her heat-stiffened hair, her sweaty, pale skin, the way she looked with fear and anger at the women in the market. *Love her. Love her. Love her for it,* I told myself. But mercy is hard to cultivate, when it's for a stranger who tells you you're only as good as what's between your legs and ignores you for hours on end.

Emmanuel must become your religion, I told myself. *Submit to him*

as you would to any preacher. It is the only way to survive here. He is your
helpmeet and your ally.

During the day, I did well enough. I sat near Ti Me in the cookhouse and tried hard to learn the language, enough so that one day I
could ask her about the gods she and Emmanuel loved.

But every night, I betrayed him, when I dreamt of being with my
mother.

Sometimes, I dreamt I was a girl, working quietly and compan-
ionably with her in her study, the heavy smell of camphor around us.
Sometimes, I dreamt I was finally driving the black carriage with DR.
SAMPSON AND DAUGHTER drawn in gold on the side. In every dream,
Emmanuel, marriage, my desire for him, was forgotten, nowhere to be
found. When I woke, I would long for her again, even as Emmanuel's
arm sat heavy across my breast, even as I felt the long naked length of
him against my back.

Sometimes, in the dreams, she held me in the softness of her lap, as
if I was a child, and swept a gold fan over us.

The drumming that had started all around us that October, that
startled me from morning sleep and afternoon rests, was a relief.
It shook my head free of grief, and to its rhythm I could sing *Love
Emmanuel,* and so forget my mother.

"The idolatrous Haitians worship the dead," Ella spat to me, the
walls of the sitting room, the sewing in her lap, whenever she heard the
drums. Emmanuel had told me that, yes, the dead here held a special
place. But what do you call it when you worship a memory of a living
person, of one who has never been completely known to you, and when
your worship is unwilling, driven not by a desire to honor but because
you have realized the world didn't make sense with her, and does not
make sense now that you are without her?

"Fet Gede is their All Souls' Day, but as with everything outside of America, the sense of humor here is keener," Emmanuel had told me in bed the night before the holiday. This was his favorite position to tell me stories—while lying down.

"Ella tells me that the men tie skeleton hands to their belts and circle their hips in lewdness," I said.

"In that, she is not wrong. If there was ever a holy day designed to speak to Ella's delusions, this is it."

Already in the night, we could hear music and laughing, louder than usual.

"It is one big celebration for the spirits of those who passed," Emmanuel said.

"It sounds macabre."

"It is not."

"If I went with you, I could see for myself if it is not."

"But then who would keep the peace with Ella and father?"

In the morning, my bed was empty.

Emmanuel had told me that he would spend Fet Gede with the houngan he was apprenticed to, a leader of a Vodoun house of worship that Ti Me had introduced him to—the very same man who had presided over his own feast of Marasa in the woods, long ago. He no longer hid the purpose of his trips from me.

The other Chases were planning to spend the day in public prayer—a pointed protest of the merriment all around them. I had already missed a chance to see how our neighbors on our street would prepare, because Emmanuel had deemed it more prudent for me to help the women clean the church and wash down the pews in preparation.

"I do not see why I cannot come with you," I'd said.

"They are already skeptical of my work," Emmanuel replied. "Your being here at least lets them see that I can be something of a family man. That my project does not exile me from any sort of decent life, which they would very much like to believe. If I were to do this work as a bachelor, they would claim I'd let my brain go foggy through lack of domestic love. If you outwardly assisted, they would claim that I was a corrupting influence on you.

"This way, they cannot discredit my work. Not if my own wife is at the front row of the choir, singing hosanna with everyone else."

"You have thought of everything," I said.

"The work is too important not to." He'd taken it as a compliment.

I took coffee with Bishop Chase and Ella, then waited as Ella went through her three shawls, deciding which one she should wear to service.

"The yellow one, I think," I said, hoping to goad her.

It worked. She quickly chose her black shawl and gave me a sly look, as if she had been triumphant. *I was learning how to manage her, at least,* I thought.

I walked with her to service, Ti Me beside us. Ella made a show of covering her ears whenever the drums seemed too close. In church, she threw herself down on her knees before the service even began, and shut her eyes tight. I did not sit beside her. What Emmanuel could not see would not hurt him. Instead, I stood at the back of the church beside Ti Me. It was not even noon, and the room was already too warm.

By the afternoon, my knees wobbled from standing and the noise outside was overwhelming. Bishop Chase raised his voice until he was hoarse, but it did not matter. Outside was a great rush of laughter and footsteps and singing.

I glanced over at Ti Me, who had stopped listening to the bishop altogether. Her face was turned toward the street. The expression on it was one of such open longing I felt a rush of pity. It did not seem fair that Ti Me should also be punished by my husband's sense of propriety.

I tapped her on the shoulder, and she startled.

I smiled, though, and whispered, "Ou vle ale la?"

She looked at me for a moment, as if deciding something.

I pointed out the doors, where a woman, her face streaked with white powder, her skirts hiked to her hips, was running past, a little boy laughing, trying to keep up with her.

Ti Me nodded, once. I took her hand and walked the two of us out of the church.

As the doors swung shut behind us, I heard the men and women inside begin to rustle, the priest call for us to return, and the whoosh of Bishop Chase's robes as he stood up from his seat.

I had finally done something to provoke a reaction from him, and I could not stop smiling as Ti Me and I ran through the streets in the sun.

"Ki kote li ye?" I panted. *Where is it?*

"Simityè a," she said. *The cemetery.* And then she squeezed my hand.

The graveyard in Jacmel was a little bit above the city, in the hills, so that the dead had a view of the ocean and the living in the town below them. In those days, it was not as big as it would become, but it was still an impressive place. The graves there were aboveground stone mausoleums. Some had columns and porticos; others were nothing more than solemn boxes with tops to shift off when the dead were buried. It was not like our graveyard back home, with its little pebbles, that I cut the grass from. *Who is cleaning father's grave now that I'm gone?* I wondered as we ran.

I thought of my mother, now left to tend two graves alone for the rest of her days, and felt a flush of shame, again—at my hasty marriage, at my foolishness. But I did not have time to feel sorry for myself, because as we drew closer, we were swept up by the crush of people at the cemetery gate, jostling one another, pressing close, hoping to get in and join their friends.

A man stood at the gate, his face dusted in white chalk, a top hat on. On his nose was balanced three pairs of spectacles, all with the glass missing. He had stuffed white cloth into his ears and mouth, like we do whenever we prepare a body for burial. He removed his cloth only to speak in a nasally, high-pitched singsong that I could not understand. Beside him was another man, taller, who was inspecting everyone who came past. All around us, everyone was eager for his scrutiny.

I nudged Ti Me. "Kiyès li ye?"

She snorted. "You talk to me in English. It will be easier."

"Who is that?"

"Papa Gede," she said. "And Brave Gede. Papa Gede, he wears the top hat, he is the first man who ever died in this world. He knows what happens to us in the land of the living, and he knows what happens to those in the land of the dead. The man next to him, that is Brave Gede. He guards the graveyard and keeps the dead inside. He keeps the living out. He decides who enters today to play with the dead."

"Will he let us in?"

Ti Me snorted again. She walked faster, through the crowd. I had no choice but to follow her.

When we reached the gate, the man in the spectacles widened his eyes and the taller man threw back his head. Both of them laughed as we approached and began to yell even louder. But whatever they were shouting did not frighten Ti Me; she began to laugh, too. And both men waved their hands, as if to say *You shall pass,* and Ti Me stepped boldly into the cemetery.

I tried to follow, but as I did, one of the men yelled something again, in that sharp, nasally voice, so strange.

Ti Me laughed to herself but kept moving.

"Why does he talk like that?" I asked her as I hesitated just past the entrance. I could feel the heat of the crowd pressing against my back.

"He speaks in the voice of the dead," Ti Me said. "The dead all sound like that."

"What did he say?"

"I will tell you after, mamselle."

In the graveyard, people were crowding around two tombs, pressing forward, laughing, singing. Some were resting against the walls of the dead, others placing bowls of food and drink on the tops. "These are the tombs of the first woman who died, Manman Briggette, and her husband," Ti Me said. "And here is the tomb of the first to die by the hand of man, and there is the first murder. They are all here to call up the dead."

All around us was the sharp smell of rum. A woman danced past, a jug held high above her head, the liquid sloshing out, down her arm, on her face. Some of it sprayed on me. I coughed when it touched my lips.

"It burns you, eh?" Ti Me laughed again. "Piman needs to be hot," she said. "You take a whole string of peppers, ten strings even, and mix them with clairin. It has to be hot enough to warm up the dead."

The woman with the jug stopped a few feet ahead of us, the crowd making room for her as she began to twirl and laugh and roll her hips. She splashed the liquid on her chest, poured it over her hands, rubbed it into her face. Someone handed her a long red pepper, and she took that, too, stuffing it into her left nostril. Another went in her ear, where it promptly fell out and onto the ground.

"That woman is ridden by a gede. The spirits found her, and she is their horse. They will move through her body. The dead are cold, but we can warm them up. He needs piman to warm him up."

The woman began to hunch down lower, to sing and to dance faster. A few people in the crowd joined her, others laughed, and some began singing another song altogether. Above us, the sun hung low in the sky, and I could see, from the cemetery gate, the harbor with the light shining bright over it, the sea turned to waves of white light in the dusk.

I had thought when I came here, I would be able to become a new person. That I would become someone for whom it did not matter that I had failed my mother. And, I supposed, that had happened. I became a wife and a sister and a daughter to people who could not see me. But was that any better than what I had been at home, beside my mother? I thought now, *It is useless.* I had thought then, *It is lost.*

I looked at the crowd rejoicing in the graves. The man closest to me pulled a femur bone from on top of one of the tombs and waved it in the air in slow circles. A few people walked with goats on leads or held in their arms. The sound of laughter kept up all around me. It had gone from a shock to a comfort to something that warmed me on the inside, that made my blood beat, that at least told me I was alive.

Ti Me had given up her role as nurse to me and was now standing by herself, watching the men and women sing. Sometimes, she sang along loudly; other times, she kept beat with hand claps.

Perhaps, I thought, I was destined to always be a child; perhaps it was silly to try to be otherwise. I thought of the life that lay ahead of me, a life of doing what my husband whispered to me late at night, of standing beside a Christian madwoman every day in church and pretending that her pronouncements were sane, of sitting across from a smelly old bishop who looked at me as the Whore of Babylon and had not spoken more than twenty words to me since I arrived. I thought of dying here, in this land, never seeing my mother's face again. I felt it, suddenly, in my chest: *I need her.*

I began to laugh. It did not start as a giggle. It was horrible. My stomach ached with it, my lips hurt from peeling back, and my bones were shaking. I was laughing so hard I could not catch my breath. My smile widened and widened until my eyes were narrowed and I felt the tiny, hot burst of tears at the corners of my eyes. The strangest thing was that I could not hear myself. I could feel the laughter bang in my throat, but in my ears was only the roar of the people around me.

Ti Me turned to look at me—both shocked and amused. "It's too much for Mamselle," she said.

"No," I gasped when I was able. "We stay." Even in my hysteria, I could see the skepticism on her face. But I wanted to do at least one part of this right.

I sat down on the dirt, against one of the tombs. Ti Me, still looking anxious, stood beside me for a bit.

She knelt down. "Do you want to know what he said at the gate?"

"Who?"

"Papa Gede. He knows everything. He knows who will die and who will be born. He said you are now with child—two, he said. I laughed because I thought he was joking. He likes to make jokes. Rude ones, especially about pretty young women," she said. "But I think—"

I began to laugh harder. I pressed my back into the tomb and rolled my neck. I could not say then if I wanted release from the moment or to be held in it forever. I was never good at deciding a side.

"No, mamselle, don't do that!" Ti Me put her hands behind my head, trying to still me. She brushed the dust out of my hair.

"If I am . . . If I am . . . If I am," I gasped, "so be it."

"Mamselle, you will hurt yourself."

"I have failed as a daughter, and I do not like being a wife. Perhaps I can be a mother," I said, and then I began to laugh even harder, until

Ti Me raised me up by the elbows, dusted off my church dress, and walked me, very carefully, out of the graveyard and back to my husband's house.

By the time we arrived, I had quieted down some. I could feel myself hiccoughing, the flutter in my diaphragm. I did not think what Ti Me and that man, whoever he had been, what they said about me—I did not believe it could be true. But by then, Ti Me was convinced. She had me lie down in my bedroom, checked the shutters to make sure they were closed against the street, and set a tincture of ginger leaves and aloe at my bedside, so bitter it made me wince.

The house was empty except for the two of us. I could hear the whisper of the bottoms of Ti Me's feet as she walked from my room, down the hall, and out to the yard. She had told me she would go to find Emmanuel, but I was not sure that I wished to see him yet.

Even in the heat, Ti Me had draped a blanket over me, and in my exhaustion I had let her. But now I tossed it off and pressed at my stomach, naming each part I imagined I felt through my skin. *The liver, the kidneys.* I imagined feeling the womb. I had not thought of this part of it, of falling pregnant without my mother there to name everything. I thought of the last day of our journey to Haiti, when we'd thrown the satchel Mama had handed me overboard and toasted to babies to come. I had done it to amuse Emmanuel, to amuse myself, really, by imagining what my mother would think if she could see me then. I had not let it occur to me that any of it could be real.

The world is only consequences, Libertie. I could hear her voice now.

"You do not always have to be right," I said to the ceiling above me.

There was a flash of light there, the reflection from the bowl of water and herbs Ti Me had left by my side. I watched as the light from the water skipped over the ceiling—back and forth, back and forth. It meant nothing. It meant everything. I was not sure where this thing called a will came from. Mama had it. Emmanuel had it. Even mad Ella, in her obsessions, had a will. But I did not. Would it come when whatever was in me was born? Or did I have a little more time to develop one, before this something else was here?

I began to laugh again, a little weakly. The heat of the graveyard was beginning to leave me. I could feel the sweat cooling on my face. By the time Emmanuel returned, led by Ti Me, both of them panting from running there, I was sitting up in bed, sipping from the bowl of water, in the last little bit of sunlight from the shutters I had thrown open wide.

"You are feeling better, at least?" Emmanuel said, his voice hesitant.

I set down my cup. "There was never anything wrong with me."

"Ti Me says you took fright."

"I was only overheated. But I am well now."

He sat down on the bed, motioned for Ti Me to leave the room.

"She told me what you heard at the cemetery."

"Do you believe it?"

"It would not be surprising."

"You do not sound delighted."

"It is only that there is so much to do, still, for the two of us," he said. He bent his head. He would not look at me.

He made as if to fall into bed beside me, but I pushed him away.

"You do not wish for this either," I said.

"There is not much to be done. It was not part of the plan, but I cannot say I can't see how it could be. Father will be satisfied, at least."

"He was about to yell at me, last time I saw him."

"You shouldn't have fled from the church like that, this is true. You could have left more discreetly," Emmanuel said. "But he forgave you when I said you might be with child. He remembers what that is like. He said, 'Women lose their minds when they are carrying. It is their burden.' But he was pleased. He will be pleased."

"Is that all?"

"I can see how it could help with a lot of things."

"I'm to raise it, to have it, here with a grandfather that hates its mother and a madwoman for an auntie."

"Don't call Ella that," he said.

I did not meet his eye. Instead, I looked at the reflection of the two of us in the mirror across from the bed—the back of his neck, red with heat, and my own reflection, dark in the shadows of the afternoon.

"I am not feeling well again," I said. "I want to rest some more."

He looked only slightly disappointed. He got up to close the shutters.

"No. Leave them open. The noise helps make the room bearable."

He tried to smile. "For tonight only," he said. Then he left me.

When I heard him walk all the way down the hall, I went to the desk and opened the drawer, the one he had told me was mine alone. The letters were crammed in until they tore, the paper crumpled into a fan. I took them out and brought them back to the bed and held them in the cradle of my lap.

Mama's need was too great. Think of that, I told myself. But who would have thought of that? I'd needed her and needed her and needed her when it was unseemly, and now here was the proof that she'd needed me back.

I tried to read her letters, but the words would not focus. My eyes would not let me take them in. I felt a pressure at my temples and suddenly very, very tired. To recognize that I had become another person for possibly a reason as foolish and flimsy as misunderstanding my mother—it was too painful to bear.

Fragments of the letters swam into clarity.

You do not write
You do not write
You do not write to me
Why?

Libertie
    I cannot think of a greater freedom than raising you from a babe in arms to a girl. You were mine, and I decided what you heard, who you listened to, what words formed on your lips. It was intoxicating to have that kind of open dominion over another, even more so because I knew you would grow to become your own person, and that person could be shaped by me.
    You do not write to me

And then the letters went back to a blur.

I closed my eyes and rapped my fist on the desk—once, twice, three times.

And then I sat down and took a fresh sheet and dipped my pen in the ink.

I wrote on one sheet, simple and direct:

    I am with child.

I called Ti Me and handed it to her to bring to the telegraph office on the Rue de Commerce. I spelled out the address carefully with my own hand. I made her repeat it back to me.

When she was gone, I looked at the pileup of my mother's love.

I'll burn it all this afternoon, I told myself in a flash of resolve. *If I burn her words, I will be free of whatever she wants of me.*

Instead, I stuffed the papers back in my drawer.

OF ALL THE things she told me about limbs and wombs and bodies, Mama did not tell me what it felt like to feel life within your own.

Within a month of the time in the graveyard, I felt it. The women in Mama's care had always described it as a flutter, but this felt more like a determined, persistent churning. As if a current was gathering inside me. The first time I felt it was in the parlor, while Ella lectured. She had been so enamored of her own words she did not see my expression, or note when I left the room. By the end of the month, the wave was steady and predictable. I imagined the child there, as faceless as the skin of the ocean, as formless as a wave.

Emmanuel was afraid I would lose it. He was convinced that what we had wished for, for so long, could be snatched from this world. It was as if all those deaths of his childhood—his mother, his brothers— were around him again and he saw winding sheets and sorrow every- where. He said it was now too dangerous for me to leave the house, even for church, even for the daily walk to the market.

"I can manage," I said. "I can help you in your work."

But he was not convinced. "It is too dangerous. You could lose it. I would not want to lose it."

"I will be as likely to lose it in this house as I am on the streets."

"This is the one thing I ask of you, Libertie," he said. "I have not asked that much."

And I thought, *This is a lie. But he truly does not know it.* And I thought, *He really has been a kind husband to you, Libertie. He could be crueler.* And I thought, again, that I was as gormless as the wave inside me if I could not make sense of any of this.

It was easier, in the end, to acquiesce. I did not think I could live in that house with everyone except for Ti Me angry with me.

"I will stay in, for now," I said.

And he smiled and kissed the top of my head. "It's lovely when you're stubborn," he said.

For the first week of my confinement, I kept my usual schedule. That is, I sat with Ella in the parlor room and the two of us pretended to work, while the other women—American and Haitian—moved in and out of the house, to Bishop Chase's study for instruction and approval.

"Emmanuel tells me you are with child?" Ella said the first morning.

"Yes."

"Well, then," Ella said. "Your work is done."

I thought we could reach a kind of peace. That, even in her madness, she would retreat in the face of this.

But Ella was cunning. She began to smother me with nostalgia. Now, alongside talk of the justice and blood she and Emmanuel had witnessed so long ago, she told me story after story of their childhood.

"When we were six, we had a pet goat who disliked me but loved Emmanuel."

"When we were fifteen, Emmanuel learned to swim and tried to teach me, but I was a lady enough to refuse," she said pointedly.

"When we were twenty, Emmanuel wished me to marry, but I asked him who was worthy, and he said, 'No one.' Just like that, my brother said, 'No one.' He has always understood me."

It seemed such a lonely way to be twins, I thought, Emmanuel always faced out to a future he was sure he could dream into existence, and Ella always turned back to a past that had meaning only for her.

For relief, I sometimes sat in the stoop of the inner courtyard, watching the hens walk across the dirt, watching them eat the dust out of boredom. But even that was not free of Ella. "Emmanuel and I had pet chickens. Two of them. They were black with red speckles, and Emmanuel loved his, but he hated mine, and he tried to pluck her feathers while she was still crowing, and . . ."

My escape was the cooking shed itself. Ella refused to enter it. "When we were ten, Ti Me told us to never enter it," she said.

"You are not ten anymore," I said.

But Ella was adamant. The shed, she was not allowed to enter.

It was quiet in there. The only sound was Ti Me's feet shuffling across the dirt and occasionally the clank of a spoon on a pot. It was hot, but when it got to be too much, I sat in the doorway and looked back at the main house. By the time I'd found the safety of the shed, my stomach and thighs had grown so much that my knees spread apart when I sat down. A rash of spots had appeared on my skin, and my underarms were always slick. I wore the same tan smock every day while Ella went about sewing me a new dress, with the waist dropped, for my final months. And still I had not heard a word from my mother.

"Have you ever been with child, Ti Me?" I said.

She sucked at her teeth, and I realized I had offended her. I felt a pang of embarrassment. I saw, in the corner of the kitchen hut, the straw pallet where Ti Me slept.

I tried again. "It feels as though my body is not my own. It feels like it belongs to whatever's growing in there."

Ti Me shifted a pot from one end of her worktable to the other. And then she began to tell me about the last time she had been ridden by lwa yo. It was a few weeks ago, she said, and she was so tired afterward she nearly did not make breakfast the next morning. Yon lwa who had mounted her turns her devotees into unruly children, begging everyone for sweets, curving their backs against the swats to come. Ti Me had stood in the circle and cried like a baby, crawled on her knees and stuffed her fingers into her mouth while the spirit acted through her.

"It isn't frightening when that happens?"

Ti Me cracked a nut on the worktable. "Why would I be scared?"

"Because you have no control over yourself. You lose yourself. You lost your freedom and died in the spirit of something else."

"Eh," Ti Me said. "Everything born dies, no?"

Emmanuel came back to me at night, but it was no longer only to me. It was a mirror of the lessons we had learned on the boat to Haiti, except that now, instead of talking to me of flowers, he manipulated the skin of my stomach, pressing hard.

"Do you remember," I said, "not so long ago, teaching me to swim?"

"Of course," he said. He was watching my stomach rise and fall with my breath.

"You could touch me like that, again, if you wished."

"The time for that is over for now," he said.

At dinner each night, as Bishop Chase and Ella listened, he questioned what I had done with my days indoors.

"What did you eat?"

"Which cistern did you drink from?"

"How many hours did you rest?"

"Did you walk the length of the hall three times, or ten?"

"I do not think," I said after the fourth night of this, "that your father and Ella want to hear every detail of my confinement."

"On that we agree," Ella said cheerfully. "I do not."

"Ella, stop." Emmanuel turned to me. "It is something we should be proud of. And it is their future, too."

"It is not," I said in a rush of anger. "It is mine."

There was a silence while Emmanuel looked down at his plate, chastened.

"You will explain to her?" Bishop Chase was speaking to Emmanuel. Never to me.

"There's nothing to explain," I said.

Bishop Chase kept chewing slowly, then swallowed and took a sip from his glass. "Ti Me, a bit more please."

"Libertie," Emmanuel said, "I will resolve it later."

I pushed myself back from the table as best I could and walked to the courtyard stoop, to stare at the night sky.

It was not clear if the face of the moon that looked down on me now was the same one that looked down on my mother. And in that loneliness, I felt a longing for her so violent that it made me rise up from the stoop and begin to pace.

"You know," I heard. "Emmanuel really does love you."

I looked up. It was Ella, standing in the light from the doorway.

"I suppose."

"You know," Ella said, "when we were sixteen—"

"I do not wish to hear childhood stories right now, Ella."

"When we were sixteen," she said, "I saw my father stick his finger in the coo coo of every serving girl up and down this street, including Ti Me. I told Emmanuel what I saw, and he said not to lie, never to lie. I told Papa what I saw, and he struck me and told me if I did not behave, I would have to stay in the house forever.

"Emmanuel said then to me what he said to you. That he would fix it with Papa. And then I knew he loved me. He told me to try very hard to forgive Papa, and he would fix it. And I did.

"Emmanuel told Papa I was sick. He told everyone I was sick. My friends have believed I was sick since we were sixteen. But he told me just to pretend. And it has been a little secret between us. I did not want you to know. You are so young, and I did not think you would understand. But you should. The world thinks you are mad . . . It's the greatest freedom I've ever known. Emmanuel gave that to me.

"I say whatever I wish to anyone. What colored woman in this world has that? Not a one, not a one anywhere on this Earth. You felt it when you first came, no? I can sew it into a million little words. I am free to speak my mind. Emmanuel did that for me, and he'll do it for you."

Ella held out her hand. "Because he really loves you."

FREEDOM WAS BEN Daisy choosing the bottom of the water over its surface, and the Graces singing, and Mama leaving me to put myself together in the loam, and the woman with the white chalked face, a pepper falling from her ear, dancing for the dead.

I knew what freedom was, and I knew I did not have it as I lay in bed beside Emmanuel, hissing in the dark, wary of what words would fall over the gaps in the ceiling above us.

"Your father is a monster. Your sister is lost."

"She is not completely lost. She told you herself."

"You would have me live that existence?"

"No. If you would be sensible. If you would trust me. If you would hold on. You would see, we only have to please him for a little while longer to be free."

"How much longer?"

"When the child is born, if it's a son, he will be more agreeable. My father and I are opposed—you know this. You cannot believe that I am the same as him."

"You've condemned your sister to . . . I am not even sure what kind of existence."

"She trusts me. As you should trust me."

"Why should I trust you if you don't even understand what is wrong?"

"You are being impossible, Libertie." He turned his back to me. The mattress creaked. "Papa . . . what he is doing is no different than what the slave masters used to do to our foremothers. Where do you think your mother's pretty color came from? Where do you think mine did?"

"But that does not make it right."

"No. But this is a new world here, with new rules. He is making his. I am making mine. You know what mine will be."

"Neither of your rules are new for me, or for your sister, or for Ti Me." I thought of the banner at Cunningham College, with its list of what made men and what made women. "We have always lived under them, whether there or here."

He turned back. I could feel his breath, hot on my face; he had brought himself as close to me as possible. "You are protected and cherished. I cherish you. And because of that, he will respect you," he said. "You have my love and devotion and my promise to always protect you. And you live in a country where I am considered man enough to make that happen. It would not be so back at your mama's house. You know that."

"You do not understand."

"What is there to understand?"

"You have freedom to define yourself, and I do not have any."

"You would not be asking for this if you loved and trusted me," he said. "It is the same with your mother. She did not trust me to wrap a bandage around a woman's arm without her oversight. But I thought you were different than her. That you had a better sense of what was possible."

I could feel his expectancy. But I did not want to give it to him. To give it to him would have been betrayal.

I sat up in bed, put my feet on the floor, and began the walk to the cooking shed.

IN THE SHED, I slept on the worktable. There was a hole in the roof, through which you could see the stars. I fell asleep looking up at them and was awakened only when Ti Me came in and gasped.

"You scared me, mamselle."

"I am sorry," I said. "But I think I will stay here with you for a while, if you wish."

"You have scared Monsieur Emmanuel. He and Ella searched the house for you and now he is walking the street, calling for you. You did not hear?"

"No." I rolled over, onto my side.

"They are trying to find you."

"Just let me rest here, please. You will not get in trouble. I will tell them I told you to let me sleep here."

"You would be more comfortable upstairs."

"Do you know, Ti Me, that when you are with child, your ribs float apart? Just like logs in a river. Float right apart."

"You are ill, mamselle."

"I only want to lie here for a little bit longer," I said. "When Monsieur Emmanuel returns, I will go back upstairs."

I could not see her expression in the dark, but I heard her turn to go back to the house. I felt the room grow cool around me. I could smell the peppers drying on strings on the wall. The grain of the worktable mixed with the blood of all the chickens cut and quartered. It was almost comforting. It reminded me of Mama.

"You will not get up?" It was Emmanuel standing over me, speaking in his softest tones.

"No."

"You would sleep better inside."

"It is good enough here for Ti Me."

"She is not with child."

You and your father see to that. "No, she is not."

"Come," he said. I felt him pull at the back of my smock.

I hunched down further, my knees bunched up against the squash of my lower belly. "I will not move. So do not try."

"You are being ridiculous."

"I am only asking to be left alone for a little while."

He said something low to Ti Me, who sucked in her teeth. Then he was gone, and it was me and her, lying there in the dark, with the chicken feathers floating around us.

I turned around again to look at her.

"Is it true, Ti Me?"

She was quiet for a long time. I could hear her breathing into the straw pallet. Then she sighed.

"Emmanuel feels like a son to me," she said. "Sometimes, he feels like a brother."

"Bishop Chase did that to you, what Ella said."

"It was not like that," she said. "Miss Ella is young and misunderstands."

"I do not think so."

Quiet again. Finally, she said, "Bishop does many things to many girls. You know what a man is like. It is no good to wish for something different. It's not possible."

I listened to Ti Me's breath slow for a long time. I listened to the night all around us. It was a queer thing that the night here in Haiti was not frightening. It was almost like a friend. I thought of lying in the Gradys' parlor, overwhelmed by loneliness. Of the night around my mother's house, always threatening to be broken by someone else's need—the knock on the door, the summons of "Doctor, come quick!"

That was not part of the night here. Sleeping in the cooking shed meant I could hear the sounds from the street more clearly. The bray of a baby goat lost for a moment from its mother. The rising and falling hum of insect wings fluttering. And far away, the roll of the ocean. I imagined I could hear the creak of a ship there, too. Would I take it, if I could? And if I did, where would it carry me? I had once believed escape was possible.

Emmanuel had always accused me of not loving the country. But as I listened to the night, I realized I loved it. I loved this land. If there was an answer to any of this, it was in the hills and the water around me. I loved it maybe even more than Emmanuel did. I loved it enough to wish more for it and my life there than what Emmanuel or his father could imagine.

HERE IS HOW you live in the cooking shed.

You make sure to wake up each morning before Ti Me, to wipe down the table you slept on. You roll off the table very carefully—your belly is heavy by then. Before you decided to live in the shed, your husband joked that perhaps you were carrying twins, and you think, each morning, more and more, that he was maybe right.

Two women cramp a shed.

You are aware you are asking a lot of your host. You wonder if you are doing the same thing you despise your husband's father for, just more politely. Sometimes, you wonder if she wishes it was she with the belly full of babies under the smock. She never looks at your body. She lets her eyes drift over it.

You find it awkward to sit in silence with her in the shed, so you try to draw her out. You talk to her in her own language, but she laughs at all the words you don't know. So sometimes you both speak in English, and sometimes you alone speak Kreyòl, and she answers that with a crack of her knuckles.

It is not a real answer.

A body cannot answer a question.

You take to making pronouncements to her. "I will never step back in that house," you tell her, "as long as the bishop lives there."

And, "I don't think he ever loved me."

And, "I think I am the silliest pickaninny who ever lived."

And, "How is it possible to become free when you do not even know who you are?"

These questions make you reckless and queasy. Saying them aloud is like sucking on the grayest gristle of fat on a stewing chicken bone. It is like smelling oxtails boiling. You feel how you used to feel when you wrote to the woman in the water, that telling the truth of what you feel is a dangerous thing, that it could invalidate your very self. Then you think of that woman in the water, and how she led this man to you. He called you one of her devotees. This man who fundamentally misunderstood you, and who you fundamentally misunderstood. You thought he was braver than he was. You thought he had a bigger imagination. His imagination was a cooking pot with the lid on, boiling.

All this takes your breath away, which is already short, because two expanding baby skulls are lovingly pressed on your lungs, making you lose your capacity for air. You are running out of air. You are not sure your husband understands this.

Gasping, you try to make yourself useful. Cooking is very much like making medicine, you think at first. There is a certain amount of drudgery in mixing and chopping and measuring, though Ti Me measures by handfuls and pinches, which makes more sense than how your mother measured, you thought bitterly. Your mother with her scales and her pipettes, and you, as a child, having to wash them each night for her. You try to do the same here, telling yourself you are useful. Ti Me looks skeptical.

You offer to gather eggs in the morning for Ti Me, and she says she supposes that you could. Sometimes, the eggs are malformed, the tops folded over onto themselves. You look at the nests, at the brooding hens, and you feel . . . nothing. You'd imagined that you would feel a great kinship with the world of mothers, now that you will shortly be one. But you do not. The pregnant nanny goat with its red swollen belly still disgusts you, and when you see another woman with child waddle past the back of the courtyard, you only feel embarrassed of how little you yourself have become a mother. Of how much you are still lacking.

Getting the eggs is tricky, because you are avoiding your husband and his family. You try to either get up before any of them or stay in the shed until your husband and his father, at least, are gone. But at night, when you lay on the worktable, you still lie as if Emmanuel was beside you. You curl to the edge and make space for this boy, as if the two of you were still in bed.

You lose count of your nights in the shed. Eventually, your husband leads his sister to the door, leads her by the hand like a child, and has her stand and call, "Libertie, Libertie, I have something to tell you."

You do not come out of the shed. You sit in the dark and call back, "You can say whatever you wish from there."

You hear them scuffle, as if someone is about to leave. Then Ella yelps. Had your husband pinched her? Ti Me, later, will confirm that he had. Just like when they were small. But after the yelp, you hear Ella, in her grudging singsong, say, "I did not mean to frighten you, sister dear. Please forgive us."

You do not shout anything back to that. You can feel the two of them out there, waiting. You will not respond. Eventually, one of them shuffles away.

A few minutes later, your husband comes into your shed and says, "Ti Me, may we have a moment."

When she is gone, you say to him, "You've forced Ti Me out of her home."

"You have," he says back, and it shocks you a bit, his willingness to do battle. You have always known him as a lover. You have always felt that power over him. You did not expect him to be willing to fight. If you do not know yourself as his lover, as the one who makes his eyes turn soft and makes his voice weak and makes him bow his head to please you:

What are you?

What power do you have here?

You are frightened then that you've lost him. That maybe he was lost to you already.

So you square your shoulders and decide, no matter. If he's lost, then maybe you are ready to be something else.

"You are a liar," you say.

"I have never lied to you," he says in a sob, and all your resolve nearly leaves you. And it is maddening that he is right. You want to go to him and hold him, to hold him as you did when you were both at sea. But in the dark shed, you think of the gleam in Ella's eye, and Ti Me's quiet voice saying:

You know what a man is like.

It is no use to wish for something different.

It is not possible.

"Do you remember," you say, "when you wooed me and told me that we were equals? That we would be companions?"

"Have we not been?"

"You did not tell me your family's history."

"I have always thought—" He stops, his voice strangled with tears. "I have always thought that I could be myself with you."

"But your self belongs to this rottenness. Your self defends it."

"I don't know what you mean."

"Which self have you been? The one who wants a million sons to build a free nation? The one who lets his father corrupt a country with his lewdness and greed? The one who calls his sister mad until maybe she's become it? The one who imagines doing all of this means he's working toward freedom?"

In the dusk, you see how slight he is, again. How pale his skin is, and how it glows. You think of how much pleasure you took in his looks, how much you took pleasure in the pleasure others took in looking at him. You were Mrs. Doctor, Mrs. Emmanuel Chase, Mrs. Chase. Your genuine desire for him was all mixed up in knowing how much he desired you, and how much anyone—Ella seething in the sitting room, his father peering at you over his glasses, your mother, shocked and scared, the high yellow American women of the colony with their faces fixed in disbelief—how all of them could see it. It was so plain they couldn't deny it.

How much it would hurt if all that certainty of who you were, at least to them, was gone.

"You are unfair, Libertie," he says. He unbends his head. And for a moment, it is as it was when the two of you were in the mountains, in the pool, his hands holding you up, through the water, to the sky.

"I do not know what to do," you say.

"There is nothing to do," he says. "You are only upset and broody."

"No," you say. "I don't know what to do."

"Come back in the house, Libertie."

"I think," you say carefully, "I will stay out here for a little while longer."

He sighs. Bends his head again.

And then he is gone.

THE BEST PART about living in the shed was being close to the fire. I no longer had to listen to the string of chicken move past Emmanuel's father's teeth, or his sister sip each teaspoon of her consommé. The only sound I missed was the fork up against my husband's tongue.

I did not eat what the family ate. I ate what Ti Me did. Sometimes, we roasted plantains in the embers of the fire. Sometimes, she cracked two raw eggs in a cup and drank it, and I drank it, too. I did not have the nausea so many women have with pregnancy. Instead, I craved the scraps of Ti Me's worktable. Sometimes, she had to slap the potato skins from my hands—she would catch me gathering them up and sucking each one as if it was honey.

"You best not start eating the dirt, mamselle," she warned me. "You do that, and I'll have Monsieur Emmanuel himself come and get you."

It was true I had been tempted, but I took Ti Me at her word, though I kept a small handful of dust in my smock pocket, to lick at when she was asleep.

"Ti Me, do you love the younger Chases?"

"Non, mamselle."

"No!" I laughed, surprised by how she'd said it without hesitation.

Her expression did not change. "They are kind. They were good to me when I came to them as a girl."

"But you don't love them?"

"What does any of that have to do with love?"

"You never loved Emmanuel and Ella, then?"

She snorted. "I never love Monsieur Emmanuel. Or Mamselle Ella. I care for them like they are my brother and sister. I care for them better than a mother. But I don't love them. When I first saw them, they were so thin. And so pale. They got spots in the sun. They were so scared—scared of everything. Emmanuel told me they see their mama pass, right in front of them. Their brothers, too. Their papa, he would always pray. The children cry, and he would tell them to pray. They would cry on me at night. I have my mother—she still living, so I did not know what to do. She told me just to hold them. So I did."

"You were not tired of them?"

"What do you mean?"

"When someone needs you that much, it doesn't make you tired?"

"You are speaking nonsense."

"I used to think that as a little girl. And I thought that was what was wonderful about Emmanuel. He wanted me without asking anything of me. I thought that at least. But now I think he asks too much."

"He asks nothing of you."

"He asks me to live with a bad man and a girl who pretends to be mad and does nothing all day."

"But the bishop and Ella can't help who they are."

"Do you think they will ever change?"

"The bishop. What would you change? He wishes for a place he cannot return to. He does what any other man would do if they were him. It is no use trying to change him."

"That's what you always say, Ti Me. Nothing is ever of any use."

"It would be cruel to try and change the bishop. You can only live beside him and turn away from him when you can. And Ella, she is still a child."

"I am to stay here and take whatever the bishop says or tries to do to me?" I said.

"You want to know why you are so restless, causing all this family trouble?"

"It is Monsieur Emmanuel who's caused the trouble."

"Bah," she said. "Men do what they do. They are like a plow, moving through dirt—they just make the way. It's women like you and your fretting that cause a mess, disturb a rut."

"What's wrong with me, then? Why am I so restless, if I should already know to do nothing like you?"

Ti Me had begun chopping up the cassava for dinner. She did not stop as she said to me, "You've been claimed by the spirit. By Erzulie. And you will be unsatisfied and miserable till you devote yourself to her."

"Have you told this to Monsieur Emmanuel?"

"I told him the first night I saw you. I said, 'Monsieur, a woman like that doesn't know herself. You should never marry a woman so lost she does not recognize herself. Can't even place her own reflection in a mirror. Can't even see her own face on top of still water.' He said you were a clever girl, you would make do. But . . . here you are." She looked up from her work to where I lay, belly-up to the soot-stained ceiling of the cookhouse.

"If you wanted to," Ti Me said while looking at the large bowl of rice, "you could change it."

"What do you mean?"

She shifted the rice—once, twice. The husking sound seemed to mock me.

"It is Monsieur Emmanuel who believes in all that," I said. "I don't."

"Wi, mamselle," Ti Me said.

"Well," I said after a moment. "What would I do? If I believed the things you did."

Ti Me finally looked me full in the face. "You would have to kouche."

I felt my cheeks grow hot, and I looked down, embarrassed. I could hear the word in Emmanuel's voice, when he'd whispered it to me in the dark, describing how we lay and died and were born together.

Ti Me laughed at my expression. "No, not like that. It means that, too, but also it means other things. You will kouche . . ." Here, she gestured to my stomach under the smock. "Give birth. But what I mean is that when you kouche, you would dedicate yourself to yon lwa. You would go to the initiation and you would kouche—it would be like you are dying. We would cry for you and grieve for you, because we would know you are passing over to another side. We would kiss you goodbye, Emmanuel and I."

I shivered.

"You would cover your eyes, and you would be made to dance in circles. Over and over. When that was done, you would be led to a small dark room, and that is where you kouche again. You would stay there. You would be reborn. You would be as a baby in a womb. You would be brought food and rubbed down, as a new baby is. You would be raised back up to become a woman again. But you would be new. When you leave the room, when you are finished, you would keep your head covered for forty days. Because you would still be like a newborn baby, and your head is soft, and the spirits within your head, even though they have finally been fed, would still be growing strong each day.

"But"—Ti Me sighed—"even though you should kouche and it would solve a lot of your restlessness, it does not matter. You will not stay here long enough to right it."

I began to sweat. "I don't understand."

"You sent me to the telegraph office. You make me send a message. You will not stay here."

"I did not ever ask to leave."

"You can leave a place in more ways than one."

THE MAIL BOAT came only on Tuesdays. The telegraph office was only open in the afternoon. Because of this, everyone knew everyone else's communications. There were the back-and-forths of the American Negro colony and the comings and goings of the white French and American merchants who stayed in the city. And then there was the continuous flow of gossip from the countryside to the market street, which wound over the mountains from Port-au-Prince. It was hard to escape this web of foreknowledge. It had already told the town that I was with child, that I had spurned my husband, that I slept among vegetable peelings.

An uppity woman, to turn a good man into a beggar in his own home.

A woman too sure of herself.

A woman that dark can't play like that.

Dr. Chase will be ruined.

Bishop Chase will, too.

I wished for any other sound to drown it out. Sometimes, I drummed my fingers on the shed's table, just to break the rhythms around me. *If only,* my index finger tapped. *If only.* It did not seem fair that my deficiencies in womanhood, in wifeliness, in Negro life, should follow me all the way to this new world, where I was supposed to be washed clean, left out of those old songs, harbinger of a different one altogether.

So it felt like a kind of dream when all this changed and began to din around the fact that we would soon all be visited by a troupe of

Negro performers. They were making a tour of the Caribbean, had come from Florida to Cuba and then to us, in Jacmel. This news was received with great excitement—even Bishop Chase seemed pleased.

The only time I saw Ti Me genuinely smile in that house was when she came to the shed and told me that Bishop Chase had given a special dispensation to everyone in the colony, allowing them to attend the performance, even though theatrics were generally considered sinful.

She shyly pulled, from under her own cot, her better shawl, all white, the one she only wore at holiday time and kept folded over, with care, in an old burlap rice sack. As I touched the gleaming white linen, I realized my dilemma. I wanted to hear something besides the sound of our alley, the sound of our animals, and Ti Me's occasional voice. I was bored in the shed by then. It was comfortable as I grew bigger and my hips grew soft, but it had lost its charm.

To leave it, though, would mean some sort of a concession. I was not sure exactly to whom. Was it to Emmanuel, or was it to myself? Lazy Libertie, without even the conviction to withstand the offer of a traveling show. Mama had stood firm for less. I felt embarrassed that I had ever criticized her as a girl. A song, it turned out, was where my resolve ended.

"They say they are bringing a man who plays a horn," Ti Me said, her voice swooping up in glee. "And another man who has trained the birds to talk to him, and can talk back to them. He can tell us their stories."

"Do you really believe that?"

"And there will be a carnival, and people will dance."

"Yes," I said. I reached for the bowl of rice Ti Me was now washing.

"And they are coming all the way from where you did."

Every evening, when Ti Me left our shed to serve dinner, I sat on the floor near the door and looked out across the yard, at the main house. Sometimes, when she returned from her duties, Emmanuel followed her. I would sit by the door, and he would tell me, again, how much I loved him, how he loved the children inside me, how I needed to only step out of the door and into the world he was building for us.

My resolve broke a bit more each time he came—because I was furious with him, with his father, but I still loved him. I still wished for him by my side, to run my hand over his pale back in the moonlight, to feel his hands underneath me, holding me up in the water. With Mama, I had held on to the anger and let the love burn away. But with Emmanuel, there was no satisfaction in this burnt space between us. It only made me lonelier, and the loneliness made me long for him more. I would be weak, I knew it, and return to him. But not yet, I hoped.

The night that word came about our visitors, I stayed for a bit longer while Emmanuel whispered all his love for me.

"I would like to see the players," I said finally.

"I do not think that is a good idea, in your condition."

"I am not so far along that I can't go."

"You are too far gone. There will surely be a crowd, and if anything were to happen to you, we would not be able to get you help in the crush of people."

"Maybe I could go but stand apart."

"You would probably," he said slyly, "be able to hear them from our bedroom window."

So that is how I found myself sitting again in my husband's room, a chair drawn up to the sill and the shutters open, straining to hear what I could past the crowd.

Ella and Bishop Chase had left to listen. Ti Me had gone, as well. It was only me and Emmanuel in the house. I sat to one side of the window; he stood to the other.

"I do not think I will be able to hear—"

"You will. They are performing on the Rue de Commerce. We can usually hear what happens there."

Outside the window, the sun was bending deeper into the sky, and we could see, just over the roofs of the trading offices, the water of the harbor moving back and forth.

I am here, far away from my mother and my father's bones, I thought, *and I am looking at a sight they will never see.*

"Do they move?" Emmanuel said.

"What?"

"Do they move, the babies? Do they move a lot? Is it painful?"

"They are sleeping at the moment," I said.

He smiled at that, his face so eager. I took a breath. Stopped. Took a breath again.

"They move the most when Ti Me speaks."

"Yes?"

"Yes. You know, she does not speak often, but when she begins to talk about something, it is almost as if they swim towards her."

"Then they know her as the rest of us know her."

I narrowed my eyes. "Do not say that."

He blushed. "I did not mean it that way."

"Your father took advantage of a girl who acted as mother to you. Who was only a few years older than you."

"Everything is not as simple as you think it is, Libertie."

"But it seems very simple. You say you want a different world than your father's. This is a chance to start making it."

He looked out the window.

"If everything you do is for the good of our people," I said, "for the country yet to come, I wonder if what he did to Ti Me, if that was part of making a nation, too."

"You are grotesque," he said.

"I am only asking questions. I want to know."

"You cannot know everything," he said. Then, "Aren't you tired of fighting, Libertie?"

I felt a heaviness in my bones that took my breath away. I felt the hang of my belly, pulling on my back, and the crook of my spine from sleeping on a wooden table. I felt the swell of my feet, the itch at the back of my knees that I could not reach. The waves, just over the horizon, moved over and over again, and even that sight exhausted me.

"You must be tired," he said again. "I know that I am. You ask me to do something that I have tried to do since I was a boy, and I tell you I will do it. When the time is right. But we have to plan, to build new things. And while we build, it would not be so bad to lie down here, in our marriage bed, which belongs half to you, after all."

He was at my elbow then, pulling it gently, and I settled into the cup of his hand. I was ready to follow him—I would have followed him, and we would have lain down, curved into each other like two rib bones in the same breathing chest. But then I heard it.

I had almost forgotten that their voices were real. I had not heard them in close to eleven months. Sometimes, in those first few nights on the ship, I had imagined that they sang to me. If I was being truthful, when I woke up in the mornings since, I was always a bit disappointed that I had not dreamt of them the night before.

Emmanuel still had his hand on my elbow, but it did not matter. I turned toward the window, and it was all I could do to keep myself from leaning out of it, from wanting to jump down to the ground below.

It was my Graces, come back to me.

I could not hear what words they were singing from so far away. But I could hear the clarity of their voices, the way they met and married in the air. I could hear how they wound their way to me. I could hear, too, how the crowd had quieted when they began.

"It's Experience and Louisa singing," I said.

Emmanuel looked exasperated. "It can't be."

But it was—I knew it was—and I listened as closely as I could until they were done, and then I heard my heart beat faster.

"You must find them. They must know I am here, but you must find them and bring them to the house."

"How will I even get close? How will I get down to them?"

"Please go!" I said.

"I will go, if it makes you happy."

And he was gone, and I thought of this man who would go out into the streets to find them for me. I thought of Ella, saying sourly, an accusation, *He really loves you.*

I sat in silence, in the darkening house, until I heard the great door downstairs open and close, and Bishop Chase and Ella purring their kindest regards, and Emmanuel laughing, and then the two voices I missed most in the world, after the voice of my mother.

LOUISA AND EXPERIENCE looked better than they had when we'd left them. Experience was a little stouter—her chin had swelled slightly, a little dimple of fat sat in the middle of it. Louisa was standing straighter. They were both in new dresses, finer fabric than I had ever seen them wear.

When they saw me, they began to shout—"Ho!" and "My!"—even Experience.

Finally, Louisa said.

"You have seen her?"

"She came to our final performance," Experience said, "before we began our engagement with the troupe."

"It was too hard," Louisa said, "to manage things on our own. We were nearly run out of town in Connecticut and robbed in Syracuse. We would have given up altogether and returned to school if we had not met Mr. Ashland and the Colored Troubadours. And then they announced their tour of the Caribbean, and that they would even come to Haiti, and we knew we had to join, if only for the chance to see you again."

"Thank God Mr. Ashland is honest," I said.

Louisa laughed. "Yes, he is a good man. We travel for six more months, and then we return to America and find another way, we suppose."

"But you must stay here," I said.

Emmanuel moved forward. "Yes, please stay."

Louisa looked quickly to Experience. "Let us send Mr. Ashland word of our plans. We were to stay two nights here and then travel on to Port-au-Prince. Mr. Ashland tells us there is an opera house there, finer than anything you can find in New Orleans, almost as fine as Paris."

"There was," Bishop Chase said. "But it burnt down."

"Mr. Ashland is not altogether honest," I said, and was rewarded with another of Louisa's laughs. I realized I had not made anyone laugh, besides Emmanuel, since I'd been here. Not kindly, anyways. Sitting at the dinner table for the first time in months, my back felt heavy against the chair.

Louisa and Experience told us all the things they had seen on their travels. It was strange to see them in front of the Chases. They did not understand the Graces' irreverence but knew enough that these women were good, because they sang the word of God. Still, the bishop mostly looked back and forth between Experience and Louisa, as if they were saying words in a language he did not understand but he knew to be indecent.

"In Florida, there is a city that is governed entirely by black men and Indians," Experience said, "and they have built an amphitheater so fine a whisper sounds like a shout."

"In Cuba, they had us sing in the market square while a man slaughtered a bull behind us," Louisa said. "We thought it would be a distraction, but no one clapped until we were done."

"They even ignored the bull's very pretty bow when he was brought down by the mace," Experience added.

"They say we will sing for the colored people in New Orleans," Louisa said, "though Mr. Ashland claims he had to take special care that we weren't engaged at a fancy house."

Ella put down her napkin at this and looked pleadingly at her father. But he shook his head slightly, as if to say *Let it pass, for our guests.*

"And," Experience said, "every penny we earn, except for incidentals, is sent back to the college, Libertie."

"We write to Alma Curtis every three weeks to assure her we are staying virtuous." Louisa winked at me, and I felt my cheeks grow hot.

"She'll be proud to know how you've turned out," Experience said.

"How I've turned out?"

"Yes, she would be proud."

"But I've done nothing I've been educated for," I said.

They both look pained.

Emmanuel looked at me sharply. "You have done very well for yourself, Libertie."

"Yes," I said. "But Alma Curtis used to say I was a girl who could have an ambition."

There was a brief, awkward silence. And then Louisa looked across the table to Ella, to compliment her on her cloak.

"It's a coat of righteousness," Ella said cheerfully. "As righteous as good brother Joseph's was."

Louisa looked at me quizzically. I shrugged.

Ella continued. "This coat is stitched with the word of the Lord."

"Is that so?" Experience said.

Emmanuel cut her off. "Ella is excellent at needlework. She really is."

"Very refined," Louisa said.

Ella narrowed her eyes at her brother.

Emmanuel smiled at the Graces. "We have not had many visitors from outside the island. Probably only once a year, and then mostly other missionaries. It is an honor to have artists in the house."

"I am an artist," Ella said.

"Enough, Ella." Bishop Chase put down his fork. "Ti Me," he called. "Ti Me!"

She appeared at the dining room door.

"Take Miss Ella to the parlor, please, to wait for us while we finish dinner."

"But I am not done!" Ella said. "I am not finished."

Bishop Chase would not look at her; he only continued to chew.

Ella rocked slightly back and forth in her chair. "You cannot make me leave," she said. But when she saw Ti Me in the doorway, Ella stood up.

"I believe I am to retire," she said. And she bowed her head—once, twice—in each Grace's direction. Then she was gone.

I felt Emmanuel's hand on mine. I had been running my fingernails down the tablecloth, in one long swipe, like the claw of an alley cat. He wrapped his hand around my wrist and squeezed it. I knew he meant it kindly, but I only wanted to pull away.

I had thought, up until that moment, with the Graces speaking warmly and Emmanuel joining them in their jokes and conversation, that maybe I could do what my husband was pleading with me to do. But then I thought of a thousand more nights in this beautiful country. Would he order me from the table, as his father did, if I said something he did not like? And would I leave with dignity, like Ella did, leave in a fiction, or would I kick and scream as I wished she would do, as I wanted to do now, and be called mad and unruly.

It was quiet for a moment. Emmanuel turned to Louisa and Experience apologetically. "Ella has not had the opportunities you have," he said. "She has never been to school. She is a bit unused to polished company, but I hope you will not hold that against her."

"I would never hold it against her," Louisa said, and Emmanuel smiled as Bishop Chase raised his head in the air. He'd heard the music in her voice, but he could not quite place it.

I had the satisfaction, at least, of seeing his expression when the world did not make sense for him. If only for a moment.

THE GRACES WERE to sleep in the parlor, on the broken-down divan that we pushed to the parlor chairs. I stood in the doorway and watched as Ti Me prepared their bed.

Experience cocked her head in Ti Me's direction as she knelt over the chairs. "This is life in Haiti, then?" she said to me. "All you do is sit up here and make sure Emmanuel is happy when he returns home?"

"You do not have to take in laundry or mending to stay afloat?" Louisa added.

"You are what those girls at school always wanted to be: a lady of leisure."

I laughed. "Leisure is stifling."

"Listen to the cheek of this girl," Louisa said, leaning over to Experience, "telling you and me, you and me, dear Louisa, that leisure is stifling."

"I would give anything to be stifled," Experience said dryly, and this set all three of us to laughing again, so loudly that Ti Me looked up, annoyed.

"Lordy," Louisa said, when we'd made a configuration of furniture that finally seemed as though it would fit the two of them. "I would never have guessed that you live such as this. Experience and I, each night, would say 'Where do you think she is now? Do you imagine she sleeps in a hammock beneath banana leaves?' And now to find you living in something like Cunningham's dining hall, but just with warmer weather . . ."

I frowned. "That is unkind, Louisa."

"Is it?" She looked up. "I did not mean it to be. I only mean, your life seems different from what you told us it would be."

"Isn't that true for all of us?" I said. "Could you have imagined traveling the world with Experience, sleeping in stagecoaches, arguing with impresarios as naturally as if you were debating the merits of philosophy back at Cunningham?"

"No," Experience said. "This is true. We could not have imagined that."

"So then life is different for all of us."

"Is that why you have not written back to your mother," Louisa said, "only sent her one telegram telling her you are with child and scaring the poor old girl half to death?"

I started. "How do you know anything of that?"

"Our last performance, before we left the North, in Manhattan, she had heard we would perform, and she came. She showed us the telegram herself. She said, 'Will you write to her? Will you find out what she means? Will you send her my word?' And I said, 'I will do you one better, madame. We will be traveling to Haiti ourselves and can deliver any message that you wish.' And so she gave us this."

And here, Louisa reached into her pocket and handed me a folded-over piece of paper, much wrinkled where it had been pressed up against her hip.

"It is from her?"

"She said to place it in your hands if you were alive, and onto your grave if you were dead."

"She thought I was dead?"

"She said you have not written her a word since your marriage. I think she is justified in thinking you had passed."

The paper was the same yellowish shade as the pages in her accounting book. I could not bring myself to open it.

"Libertie, it is very cruel of you to send a telegram like that to your mother and never write a letter," Louisa said.

"I did not know what to say." My voice came out low. "How would you explain this house to her, if you had to explain it?"

"I guess that is fair," Experience said.

"Are you safe here, Libertie?" This was Louisa. "Are you well?"

I did not know how to answer her questions. I took the letter and bowed my head and said, "Good night. I will see you in the morning."

I had promised Emmanuel, for the sake of our guests, I would not sleep in the shed that night. As I climbed the stairs to our bedroom, I felt the letter wrinkle in my hands. I did not want the ink to smear.

When I opened the door, he was there already, of course, in bed. He looked up, expectantly.

"Are they comfortable?"

"I think so."

"Will you be comfortable?"

"I do not know."

"At least lie down."

I set the letter carefully on his desk. I pulled my smock over my head and dropped it on the floor, so that I stood naked in front of Emmanuel.

He sat up in bed. "Come closer," he said. "I mean, if you please."

I kept my eyes on him as I approached. When I reached him, he held out one hand, placed it on my stomach, put the other around my waist, and let it rest at the small of my back. He rested his head on my stomach, and I felt the whisk of his eyelashes as he closed his eyes. I looked away from him, to the letter on the table. I both wanted to stand here, with his head on my stomach, with his arms holding the world, and I wanted to crouch on the floor and read every word my mother wrote me. I did not know which way to move and could not break away. So we stayed like that, for a long time, listening to the house settle around us.

Finally, he sighed. "I have missed you," he said.

"Let us sleep," I said.

A little past midnight, I heard his breath grow heavy and knew he was fully asleep. I pushed myself out of bed, carefully pulled the chair from his desk, and sat, naked, on the planks of wood, reading my mother's hand.

My Dearest Libertie,

You do not write, and that may be because you are no longer on this Earth or it may be because you are still angry at me, but either way I miss you and wish to know where you are, so I write this letter to you and send it by way of your friends, the Graces, hoping that it finds you at peace, whether you are on this Earth or below it.

The house feels truly dead now. I do not like staying here most nights. Most nights, I sleep in the waiting room of the hospital.

I write to you from the dark of the waiting room. It is about ten o'clock at night. I've just heard the church bell ring. I was to attend a lecture tonight, but I did not feel spirited enough. Besides, the topic is one I think I already know well: "The Future of the Colored Woman." It is an argument I am too old and tired to add anything to, I think.

The speaker is a very smart young woman, like your friends. She travels from city to city to talk to groups about the colored woman—a marvelous business, one that could not have existed even ten years ago. I told her this, and she seemed unimpressed by her own strangeness. She smiled and said, "Yes, mum." And I suppose that counts as progress, when a girl like her does things I could not imagine and does not stop once to think of them.

I had hoped I had made you brave like that, Libertie. Perhaps there is bravery in being a wife. Certainly, there is bravery in being a mother. I think you will learn that soon enough, if my calculations are correct.

I have delivered more babies in the last six months than I ever did when you were here with me during the war. I do not know if it is a sign of hope or a sign of desperation, that our people have gone baby mad. I think there are now more colored people in Kings County than ever before. Sometimes on the street, I do not recognize a single face, and I think how this is both a good thing and very lonely-making.

The last woman I attended, it was not here in the hospital. She was a very poor woman. Her husband came and begged me to come to her. He said she had been in labor for many days and he worried that she might not make it. I was tired. I had thought I would go

*back to the house, for once, that evening, and try to sleep there. But
the man came just as I was about to leave, so I followed him to his
home.*

*They lived in Vinegar Hill, in a small wooden building beside
a grog shop. The sounds of her laboring almost drowned out the
sounds of the sailors singing shanties next door. She was a very small
woman, but loud. I said to her husband, "It is good that she makes
so much noise. It means she has fight left in her."*

*She was doubled over, walking up and down the room, and so I
walked beside her, holding her hand. She had been laboring so long
her hand was wet with sweat and kept slipping from mine. I told
her, over and over again, what a strong woman she was. What a
wonder she was accomplishing. It was her first labor, and these were
the things she needed to hear.*

*Towards the end of it, she screamed once more, very loudly. Then
she lifted up her skirt, and what did I see, but the baby's knee sticking out, foot dangling down, almost doing a little jig.*

*And the sight of it made me laugh, Libertie, the first time I had
laughed since you had gone. I know it was a dire sight. A breeched
birth is dangerous, and the woman could have died. But I heard
the sailors singing that their love lived in the ocean, and I saw that
baby's knee jerk in time, and I saw the woman's face, her blink of
surprise, and I could only laugh. At the absurdity of the world. The
ridiculousness of your absence. The foolishness of whatever I did to
cause you to leave me.*

*You will be glad to know, the woman delivered safely. I had her
husband hold her elbows, and I squatted down between her knees,
and together we turned the baby until he was straight, and he was
delivered, just two hours ago today, by the grace of God our Creator.*

I was still laughing when I handed the boy to his mother. She and her husband must have thought me a madwoman, and I am sure they will speak to Rev. Harland about how dotty Dr. Sampson has become in her old age. But even now, as I write you, even though I know the gravest danger we were in, I cannot help laughing. And isn't that a marvel, Libertie? Is that what you would maybe call grace?

I am not sure what your answer would be. I wish I could see your face just once more, to know what your answer would be. You sent me a message that you were with child, and then nothing. I thought of closing up the hospital and traveling to Haiti myself to find you. But I prayed upon it and felt, to the bottom of my soul, that you will come to me if you are meant to. That I will hear your voice again, whether here on Earth or in heaven.

To my love, my daughter, Libertie
I love you.
Your
Dear
Mama

THE GRACES LEFT as suddenly as they came, to travel over the mountain to Port-au-Prince, in search of that burnt theater. Louisa took with her, rolled up and tied to the string of her bonnet, my letter for my mother, for whenever she saw her again.

After they left, I did not have the strength to move back down to the shed. And so it was in Emmanuel's bed, after all, where I gave birth to our children.

My labor began at dawn. I was woken from a dream of the grass on my father's grave by a sudden pain in my hips, running, like scales on a piano, up my spine.

I could smell the salt of my body all around me.

The whole day, I walked the house, while Emmanuel trotted behind me to keep up and Ella called out nonsensical advice and Bishop Chase looked, for the first time since I'd known him, genuinely nervous. By evening, I began to feel tired from the pain, and I shouted at the three of them, "Only Ti Me has any sense."

Ella was easily enough gotten rid of. She did not like the sound of pain, and she went back to her room, loudly announcing she was of better use praying for me.

But Bishop Chase did not want to leave, and he watched me, with detached interest, as I winced and Emmanuel stroked my face.

"Please," I whispered to Emmanuel. Even in pain, I did not have the courage to yell at the bishop. "Please ask your father to leave."

And he did. He went to his father and said, "Papa, go to your study."

But Bishop Chase would not. He stood in the doorway and watched me labor, and it was only when I started to undo the ties of my smock—I was so overwhelmed with the heat, with the pain, and just wanted to be free—that he turned and left the room.

I walked in pain, and Emmanuel was there each step with me. And I knew there was no other face on Earth I wished to see, at that moment, except for his.

I thought, *I have forgiven you.*

I watched him as he watched me, as his soft mouth moved, as he held my arm, as we paced the hall together. I thought of his father, whom he still did not have the power to even make leave a room.

I could hear, in the bedroom next to ours, Ella and her father praying. A whisper—they would never pray loud like the Haitians did, like the Graces dared to do. And that made me even angrier—that even now, they would scrape and keep an etiquette of God. Their hushed prayers came over the gap in the ceiling, and it nearly drove me mad. Emmanuel felt the muscles in my arm stiffen and rubbed me gently there.

"It is all right." He smiled, and I felt my love for him come back.

I have forgiven you, I thought, *but I do not think that will be enough.*

"What's wrong?" he said. "Why do you make a face like that?"

"It only hurts," I said.

At midnight, I sat up in our bed. Emmanuel lay beside me, his breath light.

The pain that was in my body was warm now. It was a pain I had seen when I attended births with Mama. The births back home in Kings County, when I was a girl—every one was a kind of celebration. Because we knew each new child meant we had a claim to the land, to our space of freedom there.

The very first birth I had seen with Mama had frightened me. I had wanted to run from the room while the woman bellowed and hissed, and the air became thick with the smell of something deep and hidden, something that smelled almost lost.

But Mama had given me a look, and I had not dared to leave her side, and on our walk home she had told me, evenly, "You will not understand until you yourself do it, but in birth is the freest you can be. You do not have to take your leave of anyone or do anything for anyone. You are even free of deciding for your body how it will go—it is deciding for you. Your only expectation is to follow, and that is a kind of freedom, if you let it be."

Now in bed, I felt the next wave of pain and wished that she were here.

The sheet beneath me became wet. Emmanuel was woken up by the damp. He cried out in joy, in excitement. And then he was up, calling for Ti Me and for boiling water and for strips of cloth and for oil.

I wanted to leave the bed again. I wanted to feel the floorboards creak beneath my feet. A line of sweat trickled from under my chin to my chest between my breasts, to the top of my stomach.

I was breathing as hard as if I was racing up the walls of the room. With Mama, sometimes, a woman insisted on laboring with a knife in the bed beside them, to cut the pain. I had thought it silly then, as silly as Mama declaring those moments an emancipation. I had never thought, fully, what it would mean for me to join them there.

"I want Mama."

"Yes," Emmanuel said. "Yes."

By then, Ti Me was there, holding my other elbow. I could feel inside me a great, deep churning. A new world was trying to break out of my body.

It felt as if my hip bones would grind apart. I looked over both their heads to the ceiling and cried up to it. I felt Emmanuel wipe my sweat and tears. My knees began to shake. My spine bore down around itself—I could name every bone as I felt each one break.

I pushed my feet on Emmanuel's shoulders, a gross inversion of all the times I used to do the same, in pleasure, at night on the boat. And then I heard nothing. Not Emmanuel crying, not Ti Me whispering, not Ella and Bishop Chase's prayers winding over the ceiling walls.

I heard only the blood rushing in my ears, as pure and steady as a river, and in that one last searing burn of pain, I heard my mother's voice, wordless, only the tone and timbre that she'd make over our family's graves.

I felt the heat of my blood between my legs, and when I looked down again, I saw Emmanuel covered in my blood and crying, and

Ti Me covered in my blood and smiling, and lying on each of my thighs, my son and my daughter, our children, my children, born into this world I would make for them.

> *My Dearest Mama,*
>
> *You have received this letter delivered to you by Louisa and Experience. Know that, as of this writing, I am alive. By the time Louisa and Experience hand this letter to you, I will have delivered your grandchildren.*
>
> *I do not know what I am or what I will have become by then. I am not sure I ever knew myself. I used to think this was a failing. Something to hide from you. How could I be a righteous woman, to serve the world as you did, if I did not know myself?*
>
> *But that seems like so little of a concern, now. I may not know myself, but I know the loneliness of love. I know what toll forgiveness takes. I know that the world is too big to be knowable.*
>
> *I have learned to swim. Emmanuel taught me at first. But I learned how to float myself. The water carries you up, even when you think you are too heavy. When I float like that, I think of you and your ledgers, I think of where you go when you order the world in your mind, and I think I am ever closer to joining you there. I wish you could see your Libertie, floating in cool water so blue it seems God would drink it, staring up at the sky. When you are worried for me, when you are scared for me, when you wish to know me, think of me like that.*
>
> *Mama, I am coming to you. I will be there maybe even before this letter arrives. When I deliver these children, I will rest for as long as I can and then I will come to you. The Graces have already agreed to help. They have left me their cut of the last leg of this tour, they have left it with a ship captain in Jacmel's port, and when I am*

*ready, I am to find out when he next sails to New York, and he will
harbor me and my children.*

*I will miss this country. I think it is here, more than anywhere
else, that is my home. But I cannot stay. What a horrible thing in
this world, to know your home and also know you can never live
in it. I will tell you what Emmanuel has done, or rather, what he
chooses to continue to have done, when I am home with you again.
Emmanuel is a man who I do not think is all bad, but he does not
have a big enough imagination to imagine me free beside him. I
have already forgiven him for it, though.*

*I will carry to you my two children. I will wear their swaddling
clothes as my own skirts. We will see you again before this world
turns in another new direction. We will, at least, turn together.*

*I learned a new saying here today. Nou bout rive nan jaden an.
We have almost reached the garden. My friend Ti Me says it to me
as she measures my belly, how far it is dropped, when I am ready
for birth. But I think of it as my song to you, my mother, when I see
you again.*

Love,

Libertie

THE BOY WAS at my breast first. He drank, and every time
I tried to look in his eyes, he closed them tight. But when I looked
away, I felt him watching me. The girl, she did not want my eyes. She
watched my mouth. She watched my lips form shapes and my tongue
vibrate as I sang to them. I watched her watch the invention of music.
Right there, I invented it for her. Being a mother means being someone's god, if only briefly. This is known, I think. But they are my gods,
too. They are my country now.

Emmanuel,

Know that I have left you because I love you. I cannot stay, though, in a house that is built on silences. I cannot pretend, as Ella does, if she is even pretending anymore.

I believe you are a strong enough man to follow. I believe you can hope for more.

I love you, I do. I love Haiti, I do. I love you enough both to leave you and hope for more.

Do you understand?

Can you follow?

Remember when I told you of Ben Daisy and how he drowned for love? And you said, in flirtation, that he and I belonged to Erzulie. Ti Me also told me, in her careful way, that I am Erzulie's, that I will always be unsatisfied, that the beauty of this world will never be enough for me and I will always long for the other side of the mirror, the more perfect world.

But I wish for a different story, I think.

So when you come to me, tell me this one. The one you told me about the water where I learned to swim. Remember the story you told me, about the pools? You said that water did not belong to us. Not to the colored people of Haiti, not to the Negroes, certainly not to the whites who caused the soil to run with blood. No, you said they belonged to Anacaona first. You said she was a Taino queen, who ruled the land here when Columbus came. She was beloved because she could sing. She could sing her people's past, she could sing her people's present, she could sing through all the way to her people's future. She led her people in revolt against the world that was descending, revolt against the world that said it was the only world possible.

The Spaniards tried to break her. They gave her the choice of death, or to be one of their wives, trapped in lust. She chose death. She went to her end with pride, even though they hanged her.

She revolted, and you said that we could still hear her cries in the water there.

That is what you told me.

When you come to find us, because I believe you will become a strong enough man to follow us, this is the first story I want to hear from your mouth, the only one I will want to hear in your voice for quite some time.

I think you can break free. I believe you can. But I cannot do it for you. You have to do it yourself. I don't know if I, myself, am free. I hope to be. Our children are already, and I leave you now to keep them that way. I leave you to keep their sovereignty intact. But do not think that you are now alone. I promise you—we are waiting for you, in the new world.

Your

Libertie

ACKNOWLEDGMENTS

There are so many people who helped me bring this book into the world. First and foremost, I would like to thank my agent, Carrie Howland, who believed that this book was possible and pushed me to write the proposal for it. I would like to thank my editor Kathy Pories, Betsy Gleick, Elisabeth Scharlatt, Michael McKenzie, and the many others at Algonquin who have so enthusiastically supported the creation of this work.

I would not have been able to complete this manuscript without the support of many generous and unexpected grants. The National Endowment for the Arts, the Whiting Foundation, the Radcliffe Institute for Advanced Study, and the Hodder Fellowship at Princeton University all provided me with the material support necessary to complete this novel. I am forever grateful and humbled to be the recipient of these fellowships. In particular, I must thank Meredith Moss Quinn at Radcliffe and Tracy K. Smith at Princeton for your support and belief in my work. Tracy also graciously connected me with a homeopath, Wanda Smith-Schick, who shared invaluable information with me.

While working on this book, I have had the good fortune of meeting so many artists and writers who inspired me, who had conversations with me, who shared with me how they saw the world and helped expand my understanding. I also had the good fortune of continuing my conversations with so many friends. This made writing less lonely and made me a better thinker. Thank you to Ja'Tovia Gary, Min Jin Lee, Lauren Groff, Mira Jacob, Bill Cheng, Tennessee Jones, Alexander Chee, Simone Leigh, Madeline Hunt-Ehrlich, Lana Wilson, Naomi Jackson, Nicholas Boggs, Tanaïs, Naima Coster, Kerry Carnahan, Evie Shockley, Andra Miller, André M. Carrington, Kinitra Brooks, Megan Mayhew Bergman, Cara Blue Adams, Mike Scalise, Margaret Garrett, Rebecca Sills, Ilana Zimmerman, Phillip Williams, Tanisha C. Ford, Molly Brown, Jessica Grose, Sheila Pundit, and Deb Reck.

I was very nervous to write about Haiti—a country I admired but that I am not from. I was scared of writing something untrue, and so I had to read and talk with as many people as I could to try not to do so. Thank you to the historians Brandon R Byrd, Kate Ramsey, Wynnie Lamour, Kendra Field and Malick Ghachem, who answered my questions and shared so many resources.

In particular, thank you to the historian Orly Clerge, who answered my questions about visiting Haiti and provided so many resources. Thank you to Edwidge Danticat and Sharifa Rhodes-Pitts, who did the same. Thank you to Patrick Sylvain, who provided expert Kreyol translations.

Thank you to Rob Field and the staff at Weeksville Heritage Center, who provided me with access to the oral history recording that inspired this novel. My time working at that historic site changed my life and I am forever grateful to those who work so hard to preserve that legacy.

Thank you to Nicole Davis.

Thank you to my family—Ariel Greenidge, Kirsten Greenidge, Kerri Greenidge, Ron Nigro, Katia Nigro and Hunter Nigro, David Dance, Suzanne Dance, Tyron Dance, Kwame Dance, Eric Davis, Candice Corbie-Davis, and Fidel and Che Corbie-Davis.

And thank you to my daughter.